Stop!

Don't turn the page until you read this!

Here's how to find the incredibly helpful things in this book:

Event Sites

How to Find Specific Sites in This Book

Sites are organized by region and city, with illustrated descriptions and details about capacities, fees and services. To find a specific site, see the alphabetical index on **page 821**.

Sites Listed by Characteristic

If a site has a special feature, like a garden, ocean view or seating capacity for over 300, you'll find it here. **See pp. 34–42**.

Find-It-Fast Chart

This matrix shows the main features of each location. You can see at a glance which sites are good possibilities for you before you read the rest of the book. **See pp. 44–55**.

Event Services

We feature Northern California's best event professionals—caterers, coordinators, photographers, florists, DJs and more. To review all of our top-rated pros, see **pages 684–819**. And to find out how they qualified to be in Here Comes The Guide, read **page 681**.

More Locations!

To access information about event sites not included in Here Comes The Guide, check out our web site, www.herecomestheguide.com.

How To Order Another Copy

If you need another copy of this book (especially if you borrowed this one), use the handy order form on **page 837**, call us at **510/525-3379** or email us at hopscotch@herecomestheguide.com.

Bridal Show Calendar

This calendar lists many Northern California bridal fairs by date and location. See **page 833**.

Our readers say...

Your book is awesome! Your descriptions are dead on—and, I love the title.
Sylvia Hendricks

This book really helped me. It gave me ideas and places I wouldn't have thought of on my own, and having all the prices was especially helpful because it narrowed down the field right off the bat.
Holly Hidalgo

I've never seen anything like this! The amount of information is amazing, and the front part with all the tips is so valuable. What you've done is not just a business venture—it's a great service that really brings something good into peoples' lives.

Carolyn Webster

Yours is not only a unique book, with a very clever name I might add, but a well-thought-out and very professional publication.
Gail Garceau, Consultant

I went out and spent the money on your book without hesitation. I'm so glad I did! I've gotten some great ideas and was able to create an outline for my budget. Not only did I find great reception locations in your book, but I think I found my rehearsal dinner place as well. It was a gold mine!
Liz Davis

I spent one night reading your book from cover to cover, and I was amazed! I can't believe all the work you did and I'm enormously grateful. Now I don't have to call up all these locations and get this information myself.
Carol Nesbaum

I couldn't believe my luck! I feel like I hit the jackpot! I had no idea *Here Comes The Guide* existed, and just want to thank you for publishing it. This book is exactly what I needed because I was feeling frantic.
Alice Pogue

I can tell you for a fact that I looked everywhere for something like your book, and I was ready to give up when I stumbled across it. You saved my life!
Karen Lee

Want more information? Check out www.herecomestheguide.com.

This is one fantastic book and you can quote me on that! It's become my bible for locations.

Dolores Michaels

Now that I've got your guidebook, I feel like an expert...well, sort of. At least when I call event sites I sound reasonably informed and intelligent. Before I had *The Guide,* I had no idea what to ask for and probably wasted a lot of time.

Wendy Woods

I've carried my *Guide* with me everywhere! I've used it so much, it's starting to fall apart. Every time I visit a location, I whip it out and check all the details. Your book has been incredibly handy. You deserve a round of applause for doing so much research for me.

Carolynn Carter

I had to plan my wedding from out of state, and I just want to tell you how much I enjoyed your book. I can't begin to express how much easier *The Guide* made it. I don't know how I would have done it without your guide.

Mary Firestein

I went to about ten locations that are in your book and found that the site descriptions were pretty accurate. I'm amazed at how well you were able to capture the feeling of a place and put it into words.

Stephanie Stevensen

All my friends told me to get this book. I didn't understand what they were raving about until I got my own copy. Boy was I ever surprised—I didn't expect your book to be so interesting and well written! Thanks, it's been a real lifesaver.

Liz Garvey

This book has been my constant companion while I've been planning my wedding. I can't imagine trying to go through this process without it.

Ann Rogers

You're quite the "Joy of Cooking" for brides and grooms. Who doesn't have your book?

Joan Freese, Event Resource & Design

Want more information? Check out www.herecomestheguide.com.

SIXTH EDITION

Copyright © 1999–2000 by Lynn Broadwell

Text, phone numbers and fax numbers for both event venues and professionals are excerpted from *Here Comes The Guide, Northern California, 6th Edition.*

Library of Congress Cataloging-in-Publication Data

Broadwell, Lynn   1951—

Here Comes The Guide, Northern California ©

Sixth Edition, Includes Index

Library of Congress Catalog Card Number Pending

ISBN 1-885355-04-1

Inside Illustrations: Michael Tse

Want more information? Check out www.herecomestheguide.com.

acknowlegements

Once again, this book would never have made it to the printer without the help of our tenacious writers: Heidi Triay, Darcy Brown-Martin, Stephanie Gold, Tracy Corrington and Martin Snapp. They visited most of the new sites for this edition of *The Guide*, and have done an admirable job of bringing these places to life for our readers.

We also must kiss the feet (figuratively, of course) of our two fabulous right arms, Meredith Jones and Jennifer Ahearn. Gathering and tracking all the information that goes into this book is a monumental task, and they handled the project with intelligence, patience and finesse. Indeed, their achievements are so great that if we had any clout with the Federal Bureau of National Monuments, we'd have their faces chiseled into Mount Rushmore next week.

And lastly, we'd like to express our appreciation to our clients and our readers, whose support over the years has made *Here Comes The Guide* a regional best-seller and, dare we exaggerate, practically a household name in Northern California.

Want more information? Check out www.herecomestheguide.com.

be a good consumer!

The information in this book is as accurate as we could make it. Keep in mind, however, that very few things stay the same over time: prices fluctuate and facilities undergo changes in ownership, decor, landscaping and services. Remember to call each location and ask what's changed since we published this book.

To help us stay current and ensure the accuracy of future editions, we'd appreciate it if you'd contact us with your comments, corrections and suggestions (or complaints) at the address and phone numbers below.

If you discover an appealing location that you think we should include in our next edition, please let us know.

HOPSCOTCH PRESS

1563 Solano Avenue, Suite 135   Berkeley, CA 94707

hopscotch@herecomestheguide.com
www.herecomestheguide.com

510·525-3379   fax 510·525-7793

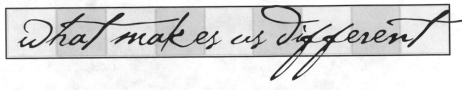
what makes us different

This is the *only* book with real solutions to finding the perfect spot! *Here Comes The Guide* offers:

■ **Comprehensive information about wedding and special event sites.** *Here Comes The Guide* includes not only a full description and an illustration for each location, but nitty-gritty details about prices, capacity, site services and amenities. By the time you call a facility, you're a thoroughly informed consumer!

■ **Access to the best wedding and special event services in Southern California.** We've knocked ourselves out doing our homework so you won't have to. The dynamite Service Directory in the back of this book will introduce you to this region's best event professionals. With *The Guide*, you can actually shop for the *right* spot and the *right* vendors without having to worry about whether you've made the right choices. Everyone we've included is outstanding—we're honored to represent them.

■ **Quality throughout!** From our lively editorials to our layout and illustrations, you can tell we've put our heart and soul into making this guidebook a top-notch resource. Readers often tell us that *Here Comes The Guide* is so well written, they actually enjoy reading it—from cover to cover! Our site descriptions are not only informative, they're accurate, often entertaining, and a refreshing change from the typical advertising copy you find in other publications.

we could use your help

We rely on you, our reader, to get the word out about our book, so we'd really appreciate your help in broadcasting how terrific *Here Comes The Guide* is. When you call places featured in it, let the sites' representatives know (loudly and clearly!) that you heard about them through *The Guide*. And if you feel we've saved you time, your sanity or even your life (don't laugh—many of our readers call up and say just that!), please tell people about it. Tell your friends. Tell your relatives. Tell your dentist. Don't hestitate to tell acquaintances you barely know what a great book this is. We'd be eternally grateful.

HERE COMES THE GUIDE

Visit our web site

www.herecomestheguide.com

Here's what you'll find—

- Easy, time-saving ways to search for the perfect spot.
- Information about new locations!
- More great wedding and special event services!
- Direct links to the event locations and services we feature.

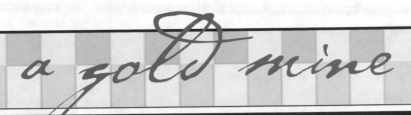

a gold mine

OF INFORMATION ON WEDDING SITES AND SERVICES

For even more information about special event sites and services, check out our web site at www.herecomestheguide.com. You'll find:

■ **An easier way to search for the perfect spot.**

We're expanding our web site database. Over time, you'll have access to hundreds of locations, many of which are not in Here Comes The Guide. By selecting your criteria, such as regional area, site type, guest count, and other requirements, you'll be able to generate a customized list of sites that fit your needs.

You can change your selection criteria any time you want and do multiple searches. And since our database of locations is regularly updated, you can dive in as often as you like to retrieve new information.

■ **Information about new locations!**

As new sites come to our attention, we'll bring you comprehensive information about them. You'll be able to read a site description, see an illustration and review nitty-gritty details about what each site offers in the way of capacity, pricing, services and restrictions.

■ **More great wedding and special event services!**

As we find out about new caterers, photographers, florists and other top-notch event professionals, we'll feature them on our web site. They'll be just as highly rated as the vendors in Here Comes The Guide, because all of them will have gone through our rigorous screening process.

■ **Direct links to other event locations and services.**

Through our web site, you'll be able to link up with the home pages of the facilities and event professionals we highlight. This means you'll get incredibly detailed information—often including photos and testimonials—to help you make the best choices.

Contents

regional areas & cities

San Francisco

North Bay

North Coast

Peninsula

East Bay

South Bay

Wine Country

Santa Cruz Area

Monterey Peninsula

San Luis Obispo Region

Gold Country & Yosemite Area

Tahoe Region

the best event professionals

regional maps

northern california

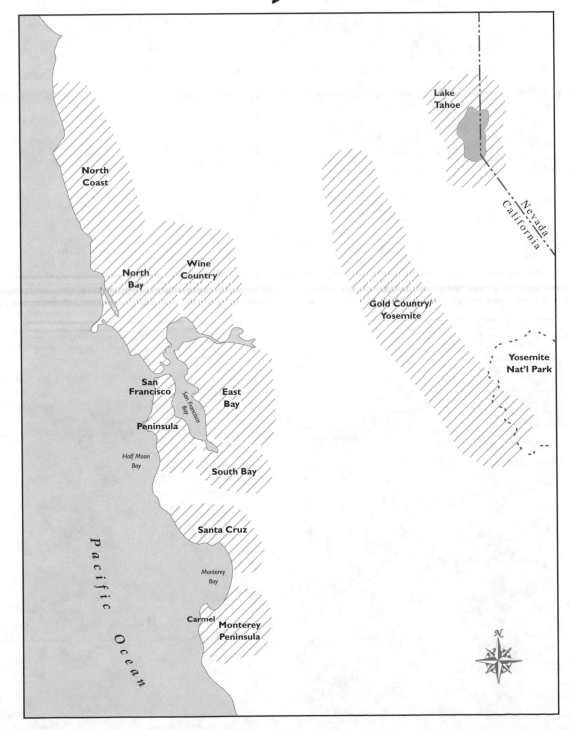

North Coast

North Bay

Wine Country

Lake Tahoe

Nevada
California

Gold Country/
Yosemite

Yosemite
Nat'l Park

San
Francisco

San Francisco Bay

East
Bay

Peninsula

Half Moon
Bay

South Bay

Santa Cruz

Monterey
Bay

Pacific Ocean

Carmel

Monterey
Peninsula

a personal note

If you're like us, you love to have really good information at your fingertips—the kind that's intelligently compiled, easy to use, and most of all, reliable.

But no matter how hard we've tried to make the information in this book completely accurate, it isn't. Facilities give us incorrect facts and figures, change ownership or management, revamp their pricing and policies and sometimes go out of business. Truth is, things in the event business can turn upside down overnight.

So how can you make sure that you're getting correct information?
It's simple:

- Bring your book with you when you hunt for locations.

- When you contact a location, show or read the information in *Here Comes The Guide* to the facility's representative to verify that it's still current.

- If it isn't, jot down the new information in your book.

- Reconfirm everything before you sign any contract!

If you use our guidebook, check the facts and get it in writing, you can't go wrong!

preface

When I graduated from college, I thought I'd never have to do another endless research project again. Boy was I wrong. Compared to looking for a place to get married, term papers were a piece of cake. I began my quest optimistically enough, but after a couple of days of frantic and fruitless networking (my wedding date was a mere three months down the road!), the enormity of my task started to sink in. It had taken me 33 years to find the right guy, and it was beginning to look like it might take an equally long time to find the right place.

Going into high gear, I reached out and touched just about everyone I knew along with quite a few total strangers. Friends and friends of friends didn't have any recommendations that suited our particular needs, and although wedding consultants had information, they were reluctant to part with their lists of sites unless I hired them to plan my wedding. I even called some caterers, florists and cake makers, but they were usually too busy to give me in-depth descriptions of places over the phone. Some chambers of commerce had organized wedding location lists ready to mail out; others had nothing and knew nothing.

After days of phoning, all I had was a patchwork quilt of information. I still hadn't found *the* place, and finally had to face the painful truth: there was no central resource or comprehensive, detailed list. I became anxious. With a full-time job I was hardly free to conduct an exhaustive search, and I realized that I would never be able to find out about the vast majority of interesting or unusual wedding sites, let alone thoroughly evaluate them! My frustration was exacerbated by the fact that it was August and the wedding date in October was drawing closer with each passing day.

As luck would have it, my sister mentioned that her hairdresser had gotten married on a yacht in San Francisco Bay. Hallelujah! That's it! I cried. What a great idea! I'd never even thought about a floating wedding and had no idea you could do such a thing.

We got married on a hot, sunny day behind Angel Island in San Francisco Bay. The captain performed the ceremony on the bow, and afterwards the yacht tooted its horn, the crew let loose multi-colored balloons, and a "just married" sign was thrown over the stern. As we swept past Alcatraz Island, Sausalito and the Golden Gate and Bay Bridges, our guests relaxed in the sun, enjoying drinks and hors d'oeuvres. What a wonderful day! Even my parents' friends had a great time, and wrote us after the wedding to let us know how much they'd loved their outing on the water.

Serendipity was largely responsible for making my wedding memorable, but you don't have to rely on luck. I wrote *Here Comes The Guide* so that others wouldn't have to experience what I went through, and I hope it makes your search for the perfect location an easy and painless one. Doug and I have been married almost twelve years now, but we wish we could do it all over again. It was the place that made all the difference.

Lynn Broadwell

introduction

Little did we know when we wrote *Here Comes The Guide, Northern California* in 1989 that it would engender such an overwhelming response from our readers. The first edition sold out in less than a year (long before expected), and as the public besieged bookstores—and kept our phones ringing with urgent requests for *The Guide*—we hustled to get the second edition in print to satisfy the demand.

So what makes this book so popular? Unlike many other publications that don't do much more than print glossy color ads, we've done all your homework for you.

■ We present comprehensive, solid information.

A full description and line drawing of each facility, along with data about fees, capacities and services enables you to examine hundreds of options and select potential sites before you ever walk out your front door. This is a reference book so we don't expect you to read it from cover to cover, but many of our readers tell us they've used *Here Comes The Guide* until it's pretty dog-eared. We've worked hard to make the information not only useful and accurate, but fun to read.

We've tried to anticipate the questions you'd ask and provide the kind of details that are important for decision-making. And we've tried to present a wide selection of facilities so that if the most popular are already booked (especially June through October), you'll still have a long list of wonderful locations from which to choose. This book is intended to open your eyes to a variety of new possibilities—delightful places that you might not have found on your own and event ideas that you might never have considered. And no matter what kind of place you finally select, *Here Comes The Guide* is designed to make all your planning efforts a lot easier.

■ This book will cut your search time by 90%.

One of the greatest benefits of using *Here Comes The Guide* is the enormous amount of time you'll save. Instead of having to call dozens of facilities and ask the same questions over and over again, you can look up all the answers in *The Guide*. Another time-saving feature is the find-it-fast chart at the front of the book. It displays most of the important information about each facility (city, capacity, main services and restrictions) in an easy-to-read matrix. You can breeze through all of the entries, pre-select those sites that match your criteria, and read the full descriptions about them later in the book.

■ We screen all our locations.

It's taken more than nine years to compile a list of over 1,200 Northern California locations and pare it down to those that offer the best ambiance, service and/or value. We personally reviewed each property in *Here Comes The Guide,* sending a professional writer to each site to make sure it met our criteria. And just in case you think that we accept every event site that comes our way, we don't. We actually turn down dozens of locations that want to be included because they don't satisfy our requirements.

■ **We're experienced.**

We've been writing and publishing the Northern California version of *Here Comes The Guide* since 1989—this is our sixth edition—so we've got a lot of experience evaluating event locations. We get calls every week from new properties that want to be in our publications, and hundreds of calls a year from people who already have *Here Comes The Guide* but want additional information about locations and services.

This publication has become the essential resource for anybody planning a wedding, party, bar mitzvah, business function—or just about any kind of event—in Northern California. *Here Comes The Guide* offers extraordinary sites for everybody and every pocketbook, and practical tips and step-by-step guidance for reviewing, selecting and evaluating both event sites and services. And since detailed information about fees, deposits and in-house catering costs are included, you can comparison shop and save money, too.

■ **Our service directory is unique—we've handpicked everyone for you!**

We know how difficult it can be to locate a first-rate caterer, DJ, florist, cake maker or photographer. How can you be sure they're really good at what they do? If they're honest and reliable? Unless you know the service provider personally or have a recommendation from a friend, you really can't. That's where we come in.

We've developed a *screened* service directory at the back of this guide in order to bring you the best services we could find, and it has grown over the years as vendors have informally discovered us, our publications and our screening process. Service providers *love* the fact that we thoroughly check them out and so do our readers. It takes a long time to get familiar with the best services available in a given region, and we're incredibly picky. The screening process is also quite time-consuming. We require 20 to 30 professional trade references to qualify each of these service providers for our publication. We call every reference and talk to them at length because we want to make sure that the people we recommend are not only technically competent, but professional, personable and serious about providing good service.

Unlike other publications that take ad dollars indiscriminately, we don't allow vendors to advertise with us until they've received great reviews from other event professionals. When you ask up to 30 people in the industry about the quality of someone's product or service, ultimately you figure out who's good and who's not. Given the enormous amount of work we've done to qualify our advertisers, we feel very confident about giving a personal endorsement to each and every one of them. We think you'll save lots of time and aggravation if you call these folks *before* you search through the Yellow Pages or elsewhere. These service providers are not just good—they're the best in the business.

■ **If you can't find the perfect spot in *Here Comes The Guide*...**

Check out our web site at www.herecomestheguide.com. You'll not only have access to *Here Comes The Guide* online, but will be able to search for special event sites and services on our database. We've set it up so you can search for locations by various criteria: city, site type, capacity, view, etc., and event professionals by service category.

As time goes on we'll be adding more and more event locations and services that are not featured in the book.

■ Create a memorable event with a memorable place.

Don't pick a place that's just so-so when you can select one that's a cut above. Take advantage of the fact that Northern California is home to some of the most outstanding facilities in the United States. There are so many locations that offer exceptional environments, top-notch cuisine and professional event services, you're sure to find a special place that suits your needs. So grab this guide and explore! Whatever your tastes, whether you're a newcomer or native to this region, we hope you'll find this an entertaining, comprehensive and indispensable guide.

understanding our information

Each location description in *Here Comes The Guide* follows the same format. To help you understand the information presented, we've provided an explanation of the main headings in the same order as they appear.

■ Description

Once you've selected a geographical area and you're clear about your needs, then thoroughly review all the sites listed in your area of preference. If you're pressed for time, you can read through the *find-it-fast* chart first to preview facilities for geographical location, capacity and other critical factors. Then, you can forge ahead to the main body of *Here Comes The Guide* and read the descriptions of *only* those sites that seem to be a good fit, based on your preliminary review. If a facility still appeals to you after you've read the description, mark it with a ✔ and then move on to capacity, etc.

■ Ceremony Capacity

Standing and seated capacities are included for ceremonies since these numbers may be totally different than the corresponding numbers for receptions.

■ Reception Capacity

By now you should have a rough idea of how many people will be attending. If not, you may be in trouble, since many facilities want a deposit based on an estimated headcount. Look at the capacity figures for each event location. Seated or sit-down capacity refers to guests seated at tables. Standing capacity refers to a function where the majority of guests are not seated, such as a champagne/hors d'oeuvres reception. Put a ✔ next to those facilities that are compatible with your guest count. If you're planning well in advance and don't have your guest list whittled down yet, then you'll just have to estimate and refine the count as the date draws near. There is a world of difference in cost and planning effort between an intimate party of 60 and a large wedding with over 200 guests. Pin down your numbers as soon as you can.

■ Meeting Capacity

We've highlighted spaces which can accommodate meetings and have listed the number of participants each space can hold. Seating configurations are: *theater-style* (auditorium row seating, with chairs arranged closely together), *classroom-style* (an organized table-and-chair arrangement, usually in rows) and *conference-style* (seating around tables).

■ Fees and Deposits

We've tried to make the information regarding costs as accurate as possible. Where we haven't mentioned the price, it may be because the facility's fee schedule was either changing at time of publication or too complicated to fit into our format. Some facilities want the flexibility to negotiate prices, and prefer not to state them until they know exactly what kind of function you have in mind.

> **Look at the information regarding fees and deposits and remember that these figures change regularly and usually in one direction—up!**

It's a good idea to confirm the information in *Here Comes The Guide* with the facility you're calling, just to make sure it's still valid. If you're planning far in advance, anticipate price increases by the time your function occurs. Once you're definite about your location, try to lock in your fees in a contract, protecting yourself from possible rate increases later. Make sure you ask about every service provided and are clear about all of the extras that can really add up. Facilities may charge you for tables, chairs, linens, plateware and silverware, glassware and additional hours for starters. Don't be surprised to see tax and service charges in fixed amounts applied to the total bill if the facility provides restaurant or catering services. Although it may seem redundant to include the phrase "tax and service charges are additional" in each entry, we find that most people forget (or just don't want to accept the painful reality) that 23%–28% will be applied to the food and beverage total.

Sometimes a deposit is non-refundable—a fact you'll definitely want to know if the deposit is a large percentage of the total bill. And even if it's refundable, you still need to read the cancellation policy thoroughly. Also make sure you understand the policies which will ensure you get your cleaning and security deposit returned in full and again, get everything in writing.

Food costs vary considerably. Carefully plan your menu with the caterer, event consultant or chef. Depending on the style of service and the type of food being served, your total food bill will vary dramatically—even if the meal is provided by the same caterer. Expect a multi-course seated meal to be the most expensive part of your event.

Alcohol is expensive, too, and you may be restricted in what you can serve and who can serve it. A facility may not allow you to bring your own alcoholic beverages, and if it does, it may limit you to wine or champagne. Many places discourage you from bringing your own (BYO) by charging an exorbitant corkage fee to remove the cork and pour. Other places have limited permits which don't allow them to serve alcohol or restrict them from serving certain kinds; some will let you or the caterer serve alcohol, others will require someone with a license. Make sure you know what's allowed. Decide what your budget is for alcohol and determine what types you're able to provide. And keep in mind that the catering fees you are quoted rarely include the cost of alcohol. A comment about trends in alcohol consumption is warranted: people are drinking less wine and hard alcohol than ever before and consumption of mineral water is on the rise; if you provide the alcohol, make sure you keep your purchase receipts so you can return any unopened bottles.

So how much will this event cost? Facility deposits are usually not large, but sometimes the rental fees plus food and beverage services can add up to $30,000 or more, depending on the site and number of guests. Be sure you have a sensible handle on your budget and read all the fine print before you sign any contract.

■ Availability

Some facilities are available 7am to 2am; others offer very limited "windows." If you'd like to save some money, consider a weekday or weeknight reception, or think about having your event in the off season (November, or January through March). Even the most sought-after places have openings midweek and during non-peak months—and at reduced costs. Facilities want your business and are more likely to negotiate terms and prices if they have nothing else scheduled. Again, read all the fine print carefully and ✔ those facilities that have time slots that meet your needs. If the date you have in mind is already booked, it doesn't hurt to ask if someone actually confirmed that date by paying a deposit or signing a contract. If they haven't, you may be in luck.

■ Services/Amenities and Restrictions

Most facilities provide something in the way of services and many have limitations that may affect your function. For instance, they may not allow you to have amplified music outdoors or bring your own caterer.

We've attempted to give you a brief description of what each location has to offer and what is restricted. Because of space limitations, we've shortened words and developed a key to help you decipher our abbreviated notations. Please refer to the *Services/ Amenities* and *Restrictions* keys for an explanation. Once you're familiar with our notation style, you'll be able to read through all the data outlined at the bottom of each entry and put a ✔ next to each facility that meets your requirements.

Selecting an Event Location:

Before you jump into the facility descriptions in *Here Comes The Guide,* identify what kind of celebration you want and establish selection criteria early. Here are some basics:

■ Is Your Site Geographically Desirable?

Your first big decision is to select a location that will make geographical sense to you, your family and the majority of your guests. Most people have special events close to home or office, so there's not much to consider. But if you pick a spot out of town, you need to think about the logistics of getting everyone to your event site.

■ Special Considerations in Northern California

Guests may be traveling a considerable distance by car to get to your party destination. Considering the Northern California freeway system and traffic congestion, you'll save them lots of time and trouble if you provide, along with the invitation, specific directions on a separate map drawn to scale. Include symbols indicating directions (north, south, etc.) and the names of the appropriate off ramps. If you're not sure about exits, landmarks or street names, take a dry run of the route to make sure everything on your map is accurate and easy to follow. And, if your function occurs after dark, do the test drive at night so you can note well-lit landmarks that will prevent your guests from getting lost—both coming to your event and going home.

If you're having a Friday evening event, take commuters into account, especially if your event site is in an area that gets bumper-to-bumper traffic. Plan to have your event after 7pm when freeways are less congested.

Even if you have few constraints when picking a location for your event, it's still worth considering the total driving time to and from your destination. When it's over two hours, an overnight stay may be necessary, and you may be limited to a Saturday night event, since your nearest and dearest won't be able to spend hours on the road during the week. If you have guests arriving by plane, it's certainly helpful if there's an airport nearby, and if your coworkers, friends or family enjoy drinking, try to house them close to the event site.

There's no reason why you can't contemplate a special event in a wine cave in Calistoga or in the Santa Cruz Mountains. Just remember that the further out you go, the more time it will take to choreograph your event—and you may end up having to delegate the details of party planning to someone else.

■ Budget

You'd think that it's an obvious consideration, but you'd be surprised how many people, especially brides and grooms, are unrealistic about what they can afford. Part of the problem is that most people aren't very experienced with event budgeting and don't know how to estimate what locations, products and services will ultimately cost.

In the early planning stages it's a good idea to talk to a professional event planner or wedding consultant to get a sense of what's feasible and what's not. You don't have to make a big financial or time commitment to use a professional; most will assist you on an hourly basis for a nuts and bolts session to determine priorities and to assign costs to items on your wish list.

Part of being realistic involves some simple arithmetic. For instance, the couple who has $5,000 dollars for 250 guests should know that $20 per guest won't go very far. Tax and gratuity combined can consume an average of 25% of the food and beverage budget (the range is 22% to 28%). If you subtract that 25% from $20, you have $15 left. If you also serve alcohol at $6/person, you're down to $9/person for food. That's not enough for a seated meal, let alone location rental fees, band, flowers, printed invitations, etc.

Before you make any major decisions or commit any of your funds for specific items, take a serious look at your total budget and make sure it can cover all your anticipated expenses. If it can't, it's time to make some hard decisions. If you have a very large guest list and a small pocketbook, you may need to shorten the list or cut back on some of the amenities you want to include. No matter who foots the bill, be advised that doing the homework here really counts. Pin down your costs at the beginning of the planning stage and get all estimates in writing.

■ Style

Do you know what kind of event you want? Will it be a formal or informal affair, a traditional wedding or an innovative party? Will it be held at night or during the day, indoors or outdoors? You can set the ambiance or tone of your function by selecting the right location, but know what you want before you start looking at locations or the sheer number of options will be overwhelming.

■ Guest Count

How many people are anticipated? Many facilities want a rough estimate 60 to 90 days in advance of your function—and they'll want a deposit based on the figure you give them. A confirmed guest count or guarantee is usually required 72 hours prior to the event. It's important to know what the numbers are early on in order to plan your budget and select the right ceremony or reception spot.

It's also important to ensure that the guest count you give the facility *before* your event doesn't change *during* your event. Believe it or not, it's possible to have more people at your reception than you expected. How? Some folks who did not bother to RSVP may decide to show up anyway. In one case we know of, the parents of the bride got an additional bill for $1,200 on the event day because there were 30 "surprise" guests beyond the guest count guarantee who were wined and dined. To prevent this from happening to you—especially if you're having a large reception where it's hard to keep track of all the guests—it's a good idea to phone everyone who did *not* RSVP. Let them know as politely as possible that you will need to have their response by a given date to finalize food and beverage totals.

■ Seasonal Differences

Northern California, for all its (pardon the expression) faults, has got some great advantages weather-wise. Outdoor special events, ceremonies and receptions can take place throughout most of the year and, from September to November, you can anticipate sunny skies and warm climes. However, when the mercury rises in areas at a distance from the coast, watch out. A canopy or tables with umbrellas are essential for screening the sun. In fact, you should ask each facility manager about the sun's direction and intensity with respect to the time of day and month your event will take place. Guests will be uncomfortable facing into the sun during a ceremony, and white walls and enclosed areas bounce light around and can hold in heat. If your event is scheduled for midday in July, for example, include a note on your location map to bring sunglasses, hat or sunscreen. If you also mention words like "poolside," "yacht deck" or "lawn seating" on the map, it will help guests know how to dress. In summer, you might want to consider an evening rather than a midday celebration. Not only is the air cooler, but you may also get an extra bonus—a glorious sunset.

If you're arranging an outdoor party November through April, or in the foothills or mountain areas, expect cooler weather and prepare a contingency plan. Despite our region's favorable Mediterranean climate, it has rained in May, June and July, so consider access to an inside space or a tent.

■ Special Requirements

Sometimes, places have strict rules and regulations. If most of your guests smoke, then pick a location that doesn't restrict smoking. If alcohol is going to be consumed, make sure it's allowed and find out if bar service needs to be licensed. If dancing and a big band are critical, then limit yourself to those locations that can accommodate them and the accompanying decibels. Do you have children, seniors or disabled guests, vegetarians or folks who want Kosher food on your list? If so, you need to plan for them, too. It's essential that you identify the special factors that are important for your event before you sign a contract.

■ Locking in Your Event Date

Let's say it's the first day of your hunt for the perfect spot, and the second place you see is an enchanting garden that happens to be available on the date you want. You really like it but, since you've only seen two locations, you're not 100% sure that this is *the* place. No problem. You decide to keep your options open by making a tentative reservation. The site coordinator dutifully pencils your name into her schedule book and says congratulations. You say thanks, we have a few more places (like 25) to check out, but his one looks terrific. Then off you go, secure in the knowledge that if none of the other sites you visit pans out, you still have this lovely garden waiting for you.

The nightmare begins a couple of weeks or perhaps months down the road when you've finished comparison shopping and call back the first place you liked to finalize the details. So sorry, the coordinator says. We gave away your date because a) oops, one of the other gals who works here erased your name by mistake (after all, it was only *penciled* in), b) we didn't hear back from you soon enough, or c) you never confirmed your reservation with a deposit.

For the tiniest instant you picture yourself inflicting bodily harm on the coordinator or at least slapping the facility with a lawsuit, but alas, there's really not much you can do. Whether a genuine mistake was made or the facility purposely gave your date to another, perhaps more lucrative party (this happens sometimes with hotels who'd rather book a big convention on your date than a little wedding), you're out of luck. To avoid the pain (and ensuing panic) of getting bumped, here's what we suggest: instead of just being penciled in, ask if you can write a refundable $100–250 check to hold the date for a limited time. If the person in charge is willing to do this but wants the full deposit up front (usually non-refundable), then you'll need to decide whether you can afford to lose the entire amount if you find a more appealing location later on. Once the coordinator or sales person takes your money, you're automatically harder to bump. Make sure you get a receipt which has the event date, year, time and space(s) reserved written on it, as well as the date your tentative reservation runs out. Then, just to be on the safe side, check in with the facility weekly while you're considering other sites to prevent any possible "mistakes" from being made. When you finally do commit to a place, get a signed contract or at least a confirmation letter. If you don't receive written confirmation within a week, hound the coordinator until you get it, even if you have to drive to the sales office and stand there until they hand it over to you. And even after you've plunked down your money and have a letter and/or contract securing your date, call the coordinator every other month to reconfirm your reservation. It pays to stay on top of this, no matter how locked in you think you are.

■ Parking

Parking is seldom a critical factor if you get married outside an urban area, but make sure you know how it's going to be handled if you're planning a party in a congested area such as downtown San Francisco, San Jose or Berkeley.

A map is a handy supplement to any invitation, and there's usually enough room on it to indicate how and where vehicles should be parked. Depending on the location, you may want to add a note suggesting carpooling or mention that a shuttle service or valet parking is provided. If there's a fee for parking, identify the anticipated cost per car and where the entry points are to the nearest parking lots. The last thing you want are surprised and disgruntled guests who can't find a place to stash their cars, or who are shocked at the $20 to $40 parking tab.

■ Professional Help

If you're a busy person with limited time to plan and execute a party, pick a facility that offers complete coordination services, from catering and flowers to decorations and music. Or better yet, hire a professional event or wedding consultant. Either way, you'll make your life considerably easier by having someone else handle the details.

■ Food and Alcohol Quality

Food and alcohol account for the greatest portion of the an event's budget; consequently, food and beverage selections are a big deal. Given the amount of money you will spend on this category alone, you should be concerned about the type, quantity and quality of what you eat and drink. If in-house catering is provided, we suggest you sample different menu options prior to paying a facility deposit. If you'd like to see how a facility handles food setup and presentation, ask the caterer to arrange a visit to someone else's party about a half hour before it starts. It's wise to taste wines and beers in advance, and be very specific about hard alcohol selections.

■ Hidden Costs

This may come as a surprise, but not all services and event equipment are covered in the rental fee, and some facilities hide the *true* cost of renting their space by having a low rental fee. It's possible to get nickeled and dimed for all the extras: tables, chairs, linens, glassware, valet service and so forth. You can also end up paying more than you expected for security and cleanup. All these additional charges can really add up, so save yourself a big headache by understanding exactly what's included in the rental fee and what's not before you sign any contract.

> ■ **The important point is that if you know what kind of event you want, and are clear about your budget, your search will be made faster and easier.**
>
> ■ **If you try to pick a location before you've made basic decisions, selection will be a struggle and it will take longer to find a spot that will make you happy.**

previewing a facility

If you plan to visit a lot of locations, here are some handy tips:

■ Make Appointments

If you reviewed a site description and liked what you read, then we recommend you make an appointment to see that location, rather than just driving by. Sometimes an unremarkable-looking building will surprise you with a secluded garden or courtyard that's hidden from the street. And sometimes the opposite is true—a stunning facade will attract you, but the interior doesn't appeal to your taste.

As you've probably discovered, we've withheld the addresses of properties that are privately owned or ones that discourage prospective clients from driving by. Should you happen to know where any of these facilities are located, we urge you to respect the owner's or manager's wishes, and resist the temptation to drop in for a visit without an appointment.

When you do call for an appointment, don't forget to ask for cross streets; some places are difficult to find without them. Try to cluster your visits so that you can easily drive from one place to another without backtracking. Get a good, detailed street map of the area, and before you go to the sites, identify each one on the map in red or another contrasting color. Schedule at least 30 minutes per facility and leave ample driving time between stops. You want to be efficient, but don't over-schedule yourself. It's best to view places when you're fresh. If you've reached your saturation point after five visits and you still have several more to go, those last places might get a bad review simply because you're looking at them through bleary eyes and can't absorb any more information. While you want to accomplish as much as you can in as brief a time as possible, you will ultimately do yourself a disservice if your judgment is clouded by fatigue.

When you're previewing a facility, make sure to check out the restrooms, dance floor and kitchen facilities. Sometimes you can get so carried away by a great view or an extraordinary gold ceiling, it's easy to overlook the fact that there's no place for a band!

■ Be Organized

Whether you're visiting a handful of facilities or canvassing an entire region, be organized. After you've decided on your requirements, selected the facilities you want to see and arranged a workable visiting schedule, there are still things you can do to make this process easy on yourself.

● **Bring along *Here Comes The Guide.*** Even though our sixth edition is pretty hefty, it's a good idea to take it with you while you're visiting locations. We've listed the street address for each site, and our illustrations will make it easier to identify the buildings you're planning to see. And if you bring the book into the facilities with you, you can double check the information in the book with the site representative and jot down changes on the appropriate page.

- **Bring a camera.** Take pictures of whatever you want to recall about a place—the front exterior, the garden, etc. A video camera is ideal because you can record the location and your thoughts about it simultaneously. A Polaroid is also wonderful because it gives you instant "memories." Just remember to bring enough film, and write the name of each facility on the back of the photo. If you're using a 35mm camera, we recommend asa 200 print film which is "fast" enough to take most interior shots. Since you won't be able to write the names of places on these pictures until after they're developed, you might want to keep a log of the shots you take. You'd be surprised how easy it is to confuse various sites when you've got a dozen of them competing for space in your mind and you can't remember which garden or dining room corresponds to which place.

- **Bring a tape recorder** if you're not videotaping everything. During or after each visit, quickly record your likes, dislikes and any other observations. You can write up your notes when you have more time. If you don't have a recorder, jot down your comments in *Here Comes The Guide* itself or in a notebook. Pay attention not only to the physical surroundings, but to how you're treated by the manager, the owner or the event coordinator. No matter how you do it, thorough note-taking is crucial if you want to be able to adequately evaluate everything you have seen and heard.

- **File everything.** Many facilities will provide you with pamphlets, menus, rate charts and other materials. One good way to handle the deluge is to put each facility's paperwork in a 9" x 12" manila envelope with its name on it. A binder with plastic pocket inserts is also handy. The idea is to avoid having to sort through a pile of things later. You want to keep your notes, photos and handouts clearly identified and easily accessible.

- **Bring snacks.** Driving from place to place can make you hungry and thirsty. If you take a little something to eat, you can munch en route and keep your energy level up.

- **Bring a checkbook or credit card.** Some of the more attractive event venues book a year to eighteen months in advance. If you actually fall in love with a location, and your date is available, plunk down a deposit to hold the date.

Working with a facility

■ Confirm All the Details

> **When you make the initial phone call, confirm that the information presented in *Here Comes The Guide* is still valid.**

We've asked each site to give us current information, but we know from long experience that facilities can change their prices and policies overnight. Show or read the information in our book to the site's representative, and have him or her inform you of any changes. If there have been significant increases in fees or new restrictions that you can't live with, cross the place off your list and move on. If the facility is still a contender, request a tour.

Once you have determined that the physical elements of the place suit you, it's time to discuss details. Ask about services and amenities or fees that may not be listed in the book and make a note of them. Outline your plans to the representative and make sure that the facility can accommodate your particular needs. If you don't want to handle all the details yourself, find out what the facility is willing and able to do, and if there will be an additional cost for their assistance. Facilities often provide planning services for little or no extra charge. If other in-house services are offered, such as flowers or wedding cakes, you need to inquire about the quality of each service provider and whether or not substitutions can be made. If you want to use your own vendors, find out if the facility will charge you an extra fee.

■ The Importance of Rapport

Another factor to consider is your rapport with the person(s) you are working with. Are you comfortable? Do they listen well and respond to your questions directly? Do they inspire trust and confidence? Are they warm and enthusiastic or cold, businesslike and aloof? If you have doubts, you need to resolve them before embarking on a working relationship with these folks—no matter how wonderful the facility itself is. Discuss your feelings with them, and if you're still not completely satisfied, get references and call them. If at the end of this process you still have lingering concerns, you may want to eliminate the facility from your list even though it seems perfect in every other way.

Working with professionals

■ Hiring a Caterer: Get References and Look for Professionalism

If you're selecting your own caterer, don't just pick one at random out of the Yellow Pages. Get references from friends and acquaintances or, better yet, call the caterers listed in the *Here Comes The Guide* service directory. We've thoroughly screened these companies and can assure you that they're in the top 5% of the industry in terms of quality and service. We keep all of their references on file, so you can call us and ask questions about them.

Every caterer is different. Some offer only preset menus while others will help you create your own. Prices and menus vary enormously, so know what you want and what you can spend. After you've talked to several caterers and have decided which ones to seriously consider, get references for each one and call them. Ask not only about the quality of the food, but about the ease of working with a given caterer. You'll want to know if the caterer is professional—fully prepared and equipped, punctual and organized. You may also want to know if the caterer is licensed, if he/she has a kitchen approved by the Department of Health, where the food is prepared, or if he or she carries workmen's compensation and liability insurance. Although this level of inquiry may seem unnecessary, responses to these questions will give you a more complete picture of how a caterer runs his or her business, and will help you determine which caterer is best suited for your event.

■ Facility Requirements for Caterers

Facilities often have specific requirements regarding caterers—they may have to be licensed and bonded, out by 11pm or fastidiously clean. Before you hire a caterer, make sure that he or she is compatible with your site. In fact, even if the facility does not require it, it's a good idea to have your caterer visit the place in advance to become familiar with any special circumstances or problems that might come up. You'll notice throughout *Here Comes The Guide* the words "provided" or "preferred" after the word *Catering*. Sites that have an exclusive caterer or only permit you to select from a preferred list do so because each wants to eliminate most of the risks involved in having a caterer on the premises who is not accustomed to working in that environment. Exclusive or preferred caterers have achieved their exalted status because they either provide consistently good services or they won the catering contract when it went out to bid. Whether you're working with one of your facility's choices or your own, make sure that your contract includes everything you have agreed on before you sign it.

■ Working with an Event Planner, Wedding Coordinator or Consultant

Opting to hire a professional planner may be a wise choice. A good consultant will ask all the right questions, determine exactly what you need, and take care of as much or as little of your affair as you want. If you'd like to feel like a guest at your own event, have the consultant manage everything, including orchestrating the day of the event. If you only want some advice and structure, hire a planner on a meeting-by-meeting basis.

Most of the principles used in selecting a caterer apply to hiring an event coordinator. Try to get suggestions from friends or facilities, follow up on references the consultants give you, compare service fees and make sure you and the consultant are compatible. The range of professionalism and experience varies greatly, so it really is to your advantage to investigate consultants' track records. Again, once you've found someone who can accommodate you, get everything in writing so that there won't be any misunderstandings down the road. Although engaging someone to "manage" your event can be a godsend, it can also be problematic if you turn the entire decision-making process over to them. Don't forget that it's your party, and no one else should decide what's right for you.

insurance considerations

Nowadays, if someone gets injured at an event or something is damaged at or near the event site, it's likely that someone will be sued. In order to protect themselves and spread the risk among all parties involved, facilities have begun to require additional insurance and/or proof of insurance from service professionals and their clients.

Event sites and service professionals (such as caterers) are very aware of their potential liability and all have coverage of one kind or another. Five years ago, less than 10% of the facilities we represented required the "renter" to obtain extra insurance coverage. That figure has more than doubled to 24.3% of our Southern California event sites, and up to 49.7% of our Northern California sites. That's a remarkable increase! This trend will probably continue, and we expect that those percentages will go much higher. The bottom line is that a large chunk of the properties we represent will require *you,* the renter, to get extra insurance.

What's funny (or not so funny) is that as more and more event sites require extra liability and/ or a certificate of insurance, fewer insurance companies are willing to issue either one, even if you're covered under a homeowner's policy. At this point, insurance carriers don't want to attach extra clauses to your policy to increase coverage for a single event, and most, if not all companies, are unwilling to add the event site's name to your existing policy as an additional insured.

Don't despair. Even though it's hard to come by, you *can* get extra insurance for a specified period of time, and it's relatively inexpensive.

■ Obtaining Extra Insurance

● **The first thing to do is read your rental contract carefully.** Make sure you understand exactly *what's* required and *when* it's required. Most facilities want $1,000,000–2,000,000 in extra liability coverage. If you don't pay attention to the insurance clauses early in the game, you'll have to play catch-up at the last moment, frantically trying to locate a carrier who will issue you additional insurance. And, if you don't supply the certificate to the facility *on time,* you may run the risk of forfeiting your event site altogether.

● **The second thing is to ask your event site's representative if the site has an insurance policy through which you can purchase the required extra coverage.** If the answer is yes, then consider purchasing it—that's the easiest route (but not necessarily the best!). The facility's extra insurance coverage may not be the least expensive and it may not provide you with the best coverage. What you need to ask is: "If one of my guests or one of the professionals working at my event causes some damage to the premises or its contents, will this extra insurance cover it?" If the answer if yes, get it in writing.

● **The third thing, if the answer is no, is to find your own coverage.** Here are two options:

1) The most time-consuming alternative is the Yellow Pages. Look under insurance, and make lots of calls. There are companies (not many) that will issue insurance for your event, but they usually charge a $300 minimum. Prices vary as does coverage— so be a good consumer and ask lots of questions about what's covered and what isn't.

2) The easiest option is to call **1-800-ENGAGED**. You'll reach **R.V. Nuccio & Associates, Inc.**, a specialty insurer of special events who can send you a brochure detailing what's offered. Rob Nuccio's coverage is underwritten by Fireman's Fund, and it's the only company in the United States we know of that offers a package policy for the following items:

- **Cancellation or postponement due to:** weather, damage to the facility, sickness, failure-to-show of the caterer or officiant, financial reasons, etc. (change of heart is not covered)

- **Photography or videography:** failure of the professional to appear, loss of original negatives, etc.

- **Lost, stolen or damaged gifts**

- **Lost, stolen or damaged equipment rentals**

- **Lost, stolen or damaged bridal gown or other special attire**

- **Lost, stolen or damaged jewelry**

- **Personal liability and additional coverage**

- **Medical payments for injuries incurred during the event**

Coverage starts at $195 per event and goes up—the total cost will depend on what you want; many of the above items are optional.

Rob offers the best deal we've found, and this is the first time we've made information about him and his company public. So don't be shy—let us know whether you're happy with his services. Call us. We'd love to get your feedback.

■ It Can't Happen To Me

Don't be lulled into the notion that an event disaster can't happen to you. It could rain when you least expect it. Or your well-intentioned aunt might melt your wedding dress while ironing out a few wrinkles. Wouldn't it be nice to know your dress, wedding photos, equipment rentals and gifts are covered? Naturally, a New Year's Eve party or a high school prom night is riskier than a wedding, but we could tell you stories of upscale parties where something did happen and a lawsuit resulted.

So even if extra insurance is not required, you may still want to consider additional coverage, especially if alcohol is being served. *You are the best predictor of your guests' behavior.* If you plan on having a wild, wonderful event, a little additional insurance could be a good thing.

■ Do Your Part

If you're wondering why we're including a brief item about recycling in a book like *Here Comes The Guide*, it's because parties and special events often generate recyclable materials and leftover food that the bride and groom don't want to take home. Nowadays, you and the caterer can feel good by donating the excess, and recycling plastic bottles, glass, metal and paper. An added benefit is that food donations are tax deductible for either you or the caterer. And, if you recycle, the cost for extra garbage containers (bins) can be eliminated or reduced.

Food donations are distributed to teenage drop-in centers, youth shelters, alcoholic treatment centers, AIDS hospices, senior centers and refugee centers throughout the region. You should also know that a 1989 state law protects the donor from liability.

Your packaged food can be picked up the day of the event or brought back to the caterer's kitchen to be picked up later on. Place food in clean plastic bags, plastic containers or boxes. Perishables should be refrigerated; other recyclable materials must be separated. Food must also be edible—if dressing has been poured over a salad, for example, it probably won't be worth eating the next day.

To recycle, call your local recycling center to arrange a pickup. To make a donation, look through your phone book to find a local Food Bank or call the following organizations to make advance arrangements.

- **San Francisco**

Food Runners	(415) 929-1866
Food Bank	(415) 957-1076
Episcopal Sanctuary	(415) 957-1076

- **Berkeley**

Daily Bread Project	(510) 540-1250

- **Oakland**

Oakland Pot Luck	(510) 272-0414

- **Santa Cruz Area**

Second Harvest	(831) 722-7110

- **San Mateo/Santa Clara Counties**

Second Harvest	(650) 266-8866

- **Marin County**

Food Bank	(415) 883-1302

- **Sacramento**

Food Bank	(916) 452-3663
Loaves & Fishes	(916) 446-0874

key to terms

key: services/amenities

CATERING

provided: the facility provides catering • *provided, no BYO:* the facility arranges catering; you cannot bring in your own • *preferred list:* you must select your caterer from the facility's approved list • *provided or BYO:* the facility will arrange catering or you can select an outside caterer of your own • *BYO, licensed:* arrange for your own licensed caterer • *provided, or BYO buy-out required:* a fee will be charged to "buy out" the facility's preferred caterer if you wish to make your own arrangements

KITCHEN FACILITIES

ample or fully equipped: large and well-equipped with major appliances • *moderate:* medium-sized and utilitarian • *minimal:* small with limited equipment, may not have all basic appliances • *setup or prep only:* room for setup and food prep, but not enough space or utilities to cook food • *n/a:* not applicable because facility provides catering

TABLES & CHAIRS

some provided or *provided:* facility provides some or all of the tables and chairs • *BYO:* make arrangements to bring your own

LINENS, SILVER, ETC.

same as above

RESTROOMS

wheelchair accessible or *not wheelchair accessible*

DANCE FLOOR

yes: an area for dancing (hardwood floor, cement terrace, patio) is available • *CBA, extra charge:* you can arrange for a dance floor to be brought in for a fee

BRIDE'S & GROOM'S DRESSING AREA

yes: there is an area for changing • *no:* there's no area for changing • *limited:* smaller space not fully equipped as changing room • *CBA:* can be arranged

PARKING

descriptions are self explanatory; *CBA:* can be arranged

ACCOMMODATIONS

if overnight accommodations are available on site, the number of guest rooms is listed • *CBA:* the facility will arrange accommodations for you

TELEPHONE

restricted: calls made on the house phone must be local, collect or charged to a credit card • *guest phones:* private phones in guest rooms • *house phone:* central phone used by all guests • *emergency only:* self-explanatory

OUTDOOR NIGHT LIGHTING

yes: indicates that there is adequate light to conduct your event outdoors after dark • *access only* or *limited:* lighting is sufficient for access only

OUTDOOR COOKING FACILITIES

BBQ: the facility has a barbecue on the premises • *BBQ, CBA:* a barbecue can be arranged through the facility • *BYO BBQ:* make arrangements for your own barbecue • *n/a:* not applicable

CLEANUP

provided: facility takes care of cleanup • *caterer:* your caterer is responsible • *caterer or renter:* both you and/or your caterer are responsible for cleanup

VIEW

we've described what type of view is available for each facility • *no:* the facility has no views to speak of

MEETING EQUIPMENT

full range: facility has a full range of audio-visual equipment, including projectors, overhead screens, etc. • *no:* no equipment is available • *BYO:* bring your own meeting equipment • *CBA:* equipment can be arranged • *CBA, extra fee:* equipment can be arranged for an extra fee

OTHER

description of any service or amenity not included in above list

key: restrictions

ALCOHOL
provided, no BYO: the facility provides alcoholic beverages (for a fee) and does not permit you to bring your own • ***BYO:*** you can arrange for your own alcohol • ***corkage, $/bottle:*** if you bring your own alcohol, the facility charges a fee per bottle to remove the cork and pour • ***WCB only:*** *(or any combination of these three letters)* only wine, champagne and beer are permitted • ***licensed server:*** the server of alcohol must be licensed

SMOKING
allowed: smoking is permitted throughout the facility • ***outside only:*** smoking is not permitted inside the facility • ***not allowed:*** smoking is not permitted anywhere on the premises • ***designated areas:*** specific areas for smoking have been designated

MUSIC
Almost every facility allows acoustical music unless stated otherwise. Essentially, restrictions refer to amplified music. ***amplified OK:*** amplified music is acceptable without restriction • ***outside only:*** no amplified music allowed inside • ***inside only:*** no amplified music permitted outside • ***amplified OK with limits or restrictions:*** amplified music allowed but there are limits on volume, hours of play, type of instruments, etc.

WHEELCHAIR ACCESS
Accessibility is based on whether the event areas (not necessarily the restrooms) of a facility are wheelchair accessible or not. ***yes:*** the facility is accessible • ***limited:*** the facility is accessible but with difficulty (there may be a step at the entrance, for example, but all of the rooms are accessible) • ***no:*** the facility is not accessible

INSURANCE
Many facilities require that you purchase and show proof of some insurance coverage. The type and amount of insurance varies with the facility, and some facilities offer insurance for a minimal charge. ***required, certificate required or proof of insurance required:*** additional insurance is required • ***not required:*** no additional insurance is required • ***may be required:*** sometimes additional insurance is required

OTHER
decorations restricted: the facility limits the use of tape, nails, tacks, confetti or other decorations

how to
find it fast

finding it fast

■ **We know your time is valuable.**

If you don't have enough time to leisurely read through all the location descriptions, use this convenient chart. It lists each facility by region and city in alphabetical order, and highlights essential information for each one. This makes it easy to quickly identify the event locations that are most appropriate for you.

Once you've identified a handful of places that seem to meet your needs, read each *Here Comes The Guide* entry for more complete information.

■ **Target your area of geographical preference first.**

Pick the cities that are best for you, your family and guests, keeping in mind the location selection advice in the "Valuable Tips" section.

■ **Identify the facilities that fit your needs.**

Scan the columns, noting which features are essential to your event. If a site seems to offer what you need, put a check mark next to it or use color highlighters (you can copy the pages first if you don't want to write in the book). Since the page numbers are listed, you can easily look up the ones you've checked and read more about them. If you still need more information, call the facility.

■ **Remember, the find-it-fast section is not perfect.**

The purpose of this chart is to reduce your searching time. However, because the information presented is abbreviated, it won't be perfect. A bullet (•) in the **Amplified Music Restricted** column, for example, may mean that amplified music is not allowed, or it may only mean that you can't have it outside or after 10pm. To find out how the restriction will affect your party, *you have to read the full description*. The following is a brief explanation of the chart headings.

chart headings

MAXIMUM CAPACITY
These numbers represent the maximum seated and standing capacities of a facility's *largest* reception and ceremony spaces. So don't discount a facility because it has a maximum capacity of 2,000 when you've only got 200 people on your guest list—it may be able to comfortably accommodate your event in one of its smaller rooms. If a location fits all your other criteria but you're just not sure about the numbers, we suggest you read the full description.

INDOOR & OUTDOOR FACILITIES
Outdoor facilities include everything from a deck to acres of gardens, so you need to read the full description to get the complete picture.

CATERING PROVIDED & BYO CATERING
Provided means that the facility will cater your event or arrange to have it catered. BYO indicates that you can make arrangements for your own caterer. Some facilities will go either way.

ALCOHOL PROVIDED & BYO ALCOHOL
If you see a • in both the *Alcohol Provided* and *Alcohol BYO* columns, it means the facility can provide alcohol *and* they will also let you bring your own. Note that many facilities charge a corkage fee if you BYO. If there's a • in the *Alcohol Provided* column, but not in the *Alcohol BYO* column, you cannot bring your own alcohol. If there isn't a • in either column it means that alcohol is not allowed.

GUEST ROOMS AVAILABLE
This column is self explanatory.

WEDDING OR EVENT COORDINATION
Many facilities provide wedding planning and/or special event coordination, everything from catering to flowers and custom party favors. This service may be free or there may be an additional charge. Be sure to ask.

SMOKING RESTRICTED
Means no smoking or smoking in designated areas only.

WHEELCHAIR ACCESS RESTRICTED
Indicates access problems ranging from a single step into a building to total inaccessibility. It doesn't mean you *can't* get into a site—it just denotes some degree of difficulty. Sometimes the event spaces are accessible but the restrooms aren't, and occasionally the reverse is true.

AMPLIFIED MUSIC RESTRICTED

Means amplified music is not allowed or is permitted with inside/outside constraints and volume or time limits.

INSURANCE REQUIRED

You need to have insurance for your event and you may be required to show proof of insurance with a certificate.

find-it-fast section

Locations by Type and Special Characteristics
and the Find-It-Fast Chart

locations by type & characteristics

gardens & parks

churches, chapels & temples

golf & country clubs

private clubs

historic, old-world

mansions, estates & private homes

bay or ocean views

waterfront properties

restaurants

appealing or historic ballrooms

wineries

yachts & boats

museums & galleries

overnight accommodations

indoor seated capacity over 300

off-site caterers allowed

find-it-fast
chart

San Francisco

	Page	Max. Seated Capacity	Max. Standing Capacity	Max. Ceremony Capacity	Max. Meeting Capacity	Indoor Facilities	Outdoor Facilities	Catering Provided	BYO Catering	Alcohol Provided	BYO Alcohol	Guest Rooms Available	Event Coordination	Smoking Restricted	Handicap Access Restricted	Amplified Music Restricted	Insurance Required
1409 Sutter Mansion	58	120	250	90	80	•		•		•	•		•	•			
42 Degrees Jazz Supper Club	60	150	300	150	100	•	•	•		•			•	•			
Archbishop's Mansion	62	100	150	50	50	•		•	•	•	•	•		•	•	•	
Atrium	64	185	350	300	150	•	•	•		•			•				
California Culinary Academy	66	280	500	250	280	•		•		•			•	•	•		
Canterbury Hotel	68	175	250	150	250	•		•		•		•		•			
✓ Carnelian Room	70	800	2000	200	200	•		•		•	•		•	•			
Chateau Tivoli	72	25	75	40	40	•		•		•	•	•		•	•	•	•
City Club, The	74	220	600	200	220	•		•		•			•	•			
Cliff House, The	76	200	300	75	125	•	•	•		•	•			•	•		
Dalla Torre Ristorante	78	70	100	70	90	•		•		•				•	•		
Delancey Street	80	300	500	325	425	•	•	•		•			•	•		•	
✓ Fairmont Hotel, The	82	1,400	2,500	500	2,500	•	•	•		•		•	•	•			
✓ Ferryboat at Pier 3	84	500	600	250	500	•	•	•		•	•		•	•	•		
Galleria at the SF Design Center	86	970	1,600	200	970	•			•				•				•
Gatewood-Keane Mansion	88	50	100	50	75	•		•		•	•		•	•	•	•	•
Grand Cafe and the Hotel Monaco	90	150	300	175	200	•		•		•		•	•	•		•	
Grand Hyatt San Francisco	92	700	1,000	700	1,000	•		•		•	•	•	•	•			
Great American Music Hall	94	350	500	350	250	•		•	•	•			•	•			•
Greens	96	150	200	200	—	•		•		•			•				
Haas-Lilienthal House	98	90	150	80	90	•		•			•			•	•	•	•
Hamlin Mansion	100	210	275	100	—	•		•			•	•		•	•		•
Hard Rock Cafe	102	180	350	—	75	•		•		•			•	•			
Hornblower Cruises & Events	104	740	900	350	350	•	•	•		•	•		•	•	•		
Hotel Majestic	106	120	180	120	100	•		•		•		•		•		•	
Hotel Rex	108	70	130	70	70	•		•		•	•	•	•	•			
James Leary Flood Mansion	110	200	400	250	300	•	•					•		•		•	
John McMullen House & Garden	112	60	120	50	50						•			•		•	
Julius' Castle	114	100	200	70	60	•	•	•		•				•	•	•	
Legion of Honor Cafe	116	210	300	350	320	•		•		•			•	•		•	
Limn Gallery	118	200	300	300	220	•		•	•				•	•	•		
MacArthur Park	120	280	500	call	280	•	•	•		•			•	•		•	
Mansions Hotel, The	122	120	150	60	120	•		•		•		•	•	•	•	•	
Marines' Memorial Club	124	300	400	300	300	•		•		•		•	•	•	•		
Mark Hopkins Inter-Continental	126	630	800	500	170	•		•		•		•		•		•	
McCormick & Kuleto's	128	220	300	100	100	•		•		•				•	•		•
✓ Merchant's Exchange Ballroom	130	400	1,000	400	430	•			•	•				•	•		•
New Main Library, San Francisco	132	210	740	210	235	•			•		•			•			•
✓ Nob Hill Hotel	134	325	546	425	641	•		•		•	•	•	•	•			•

	Page	Max. Seated Capacity	Max. Standing Capacity	Max. Ceremony Capacity	Max. Meeting Capacity	Indoor Facilities	Outdoor Facilities	Catering Provided	BYO Catering	Alcohol Provided	BYO Alcohol	Guest Rooms Available	Event Coordination	Smoking Restricted	Handicap Access Restricted	Amplified Music Restricted	Insurance Required
Old Federal Reserve Bank Bldg.	136	400	800	300	400	•				•			•				
One Market Pavilion	138	1,250	3,500	450	—	•	•			•			•			•	
Pacific Marine Yachts	140	500	500	500	500	•	•	•		•	•		•	•	•		
Palace Hotel, The	142	600	1,000	500	1,120	•	•			•	•	•	•	•			
Pan Pacific, The	144	360	500	210	465	•	•	•		•	•	•	•				
Park Hyatt San Francisco	146	250	250	150	150	•	•	•		•		•	•				
Pier 35	148	675	1,000	250	500	•	•		•	•	•		•				•
Presidio Chapel	150	—	75	175	—	•	•			•			•		•		
Queen Anne, The	152	80	150	65	80	•	•			•	•		•				
Radisson Miyako Hotel, The	154	400	600	400	500	•				•		•	•	•			
Ramada Plaza Hotel International	156	450	800	450	550	•				•		•	•	•			
RCH Lake Merced Club	158	700	900	400	500	•	•	•		•			•				
Rincon Atrium	160	500	1,000	500	—	•		•	•	•	•		•	•			•
Ritz-Carlton, The	162	600	800	500	826	•	•			•		•	•	•			
Rotunda at Neiman Marcus, The	164	175	300	125	175	•				•	•		•				
Sailing Ship Dolph Rempp	166	300	500	300	160	•	•	•		•			•	•			
San Francisco Maritime Museum	168	300	425	200	200	•	•				•		•	•	•	•	
San Remo Hotel	170	200	400	50	80	•		•	•	•	•	•	•			•	•
Savoy Hotel & Brasserie	172	98	250	48	60	•		•		•	•	•	•				
Shannon-Kavanaugh House	174	24	60	50	50	•	•	•		•	•		•	•			
Sir Francis Drake Hotel	176	250	400	250	350	•		•		•		•	•	•			
SkyDeck at Embarcadero Center	178	100	275	—	120	•				•			•			•	•
Spectrum Gallery	180	400	650	200	300	•			•	•			•				
S.S. Jeremiah O'Brien	182	150	250	150	200	•	•			•		•	•	•	•		
Studio Gallery San Francisco, The	184	200	400	—	200	•			•	•			•				
Swedenborgian Church	186	60	100	100	—	•			•	•			•	•	•		
Temple Emanu-El	188	260	600	1,700	320	•	•			•			•				•
Trinity Episcopal Church	190	150	200	450	120	•			•	•			•	•	•		
Vivande Ristorante	192	200	315	75	200	•		•		•			•	•		•	
Vorpal Gallery	194	250	250	350	250	•			•	•			•	•		•	
Wattis Room, The	196	100	200	80	80	•		•		•	•		•				
Westin St. Francis	198	1,100	1,150	700	1,500	•		•		•		•	•				

North Bay

Belvedere

	Page	Max. Seated Capacity	Max. Standing Capacity	Max. Ceremony Capacity	Max. Meeting Capacity	Indoor Facilities	Outdoor Facilities	Catering Provided	BYO Catering	Alcohol Provided	BYO Alcohol	Guest Rooms Available	Event Coordination	Smoking Restricted	Handicap Access Restricted	Amplified Music Restricted	Insurance Required
China Cabin	202	65	60	55	55	•	•		•		•			•		•	•
San Francisco Yacht Club, The	204	180	245	90	180	•	•	•		•			•	•		•	

Inverness

	Page	Max. Seated Capacity	Max. Standing Capacity	Max. Ceremony Capacity	Max. Meeting Capacity	Indoor Facilities	Outdoor Facilities	Catering Provided	BYO Catering	Alcohol Provided	BYO Alcohol	Guest Rooms Available	Event Coordination	Smoking Restricted	Handicap Access Restricted	Amplified Music Restricted	Insurance Required
Manka's Inverness Lodge	206	100	120	100	45	•	•	•				•	•	•	•	•	

	Page	Max. Seated Capacity	Max. Standing Capacity	Max. Ceremony Capacity	Max. Meeting Capacity	Indoor Facilities	Outdoor Facilities	Catering Provided	BYO Catering	Alcohol Provided	BYO Alcohol	Guest Rooms Available	Event Coordination	Smoking Restricted	Handicap Access Restricted	Amplified Music Restricted	Insurance Req.
Larkspur																	
Chai of Larkspur	208	26	—	26	50	•	•	•		•	•			•		•	•
Lark Creek Inn, The	210	200	300	150	200	•	•	•		•				•		•	
Mill Valley																	
Harbor Point Racquet & Beach Club	212	150	200	150	60	•	•	•		•				•			
Mountain Home Inn	214	60	100	30	30	•	•	•		•	•	•		•			
Outdoor Art Club, The	216	120	200	150	200	•	•		•	•				•		•	•
Olema																	
Point Reyes Seashore Lodge	218	150	150	150	25		•		•	•	•	•		•	•	•	•
Ross																	
Marin Art and Garden Center	220	300	300	300	120	•	•	•		•	•			•		•	•
Woodlands Garden	222	150	250	150	75	•	•	•		•			•	•		•	
San Rafael																	
Dominican College	224	250	400	250	250	•	•	•		•				•		•	•
Embassy Suites Marin County	226	485	650	500	500	•		•		•	•	•	•	•			
Falkirk Mansion	228	125	100	125	60	•	•			•				•		•	•
Marin Civic Center Cafe & Patio	230	350	300	125	300	•	•			•				•			
McNears Beach	232	2,000	2,000	500	—		•	•		•	•		•		•		
Sausalito																	
Alta Mira, The	234	150	300	150	88	•	•	•		•	•	•		•	•	•	•
Bay Area Discovery Museum	236	500	1,200	500	150	•	•		•	•				•			•
Bay & Delta Charters	238	49	49	49	49	•	•	•		•	•	•	•	•	•		
Campbell Hall and Garden	240	140	250	call	—	•	•		•	•				•		•	•
Casa Madrona Hotel	242	110	150	40	35	•	•	•		•		•		•		•	
Chart House Sausalito	244	220	400	110	150	•		•		•	•			•	•	•	
Discovery Yacht Charters	246	49	49	49	49		•	•					•		•		
Hawaiian Chieftain	248	47	47	47	47	•	•	•	•	•			•	•			
Sausalito Presbyterian Church	250	80	125	170	100	•	•		•	•				•			
Sausalito Woman's Club	252	150	150	150	150	•	•		•	•				•		•	•
Spinnaker Restaurant	254	160	220	160	200	•	•	•		•				•			
Stinson Beach																	
Stinson Beach Community Center	256	200	300	110	200	•	•	•	•	•				•	•		•
Tiburon																	
Corinthian Yacht Club	258	250	400	75	300	•	•	•		•	•			•	•	•	
Guaymas	260	200	250	—	20	•	•	•		•	•			•	•	•	
Old St. Hilary's	262	125	—	125	125	•		—	—	—				•			•
Tiburon Peninsula Club	264	125	250	135	125	•	•	•		•	•			•	•		•
Tutto Mare	266	150	200	—	50	•	•	•		•				•		•	

46

North Coast

Location / Venue	Page	Max. Seated Capacity	Max. Standing Capacity	Max. Ceremony Capacity	Max. Meeting Capacity	Indoor Facilities	Outdoor Facilities	Catering Provided	BYO Catering	Alcohol Provided	BYO Alcohol	Guest Rooms Available	Event Coordination	Smoking Restricted	Handicap Access Restricted	Amplified Music Restricted	Insurance Required
Albion																	
Albion River Inn	270	85	100	75	—	•	•	•		•		•	•	•			
Bodega																	
Sonoma Coast Villa	272	140	160	200	50	•	•	•		•		•	•	•			
Bodega Bay																	
Compass Rose Gardens	274	300	300	250	150		•		•		•		•	•	•	•	•
Jenner																	
Jenner Inn & Cottages	276	200	200	150	75	•	•	•		•		•	•	•	•		
Mendocino County																	
Shambhala Ranch	278	150	—	150	40	•	•	•				•	•	•	•		•
Sea Ranch																	
Sea Ranch Lodge, The	280	150	150	150	40	•	•	•		•		•	•	•	•		

Peninsula

Location / Venue	Page	Max. Seated Capacity	Max. Standing Capacity	Max. Ceremony Capacity	Max. Meeting Capacity	Indoor Facilities	Outdoor Facilities	Catering Provided	BYO Catering	Alcohol Provided	BYO Alcohol	Guest Rooms Available	Event Coordination	Smoking Restricted	Handicap Access Restricted	Amplified Music Restricted	Insurance Required
Atherton																	
Holbrook Palmer Park	284	250	250	200	200	•	•	•		•			•				•
Sacred Heart Atherton	286	450	900	450	500	•	•			•			•			•	•
Belmont																	
Ralston Hall	288	200	—	200	150	•	•			•			•				•
Burlingame																	
Kohl Mansion	290	500	1,000	500	250	•	•			•			•				•
Half Moon Bay																	
Mill Rose Inn	292	140	140	140	30	•	•	•	•	•	•	•	•	•	•		•
Hillsborough																	
Crocker Mansion, The	294	275	275	275	—	•	•			•			•		•	•	•
Los Altos Hills																	
Fremont Hills Country Club	296	200	200	—	200	•			•	•				•			
Menlo Park																	
Allied Arts Guild Restaurant	298	175	200	100	175	•	•	•		•			•	•			•
Stanford Park Hotel	300	250	250	150	150	•	•	•		•		•	•	•		•	

47

	Page	Max. Seated Capacity	Max. Standing Capacity	Max. Ceremony Capacity	Max. Meeting Capacity	Indoor Facilities	Outdoor Facilities	Catering Provided	BYO Catering	Alcohol Provided	BYO Alcohol	Guest Rooms Available	Event Coordination	Smoking Restricted	Handicap Access Restricted	Amplified Music Restricted	Insurance Req.
Millbrae																	
Terrace Cafe at El Rancho Inn	302	150	175	90	45	•	•	•		•	•	•	•	•		•	
NO Westin San Francisco Airport	304	410	600	600	700	•		•		•	•	•	•	•			
Montara																	
Montara Gardens	306	150	150	150	—	•	•		•	•		•		•			•
Palo Alto																	
Crescent Park Grill	308	200	275	—	48	•	•	•		•			•				
Gamble Garden Center, The	310	75	75	75	30	•	•		•		•		•	•		•	•
Garden Court Hotel	312	250	300	120	100	•	•	•		•	•	•	•				
MacArthur Park	314	300	300	200	222	•	•	•		•	•		•	•			
Sheraton Palo Alto	316	350	500	350	350	•	•	•		•	•	•	•	•			
Spago Palo Alto	318	200	300	50	80	•				•	•			•		•	
Vintage Room and Courtyard, The	320	200	500	200	200	•	•	•		•				•			
Woman's Club of Palo Alto	322	225	225	225	225	•			•		•			•		•	
Portola Valley																	
Ladera Oaks	324	200	500	250	200	•	•		•		•			•			
Redwood City																	
Hotel Sofitel	326	450	700	450	700	•	•	•		•		•	•	•			
Pacific Athletic Club	328	600	1,000	400	200	•	•	•		•	•		•	•			
San Mateo																	
Lark Creek San Mateo	330	250	300	160	160	•		•		•			•	•		•	
Sunnyvale																	
Historic Del Monte Building, The	332	400	700	400	450	•		•		•				•			
Palace Restaurant & Event Center	334	325	775	325	400	•		•		•	•		•	•	•		•
Woodside																	
Thomas Fogarty Winery	336	220	—	220	110	•	•			•			•	•		•	•
East Bay																	
Alameda																	
Camelot	340	48	48	48	48	•	•	•	•	•	•		•		•	•	
Commodore Dining Events	342	405	450	405	160	•	•	•	•	•	•			•	•		
O'Club & Conference Center	344	700	1,100	200	700	•	•	•		•	•		•				•
Berkeley																	
Bancroft Hotel, The	346	225	300	200	250	•				•		•	•	•	•	•	

48

	Page	Max. Seated Capacity	Max. Standing Capacity	Max. Ceremony Capacity	Max. Meeting Capacity	Indoor Facilities	Outdoor Facilities	Catering Provided	BYO Catering	Alcohol Provided	BYO Alcohol	Guest Rooms Available	Event Coordination	Smoking Restricted	Handicap Access Restricted	Amplified Music Restricted	Insurance Required
Berkeley																	
Berkeley City Club	348	300	325	300	300	•	•	•		•		•	•	•			•
Brazilian Room	350	150	225	180	225	•	•				•		•				•
Claremont Resort & Spa, The	352	450	550	180	450	•		•		•	•	•	•	•			
Faculty Club, The	354	225	325	250	225	•	•	•		•	•	•	•	•			
First Church of Christ, Scientist	356	—	—	500	500	•	•		•		•		•	•		•	
Hillside Club	358	125	200	150	150	•			•		•		•				
International House Berkeley	360	400	490	475	400	•	•	•		•	•	•	•	•	•		•
Brentwood																	
Valley Oak Nursery	362	400	400	400	—		•	•		•			•			•	•
Crockett																	
Crockett Community Center	364	350	400	350	400	•	•			•			•				•
Danville																	
Blackhawk Automotive Museum	366	450	100	450	600	•	•	•		•			•			•	•
Blackhawk Grille, The	368	75	125	—	48	•	•	•		•	•		•			•	
Crow Canyon Country Club	370	280	400	150	280	•		•		•	•		•				
Danville Station	372	150	150	150	75	•	•		•		•			•	•		•
Fremont																	
Ardenwood Historic Preserve	374	700	1,000	700	—		•	•		•			•			•	
Palmdale Estates	376	300	300	300	100	•	•	•		•			•	•			
Hayward																	
Centennial Banquet Hall/Conf. Ctr.	378	1,000	1,700	1,000	1,200	•	•	•		•			•	•			•
Kensington																	
Unitarian Universalist Church	380	250	300	400	400	•	•		•		•		•				
Lafayette																	
Lafayette Park Hotel	382	280	500	200	220	•	•	•		•	•	•	•	•		•	
Postino	384	150	200	50	30	•		•		•	•		•	•		•	
Wildwood Acres	386	275	275	275	120	•	•	•		•			•	•			
Livermore																	
Murrieta's Well	388	140	150	140	70	•	•	•		•	•		•	•			
Purple Orchid Inn	390	500	500	500	50	•	•	•		•	•	•	•	•			•
Shrine Event Center	392	450	1,000	250	1,000	•		•			•		•	•			•
Wente Vineyards Restaurant	394	500	500	500	120	•	•	•		•	•		•	•			
Montclair																	
Montclair Women's Cultural Club	396	200	300	200	200	•	•	•	•		•		•				•
Moraga																	
Hacienda de las Flores	398	100	200	200	40	•	•				•			•		•	•
Holy Trinity Cultural Center	400	350	350	450	450	•	•	•	•		•			•			•

	Page	Max. Seated Capac.	Max. Standing Cap.	Max. Ceremony Ca.	Max. Meeting Capa	Indoor Facilities	Outdoor Facilities	Catering Provided	BYO Catering	Alcohol Provided	BYO Alcohol	Guest Rooms Avail.	Event Coordination	Smoking Restricted	Handicap Access Restricted	Amplified Music Restricted	Insurance Required
Shadelands Art Center	457	300	—	450	450	•		•		•				•			
Shadelands Ranch	459	250	250	250	—		•	•		•							

South Bay

Campbell
Ainsley House & Gardens	462	200	300	200	150	•	•	•					•			•	

Los Gatos
Byington Winery	464	150	250	250	200	•	•						•	•		•	•
California Cafe	466	300	400	70	50	•	•	•		•	•		•	•		•	
Los Gatos Lodge	468	200	250	200	150	•	•	•		•		•		•			
Maison du Lac & Gardens	470	300	300	300	—		•	•		•	•		•	•	•	•	
Mirassou Champagne Cellars	472	150	200	150	80	•	•			•			•	•			•
Opera House	474	450	750	350	300	•		•		•			•			•	
Toll House, The	476	200	—	200	180	•	•	•		•		•	•	•		•	
Village Lane	470	120	120	120	75	•	•	•		•	•		•	•		•	

San Jose
Bella Mia Restaurant	480	120	—	100	120	•	•	•		•				•	•		
Briar Rose Bed & Breakfast Inn	482	150	200	150	100		•	•		•	•		•	•	•	•	•
Capital Club Athletics	484	300	400	300	350	•		•		•				•	•		
Hayes Mansion, The	486	500	1,000	1,000	350	•	•	•		•		•	•	•		•	
Hotel De Anza	488	160	160	130	130	•	•	•		•		•	•	•			
Il Fornaio at the Hyatt Sainte Claire	490	350	—	300	350	•	•	•		•	•		•	•		•	
San Jose Woman's Club	493	300	—	400	400	•			•	•				•			
Silicon Valley Capital Club	495	150	150	150	200	•	•			•			•	•			
Tech Museum of Innovation	497	500	2,500	—	300	•		•		•			•	•			•

San Juan Bautista
Arboleda	499	150	150	150	24	•	•						•	•	•	•	•

Santa Clara
Adobe Lodge	501	600	600	—	80	•	•	•		•	•			•		•	
Decathlon Club	503	600	600	200	40	•	•	•		•	•		•	•		•	
Triton Museum of Art	505	400	600	500	100	•	•	•		•				•			•

Saratoga
Chateau La Cresta	507	500	650	1,700	1,700	•	•	•		•	•			•	•	•	
Manhattans of Saratoga	510	300	500	115	280	•		•	•	•	•			•			
Plumed Horse, The	512	160	175	140	140	•		•		•	•			•		•	
Saratoga Foothill Club	514	130	150	175	175	•	•		•	•				•	•	•	•

	Page	Max. Seated Capacity	Max. Standing Capacity	Max. Ceremony Capacity	Max. Meeting Capacity	Indoor Facilities	Outdoor Facilities	Catering Provided	BYO Catering	Alcohol Provided	BYO Alcohol	Guest Rooms Available	Event Coordination	Smoking Restricted	Handicap Access Restricted	Amplified Music Restricted	Insurance Required
Savannah-Chanel Vineyards	516	300	300	300	15	•	•			•			•	•	•	•	•
Villa Montalvo	518	200	200	200	300	•	•	•		•	•			•		•	•

Wine County

Calistoga

	Page	Max. Seated Capacity	Max. Standing Capacity	Max. Ceremony Capacity	Max. Meeting Capacity	Indoor Facilities	Outdoor Facilities	Catering Provided	BYO Catering	Alcohol Provided	BYO Alcohol	Guest Rooms Available	Event Coordination	Smoking Restricted	Handicap Access Restricted	Amplified Music Restricted	Insurance Required
Hans Fahden Vineyards	522	120	120	120	60	•	•	•		•	•					•	•

Cloverdale

| Mountain House Winery & Lodge | 524 | 130 | 200 | 200 | 150 | • | • | | • | • | • | • | • | • | | • | • |

Geyserville

| Trentadue Winery | 527 | 300 | 300 | 300 | 300 | • | • | | | • | • | | • | • | | • | • |

Glen Ellen

B.R. Cohn Winery	529	300	300	300	—		•		•	•	•		•	•			•
Jack London Lodge & Cafe	531	175	200	150	—	•	•	•	•	•	•	•		•	•	•	•
Terra Cielo	533	150	150	150	150		•			•				•		•	•

Healdsburg

Hanna Winery	535	100	200	100	100	•	•		•	•	•			•			•
Healdsburg Country Gardens	537	150	—	150	—	•	•		•		•	•		•	•	•	•
Villa Chanticleer	539	300	300	300	632	•	•		•		•			•			•

Kenwood

| Annadel Winery and Gardens | 541 | 350 | 500 | 225 | 350 | • | • | | • | | • | | • | • | • | • | • |
| Landmark Vineyards | 543 | 140 | 140 | 140 | 50 | • | • | • | | • | | • | • | • | | • | |

Napa

| Churchill Manor | 545 | 150 | 150 | 150 | — | • | • | • | | | • | • | • | • | | | • |
| Embassy Suites, Napa Valley | 547 | 200 | 225 | 150 | 150 | • | • | • | | • | • | • | • | • | | | |

Petaluma

| Garden Valley Ranch | 549 | 200 | 200 | 200 | 200 | | • | • | | | • | | • | | | | • |

Rutherford

| Auberge du Soleil | 551 | 160 | 225 | 30 | 100 | • | • | • | | • | | • | | • | | • | |

Santa Rosa

| Luther Burbank Center for the Arts | 553 | 800 | 1,000 | 1,550 | 1,550 | • | • | • | • | • | | | | • | | • | • |
| Paradise Ridge Winery | 555 | 250 | 250 | 250 | 250 | • | • | • | | • | | | | • | | • | • |

	Page	Max. Seated Capacity	Max. Standing Capacity	Max. Ceremony Capacity	Max. Meeting Capacity	Indoor Facilities	Outdoor Facilities	Catering Provided	BYO Catering	Alcohol Provided	BYO Alcohol	Guest Rooms Available	Event Coordination	Smoking Restricted	Handicap Access Restricted	Amplified Music Restricted	Insurance Required
Sonoma																	
Cline Cellars	557	1,000	1,000	1,000	1,000	•	•			•			•	•		•	•
Depot Hotel, Cucina Róstica	559	150	150	150	80	•	•	•		•	•						
Garden Pavilion	561	190	250	190	150		•				•	•			•	•	•
Gloria Ferrer Champagne Caves	563	150	150	150	—	•	•					•	•			•	
Sonoma Mission Inn and Spa	565	350	350	400	200	•	•	•		•	•	•	•	•			
St. Helena																	
Bella Costa Sorrento	567	100	100	100	—	•	•			•			•			•	•
Meadowood Napa Valley	569	300	—	300	140	•	•	•		•			•			•	
V. Sattui Winery	571	350	350	200	200	•	•			•	•		•	•		•	•
Yountville																	
Napa Valley Grille	573	90	130	120	90	•	•			•	•		•	•			
Aptos																	
Bittersweet Bistro	576	125	260	125	125	•	•	•		•			•			•	
Seascape Resort	578	270	350	270	400	•	•	•		•		•	•	•		•	
Sesnon House at Cabrillo College	580	200	200	200	125	•	•	•			•		•				•
White Magnolia Restaurant	582	75	100	50	16	•	•	•		•	•		•			•	
Ben Lomond																	
Highlands House & Park	584	200	200	200	75	•	•		•	•				•	•	•	
River House, The	586	250	250	250	250		•			•			•	•		•	•
Capitola																	
Shadowbrook	588	225	—	150	225	•	•	•					•	•		•	
Felton																	
Quail Hollow Ranch	590	100	100	100	50	•	•		•	•				•	•	•	
Roaring Camp & Big Trees Railroad	592	2,000	2,500	200	500		•	•	•	•					•	•	
Santa Cruz																	
Chaminade at Santa Cruz	594	240	300	300	224	•	•	•		•		•	•	•		•	
Hollins House at Pasatiempo	596	250	250	80	50	•	•	•		•	•		•			•	
Wood Duck, The	598	150	150	150	150		•			•			•	•	•	•	•
Soquel																	
Kennolyn Conference Center	600	300	300	300	150	•	•	•				•	•	•			•
Millpond, The	602	200	200	200	200		•	•	•	•						•	•
Theo's Restaurant	604	125	125	125	55	•	•	•		•	•		•	•		•	

Santa Cruz Area

Monterey Peninsula

Big Sur Coast

	Page	Max. Seated Capacity	Max. Standing Capacity	Max. Ceremony Capacity	Max. Meeting Capacity	Indoor Facilities	Outdoor Facilities	Catering Provided	BYO Catering	Alcohol Provided	BYO Alcohol	Guest Rooms Available	Event Coordination	Smoking Restricted	Handicap Access Restricted	Amplified Music Restricted	Insurance Req.
Stone House	608	150	150	150	60	•	•		•		•	•		•	•		•

Carmel / Carmel Valley

	Page	Max. Seated Capacity	Max. Standing Capacity	Max. Ceremony Capacity	Max. Meeting Capacity	Indoor Facilities	Outdoor Facilities	Catering Provided	BYO Catering	Alcohol Provided	BYO Alcohol	Guest Rooms Available	Event Coordination	Smoking Restricted	Handicap Access Restricted	Amplified Music Restricted	Insurance Req.
Highlands Inn	610	120	180	100	130	•	•	•		•		•	•	•	•	•	
Holly Farm, The	612	200	200	200	50	•	•	•			•	•	•	•		•	•
Holman Ranch	614	450	450	250	150	•	•		•		•			•	•		•
La Playa Hotel	616	100	150	85	110	•	•	•		•		•		•		•	
Mission Ranch	618	180	180	180	200	•	•	•		•		•	•	•	•	•	
Quail Lodge Resort & Golf Club	620	500	500	500	150	•	•	•		•	•	•	•	•		•	

Monterey

	Page	Max. Seated Capacity	Max. Standing Capacity	Max. Ceremony Capacity	Max. Meeting Capacity	Indoor Facilities	Outdoor Facilities	Catering Provided	BYO Catering	Alcohol Provided	BYO Alcohol	Guest Rooms Available	Event Coordination	Smoking Restricted	Handicap Access Restricted	Amplified Music Restricted	Insurance Req.
Club Del Monte	623	600	1,000	600	600	•	•	•		•	•	•	•	•	•		•
Monterey Beach Hotel	625	350	1,000	300	650	•	•	•		•	•	•	•	•	•		
Monterey Plaza	627	350	—	400	400	•	•	•		•		•	•	•		•	
Tarpy's Roadhouse	629	300	—	50	60	•	•		•	•		•	•	•		•	

Pacific Grove

	Page	Max. Seated Capacity	Max. Standing Capacity	Max. Ceremony Capacity	Max. Meeting Capacity	Indoor Facilities	Outdoor Facilities	Catering Provided	BYO Catering	Alcohol Provided	BYO Alcohol	Guest Rooms Available	Event Coordination	Smoking Restricted	Handicap Access Restricted	Amplified Music Restricted	Insurance Req.
Martine Inn	631	125	125	125	30	•	•	•		•		•	•	•		•	

Pebble Beach

	Page	Max. Seated Capacity	Max. Standing Capacity	Max. Ceremony Capacity	Max. Meeting Capacity	Indoor Facilities	Outdoor Facilities	Catering Provided	BYO Catering	Alcohol Provided	BYO Alcohol	Guest Rooms Available	Event Coordination	Smoking Restricted	Handicap Access Restricted	Amplified Music Restricted	Insurance Req.
Lodge at Pebble Beach, The	633	250	300	250	400	•	•	•		•		•		•		•	

San Luis Obispo Area

Arroyo Grande

	Page	Max. Seated Capacity	Max. Standing Capacity	Max. Ceremony Capacity	Max. Meeting Capacity	Indoor Facilities	Outdoor Facilities	Catering Provided	BYO Catering	Alcohol Provided	BYO Alcohol	Guest Rooms Available	Event Coordination	Smoking Restricted	Handicap Access Restricted	Amplified Music Restricted	Insurance Req.
Crystal Rose Inn	636	400	400	400	60	•	•	•		•	•	•	•	•		•	

Avila Beach

	Page	Max. Seated Capacity	Max. Standing Capacity	Max. Ceremony Capacity	Max. Meeting Capacity	Indoor Facilities	Outdoor Facilities	Catering Provided	BYO Catering	Alcohol Provided	BYO Alcohol	Guest Rooms Available	Event Coordination	Smoking Restricted	Handicap Access Restricted	Amplified Music Restricted	Insurance Req.
Avila Beach Resort	638	3,000	3,000	1,000	150	•	•	•		•	•	•	•	•			•

San Luis Obispo

	Page	Max. Seated Capacity	Max. Standing Capacity	Max. Ceremony Capacity	Max. Meeting Capacity	Indoor Facilities	Outdoor Facilities	Catering Provided	BYO Catering	Alcohol Provided	BYO Alcohol	Guest Rooms Available	Event Coordination	Smoking Restricted	Handicap Access Restricted	Amplified Music Restricted	Insurance Req.
Embassy Suites Hotel	640	500	600	500	550	•		•		•	•	•		•	•		
Forum on Marsh, The	642	270	400	150	300	•	•	•		•			•	•		•	
Sycamore Mineral Springs	644	250	250	250	100	•	•	•		•		•	•	•		•	

Gold Country & Yosemite Area

	Page	Max. Seated Capacity	Max. Standing Capacity	Max. Ceremony Capacity	Max. Meeting Capacity	Indoor Facilities	Outdoor Facilities	Catering Provided	BYO Catering	Alcohol Provided	BYO Alcohol	Guest Rooms Available	Event Coordination	Smoking Restricted	Handicap Access Restricted	Amplified Music Restricted	Insurance Required
Foresthill																	
Monte Verde Inn	648	250	250	250	40	•	•			•		•	•	•			
Placerville																	
Gold Hill Vineyard	650	300	300	300	200	•	•	•				•	•			•	
Strawberry																	
Strawberry Inn & Cabins	652	200	200	200	25	•	•	•		•	•	•	•		•		
Yosemite																	
Yosemite	654	500	500	200	500	•	•	•		•	•	•	•		•	•	

Lake Tahoe Area

	Page	Max. Seated Capacity	Max. Standing Capacity	Max. Ceremony Capacity	Max. Meeting Capacity	Indoor Facilities	Outdoor Facilities	Catering Provided	BYO Catering	Alcohol Provided	BYO Alcohol	Guest Rooms Available	Event Coordination	Smoking Restricted	Handicap Access Restricted	Amplified Music Restricted	Insurance Required
Carnelian Bay																	
Gar Woods Grill and Pier	658	180	200	130	100	•	•						•	•		•	
Homewood																	
Chambers Landing	660	175	175	175	60	•	•	•		•		•	•			•	
Hope Valley																	
Sorensen's Resort	662	100	150	100	40	•	•	•		•	•	•	•	•	•		
King's Beach																	
North Tahoe Conference Center	664	300	325	350	500	•	•	•	•	•	•	•	•	•		•	
Norden																	
Sugar Bowl Resort	666	400	400	400	100	•	•	•		•		•	•	•			
Olympic Valley																	
Graham's at Squaw Valley	668	200	300	200	60	•	•	•		•		•	•		•		
PlumpJack Squaw Valley Inn	670	180	300	180	225	•	•	•		•	•	•	•	•			
Resort at Squaw Creek	672	660	950	660	936	•	•	•		•		•	•	•			
South Lake Tahoe																	
Riva Grill on the Lake	674	150	200	200	120	•	•	•		•				•			
Truckee																	
Northstar-at-Tahoe	676	200	300	350	250	•	•	•		•	•	•	•		•		

san francisco

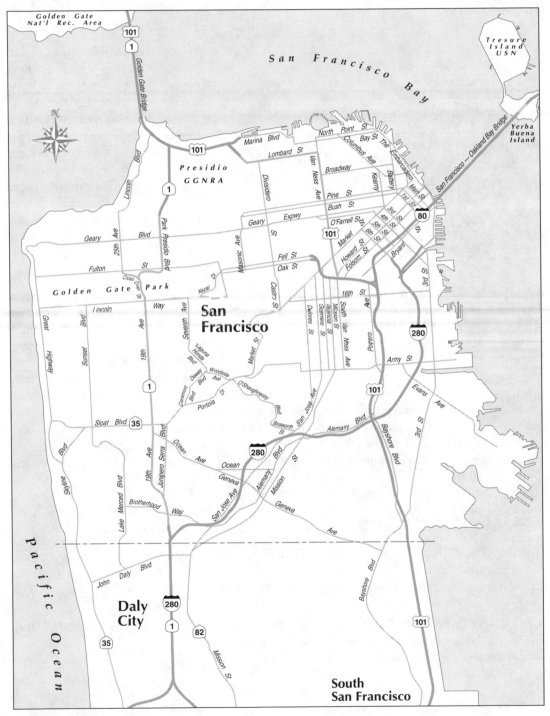

1409 Sutter Mansion

1409 Sutter Street, San Francisco
(415) 561-0869 or **561-0884, fax (415) 561-0833**
www.1409suttermansion.com
rcsutter@sirius.com

Historic Mansion

◆ Ceremonies	◆ Special Events
◆ Wedding Receptions	◆ Meetings
◆ Business Functions	Accommodations

1409 Sutter Mansion is one San Francisco address with a very long history. Built in 1881 by a forty-niner who made his fortune in business, the house is a Victorian treasure, having survived both the 1906 earthquake and subsequent fire. From the ornate, wrought-iron fence encircling the front yard to the colorful mosaic landing at the foot of impressive front doors, 1409 Sutter Mansion is a great example of Queen Anne architecture.

The formal, deep burgundy Foyer has oak wainscotting, fifteen-foot ceilings, windows with stained glass panels at the top and inlaid hardwood floors. It leads directly into the Grand Hall and Parlor which can be used independently or in combination for receptions. The Grand Hall is a very large room with a massive oak staircase, Persian rugs covering hardwood floors and brass chandeliers suspended from a high ceiling. The Parlor is slightly smaller, featuring an attractive stained glass window in a curved alcove. This floor also contains the Main Bar, a room with a long, dark mahogany bar and intricate patterned wallpaper, and the Red Room, which has striking cranberry wallpaper and another, but smaller bar. Around the corner is the Atrium, which has floor-to-ceiling glass at one end, making it the lightest room in the house. Both the Parlor and the Red Room have functioning fireplaces which, when lit, add to the mansion's Victorian ambiance.

The third floor contains a professional kitchen which supports 1409's versatile in-house chef; however, you can bring your own caterer for an additional charge. If you're looking for a one-of-a-kind mansion that imparts a sense of San Francisco history, look no further.

CEREMONY CAPACITY: The facility can accommodate up to 120 guests. The Grand Hall holds 60–90 seated; extra standing room can be arranged.

EVENT/RECEPTION CAPACITY: The entire main floor accommodates 120 seated guests, 250 for a standing reception.

MEETING CAPACITY:

Room	Theater-style	Conf-style	Classroom-style	U-Shape
Grand Hall	80	—	50	45
Atrium	—	16	—	—
Meeting Room	50	30	—	—
Board Room	—	16	—	—

FEES & DEPOSITS: Special event rental rates range $950–1,900 based on guest count, hours and season. Half the anticipated rental fee is required as a deposit to hold your date. The rental fee balance plus a $100–500 refundable security deposit are payable 60 days prior to the event. In-house catering is provided. Per-person rates are: luncheons start at $15, buffets at $25, dinners at $30, and cocktail parties at $20; alcohol, tax and service charges are additional. For ceremonies, there is a $175 fee. Full bar service is available.

For weekday meetings and business functions, rates are lower. Call for specifics.

AVAILABILITY: Year-round, daily 6am–1am, in 8-hour blocks including setup and cleanup.

SERVICES/AMENITIES:

Catering: provided or BYO, extra charge
Kitchen Facilities: fully equipped
Tables & Chairs: provided
Linens, Silver, etc.: provided
Restrooms: wheelchair accessible
Dance Floor: yes
Bride's Dressing Area: CBA
Meeting Equipment: screens, projectors & flipcharts

Parking: on street, nearby garage, valet CBA
Accommodations: no guest rooms
Telephone: pay phones
Outdoor Night Lighting: access only
Outdoor Cooking Facilities: no
Cleanup: caterer
View: no
Other: event coordination

RESTRICTIONS:

Alcohol: wine & hard alcohol provided, wine corkage $7/bottle
Music: amplified OK until midnight

Wheelchair Access: yes
Insurance: not required
Smoking: outside only

This is important! Tell facilities you're reading Here Comes The Guide and ask if our information is still current.

42 Degrees Jazz Supper Club

235 16th Street, San Francisco
(415) 777-5558, fax (415) 777-2938*51

Jazz Supper Club

◆ Ceremonies ◆ Special Events
◆ Wedding Receptions ◆ Meetings
◆ Business Functions Accommodations

The forty-second parallel is a glorious line. It traipses through Rome and Corsica, hits the Mediterranean coast of Spain near Barcelona, slices through the Spanish Pyrenees, and visits northern Portugal. Following it would make a terrific journey, but you can get a taste of these places far more easily by visiting 42 Degrees, a San Francisco jazz supper club specializing in Mediterranean fare.

Four years ago Jim Moffat took over what used to be Caffe Esprit, the stylishly renovated warehouse located behind the Esprit Outlet in San Francisco's industrial hinterland. Moffat turned it into a diamond-in-the-rough, a classy purveyor of genial warmth and award-winning cuisine.

The boxy first impression of the place doesn't prepare you for the spacious, airy feel within. The main floor is lit by a wall of floor-to-ceiling window panes, and at night delicate high-wire lights glint off the exposed pipes, casting a warm glow. Oak tables, aluminum chairs, and a zinc-topped mahogany bar add contrast and flair. Up the curving staircase (brides take note) is a cozy, retro second floor, with intimate horseshoe booths in muted orange and purple, set off by crisp white linen. Through the slatted windows are romantic views of the true San Francisco Bay—freighters, faded docks, lonely gulls, and all.

The giant-sized windows in the front of the restaurant open like elegant garage doors, leading outside to a delightful dining patio. Surrounded by a panoply of trees and flowers, street sounds are muted; birds can be heard. Concrete picnic tables and gigantic tree pots (fashioned by Buddy Rhodes, cement studio artist) look more like textured marble than what one normally associates with concrete. Large umbrellas offer shade, and heat lamps take the chill off cool days.

The meals are worth enjoying, inside or out. The chalkboard menu changes daily, but everything's available when you rent the facility for a private party. Imagine appetizers of leek and goat cheese tartlets or seared prawns with habañero chili and Pernod, platters of herb-roasted potatoes with aioli, grilled salmon with olivado, and a grapefruit and tangerine salad with fennel and black olives. The food is festive and exquisite.

Weddings at 42 Degrees tend to be as eclectic as the cuisine. Though the grand staircase will accommodate the most traditional bridal entrance and bouquet toss, the chic informality invites creativity. Hold your ceremony on the raised platform in the garden patio, then set the band there for the reception, or use the piano inside for your jazz trio. Dress the place up for a formal sit-down reception, or use the tiered space for an unstructured buffet mingle. Trendy has never been so down-to-earth and so delicious.

CEREMONY CAPACITY: The Club holds 150 seated or 200 standing guests.

EVENT/RECEPTION CAPACITY: The Club holds 150 seated or 300 standing guests indoors; 60 seated or 400 standing outdoors.

MEETING CAPACITY: The Club can seat 100 guests theater-style.

FEES & DEPOSITS: For special events, a signed contract and half of the estimated food and beverage total are required as a non-refundable deposit; the balance is due on the day of the event. A final guest count is due 48 hours prior to the event. On Sunday, Monday and Tuesday evenings, there's no room rental fee, but a $6,000 food and beverage minimum is required. Alcohol, tax and an 18% service charge are additional. Events take place in 4-hour blocks; extra time runs $500/hour. Meals run $35/person for appetizers, $45/person for buffets and $70/person for dinner. For events taking place Wednesday–Saturday, different food and beverage minimums will apply; call for specific rates.

AVAILABILITY: Year-round, daily, noon–midnight.

SERVICES/AMENITIES:

Catering: provided, no BYO
Kitchen Facilities: n/a
Tables & Chairs: provided
Linens, Silver, etc.: provided
Restrooms: wheelchair accessible
Dance Floor: yes
Bride's Dressing Area: no
Meeting Equipment: BYO

Parking: large parking lot
Accommodations: no guest rooms
Telephone: pay phones and house phones
Outdoor Night Lighting: yes
Outdoor Cooking Facilities: no
Cleanup: provided
View: garden patio, San Francisco Bay
Other: event coordination, wedding cakes

RESTRICTIONS:

Alcohol: provided, no BYO
Smoking : patio only
Music: amplified OK, entertainment subject to approval

Wheelchair Access: yes
Insurance: not required

The professionals in the back of the book are the best in the business! How do we know? Read page 681.

Archbishop's Mansion

Historic B&B Inn

1000 Fulton Street at Steiner, San Francisco
(415) 563-7872 or **(800) 543-5820, fax (415) 885-3193**

www.joiedevivre-sf.com
abm@jdvhospitality.com

◆ Ceremonies ◆ Special Events
◆ Wedding Receptions ◆ Meetings
◆ Business Functions ◆ Accommodations

It would be hard to argue with *USA Today,* which described the Archbishop's Mansion as "the most elegant in-city, small hotel on the West Coast, if not in the U.S." Built in 1904 as the residence for the archbishop of San Francisco, this landmark building is now an upscale B&B, located in a friendly residential neighborhood across from Alamo Square Park.

The Mansion's facade is impressive, and the distinguished interior is equally grand: hand-painted ceilings, detailed woodwork, Oriental carpets and fine period furnishings imbue an understated elegance. The first-floor Dining Doom and Great Hall are available for ceremonies and receptions. If you like a little drama, the Great Hall stairway allows the bride to make a grand entry and acts as a regal spot for a ceremony. And, if you take advantage of the fact that the Archbishop's Mansion is also a *très chic* bed and breakfast inn, you can spend the night or your entire honeymoon right here.

CEREMONY CAPACITY: The Entry Hall and Great Hall hold 50 seated or 75 standing, the Don Giovanni Salon 15 standing, and the Dining Room, 50 seated or 60 standing.

EVENT/RECEPTION CAPACITY: The Mansion can hold up to 50–100 seated or 75–150 standing guests, depending on exclusive use of the facility.

MEETING CAPACITY: The Dining Room can seat 24 at one large table or 50 at 5 smaller tables.

FEES & DEPOSITS: A non-refundable deposit of 50% of the estimated event total is required to secure your event date. The rental fee is $150/hour, measured from the arrival of the caterers to their departure, and based on a 4-hour minimum rental. The event balance and a $375 refundable security deposit are due 10 days prior to the wedding. Exclusive use of the Mansion runs $6,000/day (with a 2-day minimum on weekends and a $750 refundable security deposit).

For meetings or other business functions, the Dining Room rental fee is $600/day.

AVAILABILITY: Year-round, daily, any time.

SERVICES/AMENITIES:

Catering: CBA or BYO, must be licensed
Kitchen Facilities: ample
Tables & Chairs: some provided
Linens, Silver, etc.: caterer
Restrooms: not wheelchair accessible
Dance Floor: CBA
Bride's Dressing Area: yes
Meeting Equipment: flip charts & screen

Parking: on street, valet CBA
Accommodations: 15 guest rooms
Telephone: house phone
Outdoor Night Lighting: access only
Outdoor Cooking Facilities: no
Cleanup: caterer
View: of Alamo Square Park
Other: baby grand piano

RESTRICTIONS:

Alcohol: provided, corkage fee if BYO
Smoking: outside only
Music: amplified OK w/restrictions

Wheelchair Access: no
Insurance: not required
Other: decorations restricted

This is important! Tell facilities you're reading **Here Comes The Guide** and ask if our information is still current.

Atrium

Restaurant

101 California Street, San Francisco
(415) 788-4101, fax (415) 788-4593

daddydmc@aol.com

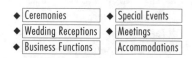

◆ Ceremonies ◆ Special Events
◆ Wedding Receptions ◆ Meetings
◆ Business Functions Accommodations

Located in the award-winning 101 California building, Atrium is one of the most elegant restaurants we've seen. As you enter the foyer, an Oriental runner leads you past a marble-topped bar into the main dining room. The soothing atmosphere created by sea-green carpet, deep mauve upholstered chairs and light peach faux marble walls is punctuated dramatically by the exotic colors of azaleas, orchids and palms. Polished marble dividers define the dining areas in this split-level room, creating separate, inviting spaces. One mirrored wall reflects the light and greenery of the atrium on the opposite side.

The glass-enclosed atrium is ideal for rehearsal or private dinners, cocktails and hors d'oeuvres or after-dinner dancing. Hanging pots of kangaroo ivy provide a lush canopy, and bud vases with colorful African daisy arrangements complete the greenhouse effect.

The adjacent granite plaza, lined with hundreds of planters overflowing with impatiens, camelias and rhododendrons, is a lovely spot for a champagne reception or a wedding ceremony. Exchange vows in front of the fountain, and take wedding photos on the sculptured granite steps in the middle of the plaza. You can also get married in the 101 California Building lobby, a six-story atrium that resembles a botanical garden.

During the Christmas season the plaza is at its most festive: a 50-foot redwood Christmas tree, aglow with 35,000 lights and surrounded by a sea of red poinsettias, creates a dazzling background display for company Christmas parties.

For very intimate dinners or a company getaway, the executive dining room offers a warm, secluded retreat. Behind plantation shutter doors, an Oriental carpet, cherrywood buffet, antique mirror and striking contemporary pastel art piece produce a rich, tasteful decor. With its special touches, imaginative cuisine, and convenient downtown location, Atrium can satisfy even the most demanding social or corporate clientele.

CEREMONY CAPACITY: The 101 California Building's Atrium lobby or Fountain Plaza can accommodate 220–300 seated or standing, each.

EVENT/RECEPTION & MEETING CAPACITY:

Area	Seated	Standing	Area	Seated	Standing
Main Dining Room	40–130	100–300	Executive Dining Room	16	20
Atrium	46	80	Entire Restaurant	185	300
Plaza	—	350–450			

FEES & DEPOSITS: A $500–1,000 non-refundable deposit (depending upon the number of guests) is required to book the restaurant and is applied towards the total bill. Payment schedules for the balance are individually arranged with the final payment due at the conclusion of the event. Buffets, luncheons and dinners range $25–40/person; beverages, tax and a 17% service charge are additional. The final guest count is due 72 hours before the event. Facility rental charge varies from $500–2,500 depending on day of week, season and guest count.

AVAILABILITY: For special events, year-round, daily, 7am–2am.

SERVICES/AMENITIES:

Catering: provided, no BYO
Kitchen Facilities: n/a
Tables & Chairs: provided
Linens, Silver, etc.: provided
Restrooms: wheelchair accessible
Dance Floor: yes, in atrium
Bride's Dressing Area: yes
Meeting Equipment: podium, screen or CBA

Parking: validated (extra charge)
Accommodations: no guest rooms
Telephone: pay phone
Outdoor Night Lighting: yes
Outdoor Cooking Facilities: no
Cleanup: provided
View: of plaza & financial district cityscape

RESTRICTIONS:

Alcohol: provided
Smoking: designated areas
Music: amplified OK

Wheelchair Access: yes
Insurance: not required

---

*This is **important!** Tell facilities you're reading **Here Comes The Guide** and ask if our information is still current.*

California Culinary Academy

Culinary Academy

625 Polk Street, San Francisco
(415) 292-8260, (415) 292-8238, fax (415) 771-2108
www.baychef.com

◆ Ceremonies ◆ Special Events
◆ Wedding Receptions ◆ Meetings
◆ Business Functions Accommodations

Founded as one of the West's first culinary teaching institutions, the California Culinary Academy has been training cooking professionals for over 20 years. While students are perfecting their skills, they put their talents to good use by cooking for the Academy's restaurants, and if you have your event here, you'll be able to enjoy the delectable fruits of their education.

Given that San Francisco is located in the center of the culinary industry, where fresh seafood, free-range meats and premium produce are available every day of the week, Academy fare is likely to be innovative as well as delicious. As one graduate put it, "We're able to taste and experiment with products that the rest of the country only reads about."

As luck would have it, you get to dine in rooms whose design and decor complement the food quite nicely. The Academy is housed in the lovely California Hall, a 1912 landmark building. The main dining room, the Carême Room, is an example of German and Flemish Renaissance architecture. It's like a formal theater: large and ornate, with an awesome 80-foot barrel-vaulted ceiling and iridescent skylights. Here you can observe chef instructors and dozens of aspiring student chefs cooking for you. The main bar area is inviting, with dark wood, mirrors and its own antique bar. The newly renovated Tavern is a relaxed and airy space, whose raspberry-colored walls are warmed by light streaming in from windows high above. For a more intimate experience, reserve the Wine Cellar, and sit amongst bottles of the Academy's award-winning wines.

By combining California's exceptional cornucopia of foods with San Francisco's multi-cultural influences, the Academy chefs don't just cook, they create art. So, if you're planning a wedding reception, banquet or corporate event, why not have it at this global culinary gem, right here in your own backyard.

CEREMONY CAPACITY: The Carême Room holds 250 seated guests.

EVENT/ CAPACITY, FEES & DEPOSITS: To secure your date, a non-refundable $1,000 deposit is required when you book this facility. A minimum of 100 people are required to open the Culinary Academy on a weekend, for which there is an additional $750 charge. The Academy office will determine when 50% of the estimated fee total is due prior to the event. Also note that for private parties, a combination of rooms with special rates can be arranged. Food service is provided. Hors d'oeuvres start at $9.50/person, luncheons at $23/person and dinners at $35/person. Alcohol, tax and an 18% service charge are additional.

Area	Standing	Seated	Rental Fee
Main Dining Room	500	280	$1,250
Main Bar	75	60	750
Private Dining Room	30	30	150
Tavern	200	150	750

AVAILABILITY: Year-round, daily. On weekdays, since the Academy operates a school, guests must arrive between 11:30am–1:30pm for lunch or 6pm–8:30pm for dinner. On weekends, 7:30am–midnight. Events have a 5-hour maximum block.

SERVICES/AMENITIES:

Catering: provided, no BYO

Kitchen Facilities: n/a

Tables & Chairs: provided

Linens, Silver, etc.: provided

Restrooms: wheelchair accessible

Dance Floor: $350 setup charge

Bride's Dressing Area: CBA

Meeting Equipment: microphone, podium

Parking: garage nearby

Accommodations: no guest rooms

Telephone: pay phone

Outdoor Night Lighting: access only

Outdoor Cooking Facilities: no

Cleanup: provided

View: no

Other: ice sculpture and wedding cakes

RESTRICTIONS:

Alcohol: provided or BYO, corkage $10/bottle

Smoking: not allowed

Music: amplified OK after 9pm on weekdays, no restrictions on weekends

Wheelchair Access: yes

Insurance: not required

The professionals in the back of the book are the best in the business! How do we know? Read page 681.

Canterbury Hotel

Murray's Glasshouse Restaurant

740 Sutter near Taylor, San Francisco
(415) 474-6464 ext. 7295, fax (415) 474-0831

www.canterbury-hotel.com
miriam@canterbury-hotel.com, jjn@canterbury-hotel.com

Hotel & Restaurant

◆ Ceremonies	◆ Special Events
◆ Wedding Receptions	◆ Meetings
◆ Business Functions	◆ Accommodations

Though newly renovated and remodeled, the Canterbury Hotel, just a few blocks from Union Square, has lost none of its genteel atmosphere. With its fabulous new restaurant and capacious event spaces, it's an appealing venue for any occasion.

Stepping into Murray's Glasshouse Restaurant, you feel as if you've traveled back to a more gracious age. Here, you could easily imagine Prince Edward having a discreet *tête-à-tête* with his mistress behind a potted palm. Formerly Lehr's Greenhouse Restaurant, the space has been completely redecorated by noted San Francisco designer Candra Scott, who wisely retained the original vaulted glass greenhouse ceiling and walls in the remodel.

Outside the windows, beds of banana trees, flowering maples, and any number of twining, vining tropical plants hide the proximity of neighboring buildings. Inside, potted palms, ficus trees and delicate orchids sustain the greenhouse ambiance. Surely the most striking feature of this incredible restaurant is the fruit-motif chandelier, where whimsical dragonflies perch on luscious-looking pears, grapes and apricots, dangling among the candle-shaped lights. Small statues are strategically placed amid the greenery, and elaborate, torch-shaped lights adorn the walls. Although the restaurant lends itself to a variety of social affairs, a wedding reception here would be breathtaking. The space can also be used for dancing, and what could be more romantic than twirling around to a Viennese waltz among the orchids and ferns?

Four other rooms can be reserved individually, or together for very large events. The Lanai Room, next door to Murray's Glasshouse Restaurant, has a floor-to-ceiling window that allows you to enjoy the beauty of the restaurant and still have privacy. The English Room has high ceilings supported by soaring columns, a large skylight that can be artificially lit at night, and a recessed area just right for a buffet, speaker's table or for the bridal party at a sit-down reception. Palm and ficus trees, brass-trimmed translucent glass chandeliers and sconces, and subtly striped wallpaper add touches of dignified elegance to the room. Garden Rooms A & B are more subdued spaces that lend themselves to business meetings and seminars.

The Canterbury Hotel may be an old San Francisco landmark, but with its fresh new look and prime location, it's a surprisingly delightful addition to the City's event sites.

CEREMONY CAPACITY:

Area	Seated	Standing	Area	Seated	Standing
English Room	80	100	Garden A	30	35
Lanai Room	50	90	Garden B	30	35
English Ballroom	150	175			

EVENT/RECEPTION CAPACITY:

Area	Seated	Standing	Area	Seated	Standing
The Glasshouse	150	175	Garden A	30	35
English Room	80	100	Garden B	30	35
Lanai Room	50	90	English Ballroom	250	150
Patio	70	90			

MEETING CAPACITY: There are also 5 suites that can accommodate 25–35 seated guests each, in addition to the rooms listed below.

Room	Theater-style	Classroom-style	Room	Theater-style	Classroom-style
English Ballroom	200	150	Garden Room A	50	35
Lanai Room	70	50	Garden Room B	50	35
English Room	80	50	The Glasshouse	250	150

FEES & DEPOSITS: For weddings, a $1,000–5,000 non-refundable rental deposit and signed contract are required to reserve your date; the anticipated event balance is payable 10 days prior to the event. In-house catering is provided, with menus ranging from $42–125/person. Alcohol, tax and a 17% service charge are additional. Wedding packages include a complimentary wedding night suite for the bride and groom with champagne, chocolates and breakfast buffet; and a suite for one night on the couple's first anniversary. Wedding receptions are allowed a 4-hour block; each additional hour is $6/person per hour.

For business functions or meetings, a $100–2,000 non-refundable deposit and signed contract are required; the event balance is due 72 hours prior to the function. Room charges are based on minimum food and beverage totals, depending on room capacity. Breakfast meetings can be arranged; luncheons run $15–24/person and dinners $28–38/person. Tax and service charges are additional.

AVAILABILITY: Year-round, daily, 7am–midnight.

SERVICES/AMENITIES:

Catering: provided, no BYO
Kitchen Facilities: n/a
Tables & Chairs: provided
Linens, Silver, etc.: provided
Restrooms: wheelchair accessible
Dance Floor: CBA, extra fee
Bride's & Groom's Dressing Area: yes
Meeting Equipment: full range

Parking: garages nearby, valet CBA
Accommodations: 250 guest rooms
Telephone: pay phones
Outdoor Night Lighting: access only
Outdoor Cooking Facilities: no
Cleanup: provided
View: garden view from Grill Room
Other: ice sculpture, in-house florist

RESTRICTIONS:

Alcohol: provided, or corkage $10/bottle
Smoking: outside only
Music: amplified OK until midnight

Wheelchair Access: yes
Insurance: not required

Carnelian Room

Restaurant

555 California Street, 52nd Floor, San Francisco
(415) 433-7500, fax (415) 291-0815

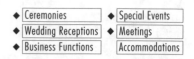

◆ Ceremonies   ◆ Special Events
◆ Wedding Receptions   ◆ Meetings
◆ Business Functions   Accommodations

The Carnelian Room is truly a "room with a view." Occupying an enviable location on the top floor of the Bank of America building, it overlooks the Bay, both bridges, the Embarcadero and the East Bay hills.

At night, a carpet of sparkling lights spreads out below you. Inside, the atmosphere is reminiscent of an English manor—warm and elegant with rich walnut paneling and masterworks of 18th- and 19th-century art. Complementing the view from the main dining room is an equally imposing backdrop: one of the West's finest wine cellars, housing some 40,000 bottles in all. Imaginative menus are available featuring contemporary California cuisine, or consult with the catering director and create your own. Experienced staff are also on hand to coordinate all the details of your special event.

CEREMONY CAPACITY:

Room	Seated	Standing	Room	Seated	Standing
Pacific Room	110	200	Belvedere Room	90	180
Rooms Combined	230	350			

EVENT/RECEPTION CAPACITY: The Main Dining Room and 10 private suites, each with a glittering vista of the Bay Area, can be scaled for groups as small as 2 or as large as 800 seated or 2,000 standing guests.

MEETING CAPACITY: The Giannini Auditorium holds 180 seated theater-style.

FEES & DEPOSITS: A $100–500 refundable deposit is required when the function is booked. The rental fee for the Giannini Auditorium ranges $700–1,400 depending on event duration and day of week. The rental fee for small suites is $75/event; the large suites start at $200/event. Menus are developed in advance of any event. Dinners start at $41/person and substantial hors d'oeuvres start at $20/person. 75% of the estimated event total is payable 10 days prior to the function; the balance is due the day of the event. Alcohol, tax and an 18% service charge are additional.

For business functions, fees vary depending on what services are selected. Services include full audio/video support and satellite hookups.

AVAILABILITY: Year-round, Monday–Friday from 3pm, Saturday and Sunday all day. Closed most major holidays.

SERVICES/AMENITIES:

Catering: provided, no BYO

Kitchen Facilities: n/a

Tables & Chairs: provided

Linens, Silver, etc.: provided

Restrooms: wheelchair accessible

Dance Floor: CBA

Bride's Dressing Area: CBA

Meeting Equipment: full range CBA

Parking: garage, $7 after 5pm or on weekends

Accommodations: no guest rooms

Telephone: pay phones

Outdoor Night Lighting: access only

Outdoor Cooking Facilities: no

Cleanup: provided

View: San Francisco Bay and skyline

Other: full event coordination

RESTRICTIONS:

Alcohol: provided, corkage $15/bottle

Smoking: not allowed

Music: amplified OK

Wheelchair Access: yes

Insurance: not required

This is important! Tell facilities you're reading Here Comes The Guide and ask if our information is still current.

71

Chateau Tivoli

Historic Victorian

1057 Steiner Street, San Francisco
(415) 776-5462, (800) 228-1647, fax (415) 776-0505
www.chateautivoli.com

- ◆ Ceremonies
- ◆ Wedding Receptions
- ◆ Business Functions
- ◆ Special Events
- ◆ Meetings
- ◆ Accommodations

Chateau Tivoli is one of the Grand Dames of the Victorian era, as rich with romance and cultural history as she is with luminous oak and period antiques. The mansion began as a mistress' hideaway back in 1892 when Oregon lumber baron Daniel Jackson had it designed for his paramour by renowned San Francisco architect William Armitage. After Jackson died, the house was purchased by Ernestine Kreling, owner of the Tivoli Opera House. From 1898 to 1917 Kreling held elaborate parties and hosted struggling young opera singers. In the following half century, Chateau Tivoli was home to orphaned girls, the Yiddish Literary and Dramatic Society, a group of pagan hippies, and New Age Druids. Murals of lotus flowers and unicorns adorned the hallowed walls, and Tibetan bells and chanting filled the air.

Then the winds changed again in 1985, when the building got a new owner and an extensive restoration. Numerous coats of paint were stripped from the grand oak staircase, hardwood floors were replaced and refinished, plaster detailing was recreated, and a new slate roof was installed in decorative stripes. The results are impressive! Any centenarian would be happy to look one quarter as good as the Chateau Tivoli does now.

Needless to say, this is a great place for a wedding, rehearsal dinner or shower. Walk past the peacock mural outside and through the grand portals, and you enter an oasis of turn-of-the-century elegance. The Parlor to the right of the lobby is lovely for ceremonies, with a rounded bay window for the minister, and a lustrous Weber piano for the processional. The Grand Staircase of gleaming oak leads into the lobby and makes for a dramatic bridal entrance. After the ceremony, the whole downstairs (split parlor, lobby, and dining room) is available for a reception in Renaissance Revival splendor. With gem-toned stained glass, fine Oriental rugs, and a fetching Pan statue with twin trumpets raised in exaltation, Chateau Tivoli wears her age with a dignified joie de vivre.

Upstairs is an assortment of beautiful bedrooms. Start your marriage off in style by spending the night in one of them, such as the Luisa Tetrazzini Suite. It has a working fireplace in the parlor, a valanced bed, and bay windows. A chilled bucket of champagne, courtesy of the House, only adds to the charm of it all.

CEREMONY CAPACITY: The Parlor holds 40 seated or up to 75 with additional standing guests.

EVENT/RECEPTION CAPACITY: Chateau Tivoli can accommodate up to 25 seated guests or 75 for a cocktail reception.

MEETING CAPACITY: The Parlors hold 40 seated, the Louisa Tetrazzini Suite and the Mark Twain Suite hold 15 seated guests, each.

FEES & DEPOSITS: A refundable $250 security deposit is required to secure your date; the $250/hour use fee is payable at the event's conclusion. Catering can be provided in-house: luncheons start at $20/person, dinners at $40/person; tax, service charges, alcohol and set up fees are additional. For business-related events, special breakfast and lunch/break services can be arranged; call for more information.

AVAILABILITY: Year-round, daily, any time, including holidays.

SERVICES/AMENITIES:

Catering: provided or BYO
Kitchen Facilities: fully equipped
Tables & Chairs: provided, extra charge
Linens, Silver, etc.: provided, extra charge
Restrooms: not wheelchair accessible
Dance Floor: no
Bride's & Groom's Dressing Area: CBA
Meeting Equipment: BYO

Parking: on street or nearby lot
Accommodations: 9 guest rooms; 4 suites
Telephone: with approval or guest phones
Outdoor Night Lighting: access only
Outdoor Cooking Facilities: n/a
Cleanup: provided
View: urban skyline
Other: floral arrangements

RESTRICTIONS:

Alcohol: provided, or BYO w/corkage fee
Smoking: designated areas outdoors
Music: acoustic only

Wheelchair Access: not accessible
Insurance: extra liability required

The professionals in the back of the book are the best in the business! How do we know? Read page 681.

The City Club

155 Sansome Street, San Francisco
(415) 362-2480, fax (415) 362-0965

sheldon.sloan@ourclub.com
rebekah.bridges@ourclub.com

◆ Ceremonies ◆ Special Events
◆ Wedding Receptions ◆ Meetings
◆ Business Functions Accommodations

Just walking into the lobby of this former Stock Exchange Tower, situated in the heart of the financial district, gives you an inkling of what's to follow. One glance at the highly polished black-and-green marble floors, black-and-white marble walls and gold ceiling and you feel instantly surrounded by glamour.

Elevators whisk you up to the 10th floor, and the entrance to the City Club itself. Here, even the elevator doors—framed in bronze and decorated in silver, bronze and brass appliqué—offer an elegant example of this facility's attention to detail. The Club (which occupies the 10th and 11th floors) features one of the most striking and exquisite Art Deco interiors we've seen, including a remarkable stairwell painted with an original 30-foot-high Diego Rivera fresco. Furnishings are original Art Deco pieces and appointments are generously clad in black marble, silver and brass. The ceiling is stunning, covered with burnished gold leaf squares, and there's even a white baby grand piano. Sophisticated with just the right amount of glitz, this is an exceptional place for a wedding reception or corporate special event.

CEREMONY CAPACITY: The 10th floor (cafe) can accommodate 120 seated or 250 standing; the 11th floor (main dining room) 200 seated or 300 standing guests.

EVENT/RECEPTION & MEETING CAPACITY: For receptions, the entire club (10th and 11th floors) may be reserved. The Club holds 220 seated or 600 for a standing reception.

Room	Seated	Standing	Room	Seated	Standing
Wine Room	20	30	Bechtel Room	50	60
Game Room	30	50	Empire Room	6	—
Stackpole Room	10	—	Entire Club	220	600

FEES & DEPOSITS: 25% of the estimated event total is the non-refundable deposit required when reservations are confirmed. Half the event total is payable 60 days prior to the event; the balance is payable 1 week prior. For Saturday or Sunday parties, the minimum rental fee is $1,300 for a 4-hour block. Extra hours run $250/hour. On week nights, Monday–Friday, the fee for the Main Dining Room is $300, and for both floors, $500. In-house catering is provided.

Seated luncheons run $25–35/person, dinners or food stations $30–50/person; alcohol, tax and a 20% service charge are additional. The catering balance is payable 1 week prior to the event. An $8,000 food and beverage minimum applies on weekends, and varies midweek depending on which room is reserved.

For business meetings, room rentals plus food and beverage minimums will apply.

AVAILABILITY: Year-round, daily, 4pm–2am. On Saturdays and Sundays, 8am–2am.

SERVICES/AMENITIES:

Catering: provided, no BYO

Kitchen Facilities: n/a

Tables & Chairs: provided up to 180 guests

Linens, Silver, etc.: provided

Restrooms: wheelchair accessible

Dance Floor: yes

Bride's Dressing Area: yes

Meeting Equipment: VCR; flip charts; overhead, slide and screen projectors

Parking: CBA

Accommodations: no guest rooms

Telephone: pay phone

Outdoor Night Lighting: access only

Outdoor Cooking Facilities: no

Cleanup: provided

Other: white baby grand piano, wedding and event coordination

View: of San Francisco skyline

RESTRICTIONS:

Alcohol: provided

Smoking: outside only

Music: amplified OK

Wheelchair Access: yes

Insurance: not required

This is important! Tell facilities you're reading **Here Comes The Guide** and ask if our information is still current.

The Cliff House

1090 Point Lobos, San Francisco
(415) 666-4017, fax (415) 387-7837

www.cliffhouse.com
info@cliffhouse.com

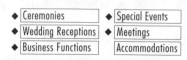

- Ceremonies
- Wedding Receptions
- Business Functions
- Special Events
- Meetings
- Accommodations

The Cliff House has become a San Francisco institution for a number of reasons: it's built at the edge of the City, overlooking the vast Pacific; it was once located next to the famous turn-of-the-century Sutro Baths; and it's become synonymous with San Francisco due to its longevity. Its historic location has actually been the home of several Cliff Houses: the first, a modest 1863 structure, the second a grand and elaborate Victorian resort built in 1896, and the current structure, built in 1909, which is now part of the Golden Gate National Recreation Area.

The upstairs dining rooms are favorite destinations for both tourists and locals to eat (and have a few cocktails) while experiencing a glorious California sunset. Downstairs, you'll find the Terrace Room, a private dining room which can be reserved for rehearsal dinners, wedding receptions, private dinners or meetings. It has a marble entryway and is decorated with Victorian-style wallpaper and silk draperies in dusty rose, green and gold.

You'll appreciate that three sides of the Terrace Room have multiple windows which overlook the ocean. There's also a small outdoor terrace for cocktails or ceremonies, where you can smell the salt air, feel the ocean breezes and watch the sea lions cavort on the rocks below. The room is large enough to handle a crowd and it's separated from the rest of the Cliff House's public spaces, so it's completely private and quiet. If you've been searching for a special spot next to the ocean, the Terrace Room is worth a look.

CEREMONY CAPACITY: The Terrace Room or Terrace can accommodate 75 seated or 135 standing.

EVENT/RECEPTION CAPACITY: The Terrace Room holds 140 seated or 200 standing guests.

MEETING CAPACITY: The Terrace Room holds 125 theater-style or 95 classroom-style.

FEES & DEPOSITS: To reserve for events, a $500 non-refundable deposit (which is applied towards the final bill) is required when reservations are confirmed. 75% of the estimated event total is due 4 weeks prior to the event; the balance payable at the end of the function. A guest count confirmation is due 72 hours in advance. Food service is provided. Per person costs are approximately $39 for buffets, $29.50–65 for seated dinners. Alcohol, tax and a 17% service charge are additional.

For business meetings, an $800 room rental fee may apply. The fee will vary depending on day of week, event duration and food and beverage total.

AVAILABILITY: Year-round, daily, 6am–1:30am. The Terrace Room is not available Sunday before 6pm or on major holidays.

SERVICES/AMENITIES:

Catering: provided, no BYO
Kitchen Facilities: n/a
Tables & Chairs: provided
Linens, Silver, etc.: provided
Restrooms: wheelchair accessible
Dance Floor: CBA, extra charge
Bride's Dressing Area: CBA
View: Pacific Ocean & coastline

Parking: on street, 2 free lots, valet CBA
Accommodations: no guest rooms
Telephone: pay phones
Outdoor Night Lighting: yes
Outdoor Cooking Facilities: no
Cleanup: provided
Meeting Equipment: podium, microphone, monitor and VCR

RESTRICTIONS:

Alcohol: provided, or WC corkage $12/bottle
Smoking: allowed on Terrace only
Music: amplified OK

Wheelchair Access: limited
Insurance: not required
Other: no rice or birdseed

The professionals in the back of the book are the best in the business! How do we know? Read page 681.

Dalla Torre Ristorante

Restaurant

1349 Montgomery Street, San Francisco
(415) 296-1111, (800) 733-6218, fax (415) 986-8197

www.dallatorreristorante.com
dlatorre@ix.netcom.com

◆ Ceremonies	◆ Special Events
◆ Wedding Receptions	◆ Meetings
◆ Business Functions	Accommodations

Nestled on the shoulder of Telegraph Hill, adjacent to Coit Tower, Dalla Torre (which means "at the tower" in Italian) commands an extraordinary view of San Francisco Bay. The building, which is over 100 years old, was formerly The Shadows restaurant, which was established in 1932. It remained The Shadows until its recent renovation, during which it received a new name, a new chef, and a new interior.

And what a delightful interior it is. Just inside the front door, there is a cozy cocktail bar, with a large picture window overlooking a tropically lush garden. From here you can look down a half-flight of stairs into the Main Dining Room, a warm, inviting space with a peaked ceiling that makes you feel like you're in a big Italian family kitchen. The atmosphere is decidedly Mediterranean: white and earth tones mix with natural wood accents and stone floors; a mural depicting an Italian country scene adds regional color, while occasional exposed bricks in the walls provide a rustic touch. Windows on one side overlook the garden, while those on the other side provide glimpses of the bay and Treasure Island between the Art Deco buildings across the street. And, of course, everyone loves being able to watch the chefs at work in the exhibition kitchen.

The Roof Top Room upstairs is one of the City's nicest spots for a rehearsal dinner, small ceremonies, receptions or business functions. Windows on two sides offer an unobstructed panorama stretching from Treasure Island and the Bay Bridge to Mt. Diablo—all of which is reflected by a mirrored third wall. The effect is quite remarkable, giving diners the impression they're completely surrounded by glorious bay views.

In the world of real estate, the mantra is "location, location, location." In the restaurant business it's "good food, good food, good food." Here at Dalla Torre, you get both, with a lot of Italian charm thrown in for good measure.

CEREMONY CAPACITY: The Roof Top Dining Room holds 40 seated or 60 standing guests; the Main Dining Room holds 70 seated guests.

EVENT/RECEPTION CAPACITY:

Area	*Seated*	*Standing*	*Area*	*Seated*	*Standing*
Roof Top Room	40	60	Main Dining Room	70	100

MEETING CAPACITY: The Roof Top Room holds 30 seated conference-style or 50 theater-style; the Dining Room holds 60 seated conference-style or 90 theater-style.

FEES & DEPOSITS: A $500–2,000 non-refundable food and beverage deposit, depending on the size of your party, is required to book your event; the balance is due at the end of the function. No rental fee is required. Menus range from hors d'oeuvres at $2/piece to full meals at $25–45/person. Alcohol, tax and a minimum 15% service charge are additional. A $25/person food charge is required Sunday–Thursday, $35/person Friday, Saturday and holidays.

AVAILABILITY: Year-round, daily, 9am–midnight.

SERVICES/AMENITIES:

Catering: provided, no BYO

Kitchen Facilities: n/a

Tables & Chairs: provided

Linens, Silver, etc.: provided

Restrooms: not wheelchair accessible

Dance Floor: no

Bride's & Groom's Dressing Area: yes

Meeting Equipment: BYO

Parking: valet $5/car

Accommodations: no guest rooms

Telephone: restaurant phone

Outdoor Night Lighting: access only

Outdoor Cooking Facilities: no

Cleanup: provided

View: SF Bay, Bay Bridge, Treasure Island, Mt. Diablo and beyond

RESTRICTIONS:

Alcohol: provided, no BYO

Smoking: outside only

Music: CDs only w/approval

Wheelchair Access: no

Insurance: not required

---

*This is important! Tell facilities you're reading **Here Comes The Guide** and ask if our information is still current.*

Delancey Street

Special Event Facility

600 Embarcadero, San Francisco
(415) 945-0487, (415) 512-5104, fax (415) 924-4889

◆ Ceremonies ◆ Special Events
◆ Wedding Receptions ◆ Meetings
◆ Business Functions Accommodations

Named after the part of New York City's Lower East Side where immigrants congregated at the turn of the century, Delancey Street has evolved over the last 20 years into "the world's greatest halfway house." Constructed almost entirely by the residents, it includes a variety of spaces that are available for special events.

The gated complex feels like a contemporary Mediterranean-style "village." All the buildings are painted earthy shades of terra cotta or adobe, and have tile roofs. Windows often overlook small balconies, or white planter boxes brimming with red and pink geraniums. The wide, tiled walkways that thread between the buildings are kept impeccably clean, and it's so quiet you'd never guess that quite a few people live here.

Delancey's Town Hall has been designed for all types of events, and has hosted its share of weddings, receptions, bar mitzvahs, seminars and large private parties. While you may be wondering why anyone would have their celebration in a "town hall," you have only to walk through this one to understand its appeal. It's a grand, triangular room with a vaulted, beamed ceiling made entirely of natural pine. The hardwood floor gleams, and there's a huge river rock fireplace in one corner. Two of its three walls each have half a dozen glass double doors that let in an abundance of natural light; the third has a large barn door that slides open to reveal a sunny, tiled courtyard with a bubbling fountain.

Cocktail parties flourish in the courtyard, especially in the evening when stars are visible in a clear sky. Many couples get married here too, in front of the fountain. Trees planted in terra cotta pots and placed around the perimeter of the space add greenery, while the buildings, which enclose the area on three sides, make it feel private and intimate. After the ceremony, guests have only to stroll back through the barn door for the reception in the Town Hall.

Another popular facility facing the courtyard is the Theatre, a real gem featuring plush seating, a stage, and state-of-the-art lighting, screen and projector. Serve cocktails and hors d'oeuvres in the Theatre foyer, then treat your guests to a "this is your life" film or video. For smaller cocktail parties, awards ceremonies or dinners, reserve the Club Room, a spacious gathering spot just a short walk from the courtyard. The atmosphere is more casual here: white walls are covered with photos depicting the remarkable history of Delancey Street, and a variety of pool, ping pong and shuffle board tables are available if you and your guests are in the mood for a little sport. If not, have those tables removed, and set the room up with linen-clad replacements for a not-too-formal reception. No matter how you use the room, you'll love the view. The entire front wall has large picture windows that overlook the bay, and the Bay Bridge. If you'd like a better vantage and a little sea air, step out onto the balcony which runs along the length of the room.

Delancey Street may be the world's greatest halfway house, but its creators haven't done anything half way. The facility offer lots of possibilities (you'll need an appointment to view them), and once you've booked your event here, you'll have the added pleasure of knowing that your rental dollars will help maintain one of the City's most impressive success stories.

CEREMONY CAPACITY: The Town Hall holds 300, the patio 325 and the garden, 200 seated.

EVENT/RECEPTION CAPACITY:

Area	Seated	Standing	Area	Seated	Standing
Town Hall	50–300	500	Gallery	60	100
Theatre	150	—	Club Room	80	80–200

MEETING CAPACITY:

Room	Theater-style	Conference-style	Room	Theater-style	Conference-style
Town Hall	325	425	Garden	150	—
Club Room	150	150			

FEES & DEPOSITS: Facility rental fees range from $750–2,000 depending on the room used. Half of the rental fee is required as a non-refundable deposit when the final booking is made, and is applied to the total. 80% of the anticipated cost of the event is due 2 weeks prior to the event, and the balance is payable at the conclusion. Dinner starts at $18/person; alcohol, tax and an 18% gratuity are additional.

AVAILABILITY: Year-round, daily, 8:30am–2am. Closed Thanksgiving, Christmas and New Year's Days.

SERVICES/AMENITIES:

Catering: provided, no BYO
Kitchen Facilities: n/a
Tables & Chairs: provided
Linens, Silver, etc.: caterer
Restrooms: wheelchair accessible
Dance Floor: CBA, extra fee
Bride's Dressing Area: yes
Meeting Equipment: CBA, extra fee

Parking: on street, nearby garages
Accommodations: no guest rooms
Telephone: pay phone
Outdoor Night Lighting: yes
Outdoor Cooking Facilities: n/a
Cleanup: caterer
View: San Francisco Bay and Bay Bridge
Other: event coordination

RESTRICTIONS:

Alcohol: provided or corkage $7/bottle
Smoking: outside only
Music: amplified OK in Town Hall only

Wheelchair Access: yes
Insurance: not required

The Fairmont Hotel

Atop Nob Hill, San Francisco
(415) 772-5186, fax (415) 249-7726

bdiapoulos@fairmont.com

◆ Ceremonies ◆ Special Events
◆ Wedding Receptions ◆ Meetings
◆ Business Functions ◆ Accommodations

From the moment you walk into the Fairmont's lobby, you know you're in for a special treat. Red velvet furnishings, massive marble pillars topped with gold capitals and high ceilings covered with gilded bas relief create an extravagant Victorian ambiance, an authentic reminder of San Francisco's 19th-century past.

This historic landmark has a collection of one-of-a-kind banquet rooms that have a grand, glamorous style. The dazzling Gold Room glitters with French Provincial detailing. Ornate, gold-leaf bas reliefs decorate walls, indoor balconies and the eighteen-foot, coffered ceiling. Crystal chandeliers and wall sconces, and hand-painted murals add authentic turn-of-the-century accents. Recreating the splendor of 17th-century Spanish palaces, the Venetian Room's 24-foot ceiling, wall-length murals, red velvet curtains and black walls embellished with gold-leaf ornamentation create a sumptuous space. The Pavilion Room features picture windows that overlook the Fairmont's rooftop garden, a sublime spot for taking vows. If your guest list tops 600, be sure to take a peek at the Grand Ballroom. Hues of yellow and gold, a custom-designed Victorian carpet and a garland of flowers hand-painted on the wraparound balcony give the Grand Ballroom a warm, festive ambiance.

If your reception is on a more intimate scale, the Fairmont has many smaller, but equally exquisite banquet rooms from which to choose. Upscale events are easily accommodated here, and the Fairmont's well preserved, vintage decor along with its tradition of personalized service place this deluxe hotel in the five-star category.

CEREMONY CAPACITY:

Room	Seated	Room	Seated	Room	Seated
French Room	130	Penthouse	80	Vanderbilt Room	50
Gold Room	500	Terrace Room	500	Pavilion Room	170
Roof Garden	150	Squire Room	80		

EVENT/RECEPTION CAPACITY:

Room	Seated	Standing	Room	Seated	Standing
Gold Room	350	800	Venetian Room	300	800
Pavilion Room	150	300	Grand Ballroom	900	2,500
Terrace Room	350	800	Vanderbilt Room	40	150
Squire Room	80	100	Penthouse	80	200

MEETING CAPACITY: There are 19 rooms that can accommodate 35–2,500 seated guests theater-style or 12–1,000 seated classroom-style.

FEES & DEPOSITS: A non-refundable deposit is required when reservations are confirmed. Catering is provided: luncheons start at $40/person, dinners at $55/person and buffets at $58/person. Half of the estimated event total is due 30 days prior to the event; the balance is payable 14 days prior. Alcohol, tax and a 20% service charge are additional. For weddings, a $350–1,500 ceremony setup fee is charged depending on room(s) selected and extent of setup.

Bride and groom receive a complementary suite. Group rates for overnight guests can be arranged.

Fees for business functions start at $250, and vary depending on room(s) and services selected.

AVAILABILITY: Year-round, daily, 8am–2am.

SERVICES/AMENITIES:

Catering: provided, no BYO
Kitchen Facilities: n/a
Tables & Chairs: provided
Linens, Silver, etc.: provided
Restrooms: wheelchair accessible
Dance Floor: provided
Bride's & Groom's Dressing Area: yes
Meeting Equipment: full range CBA
Other: event planning, ice sculpture

Parking: adjacent garages, valet CBA
Accommodations: 600 guest rooms
Telephone: guest or pay phones
Outdoor Night Lighting: n/a
Outdoor Cooking Facilities: no
Cleanup: provided
View: SF Bay, city skyline, Bay and Golden Gate Bridges

RESTRICTIONS:

Alcohol: provided, no BYO
Smoking: outdoors only
Music: amplified OK indoors

Wheelchair Access: yes, elevator
Insurance: not required

The professionals in the back of the book are the best in the business! How do we know? Read page 681.

Ferryboat at Pier 3

Historic Ferryboat

Pier 3 at the Embarcadero, San Francisco
(415) 788-8866 ext. 279, fax (415) 434-0425

www.hornblower.com
jmiller@hornblower.com

◆ Ceremonies ◆ Special Events
◆ Wedding Receptions ◆ Meetings
◆ Business Functions Accommodations

Docked just north of the Ferry Building is one of San Francisco's great party sites: the Ferryboat at Pier 3. She's been a part of the City since 1927, when she began ferrying passengers between San Francisco and Santa Rosa. After four decades of linking the two cities, she was retired from active duty in 1968. But now she supplies another kind of essential service—hosting conventions, corporate parties, weddings and a variety of special events.

Her entrance buffered from the Embarcadero by a covered hanger, this 216-foot historic ferry sits permanently moored at Pier 3. Just a ramp away from shore, the lower level is an impressive space for a celebration. The West Deck features a spacious parquet dance floor, a bandstand, and windows that look out over the water and Pier 5—all the way to Coit Tower, and the Roof Deck offers a panorama of the entire bay. The East Deck offers a spectacular vista of Treasure Island and sweeping views of the water. At night, the twinkling lights of the Bay Bridge add a festive touch. But no matter what time of day you hold your event, you can hear the water lapping against the hull, smell the salt air, and feel the sea breeze easing your cares away.

Because it's so close to the Financial District, the Ferryboat is ideal for after-work celebrations. After a day closeted in a board room, you can cut loose on the dance floor, sip champagne on the Roof Deck, and watch the lights of the City reflect off the Bay. And because you're docked, you can come and go as you please.

With all its decks and vistas, the Ferryboat is remarkably versatile. It can be dressed up or down to create any ambience you want: tropical plants can be "planted" around the support poles for an Islands motif or perhaps you could set up a backdrop behind the stage—say a New York City skyline or a tropical island vista—to enhance whatever theme you've chosen.

The Ferryboat has been the site of sock hops, high school proms, cocktail parties and elegant formals. It's also been home to hundreds of weddings. Ceremonies often take place in the open air of the Roof Deck, followed by a reception on the lower decks. The Ferryboat is unsurpassed, however, for convention socials and corporate cocktail parties. Its on-the-water location and nautical flavor give you a wonderful sense of getting away, while its permanent dock access gives you on-shore convenience. And after a day of windowless meetings, there's nothing more refreshing to the soul than a sparkling expanse of open water.

CEREMONY CAPACITY: The Sundeck holds 50 seated or 150 standing; the East or West deck 250 seated or 300 standing.

EVENT/RECEPTION & MEETING CAPACITY:

Area	Seated	Standing	Area	Seated	Standing
Entire Ferryboat	500	600	West Deck	250	300
East Deck	250	300			

FEES & DEPOSITS: A $2,000 deposit is required within 7 days after booking, and the balance is due 5 days before the event. On-board charges must be paid the evening of the function. Rental fees are as follows:

Day	Hours	Fee	Minimum Rental
Mon–Fri	before 5pm	$200–250/hr	3 hours
Sun–Thurs	after 5pm	$400–600/hr	3 hours
Weekends	5pm Fri–5pm Sun	$500–700/hr	4 hours Saturday eve
			3 hours Sunday
Holidays	anytime	$800/hr	4 hours

AVAILABILITY: Year-round, daily, any time.

SERVICES/AMENITIES:

Catering: provided or select from list
Kitchen Facilities: setup only
Tables & Chairs: provided, extra fee
Linens, Silver, etc.: linens provided, extra fee other tableware through caterer
Restrooms: wheelchair accessible
Dance Floor: yes
Bride's Dressing Area: private ladies room
Other: event coordination

Parking: on street or lot, extra charge
Accommodations: no guest rooms
Telephone: boat phone
Outdoor Night Lighting: CBA, extra charge
Outdoor Cooking Facilities: BYO
Cleanup: provided
View: San Francisco Bay, skyline, bridges
Meeting Equipment: CBA, extra fee

RESTRICTIONS:

Alcohol: provided, or corkage $10/bottle
Smoking: outdoors only
Music: amplified OK

Wheelchair Access: main deck only
Insurance: required with own caterer

This is important! Tell facilities you're reading **Here Comes The Guide** *and ask if our information is still current.*

Galleria at the San Francisco Design Center

Event Facility

101 Henry Adams Street, San Francisco
(415) 490-5800, fax (415) 490-5885

www.sfdesigncenter.com
mcasey@sfdesigncenter.com

◆ Ceremonies ◆ Special Events
◆ Wedding Receptions ◆ Meetings
◆ Business Functions Accommodations

The exterior of the Galleria building at the San Francisco Design Center gives you no clue as to what's inside—all you see is sky and trees, reflected in a gleaming, four-story facade of more than 700 individual glass panes. Walk through the front doors, however, and you see the world as it would be if top designers were in charge.

The main event space is directly ahead of you, and it becomes immediately clear that the building's architects have made excellent use of the four stories they had to play with. They've created a soaring atrium with a retractable skylight, that literally brings the outdoors inside: on nice days, *real* air and sunshine floods in. The whole space radiates cosmopolitan techno-chic, with its open, airy feel and exposed brick walls. The only decoration is a couple of gorgeous fishtail palms, sprouting luxuriantly in the natural light.

Just about any kind of event would feel at home here. The polished hardwood floor in the center can be used for meetings, dining or dancing; the elevated stage for speakers, a band or a performance. To the right is a raised terrace for a few tables, to the left is the beverage bar. And rising from all sides are three stylish tiers, where tête-a-tête tables provide extra seating, command a great view of the dance floor below, and give guests a delicious opportunity to people watch.

On weekdays, the Galleria showcases classy furniture, but on weeknights and weekends it comes into its own as a party venue. With its state-of-the-art sound and light system, its stage and dance floor, and its versatile seating options it's especially suitable for corporate galas, award ceremonies and cocktail parties. Past events have totally transformed the place: for a party with a Napa Valley theme, columns and the bar area were festooned with real grapes; for a Casablanca night, guys sporting fezzes and women draped in 40s-style gowns watched the movie, which was screened over the stage; a Phantom of the Opera bash featured shields made to look like opera boxes attached to the railings, and a huge chandelier which dropped onto the stage. They've even filled the place with "snow" and frosted Christmas trees for a "White Christmas" party.

As an added plus, the Galleria offers *idea house* for after hours tours. The *idea house* is three complete "homes" filled with great decorating ideas and the best designer furnishings, all available for ogling, touching and dreaming about. Currently on tap are a Napa Valley cottage (with exquisite silk wallcovering), a Berkeley Hills home (with enormous blackboard for creative family communication), and a Silicon Valley house (sporting a waterfall in the shower). These changing displays make for an inspiring, entertaining, and unusual event diversion.

The Galleria at the San Francisco Design Center is also a tremendous site for a wedding. Picture the atrium awash in rose petals...or maybe palm trees and toucans for that tropical island ambiance... or hey, that snow idea sounds pretty good for a winter celebration. Go ahead and fantasize—truth is, for any event where you want a quality production with endless possibilities, the Galleria has got the resources, the space, and above all, the style.

CEREMONY CAPACITY: The Galleria holds 200 seated guests.

EVENT/RECEPTION & MEETING CAPACITY: The Galleria can accommodate 200–970 seated or 1,600 standing guests; the first floor holds 370 seated or 1,000 standing, and three additional floors can accommodate 200 more seated guests per floor.

FEES & DEPOSITS: 50% of the rental fee is required as a partially refundable deposit to secure your date; the balance is payable 30 days prior to the event. The rental fee ranges $4,500–6,500 (6-hour minimum), depending on which floors are reserved. Sound and light technicians at $30/hour per technician are available. A facility manager and security guard may be required depending on the event's time frame; call for specific rates.

AVAILABILITY: Year-round, weekday evenings 3pm–2am, and weekends 8am–2am.

SERVICES/AMENITIES:

Catering: BYO
Kitchen Facilities: no
Tables & Chairs: provided for up to 300 guests
Linens, Silver, etc.: through caterer
Restrooms: wheelchair accessible
Dance Floor: yes
Bride's Dressing Area: yes
Meeting Equipment: microphone, podium

Parking: on street, pay garages
Accommodations: no guest rooms
Telephone: pay phones
Outdoor Night Lighting: access only
Outdoor Cooking Facilities: n/a
Cleanup: provided
View: no view

RESTRICTIONS:

Alcohol: provided, no BYO
Smoking: outside only
Music: amplified OK

Wheelchair Access: yes
Insurance: liability insurance required

The professionals in the back of the book are the best in the business! How do we know? Read page 681.

Gatewood-Keane Mansion

Address withheld to ensure privacy. San Francisco
(415) 861-3287, fax (415) 861-3287

◆ Ceremonies ◆ Special Events
◆ Wedding Receptions ◆ Meetings
◆ Business Functions Accommodations

Beautifully preserved Victorian homes, such as the Gatewood-Keane Mansion, are part of San Francisco's rich cultural heritage. With its Italianate architecture and Corinthian-columned porch and bay windows, the mansion's exterior is impressive in its own right, but what the building contains may intrigue you even more. Inside, a treasure trove of Victorian, Renaissance Revival, Oriental, Italianate and contemporary design elements creates a visually striking environment. Craig Williams, the event coordinator and caterer at the Gatewood-Keane Mansion, says "Every single part of this venue is eye-catching," and that's no exaggeration.

Built in 1875 by Pierre Cornwell, coal-mine owner, stockbroker and U.C. Regent, the mansion was sold to Peter Difley in 1877. Difley gave it to his daughter, Mary, upon her marriage to Thomas Keane. The mansion was turned into rental units in 1905, but fortunately in 1982 it was purchased by the internationally known artist William Gatewood, who completely restored it over the next ten years. During his extensive travels in Asia, Gatewood acquired the Oriental antiques that are seen throughout the house, which complement the many displays of his own kimono-influenced art. Gatewood died in 1994, but the Gatewood Trust insures that the mansion will be preserved in accordance with Gatewood's vision.

The Double Gentlemen's Parlor is the preferred place for weddings. Just a few of the outstanding features of this room are a marble fireplace topped by an intricately carved Italianate mirror, two crystal chandeliers (one is actually candle-lit), a harpsichord, and stately gold-leafed Corinthian columns. Ceremonies are held in the generous bay window overlooking Page Street and Koshland Park. Opening onto the Double Gentlemen's Parlor is the Ladies' Parlor, where the buffet and bar are set up. Mirrors set into the walls and the oval mirror above the marble fireplace reflect the room's glittering crystal chandelier. The walls are almost entirely covered with gold leaf, with stenciled columns and arches around the mirrors.

The front second-floor suite, which includes an elegant bathroom, is reserved for the bride and her attendants. Should the nervous bride (or groom, for that matter) feel overcome by her impending nuptials, she can recover her composure in the Fainting Room. This small room was originally a place for women to loosen their tight whalebone corsets. Now it serves as an intimate space for a small cocktail party, an overflow area for those waiting for the ceremony to begin, or a cloakroom. The walls are a relaxing sombre blue surrounded by maroon and gold friezes, above which Gatewood's "Skyfan" designs are painted. Antique bird cages are hung in front of a long etched window, adding to the light, airy feeling of the room.

Even if you don't have a traditional event coming up in the near future, use any excuse to have a celebration at this outstanding location. A rehearsal dinner, an office get-together or company Christmas or New Year's Eve gala—all of these are great reasons to have a party at the Gatewood-Keane Mansion.

CEREMONY CAPACITY: The mansion holds 50 seated guests.

EVENT/RECEPTION CAPACITY: 50 seated or 100 standing guests.

MEETING CAPACITY: Theater-style, 75 guests, depending on table and chair layout.

FEES & DEPOSITS: When you make reservations, 25% of the anticipated total is due as a non-refundable deposit. Half of the remaining balance is payable 150 days prior; the balance and a $500 refundable security deposit are payable 30 days prior to the event. January–August, the rental fee is $1,800; September–December, $2,500. In-house catering is provided: luncheons range $30–50/person, and dinners $50–85/person. Alcohol, bar service, tax and a 19% service charge are additional. Packages are available; call for quotes. Valet parking is required.

AVAILABILITY: Year-round, daily until 11pm.

SERVICES/AMENITIES:

Catering: provided, no BYO
Kitchen Facilities: n/a
Tables & Chairs: CBA, extra charge
Linens, Silver, etc.: CBA, extra charge
Restrooms: not wheelchair accessible
Dance Floor: hardwood floor
Bride's & Groom's Dressing Area: yes
Meeting Equipment: CBA

Parking: valet required
Accommodations: no guest rooms
Telephone: emergency use only
Outdoor Night Lighting: access only
Outdoor Cooking Facilities: no
Cleanup: provided
View: no
Other: full event planning

RESTRICTIONS:

Alcohol: BYO or CBA
Smoking: outdoor enclosed garden only
Music: amplified w/restrictions

Wheelchair Access: no
Insurance: extra required

---

*This is important! Tell facilities you're reading **Here Comes The Guide** and ask if our information is still current.*

Grand Cafe and the Hotel Monaco

501 Geary Street, San Francisco
(415) 292-0100 ext. 234, fax (415) 292-0149

Hotel & Restaurant

◆ Ceremonies   ◆ Special Events
◆ Wedding Receptions   ◆ Meetings
◆ Business Functions   ◆ Accommodations

Like the diminutive country it was named for, the Hotel Monaco combines French sophistication and Mediterranean charm, and it offers the added attraction of American efficiency and modern conveniences. Its eclectic decor harmonizes with almost any wedding style, whether you're wearing yards of tulle and seed pearls, or sporting a linen suit and a single calla lily. And this versatile hotel also welcomes business or social gatherings of all types.

Situated in San Francisco's bustling theater district two blocks from Union Square, the Hotel Monaco was built in 1910, but has recently undergone a complete renovation. The new owners kept many of the hotel's original Beaux-Arts features, such as tall, arched windows, stately columns, and black marble and bronze filigree staircases perfect for a bride to float down. Fanciful *trompe l'oeil* ceiling domes, hand-painted geometrical friezes, and a tasteful selection of modern art keep the look contemporary.

The Paris Ballroom is the hotel's largest reception space. Red velvet screens, black marble buffet tables topped with miniature topiaries, and wrought-iron chandeliers provide warm elegance. Smaller groups can choose either the Vienna or Athens Room, both similar in style to the Paris Ballroom. All three rooms can be divided, if desired.

For intimate celebrations, the Foyer is ideal. A striking white inglenook fireplace, graceful potted palms, and *trompe l'oeil* ceiling domes depicting fluffy clouds and hot-air balloons give the room a soaring, airy quality. The Sydney Lounge, on the lower lobby level of the hotel, manages to extend the open feeling of the Foyer through the clever use of mirrors, more potted palms and graceful Empire love seats. It even has its own scaled-down marble staircase, so necessary for that grand entrance.

If money is no object, rent the Grand Cafe Restaurant next door. Decorated in a lively Art Deco/Nouveau style in earthy shades of gold, brown, and maroon, its cozy ambiance and cheerful *fin de siècle* posters are guaranteed to take the chill out of the gloomiest San Francisco day. We don't know if Prince Ranier has ever graced the Hotel Monaco with his presence, but we're sure he'd feel quite comfortable here and so will you.

CEREMONY CAPACITY: The Sydney Lounge holds 50 standing guests; the north section of the Paris Ballroom 175 seated or 250 standing guests.

EVENT/RECEPTION CAPACITY:

Room	Seated	Standing	Room	Seated	Standing
Paris Ballroom	150	250	Sydney Lounge	—	75
Vienna Room	125	160	Athens Room	125	160
Sydney & Vienna	—	225	Grand Cafe	170	300

MEETING CAPACITY:

Room	Theater-style	Conf-style	Room	Theater-style	Conf-style
Paris Ballroom	200	35	Athens Room	120	30
Vienna Room	120	30			

FEES & DEPOSITS: The room rental fee varies from $250–1,000 depending on the number of guests and rooms rented; the fee may be waived if the event total exceeds a certain amount; call for details. To reserve your date, 25% of the estimated total is required as a refundable deposit; the balance is payable within 72 hours of the event date. Catering is provided through the Grand Cafe. Seated luncheons start at $30, dinners at $39.50/person. There is a $100 bartender fee; a $2/person fee will apply if you bring in your own wedding cake. Tax and an 19% service charge are additional. For business meetings, the room rental fee starts at $100 per half-day block; catering costs, tax and service charges are additional.

AVAILABILITY: Year round, daily until midnight. Early morning hours by arrangement.

SERVICES/AMENITIES:
Catering: provided, no BYO
Kitchen Facilities: n/a
Tables & Chairs: provided
Linens, Silver, etc.: provided
Restrooms: wheelchair accessible
Dance Floor: CBA, extra charge
Bride's & Groom's Dressing Area: yes
Meeting Equipment: BYO or CBA

Parking: nearby garages or valet, extra fee
Accommodations: 201 guest rooms
Telephone: pay phones
Outdoor Night Lighting: access only
Outdoor Cooking Facilities: no
Cleanup: provided
View: no
Other: event coordination

RESTRICTIONS:
Alcohol: provided, or WC corkage $15/bottle
Smoking: designated areas
Music: amplified OK within limits

Wheelchair Access: yes
Insurance: not required
Other: no rice, glitter, birdseed or confetti

The professionals in the back of the book are the best in the business! How do we know? Read page 681.

Grand Hyatt San Francisco

On Union Square

Hotel

345 Stockton Street, San Francisco
(415) 398-1234 ext. 4260, fax (415) 392-2536
www.hyatt.com
ncarrier@sfouspo.hyatt.com

◆ Ceremonies ◆ Special Events
◆ Wedding Receptions ◆ Meetings
◆ Business Functions ◆ Accommodations

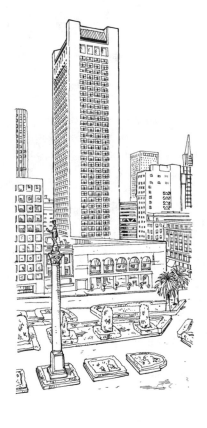

The Grand Hyatt Hotel soars 36 stories above Union Square. Outside, it's a distinctive landmark, with its tall tower, sprawling red brick terrace, and famous Ruth Asawa fountain, with its 41 bronze plaques covered with thousands of sculptured San Francisco figures. Inside, its variety of spaces and options make it extremely versatile, with appropriate settings for weddings, business meetings, conventions, and corporate events.

Starting at the top, the 36th floor is a great place for any type of celebration. The Bayview Room stretches 90 feet long, with one entire side of windows offering a commanding view of San Francisco, from Twin Peaks to Moscone Center and from the Bay Bridge to Coit Tower. Standing level with the top of the Pyramid Building, you have a bird's-eye view of the Square. And at night, the city lights below and the stars up above provide a double dose of sparkle. People often host a cocktail party here, then flow into the adjacent Union Square Room for an elegant sit-down dinner and more of the same exhilarating views. As in the Bayview Room, windows line the southern wall. But in the Union Square Room, the northern wall is set with mirrors, which reflect the vista and add a spacious feel. After you dine, stroll back to the Bayview Room for more festivities and dancing.

For a completely different ambiance, reserve the Grand Terrace on the Mezzanine. Even though it's a smaller, more intimate space, it looks out over the lobby and has an open, uninhibited glamour. Have your private party beneath high ceilings, and among luxurious brocade drapes and green ferns. Through plate glass windows you can see Sutter Street, but for a more intriguing view, peer over the railings onto the sumptuous Oriental fixtures and interesting parade of people in the lobby. The Grand Terrace offers an unusual combination: a sophisticated party atmosphere, the luxury of a floor to yourself, and a public edge.

And finally, on the Lower Level, there's the Ballroom. The leisurely escalator ride down sets an anticipatory tone, and the first thing you see in the Ballroom Foyer is its stupendous chandelier, an impressive work of art composed of 6,000 individual crystal pendants all reflecting and diffusing a beautiful light. With its marble walls and elegant ceiling, the space doesn't need any dressing up to look classy. After cocktails in the Foyer, you can proceed to the Ballroom itself, a large room with a stage, another grand crystal chandelier, and wall sconces that provide the room with a soft, warm glow. Dimmer lights enable you to create just the right the mood, from corporate meeting bright to romantic wedding subtle. The stage can be used for a speaker or a band, and any portion of the floor can be used for dancing. In addition, the Grand Hyatt staff can place a backdrop behind the stage or procure whatever props you need for a particular theme. And for a wedding, the escalator makes for an unexpected and spectacular entrance.

More than anything else, what the Grand Hyatt offers is unbeatable service. In addition to receiving the American Automobile Association's Four Diamond Award eight years in a row, the hotel is the only one in San Francisco staffing five members (including the president) of Les Clefs d'Or, the prestigious concierge organization. For caring, experienced staff, versatile facilities and a prime location in the heart of San Francisco, you can't do better than the Grand Hyatt.

CEREMONY & EVENT/RECEPTION CAPACITY:

Room	Seated	Standing	Room	Seated	Standing
Grand Plaza Ballroom	700	1,000	Bayview Room	80	150
Union Square Room	100	150			

MEETING CAPACITY: There are 19 meeting rooms (22,000 sq. ft.) which can accommodate a board meeting of 10 to gatherings of 1,000 guests.

FEES & DEPOSITS: For special events, a $500–1,000 non-refundable deposit is required to secure your date. Room rental fees may apply depending on food and beverage minimums. Luncheons start at $28/person, dinners at $38/person; alcohol, tax and a 19% service charge are additional. Custom menus are available on request. For weddings, a $1.50/person cake-cutting fee applies. A deluxe bridal suite can be arranged; the hotel offers group discounts for overnight guests.

For meetings and business functions, room rental fees run $300–10,000 depending on room(s) selected.

AVAILABILITY: Year-round, daily, 7am–1am.

SERVICES/AMENITIES:

Catering: provided, no BYO
Kitchen Facilities: n/a
Tables & Chairs: provided
Linens, Silver, etc.: provided
Restrooms: wheelchair accessible
Dance Floor: yes
Bride's & Groom's Dressing Area: yes
Meeting Equipment: full service AV dept.

Parking: valet only, extra charge
Accommodations: 685 guest rooms
Telephone: pay phones
Outdoor Night Lighting: no
Outdoor Cooking Facilities: n/a
Cleanup: provided
View: SF Bay and skyline, bridges, Alcatraz, Union Square and Coit Tower

RESTRICTIONS:

Alcohol: provided or corkage $10/bottle
Smoking: designated areas
Music: amplified OK

Wheelchair Access: yes
Insurance: not required

Great American Music Hall

859 O'Farrell Street, San Francisco
(415) 202-9812 ext. 833, fax (415) 885-5452

www.musichallsf.com
cp@gamh.com

Historic Music Hall

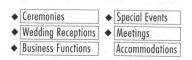

◆ Ceremonies   ◆ Special Events
◆ Wedding Receptions   ◆ Meetings
◆ Business Functions   Accommodations

Standing beneath marble columns, ornately gilded balconies and an elaborate frescoed ceiling, it's easy to envision this building in its original incarnation—a flashy French restaurant/bordello with fine food, gambling and fast women. Built in 1907, it soon got a reputation as the place to go (for men only, of course), and it flourished for a quarter century, closing in 1933. Since then it's served as the backdrop for Sally Rand's fan dancing, a Moose Lodge club and yet another French restaurant.

In 1972 it was reborn as the Great American Music Hall, and in 1994 a complete facelift restored the Club to its original rococo grandeur. Modern amenities, such as additional restrooms and a handicap accessible ramp, were also installed to keep customers happy. For more than twenty years, the hall has showcased the talents of music and comedy greats such as Ray Charles, the Grateful Dead, Bonnie Raitt, Jay Leno, Whoopi Goldberg and Robin Williams. With its large stage, two full bars, state-of-the-art lighting and sound system (complete with technicians), the hall can most likely accommodate your every desire. The only building of its kind in the City, the Great American Music Hall offers a unique window into San Francisco's colorful, exuberant past.

CEREMONY & EVENT/RECEPTION CAPACITY: The Hall can accommodate 50–350 seated and up to 500 standing guests for a reception. Ceremonies can take place on the stage.

MEETING CAPACITY: Up to 250 seated guests.

FEES & DEPOSITS: Half the anticipated total is due when reservations are confirmed; the balance plus a $500 refundable security deposit are payable the business day prior to the event. Facility rental rates are as follows: Daytime rates (6am–4pm) run $1,600 for a 4-hour minimum, and $400 for each additional hour. Evening rates (4pm–1am) run $2,800 Sunday–Wednesday, plus a $2,500 bar minimum; $4,500 Thursday–Saturday, plus a $4,000 bar minimum. Holiday rates are higher.

There are additional fees for miscellaneous services as well as a 17% gratuity for an open or hosted bar. Evening rates include house manager, bar and janitorial staff, and sound and lighting technicians. If you use the in-house caterer, hors d'oeuvres start at $15/person, luncheons and dinners at $20/person; alcohol, tax and a 17% service charge are additional.

AVAILABILITY: Year-round, daily, 6am–4pm or 4pm–2am. Other blocks of time can be arranged.

SERVICES/AMENITIES:

Catering: provided or BYO
Kitchen Facilities: fully equipped
Tables & Chairs: cocktail tables & chairs are provided or BYO
Linens, Silver, etc.: provided or BYO
Restrooms: wheelchair accessible
Dance Floor: yes
Bride's Dressing Area: 3 dressing rooms
Meeting Equipment: microphones, stage
View: no

Parking: valet, garage & nearby lots, on street
Accommodations: no guest rooms
Telephone: pay phone
Outdoor Night Lighting: access only
Outdoor Cooking Facilities: no
Cleanup: provided
Other: event coordination, state-of-the-art sound & lighting systems, entertainment bookings

RESTRICTIONS:

Alcohol: provided
Smoking: CBA for private parties
Music: amplified OK

Wheelchair Access: yes
Insurance: negotiable
Other: no birdseed, rice or confetti; no stick-on name tags

This is important! Tell facilities you're reading Here Comes The Guide and ask if our information is still current.

95

Greens

Waterfront Restaurant

Fort Mason, Building A, San Francisco
(415) 771-1635, fax (415) 771-3472

rjgreens@aol.com

◆ Ceremonies ◆ Special Events
◆ Wedding Receptions Meetings
Business Functions Accommodations

Greens is a special restaurant, not just because of its waterfront location at Fort Mason, or because it's owned by a Zen Buddhist organization, or because it serves gourmet vegetarian fare with flair. This place is special because the space makes you feel so good.

Greens has enormous multi-paned windows extending the entire length of the restaurant. These windows have superb views of the Golden Gate Bridge and of the boat harbor just beyond the building. At sunset, the waning light reflected off the bridge and boats is a stunning sight to see. The interior of Greens is also exceptional, with excellent original artwork, unusual carved wood seating and tables, and a high, vaulted ceiling. The overall impression is light, airy and comfortable.

And just in case you think Greens serves bean sprouts and tofu, think again. Their menus are diverse, with wide-ranging entrees that appeal to vegetarians and non-vegetarians alike. Mouth-watering hors d'oeuvres, savory vegetable tarts, hearty pasta and filo dishes and an extensive wine list help make Greens one of the most popular places in San Francisco. We have a feeling that long after the party's over, your wedding guests will return to sample Greens' other culinary delights on their own.

CEREMONY CAPACITY: The main dining room holds 200 standing with 18 seated guests.

EVENT/RECEPTION CAPACITY: Greens can accommodate 150 for a seated meal or 200 for an hors d'oeuvres reception.

FEES & DEPOSITS: A $500 non-refundable deposit is required when the event is booked, and is credited to the final billing. Full meal service is provided. Rates vary according to group size: $50–60/person for a 50-person dinner; $40–50/person for 100 guests. These figures include space rental for 4 hours, labor, linens, flowers and candles. Alcohol, tax and a 17% service charge are additional. Beyond 4 hours, there's a $200/hour fee.

AVAILABILITY: Year-round, Sundays after 5pm.

SERVICES/AMENITIES:

Catering: provided, no BYO
Kitchen Facilities: n/a
Tables & Chairs: provided
Linens, Silver, etc.: provided
Restrooms: wheelchair accessible
Dance Floor: CBA, extra cost
Bride's Dressing Area: CBA
Meeting Equipment: n/a

RESTRICTIONS:

Alcohol: provided, WBC only
Smoking: outside only
Music: amplified OK

Parking: large lot
Accommodations: no guest rooms
Telephone: pay phone
Outdoor Night Lighting: access only
Outdoor Cooking Facilities: no
Cleanup: provided
View: Golden Gate & Bay bridges, San Francisco Bay and marina

Wheelchair Access: yes, ramp
Insurance: not required

The professionals in the back of the book are the best in the business! *How do we know? Read page 681.*

Haas-Lilienthal House

2007 Franklin Street at Washington, San Francisco
(415) 441-3011, fax (415) 441-7735

www.sfheritage.org
info@sfheritage.org

◆ Ceremonies   ◆ Special Events
◆ Wedding Receptions   ◆ Meetings
◆ Business Functions   Accommodations

The Haas-Lilienthal House is a stately gray Victorian located in Pacific Heights, and it's one of the few houses in the City that remains largely as it was when it was first occupied by the Haas and Lilienthal families in 1886 (they lived in the home until 1972).

Wednesday and Sunday afternoons, there are tours through this grand home, showing what it was like to live in San Francisco at the turn of the century, and if you like, you can schedule a docent to give you a tour of the house during your event.

The house provides an unusual and intimate environment for weddings. The main floor has thirteen-foot ceilings, two large parlors, a formal dining room and a foyer and hall. Downstairs, there's a ballroom for larger parties. The interior is very attractive, with subtle colors, Oriental carpets, rich woodwork and many of the original furnishings from the early 1900s. This architectural treasure is very comfortable and warm inside, and would be a most interesting place for your celebration.

CEREMONY CAPACITY: The front and middle parlors, combined, hold 80 seated or standing.

EVENT/RECEPTION CAPACITY: The house can accommodate up to 90 seated guests, or up to 150 standing.

MEETING CAPACITY: The house holds up to 90 seated guests.

FEES & DEPOSITS: A $500 refundable security deposit is required and is returned 30 days after the event. The rental fee runs $2,000–2,5000 and includes use of the entire house, tables and chairs, and dressing rooms. At Christmas time, the house is completely decorated for the holidays. For wedding rehearsals, there is an extra $100 fee, which is subtracted from the security deposit.

Rates for business functions and meetings vary depending on services selected; please call.

AVAILABILITY: Year-round, daily. Monday, Tuesday and Thursday until 10pm; Friday and Saturday until 11pm; Wednesday and Sunday 5pm–10pm.

SERVICES/AMENITIES:

Catering: provided, BYO w/approval

Kitchen Facilities: moderately equipped

Tables & Chairs: provided

Linens, Silver, etc.: through caterer or BYO

Restrooms: not wheelchair accessible

Dance Floor: yes

Bride's Dressing Area: provided

Meeting Equipment: fax, copier

Parking: on street, valet CBA

Accommodations: no guest rooms

Telephone: emergency only

Outdoor Night Lighting: access only

Outdoor Cooking Facilities: w/approval

Cleanup: caterer

View: no

RESTRICTIONS:

Alcohol: BYO

Smoking: outside only

Music: amplified OK w/restrictions

Wheelchair Access: no

Insurance: extra liability required

This is important! *Tell facilities you're reading* **Here Comes The Guide** *and ask if our information is still current.*

Hamlin Mansion

2120 Broadway, San Francisco
(415) 331-0544, fax (415) 331-9161

parties@wenet.net

Historic, Pacific Heights Mansion

◆ Ceremonies   ◆ Special Events
◆ Wedding Receptions   Meetings
◆ Business Functions   Accommodations

The Hamlin Mansion, located in one of San Francisco's more prestigious neighborhoods, is an impressive structure inside and out.

The interior features the elegant and spacious Foyer and the two-story Great Hall, complete with ornate oak columns, herringbone hardwood floors and a richly detailed leaded glass skylight. The magnificent staircase, backed on the landing by a huge leaded glass window, is perfect for presenting the bride. The Main Dining Room has a striking black marble and gold fireplace and great views of the Bay. With Italian hand-laid mosaic tile on its floor and walls plus lovely leaded Tiffany-style skylights, the Solarium is a jewel of old-fashioned craftsmanship. Upstairs are several rooms with sensational ornate plaster ceilings, painted detailing and fireplaces. With classic lines and plenty of rich appointments, the Mansion makes a wonderful place for an upscale, elegant wedding, party or corporate event.

CEREMONY CAPACITY: The Great Hall holds 100 seated, with space around the balcony for an additional 80 standing guests.

EVENT/RECEPTION CAPACITY: The Mansion can hold up to 210 seated guests or 275 for a standing reception.

FEES & DEPOSITS: A refundable $1,000 security/cleaning deposit is required when the contract is signed. For weddings, a $3,000 rental fee covers use of the facility for 4 hours and is payable 2 months prior to the event. Food services are provided: an hors d'oeuvres buffet starts at $40/person, buffet dinners at $47/person and seated dinners at $55/person. Prices include staff, service and equipment. Tax and alcohol are additional. Brunch and luncheon menus, and full event-planning services are also available. Valet service runs $400–1,500 and a security guard $175–525/event; both price ranges depend on guest count.

For corporate events, the rental fee runs $3,500 for groups under 100 guests or $4,000 for groups over 100 guests.

AVAILABILITY: Year-round, weekdays after 4pm, weekends and school holidays all day.

SERVICES/AMENITIES:

Catering: provided, no BYO
Kitchen Facilities: n/a
Tables & Chairs: some provided
Linens, Silver, etc.: provided, extra charge
Restrooms: wheelchair accessible
Dance Floor: yes
Bride's Dressing Area: yes
Meeting Equipment: n/a

Parking: valet required, extra charge
Accommodations: no guest rooms
Telephone: CBA
Outdoor Night Lighting: access only
Outdoor Cooking Facilities: no
Cleanup: caterer
View: panoramic view of SF Bay
Other: baby grand piano, coordination

RESTRICTIONS:

Alcohol: BYO or CBA
Smoking: outdoors only
Music: amplified OK, music curfew 10pm
Sunday–Thursday, 11:30pm Friday–Saturday;
bands have 5-piece instrument max.

Wheelchair Access: limited, elevator
Insurance: recommended
Other: no rice, rose petals or bubbles

The professionals in the back of the book are the best in the business! *How do we know? Read page 681.*

Hard Rock Cafe

1699 Van Ness Avenue, San Francisco
(415) 885-1611, fax (415) 885-0701

www.citysearch.com

Restaurant

Ceremonies	◆ Special Events
◆ Wedding Receptions	◆ Meetings
◆ Business Functions	Accommodations

The entrance to San Francisco's local outpost of the globe-trotting Hard Rock Cafe conglomerate doesn't give much away—provided you overlook the life-size fiberglass cow placidly eyeing foot traffic from her post on the sidewalk. A green awning sporting the trademark logo juts out over gleaming brass-and-glass doors with guitar-shaped pulls; two white Hard Rock flags flutter in the bay breeze; large plate-glass windows, partly shuttered, reflect the Old First Presbyterian Church on the opposite corner of Van Ness, and reveal little of what's inside.

But just beyond the mild facade—are you ready? POW! Visual overload! Aural ecstasy! Long live rock 'n' roll!

The Hard Rock is no place for a sedate event. But for a rockin' bar mitzvah, a swinging bachelor party, a full-tilt wedding shower, or a high-energy corporate event—you have arrived. At 10 am, the stereo is cranking. Speakers angle out from giant floor-to-ceiling posts and dangle from the ceiling at regular intervals; sound booms around the large, rectangular room. Jimi Hendrix's outsize multi-color mohair coat gleams dully from an enormous gilt-edged glass case in the center of the left-hand wall. In a photo over the bar, the Red Hot Chili Peppers march single file across a stand-in Abbey Road, naked save for tube socks dangling over their private parts. (Could these be those very socks encased in glass in the back hallway? The accompanying placard gives nothing away...) Here's Keith Richards in overblown drag, with filmy tulle hat, flowered dress, and handbag dangling indelicately from one wiry arm. Madonna's sequined tuxedo-style jacket and short-shorts, circa the "Truth or Dare" tour, shimmer in the back hallway (she's tiny!). Guitars of every imaginable size, shape, and color protrude from the posts, bearing the famous scrawls of musicians from Jerry Garcia to Courtney Love. No single inch of space has been left unadorned.

Beneath the eye-popping decor, this museum of memorabilia is a simple space. At the center of the room is a giant four-sided bar, surmounted by a raised ceiling of celestial blue. Table seating ranges around the bar, with two levels rising a few steps each on the right-hand sides of the space. These are ideal for creating separate areas for adult and teenager partygoers, which suits many bar mitzvah celebrants perfectly; or the uppermost level can be converted to a bandstand, providing every guest with an unobstructed view of the entertainment. At the back of the room, counter seating in front of the open kitchen allows guests to spy on busy chefs as they prepare platters of hearty American fare; alternatively, during private parties, the kitchen can be screened off with a thick hedge of potted trees.

Larger parties will want to rent the entire restaurant for the evening; smaller groups can arrange to have a seating area roped off for their private use. Either way, an event held at the Hard Rock is sure to be an unabashed, uninhibited celebration. Rock on!

CEREMONY CAPACITY: Ceremonies don't take place at this venue.

EVENT/RECEPTION CAPACITY: The entire restaurant holds 180 seated or 350 standing guests.

MEETING CAPACITY: One section of the restaurant holds 75 seated guests, theater-style.

FEES & DEPOSITS: To reserve the restaurant for a private event, half of the anticipated event total is required as a refundable deposit; the event balance is payable 1 week prior to the function. The rental fee includes exclusive use for up to a 4-hour event, setup and take down. Luncheons start at $12/person, dinners at $16/person; tax, and 18% service charge and alcohol are additional. For groups with less than 75 guests, no minimums apply; for events up to 350 guests, food and beverage minimums run $15,000–35,000 depending on the day of week and season. Menus can be customized; fully themed parties and Hard Rock Cafe merchandise can be included as part of the event package.

AVAILABILITY: Year-round, daily, anytime, including holidays.

SERVICES/AMENITIES:

Catering: provided, no BYO
Kitchen Facilities: n/a
Tables & Chairs: provided
Linens, Silver, etc.: provided
Restrooms: wheelchair accessible
Dance Floor: hardwood floor
Bride's Dressing Area: no
Meeting Equipment: video monitors, sound system

Parking: valet CBA
Accommodations: no guest rooms
Telephone: pay phones
Outdoor Night Lighting: access only
Outdoor Cooking Facilities: n/a
Cleanup: provided
View: no
Other: event coordination, themed events, CD music library

RESTRICTIONS:

Alcohol: provided, no BYO
Smoking: outside only
Music: amplified OK

Wheelchair Access: yes
Insurance: not required
Other: decorations require approval

This is important! Tell facilities you're reading **Here Comes The Guide** and ask if our information is still current.

Hornblower Cruises & Events

San Francisco and Berkeley
(415) 788-8866 ext. 6, fax (415) 434-0425
www.hornblower.com
brides1@hornblower.com

◆ Ceremonies	◆ Special Events
◆ Wedding Receptions	◆ Meetings
◆ Business Functions	◆ Accommodations

From sleek yachts to a replica of a turn-of-the-century coastal steamer, Hornblower Cruises & Events offers a wide range of vessels that combine the facilities of a fine hotel with the excitement of a bay cruise. Whether you're planning a fabulous formal affair or a blow-out blast for 900 of your closest friends, one of Hornblower's San Francisco Bay-based fleet will provide a spectacular setting for your celebration.

The *Captain Hornblower* and the *Admiral Hornblower* are similar, 60-foot fiberglass Carricraft catamarans that each have two decks, a bar and a dance floor. The *Commodore Hornblower* is a sleek, 90-foot custom-built wood yacht with two decks and two bars. The *Empress Hornblower* is a triple-decked, 100-foot vessel reminiscent of river ferryboats. Outfitted with the rich woods and shining brass typical of the Hornblower fleet, she features indoor decks, an expansive, awning-covered outdoor deck, two dance floors and two bars. The 183-foot *California Hornblower* is patterned after early 19th-century steamships and is the largest capacity dining yacht on the West Coast. Featuring three decks, three dining salons, three mahogany bars, spacious promenade decks and multiple dance floors, she can handle even the largest gathering with style. The 72-foot *Papagallo II* is a superb choice for intimate gatherings; her salons, lower-deck staterooms and master suite with spa create a luxurious ambiance—just the style you'd want for your own, private yacht. And since the *Papagallo II* can be reserved for overnight stays, you can drop off your guests after the reception and sail away for a honeymoon cruise.

Standard amenities include white linens, china and silver, and the Hornblower staff can handle as many of your wedding details as you desire—from personalized menus and invitations to photography and custom floral displays. And if you get married on board, note that all of Hornblower's captains are licensed ministers. With over 50,000 special events and private parties to their credit, Hornblower Cruises & Events knows how to create an unforgettable setting and provides all the finery to make your celebration truly memorable.

CEREMONY, EVENT/RECEPTION & MEETING CAPACITY:

Vessel	Seated	Standing	Vessel	Seated	Standing
Captain Hornblower	52	65	Admiral Hornblower	52	65
Commodore Hornblower	100	135	Empress Hornblower	230	400
California Hornblower	740	900	Monte Carlo	300	450
Papagallo II	24	45			

The largest seated meeting capacity on one deck is 350 people.

FEES & DEPOSITS: A $1,500–9,000 deposit is required to book a vessel; the amount varies depending on the vessel selected. Wedding packages start at $53/person and include a 3–4-hour cruise, meal, bar program, champagne and wedding cake. Tax and a 19% service charge are additional. Customized weddings can be arranged; the total cost will include an hourly rate for vessel charter and per person charges for individualized menus. A confirmed guest count is due 7 working days prior to the event; the final balance 5 working days prior. The captain performs ceremonies at no extra charge. Hornblower's Charter Coordinators offer a multitude of special services, including entertainment.

AVAILABILITY: Year-round, daily, any time.

SERVICES/AMENITIES FOR ALL VESSELS:
Catering: provided
Kitchen Facilities: n/a
Tables & Chairs: provided
Linens, Silver, etc.: provided
Restrooms: wheelchair accessibility varies per each vessel
Dance Floor: provided, except *Papagallo II*
Bride's Dressing Area: CBA
Meeting Equipment: full range CBA

Parking: various locations
Accommodations: *Papagallo* only
Telephone: varies per vessel
Outdoor Night Lighting: varies
Outdoor Cooking Facilities: no
Cleanup: provided
View: the entire San Francisco Bay and skyline, Alcatraz and all bridges
Other: full event planning

RESTRICTIONS:
Alcohol: provided w/packages, corkage $10/bottle
Smoking: allowed on outside decks
Music: provided or BYO; amplified OK

Wheelchair Access: varies per vessel
Insurance: not required
Other: no rice on boats

---

*This is important! Tell facilities you're reading **Here Comes The Guide** and ask if our information is still current.*

Hotel Majestic

1500 Sutter Street at Gough, San Francisco
(415) 441-1100 ext. 240, fax (415) 673-7331
www.sidewalk.com, www.expedia.com
hotelmaj@pacbell.net

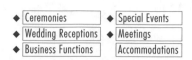

◆ Ceremonies   ◆ Special Events
◆ Wedding Receptions   ◆ Meetings
◆ Business Functions   Accommodations

Built in 1902 and authentically restored, Hotel Majestic is an appetizing restaurant in both cuisine and ambiance. For social or business receptions and rehearsal dinners, this is a splendid spot.

The first thing you'll notice as you enter the dining room is a dramatic floral arrangement designed by Jenny Martin, one of San Francisco's premier floral designers. It sets the tone for the restaurant, an elegant space with a distinctively European flavor. The refreshing and airy interior has peach walls, a high ceiling and tall windows along the street side of the room; the warm wall color contrasts nicely with the light teal wainscotting, shutters and trim. Palms placed in each corner frame the room softly, and provide a bright green counterpoint to the crisp white table settings. Wall sconces cast a honeyed, romantic glow throughout.

For meetings or small luncheons or dinners, reserve the Board Room or Hearst Room. Both feature Edwardian-style furnishings, 18th-century art and shuttered windows. The Board Room, with its antique Old English conference table and fireplace, is particularly well suited for business-oriented functions, while the Hearst Room can be set up any way you like and decorated with flowers and candles for more festive celebrations.

Hotel Majestic offers California cuisine with an Asian touch, using the freshest local ingredients in an unusual blend of flavors and textures. And in addition to its charming atmosphere and superb food, the Hotel offers an added benefit: once the party's over, you can spend the night right here in the Hotel Majestic.

CEREMONY CAPACITY: The dining room holds 120 seated guests, the lobby area 70 standing.

EVENT/RECEPTION CAPACITY: The main dining room holds 120 seated or 180 standing; the Board Room holds 14 seated or 20 standing, the Hearst Room, 20 seated guests.

MEETING CAPACITY: The Board Room holds 14 seated, the Hearst Room 38 seated and the Cafe Majestic, 100 seated guests theater-style.

FEES & DEPOSITS: For special events, up to 50% of the estimated charges is required as a refundable deposit to book your date; the estimated balance is payable 1 week prior to the event. Luncheons and dinners run approximately $28–40/person; alcohol, tax and a 19% service charge are additional. If you'd like to have exclusive use of the dining room and bar, a rental fee may apply depending on the day of week, event duration and season.

AVAILABILITY: Year-round, daily, 7am–11pm. The entire restaurant and bar can be reserved for exclusive use Saturday or Sunday, noon–11pm. Other hours can be arranged.

SERVICES/AMENITIES:

Catering: provided, no BYO

Kitchen Facilities: n/a

Tables & Chairs: provided

Linens, Silver, etc.: provided

Restrooms: wheelchair accessible

Dance Floor: yes

Bride's Dressing Area: no

Meeting Equipment: AV and office equipment

Parking: valet, extra charge

Accommodations: 57 guest rooms

Telephone: pay phone

Outdoor Night Lighting: access only

Outdoor Cooking Facilities: no

Cleanup: provided

View: no

Other: pianist available, grand piano

RESTRICTIONS:

Alcohol: provided, no BYO

Smoking: outside only

Music: amplified OK with restrictions

Wheelchair Access: yes

Insurance: not required

The professionals in the back of the book are the best in the business! **How do we know? Read page 681.**

Hotel Rex

562 Sutter Street, San Francisco
(415) 433-4434, (800) 433-4434, fax (415) 433-3695
www.citysearch7.com

Boutique Hotel

◆ Ceremonies   ◆ Special Events
◆ Wedding Receptions   ◆ Meetings
◆ Business Functions   ◆ Accommodations

Hotel Rex is different! Referred to as the "West Coast Algonquin" (after the famous New York literary hotel), Hotel Rex is the only literary and arts hotel in San Francisco—and its appeal lies in how charmingly well it succeeds at that.

First impressions count, and you're likely to get a favorable one at the reception desk, manned by genuinely friendly and caring staff. A step past the desk and you're in the lobby, with its inviting and comfortable club chairs, and its collection of oil paintings—an interesting assortment of portraits in various poses of reflection. Besides the paintings, the lobby presents striking hand-painted lamp shades, book shelves full of real books, and a glittering bar at the far end. Muted cantelope-colored walls, and molding trim of sable-brown, burgundy, and gold add to the warm aura. The feel is an international mix of French salon chic, British club comfort, and American hospitality. Cocktail parties begin here, and then flow into the Salon, the private room just off the lobby where special events are held.

The Salon is a beautiful space, with a rich ruby-red rug, cheerful gold-toned lamp chandeliers and absolutely terrific caricature drawings by Jack Keating. Done in charcoal with the occasional touch of color, his broad strokes animate the walls with Isadora Duncan, Jack London, Dashiell Hammet, the Fitzgeralds, and other literary and artistic luminaries. It's worth renting the room just to enjoy Keating's art, but that's not the only reason. Its elegant, yet relaxed 1920s literati atmosphere lends real panache to any gathering.

Corporate meetings, wedding receptions, rehearsal dinners, showers, brunches, and private parties have all been hosted in the Salon. With its state-of-the-art lighting, the Rex can create different moods, from businesslike to intimate and romantic. A dance floor can go down; a band stage can go up. Planning a late-night affair? The Salon is available until 1am, if you like. Now, at 1am, you and your guests (especially the out-of-town ones) probably won't want to drive anywhere, and you don't have to! This is, after all, a hotel, and a lovely one at that. The comfortable guest rooms all have an artistic flair, and you can't beat the Union Square location. The suites (with bedroom, living room, two bathrooms, and lots of color and style) are also perfect for small corporate meetings or bridal preparations.

The Rex is known for its poetry readings, book signings, and musical and art events. But other types of events also receive the hotel's very personal touch. For corporate groups who want to get away from the big hotel feel, or brides and grooms who want to be surrounded by an artistic, cozy ambiance, the Hotel Rex is a delightful choice.

CEREMONY CAPACITY: The Salon holds 70 seated guests.

EVENT/RECEPTION CAPACITY: The Salon holds 70 seated or 130 standing; the Lobby Bar holds 75 standing guests.

MEETING CAPACITY: The Salon can accommodate 40 seated U-shape, 30 seated conference-style, 40 seated classroom-style, and 70 seated theater-style. Two suites are available for small corporate conferences or production gatherings for up to 8 people, each.

FEES & DEPOSITS: For social functions, a non-refundable $1,000 deposit is required to secure your date. The balance, along with a guest count guarantee, is due 3 business days prior to the event. The Salon's room rental fee is $1,000. Catering is provided in-house: a 3-course luncheon starts at $25/person and 3-course dinners at $36/person; tax, gratuities, service charges and alcohol are additional.

A full range of business packages are available and are customized per event, including breakfasts, beverage service, mid-morning and mid-afternoon breaks. Full audio visual services are provided. Prices will vary depending on what services are selected; call for more information.

AVAILABILITY: Year-round, daily, 6am–midnight, including holidays. Later hours can be negotiated.

SERVICES/AMENITIES:

Catering: provided
Kitchen Facilities: fully equipped, commercial
Tables & Chairs: provided
Linens, Silver, etc.: provided
Restrooms: not wheelchair accessible
Dance Floor: CBA, extra fee
Bride's & Groom's Dressing Area: CBA
Meeting Equipment: wide range CBA, extra fee

Parking: nearby garages; valet services CBA
Accommodations: 94 guest rooms
Telephone: pay phones
Outdoor Night Lighting: access only
Outdoor Cooking Facilities: n/a
Cleanup: provided
View: no
Other: wedding cakes, event coordination

RESTRICTIONS:

Alcohol: provided or BYO w/corkage fee
Smoking: outside only
Music: amplified OK indoors until midnight

Wheelchair Access: yes
Insurance: not required

The professionals in the back of the book are the best in the business! ***How do we know? Read page 681.***

James Leary Flood Mansion

Historic Mansion

2222 Broadway, San Francisco
(415) 563-2900, fax (415) 292-3183

www.sacred.sf.ca.us/flood_mansion
hackman@sacred.sf.ca.us

◆ Ceremonies ◆ Special Events
◆ Wedding Receptions ◆ Meetings
◆ Business Functions ☐ Accommodations

The Flood Mansion is a symphony of classical styles—Italian Renaissance, Rococo, Tudor and Georgian. This elegant building, constructed in 1915, has remained well-preserved since Mrs. Flood donated her home to the Religious of the Sacred Heart in 1939. Although the building is now used as a private school, it's available for special events after school hours and on weekends.

The Mansion is impressive: its Grand Hall is 140 feet long with marble floors and great views of the Bay; the Adam Room, near the entry, has a high, ornate ceiling, specially designed wood tables and chairs, and a marble fireplace; the architecturally complex Reception Room boasts a magnificent coffered ceiling, painted murals in golds, blues and greens, and a parquet floor. And weather permitting, a pretty enclosed courtyard off of the Grand Hall is available for outdoor gatherings. The Flood Mansion is definitely the place for a stately and elegant party.

CEREMONY CAPACITY: The courtyard holds 125–150 seated, 150 standing; the Grand Hall 250 seated; and the Adam Room 80 seated guests.

EVENT/RECEPTION CAPACITY: The entire main floor can hold 200 seated or 400 standing guests. Individual seated capacities: the Grand Hall, 200; the Adam Room, 60; the Reception Room, 80–100 people; and the Duchesne Room, 80 seated. In addition, there's a theater area downstairs which can hold up to 300 seated guests. The courtyard holds 200 standing guests.

MEETING CAPACITY: The main floor can accommodate 200 seated and the theater area on the lower floor, 300 seated.

FEES & DEPOSITS: The $6,000 rental fee includes security and custodial fees. A $3,000 non-refundable deposit is required to secure your date; the rental balance and a certificate of insurance are due 2 weeks prior to the event date.

AVAILABILITY: Year-round, Fridays after 3:30pm, Saturday and Sunday all day. Guests and catering staff must vacate the premises by 12:30am.

SERVICES/AMENITIES:

Catering: select from preferred list
Kitchen Facilities: ample
Tables & Chairs: BYO
Linens, Silver, etc.: BYO
Restrooms: wheelchair accessible
Dance Floor: yes
Bride's Dressing Area: CBA
Meeting Equipment: BYO

Parking: valet parking required
Accommodations: no guest rooms
Telephone: pay phone
Outdoor Night Lighting: access only
Outdoor Cooking Facilities: no
Cleanup: caterer
View: SF bay, Golden Gate bridge & Alcatraz
Other: 2 baby grand pianos

RESTRICTIONS:

Alcohol: BYO, must use licensed server
Smoking: courtyard only
Music: amplified OK Sunday–Thursday until 10pm;
Friday–Saturday until 11pm

Wheelchair Access: yes
Insurance: extra liability required

This is important! Tell facilities you're reading **Here Comes The Guide** *and ask if our information is still current.*

John McMullen House & Garden

827 Guerrero, San Francisco
(415) 282-2168, fax (415) 282-4310
kasl@aol.com

◆ Ceremonies ◆ Special Events
◆ Wedding Receptions ◆ Meetings
◆ Business Functions Accommodations

The John McMullen House and Garden, set back majestically from Guerrero Street, is an 1881 eclectic Queen Anne beauty that manages to combine polished period grace with intimate family charm. And while each room has its own personality, there's an easy flow between them, making the house a comfortable space for wandering and mingling.

Once up the flower-fringed front steps, through the wrought-iron gate, and past the heavy oak doors, you enter a foyer that welcomes you with the warm wood hues that permeate the entire house. Polished amber tones reflect off stained glass windows and hand-stenciled wallpaper, creating a breathtaking entrance. To the left is an adorable yet formal parlor lit by a crystal chandelier above; to the right is a vestibule, with stained glass windows and brilliant oak walls under a Samuel Newsom Moorish arch. Forward through the foyer is another parlor, with opulent wallpaper and deep mahogany accents. It's great for cocktails and hors d'oeuvres, especially when paired with the little room adjacent to it, a picturesque space with its original fireplace and Garfoli oil painting, that's just the right size for a bar.

Further on is the McMullen Room, with an Irish court cupboard from the 1600s—made of oak, cherry, and wormwood—polished to a luster and beautifully engraved with flowers and swirls. From this dining room, a door leads out to the landscaped garden filled with Japanese maple, Tasmanian tree fern, Dalmatian bellflowers and creeping fig vines; lavender, rosemary, gardenia and climbing roses add fragrance. With its fountain, lattice enclosure and plenty of room for a tent, the garden is a lovely area for an outdoor gathering.

Another dining room features a George VI-style mahogany table that matches the Honduras mahogany wood walls and fireplace mantle, while peacock wallpaper, a terra cotta-tiled fireplace, and stained glass windows add to the color and ambiance.

Although the house is a splendid place for corporate parties and weddings (brides note the grand oak staircase, and the dressing room upstairs), hosting special events is not its only purpose. In fact, the house has long had an interesting history and a laudable focus. From the

1960s through 1994 when a fire ravaged it, the McMullen House served as a boarding home for the mentally ill. When owners Leroy and Kathy Looper purchased it, they not only brought the building back to life, they renewed their commitment to the disabled community as well. Along with making their home almost completely handicap-accessible, they are training disabled individuals to participate in the catering process during events. This partnership benefits everyone: enhanced wallets and self-esteem for the disabled, a healthier budget for Kathy and Leroy to continue their admirable efforts, and a warm feeling for the people whose rental dollars are going to such a good cause. How fortunate can you get?—all this on top of landing one of the loveliest, most sumptuous historic house and garden venues in San Francisco. It's a rare marriage of beauty and heart.

CEREMONY CAPACITY: The Garden holds 50 seated, and a few extra standing guests.

EVENT/RECEPTION & MEETING CAPACITY: The Dining Room holds 50 seated, the McMullen Room 15 seated, the Grand Parlor 30 seated, and the Front Parlor 10 seated. The entire house can accommodate 60 seated or 120 for a cocktail reception.

FEES & DEPOSITS: A partially refundable $500 rental deposit and a refundable $500 cleaning/damage deposit are required to secure your date. The rental balance is due 30 days prior to the event. The rental fee, for an 8-hour event, is $1,800 from January to November or $2,200 December 1 to January 1.

AVAILABILITY: Year-round, daily, Sunday–Thursday 8am–10:30pm, or Friday and Saturday 8am–11:30pm.

SERVICES/AMENITIES:

Catering: select from preferred list
Kitchen Facilities: fully equipped, commercial
Tables & Chairs: renter or caterer
Linens, Silver, etc.: renter or caterer
Restrooms: wheelchair accessible
Dance Floor: in Grand Parlor
Bride's Dressing Area: yes
Meeting Equipment: BYO

Parking: public parking garage nearby
Accommodations: no guest rooms
Telephone: office phone with approval
Outdoor Night Lighting: yes
Outdoor Cooking Facilities: BYO
Cleanup: caterer
View: no view

RESTRICTIONS:

Alcohol: BYO, licensed server
Smoking: outside only
Music: acoustic only; indoors until 10pm weekdays, 11pm weekends; outdoor curfew 8:30pm

Wheelchair Access: yes
Insurance: extra liability required
Other: no bottled beverages outdoors; no rice or birdseed

The professionals in the back of the book are the best in the business! **How do we know? Read page 681.**

Julius' Castle

1541 Montgomery Street, San Francisco
(415) 392-2222, (800) 733-6218, fax (415) 986-8197

www.juliuscastlerestaurant.com
j.castle@ix.netcom.com

◆ Ceremonies	◆ Special Events
◆ Wedding Receptions	◆ Meetings
◆ Business Functions	Accommodations

Perched high atop Telegraph Hill, adjacent to Coit Tower, Julius' Castle is one of San Francisco's most famous landmarks. It was built in 1922 by Julius Roz, an Italian immigrant and one-time restaurant counterman who dreamed of having a spectacular house on a hill. Well, not only did he make his dream come true, he did such a fantastic job, it's wowed San Franciscans and visitors from all over the world for nearly a century.

Constructed of materials from the 1915 Panama-Pacific Exposition, the restaurant is designed to look like a medieval castle. The Main Dining Room, warmed by rich, dark wood and candlelight, has a romantic, Old-World feeling, and the view is definitely fit for a king. No matter where you sit, you can see the Bay, and from most tables the vista includes the wharf, Alcatraz, the Bay Bridge, and the East Bay.

You can reserve the entire restaurant for your wedding or special event (IBM, Genentech and the band, Journey, have done just that) or host it in the Penthouse, a private room upstairs with its own terrace. The former living quarters of Julius Roz, the Penthouse has been transformed into an intimate spot for a wedding, rehearsal dinner or elegant cocktail party. Antique beige, textured walls contrast with the rich burgundy of the carpet and upholstery, the dark wood trim, and the floor-to-ceiling mahogany fireplace. Natural light floods the room during the day, and at night, faux-candle chandeliers and wall sconces provide a soft glow. French doors lead out to a slate-tiled terrace with heaters, a lovely spot for a ceremony or *al fresco* luncheon. The view from the Penthouse is breathtaking, especially from Table 34, one of the most coveted dining spots in the City. This totally private, hexagonal niche is separated from the rest of the room by wine-colored velvet drapes. From here, you have your own exclusive vantage of the glittering sea below and all the familiar landmarks.

Julius' Castle is not only a mecca for those seeking romance (voted the best romantic restaurant and view by readers of *San Francisco Focus Magazine*), but it also delivers great food, wine and service. (*Gourmet Magazine Reader's Poll* voted Julius' Castle as one of the top 20 Bay Area restaurants). You can't miss the wall full of *Wine Spectator* awards as you enter through the bar area downstairs, and the waiters—some of whom have been at the Castle for twenty years— admit to loving the Castle as much as the guests do. Dinner may no longer cost a mere $2.00, as it did on a 1928 menu displayed on the wall, but when you dine at Julius' Castle, you'll have an experience you won't soon forget.

CEREMONY CAPACITY: The Terrace holds 60 seated guests with room for 10 additional standing guests.

EVENT/RECEPTION CAPACITY: The Castle can accommodate 100 on the main floor or 100 in the Penthouse. The restaurant holds 200 guests, maximum.

MEETING CAPACITY: The main dining room holds 60 seated conference-style or theater-style. The Penthouse holds 40 seated conference-style or 50 seated theater-style.

FEES & DEPOSITS: A $500–3,000 non-refundable food and beverage deposit is required to reserve your date; the amount varies depending on guest count. Hors d'oeuvres average $2 each. Sunday–Thursday, the minimum food charge is $35/person, Friday, Saturday and holidays, $45/person. Tax and a minimum 15% service charge are additional; alcohol charges are based on consumption. The balance is payable at the end of the function.

AVAILABILITY: Year-round, daily, 9am–midnight.

SERVICES/AMENITIES:

Catering: provided, no BYO
Kitchen Facilities: n/a
Tables & Chairs: provided
Linens, Silver, etc.: provided
Restrooms: not wheelchair accessible
Dance Floor: no
Bride's Dressing Area: yes
Meeting Equipment: BYO

Parking: valet only, $6/car
Accommodations: no guest rooms
Telephone: restaurant phone
Outdoor Night Lighting: access only
Outdoor Cooking Facilities: n/a
Cleanup: provided
View: panoramic view of SF Bay, bridges, Alcatraz, Treasure Island and beyond

RESTRICTIONS:

Alcohol: wine provided, no BYO
Smoking: on Terrace only
Music: acoustical only

Wheelchair Access: no
Insurance: not required

---

*This is important! Tell facilities you're reading **Here Comes The Guide** and ask if our information is still current.*

Legion of Honor Cafe

Lincoln Park, 34th Ave. and Clement St., San Francisco
(415) 221-2233, fax (415) 221-3197

www.edible-art.com
cafe@famsf.org

Landmark Museum

◆ Ceremonies   ◆ Special Events
◆ Wedding Receptions   ◆ Meetings
◆ Business Functions   Accommodations

The striking natural setting of the Presidio and the classical French design of the Palace of the Legion of Honor have long been a favorite backdrop for special events, and now there's another reason to choose this European fine art museum. After a top-to-bottom renovation, the Legion of Honor Cafe's newly refurbished space is just right for upscale private events, wedding receptions and business functions.

Located on the garden level of the museum, the Cafe occupies its own, private niche. It opens onto a sculpture garden where the sculptures change regularly. Overlooking the Lincoln Park Golf Course dotted with numerous cypresses and Monterey pines, the garden's granite patio and mature olive trees create a classically inspired setting; at night, outdoor lighting brings heightened drama to the scene.

Large picture windows and multiple sets of French doors bring views of the sculpture garden and lots of sunlight into the Cafe. Its high ceiling, hardwood floor, glazed plaster walls, and antiqued mirror panels give it a gallery-like ambiance. Silver-leaf sliding doors can divide the 3,000-square-foot cafe into a variety of configurations, accommodating parties large or small. A European-style jewel in a park setting, the Palace of the Legion of Honor Cafe is as elegant as its artistic surroundings.

CEREMONY CAPACITY: The outdoor courtyard holds up to 250 seated guests.

EVENT/RECEPTION CAPACITY: The facility holds 210 seated or 300 standing guests. The Board Room, available during operating hours, seats 80.

MEETING CAPACITY: The Museum's Gould Theater holds 320 seated, theater-style.

FEES & DEPOSITS: A $2,500 rental fee as well as a $1,000 catering deposit are required to reserve your date. An additional payment, bringing the catering deposit to 75%, is payable 60 days prior to the event; the catering balance and a confirmed guest count guarantee are due 10 days prior. Formal seated dinners start at $50/person; 4-hour hors d'oeuvres receptions at $40/person. Alcohol, tax and an 18% service charge are additional.

The Board Room rental fee is $500 for a 2-hour event. Call for information regarding all-day meetings.

AVAILABILITY: Year-round, daily, 6pm–10pm; business meetings 9am–5pm. Additional hours may be negotiated for an extra fee. Closed on major holidays.

SERVICES/AMENITIES:

Catering: provided, no BYO
Kitchen Facilities: n/a
Tables & Chairs: provided
Linens, Silver, etc.: provided, extra fee
Restrooms: wheelchair accessible
Dance Floor: Cafe hardwood floor
Bride's Dressing Area: CBA, extra fee
Meeting Equipment: CBA, extra fee

Parking: large lot
Accommodations: no guest rooms
Telephone: pay phones
Outdoor Night Lighting: yes
Outdoor Cooking Facilities: n/a
Cleanup: provided
View: Lincoln Park, Pacific Ocean
Other: event coordination CBA

RESTRICTIONS:

Alcohol: WB and hard alcohol provided, WC corkage $9/bottle
Smoking: not allowed

Wheelchair Access: yes
Insurance: certificate required
Music: amplified OK with volume restrictions

The professionals in the back of the book are the best in the business! **How do we know? Read page 681.**

117

Limn Gallery

292 Townsend at Fourth, San Francisco
(415) 977-1300, fax (415) 543-5971

www.limn.com

Art & Events Gallery

◆ Ceremonies	◆ Special Events
◆ Wedding Receptions	◆ Meetings
◆ Business Functions	Accommodations

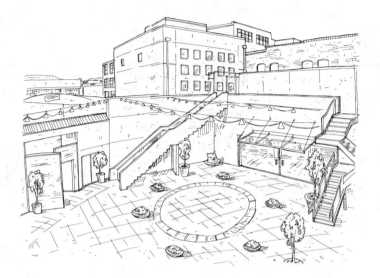

Specially designed to showcase events as well as art, Limn Gallery is sure to be one of San Francisco's hottest new special event venues. The complex, an enclosed courtyard and gallery building, is *really* brand new, finished in late 1996. But based on owner-architect Dan Friedlander's design track record—which includes 30 restaurants, among them Napa Valley's Tra Vigne and San Francisco's BIX—we have no doubt that Limn Gallery is going to be a high-style urban oasis.

The Gallery is sophisticated and stylish without being stuffy. You enter through an enclosed courtyard where touches of European craftsmanship and design abound. The courtyard is paved in hand-cast stones, each one made for its own individual spot. A decorative gate, potted trees and climbing vines with bright flowers will make you feel like you're in a private piazza in Tuscany, enjoying a summer night. The evening air can be warmed by a large soapstone fireplace that also moonlights as a pizza oven, grill and rotisserie. A kitchen and food-prep area opens onto the courtyard through wooden barn-style doors that make for easy alfresco service, and add a dash of rustic Mediterranean charm to the setting. If you're concerned about weather, the courtyard can be tented to provide protection from the elements.

The gallery building, two spacious rooms on either end of a large central hall, wraps around three sides of the courtyard. It's sleek and contemporary, and showcases museum-quality art and design exhibits. Floors are sealed concrete and walls are natural plaster. An elaborate track lighting system throughout enables you to add drama and atmosphere to either an elegant sit-down affair or a lively dance party. There's a built-in, indoor-outdoor sound system, and Limn Gallery can provide you with lots of floor-plan ideas drawn up on paper to help you stage your event. Ample parking, public transit and freeway access from all directions are close by, making it super easy to find Limn Gallery—your ticket to an event with European flair and a South-of-Market twist.

CEREMONY, EVENT/RECEPTION & MEETING CAPACITY: The gallery area holds 200 seated or 300 standing; the courtyard holds 80 seated or 200 standing. The facility can accommodate 300 guests, maximum.

FEES & DEPOSITS: The non-refundable $2,000–5,000 rental fee varies according to guest count and use of the space. To secure your date, half of the rental fee and a refundable security deposit (25% of the rental fee) are required. The rental balance is payable 2 days prior to the event. An extra charge will be incurred if more guests than scheduled attend.

AVAILABILITY: Year-round, daily. Hours are by arrangement.

SERVICES/AMENITIES:

Catering: preferred list or CBA

Kitchen Facilities: limited

Tables & Chairs: CBA

Linens, Silver, etc.: BYO

Restrooms: wheelchair accessible

Dance Floor: CBA

Bride's Dressing Area: CBA

Meeting Equipment: PA, microphones

View: of garden

Parking: nearby garages, 60-space lot CBA

Accommodations: no guest rooms

Telephone: emergency use only

Outdoor Night Lighting: yes

Outdoor Cooking Facilities: BBQ, rotisserie, pizza warmer CBA

Cleanup: caterer

Other: courtyard tent, event coordination, espresso bar, flowers, entertainment

RESTRICTIONS:

Alcohol: BYO, licensed & insured

Smoking: not allowed indoors or outdoors

Music: amplified OK w/volume restrictions

Wheelchair Access: yes

Insurance: certificate/rider required

Other: wall decorations restricted

---

*This is important! Tell facilities you're reading **Here Comes The Guide** and ask if our information is still current.*

MacArthur Park

607 Front Street, San Francisco
**(415) 398-5700, (415) 217-3891 ext. 232,
fax (415) 296-7827**

macparksf@aol.com

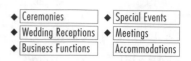

◆ Ceremonies ◆ Special Events
◆ Wedding Receptions ◆ Meetings
◆ Business Functions Accommodations

Housed in a pre-1906 brick ware-house—built when the area was the infamous Barbary Coast—MacArthur Park is located just blocks from the financial district. The Main Dining Room is light and airy with an eighteen-foot ceiling, skylights and a couple of towering indoor trees. The lower level of the room, called The Arcade, is frequently used for cocktails and hors d'oeuvres. It features brick arches and an expanse of tall windows that overlook the park across the street.

The Aviary, once a roosting place for peacocks and other tropical birds, offers a private and soothing atmosphere for small rehearsal dinners. A skylight ceiling, tile floor and brick walls hung with modern prints create warmth and intimacy. The adjacent Patio provides a setting for open-air events, particularly luncheons and cocktail receptions. Guests can enjoy the fresh air and stay comfortable outdoors thanks to a bank of heaters. The West Room accommodates larger groups, with wood-paneled walls featuring limited-edition American watercolors, windows that open out onto an ivy-covered courtyard and a large brick fireplace. Connected by French doors, these three rooms can be used individually or in combination. Blending rustic and sophisticated elements, MacArthur Park is a genial location for your wedding event, company party or personal celebration.

CEREMONY CAPACITY: Small, intimate ceremonies can take place in the restaurant; larger ones can occur outdoors, across the street in Waldon Park.

EVENT/RECEPTION & MEETING CAPACITY:

Space	Seated	Standing	Space	Seated	Standing
Arcade	60	100	West Room	75	125
Aviary	34	50	Main Dining Room	120	200
Bar Area	50	250	Entire Restaurant	280	500
Patio	25	30			

FEES & DEPOSITS: A signed contract and half the anticipated food and beverage total is required as deposit are required when the event is booked; the balance is due the day of the event. Per-person food costs are $21–34 for luncheons or $28–42 for dinners. Alcohol, tax and a 20% service charge are additional.

AVAILABILITY: Year-round, Sat & Sun 10–4pm, weekday evenings 5pm–11pm. With a buyout, more flexible hours can be negotiated.

SERVICES/AMENITIES:

Catering: provided, no BYO

Kitchen Facilities: n/a

Tables & Chairs: provided

Linens, Silver, etc.: provided

Restrooms: wheelchair accessible

Dance Floor: yes

Bride's Dressing Area: CBA

View: of Waldon Park, across the street

Parking: complimentary valet (dinners only), on street

Accommodations: no guest rooms

Telephone: pay phone

Outdoor Night Lighting: access only

Outdoor Cooking Facilities: no

Cleanup: provided

Meeting Equipment: full range AV

RESTRICTIONS:

Alcohol: provided, corkage $10/bottle

Smoking: outside only

Music: amplified OK if entire restaurant reserved

Wheelchair Access: yes, except Aviary

Insurance: not required

The professionals in the back of the book are the best in the business! **How do we know? Read page 681.**

The Mansions Hotel

Hotel & Restaurant

2220 Sacramento Street, San Francisco
(415) 929-9444, fax (415) 824-1945

www.themansions.com

◆ Ceremonies ◆ Special Events
◆ Wedding Receptions ◆ Meetings
◆ Business Functions ◆ Accommodations

Where can you find Richard Nixon's letter of resignation, the typewriter on which Jack London wrote *Call of The Wild*, and a major collection of Beniamino Bufano sculptures—all displayed in a setting of Victorian elegance? At the Smithsonian, perhaps? No, at the historic Mansions Hotel, right here in San Francisco's prestigious Pacific Heights.

The Mansions is really two landmark Victorian homes joined into one remarkable hotel and restaurant. Twelve lavishly appointed public rooms (including two parlors, three dining rooms, a banquet room and a billiard room) are available for events, and between them they contain thousands of beautiful, fascinating and downright surprising things. Period furnishings are accented by crystal chandeliers, gilded picture frames and flower arrangements throughout. Walls come alive with murals depicting a century of The Mansions' history, and the main dining room glows with its own mural, this one a 32-foot continuous panel of stained glass. Oil paintings, including an important work by J. M. Turner, keep company with an unusual array of items displayed in several mini-museums. The Historic Document Museum showcases handwritten letters and documents signed by Washington, John Hancock and Lincoln, just to name a few, while the Magic Museum displays magic memorabilia, including Houdini letters and artifacts. There's even an International Pig Museum, a whimsical tribute to Claudia, the niece of the Mansions' original owner—and resident ghost—who happened to have a passion for pigs.

While you can hold your event in any or all of a dozen rooms, the Victorian Cabaret Theater is probably the hotel's most unique attraction. World-class illusionists perform magic shows personalized for your wedding party or corporate group, and the performance ends with an actual "snowstorm" in the theater.

In addition to nourishing one's aesthetic sensibilities, The Mansions is also noted for its excellent cuisine. Described by *Inside San Francisco* as "one of San Francisco's ten top dining spots," its culinary staff offers a full-spectrum food service, from simple passed hors d'oeuvres to a sumptuous banquet. And after being wined and dined here, you'll naturally want to spend the night. Newlyweds are particularly fond of the Josephine Room, with its canopied bed, fireplace and private balcony overlooking the patio and sculpture garden.

The *Christian Science Monitor* said that when you come to The Mansions, "you jump back a century, slow down a bit and breathe an atmosphere of forgotten elegance." Guests such as Robin Williams, Barbra Streisand and John F. Kennedy, Jr. have been charmed by this place and we're confident that you will be too.

CEREMONY CAPACITY: Small ceremonies for up to 60 guests can be arranged.

EVENT/RECEPTION CAPACITY: The Mansions holds 150 for a standing reception or 120 for seated meals.

MEETING CAPACITY: The Conference Room holds 20 seated, the Cabaret Theater 55 seated, the Dining Room 120 seated, and the public parlors, 150 standing guests.

FEES & DEPOSITS: Half of the estimated event total is required when the site is booked; the balance is payable the day of the event. Catering is provided. Receptions with hors d'oeuvres, multi-course, seated dinner, 1-hour personalized magic show or live music for dancing, and full beverage service run $89/person. A $99/person wedding package includes flowers, wedding cake, ceremony, seated meal, an excellent wine and champagne list, plus a magic show or dancing with live music. Events can be customized; prices vary depending on the services selected. Tax and an 18% service charge are additional.

For business meetings, the Conference Room rental fee is $300, which may be waived with a food and beverage minimum.

AVAILABILITY: Year-round, daily, 7am–11pm. Weddings and receptions are usually held 11am–4pm on Saturdays, noon–10pm Sundays. Saturday night bookings are negotiable.

SERVICES/AMENITIES:

Catering: provided, no BYO
Kitchen Facilities: n/a
Tables & Chairs: provided
Linens, Silver, etc.: provided
Restrooms: not wheelchair accessible
Dance Floor: yes
Bride's Dressing Area: CBA
Meeting Equipment: CBA, extra fee

Parking: Webster/Clay garage and valet
Accommodations: 21 guest rooms & suites
Telephone: house phone
Outdoor Night Lighting: yes
Outdoor Cooking Facilities: no
Cleanup: provided
View: no
Other: pianos and billiard room

RESTRICTIONS:

Alcohol: BWC provided or corkage $10/bottle
Smoking: restricted
Music: amplified OK until 10pm

Wheelchair Access: no
Insurance: not required

*This is important! Tell facilities you're reading **Here Comes The Guide** and ask if our information is still current.*

123

Marines' Memorial Club

609 Sutter Street, San Francisco
(415) 673-6672 ext. 264, fax (415) 928-4513

www.marineclub.com
catering@marineclub.com

Historic Club and Hotel

- ◆ Ceremonies
- ◆ Wedding Receptions
- ◆ Business Functions
- ◆ Special Events
- ◆ Meetings
- ◆ Accommodations

Marines' Memorial Club is a hidden jewel in the heart of downtown San Francisco. Built in 1910 as a formal women's club, it was transformed in 1946, as a memorial to Marines who lost their lives during World War II.

The nonprofit Club has a restaurant, health club, indoor pool, library, museum, suites and wonderful banquet rooms. What you might not know is that the Club has an exquisite, take-your-breath-away Crystal Ballroom that is available for grand parties. Ornate chandeliers, a detailed ceiling, raised stage and a gleaming parquet floor all create an exceptional venue for wedding receptions. The Heritage Room, Commandants Room and the Regimental Room are also available for weddings. The latter has a vaulted, painted ceiling, marble fireplace and lots of wood detailing. Not only are the rooms lovely, but the prices are attractive, too. If you're going to have a reception in the City, make sure you don't overlook this facility.

CEREMONY & EVENT/RECEPTION CAPACITY:

Room	Seated	Room	Seated
Heritage Room	20–50	Regimental Room	20–60
Crystal Ballroom	150–200	Commandants Room	50–300

MEETING CAPACITY:

Room	Theater-style	Conf-style	Room	Theater-style	Conf-style
Heritage Room	50	40	Regimental Room	60	40
Crystal Ballroom	250	100	Commandants Room	300	100
Lounge	30	30			

FEES & DEPOSITS: For weddings, a $1,000 refundable deposit is required within 14 days of reserving a banquet room. There's no rental fee if you meet a food and beverage minimum, however house catering is required. A guest count along with the estimated event balance is required 72 hours prior to the event. Seated luncheons start at $19/person and dinners at $27/

person. Hors d'oeuvres start at $8/person and buffets (min. 75 people) at $30/person. Alcohol, tax and a 17% service charge are additional.

For meetings and business functions, fees for meeting rooms range from $200–2,000, depending on room(s) and/or services selected. Call for additional information regarding food and beverage charges.

AVAILABILITY: Year-round, daily, 7am–11pm. There are overtime charges for events running more than 5 hours.

SERVICES/AMENITIES:

Catering: provided, no BYO
Kitchen Facilities: n/a
Tables & Chairs: provided
Linens, Silver, etc.: provided
Restrooms: wheelchair accessible
Dance Floor: yes
Bride's Dressing Area: CBA
Meeting Equipment: provided

Parking: nearby garage
Accommodations: 137 guest rooms
Telephone: pay and guest phones
Outdoor Night Lighting: access only
Outdoor Cooking Facilities: no
Cleanup: provided
View: of Nob Hill and SF Bay
Other: full event coordination

RESTRICTIONS:

Alcohol: provided, corkage $8/bottle
Smoking: designated areas
Music: amplified OK

Wheelchair Access: yes, elevator
Insurance: not required

The professionals in the back of the book are the best in the business! **How do we know? Read page 681.**

125

Mark Hopkins Inter-Continental Hotel

Hotel

Number One Nob Hill, San Francisco
(415) 616-6935 Catering Dept., fax (415) 616-6970

www.interconti.com
roxane_hoey@interconti.com

◆ Ceremonies ◆ Special Events
◆ Wedding Receptions ◆ Meetings
◆ Business Functions ◆ Accommodations

Since it opened in 1926, the Mark Hopkins has been one of San Francisco's premier hotels. Poised at the crest of Nob Hill, it rises nineteen stories and is as much a San Francisco icon as the cable cars that clang past its grand entrance. So it's no surprise that it evokes lots of romance and history. During WWII, the Top of the Mark was the site of many farewell rendezvous where couples met for a last drink before the men shipped out. Wives and girlfriends stayed behind to watch from the top-story windows as their sweethearts' ships slipped through the Golden Gate.

The Mark Hopkins is still a perfect place for a romantic rendezvous—happily without a tearful farewell. Hold your ceremony in the Room of the Dons, notable for its twenty-six-foot ceiling and nine vibrant murals (by Maynard Dixon and Frank Van Sloun) depicting scenes from early California. Painted in a rich medley of reds, blues and browns against gold leaf, they were completed in 1926 for the hotel's grand opening. The seven-foot-high murals, set off by the subtle cream-and-taupe walls and ceiling, create a colorful banner around the room's perimeter. While you're admiring their artistry, say your vows in front of a towering arched window, which is gracefully draped in silk brocade.

Receptions are often held in the Peacock Court, a light, palatial ballroom befitting a grand hotel. Complete with its own stage, its classical details include soft beige walls with delicately carved plaster moldings, arched windows draped in layers of teal and gold silk brocade, and a ceiling with intricate plaster work. After the festivities, retire to one of the hotel's luxurious honeymoon suites where you'll savor views from your private glass solarium—a knockout spot for sipping champagne by moonlight and for enjoying your first breakfast as husband and wife.

The Mark Hopkins has two smaller event rooms as well, both of which reflect the hotel's grace and elegance and provide flexible event-planning options. Or for a world class treat, reserve the Top of the Mark, with its breathtaking 360-degree view of San Francisco and much of the Bay Area. A recent one-million-dollar renovation has provided a twenty-foot vaulted ceiling and a split level floor that promises unobstructed views from every seat. Literally one of the City's high points, it's an exceptional spot for receptions and business functions. Whatever type of event you have, the Mark Hopkins will leave you and your guests walking on air.

CEREMONY CAPACITY: Five rooms hold 45–500 seated or 50–600 standing guests.

EVENT/RECEPTION CAPACITY:

Room	Seated	Standing	Room	Seated	Standing
Golden Gate Room	160	220	Peacock Court	450	600
Room of the Dons	220	350	Peacock & Dons	630	800

MEETING CAPACITY: The Hotel has 14 rooms with 14,500 square feet of meeting space; many rooms can be combined.

Room	Seated	Room	Seated	Room	Seated
Florentine Room	20–40	Garden Room	20–40	Board Room	16
Harvard Room	15–30	Emerald Room	26–50	Six Continents	40–120
George D. Smith	30–100	Barclay 1&2	20–40 ea.	Willard 1 & 2	20–40 ea.
Top of the Mark	100–170	Nob Hill Terrace	70		

FEES & DEPOSITS: A 10% deposit is payable when the contract is submitted; the event balance along with a guest count guarantee are due 72 hours prior to the event. Rental fees from $125–6,000 may apply to corporate meetings and wedding ceremonies, depending on room(s) selected, catering fees, guest count and season. Any menu can be customized. Luncheons start at $28/person, buffets at $40/person, and dinners at $39/person; alcohol, tax and a 19% service charge are additional. Several wedding packages are available that include hors d'oeuvres, open bar, 4-course seated meal, wine with dinner, wedding cake, champagne toast, and Terrace Suite for the bride and groom. Prices start at $140/person inclusive of tax and service charges. Seasonal discounts may be available for group accommodations.

AVAILABILITY: Year-round, daily, any time. Weddings take place in 5 1/2-hour blocks, with additional time negotiable.

SERVICES/AMENITIES:

Catering: provided, no BYO
Kitchen Facilities: n/a
Tables & Chairs: provided
Linens, Silver, etc.: provided
Restrooms: wheelchair accessible
Dance Floor: provided
Bride's & Groom's Dressing Area: CBA
Meeting Equipment: full range

Parking: hotel garage, nearby garages
Accommodations: 392 guest rooms, 28 suites
Telephone: pay and guest phones
Outdoor Night Lighting: access only
Outdoor Cooking Facilities: no
Cleanup: provided
View: of Nob Hill, San Francisco & Bay
Other: baby grand, ice sculptures

RESTRICTIONS:

Alcohol: provided, no BYO
Smoking: designated areas
Music: amplified OK w/volume restrictions

Wheelchair Access: yes, elevator
Insurance: not required
Other: decorations restricted

---

*This is important! Tell facilities you're reading **Here Comes The Guide** and ask if our information is still current.*

McCormick & Kuleto's

900 North Point, San Francisco
(415) 929-8374, fax (415) 567-2919

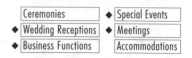

Restaurant

Ceremonies	◆ Special Events
◆ Wedding Receptions	◆ Meetings
◆ Business Functions	Accommodations

If it's true that good food tastes even better when it's served up with a great view, then eating at McCormick & Kuleto's is bound to be a delectable experience. This three-tiered restaurant in Ghirardelli Square specializes in impeccably fresh seafood from all over the world. It overlooks the bay—which just happens to be right across the street—and almost every diner has an unobstructed view of Alcatraz, Marin and a variety of historical ships that are docked at Hyde Street Pier.

The interior scenery is also captivating. In the Main Dining Room, fantastic tortoise shell "boat" chandeliers drop from the vaulted ceiling. Wood-and-copper railings flow from tier to tier, defining each level. The Captain's Room derives its warmth from sumptuous burled redwood paneling throughout, and elegant, hand-crafted glass lighting fixtures. The Bay View Room, which has its own bar, is a favorite for cocktail receptions. Both the Bay View and Captain's Rooms can be reserved individually or in conjunction for seated receptions. The Dolphin Room, with its mirrored walls and views of the bay, is a nice spot for intimate rehearsal dinners and receptions, as is the adjoining patio. For smaller receptions, the Alcatraz Room is a more informal space with redwood paneling and pictures of historic ships decorating the walls.

And if you'd like your event outdoors, there's an intimate brick patio with the same great bay vistas. Suffused with sunlight or enhanced by the nighttime glitter of boats docked below, McCormick & Kuleto's provides a generous helping of visual as well as gastronomic appeal.

CEREMONY CAPACITY: This venue does not host ceremonies.

EVENT/RECEPTION CAPACITY:

Area	*Seated*	*Standing*		*Area*	*Seated*	*Standing*
Captain's Room	50–120	200		Bay View Room	80	100*
Alcatraz Room	20–60	80		Bay View & Captain's Rms	150–220	300
Dolphin Room	20–60	90		*Seasonal availability.*		

MEETING CAPACITY:

Area	*Theater-style*		*Area*	*Theater-style*
Captain's Room	50–100		Bay View Room	60–80
Alcatraz Room	20–60		Dolphin Room	20–60

FEES & DEPOSITS: A $500 deposit is due when reservations are made, and the balance is payable the day of the event. Any menu can be customized; catering costs run $15–26/person for luncheons and $25–40/person for dinners. Tax and a 17% service charge are additional.

Rates for business functions vary, call for more specifics.

AVAILABILITY: Year-round, daily, 11:30am–midnight.

SERVICES/AMENITIES:

Catering: provided, no BYO
Kitchen Facilities: n/a
Tables & Chairs: provided
Linens, Silver, etc.: provided
Restrooms: wheelchair accessible
Dance Floor: CBA, extra charge
Bride's Dressing Area: no
Meeting Equipment: CBA, extra charge
Other: event coordination

Parking: garage, on street, valet CBA
Accommodations: no guest rooms
Telephone: pay phone
Outdoor Night Lighting: on patio
Outdoor Cooking Facilities: CBA
Cleanup: provided
View: SF Bay, Maritime Museum, historic ships, Angel Island

RESTRICTIONS:

Alcohol: provided
Smoking: outdoors only
Music: amplified OK until midnight, volume restrictions

Wheelchair Access: yes
Insurance: may be required

The professionals in the back of the book are the best in the business! **How do we know? Read page 681.**

129

Merchant's Exchange Ballroom
and Conference Center

465 California Street, 15th Floor, San Francisco
(415) 421-7730, fax (415) 421-6726

www.clintonreilly.com
ken@clintonreilly.com

Historic Landmark

◆ Ceremonies ◆ Special Events
◆ Wedding Receptions ◆ Meetings
◆ Business Functions Accommodations

The Merchant's Exchange Building may be located in San Francisco's financial district, but an event held in this historic gem will not be business as usual. Designed by Willis Polk and Julia Morgan, it's a landmark, and its classic Beaux Arts style is the same as that of San Simeon, Morgan's more famous architectural creation.

The moment you pass through the street-level doors, you know you've arrived somewhere special. The barrel-vaulted lobby is a gorgeous entrance that sparkles with marble, gold leaf and bronze, with a crosshatch glass ceiling. Although all events are held on the Fifteenth Floor, this area can be used in conjunction with your rental.

The Fifteenth Floor retains the flavor of its tenure as a private men's club, which only recently closed its doors. The rooms have been refurbished and lightened, but the sense of privacy remains: there are no busy hotel corridors to contend with, no intrusions from the outside world. The space is so expansive and fluid that it's easy to imagine any event being held here, from an elegant formal wedding or holiday party to an annual corporate sales event or training seminar.

The lounge has its own classic coat-check room and opens onto what was once called the cardroom. Both rooms are paneled in rich mahogany and have gilded ceilings, and used together they form a comfortable hall with large matching fireplaces of carved, creamy stone at either end. The cardroom has a 25-foot curved mahogany bar that sweeps you toward the ballroom, a room that is nothing short of grand, with over 4,300 square feet of elegance. Light flows in through a wall of soaring floor-to-ceiling arched windows that afford a view of the heart of San Francisco's skyline; arched mirrors on the opposite wall reflect and reciprocate the light. The view overhead is also impressive—the ceiling is a honeycomb of mahogany octagonals. Like the other rooms, the ballroom is paneled in mahogany, but here the walls showcase classic columns worked into the wood. At the far end, a 20-foot fireplace of the same creamy stone used elsewhere creates the final touch of majesty.

The lounge and bar area (over 1,600 square feet) can be rented exclusively, but when you reserve the ballroom, you can use the entire floor. This gives you access to several smaller rooms, perfect for bridal dressing areas or meetings. One bride hired a clown and used one of the small rooms for entertaining the children on her guest list. If you're looking for a special place to hold an event in the grand tradition, the Fifteenth Floor of the Merchant's Exchange is not to be missed. Like San Simeon, it has grace and opulence, but unlike San Simeon, it can be yours for a day or night.

CEREMONY & EVENT/RECEPTION CAPACITY: Ceremonies and receptions can be held in the ballroom or lounge area. The ballroom holds up to 400 seated or 800–1,000 standing. The lounge area holds 100 seated or 300 standing.

MEETING CAPACITY: For large meetings, the ballroom can hold 430 theater-style or 350 conference-style. There are 3 smaller seminar rooms which can accommodate 12–40 seated conference-style.

FEES & DEPOSITS: The rental fee for use of the entire 15th floor starts at $3,750. The rental fee for only the lounge area is $1,500. The fee for smaller meeting rooms starts at $350. To secure your date, half the non-refundable rental fee is required as well as a $500 refundable security deposit. Prices will vary during the holiday season and special holiday weekends.

AVAILABILITY: Year-round, daily. Hours are by arrangement.

SERVICES/AMENITIES:

Catering: BYO, licensed, insured & bonded
Kitchen Facilities: prep only
Tables & Chairs: provided, extra charge
Linens, Silver, etc.: BYO
Restrooms: wheelchair accessible
Dance Floor: provided, extra charge
Bride's & Groom's Dressing Area: yes
Meeting Equipment: AV equipment CBA

Parking: nearby garages
Accommodations: no guest rooms
Telephone: pay phone
Outdoor Night Lighting: no
Outdoor Cooking Facilities: no
Cleanup: caterer
View: downtown San Francisco
Other: event coordination, flowers, cake, music CBA

RESTRICTIONS:

Alcohol: provided, no BYO
Smoking: outdoors only
Music: amplified OK

Wheelchair Access: yes
Insurance: certificate required
Other: no rice, birdseed, glitter

---

*This is important! Tell facilities you're reading **Here Comes The Guide** and ask if our information is still current.*

New Main Library, San Francisco

Library

100 Larkin Street, San Francisco
(415) 437-4856, fax (415) 437-4855

sfpl.lib.ca.us/page/index.html
cindylf@sfpl.lib.ca.us

◆ Ceremonies ◆ Special Events
◆ Wedding Receptions ◆ Meetings
◆ Business Functions ☐ Accommodations

The grand limestone edifice of San Francisco's New Main Public Library looms large and elegant across from City Hall. The light sheen of the stone, the soaring windows and solid construction announce a major, enduring public space with a fine arts sensibility. Just two years old, this structure has already become the new heart of San Francisco's cultural community.

There are many entrances, but the grandest is through the portals across from City Hall, opening onto the Larkin Street Bridge. The Bridge, itself a rentable space that works well for cocktail parties, leads to an elegant stairway that takes you down to the Library's main event space: the Atrium. As you stand on the ground floor looking up, you see the five tiers of the library circling towards the asymmetrical Atrium dome. During the day, windows diffuse a natural light, but at night, the atmosphere becomes much more glamorous. Candlelight reflects beautifully off the interior finish, and the "Constellation" sculpture by Nayland Blake really glows and glitters like stars in the night sky.

There are lots of party options. The Atrium, filled with linen-draped tables and roving waiters instead of the book-borrowing public, is transformed into a formally elegant setting, with its polished chrome railings, limestone floor, and wax-on-plaster walls. Note that the walls achieve their unique look thanks to hundreds of pounds of coffee beans that, when added to the mix, create tone, texture and warmth. Then there's the sixth floor Skylight Gallery, with its open-air terrace, intriguing sculptures, and atrium-top views; it's a popular space for after-dinner coffee and dessert, or for smaller functions that don't need the atrium expanse. Downstairs, the informal Gallery Foyer is an architecturally fascinating, dramatic spot, with lots of angles and curves, windows and pillars. It makes for a nice reception area outside the Koret Auditorium, which is blessed with excellent acoustics, top technical equipment, an intimate feel and extraordinary wall sconces that look like light-emitting screens.

Though by day the library is a hub of research and a lender of books, by night it's surprisingly versatile. Now that the library has opened its doors to private after-hours functions, it hopes to further its public role by appealing to the broadest group of people and events possible. And proceeds derived from your tax-deductible contributions go toward the continued upkeep of the library. Many corporate events have been hosted here, plus non-profit and alumnae parties, exhibitions and fund-raisers, not to mention Vice President Gore and scads of mayors during the U.S. Conference of Mayors. The library has also been featured in the Hollywood feature film "City of Angels" and the television series "Nash Bridges." Given its growing popularity, it's a little surprising that the one special event that hasn't been held here so far is a wedding—this despite the Atrium's grand, curved staircase, designed as though with a bride in mind. Yours could just be the first.

CEREMONY CAPACITY: The Atrium can seat 210 guests. The Skylight Gallery seats 180.

EVENT/RECEPTION CAPACITY: The Atrium can accommodate 210 seated guests or 440 standing; in combination with the adjacent Larkin Street Bridge, the space can accommodate up to 740 standing guests. The Skylight Gallery can hold 180 seated or 485 standing.

MEETING CAPACITY: The Community Meeting Room seats 100 guests conference-style or 150 theater-style. The Koret Auditorium can seat 235 guests theater-style.

FEES & DEPOSITS: A 30% non-refundable rental fee deposit is required to secure your date. The balance of the rental fee is due 2 weeks prior to the event. Rental fees are as follows:

Area	*Fee*	*Area*	*Fee*
Atrium	$7,500–9,000	Community Mtg. Rm.	$1,000
Skylight Gallery	$5,500	Koret Auditorium	$1,500

AVAILABILITY: Year round, Friday–Monday, 6pm–midnight. Friday and Sunday morning, 6am–11am.

SERVICES/AMENITIES:

Catering: BYO
Kitchen Facilities: ample, no cooking indoors
Tables & Chairs: chairs only in Comm. Mtg. Rm.
Linens, Silver, etc.: BYO
Restrooms: wheelchair accessible
Dance Floor: yes
Bride's Dressing Area: no
Meeting Equipment: a/v equipment

Parking: paid parking on street or garage
Accommodations: no guest rooms
Telephone: pay phone
Outdoor Night Lighting: no
Outdoor Cooking Facilities: no
Cleanup: caterer
View: no view

RESTRICTIONS:

Alcohol: BYO
Smoking: not allowed
Music: amplified OK

Wheelchair Access: yes
Insurance: liability required
Other: no rice, birdseed or red wine

The professionals in the back of the book are the best in the business! **How do we know? Read page 681.**

Nob Hill Hotel & Event Center

Hotel & Event Center

827 Hyde Street, San Francisco
(415) 921-2324 x609, fax (415) 567-1585
www.nobhilleventcenter.com
info@nobhilleventcenter.com

◆ Ceremonies ◆ Special Events
◆ Wedding Receptions ◆ Meetings
◆ Business Functions ◆ Accommodations

Surveying the beautifully renovated Nob Hill Hotel and Event Center, you'd never guess that this historic building almost met a fiery end in the 1906 earthquake. Built just two years before to house the Eastern Exchange Telephone company, it survived, and after a quick refurbishing, was once again able to fulfill its original purpose: providing telephone service to the community—this time to thousands of post-quake survivors.

Now the facility has a new purpose: hosting a wide range of special events. Although its nicely detailed Neoclassical facade is still intact—complete with gold-leafed lion heads gazing down from the top—the interior has been updated with an Italian motif. You get your first glimpse of this in the cozy vestibule, just in front of the hotel lobby. This marble entry, with its pale terra cotta walls, elaborate molding and *trompe l'oeil* sky full of clouds overhead is a charming introduction to the rest of the building.

Actually, we should probably say two buildings. The hotel and the Event Center exist side by side, connected at the first-floor lobby level by an arched doorway. It's a very convenient arrangement: after your festivities in the Event Center, you and your guests have only to go next door to stay overnight in the quaint guest rooms, all furnished with Victorian antiques.

Nob Hill's event spaces give you a surprising number of options, because you can reserve any or all of them and use them in whatever way best suits you. Say you're getting married here. You could have a small ceremony in the Oak Room, an intimate oak-paneled room, with a tall brick fireplace and beveled-glass windows. Or you could tie the knot in the Theatre Room, a theatrical space with a turn-of-the-century stained-glass doorway, heavy velour curtains, faux-marble pillars and a hand-crafted oak bar. The Event Center's second-floor lobby offers another possibility, including gilded mirrors, plants and an eight-foot statue of the winged woman of Avalon, plus a staircase that comes in handy for a bridal entrance.

All large receptions and parties are held upstairs in the Avalon Ballroom. Tasteful glitz gives the Ballroom an exciting ambiance, especially for evening affairs. Thirteen crystal chandeliers drop from a high ceiling, reflecting light off the mirrored walls, covered in shimmery gold-patterned wallpaper. In soft contrast, swags of ivory fabric are draped between gold-painted wall columns, and the floor is carpeted in a rich black, delicately threaded with gold swirls.

Two large ficus trees and ferns placed throughout provide a bit of nature indoors. The room has its own bar, a raised stage, and a hardwood dance floor. It's also equipped with a full stage, state-of-the-art lighting and PA systems, and a white-and-gold baby grand piano.

More intimate affairs are accommodated in the Roman Room, another sophisticated space featuring faux-marble columns, marble pedestals topped by lush ferns, five crystal chandeliers and gilt mirrors on the walls. Thursday through Saturday nights it's used for a comedy club, but any other time of the week you can reserve it for your rehearsal dinner, small reception, or meeting.

And if you'd like help planning your event, the in-house coordinator will take care of all the worrisome details so you don't have to. The Nob Hill Hotel and Event Center may be a new player in the world of San Francisco event facilities, but with its great location, flexibility and friendly staff it won't be long before it's won over a devoted following.

CEREMONY CAPACITY: The Ballroom holds 425 seated, the Roman Room holds 222 seated and the Oak Room 83 seated.

EVENT/RECEPTION CAPACITY: The Oak Room holds 56 seated or 105 standing, the Roman Room 160 seated or 286 standing, and the Ballroom 325 seated or 546 standing guests.

MEETING CAPACITY: There are three rooms available for meetings, which can accommodate up to 641 seated guests.

FEES & DEPOSITS: 50% of the event total is the deposit required to secure your date. The rental fee balance is due 60 days prior to the event. Hors d'oeuvres start at $15/person, luncheons at $18/person and dinners at $35/person; tax, alcohol and an 18% service charge are additional. Rental fees are as follows:

Area	Mon–Thurs	Fri–Sun		Area	Mon–Thurs	Fri–Sun
Ballroom	$1,950	$3,200		Oak Room	550	700
Roman Room	650	850				

AVAILABILITY: Year-round, daily; 8am–2am.

SERVICES/AMENITIES:

Catering: provided, or BYO w/approval

Kitchen Facilities: yes

Tables & Chairs: some prov., more CBA, extra fee

Linens, Silver, etc.: some prov., more CBA, extra fee

Restrooms: wheelchair accessible

Dance Floor: yes

Bride's Dressing Area: yes

Meeting Equipment: some provided, CBA, extra fee

Parking: on street or garage, valet CBA

Accommodations: 48 guest rooms

Telephone: pay phones

Outdoor Night Lighting: no

Outdoor Cooking Facilities: no

Cleanup: caterer or renter

View: no view

Other: event coordination, baby grand piano, state-of-art lighting & PA system, entertainment bookings

RESTRICTIONS:

Alcohol: provided, or corkage $7.50/bottle

Smoking: not allowed

Music: amplified OK

Wheelchair Access: yes

Insurance: extra liability required

Old Federal Reserve Bank Building

400 Sansome Street, San Francisco
(415) 392-1234, fax (415) 296-2919

bpeters@sfophpo.hyatt.com

Historic Bank Foyer

◆ Ceremonies ◆ Special Events
◆ Wedding Receptions ◆ Meetings
◆ Business Functions ◆ Accommodations

We always get asked about mansions in San Francisco, and to tell you the truth, there aren't many which can accommodate large wedding receptions indoors. Although the Old Federal Reserve Bank Building is not a mansion, it possesses the stately, elegant and understated grandeur you'd expect from a palatial estate. And it can handle quite a crowd.

Originally part of the lobby of the 1924 Federal Reserve Bank, the event space has been fully restored and the building in which it's housed is included in the National Register of Historic Places. The Old Federal Reserve is a fine example of San Francisco's "banking temple" tradition and the government's penchant for monumental classical architecture during that era. Inside, you'll find one of the most dramatic staircases we've ever seen. If you'd like to make a theatrical entrance, descend the bronze and marble double stairway which starts from two separate places and curves seamlessly down onto the gleaming marble floor below. Everywhere you look, you'll see French and Italian marble (or a close facsimile). Expertly painted faux marbling has transformed the two rows of twenty-five-foot-tall Ionic columns that flank the room into "rock-solid" architectural elements. The entry doors are solid bronze, and two original bronze chandeliers (designed by the architect) draw your eyes up to the awe-inspiring 34-foot ceiling overhead. All in all, if you have an extended guest list and are searching for a grand location in the City, you couldn't ask for a better spot.

CEREMONY CAPACITY: The main foyer holds 300 seated guests.

EVENT/RECEPTION & MEETING CAPACITY: The building can hold 150–400 seated or 800 for a standing reception.

FEES & DEPOSITS: The rental fee is $4,000 on weekdays, $4,500 on weekends. A deposit, also based on event size, is due when the space is booked. The balance of all fees is due 14 days prior to the event.

AVAILABILITY: Year-round, daily from 5pm–1am. For day use, special arrangements must be made.

SERVICES/AMENITIES:

Catering: select from preferred list
Kitchen Facilities: no
Tables & Chairs: caterer
Linens, Silver, etc.: caterer
Restrooms: wheelchair accessible
Dance Floor: CBA
Bride's Dressing Area: CBA
Cleanup: provided
Meeting Equipment: full range CBA

Parking: adjacent garage, discounted on evenings and weekends
Accommodations: 360 guest rooms at adjacent Park Hyatt San Francisco, including 37 suites
Telephone: pay phones
Outdoor Night Lighting: access only
Outdoor Cooking Facilities: no
View: no
Other: health club

RESTRICTIONS:

Alcohol: provided, corkage $10/bottle
Smoking: outside only
Music: amplified OK

Wheelchair Access: yes
Insurance: not required

This is important! Tell facilities you're reading **Here Comes The Guide** *and ask if our information is still current.*

One Market Pavilion
Concourse & Bay View Terrace

One Market, San Francisco
(415) 777-2233, fax (415) 777-4411

Special Event Facility

◆ Ceremonies   ◆ Special Events
◆ Wedding Receptions   ◆ Meetings
◆ Business Functions   Accommodations

One Market Pavilion and the Concourse include some of the most architecturally dramatic spaces in The City. Located at the foot of Market Street, both showcase the sophisticated glitz of the building's recent $37-million transformation.

Although there are four entrances to the Pavilion, the most intriguing is on Mission Street, where a seven-story, white metal gate tower clues you in to what you'll find inside. The first thing you see is a stunning, block-long Concourse that makes you stop in your tracks: a sea of gleaming cream- and rust-colored Italian marble flows beneath your feet; glass-and-metal light trees "grow" along both sides, forming a high-tech canopy overhead; domed skylights 80 feet above bathe the entire space in natural light. And as vast as this area seems, its boundaries are extended even further by the adjacent, sleek Steuart and Spear Tower lobbies.

At the far end of the Concourse is the Pavilion. Named for the striking hexagonal structure in its center, it's actually a courtyard atrium enclosed on four sides. The central sculpture is an avant-garde gazebo, with an intricate latticework of enormous white steel beams, soaring 132 feet towards a skylit dome. A translucent water fountain sculpture, deep terra-cotta-colored walls and a mosaic marble floor give the space a distinctive Italian flavor, and computer-controlled lighting allows the mood to be varied. You can host an intimate party within the structure itself, or a gala event for thousands if you reserve the Concourse and lobbies along with the Pavilion. With its grand scale and innovative design, this is one event site that's bound to favorably impress all your guests.

CEREMONY CAPACITY: The 7th floor rooftop Bay View Terrace holds 400 seated or 450 standing. Other areas can be arranged.

EVENT/RECEPTION CAPACITY: The Pavilion holds 750 seated or 1,000 standing; the Pavilion and Concourse, combined, 1,250 seated or 2,000 standing; the Pavilion, Concourse and outer lobbies, combined, 3,500 standing.

FEES & DEPOSITS: To reserve your date, the entire rental fee is required: $5,500 for the Pavilion; $7,500 for the Pavilion with Concourse and lobbies, or $1,200 for the Bay View Terrace. The anticipated catering total is payable 10 days prior to the event.

In-house catering is provided by One Market Restaurant in concert with *Taste Catering, Paula LeDuc Fine Catering* or *McCall & Associates;* each menu is customized and prices will vary depending on guest count and menu items selected. Alcohol, tax and service charges will be additional.

AVAILABILITY: Year-round, weekdays 5:30pm–1am; weekends 8am–1am.

SERVICES/AMENITIES:

Catering: provided, no BYO

Kitchen Facilities: n/a

Tables & Chairs: provided, extra charge

Linens, Silver, etc.: provided, extra charge

Restrooms: wheelchair accessible

Dance Floor: CBA, extra fee

Bride's Dressing Area: CBA

View: San Francisco Bay and Bay Bridge from Bay View Terrace

Parking: valet required, extra fee

Accommodations: no guest rooms

Telephone: pay phones

Outdoor Night Lighting: access only

Outdoor Cooking Facilities: n/a

Cleanup: provided

Meeting Equipment: CBA, extra charge

Other: stage and lighting CBA, extra fee; variety of theme decor CBA

RESTRICTIONS:

Alcohol: provided, no BYO

Smoking: outside only

Music: amplified OK w/approval

Wheelchair Access: yes

Insurance: certificate required

Other: no confetti, rice, birdseed, or glitter; decorations w/approval

---

The professionals in the back of the book are the best in the business! **How do we know? Read page 681.**

Pacific Marine Yachts

Yachts

Charter & Dining Cruises

Berthed at Pier 39, San Francisco
(415) 788-9100, (800) 292-2487, fax (415) 788-5445

www.pacificmarineyachts.com
sales@pacificmarineyachts.com

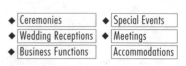

◆ Ceremonies	◆ Special Events
◆ Wedding Receptions	◆ Meetings
◆ Business Functions	Accommodations

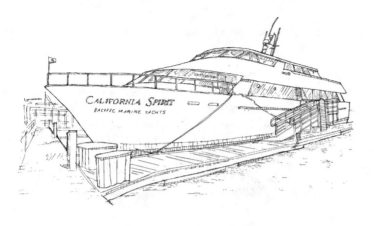

Lots of places boast about their spectacular views, but how many can claim a view that encompasses the entire San Francisco Bay? We immediately think of three, and all belong to Pacific Marine Yachts. On Pacific Marine's fleet you'll celebrate while sailing over blue waters and seeing the skylines, bridges and islands of the Bay as you've never seen them before. While you're enjoying the sights, you'll be treated to a vast array of services, all supplied by this company's experienced staff. You don't have to think twice about having your event here: Pacific Marine handles both private parties and corporate clients with ease, from meetings and executive retreats to dinner parties and awards ceremonies. And if you're tying the knot on board, they make the wedding experience so easy, you won't have to worry about anything at all except keeping a hand on your veil while strolling 'round the decks.

Pacific Marine's 150-foot San Francisco Spirit is the equivalent of a sophisticated, floating ballroom with unparalleled views of the Bay. Here, even the biggest celebrations will have plenty of room for informal mingling and formal dining; the yacht's three decks offer well-designed areas for bar and food stations, marble dance floors and seated dining. There are even spots for wedding ceremonies—performed by the captain or an officiant of your choice. The 100-foot California Spirit was custom designed by Pacific Marine's owner, Marti McMahon. Stunningly refurbished in 1998, the yacht features warm, teak interiors throughout its three spacious salons. This vessel has ample open deck space, and a posh environment that includes a luxurious combination of textured fabrics, leather upholstery and granite tables. Banquettes have been specifically designed for comfort and versatility. The sleek Golden Sunset, a 75-foot Westport Motor Yacht, features two decks with wet bars and an open air fly bridge. Rich mahogany, macassar ebony and teak woods accent the plush interior. A granite bar and tables with custom seating create an intimate clubroom atmosphere of understated elegance. Downstairs, the stateroom comes complete with queen bed, VCR and marble bath with Jacuzzi tub—accoutrements that you wouldn't expect to see or experience on a boat!

So climb aboard and enjoy the tang of salt breezes and the exhilaration of cruising the Bay. And if you'd like to sail away from another location of your choice, note that alternative pickup points can be arranged for a modest additional charge.

CEREMONY, EVENT/RECEPTION & MEETING CAPACITY:

Vessel	Seated	Standing	Vessel	Seated	Standing
San Francisco Spirit	500	700	California Spirit	107	149
Main Salon	250	300	Golden Sunset	50	70
Mid-deck Salon	130	175			

FEES & DEPOSITS: A charter deposit is due within 7 days of making reservations. Half the food and beverage total is payable 30 days prior to the event; the balance is due 5 days prior. Wedding receptions start at $70–75/person and include the charter, food, beverages, bar service, captain, crew, tax and service charges. Any menu or wedding service can be customized. For other special events and business functions, prices vary depending on services selected; call for more specifics.

Vessel	Deposit	Vessel	Deposit
San Francisco Spirit	$6,000	California Spirit	3,000
Main Salon	5,000	Golden Sunset	2,000
Mid-deck Salon	5,000		

AVAILABILITY: Year-round, daily, any time.

SERVICES/AMENITIES:

Catering: provided, no BYO
Kitchen Facilities: n/a
Tables & Chairs: provided
Linens, Silver, etc.: provided
Restrooms: wheelchair access varies/vessel
Dance Floor: provided on most vessels
Bride's Dressing Area: yes
Meeting Equipment: podium, microphone
Other: event coordination, ice sculpture, sound systems, CD & cassette players

Parking: Pier 39 garage, discount validation CBA for groups
Accommodations: no guest rooms
Telephone: cellular only
Outdoor Night Lighting: yes
Outdoor Cooking Facilities: no
Cleanup: provided
View: San Francisco Bay, bridges, islands

RESTRICTIONS:

Alcohol: provided, corkage $10/bottle
Smoking: on decks only
Music: amplified OK

Wheelchair Access: varies per vessel
Insurance: not required
Other: no glitter, rice or birdseed

This is important! Tell facilities you're reading **Here Comes The Guide** *and ask if our information is still current.*

The Palace Hotel

Hotel

2 New Montgomery Street, San Francisco
(415) 512-1111, fax (415) 243-8062

www.sfpalace.com
melissa_watro@ittsheraton.com

◆ Ceremonies ◆ Special Events
◆ Wedding Receptions ◆ Meetings
◆ Business Functions ◆ Accommodations

There is nothing quite like the Palace. Following a stunning multimillion-dollar renovation, it has reclaimed its role as San Francisco's premier historic hotel. If you've dreamed of an elegant wedding in a royal setting, the Palace is the perfect location. You can host a bridal tea in the world-renowned Garden Court, one of the most exquisite rooms we've ever seen. The magnificent domed ceiling of pale yellow leaded glass floods the restaurant with warm natural light, and the original crystal chandeliers add old-world sparkle. Wedding ceremonies are often held in the Ralston Room, which served as The Men's Grille at the turn of the century. Reminiscent of a Gothic cathedral, this room soothes with its cream, gold and jewel tones.

For large wedding receptions, the Grand Ballroom lives up to its name. English classical in style, its charm comes from unique lace plasterwork and shimmering chandeliers decorated with carved crystal pears and apples. The Gold Ballroom is the most popular reception site. Once the Hotel's music room, it has the feel of a ballroom in a manor house. Tall draped windows highlight the intricate lattice plasterwork and gold leaf detailing throughout. An antique orchestra balcony, grand fireplace, and rich blue and gold carpet complete the lovely decor. For smaller ceremonies or receptions, the French Parlor features stained glass skylights, crystal chandeliers, marble fireplaces and a birds-eye view of the Garden Court ceiling that is guaranteed to take your breath away. And for a more contemporary space, the Sunset Court accommodates intimate gatherings and ceremonies beneath an arched glass dome. Grand and gorgeous, the Palace Hotel is a place worth visiting even if you're not planning a wedding. Come and see for yourself why it's been a San Francisco landmark for over 100 years.

CEREMONY CAPACITY:

Room	Seated	Room	Seated
Sunset Court	300	California Parlor	50
Ralston Room	500	French Parlor	70

EVENT/RECEPTION CAPACITY:

Room	Seated	Standing
Grand Ballroom	600	1,000
Gold Ballroom	275	600
Ralston Room	275	600

Room	Seated	Standing
French Parlor	100	150
Sunset Court	200	600

MEETING CAPACITY: The Palace has over 20 rooms that can accommodate meetings, seminars, conferences and lectures. This is a brief list of some of the larger spaces:

Room	Theater-style	Classroom-style
Grand Ballroom	1,120	550
Gold Ballroom	550	300
Ralston Room	600	300
Sea Cliff	150	75

Room	Theater-style	Classroom-style
Rose	500	288
Concert	500	288
Pacific Heights	150	75
Twin Peaks	320	150

FEES & DEPOSITS: A non-refundable deposit in the amount of 10% of the estimated cost is required with the signed contract; the balance is due 48 hours prior to the event. There's a $500–1,500 fee for ceremonies only. Per-person food service rates are: $30–40 for luncheons, $40–56 for dinners and $50–70 for buffets. Alcohol, tax and a 17% service charge are additional.

AVAILABILITY: Year-round, daily, 6am–1am.

SERVICES/AMENITIES:

Catering: provided
Kitchen Facilities: n/a
Tables & Chairs: provided
Linens, Silver, etc.: provided
Restrooms: wheelchair accessible
Dance Floor: yes
Bride's Dressing Area: yes
Meeting Equipment: full range CBA

Parking: valet CBA at a charge, or lot
Accommodations: 550 guest rooms
Telephone: pay phones
Outdoor Night Lighting: access only
Outdoor Cooking Facilities: no
Cleanup: provided
View: no
Other: coordination

RESTRICTIONS:

Alcohol: provided, corkage $12/bottle
Smoking: allowed for private parties
Music: amplified OK

Wheelchair Access: yes
Insurance: provided by Hotel

The professionals in the back of the book are the best in the business! **How do we know? Read page 681.**

The Pan Pacific

500 Post Street, San Francisco
(415) 771-8600, fax (415) 398-0267

www.panpac.com

◆ Ceremonies   ◆ Special Events
◆ Wedding Receptions   ◆ Meetings
◆ Business Functions   ◆ Accommodations

Elegant. Sophisticated. Tasteful. The Pan Pacific is all of these and then some. World-renowned architect John Portman has successfully blended Asian and American elements, warm colors and graceful design themes in this twenty-one-story architectural gem. Eye-pleasing arches abound, from the exterior windows to interior entryways. Portuguese rose marble is used for flooring and columns throughout, and Oriental antiques and art lend a timelessness to an otherwise contemporary structure.

Couples looking for a swank wedding and reception site are invariably impressed with the Olympic Ballroom which, with its spacious foyer and four auxiliary rooms, takes up the entire second floor. The foyer is lovely, featuring a marble floor and brilliant cut-glass columns. You'll find even more glamour in the Ballroom, thanks to four enormous brass-and-crystal chandeliers, and a rear wall of beveled glass panels that sparkle as sunshine passes through them, bathing the room in natural light. Recently refurbished, the Ballroom has a sumptuous new look: golden coffers give the ceiling a rich, subtle sheen; walls are textured in ivory fabric; and the new carpet—custom woven in England—covers the floor in earth tones of sage, terra cotta and bisque. All the rooms on this floor flow conveniently into one another, so you can use them in any combination.

Upstairs on the third floor is the main lobby, including The Bar and conversation areas anchored by two imposing rectangular fireplaces. The focal point of the room is the hotel's signature bronze sculpture entitled "Joie de Danse," four fluid, larger-than-life dancers circling round a marble fountain. Have your guests gather here for cocktails and mingling, or use the fountain as a striking backdrop for photos. You can also host your rehearsal dinner on this floor, in the award-winning *Pacific* restaurant.

A swift trip by elevator takes you to the 21st-floor Terrace Room, where smaller receptions are often held. Wraparound windows offer spectacular views—especially at sunset, when the light reflected off thousands of high-rise windows can take your breath away. A coffered ceiling, rosewood bar, and arched fireplaces are complemented by new decor: freshly painted ivory walls, a custom carpet and oversized club chairs. From the Terrace Room, guests can stroll into the adjacent Solarium, an open-air brick patio that also provides a delightful spot for cocktails and conversation. The Penthouse, which is only a few steps away, can extend your reception space, host an intimate reception by itself, or simply offer one of the most luxurious overnight stays in San Francisco. More like a gracious home than a hotel suite, it features two bedrooms, custom-designed furniture, a baby grand piano and a terrific view.

All of the aforementioned event spaces are also available for corporate parties and meetings. In addition, the hotel actually has a separate Executive Conference Center with its own dining area and staff, as well as a full range of business services and equipment. And unlike most hotels, the Pan Pacific has a very high staff to guest ratio, making service its top priority. What more could you ask for?

CEREMONY CAPACITY:

Space	*Seated*	*Standing*	*Space*	*Seated*	*Standing*
Olympic Ballroom (half)	210	—	Solarium	30	50
Terrace	50–60	—	Luxury Suites	—	20–25

EVENT/RECEPTION CAPACITY:

Space	*Seated*	*Standing*	*Space*	*Seated*	*Standing*
Olympic Ballroom	120–300	100–500	Executive Center	30–50	35–125
(can be sectioned)			The Terrace	50–100	175
Prefunction Foyer	180	300	Solarium	30	50
Penthouse	10	60–80			

MEETING CAPACITY: There are 9 rooms and an Executive Conference Center that can accommodate 10–78 seated conference-style, 20–465 theater-style or 12–265 classroom-style.

FEES & DEPOSITS: For weddings, a non-refundable deposit of 30% of the event total is required 30 days after booking to secure your date, and the balance is due 72 hours prior to the event. A ceremony fee is additional. There is no rental fee for over 150 guests. Per-person food costs range from $35–80 for lunch and $45–140 for dinner. Beverage, tax and an 18% gratuity are extra.

For business functions and meetings, fees vary depending on rooms and services selected.

AVAILABILITY: Year-round except Christmas and New Year's Day.

SERVICES/AMENITIES:

Catering: provided, no BYO
Kitchen Facilities: n/a
Tables & Chairs: provided
Linens, Silver, etc.: provided
Restrooms: wheelchair accessible
Dance Floor: yes
Bride's Dressing Area: complimentary suite
View: SF Bay & skyline from upper floors
Other: event coordination, fitness center

Parking: valet and nearby lots
Accommodations: 328 guest rooms
Telephone: pay & guest phones, house phones & business lines
Outdoor Night Lighting: Terrace Solarium only
Outdoor Cooking Facilities: no
Cleanup: provided
Meeting Equipment: full service AV, built-in projector screens, white boards

RESTRICTIONS:

Alcohol: provided, or corkage $8–12/bottle
Smoking: designated areas
Music: amplified OK, music in the Terrace Room ends at 11pm

Wheelchair Access: yes
Insurance: not required

Park Hyatt San Francisco

Hotel

333 Battery Street, San Francisco
(415) 392-1234 Catering, fax (415) 296-2919

bpeters@sfophpo.hyatt.com

◆ Ceremonies   ◆ Special Events
◆ Wedding Receptions   ◆ Meetings
◆ Business Functions   ◆ Accommodations

The Park Hyatt is a different kind of hotel. Upscale yet understated, it provides an environment conducive to elegant affairs. Along with its tasteful interior, the hotel's professional staff is one of the best we've encountered. From the doorman to the catering manager, each employee offers the kind of friendly, impeccable service that's rare in today's world. No matter what type of function you have here, you'll be able to relax and enjoy it knowing that this hostelry's staff bends over backwards to provide a worry-free experience.

Receptions or rehearsal dinners are held in the Park Grill on the third floor or downstairs on Level Two. Brides who'd like to make a dramatic entry can arrive at either level via a spiral staircase. Level Two has an exclusive club-like atmosphere throughout its nine rooms. The Consortium I and II are the largest spaces, featuring a warm and sumptuous decor, with rich polished wood, translucent onyx fixtures and a detailed ceiling. The Park Grill, a popular restaurant with a strong culinary as well as visual appeal, can host receptions or rehearsal meals. This is a top-notch eatery, with lounge alcoves and a beautiful bar. For outdoor entertaining, the adjacent patio can be dressed up with black tables, white linens and large umbrellas. A sophisticated place with flawless style and service, the Park Hyatt actually delivers what most other places just talk about.

CEREMONY CAPACITY: Level B holds 150 seated, Level Two 125 seated and the Consortium I/II holds 125 seated guests.

EVENT/RECEPTION CAPACITY: Level Two can accommodate 8–350 guests; the Park Grill holds up to 175 guests; the outside patio holds 250 seated or standing.

MEETING CAPACITY: The Park Hyatt can accommodate 8–30 seated conference-style, 8–100 seated classroom-style, and 8–150 guests seated theater-style.

FEES & DEPOSITS: A deposit of 25% of the total estimated food and beverage cost is due when reservations are made. The balance is due 2 weeks prior to the event.

AVAILABILITY: Year-round, daily, 6am–2am.

SERVICES/AMENITIES:

Catering: provided
Kitchen Facilities: n/a
Tables & Chairs: provided
Linens, Silver, etc.: provided
Restrooms: wheelchair accessible
Dance Floor: yes
Bride's Dressing Area: yes
Outdoor Cooking Facilities: no
Meeting Equipment: full range AV

Parking: adjacent garage, discounted on weekends and evenings
Accommodations: 360 guest rooms, including 37 suites
Cleanup: provided
Telephone: pay phones
Outdoor Night Lighting: access only
View: no

RESTRICTIONS:

Alcohol: provided
Smoking: designated areas
Music: amplified OK

Wheelchair Access: yes
Insurance: not required

This is important! Tell facilities you're reading **Here Comes The Guide** *and ask if our information is still current.*

Pier 35

Pier 35, San Francisco
(415) 433-7363, fax (415) 346-2362

www.akeps.com
p35@akeps.com

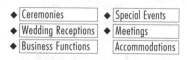

- ◆ Ceremonies
- ◆ Wedding Receptions
- ◆ Business Functions
- ◆ Special Events
- ◆ Meetings
- Accommodations

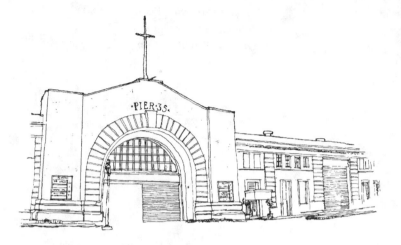

Who would have thought that a cruise ship passenger terminal could be such an outstanding event space? Located at Pier 35, the terminal sits right on the water's edge and has wide open, unobstructed views of the bay, Treasure Island and the Bay Bridge. Two spacious rooms on the upper level are the *pièce de résistance* of the complex. Both are light and airy, thanks to a wall of floor-to-ceiling windows which faces San Francisco Bay. Scarlet, yellow, purple and blue banners suspended from an open, beamed ceiling create a festive atmosphere. Each room opens out onto a wide deck which runs the length of the building. Dine in the banquet room and dance on the parquet floor of the reception area, or treat your guests to an al fresco lunch or dinner on the deck. It's easy to imagine a balmy afternoon party with the sun sparkling on the water and the waves gently lapping below. Or picture an evening affair—the deck aglow with lights, a sprinkle of stars overhead and the illuminated outline of the Bay Bridge off in the distance.

There's also easy access to another area downstairs that can handle a crowd by itself, or provide additional space for a bash that's too big for the upper floor alone. Roll-up doors and a deck give guests here the same vistas and sea breezes they'd enjoy up above. All three rooms can be reserved individually or in combination, and there's plenty of sheltered parking available downstairs on the main floor of the terminal. And if you just happen to be looking for a place to hold a very large function, Pier 35 has an additional 218,000 square feet of event space for sizable events.

CEREMONY CAPACITY: The Main Ballroom holds 250 seated, the Parquet Reception Area 200 seated and the covered Observation Deck, 75 seated guests.

EVENT/RECEPTION & MEETING CAPACITY:

	Area	*Seated*	*Standing*	*Area*	*Seated*	*Standing*
Upper Level	Banquet Room	250	400	Deck	175	300
	Reception Area	200	400	Entire Upper Level	625	1,000
Lower Level		600	1,000			

FEES & DEPOSITS: Rental rates run $1,000–3,500 depending on the spaces selected and the time of year. Half the rental fee is payable as a deposit when the contract is signed; the balance is due 10 days prior to the event. Call for information regarding rental of the entire pier.

AVAILABILITY: Year-round, daily 6am–2am, subject to cruise ship schedules.

SERVICES/AMENITIES:

Catering: select from preferred list or BYO
Kitchen Facilities: prep only
Tables & Chairs: caterer or CBA, extra fee
Linens, Silver, etc.: caterer or CBA, extra fee
Restrooms: wheelchair accessible
Dance Floor: BYO or CBA, extra charge
Bride's Dressing Area: yes
Meeting Equipment: BYO or CBA, extra fee
Other: event coordination

Parking: 144 spaces inside terminal for a nominal fee
Accommodations: no guest rooms, but CBA
Telephone: pay phones
Outdoor Night Lighting: access only
Outdoor Cooking Facilities: no
Cleanup: provided, extra fee
View: San Francisco Bay and Bridge

RESTRICTIONS:

Alcohol: provided or BYO, licensed server required
Smoking: on deck only
Music: amplified OK

Wheelchair Access: yes
Insurance: extra liability required

The professionals in the back of the book are the best in the business! **How do we know? Read page 681.**

Presidio Chapel

Historic Chapel

Fisher Loop, Presidio, San Francisco
(415) 561-3930, fax (415) 771-8681

www.interfaith-presidio.org
icpwebmaster@yahoo.com

◆ Ceremonies   Special Events
◆ Wedding Receptions   Meetings
   Business Functions   Accommodations

For years this graceful Spanish-style chapel has been an inspirational place for couples—those with military connections, that is—to say their vows. With the Presidio's transfer to the National Park System, however, it's now available to the public as an interfaith chapel. Built in 1931 on the crest of a wooded hill, it stands sentry over a glorious panorama that extends from the Golden Gate Bridge to the San Francisco skyline. Architecturally, the chapel is a descendent of the old California mission churches with its tiled roof, three-story bell tower, and textured stucco exterior. Long considered sacred ground, the site was revered by the Ohlone Indians before the Spanish established the Presidio in 1776.

In fair weather, gather for pre-ceremony refreshments in the memorial garden, a flower-lined, tiled patio that overlooks the Presidio grounds and the Bay. Views of Angel and Alcatraz Islands are framed by sweeping branches of pine and eucalyptus. Here guests await the peal of the church bell summoning them to the sanctuary for the ceremony. Inside the chapel, a soaring redwood-beamed ceiling hung with wrought-iron chandeliers, twelve arched stained glass windows, and heavy oak doors all contribute to a strong "old world" flavor. The Chaplain's office serves as a comfortable private dressing area, and there's even a pipe organ for that traditional rendition of Here Comes The Bride.

Adjacent to the sanctuary, the mural room feels like a long, glass-enclosed sun porch. It overlooks the garden and hillside, but its most notable feature is the mural from which it derives its name. Painted by the same artist who created the famed Coit Tower murals, it depicts St. Francis at its center—a fitting picture considering the variety of wildlife that lives around the chapel and the fact that St. Francis is the patron saint of animals. The room makes a tranquil spot for an intimate reception or post-wedding mingling while the bride and groom get their photos taken in the picturesque memorial garden.

The Chapel is now in the care of the Interfaith Center at the Presidio, a nonprofit organization dedicated to inter-religious friendship. The passing of the chapel into public hands as part of the Golden Gate National Recreation Area is being celebrated not only by the Bay Area's diverse religious community, but by everyone who appreciates the sanctity and beauty of this historic spot.

CEREMONY CAPACITY: The Chapel holds 175 seated guests, the patio area 20 seated or standing.

EVENT/RECEPTION CAPACITY: The mural room is used for small standing receptions of up to 75 people.

FEES & DEPOSITS: The main chapel space, mural room and patio area are rented together. On weekends, the rental fee is $1,000, weekdays, $600; the fee usually covers a 2-1/2 hour rental period. Rehearsals run $100/hour. To reserve your date, a $100 non-refundable deposit is required. Half the rental balance is due 60 days after submitting your first deposit; the remainder is payable 30 days prior to the event. No security or cleaning deposit is required.

AVAILABILITY: Year-round, daily, 7am–11pm. Weddings occur in 2-1/2-hour blocks; additional hours can be arranged.

SERVICES/AMENITIES:

Catering: BYO
Kitchen Facilities: no
Tables & Chairs: 3 tables, 32 chairs
Linens, Silver, etc.: BYO
Restroom: wheelchair accessible
Dance Floor: no
Bride's & Groom's Dressing Area: yes
View: panoramic vistas of San Francisco, Bay & bridges

Parking: ample, large lot
Accommodations: no guest rooms
Telephone: emergency use only
Outdoor Night Lighting: access only
Outdoor Cooking Facilities: no
Cleanup: caterer or renter
Meeting Equipment: n/a

RESTRICTIONS:

Alcohol: BYO, server required, unlicensed OK
Smoking: outside only
Music: acoustic only

Wheelchair Access: yes
Insurance: not required
Other: no glitter, confetti, birdseed, rice or balloon releases; some decoration restrictions

*This is important! Tell facilities you're reading **Here Comes The Guide** and ask if our information is still current.*

151

The Queen Anne

Hotel

1590 Sutter Street, San Francisco
(415) 621-3223, (800) 227-3970

www.queenanne.com

- ◆ Ceremonies
- ◆ Wedding Receptions
- ◆ Business Functions
- ◆ Special Events
- ◆ Meetings
- ◆ Accommodations

Built in 1890 by Comstock silver king Senator James G. Fair, this landmark building has had almost as many lives as a cat. It started out as Miss Mary Lake's School for Girls, and later became an exclusive gentleman's club and then the Girls Friendly Society. In 1906, it narrowly escaped destruction from the quake. Somehow, even though it was a mere three blocks from the firestorm that swept through San Francisco, the hotel survived intact.

Many of the Queen Anne's notable architectural features have endured, and except for contemporary elements like telephones, elevators and private bathrooms, not much has changed over the last hundred years. In 1980, the structure was renovated and restored, retaining as much of the original as possible: marble sinks, wood moldings, leaded glass windows and even Victorian doorknobs.

When you walk into the hotel, the entry hallway makes an immediately favorable impression. It has a lovely inlaid parquet floor designed in a geometric pattern, and five-foot-high paneling of carved oak. The first floor is handsomely furnished with Victorian antiques, including the front desk, public telephone booth and pot bellied stove. Both ceremonies and receptions are held in the Parlor, a rich repository of Victorian influence. It's not only filled with antiques, but has two fireplaces—one gas and the other wood-burning. The windows are framed with heavy swag drapes, and hung with Irish lace which diffuses incoming sunlight. Above the room's wainscotting, walls are painted a deep burgundy. For ceremonies, a grand oak staircase off to one side has enabled many a bride to make a picture-perfect entry.

The Salon, the Hotel's original dining room, is also vintage 1890s, with gold-and-burgundy wallpaper, heavy swag drapes gracing tall windows, mirrors, chandeliers and a fireplace. Two sets of doors lead to the Courtyard, a covered space with wooden decking, which can be used for a cocktail reception or for a meeting break, if you're having a business function here. Of all the Queen Anne's lives, we think her present one just may be the best: by opening her doors to all types of events, she offers each one of us a chance to glimpse a little of the City's past.

CEREMONY CAPACITY: The Parlor can accommodate 80 standing guests.

EVENT/RECEPTION CAPACITY: The Hotel can serve 80 guests for a seated meal and up to 150 for a standing reception. The covered, outdoor courtyard holds an additional 24 seated guests.

MEETING CAPACITY:

Room	Theater-style	Classroom-style	Conference-style
Salon	—	55	20–40
Board Room	15	12	10
Library	—	—	10

FEES & DEPOSITS: To secure your date, 50% of the anticipated event total is required as a non-refundable security deposit; it will be applied towards the total charge. For wedding receptions, the rental fee is $1,500, or $1,000 for smaller receptions. If you or your party stay overnight, special rates may apply for group stays.

Fees for business functions or meetings vary depending on guest count and room(s) selected; call for more specifics.

AVAILABILITY: Any day, any time up to 11pm.

SERVICES/AMENITIES:

Catering: provided, no BYO
Kitchen Facilities: fully equipped
Tables & Chairs: provided
Linens, Silver, etc.: caterer
Restrooms: wheelchair accessible
Dance Floor: CBA, extra charge
Bride's Dressing Area: CBA
Meeting Equipment: full range CBA

Parking: valet recommended
Accommodations: 48 guest rooms
Telephone: pay phone
Outdoor Night Lighting: yes
Outdoor Cooking Facilities: no
Cleanup: caterer
View: no

RESTRICTIONS:

Alcohol: provided by caterer
Smoking: allowed, designated areas
Music: amplified OK until 10pm

Wheelchair Access: yes
Insurance: not required

The professionals in the back of the book are the best in the business! ***How do we know? Read page 681.***

The Radisson Miyako Hotel

1625 Post Street, San Francisco
(415) 922-3200 ext. 7285, fax (415) 922-0503

www.miyakosf.com
miyakosf@slip.net

Hotel

◆ Ceremonies ◆ Special Events
◆ Wedding Receptions ◆ Meetings
◆ Business Functions ◆ Accommodations

The Radisson Miyako Hotel, located at the base of Pacific Heights in Japantown, reflects an interesting blend of Eastern and Western cultures. The Imperial Ballroom, with its original, hand-painted Japanese murals, is an elegant, formal space for special events, business functions or wedding receptions. A custom-designed carpet adds vibrance, taking its rich blue and coral tones from antique *obi* sashes. More relaxed in style, the Sakura Ballroom can also host smaller receptions. Its Japanese ambiance is enhanced by a shoji-panel-coffered ceiling and a floor-to-ceiling view of a Japanese tea garden called the Summer Garden. Intimate receptions are often held in the Spring Room, a serene space with a spring garden vista. The secluded Kyoto Suite, with its antique kimonos, shoji screens and garden view is perfect for showers, rehearsal dinners or small parties.

For a culinary treat, have your rehearsal dinner in YOYO Bistro, the Hotel's restaurant, specializing in authentic Asian cuisine. Painted in striking colors, it features changing art exhibits, sculpture and light fixtures created by local artisans. Whether you're planning a company party, an intimate gathering or a large wedding, The Radisson Miyako Hotel's multilingual staff and emphasis on personalized service will make it a success.

CEREMONY CAPACITY:

Room	Seated	Standing	Room	Seated
Sakura Ballroom	250	—	Imperial Ballroom	400
Osaka Room	100	—	Spring Room	120

EVENT/RECEPTION CAPACITY:

Room	Seated	Standing	Room	Seated	Standing
Imperial Ballroom*	250–350	300–600	Spring Room	60–100	75–150
Sakura Ballroom*	60–200	75–400	Kyoto Suite	15–60	30–100
YOYO Bistro	20–120	20–150	*These rooms can be sectioned		

MEETING CAPACITY:

Room	Classroom-style	Theater-style	Room	Classroom-style	Theater-style
Sakura Ballroom	198	400	Osaka Rm	50	120
Imperial Ballroom	300	500	Garden A	30	50
Spring Room	60	150	Garden B	18	30
Kyoto Suite	48	100			

FEES & DEPOSITS: A $500 deposit is required to reserve your date, and is applied to the balance, due 72 hours prior to the event. Per-person food costs, not including wine, are $30–40 for lunch or $35–50 for dinner. Alcohol, tax and an 18% service charge are additional.

AVAILABILITY: Year-round, daily, any time.

SERVICES/AMENITIES:

Catering: provided, no BYO
Kitchen Facilities: n/a
Tables & Chairs: provided
Linens, Silver, etc.: provided
Restrooms: wheelchair accessible
Dance Floor: yes
Bride's & Groom's Dressing Area: CBA
Meeting Equipment: full service AV & business center

Parking: Japan Center garage or valet, extra charge
Accommodations: 218 guest rooms
Telephone: pay phones, guest phones
Outdoor Night Lighting: access only
Outdoor Cooking Facilities: n/a
Cleanup: provided
View: some rooms face Japanese tea gardens
Other: event coordination, piano, stage

RESTRICTIONS:

Alcohol: provided, corkage negotiable
Smoking: outside only
Music: amplified OK

Wheelchair Access: yes
Insurance: not required

This is important! Tell facilities you're reading **Here Comes The Guide** *and ask if our information is still current.*

Ramada Plaza Hotel International

Hotel

1231 Market Street, San Francisco
(415) 487-4463, (415) 487-4439, fax (415) 487-4489

◆ Ceremonies   ◆ Special Events
◆ Wedding Receptions   ◆ Meetings
◆ Business Functions   ◆ Accommodations

San Francisco's Market Street is a pretty busy place, and downtown isn't exactly known for cathedral ceilings and lovely interiors, but walk through the front doors of the Ramada Plaza and that's what you'll see. The spacious lobby, with its polished Italian marble, wood paneling and flowers is sublimely refreshing to the soul.

But creating a beautiful environment is not this hotel's only talent. While preserving and capitalizing on its historic grandeur, the Ramada Plaza has also managed to provide the best of modern amenities, and make the whole elegant package surprisingly affordable.

Its history makes the Ramada Plaza special in both structure and aura. The hotel was still under construction during the 1906 earthquake, which devastated the City and ruined City Hall. City officials decided that the hotel would be perfect for a temporary City Hall, and after it was completed, it served as San Francisco's seat of government from 1912 to 1915. In fact, some of the old jail cells in the basement are still intact, and curious guests can arrange to see them if they ask in advance.

Nowadays, along with the grand lobby, marble pillars, Tiffany glass, and hand-carved wood that are part of its legacy, the Ramada Plaza also enjoys a Starbucks Cafe, a health club, and all the space and equipment to support business meetings in the electronic age. On either side of the Lobby, enormous doors take you into the main event spaces: the Whitcomb Ballroom and the Girardelli Room. The Ballroom is where ceremonies usually take place, but receptions are held here too. There's a grand stairway entrance for brides, a mezzanine for photographers, one of the largest parquet dance floors in The City, and a ritzy ambiance created in part by leaded glass and gold leaf. The Girardelli Room, smaller though no less elegant, is often used for rehearsal dinners, and intimate receptions. If both rooms are reserved, wedding guests can flow between them and the Lobby, enjoying the flavors of the different settings.

These rooms, however, are not just for weddings. If you're putting on a business function, the Ballroom is perfect for large keynote speeches, while the Girardelli Room is great for board meetings; there are smaller breakout rooms and plenty of overnight accommodations, too.

Regardless of the type of event you hold here, your guests will appreciate the hotel's proximity to everything San Francisco is known for: Union Square and all its stores (hey, you never know when someone will need to rush out for a new pair of stockings or a replacement computer), the theater district, Chinatown and Fisherman's Wharf. At the Ramada Plaza, you can reap big city rewards, surrounded by the options and elegance of a historic hotel—truly the best of both worlds.

CEREMONY CAPACITY: The Whitcomb Ballroom holds 450 seated, the Ghirardelli Room 80 seated guests. Some standing guests can also be accommodated.

EVENT/RECEPTION CAPACITY:

Room	Seated	Standing	Room	Seated	Standing
Whitcomb Ballroom	300	600	Ghirardelli Room	100	150
Ballroom & Mezzanine	450	800			

MEETING CAPACITY: In addition to the rooms below, there are seven other rooms which can accommodate 8–20 guests seated conference-style or 30–75 guests seated theater-style.

Room	Theater-style	Classroom-style	Room	Theater-style	Classroom-style
Whitcomb Ballroom	450	250	Ghirardelli Room	80	60
Whitcomb & Mezz.	550	250			
Mezzanine	100	—			

FEES & DEPOSITS: For weddings, a $1,000 non-refundable deposit is required. The event balance is payable 72 hours prior to the event along with a guest count guarantee. There are 2 wedding packages (100 guests minimum) which run $45–55/person, including champagne reception, wine with meal, tax and service charge. Menus can be customized.

For other special events and business functions, a deposit is required, and varies depending on the services and menu selected. Room rental fees may apply depending on food and beverage totals. Call for more specific information.

AVAILABILITY: Year-round, daily, any time including holidays.

SERVICES/AMENITIES:
Catering: provided, no BYO
Kitchen Facilities: n/a
Tables & Chairs: provided
Linens, Silver, etc.: provided
Restrooms: wheelchair accessible
Dance Floor: provided
Bride's & Groom's Dressing Area: suite provided with package
Meeting Equipment: full range, extra CBA

Parking: garage or adjacent parking CBA, extra charge
Accommodations: 460 guest rooms
Telephone: pay phones, guest phones
Outdoor Night Lighting: access only
Outdoor Cooking Facilities: n/a
Cleanup: provided
View: no
Other: ice carvings, event planning

RESTRICTIONS:
Alcohol: provided, or corkage $7.50/bottle
Smoking: outside only
Music: amplified OK, midnight curfew

Wheelchair Access: yes
Insurance: not required

RCH Lake Merced Club

Lakeside Facility

Address withheld to ensure privacy. San Francisco
(415) 927-4721

www.celebrat.com

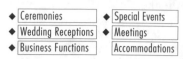

◆ Ceremonies   ◆ Special Events
◆ Wedding Receptions ◆ Meetings
◆ Business Functions   Accommodations

If you've never been to the forested fringe of San Francisco, you might want to take a little trip out to the RCH Club. Set on five and a half wooded acres, a stone's throw from Lake Merced, this quiet, relaxed facility is a refreshing place for wedding receptions and private parties.

The Main Hall is a very large room, made light and airy by roofline windows all around the perimeter, a wall of glass overlooking the lake, and a bank of skylights along the lake side. A high, open-beamed ceiling only increases the feeling of spaciousness. In winter and on cool summer evenings when the fog rolls in from the ocean, a blazing fire adds warmth and intimacy to the space.

Thanks to its size and openness, the Hall can be set up in a variety of ways. During wedding receptions, couples often put the head table on the lake side of the room, where they have the best view of Lake Merced through a grove of eucalyptus trees. A raised, hardwood stage is the perfect spot for a band, and a pulldown screen, piano, and an excellent sound and lighting system give you plenty of options for creative entertainment ("this is your life" movies of the bride and groom are always a hit!).

The hall is also a favorite for meetings, private parties and other functions. During very large events, such as fundraisers, crab feeds and casino nights, it's frequently used in conjunction with the adjacent auditorium. Guests usually gather in the auditorium for the banquet, games or other activities, then flow into the Hall for dancing and mixing. Additional rooms in the complex are available for smaller meetings.

Everyone who hosts an event here appreciates the easy access, abundance of free parking and, of course, the trees all around. There is one more perk, however: the satisfaction of knowing that all funds acquired from special events are funneled back into wonderful programs that RCH runs for children and adults with disabilities. So, go ahead and have your reception, your gala or your seminar—while you're having the time of your life, you'll also be making an important contribution to the community.

CEREMONY CAPACITY: The Auditorium holds 400 seated, the Main Hall 400 seated. A garden, which will hold 150 guests, is projected for summer 1999.

EVENT/RECEPTION CAPACITY: The Main Hall can accommodate 300 seated (250 seated with dancing) or 400 for a cocktail reception. The adjoining Auditorium holds 400 seated or 500 standing. Both rooms, combined, hold 700 seated or 900 standing.

MEETING CAPACITY:

Room	Theater-style	Classroom-style	Conference-style
Main Hall	450	350	300
Auditorium	450–500	400	200
Conference Room	10–15	10–15	10

FEES & DEPOSITS: To secure your date, a $300 non-refundable deposit is required. The rental fee for the Main Hall is $1,200; for both Hall and Auditorium, $1,500. The rental balance and a $500 refundable security/damage deposit are payable 1 week prior to the event.

Catering is provided by *Event of the Season*. All menus are customized; luncheons start at $35/person, dinners at $40/person. Tax is additional.

AVAILABILITY: Year-round; Saturdays 9am–2am, Sundays 9am–midnight, Monday and Wednesdays, 2pm–midnight.

SERVICES/AMENITIES:

Catering: provided
Kitchen Facilities: n/a
Tables & Chairs: chairs provided, some tables
Linens, Silver, etc.: through caterer
Restrooms: wheelchair accessible
Dance Floor: provided
Bride's & Groom's Dressing Area: CBA
Meeting Equipment: sound system, microphone, podium, screen

Parking: on and off-street parking
Accommodations: no guest rooms
Telephone: pay phones
Outdoor Night Lighting: access only
Outdoor Cooking Facilities: through caterer
Cleanup: caterer
View: Lake Merced

RESTRICTIONS:

Alcohol: BYO, service by caterer or licensed server
Smoking: outside only
Music: amplified OK indoors

Wheelchair Access: yes
Insurance: not required
Other: no confetti; auditorium requires rented floor covering

---

The professionals in the back of the book are the best in the business! **How do we know? Read page 681.**

Rincon Atrium

101 Spear Street, San Francisco
(415) 512-0450, fax (415) 896-5548

www.chalkers.com
iratask@aol.com

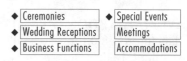

- Ceremonies
- Wedding Receptions
- Business Functions
- Special Events
- Meetings
- Accommodations

If fun is a top priority, whether your guest list ranges from 20 to 1,000, the Rincon Atrium and Chalkers Billiard Club provide an interesting combination of spaces in an upscale, downtown location. The Atrium is at the heart of the Rincon Center, an impressive historic building that houses everything from businesses to federal offices to apartments; Chalkers is one of the site's marquee businesses.

The Atrium presents a vibrant contrast to its serious Financial District surroundings. It's a dramatic indoor courtyard that soars five stories and is topped with a glass ceiling. Built of polished granite with rich wood touches, its contemporary design is softened by an abundance of greenery: potted palms all around, and lush plants cascading off the balconies above. The focal point is a unique fountain, whose five-story free fall begins at the ceiling and ends in a simple pool, set flush with the floor. And while this is a public use area, a sense of privacy is created by having the storefronts (all done in polished cherry wood) tucked unobtrusively around the outer circumference of the space. Four separate eating areas off the main walk-through also provide intimate gathering places. On weekends and after business hours, the Atrium is virtually empty and chances are good you'll have it completely to yourself. Events here have included everything from corporate holiday parties and elegant civic functions to weddings staged in front of the dramatic backdrop of the fountain.

Chalkers—just a few steps from the Atrium—may be technically a billiards room, but it feels more like an English country estate drawing room. All 30 pool tables are made of polished cherry or antique walnut. The walls are painted mustard yellow and feature ornately framed oil reproductions, one of which catches Mona Lisa holding a cue stick. A house pro is on hand to entertain with trick-shot exhibitions and informal instruction, and tableside food and drink service keeps everyone well fortified. If your group is small, you can reserve the private VIP room exclusively.

The Rincon Atrium and Chalkers are available separately or together, depending on the size and focus of your event. If you decide to take over both facilities, rest assured that this is one of the few places where you can host an elegant formal affair or a casual pool-playing party—and it will feel perfectly natural to have a champagne flute in one hand and a pool cue in the other.

CEREMONY & EVENT/RECEPTION CAPACITY: The Atrium can accommodate up to 500 seated or 1,000 standing, depending on the event's setup.

FEES & DEPOSITS: Half of the anticipated event total is required when the event is booked; the balance is payable at the event's completion. The rental fee for the Atrium is $1,500–2,000 Sunday–Thursday or $1,950–2,500 Friday and Saturday. Catering can be provided in house, ranging $20–85/person depending on menu and services selected. Alcohol, tax and a 15% service charge are additional.

If you'd like to provide entertainment for your guests, the adjacent Chalkers Billard Club can be rented in conjunction with the Atrium for a substantial discount; call for more details.

AVAILABILITY: Year-round, daily, 11am–2am.

SERVICES/AMENITIES:

Catering: provided or BYO w/approval
Kitchen Facilities: no
Tables & Chairs: provided up to 500 guests
Linens, Silver, etc.: provided
Restrooms: wheelchair accessible
Dance Floor: provided
Bride's Dressing Area: no
Meeting Equipment: CBA
Other: complete event planning, entertainment

Parking: valet recommended for large events; garages nearby
Accommodations: no guest rooms
Telephone: pay phones
Outdoor Night Lighting: n/a
Outdoor Cooking Facilities: n/a
Cleanup: provided
View: no

RESTRICTIONS:

Alcohol: provided, or wine corkage $10/bottle
Smoking: not allowed
Music: amplified OK w/volume limits

Wheelchair Access: yes
Insurance: additional may be required
Other: no glitter or confetti

---

*This is important! Tell facilities you're reading **Here Comes The Guide** and ask if our information is still current.*

The Ritz-Carlton

Hotel

600 Stockton at California, San Francisco
(415) 296-7465, fax (415) 788-2824

www.ritzcarlton.com

◆ Ceremonies ◆ Special Events
◆ Wedding Receptions ◆ Meetings
◆ Business Functions ◆ Accommodations

Set atop prestigious Nob Hill, The Ritz-Carlton is housed in one of San Francisco's finest examples of Neo-classical architecture. Originally built in 1909, the block-long structure has an impressive and stately facade. As you step inside, you're surrounded by The Ritz-Carlton's signature style—handsome, classically de-signed spaces graced by 18th- and 19th-century museum-quality art and antiques. Gold framed seascapes and landscapes, Persian carpets, crystal chandeliers, silk wall coverings and enormous, fresh floral arrangements lend a sophisticated, yet understated quality to the hotel's public spaces.

Large parties take place in the Ballroom, which is often used in tandem with several adjacent galleries. The galleries themselves are perfect for cocktails and hors d'oeuvres—spacious, with high, vaulted ceilings, ornate woodwork, large oil paintings and silk-covered walls in mauve, peach and subdued blue tones. Seated receptions follow in the Ballroom, a sizable and regal space which can be partitioned into smaller segments. The room is warm: light glows from crystal chandeliers suspended from a recessed oval ceiling and walls are softened by panels of patterned, muted peach silk.

The hotel has more event spaces on the second and third levels, each of which can be used for a private rehearsal dinner or small reception. All are nicely designed with floral arrangements, tasteful artwork and light wood molding and wainscotting. For outdoor parties, there's a beautiful red-brick courtyard, which has a terrific cityscape and is enclosed by an impeccably manicured garden of roses, herbs, ivy and flowers. Glass-topped tables with umbrellas and wrought-iron chairs dot the courtyard, and the central portion can be tented if the weather doesn't cooperate. After the celebration there's no need to rush off—the bride and groom can unwind in a honeymoon suite, and be whisked off to the airport the next day by a hotel-arranged limousine service.

CEREMONY CAPACITY:

Area	Seated	Standing	Area	Seated	Standing
Courtyard	350	400	Small Reception Rooms (9)	10–60	25–75
Ballroom	100–500	200–800			

EVENT/RECEPTION CAPACITY:

Area	Seated	Standing	Area	Seated	Standing
Courtyard	170	200	Prefunction Area	—	500
Ballroom	100–600	200–800	Small Reception Rooms (9)	16–50	26–70

MEETING CAPACITY: There are 13 spaces that can accommodate 26–826 guests seated theater-style, 12–122 conference-style or 16–475 classroom-style.

FEES & DEPOSITS: For weddings, a $2,000–5,000 non-refundable deposit, which varies depending on guest count and room selection, is due when your contract is submitted. The ceremony setup charge is approximately $2,000. For reception meals the approximate rate per person is: buffet luncheons $32–45, seated luncheons $45–52 and seated dinners $65–72. Tax and service charges are additional. The estimated food and beverage total is payable 10 days prior to the event.

For business functions or meetings, fees vary depending on rooms and services selected. Call for specifics.

AVAILABILITY: Year-round, daily including holidays, 8am–2am.

SERVICES/AMENITIES:

Catering: provided, no BYO
Kitchen Facilities: n/a
Tables & Chairs: provided
Linens, Silver, etc.: provided
Restrooms: wheelchair accessible
Dance Floor: provided
Bride's Dressing Area: yes
Meeting Equipment: full range CBA

Parking: valet at $22/car
Accommodations: 336 guest rooms
Telephone: pay & guest phones
Outdoor Night Lighting: CBA
Outdoor Cooking Facilities: CBA
Cleanup: provided
View: SF Bay & skyline from upper floors
Other: event coordination

RESTRICTIONS:

Alcohol: provided, no BYO
Smoking: designated areas only
Music: amplified OK

Wheelchair Access: yes
Insurance: not required
Other: no rice indoors

---

*The professionals in the back of the book are the best in the business! **How do we know? Read page 681.***

The Rotunda at Neiman Marcus

Restaurant

150 Stockton Street, San Francisco
(415) 362-4777

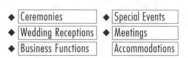

◆ Ceremonies   ◆ Special Events
◆ Wedding Receptions   ◆ Meetings
◆ Business Functions   Accommodations

You say you love the gracious decor of the gilded age, but the only places you can find it are in a period movie, a museum or your great aunt's house? Well, we've discovered just the setting you're looking for in, of all places, a department store. Not just any department store, mind you, but the one whose catalogs once offered his & hers Lear Jets: Neiman Marcus.

High up on the top floor of NM, the Rotunda Restaurant is one of the more unusual event spaces we've come across. It's crowned by a stunning glass dome, constructed of 2,600 pieces of white, soft rust and yellow glass. During the day, sunlight filters through it, casting a warm, golden glow; at night it's a striking focal point, backlit and rimmed with sparkling globe lights. Natural light also streams in through a curved expanse of floor-to-ceiling windows, overlooking the fine hotels and chic stores of Union Square.

The room itself curves gracefully around a central atrium that descends four stories to the ground floor. (It's interesting to note that the clever design of the building allows you to watch shoppers bustling about below, while you're completely invisible to them.) Multilevel seating gives each booth a "box seat" quality: no matter where you sit you have an excellent view of the dome, the glass wall and all the festivities.

There's an elegance to the room's furnishings that comes of using a time-honored harmonizer, the curve. You see it not only in the shape of the room, but in the booths, the railings and the cherrywood bar. Victorian influences such as the undulating baroque plasterwork and gold-leafed molding around the dome are complemented by more modern accents, like brass railings and vivid contemporary watercolors which line the walls.

The Rotunda has a private entrance for special event guests, complete with an express elevator that whisks them straight up to the restaurant. This is particularly handy for any bride who wants to surprise her "audience" with a well-timed, sweeping entrance around the atrium.

While wedding receptions are frequently held at the Rotunda, some very colorful corporate and fundraising events have had their day here, too. There was a Caribbean Night with steel drums and costumed dancers (not to mention goldfish bowls on the bar), and Showboat Night with guests gambling in 1890s period garb. It's also been a great place for art and collectibles auctions, where buffet fare is served and items are displayed all around in the booths. Christmas parties—especially for kids—are not to be missed. Santa sits on his throne in the restaurant, presiding over a four-story-high Christmas tree, decorated as only Neiman Marcus can do it. (And hey, if you need a last-minute gift, all you have to do is make a quick trip downstairs.) So when you want an event location that truly rises above the ordinary, come to the Rotunda. They'll take care of everything for you, so you'll have extra time to—you guessed it!—go shopping.

CEREMONY CAPACITY: The area in front of the center window holds 125 standing guests.

EVENT/RECEPTION & MEETING CAPACITY: The Rotunda can hold 50–175 seated guests or 50–300 for a standing reception.

FEES & DEPOSITS: A $500 non-refundable deposit is required to secure your date. There is no rental fee with food service, however the food and beverage minimum is $2,500. Catering is provided. Dinners are à la carte, with entrees starting at $17.50/person, buffets at $29/person and hors d'oeuvres selections at $2–5 each. Alcohol, tax and an 18% service charge are additional. For Neiman Marcus cardholders, note that you can make payment using your NM card to gain *Incircle* points.

AVAILABILITY: Year-round, daily, 6pm–midnight.

SERVICES/AMENITIES:

Catering: provided, no BYO

Kitchen Facilities: n/a

Tables & Chairs: provided

Linens, Silver, etc.: provided

Restrooms: wheelchair accessible

Dance Floor: yes

Bride's Dressing Area: yes

Meeting Equipment: BYO

Parking: Union Square garage

Accommodations: no guest rooms

Telephone: pay phone

Outdoor Night Lighting: access only

Outdoor Cooking Facilities: no

Cleanup: provided

View: of downtown & City skyline

RESTRICTIONS:

Alcohol: provided, or corkage $6/bottle

Smoking: outdoors only

Music: amplified OK

Wheelchair Access: yes

Insurance: not required

This is important! Tell facilities you're reading **Here Comes The Guide** *and ask if our information is still current.*

Sailing Ship Dolph Rempp

Historic Vessel, Restaurant

*Pier 42–44 on the Embarcadero,
South of Market Street, San Francisco*
(415) 777-5771 or **(415) 543-4024, fax (415) 957-1470**

◆ Ceremonies   ◆ Special Events
◆ Wedding Receptions   ◆ Meetings
◆ Business Functions   Accommodations

This impressive, hundred-year-old three-masted schooner offers all the advantages of being "out to sea" without any of the disadvantages. Because the vessel rests in an earthquake-proof concrete cradle at the southwest end of San Francisco's waterfront, guests will never miss the boat no matter how late they are, can leave whenever they want to, and can enjoy the salt air, the sights and sounds of being on the water—all while remaining motionless.

The *Sailing Ship Dolph Rempp* was built in 1884 as a trading vessel in the Baltic Sea, and has had an illustrious career. Jules Verne was aboard for exploratory journeys and used the schooner as inspiration for his novels. It was also a rum runner, a pleasure craft and a World War I supplies carrier (used for espionage!). You and your guests will feel like stars in your own movie production when you board the *Sailing Ship,* since it's been featured in more than 100 Hollywood films.

There's a full restaurant indoors, and you can sip cocktails or relax outdoors as well, thanks to several helpful features. The back deck has an extra bar, a canopy and butane heaters strategically placed to keep guests warm. And if you want to expand your guest list or have more room for a ceremony or dancing, you can tent the front deck. For brides who want to get ready while socializing with friends and family, there's even a "hidden" wine cellar outfitted with bathroom, mirrors, bar and couches.

So when you want to feel like you're ocean bound, but don't really want to go for a cruise, consider *Sailing Ship Dolph Rempp.* It now combines its rich history with elegant dining and fabulous views of the City, the Bay Bridge and the colorful South Beach Harbor Marina.

CEREMONY CAPACITY:

Space	*Seated*	*Standing*	*Space*	*Seated*	*Standing*
Captain's Deck Area	80	200	Front Deck	300	500
Main Salon	110	200	Back Deck	125	200
			Side Deck	200	300

EVENT/RECEPTION & MEETING CAPACITY:

Space	Seated	Standing	Space	Seated	Standing
Captain's Deck Area	60	200	Cabaret	53	200
Main Salon	110	200	Back Deck	125	200
Outside Front Deck	300	500	Wine Cellar	20	30

FEES & DEPOSITS: A $500 non-refundable deposit is required to secure your date; the balance is payable the week of the event. A $5/person rental fee ($2.50 for children) or $500 minimum is required for weddings and other special events that make use of the entire ship. Hors d'oeuvres run $6–16.50/person, luncheons or dinners $15.50–55/person; beverages, tax and an 18% service charge are additional.

AVAILABILITY: Year-round, daily, 8am–1:45am, including major holidays.

SERVICES/AMENITIES:

Catering: provided, no BYO
Kitchen Facilities: n/a
Tables & Chairs: provided
Linens, Silver, etc.: provided
Restrooms: wheelchair accessible
Dance Floor: yes
Bride's Dressing Area: yes
Meeting Equipment: CBA, extra charge
Other: canopies or tenting CBA

Parking: on street and adjacent lot
Accommodations: no guest rooms
Telephone: pay phone
Outdoor Night Lighting: yes
Outdoor Cooking Facilities: BBQ CBA
Cleanup: provided
View: City skyline, Bay Bridge, So. Beach Marina, San Francisco Bay

RESTRICTIONS:

Alcohol: provided, corkage $10–13/bottle
Smoking: restricted to back deck
Music: amplified OK

Wheelchair Access: limited
Insurance: not required

The professionals in the back of the book are the best in the business! **How do we know? Read page 681.**

San Francisco Maritime Museum

San Francisco Maritime National Historic Park
900 Beach Street (at the foot of Polk), San Francisco
(415) 561-6662 ext. 18, fax (415) 561-6660

www.maritime.org
sfnmma@aol.com

Historic Maritime Museum

◆ Ceremonies   ◆ Special Events
◆ Wedding Receptions   ◆ Meetings
◆ Business Functions   Accommodations

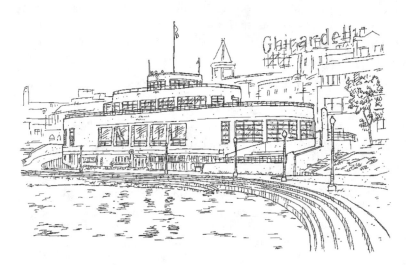

Imagine your event held a stone's throw from the water's edge! Make your vision a reality by renting the San Francisco Maritime Museum, located across from Ghirardelli Square in the heart of Aquatic Park.

In addition to housing hundreds of artifacts, photographs and documents of West Coast seafaring history, the building was cleverly designed to actually resemble a cruise ship, even down to the nautical-looking air vents! The Museum's design will take you back about sixty years—it's a marvel of Art Deco style with terrazzo floors, murals and chrome detailing that are classic 1930s. Loaded with marine artifacts and historic memorabilia, the main exhibit room is terrific.

Also of note is the Bayview Room, situated at the east end of the building. Constructed in the round, the space has a high ceiling, inlaid terrazzo floor and large glass windows on almost all sides providing sensational views of the Aquatic Park pier, Alcatraz, Sausalito and historic ships berthed nearby. An additional benefit is the adjacent open-air loggia (balcony), which resembles a long, narrow deck except that it has a tile floor. Bay breezes will enliven any celebration and the loggia's nautical paraphernalia will capture your guests' attention. They'll be able to touch parts from old ships, and marvel at the dry-docked nineteen-foot sloop *The Mermaid,* Benny Buffano sculptures and unblemished examples of 1930s Art Deco tile murals along the wall facing the Bay. You can extend your party by bringing tables onto the loggia—or just have the bar set up here so everyone can enjoy the sights and sounds of San Francisco Bay.

From the loggia, the views of the harbor and Alcatraz are unobstructed, and the water is so close you can hear the waves lapping against the sand. Do yourself a favor and ask for a tour. This is a real find.

CEREMONY CAPACITY: The Bayview Room holds 150 seated or 200 standing, the second floor roof deck 200 seated or 250 standing.

EVENT/RECEPTION CAPACITY: The Museum holds 100 seated or 250 standing, the Bayview Room 175 seated or 200 standing, the Loggia 100 seated or 150 standing. The Bayview Room and Museum, combined accommodate 300 seated or 425 standing guests.

MEETING CAPACITY: The Bayview Room holds 200 seated theater-style or 150 conference-style.

FEES & DEPOSITS: A non-refundable $200 deposit is required to confirm your date. The rental fee ranges from $1,150–2,500, depending on guest count and spaces used. The rental fee balance and a $500 refundable security deposit are payable 10 days prior to the event.

AVAILABILITY: Year-round, daily, 5pm–midnight.

SERVICES/AMENITIES:

Catering: select from preferred list
Kitchen Facilities: fully equipped
Tables & Chairs: some provided
Linens, Silver, etc.: BYO
Restrooms: wheelchair accessible
Dance Floor: in Bayview Room
Bride's Dressing Area: CBA
Meeting Equipment: BYO

Parking: on street, nearby garage
Accommodations: no guest rooms
Telephone: pay phone
Outdoor Night Lighting: access only
Outdoor Cooking Facilities: no
Cleanup: caterer
View: SF Bay, Alcatraz, historic ships docked at Hyde Street Pier

RESTRICTIONS:

Alcohol: BYO
Smoking: outside only
Music: amplified OK until 11pm

Wheelchair Access: partial access
Insurance: included in rental fee

This is important! Tell facilities you're reading **Here Comes The Guide** *and ask if our information is still current.*

San Remo Hotel

Historic Hotel

2237 Mason Street, San Francisco
(415) 776-8688, fax (415) 776-2811

www.sanremohotel.com
info@sanremohotel.com

◆ Ceremonies   ◆ Special Events
◆ Wedding Receptions   ◆ Meetings
◆ Business Functions   ◆ Accommodations

With its cream-colored pressed tin ceilings, converted gas lamps and wood detailing, the San Remo Hotel's romantic elegance derives from its colorful past. It was built by Bank of America founder, A.P. Giannini, just after the 1906 earthquake. Early on, the hotel housed a variety of guests in the quaint rooms upstairs, such as sailors and stevedores; during the Depression, it served enormous family-style meals downstairs to hungry crowds. Recently restored and filled with antiques, plants and Art Nouveau posters, this Italianate Victorian is a thoroughly charming setting for all types of events.

The pride of the San Remo is the mahogany Victorian bar, the focal point of the banquet space on the first floor. Older than the hotel itself, this intricately carved masterpiece was brought around Cape Horn by ship more than a century ago. Adjoining the bar area are the Victorian banquet room and front dining room, each featuring a large antique buffet, redwood wainscotting, beveled glass windows, and those ornate pressed tin ceilings you so rarely see these days. The whole ambiance is one of cozy, polished refinement.

All rooms open to each other, which gives your event ample space, and allows your guests to flow comfortably from room to room. The San Remo is a terrific choice for an office party or anniversary celebration, and for weddings it's a truly special place. If you're planning a small ceremony and you're not in the mood for a church, consider the Victorian banquet room. It's a warm and intimate space that doesn't need any decoration, but you can bring in a gazebo if you wish. If you get married somewhere else in San Francisco, add a little excitement to your exit by having San Remo staff pick you up after the ceremony, and chauffeur you back to the hotel in their trademark 1941 Ford "Woody" station wagon.

When the festivities have ended, treat yourselves to one last San Remo experience: a penthouse honeymoon. Take the stairway to the top of the hotel, where your private room and deck await. From your outdoor perch you can enjoy a 360-degree view of San Francisco, watch the twilight fall, and treat yourself to an *al fresco* breakfast (or lunch or dinner) the next day. The San Remo is a delight, and if A.P. Giannini were to set foot inside today, he'd undoubtedly agree that his little hotel has become a surprisingly romantic place.

CEREMONY CAPACITY: The Victorian Room holds 50 seated with an additional 20 standing guests.

EVENT/RECEPTION CAPACITY: The Bar/Bistro holds 60 seated or 100 standing, the front banquet room holds 80 seated or 150 standing, and the Victorian Room holds 80 seated or 150 standing guests.

MEETING CAPACITY: The front banquet room holds 36 seated boardroom style, the Victorian Room holds 30 seated boardroom-style, 80 seated U-shape or 50 seated theater-style.

FEES & DEPOSITS: For special events, a $500 refundable security/cleaning deposit is required to reserve your date. The rental fee is payable 1 month prior to the event and runs $200–500 per room, depending on the event. For business functions, the fee is $150–250/room. During the holiday season, rates may be higher.

AVAILABILITY: Year-round, daily, 8am–11pm, including holidays.

SERVICES/AMENITIES:

Catering: select from preferred list or BYO w/approval
Kitchen Facilities: fully equipped
Tables & Chairs: provided
Linens, Silver, etc.: caterer
Restrooms: wheelchair accessible
Dance Floor: CBA, extra charge
Bride's & Groom's Dressing Area: CBA
Other: upright piano, 1941 Woody stationwagon

Parking: garages nearby or valet CBA
Accommodations: 20 guest rooms
Telephone: pay phones
Outdoor Night Lighting: n/a
Outdoor Cooking Facilities: n/a
Cleanup: caterer or renter
View: no
Meeting Equipment: CBA, extra fee

RESTRICTIONS:

Alcohol: provided, or BYO wine corkage $10/bottle
Smoking: outside only
Music: amplified OK w/volume limits, curfew 10pm

Wheelchair Access: yes
Insurance: certificate required
Other: no glitter or confetti; no open flames

The professionals in the back of the book are the best in the business! **How do we know? Read page 681.**

Savoy Hotel & Brasserie

Hotel & Brasserie

580 Geary Street, San Francisco
(415) 441-2700 ext. 221, (800) 227-4223
fax (415) 441-0124

◆ Ceremonies ◆ Special Events
◆ Wedding Receptions ◆ Meetings
◆ Business Functions ◆ Accommodations

From the sign on the awning advertising *"Homards, Coquilles, Moules,"* to the down-filled featherbeds in all 83 rooms, the Savoy Hotel seems like a little bit of Paris transported to the heart of San Francisco. Originally built in 1913, and renovated in a French Provincial style in 1998, the Savoy can claim an ideal location. Perfect for the business person with a few free hours between meetings, or out-of-town theatergoer spending the weekend in the City, it's a mere two-and-a-half blocks from Union Square, the theater district, and cable car lines that can take you to Fisherman's Wharf or North Beach. Chinatown is within walking distance, as is Nob Hill (but you'd better be in shape for that walk).

The hotel also features two banquet rooms, suitable for business or pleasure. Oenophiles will enjoy the Wine Room, named after the large, open wine rack covering one wall. Shades of beige and cream with dark wood paneling give the Wine Room a cozy clubbiness. Watercolor paintings of musicians and other denizens of the *demi-monde* add a touch of drama. The L-shaped Terrace Room with its rich, Oriental-style carpeting and mellow ivory walls overlooks the bustling Brasserie Savoy below. You can host a party or meeting in either room, and both can be set up with individual tables or a long banquet table for sit-down events.

The hotel's restaurant, the Brasserie Savoy, can also be rented for special events. It features black-and-white marble floors, an inviting wooden bar and sprightly black-and-white woven bamboo chairs. With its proximity to the theater district, the Brasserie is ideal for pre- or post-theater dining. And even though you may think the Champs-Elysees is right outside the front door, you won't need a French dictionary; despite all evidence to the contrary, English is definitely spoken here.

CEREMONY CAPACITY: The Wine Room holds 26 seated or 50 standing and the Terrace Room holds 48 seated or 100 standing.

EVENT/RECEPTION CAPACITY: The restaurant holds 98 seated, or up to 250 standing guests.

MEETING CAPACITY: The Terrace Room holds 60 seated theater-style and up to 25 conference-style; the Wine Room seats 30 theater-style and 12 conference-style.

FEES & DEPOSITS: Room rental fees range $150–500 depending on rooms selected and event duration. To secure your date, half of your room rental fee is required; the balance is due 10 days before the event. In-house catering is provided. Luncheons run $25–30/person; 3-course dinners $40–60/person. Alcohol, tax and a 19% service charge are additional.

AVAILABILITY: Year-round, daily, 6:30am–11pm. Other hours can be arranged.

SERVICES/AMENITIES:

Catering: provided, no BYO
Kitchen Facilities: n/a
Tables & Chairs: provided
Linens, Silver, etc.: provided
Restrooms: wheelchair accessible
Dance Floor: in Terrace Room
Bride's Dressing Area: CBA
Meeting Equipment: full range

Parking: valet service $7/day, $18 with an overnight stay
Accommodations: 83 guest rooms & suites
Telephone: pay phones
Outdoor Night Lighting: no
Outdoor Cooking Facilities: no
Cleanup: provided
View: no

RESTRICTIONS:

Alcohol: provided, corkage $10–20/bottle
Smoking: outside only
Music: amplified OK

Wheelchair Access: yes
Insurance: not required

---

*This is important! Tell facilities you're reading **Here Comes The Guide** and ask if our information is still current.*

Shannon-Kavanaugh House

722 Steiner Street, San Francisco
(415) 563-2727, fax (415) 563-0221
www.s-j.com/bed&breakfast/html

Historic, Victorian Mansion

◆ Ceremonies ◆ Special Events
◆ Wedding Receptions ◆ Meetings
◆ Business Functions ◆ Accommodations

There's nothing quite like a home wedding for intimacy and warmth. But let's say you also want more elegance, luxury and space than your home's got, and don't want to be bothered with setup or cleanup duties. How do you satisfy all your desires? Hold the affair in someone else's house, preferably one with style, impeccable taste and a charming host.

Michael Shannon is that flawless host, and The Shannon-Kavanaugh House is that home. Behind its lovingly restored and refurbished facade lies a lot of history, lending a personal touch to the business of entertaining. The story starts in 1892, when Matthew Kavanaugh built this Queen Anne-style home. He sold it to Frederic Klopper in 1900, and Klopper's daughter got married here that same year, followed later by ceremonies for Michael Shannon's mother and nieces. Thus a tradition of hosting beautiful weddings was established.

But hosting weddings was probably the last thing on Shannon's mind when he first saw the house in 1975. It was not a pretty site: condemned and boarded up, it was about to be razed for a parking lot. Committed to restoring it, however, he took a deep breath and plunged into the transformation. Today, the Shannon-Kavanaugh House radiates eclectic quality. As you walk in the front door, notice the stairs leading to the second floor—they're lit from above by a stained-glass skylight salvaged from a St. Louis church, and by a working gaslight affixed to the banister. To the right is the parlor, where Country French reproductions mingle with Victorian authentics, and hand-carved teak tables from Japan fraternize with a gilded mirror shipped from New York via Cape Horn in 1870. Windows overlook Alamo Square Park, the finishing touch on a setting that's just right for a ceremony or reception.

In back of the parlor is a beautifully designed kitchen, where red granite counters, an oak parquet floor and a redwood ceiling gleam. The formal dining room off the kitchen is another jewel, with a reproduction 18th-century Irish fireplace, somberly vibrant Dutch portraits, warm terra cotta-hued walls and a gaslight chandelier (Shannon just loves authentic gaslights). The rest of the house is equally lovely. An upstairs bedroom (fireplace, brocades, silver wallpaper) can be used as the bridal staging area, or reserved for a luxury honeymoon. Accommodations are also available in a garden apartment, or in the two-bedroom, two-bath cottage next door, with its own English garden in back.

Shannon is justifiably pleased with what he's wrought, and he likes sharing his home's splendor. Since 1984 the house has been featured in movies (Maxie, Junior, and Invasion of the Body Snatchers), TV series (Hawaii Five-O, Trapper John, MD, Streets of San Francisco), commercials (Macy's, Kool Aid, and Toyota), and countless "Postcard Row" photos; it's also hosted private parties, innumerable weddings, and special corporate events for the likes of Ford, Apple Computer and Charles Schwab. A genial and gifted host, Shannon utilizes his capable staff and employs top local chefs to cater events, leaving him free to take part in the festivities and make sure everything runs without a hitch. Yes indeed, there's nothing quite like a home wedding.

CEREMONY CAPACITY: The Double Parlor holds 50 guests; the Garden 20 seated guests.

EVENT/RECEPTION CAPACITY: The Dining Room can accommodate 24 seated guests or 60 standing; the Victorian Garden Cottage can hold 12 seated or 30 standing.

MEETING CAPACITY: The Dining Room holds 30 guests; the Double Parlor can seat 50 guests.

FEES & DEPOSITS: A $650 non-refundable deposit is required to reserve your date. The balance is due 2 weeks prior to the event. The rental fee ranges from $750–1,500 depending on the time of year. Luncheons run $35–75/person; dinners from $50–150/person and include a formal sit-down meal with non-alcoholic beverages and dessert. Tax, alcohol and a 17% service charge are additional.

AVAILABILITY: Year-round, daily, 8am–11pm.

SERVICES/AMENITIES:

Catering: provided or BYO
Kitchen Facilities: ample
Tables & Chairs: provided
Linens, Silver, etc.: provided
Restrooms: not wheelchair accessible
Dance Floor: no
Bride's & Groom's Dressing Areas: yes
Meeting Equipment: BYO
Other: player piano

Parking: on street or valet, extra charge
Accommodations: 2-bedroom cottage, 1-bedroom apartment, 1 master suite
Telephone: house phones
Outdoor Night Lighting: access only
Outdoor Cooking Facilities: no
Cleanup: provided or through caterer
View: San Francisco skyline

RESTRICTIONS:

Alcohol: provided, or BYO, corkage $5/bottle
Smoking: outside only
Music: amplified OK indoors

Wheelchair Access: no
Insurance: not required
Other: children under 6 require adult supervision

*The professionals in the back of the book are the best in the business! **How do we know? Read page 681.***

Sir Francis Drake Hotel

Hotel

450 Powell Street, San Francisco
(415) 395-8506 Catering Dept., fax (415) 677-9341

www.sirfrancisdrake.com
citysearch7.com

- ◆ Ceremonies   ◆ Special Events
- ◆ Wedding Receptions   ◆ Meetings
- ◆ Business Functions   ◆ Accommodations

The Sir Francis Drake Hotel's 21-story, Gothic-style tower just off Union Square and its Beefeater-attired doormen have been beloved San Francisco attractions since 1928. Happily for those of us who appreciate architectural gems, hotelier Bill Kimpton purchased the Drake in 1993, and spent $10 million restoring its splendid interior.

Stepping into the Drake's opulent, Italian Renaissance lobby is just like stepping back into 1928. Marble staircases, walls and pillars convey a stately air, crystal chandeliers shine and its lofty, ornately detailed ceilings sparkle with gold leaf. The main event spaces, the Empire Ballroom and the Franciscan Room, have a high society, *Age of Innocence* ambiance. The gold-and-white Empire Room features very pretty, hand-painted murals. Three crystal chandeliers suspended from a vaulted ceiling painted with ribbons of gold leaf give the room a delicate, amber glow. The adjoining wood-paneled Walnut Room, with its club-like, Edwardian atmosphere and built-in bar, makes a great pre-function space.

Located just off the mezzanine, the spacious and grand Franciscan Room is an excellent choice for formal weddings. A 21-foot ceiling aglow with intricate gold embossing, windows draped with blue silk curtains, columns with carved, gold capitals and hand-painted murals make this an exceptional space for indoor ceremonies. The adjoining anteroom is equally impressive, with a 21-foot, coffered ceiling and floor-to-ceiling windows. You can use the anteroom as a bride's dressing room, and make your grand entrance through the ten-foot-tall, double doors. After the ceremony, guests can mingle on the mezzanine while white-gloved butlers pass trays of hors d'oeuvres and serve champagne, then return to the Franciscan Room for a seated meal.

And for those who have a yen for a panoramic, 180-degree view of San Francisco, try Harry Denton's Starlight Room, located on the 21st floor. Recently renovated, it not only has a built-in dance floor and a shiny baby grand piano, it features floor-to-ceiling windows that wrap around the entire room, making it seem like you're floating in the clouds.

If you haven't seen the Sir Francis Drake in a long time, we suggest you come by for a visit. Like a phoenix, the Sir Francis Drake has risen again to reclaim its standing among San Francisco's vintage landmark hotels.

CEREMONY & EVENT/RECEPTION CAPACITY:

Room	Seated	Standing	Room	Seated	Standing
Empire Ballroom	250	350	Harry's Starlight Room	150	200
Franciscan Room	140	200			

MEETING CAPACITY: The Hotel has 20,000 square feet of meeting and conference space with 15 different rooms accommodating groups from 10 to 350 people.

FEES & DEPOSITS: For weddings, a non-refundable $1,000 deposit is required to confirm your date. Half the total food and beverage payment is payable 60 days prior to the event; the balance and guest count guarantee is due 3 days prior. Per-person prices for seated meals are as follows: luncheons start at $25, dinners at $32, luncheon buffets at $32, and dinner buffets at $45. Alcohol, tax and an 19% service charge are additional. Bride and groom receive a complimentary suite and group discounts for overnight guests can be arranged.

Fees for meetings and business functions vary depending on rooms and services selected; call for specifics.

AVAILABILITY: For special events and business functions, year-round, daily, 6am–11pm. Weddings usually take place on Saturdays 11am–5pm or 6pm–midnight; other days have more flexible time frames. The Starlight Room is available Saturday 10am–4pm, and all day Sunday until midnight.

SERVICES/AMENITIES:

Catering: provided, no BYO
Kitchen Facilities: n/a
Tables & Chairs: provided
Linens, Silver, etc.: provided
Restrooms: wheelchair accessible
Dance Floor: provided
Bride's & Groom's Dressing Area: yes
Meeting Equipment: AV

Parking: nearby garages or valet, extra fee
Accommodations: 417 guest rooms
Telephone: guest and pay phones
Outdoor Night Lighting: n/a
Outdoor Cooking Facilities: n/a
Cleanup: provided
View: Starlight Room has 180° view of SF skyline
Other: event coordination, baby grand piano

RESTRICTIONS:

Alcohol: provided, no BYO
Smoking: designated areas
Music: amplified OK

Wheelchair Access: yes, elevator
Insurance: not required
Other: no rice

---

*This is important! Tell facilities you're reading **Here Comes The Guide** and ask if our information is still current.*

SkyDeck at Embarcadero Center

Events Facility

One Embarcadero Center, 41st Floor, San Francisco
(415) 772-0589, fax (415) 982-1780

www.sfskydeck.com

Ceremonies	◆ Special Events
Wedding Receptions	◆ Meetings
◆ Business Functions	Accommodations

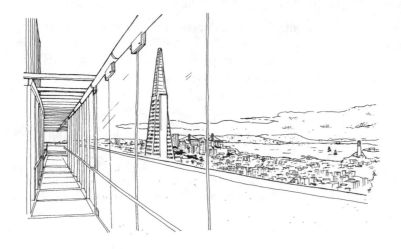

Ever wonder where they shoot those spectacular panoramic views of San Francisco you see on picture postcards? For professional photographers, the best spot is the SkyDeck on the 41st floor of One Embarcadero Center, the only indoor/outdoor viewing observatory in The City. On a clear day you can see way beyond Mt. Diablo and the Marin Headlands. And at night the view is even more magical, with the lights of the City playing counterpoint to the lights on the Golden Gate and Bay Bridges.

Since the SkyDeck opened in 1996, it's been the site of some extraordinary evenings, and breakfast and lunch gatherings: Mayor Willie Brown's Osaka Sister City event; Dreamworks exhibitors' lunch; opening night cast parties for Broadway productions; and press previews for the San Francisco Film Festival. For sheer San Francisco sophistication, there's nothing quite like an event on the SkyDeck.

Picture your guests strolling through the SkyDeck's three flow-through adjoining rooms, gazing at The City's celebrated skyline through what is essentially a 360-degree wall of glass. Those who want an even more glorious view can step outside and take in the scene from the outer deck, which runs around the perimeter. (Not to worry; they'll be protected from the elements by sheets of crystal-clear glass.)

For anyone who wants to know more about what they're looking at, six interactive touch-screen computer kiosks are placed at strategic viewing points. Touch the screen overlooking North Beach, and a clever multimedia presentation tells you about the Beat generation. Touch the screen overlooking Nob Hill, and you'll learn about Leland Stanford and Mark Hopkins and that famous eccentric, Emperor Norton. And for those who want to know even more, the SkyDeck's docents can draw on their seemingly inexhaustible supply of fascinating anecdotes about San Francisco history.

Don't overlook one of the SkyDeck's biggest assets: the parking. Finding a place to park in San Francisco is a notoriously difficult task, but the Embarcadero Center sits on top of 2,000 underground parking spaces. And major bus and cable car lines intersect right outside.

The SkyDeck is a favorite for anniversaries, office parties and corporate functions. If you're looking for something different, this is truly a room with a view.

CEREMONY CAPACITY: The SkyDeck does not host ceremonies.

EVENT/RECEPTION CAPACITY: The SkyDeck can accommodate 100 seated or 275 standing guests.

MEETING CAPACITY: The SkyDeck can hold 120 guests seated theater-style.

FEES & DEPOSITS: A $500 refundable security deposit and the entire facility rental fee are due with the signed contract. Rental fees for evening events run $3,000–4,000; daytime events run $850–1,000.

AVAILABILITY: Year-round, Monday–Friday, 7am–midnight; Saturday and Sunday evenings, 6pm–midnight.

SERVICES/AMENITIES:

Catering: select from preferred list
Kitchen Facilities: prep only
Tables & Chairs: provided
Linens, Silver, etc.: through caterer
Restrooms: wheelchair accessible
Dance Floor: BYO
Meeting Equipment: BYO
Other: docent tour guide

Parking: adjacent garages
Accommodations: no guest rooms
Telephone: no
Outdoor Night Lighting: yes
Outdoor Cooking Facilities: n/a
Cleanup: provided
View: panoramic view of SF skyline

RESTRICTIONS:

Alcohol: through caterer
Smoking: deck only
Music: amplified OK upon approval

Wheelchair Access: yes
Insurance: liability required
Other: no decorations on walls

The professionals in the back of the book are the best in the business! **How do we know? Read page 681.**

Spectrum Gallery

511 Harrison Street, San Francisco
(415) 495-1111, fax (415) 882-9999

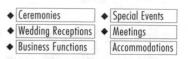

- ◆ Ceremonies
- ◆ Wedding Receptions
- ◆ Business Functions
- ◆ Special Events
- ◆ Meetings
- Accommodations

Designed and built by an event professional, this spacious fine art gallery has a twenty-foot-high wall of windows facing the entire downtown skyline. At night, the view sparkles with thousands of lights twinkling just four blocks away. Spectrum also offers almost every amenity you could want: a state-of-the-art lighting and dimming system that can pin-spot anything from dining tables to the wedding cake, a whisper-clear P/A system for background music and toasts, a portable stage and dance floor, a private bride's dressing room, a 1,200-square-foot caterer's area, huge restrooms and abundant free parking nearby.

Adaptable and adjustable, as few as 100 or as many as 400 can be seated comfortably, all in the same room. The museum-quality paintings and sculpture and the wide range of amenities create an environment that's unique, dramatic and truly memorable. Ceremonies are welcome, and Spectrum's experienced "hands-on" staff are always available to help with planning and coordination.

CEREMONY CAPACITY: Spectrum holds 200 seated or 300 standing guests.

EVENT/RECEPTION CAPACITY: This facility can hold 100–400 seated guests (with stage and dance floor), 150–650 guests for a standing reception.

MEETING CAPACITY: Spectrum Gallery holds up to 300 seated theater-style or 175 seated classroom-style.

FEES & DEPOSITS: Half the rental fee is the non-refundable deposit due when reservations are confirmed; the balance is due 90 days prior to your event. The rental fee is $3,250 for weddings, $3,500 for business functions. A fully refundable $1,000 cleaning/damage deposit is due 5 days prior to your function. During December, the rental fee is higher. For daytime, Monday–Friday special events or business functions, the rental fee is $1,750.

AVAILABILITY: Year-round, daily, 8am–2am.

SERVICES/AMENITIES:

Catering: any insured caterer
Kitchen Facilities: moderate
Tables & Chairs: provided
Linens, Silver, etc.: BYO
Restrooms: wheelchair accessible
Dance Floor: yes
Bride's Dressing Area: yes
Meeting Equipment: full range

Parking: abundant on-street
Accommodations: no guest rooms
Telephone: pay phones
Outdoor Night Lighting: access only
Outdoor Cooking Facilities: no
Cleanup: caterer and Spectrum
View: of SF financial district & skyline
Other: stage, riser, projection screen, lighting/dimming & sound systems

RESTRICTIONS:

Alcohol: provided
Smoking: outside only
Music: amplified OK

Wheelchair Access: yes
Insurance: required, available

This is important! Tell facilities you're reading **Here Comes The Guide** *and ask if our information is still current.*

S.S. Jeremiah O'Brien

Pier 32, San Francisco
(415) 822-3710, fax (415) 822-0534

dailypi@aol.com

WWII Merchant Ship

◆ Ceremonies   ◆ Special Events
◆ Wedding Receptions   ◆ Meetings
◆ Business Functions   Accommodations

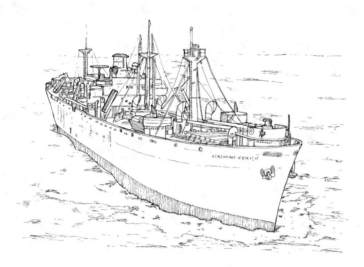

If you get nostalgic remembering the days of victory gardens, the Andrews Sisters, and movie newsreels, or if you just like being out on the bay, you won't be disappointed by the *S.S. Jeremiah O'Brien*, docked at Pier 32 just south of the San Francisco Bay Bridge anchorage. Climb the gangway to the main deck, twenty feet above the water, and you're surrounded by booms, gun tubs, and rising tiers of decks. From this vantage point the Bay Bridge seems almost close enough to touch.

Built in 57 days during World War II's emergency shipbuilding program, the *S.S. Jeremiah O'Brien* is one of only two working vessels that remain from her original fleet of 2,700. The *O'Brien* carried everything from troops to trains, and she's still sturdy and spirited. Restored to working order and maintained by a loyal crew of over 200 volunteers, she was the only American ship from the original D-Day armada to return to Europe for the commemorative D-Day + 50 celebration.

Today, however, the ship is more likely to host visitors and events than sail the seas. You can rent the Officers' Mess for a small sit-down dinner or cocktails for up to 35 guests. It's an intimate room on the main deck with built-in tables, deep-green upholstered bench seats, and varnished oak trim touches.

Events from corporate luncheons and meetings to association dinners and weddings are held in the cargo hold (No. 2 Hold), an auditorium-sized area below the main deck. Walls are painted white, the floor red, and you can decorate according to your theme or taste. The hatch, which takes up a good portion of the room, makes a perfect dance floor, and the acoustics are great. One couple bedecked the entire cargo hold with hundreds of colorful spinnakers, and another couple mutinied against plans for a formal wedding in favor of holding their ceremony aboard the *O'Brien*. Other couples have used the in-house event planning company, *Daily Plan It,* to transform the ship into a totally themed environment. You can stretch your imagination (or have *Daily Plan It* stretch it for you!) by offering a Beauty and the Beast party, a murder mystery, a gaming ship event (like a floating Monaco casino), a Caribbean cruise theme, or an interactive, pseudo-military "disco bonding" party. And there's another bonus: you and your guests can be treated to tours of the ship, which is especially appealing to ship lovers.

CEREMONY & EVENT/RECEPTION CAPACITY: No. 2 Hold can accommodate 150 seated or 250 standing guests (250 guests is the ship's maximum). The Officers' Mess holds 16 seated or 35 standing guests.

MEETING CAPACITY: The Gunners' Mess holds 12 seated guests conference-style, the Officers' Mess 16 seated theater-style, and the No. 2 Hold, 200 seated theater-style or 80 seated conference-style.

FEES & DEPOSITS: To secure your date, a $150 cleaning fee is required. The rental fee for the No. 2 Hold is $5/person (100-guest minimum), the Officers' Mess is $75 plus $5/person. To rent the Gunners' Mess, the fee is $30 plus cost of admission to the ship/person. The admission price varies depending on age and/or military status.

AVAILABILITY: Year-round, 8am–11pm if the ship is in port. Call to check schedule.

SERVICES/AMENITIES:

Catering: provided by *Arguello Catering*
Kitchen Facilities: minimal prep, steam table, bar
Tables & Chairs: provided
Linens, Silver, etc.: BYO
Restrooms: not wheelchair accessible
Dance Floor: in No. 2 Hold
Bride's Dressing Area: CBA
Meeting Equipment: PA, microphones

Parking: ample on pier
Accommodations: no guest rooms
Telephone: emergency use only
Outdoor Night Lighting: access only
Outdoor Cooking Facilities: no
Cleanup: provided, extra charge
View: San Francisco & bridges
Other: docent tours CBA, event planning by *Daily Plan It*

RESTRICTIONS:

Alcohol: BYO, licensed & insured server
Smoking: on deck only
Music: amplified OK

Wheelchair Access: no
Insurance: certificate required
Other: no rice, birdseed, confetti or glitter

The professionals in the back of the book are the best in the business! ***How do we know? Read page 681.***

The Studio Gallery San Francisco

Art Gallery

654 Mission Street, San Francisco
(888) 643-8670, fax (415) 243-8671

www.studiogallery.com
info@lje.com

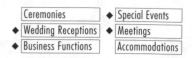

Ceremonies	◆ Special Events
◆ Wedding Receptions	◆ Meetings
◆ Business Functions	Accommodations

It's a rare gallery that manages to appeal to both your serious and silly sides, but this one definitely does. Owned by the family of world-famous animator Chuck Jones, the Studio Gallery is filled with powerful photography and whimsical animation art, all of which will keep your guests intrigued and entertained for hours. Its prime location, just a block from Moscone Center and around the corner from the San Francisco Museum of Modern Art, also makes it a convenient meeting or reception site for conventioneers and locals, looking for something out of the ordinary.

Two spacious floors are available for events, and you can use either or both. Each one has a high ceiling, track lighting, white walls and grey carpet—the neutral, spare decor that's conducive to showcasing art. The main floor, with multiple exhibit areas, is most often used for cocktail receptions. Here you get a chance to revisit your childhood: Bugs Bunny, Daffy Duck, Elmer Fudd, Wile E. Coyote and the many other characters created by Chuck Jones cavort in animation cels, original drawings, oils and watercolors. Joining that crew are Snoopy, Charlie Brown and Woodstock, who come to life in the work of Charles Schulz and Bill Melendez, animators of the popular Peanuts gang. There's also a little something for fans of Rocky and Bullwinkle, and Dr. Seuss. In a separate area, you'll find the mesmerizing images of internationally acclaimed photographer and author Phil Borges, whose haunting portraits of indigenous peoples go beyond the surface to find the inner spirit of those he captures on film. On the day we visited, they had just installed a temporary exhibit of Beatles photos, which we found fascinating.

The second floor gallery is perfect for an intimate reception, party or meeting. During the day, the large room is bright and cheery, thanks to natural light pouring in from three oversized skylights, and multipaned windows at both ends. At night, the track lighting can be adjusted to create the kind of ambiance you want. Exhibits up here change periodically and, if you like, staff members are available to answer questions about the artwork.

Because the spaces are flexible, you can host a wide range of events, from a casual evening lecture to a holiday party or formal wedding reception. And in case you're wondering where food preparation takes place, there's a private mezzanine for your caterer.

The Studio Gallery is a fresh alternative to standard event sites, but you don't have to be planning an event to enjoy its exhibits. Just stop in on a weekday and take a leisurely stroll through the galleries—it will be time well spent.

CEREMONY CAPACITY: Ceremonies don't take place at this venue.

EVENT RECEPTION & MEETING CAPACITY: There are 2 floors; you can rent either individually, or both floors combined for special events. Each floor holds 75–100 seated or 150–200 standing guests. The maximum site capacity is 200 seated or 400 standing guests.

FEES & DEPOSITS: Half of the rental fee is a non-refundable deposit required when reservations are confirmed; the balance is payable 30 days prior to the event. The rental fee is $1,500 per floor; during peak periods, the rental fee is higher. A $750 refundable cleaning/damage deposit is due 7 days prior to the event.

AVAILABILITY: Year-round, daily, except major holidays; 6pm–midnight.

SERVICES/AMENITIES:

Catering: BYO
Kitchen Facilities: minimal prep
Tables & Chairs: BYO
Linens, Silver, etc.: BYO
Restrooms: wheelchair accessible
Dance Floor: CBA, extra charge
Bride's Dressing Area: n/a
Meeting Equipment: CBA, extra charge

Parking: garages nearby
Accommodations: no guest rooms
Telephone: emergency use only
Outdoor Night Lighting: access only
Outdoor Cooking Facilities: no
Cleanup: through caterer
View: no
Other: art consultants, choice of variety of artists' work

RESTRICTIONS:

Alcohol: BYO, licensed server
Smoking: outside only
Music: amplified OK indoors

Wheelchair Access: yes
Insurance: not required
Other: no red wine or children under 6

---

*This is important! Tell facilities you're reading **Here Comes The Guide** and ask if our information is still current.*

185

Swedenborgian Church

Landmark Chapel

2107 Lyon Street at Washington, San Francisco
(415) 346-6466, fax (415) 474-0172

◆ Ceremonies   Special Events
◆ Wedding Receptions   Meetings
Business Functions   Accommodations

Built in 1895 in Pacific Heights by a coterie of artists, architects and spiritual seekers, the historic Swedenborgian Church is rustic and charming in the Arts and Crafts tradition. There's a huge brick fireplace inside and, lit with candles, the interior is exceptionally beautiful and serene. Floors, walls and ceilings are wood, and the arching overhead beams are good-sized madrone tree trunks. In lieu of conventional pews, handmade maple chairs are provided.

Many of San Francisco's most important (if not famous!) personages were once affiliated with this church, such as Robert Frost, who went to Sunday School here. The founders of the Sierra Club were all members, including John Muir. The Sierra Club's legendary landscape painter, William Keith, painted four large murals that line the north wall of the sanctuary, and Phoebe Hearst (William Randolph Hearst's better half) is represented by her donation of a rare, cast-iron copy of Peter Vischer's 15th-century "Praying Madonna."

Adjacent to the chapel is a turn-of-the-century house whose living, dining and garden rooms are used for receptions. In front of the house, a quiet garden with a small pool, trees, benches and flowers provides a pretty spot for gatherings.

The Swedenborgian Church offers traditional, contemporary and interfaith ceremonies, with weddings usually scheduled two hours apart. Reception space is limited, so the reception facilities are available only after the last wedding of the day on Saturday and Sunday. If you're willing to get married on a weekday there's much greater flexibility.

CEREMONY CAPACITY: The chapel holds 100 seated or 125 standing.

EVENT/RECEPTION CAPACITY: The house holds up to 60 seated or 100 standing guests.

FEES & DEPOSITS: A $250 deposit is required to secure your wedding date and time. For receptions, a refundable security deposit of $250 is also required. A donation of $950 is required for Friday, Saturday, Sunday and holiday wedding ceremonies. Monday–Thursday ceremonies with fewer than 20 guests cost $350; with over 20 guests, the fee is $550. The rental fee for the reception area is $300/hour, not including setup and cleanup time. Full payment is due 1 month before the wedding. The donation includes a minister's services, staff musician, the assistance of a wedding hostess, a large floral arrangement, bridal dressing room and use of the garden for wedding photos.

AVAILABILITY: Saturday receptions are possible only after the 5pm wedding; Sundays, after the 4pm wedding. Weekday receptions can be scheduled by arrangement. Guests must vacate the premises by 9pm.

SERVICES/AMENITIES:

Catering: BYO
Kitchen Facilities: modest
Tables & Chairs: provided
Linens, Silver, etc.: BYO
Restrooms: not wheelchair accessible
Dance Floor: yes, small receptions only
Bride's Dressing Area: yes

Parking: on street
Accommodations: no guest rooms
Telephone: house phone
Outdoor Night Lighting: access only
Outdoor Cooking Facilities: no
Cleanup: caterer
View: of Pacific Heights neighborhood

RESTRICTIONS:

Alcohol: BYO wine or champagne
Smoking: outside only
Music: no amplified

Wheelchair Access: no
Insurance: not required
Other: no rice or seeds

The professionals in the back of the book are the best in the business! **How do we know? Read page 681.**

Temple Emanu-El

Temple

2 Lake Street, San Francisco
(415) 751-2535, fax (415) 751-2511

mail@emanuelsf.org

◆ Ceremonies ◆ Special Events
◆ Wedding Receptions ◆ Meetings
◆ Business Functions ☐ Accommodations

It's easy to see why Temple Emanu-El is a San Francisco landmark—its huge dome is visible for blocks around. Built in 1925, its Mediterranean and Middle Eastern influences are reflected in the tiled roof, columns and numerous arched entryways and windows. The main entrance is imposing, with a set of massive arches curving high overhead as you ascend the staircase and walk into an open-air courtyard. If you're willing to take a chance on the weather, this is a delightful spot for a reception or cocktail party. A mosaic-tiled fountain bubbles in the center of a brick terrace, enclosed on all sides by the building's graceful, arched corridors. Pine, olive and fig trees fill the corners of the courtyard, and planters overflow with colorful flowers.

Elevators take guests to the Guild Hall, a large ballroom with a state-of-the-art lighting system, as well as an optional dance floor and stage. Subtle tones of beige, cafe au lait and teal provide a neutral backdrop, and simple alabaster chandeliers add a touch of elegance. The Guild Hall can also be divided to produce two smaller spaces of equal beauty, accommodating either receptions or meetings.

The Martin Meyer Reception Room, designed in distinctive shades of teal, burgundy and ocher, handles smaller receptions, luncheons or cocktail events. It features coffered ceilings and a bank of arched doors which lead into the center outdoor courtyard. Adjoining this room is the Martin Meyer Sanctuary. Popular for wedding ceremonies, musical events and lectures, this space highlights a state-of-the-art sound system and highly acclaimed acoustics.

The Temple Foyer, which is often used for cocktail receptions, is a classic marble columned room featuring an arched, hand-painted ceiling. One wall accesses the outdoor brick courtyard through a bank of double doors. Bordering this room is the Main Sanctuary where larger concerts and weddings take place. Its soaring interior is capped by the Temple's magnificent and famous dome. Soft light is cast by the black-and-gold chandeliers and two stunning stained glass windows that glow on either side of the room.

This venue is used by the whole community for a variety of events including wedding receptions, concerts, lectures, conferences and meetings. Its range of event spaces and its elegance make Temple Emanu-El well worth your consideration.

CEREMONY CAPACITY: The Main Sanctuary seats 1,700 guests, the Chapel seats 100, and the Martin Meyer Sanctuary 250 seated on the main floor.

EVENT/RECEPTION CAPACITY:

Area	Seated	Standing	Area	Seated	Standing
Guild Hall 1 or 2	120	300	Guild Hall 1 & 2	260	600
Martin Meyer Reception Room	80	200	Foyer	130	250

MEETING CAPACITY:

Area	Theater-style	Area	Theater-style
Guild Hall 1 or 2	180	Meyer Auditorium Balcony	96
Meyer Auditorium	280		

FEES & DEPOSITS: One third of the anticipated total is due when rooms are booked; prices vary depending on time of day and day of week rented. Higher fees are charged for weekend use. The rental fee for Guild Hall 1 or 2 runs $250–900 for nonmembers. The fee for the entire Guild Ballroom is $500–1,200, and the Martin Meyer Reception Room, $500–1,000. Discount packages are available for weekday functions.

AVAILABILITY: Year-round, 8am–1am

SERVICES/AMENITIES:

Catering: select from preferred list
Kitchen Facilities: fully equipped
Tables & Chairs: provided
China, Silver, etc.: provided
Restrooms: wheelchair accessible
Dance Floor: yes; stage extra fee
Bride's Dressing Area: provided
View: no

Parking: on-street or garage nearby
Accommodations: no guest rooms
Telephone: pay phone
Outdoor Night Lighting: courtyard
Outdoor Cooking Facilities: no
Cleanup: provided, setup provided
Meeting Equipment: podium, projectors, wireless microphones

RESTRICTIONS:

Alcohol: BYO or through caterer
Smoking: outside only
Music: amplified OK

Wheelchair Access: yes, elevator
Insurance: may be required
Other: no pork or shellfish may be served

---

*This is important! Tell facilities you're reading **Here Comes The Guide** and ask if our information is still current.*

Trinity Episcopal Church

Historic Church

1668 Bush Street (corner of Bush & Gough), San Francisco
(415) 775-1117, fax (415) 775-3976

trinitysf@earthlink.net

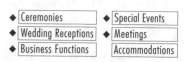

◆ Ceremonies   ◆ Special Events
◆ Wedding Receptions   ◆ Meetings
◆ Business Functions   Accommodations

Trinity Episcopal Church appears to have been lifted, lock, stock and stained-glass windows, from a quaint village in England. Even the rector, Reverend Robert Cromey, looks as if he answered a call from Central Casting for a "dignified English vicar." But don't let the imposing Norman-Romanesque architecture fool you. Beneath the church's 104-year-old Colusa sandstone exterior beats a progressive heart. This church may look old-fashioned, but the attitudes of its clergy and congregation are firmly rooted in the 1990s.

Trinity is the oldest Episcopal church west of the Rockies, and was staunchly conservative until the arrival of Father Cromey in 1981. Now, it's a thriving cornerstone of the community, with a diverse, inclusive congregation. Project Open Hand, a service that brings free, hot meals to AIDS patients, got its start here. Theater companies and recovery groups rent space from Trinity, and the church hosts such innovative workshops as "Exploring Christian Yoga." More important to those planning a wedding, the church places no restrictions on who can get married here. You need not be a member of the congregation, you need not be baptized and you can bring your own clergy or design the ceremony yourself. Same-sex blessings are permitted, and the participation of family members in the ceremony is encouraged. The staff has many innovative ways to include children in a wedding. This is especially nice for couples who are "blending" families, as it gives them a chance to give everyone an active role in starting their new life together.

The main church features rainbow-hued stained-glass windows, an 86-foot-long aisle, an antique Skinner organ (one of only four on the West Coast), and a grand piano. The pulpit is carved in the shape of an angel, and has a PA system for readings by family members or friends. The altar, which is decorated with brass candlesticks for wedding ceremonies, is inlaid with intricate mosaic designs. The church's ornateness makes very elaborate decorations unnecessary, which is nice for those on a tight budget.

The reception facilities consist of two rooms with hardwood floors and dark, wood-paneled walls. One of the rooms is enlivened by five arched windows that overlook lush plantings of ferns and impatiens. The two rooms can be opened to make one large room.

Trinity Episcopal Church is ideal for couples who want the dignified beauty, but not the stuffy rigidity, of a traditional church wedding. Who says you can't have your wedding cake, and eat it, too?

CEREMONY CAPACITY: The church holds up to 450 seated guests.

EVENT/RECEPTION CAPACITY: The Social Hall accommodates 120 seated or 200 standing guests.

MEETING CAPACITY: The Social Hall holds 120 seated theater-style or conference-style.

FEES & DEPOSITS: A $250 rental deposit ($150 of it is non-refundable) is required to reserve your date; the balance is due 2 weeks prior to the event. The church rental fee is $850. The fee covers a 3-hour block plus a 1-hour rehearsal; additional hours are available at $100/hour. The Social Hall base rental fee is $500 for 3 hours; additional hours can be arranged at $150/hour. Business meeting rates vary depending on use; call for specifics.

AVAILABILITY: Year-round, daily, any time. The Church is not available Sundays until 1pm or the first Saturday of each month until 1pm.

SERVICES/AMENITIES:

Catering: BYO
Kitchen Facilities: fully equipped, no utensils
Tables & Chairs: 12 tables, 120 chairs provided
Linens, Silver, etc.: BYO
Restrooms: not wheelchair accessible
Dance Floor: BYO
Bride's Groom's Dressing Area: yes
Meeting Equipment: PA system, other BYO

Parking: local garages or on street
Accommodations: no guest rooms
Telephone: emergency use only
Outdoor Night Lighting: access only
Outdoor Cooking Facilities: no
Cleanup: caterer or renter
View: no
Other: some coordination

RESTRICTIONS:

Alcohol: BYO; inquire about restrictions
Smoking: not allowed
Music: no amplified; recorded or acoustic only

Wheelchair Access: limited
Insurance: not required
Other: no rice, confetti or birdseed; decorations restricted

The professionals in the back of the book are the best in the business! **How do we know? Read page 681.**

Vivande Ristorante

Italian Restaurant

670 Golden Gate Avenue, San Francisco
(415) 673-9245, fax (415) 673-2160

www.citysearch.com/sfo/vivanderistoran

◆ Ceremonies ◆ Special Events
◆ Wedding Receptions ◆ Meetings
◆ Business Functions ◆ Accommodations

The entrance to Vivande couldn't be more unusual or more fitting: a 15-foot face, modelled after a 19th-century Italian frieze in Rome, has an arched door for an open mouth. Step through the "mouth" and, like Alice in Wonderland, you'll find yourself in a rather interesting place—one with the gracious feel of an Italian villa. It could almost be someone's home—someone with superb taste, a penchant for Italian antiques and artistic touches. Someone who cooks really well. The open kitchen and brick wood-burning oven fill the restaurant with the sounds and smells of gourmet dinners in the making, while the slate and marble floors, ochre walls, glorious ceramic urns, and striped lamps all create an atmosphere that is at once sophisticated and festive.

This is a restaurant your friends will definitely enjoy. The main dining room affords a clear view of the open kitchen, while the adjacent bar and lounge offers a more subdued "nook" for cocktails and conversation. For small, more private parties, the Gate Room is a lovely, intimate enclosure with richly textured amber-colored walls, soft lighting and wonderful old sepia-tone Italian photographs. Even the restrooms are aesthetically pleasing, with their amber wall frescoes of angels and tasteful nudes from Pompei.

Vivande hosts all sorts of events, including jazz brunches, corporate parties and rehearsal dinners. They once orchestrated an elaborate evening with a Carnival theme—complete with waiters outfitted with Carnival masks. Weddings are a specialty, and Vivande's particularly well-suited for Jewish weddings, since it's easier to reserve the restaurant on a Sunday than the busier Friday or Saturday nights. They are also known for their literary fêtes (in conjunction with author readings from A Clean Well-Lighted Place for Books, the bookstore around the corner) and parties put on by San Francisco's music and art elite.

Vivande can do more, however, than just put on a great party. Their other restaurant, Vivande Porta Via has been making gourmet carry-out Italian cuisine since 1981. If you want their food and accommodating service but not their restaurant space, Vivande is happy to prepare an elegant feast to whatever your specifications might be: with staff service or drop-off, packaged for a bridal picnic or a sailboat soirée, delivered to private jets (a service enjoyed by Henry

Kissinger, Goldie Hawn, and Barbra Streisand), or done up in gift baskets and delivered to the hotels for the visiting aunts and uncles and cousins.

The bottom line at Vivande Ristorante, underlying their gracious restaurant atmosphere and delectable food, is their sensitivity to the customer. The staff are experienced in the art of designing an evening that runs smoothly, and they delight in working with special requests for an unusual theme or idiosyncratic need. It's as much a pleasure to work out the details with them as it is to enjoy the results.

CEREMONY CAPACITY: The restaurant can hold up to 75 seated or 100 standing.

EVENT/RECEPTION CAPACITY: For cocktail receptions, Vivande holds up to 150 standing guests; the outdoor courtyard up to 100 standing guests. With a buyout, the entire restaurant can accommodate 200 seated or 315 standing.

MEETING CAPACITY: The Gate Room seats 30 guests, conference style. The restaurant can accommodate up to 200 with a buyout.

FEES & DEPOSITS: To secure your date, a $200 non-refundable deposit is required. Half of the estimated food and beverage total is payable, along with a signed contract and guest count guarantee, 2 weeks prior to the event. The balance is due at the event's conclusion.

Any menu can be customized for private parties: luncheons start at $25/person, dinners at $35/person, and hors d'oeuvres at $25/person; alcohol, tax and a 20% service charge are additional. Exclusive use of Vivande can be arranged; call for more specific information about what is required for a buyout.

AVAILABILITY: Year-round, daily, 11:30pm–1am.

SERVICES/AMENITIES:

Catering: provided, no BYO
Kitchen Facilities: n/a
Tables & Chairs: provided
Linens, Silver, etc.: provided
Restrooms: wheelchair accessible
Dance Floor: tile floor in dining room, or CBA
Bride's & Groom's Dressing Area: yes
Meeting Equipment: microphone

Parking: 24-hour Opera Plaza garage
Accommodations: no guest rooms
Telephone: pay phone
Outdoor Night Lighting: yes
Outdoor Cooking Facilities: no
Cleanup: provided
View: no
Other: event planning

RESTRICTIONS:

Alcohol: provided, or BYO corkage $10–15/bottle
Smoking: outside only
Music: amplified OK w/volume limits

Wheelchair Access: yes
Insurance: not required
Other: no rice or birdseed

---

*This is important! Tell facilities you're reading **Here Comes The Guide** and ask if our information is still current.*

Vorpal Gallery

Art Gallery

393 Grove Street, San Francisco
(415) 397-9200, fax (415) 864-8335

vorpal@concentric.net

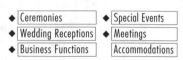

◆ Ceremonies ◆ Special Events
◆ Wedding Receptions ◆ Meetings
◆ Business Functions Accommodations

Our visit to the Vorpal Gallery took a lot longer than we expected. Instead of breezing through the various spaces, we found ourselves meandering slowly from room to room, lingering in front of dozens of works of art that grabbed our attention. We simply couldn't pass them by.

Some of the most riveting pieces are the mind-bending creations of Dutch graphic artist, M.C. Escher. In 1970 the Vorpal mounted a major exhibition of the artist's work, introducing him to the American public. The show was a triumph for both Escher and the gallery, which still has one of the world's most extensive collections of his paintings, drawings, woodcuts, lithographs and etchings. For decades, you've seen reproductions of his graphics in books and on posters; here at the Vorpal you can wrap your eyes around the originals (or at least you can try to!).

But Escher is not the gallery's only attraction. The Vorpal represents artists from all over the world, and has been doing so since 1962. In addition to temporary exhibits of contemporary artists, you'll find works of some of the Old Masters, like Rembrandt, Renoir, Gauguin and Durer. The art is displayed throughout 15,000 square feet of exhibition space on two floors, and collectively it makes an extraordinary backdrop for a special event.

The main floor, with its labyrinth of angular "rooms," is wonderful for cocktail receptions. The spaces vary in size; larger ones can accommodate a group gathering, while the smaller ones encourage private conversations between two or three people. The rooms all flow together, but in a curiously mysterious way, so you enter each new area with a sense of anticipation. The second floor is one grand gallery that's often used for receptions, private parties, sit-down dinners, conferences, lectures and concerts. It's spacious enough for a long guest list, but if you want to trim its dimensions a bit, several movable walls can be reconfigured to suit your needs.

As with most galleries, the interior is spare, and very effective in its simplicity. Both floors have white walls and fifteen-foot-high, black ceilings supported by natural wood posts and beams. The flooring is maple, stained a rich mahogany and varnished to a soft sheen. Spot lights throughout are expertly trained on paintings and sculptures, making them come to life. You can use the lighting to your own advantage, too, to enhance a productions or bring out the sparkle in crystal and silver on your elegantly set tables.

Located just one block from the Opera House and Davies Symphony Hall, the Vorpal Gallery has hosted events for both of those illustrious entities, as well as dozens of other art-loving clients. Their knowledgeable staff is on hand during your event to greet guests, talk about the art and change the occasional light bulb. By the way, if you can manage it, spend a little time chatting with gallery owner, Muldoon Elder. He's a veritable encyclopedia of art history and anecdote, whose insights will make your experience at the Vorpal that much richer.

CEREMONY CAPACITY: The Gallery can accommodate up to 350 seated guests.

EVENT/RECEPTION CAPACITY: This facility holds 250 seated guests.

MEETING CAPACITY: The Gallery can accommodate 250 guests seated theater-style.

FEES & DEPOSITS: A deposit of 50% of the rental fee, along with a $500 damage deposit, is required to reserve the date. The balance is due 12 weeks prior to the event. The facility rental fee is $3,000 plus $150/hour. Fees are higher in December.

AVAILABILITY: Year-round, Tuesday–Sunday, 11am–6pm.

SERVICES/AMENITIES:

Catering: BYO
Kitchen Facilities: small kitchen
Tables & Chairs: BYO
Linens, Silver, etc.: provided
Restrooms: wheelchair accessible
Dance Floor: tile floor in dining room, or CBA
Bride's Dressing Area: no
Meeting Equipment: microphone

Parking: 2 lots and 24 hour garage
Accommodations: no guest rooms
Telephone: house phone
Outdoor Night Lighting: yes
Outdoor Cooking Facilities: no
Cleanup: renter or caterer
View: no
Other: event planning

RESTRICTIONS:

Alcohol: BYO
Smoking: outside only
Music: amplified OK w/volume limits

Wheelchair Access: yes
Insurance: not required
Other: no rice or birdseed

---

*The professionals in the back of the book are the best in the business! **How do we know? Read page 681.***

The Wattis Room

at Davies Symphony Hall

201 Van Ness Avenue, San Francisco
(415) 255-6355 ext. 208, fax (415) 255-6377
www.nowcook.com
kathleen@nowcook.com

Banquet Room

◆ Ceremonies	◆ Special Events
◆ Wedding Receptions	◆ Meetings
◆ Business Functions	Accommodations

Most people don't know that the Wattis Room is available for social and corporate events. Maybe that's because it's a private club for major donors of the San Francisco Symphony or perhaps because it's tucked away on the first floor, accessible only through the main doors on Grove Street.

It's a medium-sized, contemporary space with subdued lighting and tasteful decor. Splashes of color come from a hanging tapestry and multiple, large paintings on the walls, all pieces of art from the San Francisco Museum of Modern Art's rotating exhibits. From rehearsal dinners to formal seated receptions, this location is versatile enough to handle any type of crowd.

CEREMONY & EVENT/RECEPTION CAPACITY: The Wattis Room holds 25–100 seated guests or 200 standing guests.

MEETING CAPACITY: The Room accommodates 80 seated theater-style. Other seating configurations can be arranged.

FEES & DEPOSITS: To secure your date, a 50% rental deposit is required. The $1,000 rental fee covers a 4-hour event and includes flowers, piano and custodial services. Any time over 4 hours runs an additional $100/hour. Customized menu planning and full-service event production (including event planning, thematic decor and entertainment) is provided by *Now We're Cooking!* Luncheons start at $25/person, dinners at $30/person and hors d'oeuvres at $20/person. Staff, rental equipment, alcohol, tax and a 15% production charge are additional.

AVAILABILITY: Year-round, daily, any time. Dates in June, July, August and Christmas holidays are more available because the Symphony is in recess. Overtime will be charged for functions past midnight.

SERVICES/AMENITIES:

Catering: provided by *Now We're Cooking!*
Kitchen Facilities: n/a
Tables & Chairs: some provided

Parking: nearby garages & lots or on street
Accommodations: no guest rooms
Telephone: pay phone

Linens, Silver, etc.: some provided
Restrooms: wheelchair accessible
Dance Floor: CBA
Bride's Dressing Area: restroom
Meeting Equipment: CBA

Outdoor Night Lighting: access only
Outdoor Cooking Facilities: no
Cleanup: provided
View: no

RESTRICTIONS:

Alcohol: provided, corkage negotiable
Smoking: outside only
Music: amplified OK w/approval; CBA

Wheelchair Access: yes
Insurance: not required
Other: no red wine at standing functions

This is important! Tell facilities you're reading **Here Comes The Guide** *and ask if our information is still current.*

Westin St. Francis

335 Powell Street, Union Square, San Francisco
(415) 774-0126, fax (415) 403-6891

www.westin.com
stfrancis_sales@westin.com

◆ Ceremonies ◆ Special Events
◆ Wedding Receptions ◆ Meetings
◆ Business Functions ◆ Accommodations

The Westin St. Francis has so many rooms in which to hold an elegant wedding ceremony, a grand reception, or a banquet, brunch or business bash of any kind, that they cannot all be fully described on these two little pages. They can, however, be divided into just two categories: Grand Old Hotel Elegance and Thoroughly Modern Luxury.

In the first category, one finds the numerous event rooms of the original 1904 and 1907 hotel towers—rooms with original marble floors, gilt pillars, lacy wrought-iron balconies, intricately carved ceilings, rich furnishings, and nearly a century's worth of history. They include, among others: the Borgia Room, a jewel-box chamber with oak-paneled walls, a six-foot-tall marble fireplace, and a vaulted, delicately painted ceiling (originally the hotel's chapel, it's ideally suited for wedding ceremonies); the Oak Room, a warm, clubby space decorated with large oil paintings of turn-of-the-century diners (just right for a smaller ceremony and reception in one space); and the Colonial Room, a ballroom with Italianate murals, triple-branched standing candelabras, and gold-leafed columns separating little individual balconies.

The rooms in the second category, Thoroughly Modern Luxury, are especially appropriate for those searching for two things—space and splendor. For the most part, they are located in the "new" (circa 1967) hotel Tower, and include such features as sparkling crystal chandeliers, rich carpeting, and up-to-the-minute audio-visual equipment that will make business presentations a snap. A few of these rooms, such as the Grand Ballroom, are large and straightforward, best suited to business functions or weddings where the size of the room is its most important feature.

However, "straightforward" is the exception rather than the rule at the St. Francis, and the two most glamorous event rooms in the new Tower are simply sumptuous. Located on the 32nd floor and accessed by five glass elevators with fine views of downtown, they are known collectively as the Imperial Floor. Glowing, translucent blue-glass chandeliers with matching 8-foot tall torchieres combine with hundreds of tiny pin-spot lights to provide illumination. Floors and walls have been hand-stenciled with soft celadon and gold decorations by Bay Area artists. Wraparound San Francisco views—from the Bay Bridge to the Golden Gate—are framed in 14-foot-high bay windows draped with floor-to-ceiling silk curtains. Victor's Palace, as the left-hand room is known, is fitted with a Regency-style armoire of glowing burl veneer that opens to serve as a bar. The brand new Alexandra's, on the right, is finished with peach drapes whose inner linings have been hand-painted by a San Francisco set designer. Access to the room is through a set of ten-foot-high red-leather doors. Wedgewood china, crystal goblets, and floor-length satin table linens complete the package.

Old San Francisco glamour or modern opulence? The range and quality of options at the Westin St. Francis is astonishing, and your choice will not be easy. You might decide to combine both eras, with a ceremony in the Borgia Room followed by dinner and dancing in Alexandra's. Whichever room plays host to your event, the setting will most certainly be splendid.

CEREMONY CAPACITY: The hotel can accommodate 20–700 seated guests.

EVENT/RECEPTION CAPACITY: The St. Francis has 30 banquet rooms with 45,000 square feet of event space; some of the larger rooms are noted below.

Room	Seated	Standing	Room	Seated	Standing
Colonial Room	150–320	350	Victor's Palace	100–190	190
Alexandra's	200–290	300	Grand Ballroom	800–1,100	1,500

MEETING CAPACITY: The St. Francis has 30 rooms and over 45,000 square feet of meeting space that can accommodate 20–1,500 theater-style, 15–800 classroom-style or 10–50 seated conference-style.

FEES & DEPOSITS: For social events, 1/3 of the estimated event total is required as a non-refundable deposit when the contract is signed; the remaining balance with a final guest count are due 72 business hours prior to the event. Catering is provided in house: luncheons start at $30/person, dinners at $45; alcohol, tax and a 20% service charge are additional. Wedding packages start at $110/person, and include hors d'oeuvres, bar, 3-course meal, wedding cake, champagne toast, wine with meal, and suite for the bride and groom. Ceremony setup fees start at $1,500. Customized wedding and bar mitvah packages can be arranged; kosher catering, under strict Rabbinical supervision, is available.

For business-related functions, deposits will vary. Corporate direct billing is available. Meeting packages include a full range of meals and services; in-house audio visual services and electronic/communication equipment can be arranged through the Business Center. For rates, call for specific information.

AVAILABILITY: Year-round, daily, any time, including holidays.

SERVICES/AMENITIES:

Catering: provided, no BYO
Kitchen Facilities: n/a
Tables & Chairs: provided
Linens, Silver, etc.: provided
Restrooms: wheelchair accessible
Dance Floor: provided
Bride's & Groom's Dressing Area: suite provided
Meeting Equipment: full range; AV extra charge
Other: pianos, kosher catering, wedding cakes

Parking: limited in-house; many nearby garages
Accommodations: 1,189 guest rooms
Telephone: pay phones
Outdoor Night Lighting: n/a
Outdoor Cooking Facilities: n/a
Cleanup: provided
View: sweeping cityscape from upper floors

RESTRICTIONS:

Alcohol: provided, no BYO
Smoking: outside only
Music: amplified OK

Wheelchair Access: yes
Insurance: not required

north bay

© GeoGraphics 1995

Healdsburg

128   29

Calistoga

Windsor

Guerneville

Silverado Trail

St Helena

29

1   116   River Rd

116   Fulton   101

Jenner   Russian   River

Santa Rosa

12   Rutherford

128

Kenwood   Yountville

1   12   Sebastopol

Bodega Hwy   116   Rohnert Park   Glen Ellen

Bodega Bay   Petaluma Valley Ford Rd   12

Bodega Bay   Sonoma

1   Tomales   Tomales Petaluma Rd   Petaluma   116   121   12

Bodega Ave   116   121

Tomales Bay   101   Lakeville Rd

Pt Reyes–Petaluma Rd   Novato Blvd   37

1   Inverness   Nicasio Valley Rd   Novato   San Pablo Bay

Drakes Bay   Olema   Str Francis Drake Blvd   Lucas Valley Rd   101

Woodacre   San Rafael   San Pablo

1   Fairfax   Ross   Richmond

Kentfield   580

Larkspur   101

Pacific   Stinson Beach   1   Tiburon

N   Ocean   Mill Valley   Belvedere Sausalito

101

1   101

San Francisco   80

201

China Cabin

54 Beach Road, Belvedere
(415) 435-1853

Historic, Waterfront Landmark

◆ Ceremonies   ◆ Special Events
◆ Wedding Receptions   ◆ Meetings
◆ Business Functions   Accommodations

In 1866, the Pacific Mail Steamship Company commissioned W. H. Webb to construct a sidewheel steamer. Unfortunately, with a wood hull, the ship was destined for a short career and was burned for scrap metal in 1886. The China Cabin, the first class Social Saloon, was removed intact from the ship and set on pilings in the Belvedere Cove.

The Cabin consists of a large room and two small staterooms. Its plain exterior belies the ornate and regal appointments inside. This place is impressive. The walls and arched ceiling are panels of elaborately decorated wood that have been painted a crisp white and highlighted with gold leaf. Along the sides of the Cabin are a series of small, delicately etched glass windows; handsome crystal chandeliers hang at each end of the room. The Cabin also has decks on three sides that have wonderful views of the San Francisco skyline and of the colorful boats berthed at the nearby yacht harbor. The China Cabin offers a glimpse of old-world elegance and attention to detail; the result is a rich, sophisticated appearance that makes this a very unique setting for a special wedding, anniversary, corporate party or business meeting.

CEREMONY CAPACITY: Indoors, 55 including staff.

EVENT/RECEPTION & MEETING CAPACITY: Indoors, 55 including staff; with deck (weather permitting) 65 maximum.

FEES & DEPOSITS: A $100 deposit is required when you make your reservation and a $250 refundable damage deposit is also required. The rental fee is $700 for a 5-hour minimum rental block and $140 for each additional hour. The total fee is due 30 days prior to your party. Fees for meetings, chamber concerts, photo shoots and some other functions are negotiable.

AVAILABILITY: Year-round, daily until midnight; not available Wednesday or Sunday 1pm–4pm, April–October.

SERVICES/AMENITIES:

Catering: BYO, must be approved
Kitchen Facilities: pantry only
Tables & Chairs: provided, extra fee
Linens, Silver, etc.: CBA, extra fee
Restrooms: not wheelchair accessible
Dance Floor: yes
Bride's Dressing Area: CBA
Meeting Equipment: BYO

Parking: CBA
Accommodations: no guest rooms
Telephone: house phone
Outdoor Night Lighting: deck only
Outdoor Cooking Facilities: no
Cleanup: caterer and renter
View: Bay Bridge, San Francisco skyline

RESTRICTIONS:

Alcohol: BYO
Smoking: not allowed indoors or on deck
Music: no amplified

Wheelchair Access: yes
Insurance: proof of liability required
Other: decorations restricted; no rice, seeds, grains, petals or confetti

---

*This is important! Tell facilities you're reading **Here Comes The Guide** and ask if our information is still current.*

The San Francisco Yacht Club

98 Beach Road, Belvedere
(415) 435-9133, fax (415) 435-8547

sf4russ@aol.com

Yacht Club

◆ Ceremonies   ◆ Special Events
◆ Wedding Receptions   ◆ Meetings
◆ Business Functions   Accommodations

The San Francisco Yacht Club, established in 1869, is the oldest yacht club on the West Coast. Located at the edge of Belvedere Cove, the Club offers an enchanting view of blue-trimmed sailboats on the bay. Its variety of settings for private parties has made the Club a popular choice for sailors and their friends. (You need a sponsoring Club member to hold an event here.)

If you desire a traditional club environment, the warm, dark woods and nautical memorabilia of the Main Dining Room and the Commodore Room will appeal to you. The former's ample proportions and expansive marina view provide large receptions with an upbeat, maritime ambiance, and the latter is a good choice for intimate gatherings. Both rooms open onto the club's wide, redwood deck overlooking the marina, where you can sip cocktails in the refreshing ocean air.

The Cove House is separate from the clubhouse, and set in its own private enclave. A dusky-rose-colored lattice fence and high box hedge border a small, sloping lawn and a diamond-shaped patio with steps that lead up to the front terrace of the house. Originally built for the 1915 Panama Exhibition, the Neoclassic-style Cove House is as pretty as a wedding cake. Constructed of dusky pink and cream-colored stone, its three graceful center arches frame an exterior foyer that opens into the main room. A fourteen-foot ceiling, peach-colored walls accented with white millwork, a wood-burning fireplace and gleaming hardwood floors create an exceptionally lovely, sophisticated space. Take your vows on the steps leading to the front terrace or, if the ocean breeze brings in a bit of fog, step inside and have your ceremony in front of the fireplace. With the club's experienced coordinator, Cathy Larson, on site to help with all the details, The San Francisco Yacht Club promises to make your event smooth sailing.

CEREMONY CAPACITY: The Cove House deck and courtyard hold 90 seated or 150 standing.

EVENT/RECEPTION & MEETING CAPACITY:

Area	Seated	Standing	Area	Seated	Standing
Main Dining Room & Bar	180	245	Commodore Room (winter)	40	40
Cove House Only	60	50–75	Commodore Room (summer)	40	60
Cove House w/piazza	90	150			

FEES & DEPOSITS: Half the rental fee is a refundable deposit required to secure your date. The rental fee for the Commodore Room is $250, the Cove House interior and deck, $400, and the Cove House, deck and piazza $2,800. Food service is provided by the Club, with hors d'oeuvres starting at $18.50/person, luncheons at $15/person, buffets at $34/person and dinners at $22/person. Bar service and bartender run an additional $50/event. The food and beverage balance is payable 1 week prior to the event; alcohol, tax and a 18% service charge are additional.

AVAILABILITY: The Main Dining Room and Bar are available Monday, Tuesday and Wednesday after 11am. The Commodore Room is available 9am–9pm, and the Cove House 11:30am–7pm, daily.

SERVICES/AMENITIES:

Catering: provided, no BYO
Kitchen Facilities: n/a
Tables & Chairs: provided
Linens, Silver, etc.: provided
Restrooms: wheelchair accessible
Dance Floor: provided
Bride's Dressing Area: no
Meeting Equipment: some provided

Parking: large lot or on street
Accommodations: no guest rooms
Telephone: pay phones
Outdoor Night Lighting: Cove House only
Outdoor Cooking Facilities: BBQs
Cleanup: provided
View: San Francisco, Angel Island, Alcatraz
Other: wedding cakes, banquet coordinator

RESTRICTIONS:

Alcohol: provided, no BYO
Smoking: outdoors only
Music: amplified OK indoors until 10pm

Wheelchair Access: yes
Insurance: not required

The professionals in the back of the book are the best in the business! **How do we know? Read page 681.**

Manka's Inverness Lodge

30 Callendar Way off Argyle, Inverness
(800) 585-6343, (415) 669-1034, fax (415) 669-1598
www.mankas.com

Lodge, Restaurant & Boathouse

◆ Ceremonies   ◆ Special Events
◆ Wedding Receptions   ◆ Meetings
◆ Business Functions   ◆ Accommodations

Tucked into the hills of the tiny village of Inverness, and surrounded by 80,000 acres of the Point Reyes National Seashore, Manka's is one of those charming, hidden inns that, once known, becomes a place you want to return to over and over again. It was built in the early 1900s as a hunting and fishing lodge, and this legacy continues in both cuisine and decor.

Walk into the lodge's parlor and chances are you'll be greeted by the savory aroma of wild game or fish caught that day, roasting over an open fire. The room is "rustically elegant," furnished with old hickory rockers, authentic Craftsman pieces, and an assortment of fishing gear. With its warm, Arts and Crafts ambiance, the parlor is an ideal setting for an intimate wedding.

If you'd prefer an outdoor ceremony, the natural beauty of the lodge and its surroundings provides numerous options. Tie the knot at the edge of a cliff overlooking the ocean, or on the beach. You can also get married right at Manka's, either on the second-floor decks amidst the treetops, or in the bright-blooming flower garden below. For bigger bashes you'll want to reserve the Boathouse, a weathered 1911 structure built over the water. Once a boat maker's shop, it's been renovated into a sleek event space with twelve-foot glass doors that open onto large decks, a long pier, the water and open hills beyond. Still another site is a small, 1850s cottage known as Chicken Ranch *(shown above)*. Set on a couple of very private beachfront acres, its windblown beauty makes it one of the most romantic settings we've seen. Here couples say their vows in a small meadow filled with wildflowers. After the ceremony, guests move to the cottage's wraparound deck where they can sip champagne under a trellis tangled with roses and grape vines. This delightful hideaway is often where the bride and groom tuck in for the evening, too.

Receptions are usually held at the lodge. For large gatherings (and especially for dancing), you can tent the parking area on the western side of the building. Smaller parties rendezvous in the dining room, a delightful light-infused space with wraparound Craftsman-style windows framing a tableau of liquid amber, hawthorn and magnolia trees. Here, as they wait for one of Manka's delicious meals (the lodge is renowned for its wild game, line-caught fish and fresh produce), guests will be captivated by interior artistic touches: a gorgeous sunburst of flowers on a block pedestal in the room's center; a mural portraying Tomales Bay in an earlier era; and anecdotal quotes about the "essence of dining" stenciled on the walls.

Manka's has fourteen accommodations including the Boathouse and Chicken Ranch, each decorated in the appealing homespun style of the parlor. What's more, recognizing that people and their dogs are not easily parted, the lodge invites dogs to spend the night as well! Warm gestures like this one, coupled with Manka's exquisite aesthetic sense, give the lodge its excellent, well-deserved reputation.

CEREMONY CAPACITY: Manka's indoor space holds 100 guests; the garden with gazebo or Boathouse can hold up to 80 seated, each. The Chicken Ranch holds 25 seated; the private decks, 25 seated.

EVENT/RECEPTION CAPACITY: The Dining Room holds 100 seated; the Boathouse holds 80–120 seated guests. For larger parties, the parking lot can be tented which increases the capacity to 140 seated guests.

MEETING CAPACITY: The Chicken Ranch and Manka's Cabin each hold 12 seated, the Boathouse, 45 seated guests, classroom-style.

FEES & DEPOSITS: For special events, a $1,500 non-refundable deposit is required to reserve your date; the event balance is payable the day of the event. The rental fee for the Chicken Ranch is $850, for the boathouse, $1,500. A room fee for exclusive use of Manka's Dining Room may apply, and the amount will depend on when the event takes place and guest count. Exclusive use requires an overnight guest room minimum. Extra staffing and cleanup charges also may apply. Three-course luncheons run $35–65/person, 3- to 6-course dinners run $50–95/person; alcohol, tax and an 18% service charge are additional.

AVAILABILITY: Year-round, daily. For non-exclusive events taking place in the dining room, 11am–4pm; with exclusive use, 11am–midnight. Events and meetings in the Boathouse can take place 4pm–11am the following day. If you reserve additional overnight accommodations, you can increase the number of hours.

SERVICES/AMENITIES:

Catering: provided, no BYO
Kitchen Facilities: n/a
Tables & Chairs: provided, more chairs CBA, extra fee
Linens, Silver, etc.: provided
Restrooms: wheelchair accessible
Dance Floor: no unless tent used
Bride's & Groom's Dressing Area: guest room
Meeting Equipment: anything CBA

Parking: medium-sized lot or on street
Accommodations: 14 guest rooms
Telephone: pay phone
Outdoor Night Lighting: yes
Outdoor Cooking Facilities: BBQs
Cleanup: provided
View: Tomales Bay & Inverness hills
Other: cakes, coordinator, flowers

RESTRICTIONS:

Alcohol: BW provided, no BYO
Smoking: outdoors only
Music: amplified OK outdoors until 10pm

Wheelchair Access: limited, CBA
Insurance: not required

---

*This is important! Tell facilities you're reading **Here Comes The Guide** and ask if our information is still current.*

Chai of Larkspur

Restaurant & Tea Salon

25 Ward Street, Larkspur
(415) 945-7161, fax (415) 945-7164

www.chaioflarkspur.com
betty@chaioflarkspur.com

- ◆ Ceremonies
- ◆ Wedding Receptions
- ◆ Business Functions
- ◆ Special Events
- ◆ Meetings
- Accommodations

Named after the word for "tea" in a variety of languages, Chai is not only a unique tea house and restaurant, but a delightful, intimate spot for receptions, parties, showers and meetings.

As soon as you step through the door, it's obvious this isn't your typical dining establishment. Rich, creamy tomato colored walls, accented by black columns and trim, Kentia palms in dragon-embossed green jardinières, and Chinese-red tea canisters give the parlour an exotic touch; sage-green wicker chairs, black magnolia-printed drapes, and starched, champagne napery add traditional charm. Other striking features include a black fireplace with antique mantelpiece, vintage chandeliers, and lamps with hand-embroidered, fringed silk lampshades. The intricately-patterned Axminster carpet was custom-made in England, and the colorful fire screen is actually an antique card table hand-painted with flowers. Of special interest is an Oriental black cabinet, elaborately painted with flowers, and the unusual collection of teapots (including Yixing, Wedgwood, Belleek) lining the walls. This room can be arranged in a variety of ways to accommodate your particular event.

Outside, the diminutive lattice-walled courtyard can be rented separately or in conjunction with the parlour. Sitting there is like sitting in a rose-painted teacup, thanks to a bevy of rose bushes, including Sterling Silver, Double Delight and Don Juan, that clamber up the lattices. Other blooms, such as bougainvillea, honeysuckle and pink bower trumpet vines, add their color and fragrance to the flower-filled atmosphere, while market umbrellas cast a cooling shade over aubergine wicker chairs and champagne-clad tables set with fine china. It is most definitely a lovely spot for an intimate wedding or bridal shower.

Another thing that sets Chai apart from its peers is its cuisine, whose delectable blend of unconventional and familiar elements is as original as the decor. You'll find not only classic Afternoon and High Teas, but internationally-themed menus as well. Choose from dishes with French, Middle Eastern, Latin and Mediterranean influences, each with generous portions that can satisfy even a manly appetite. Naturally, all are served on delicate china, and the food is presented on elegant, tiered serving trays.

Chai's fans are numerous and, as their comments in its guest book indicate, they consider the restaurant "magical," "exquisite," and "a little bit of heaven." Host your event in this oasis of serenity and style, and you'll find out why they keep coming back.

CEREMONY CAPACITY: The Parlor seats 26; the Garden holds 24 seated guests.

EVENT/RECEPTION CAPACITY: The entire restaurant can accommodate 50; the Courtyard 24 seated guests.

MEETING CAPACITY: The restaurant, indoors and outdoors, can accommodate 50 seated theater-style or conference-style, the Courtyard 24 seated theater-style or conference-style.

FEES & DEPOSITS: The rental fee is the non-refundable deposit required to secure your reservation. The Courtyard rental fee ranges $125–350; the fee for the entire restaurant ranges $650–1,300 depending on the season, guest count, day of week and time frame. In-house catering is provided with meals starting at $16/person; alcohol, beverages, tax and a 20% service charge are additional. A confirmed guest count guarantee is due 14 days prior to the event; any remaining rental balance is payable 7 days prior. The catering balance is payable the day of the function. The fee for ceremonies in the Courtyard ranges $700–1,000, which includes rehearsal and setup.

Fees for meetings, concerts, photo shoots and other functions are negotiable.

AVAILABILITY: Year-round, daily, 8am–midnight.

SERVICES/AMENITIES:
Catering: provided
Kitchen Facilities: n/a
Tables & Chairs: provided
Linens, Silver, etc.: provided
Restrooms: wheelchair accessible
Dance Floor: CBA, extra charge
Bride's Dressing Area: no
Meeting Equipment: BYO or CBA, extra charge

Parking: on street or in lot; valet CBA
Accommodations: no guest rooms
Telephone: house phones w/restrictions
Outdoor Night Lighting: in courtyard
Outdoor Cooking Facilities: no
Cleanup: provided
View: garden

RESTRICTIONS:
Alcohol: provided or BYO, corkage $10/bottle
Smoking: restricted
Music: amplified OK w/restrictions

Wheelchair Access: yes
Insurance: may be required
Other: no rice, birdseed, confetti; decorations must be approved

---

The professionals in the back of the book are the best in the business! **How do we know? Read page 681.**

The Lark Creek Inn

Restaurant & Garden

234 Magnolia Avenue, Larkspur
(415) 924-1602, fax (415) 924-7117

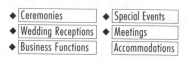

- ◆ Ceremonies
- ◆ Wedding Receptions
- ◆ Business Functions
- ◆ Special Events
- ◆ Meetings
- Accommodations

The Lark Creek Inn, one of the most popular restaurants in the Bay Area, is a delightful place for a wedding or reception. Built in 1888, this former Victorian country home is nestled in a grove of redwoods, next to a flowing creek. Sunlight filters through trees and windows, warming the tables in the Main Dining Room. Overhead, an enormous skylight creates an open, airy ambiance. Muted colors, rich wood paneling and rotating original art complete the tasteful interior. Outdoors, the Creekside Patio is perfect for a romantic outdoor ceremony, and the formal front garden with fountain provides a lovely backdrop for photographs.

The Lark Creek Inn has received national acclaim as well as local restaurant awards, and we have found the food here to be some of the best we've ever tasted. Note that the special events manager is available to coordinate all aspects of your party, including rehearsal, ceremony and reception. Add to that the outstanding atmosphere and you'll understand why your wedding celebration here will receive rave reviews.

CEREMONY CAPACITY: The Creekside Patio holds 80 seated or 150 standing guests.

EVENT/RECEPTION & MEETING CAPACITY:

Area	Standing	Seated	Area	Standing	Seated
Private Dining Room	40	24	Creekside Patio	120	70
Entire Restaurant (incl. patio)	300	200	Sunroom	60	48

FEES & DEPOSITS: Room rental fees are $75 for the Private Dining Room, $100 for the Sunroom, $150 for the Creekside Patio or $500 for the entire restaurant. Food and beverage minimums are as follows: for the entire restaurant, Saturdays 11am–4pm, $6,000 May–October, $5,000 November–April (other times are available and minimums will vary); Private Dining Room, Friday and Saturday, 5:30–11pm, $1,000 (other times are available and with no minimums). The fees for the Creekside Patio (available May–October) and Sunroom (November–April) vary, call for rates. Tax and service charged are additional. A $300–4,000 deposit, based on the space(s), day and time reserved, is required to book your date. The balance is payable the day of the function.

AVAILABILITY: Year round, daily for dinners, 5:30pm–11pm, except Christmas and New Year's day. Monday–Friday luncheons, 11:30am–3:30pm; Sunday 10am–3:30pm. Saturday 11am–4pm only, but you must reserve the entire restaurant. Breakfast meetings by special arrangement.

SERVICES/AMENITIES:

Catering: provided, no BYO
Kitchen Facilities: n/a
Tables & Chairs: provided
Linens, Silver, etc.: provided
Restrooms: wheelchair accessible
Dance Floor: yes
Bride's Dressing Area: yes
Meeting Equipment: CBA, extra fee

Parking: large lot, valet CBA
Accommodations: no guest rooms
Telephone: pay phone
Outdoor Night Lighting: yes
Outdoor Cooking Facilities: n/a
Cleanup: provided
View: of garden, redwoods and creek
Other: in-house pastry chef

RESTRICTIONS:

Alcohol: provided, no BYO
Smoking: designated area only
Music: amplified OK w/approval

Wheelchair Access: yes
Insurance: not required

---

*This is important! Tell facilities you're reading **Here Comes The Guide** and ask if our information is still current.*

211

Harbor Point Racquet & Beach Club

475 East Strawberry Drive, Mill Valley
(415) 388-4036, fax (415) 388-5183

Waterfront Club & Restaurant

- ◆ Ceremonies
- ◆ Wedding Receptions
- ◆ Business Functions
- ◆ Special Events
- ◆ Meetings
- Accommodations

If you're a tennis buff, and the word "love" tugs at more than your heart strings, the Harbor Point Racquet and Beach Club may be the perfect place to celebrate your love match. And even if you're not a tennis aficionado, you can still score a winning shot holding an event here.

Tucked at the base of Mill Valley's rolling hills, the clubhouse is unpretentious and, with its peaked, shake-shingled roof, looks almost like a private residence—albeit one surrounded by tennis courts and a large lap pool. There isn't actually a beach here as the name suggests, but the glass-and-wood clubhouse sits right at the edge of an estuary in a quiet unhurried corner of the bay, where sea birds from a nearby preserve loll offshore and there are few reminders of city life.

The main room is intimate and relaxed yet feels spacious, thanks to an open-beam ceiling and floor-to-ceiling windows. There's an expansive bayview panorama, and if you prefer to do your viewing outside, slip out onto one of the wide decks surrounding the building. For those evenings when it can get chilly on the bay, there are two large stone fireplaces—one in the main room and the other in a smaller adjoining room, an ideal spot in which to set up a buffet.

While most people use the clubhouse for anniversary parties, fund-raising events, and wedding receptions, small, intimate ceremonies can also be held here. The club manager will happily assist you in tying the knot center court, where you'll exchange rings and vows instead of passing shots.

CEREMONY & EVENT/RECEPTION CAPACITY: The Main Room and Tented Room, combined, hold 150 seated or up to 200 for a cocktail reception.

MEETING CAPACITY: The Main Room accommodates up to 60 seated guests, theater-style or conference-style.

FEES & DEPOSITS: To reserve your date, a $100 non-refundable reservation fee is required. A $250 refundable security/cleaning deposit and the rental balance are due 60 days prior to the event. Rental fees are: $500 for up to 50 guests, $600 for 51–100 guests, $700 for over 100 guests. A $100 discount applies if the in-house caterer is used.

In-house catering is provided: $8+/person for hors d'oeuvres; $15+/person for buffets or seated meals; alcohol, tax and a 15% service charge are additional. The food and beverage balance is payable at the end of the event. A $250 charge is extra if you want to bring your own caterer.

AVAILABILITY: Year-round, Mon–Thurs, 6pm–11pm; Sat–Sun, 6pm–11pm. For $100, you can arrange an additional hour to midnight. The Club is not available for private parties on Friday night, but dinner party reservations for small parties or groups can be arranged

SERVICES/AMENITIES:

Catering: provided or BYO, licensed & insured
Kitchen Facilities: fully equipped
Tables & Chairs: provided
Linens, Silver, etc.: can provide or BYO
Restrooms: some wheelchair accessible
Dance Floor: provided
Bride's & Groom's Dressing Area: yes
Meeting Equipment: PA, lectern, easels, screen, TV, VCR

Parking: large lot or on street
Accommodations: no guest rooms
Telephone: pay phones
Outdoor Night Lighting: yes
Outdoor Cooking Facilities: BBQs
Cleanup: provided or through caterer
View: San Francisco Bay
Other: CDs and tape player available

RESTRICTIONS:

Alcohol: provided, or wine corkage $7/bottle
Smoking: outside decks or tented (& heated) area
Music: amplified OK

Wheelchair Access: yes
Insurance: not required

The professionals in the back of the book are the best in the business! **How do we know? Read page 681.**

Mountain Home Inn

Restaurant & Inn

810 Panoramic Highway, Mill Valley
(415) 381-9000, fax (415) 381-3615
www.mtnhomeinn.com

- ◆ Ceremonies
- ◆ Wedding Receptions
- ◆ Business Functions
- ◆ Special Events
- ◆ Meetings
- ◆ Accommodations

Perched on the eastern slope of Mt. Tamalpais, this modern wooden structure has spectacular views of Marin, San Francisco Bay and Mt. Diablo. The decor in the main dining room is simple, but elegant. Furnishings and rugs are in muted pastels and a large stone fireplace enhances the feeling of cozy intimacy.

The Mountain Home Inn also features a light and airy bar area, with high ceilings adorned with natural redwood tree trunks. Nearby is a large deck that takes full advantage of the panoramic views below. An additional dining room downstairs uses mirrors to reflect the light coming in from the neighboring deck, and is a terrific spot for rehearsal dinners, small receptions or company parties. For a redwood tree and blue sky ceremony, try the downstairs dining area deck.

CEREMONY CAPACITY: The lower deck holds 10 seated or 20–30 standing; the upper deck 30 seated or 100 standing guests.

EVENT/RECEPTION CAPACITY:

Area	Seated	Standing
Upper & Lower Dining Rooms and Deck	40–60	80–100
Downstairs Dining Room	20–30	30

MEETING CAPACITY: The Inn can accommodate 20–30 seated conference-style.

FEES & DEPOSITS: A non-refundable deposit in the amount of your rental fee is required to secure your date. The Upper & Lower Floor rental rate is $1,500. The Lower Floor rental fee is $250. The rate for each of the 10 guest rooms ranges from $139–259/night. Food service is provided. Food costs run $20–25/person for hors d'oeuvres or light meals, $25–40/person for buffets and seated meals. Bar service, sales tax and a 20% gratuity are added to the final bill. The Honeymoon Suite runs $259/night.

AVAILABILITY: The Upper Dining Room is available Monday through Thursday, 11:30am–4pm or 5:30–9pm; the Downstairs Dining Room is available on weekends, 11:30am–4pm or 4:30–9pm.

SERVICES/AMENITIES:

Catering: provided, no BYO
Kitchen Facilities: n/a
Tables & Chairs: provided
Linens, Silver, etc.: provided
Restrooms: wheelchair accessible
Dance Floor: upstairs Dining Room
Bride's Dressing Area: CBA, extra charge
View: Marin hills, SF Bay and Eastbay hills

Parking: on-street; easy evenings, difficult weekends
Accommodations: 10 guest rooms
Telephone: in guest rooms
Outdoor Night Lighting: yes
Outdoor Cooking Facilities: no
Cleanup: provided
Meeting Equipment: screen, flip chart stand

RESTRICTIONS:

Alcohol: provided, WBC only, corkage $8/bottle
Smoking: not allowed
Music: amplified OK until 11pm

Wheelchair Access: yes
Insurance: not required

---

*This is important! Tell facilities you're reading **Here Comes The Guide** and ask if our information is still current.*

The Outdoor Art Club

1 West Blithedale, Mill Valley
(415) 383-2582

Historic Landmark

◆ Ceremonies   ◆ Special Events
◆ Wedding Receptions   ◆ Meetings
◆ Business Functions   Accommodations

The Outdoor Art Club, located in downtown Mill Valley, is one of Marin's favorite event spots. You enter through a quaint, English garden gate into a restful garden courtyard that immediately removes you from the bustle of everyday life. A sprawling native oak tree rests in the middle, providing a leafy canopy and allowing dappled light to filter through onto the courtyard floor. Guests can informally mingle under the oak with cocktails and hors d'oeuvres, or they can be seated in the courtyard for more formal receptions. Annuals, perennials and a backdrop of green shrubbery around two sides of the patio area add to the feeling of serenity.

The clubhouse, which borders two sides of the courtyard, is a charmer with a capital "C". Designed in 1904 by Bernard Maybeck, this classic Arts and Crafts structure has a rustic, brown-shingled exterior, multi-paned windows and multiple sets of French doors that bring the outside in when they're all opened. The interior is spacious, with a beamed, vaulted ceiling, hardwood floor and raised stage along one end, perfect for a head table or band setup. The Sun Porch, a smaller space running almost the full length of the clubhouse, is suitable for buffets or for the cake table.

Behind the clubhouse is a delicate, sheltered garden, the optimal spot for a ceremony. Guests can be seated in rows on the lawn and the bride and groom can say their vows in front of a wall of dense trees and shrubbery. It's no mystery why the Outdoor Art Club is so popular—it has an old-world appeal that's hard to resist.

CEREMONY CAPACITY: The garden can hold 100 seated or 150 standing; the courtyard can accommodate 150 seated or 200 standing guests.

EVENT/RECEPTION CAPACITY: The facility can hold up to 200 standing or 120 seated guests. The Sun Porch holds an additional 40 seated guests.

MEETING CAPACITY: The Main Room holds 200 seated in rows, the Sun Porch 40 and the Library 40.

FEES & DEPOSITS: A deposit of half the rental fee is required to reserve a date (if you cancel, it's refundable only if the date is rebooked); the balance is due 10 days before your function. A $500 security deposit is also required and is refunded after the keys are returned. The Club's rental fee is $1,500.

AVAILABILITY: Weekends 8am–1am. Weekday times are negotiable.

SERVICES/AMENITIES:

Catering: BYO
Kitchen Facilities: fully equipped
Tables & Chairs: provided for 180
Linens, Silver, etc.: silver/china provided for 180
Restrooms: not wheelchair accessible
Dance Floor: yes
Bride's Dressing Area: yes
Meeting Equipment: no

Parking: on street only
Accommodations: no guest rooms
Telephone: pay phone
Outdoor Night Lighting: yes
Outdoor Cooking Facilities: no
Cleanup: caterer
View: garden
Other: custodian provided

RESTRICTIONS:

Alcohol: BYO
Smoking: outdoors only
Music: amplified OK inside until midnight, volume limits

Wheelchair Access: yes
Insurance: certificate required or provided, extra fee

*The professionals in the back of the book are the best in the business! **How do we know? Read page 681.***

217

Point Reyes Seashore Lodge

10021 Highway 1, Olema
(415) 663-9000, fax (415) 663-9030

www.pointreyesseashore.com
prsl@worldnet.att.net

Lodge & Retreat

◆ Ceremonies	◆ Special Events
◆ Wedding Receptions	◆ Meetings
◆ Business Functions	◆ Accommodations

With a setting you're likely to see in one of those gorgeous photographic coffee table books, the Lodge has long maintained a reputation as a terrific romantic hideaway. It's on one of the prettiest sections of the Northern California coast, flanked by giant redwoods and Point Reyes National Seashore Park, and its guest rooms feature fireplaces, feather beds and whirlpool tubs with pastoral views of the Lodge's landscaped grounds and the Park's meadows and mountains beyond (yes, you can see the view from the tub!). Given its natural appeal, the Lodge has now increased its romantic possibilities by hosting weddings and receptions.

With the Lodge as a backdrop and the expansive, sloping lawn of the hotel grounds before you, garden weddings here are a special treat. You can tie the knot under the branches of a blossoming magnolia tree, or any one of the mature olive, oak and pine trees that border the grounds.

Another option is the Lodge's Casa Olema Retreat, which includes a cottage and lawn. Walk down a flagstone path behind the Lodge and under a redwood arch, and you'll be in a separate grass-covered area, surrounded by a formal herb and flower garden and apple, fig, pear and magnolia trees. At one side of the lawn is an arbor containing a built-in table and benches. Crafted from the Lodge's trademark golden fir, and thickly draped with ivy, it's a charming and intimate setting. For larger gatherings, you can set up tables and chairs on the lawn itself.

The adjacent, recently renovated cottage provides both a small kitchen for caterers and a bride's dressing room. Deep-rose-colored carpet, Laura Ashley-style furnishings, a fir-mantled fireplace and wainscotting create a room as quaint and personable as any one of the Lodge's guest rooms. The cottage's eight-person outdoor whirlpool tub, set within an enclosed brick patio, is a relaxing treat for bride and groom or members of the wedding party. If you're inviting out-of-town guests, you're in luck—the entire Lodge can be rented. You'll have the exclusive use of its cozy breakfast room, where you can warm yourself in front of a massive, stone fireplace, and the downstairs game room, outfitted with antique billiard and card tables. The Point Reyes Seashore Lodge makes it possible to combine getting married and getting away in one of the state's most scenic and secluded areas.

CEREMONY CAPACITY: The Casa Olema Retreat lawn and the lawn behind the Lodge each hold 150 seated or standing.

EVENT/RECEPTION CAPACITY: The Casa Olema Retreat lawn can accommodate 150 seated or standing for a variety of events including picnics and barbecues. Tents may be advisable depending on weather conditions.

MEETING CAPACITY: The Casa Olema Retreat can accommodate 20 seated conference-style and 25 theater-style.

FEES & DEPOSITS: For weddings or special events, a non-refundable deposit in the amount of 50% of rental fee is required to secure your date. The rental fee ranges $2,500–3,500 depending on guest count, and includes tables and chairs, and two nights' lodging at the Casa Olema Retreat. The rental balance, a refundable $500 cleaning/damage deposit and a certificate of insurance are due 6 weeks prior to the event. If the Casa Olema Retreat and all guest rooms are not reserved, you will be restricted to the Casa Olema grounds. A $250 rental fee is charged for ceremonies without receptions. Some flexibility in fees for midweek ceremonies and receptions.

For business functions, fees are based upon date reserved, number of rooms booked and services requested. Please call for rates.

AVAILABILITY: Mid-May through mid-October, weather permitting. A 6-hour block is allowed for ceremonies and receptions between 1pm and 7pm.

SERVICES/AMENITIES:

Catering: select from preferred list or BYO w/approval
Kitchen Facilities: prep only
Tables & Chairs: provided
Linens, Silver, etc.: BYO
Restrooms: Casa Olema has wheelchair access
Dance Floor: provided, extra charge
Meeting Equipment: VCR, TV, projector; secretarial services CBA

Parking: in the field next to the Lodge
Accommodations: 22 guest rooms
Telephone: emergency use only
Outdoor Night Lighting: access only
Outdoor Cooking Facilities: BBQ
Cleanup: caterer or renter
Bride's Dressing Area: yes
View: coastal mtns, creek, meadows

RESTRICTIONS:

Alcohol: provided or BYO, BWC only
Smoking: outdoors only
Music: acoustic only

Wheelchair Access: limited
Insurance: certificate required
Other: no confetti, rice or birdseed

---

*This is important! Tell facilities you're reading **Here Comes The Guide** and ask if our information is still current.*

Marin Art and Garden Center

30 Sir Francis Drake Boulevard, Ross
(415) 454-1301, fax (415) 454-0650

- ◆ Ceremonies
- ◆ Wedding Receptions
- ◆ Business Functions
- ◆ Special Events
- ◆ Meetings
- Accommodations

The Marin Art & Garden Center, a ten-acre historic estate in the exclusive town of Ross, is a dream come true for anyone seeking exquisitely landscaped gardens and a serene, private atmosphere. Within the Center's lush, tree-shaded grounds are various indoor and outside sites available for weddings, parties, meetings, workshops and other special events.

The Center's primary indoor facility is the Caroline Livermore Room, which features a beamed ceiling, an indoor/outdoor fieldstone fireplace, and sliding glass doors that open onto an awning-shaded deck. Just beyond, you'll find the Stratford Garden. Consisting of a raised, crushed-rock area shaded by ginkgo, elm, oak and tulip trees, with plantings of ferns, impatiens, rhododendrons and Japanese maples, this garden is a lovely spot for weddings. Together, the Stratford Garden and Livermore Room make an all-purpose venue for large affairs. Events such as small meetings, teas, showers or birthday parties sometimes take place in the Garden House, a quaint cottage with plenty of rustic charm.

Within the Center's expansive, woodsy grounds are a host of attractive ceremony sites. The Fountain area is the loveliest of these, and is perfect for an elegant outdoor ceremony, reception or party. Here, a large fountain pool, containing four life-like bronze cranes, sends its spray of glittering droplets into the air. A floral rainbow of daylilies, blue catnip, verbena, Santa Barbara daisies and iris blooms around the fountain, all enclosed by an aggregate-concrete path. On one side, a forest of mature elms, Lombardy poplars, deodar cedars and honey locusts forms a backdrop behind a curving wooden bench shaded by a pergola. To the left, couples tie the knot in the Memory Garden, a shady glade decorated with garden ornaments. Other spots for ceremonies include the Sequoia Tree Garden; the Magnolia Tree Lawn with its 125-year-old magnolia tree, and the Meadow Lawn, a large swath of velvety grass graced by a rare dawn redwood, elm and horse chestnut trees.

Though its fabulous gardens and tranquil atmosphere make the Marin Art & Garden Center seem a world away, it's centrally located near Highway 101, and only twenty minutes from San Francisco. When you have your event here you not only get a chance to "get away from it all," you get to discover a little piece of Paradise close to home.

CEREMONY CAPACITY:

Area	Seated Guests	Area	Seated Guests
Stratford Garden	300	Magnolia Tree Lawn	120
Meadow Lawn	300	Garden House	75
Fountain Garden	150	Memory Garden	50
Caroline Livermore Room	120		

EVENT/RECEPTION CAPACITY:

Area	Seated	Standing	Area	Seated	Standing
Caroline Livermore Room	120	200	Fountain Garden	150	200
in comb. w/Stratford Garden	300	300			

MEETING CAPACITY: The Caroline Livermore Room can accommodate 70 guests seated classroom-style or 120 guests theater-style. The Garden House can seat 12 guests conference-style.

FEES & DEPOSITS: Half of the total rental fee is required to secure your date; the rental balance and a $300 refundable cleaning/security deposit are due one month prior to the function. The rental fee for winter weekend functions in the Caroline Livermore Room is $1,000. The summer weekend rental fee is $1,500 for either the Livermore Room and Stratford Garden or the Fountain Garden. Use of any additional site runs an extra $200. Rates for weekday meetings start at $100–150. Breakfasts and luncheons run $10–25/person; dinners run $18–50/person; tax, alcohol, waitstaff and a 15% service charge are additional.

AVAILABILITY: Year-round, weekends 8am–8pm or dusk, whichever is earlier.

SERVICES/AMENITIES:

Catering: provided, no BYO
Kitchen Facilities: n/a
Tables & Chairs: provided
Linens, Silver, etc.: CBA, extra charge
Restrooms: wheelchair accessible
Dance Floor: yes
Bride's Dressing Area: yes
Meeting Equipment: BYO
Other: security guard CBA

Parking: large lot
Accommodations: no guest rooms
Telephone: pay phone
Outdoor Night Lighting: access only
Outdoor Cooking Facilities: no
Cleanup: provided for social events; renter's responsibility for business functions
View: garden

RESTRICTIONS:

Alcohol: provided or BYO corkage $7/bottle
Smoking: outdoors only
Music: acoustic only outdoors; amplified OK indoors w/restrictions

Wheelchair Access: yes
Insurance: liability required
Other: no rice or birdseed; decorations restricted

The professionals in the back of the book are the best in the business! **How do we know? Read page 681.**

Woodlands Garden
at the Marin Art & Garden Center

Restaurant

30 Sir Francis Drake Boulevard, Ross
(415) 457-3793, fax (415) 453-3663

www.woodlandsmarket.com
santawood@aol.com

◆ Ceremonies	◆ Special Events
◆ Wedding Receptions	Meetings
◆ Business Functions	Accommodations

This charming restaurant calls itself "Woodlands Garden," and we're happy to report that, unlike some establishments we've seen, the name is delightfully accurate. Located within the environs of the Marin Art & Garden Center, Woodlands Garden takes full advantage of its woodsy surroundings, and so can you.

At the entrance to Woodlands Garden, an intriguing gate of brick, wood, and pierced metal invites you into the principal outdoor venue, a large area enclosed by sheltering live oaks, redwoods, Japanese maples and ivy-covered walls. Below these trees, huge mossy boulders, heavenly bamboo and flourishing shrubs heighten the woodsy atmosphere. A lava rock fountain whispers to itself in one corner; a Japanese stone lantern sits serenely in another. Tables with white umbrellas provide seating in the sun-dappled center of the space. Immediately adjacent is a slightly raised area, shaded by redwoods, for buffet service or a string quartet. Evening events are made magical by discreet lighting, the bubbling fountain, and hurricane lamps placed on tables and hung on poles throughout the garden.

For indoor events, the restaurant itself is an elegant, yet relaxing spot, whose soft, light color scheme, French doors and generous skylights almost convince you you're seated outdoors. This blending of indoor/outdoor ambience is enhanced by faux-finished walls, painted in a montage of Impressionist-style colors. Other tasteful features include a generous fireplace, glass wall sconces twined with metal grapevines and paintings in opulent gold frames.

Behind the restaurant, you'll find a diminutive brick-walled flower garden containing a lawn, rose, hydrangea and camellia bushes, and a seashell fountain. Though most couples exchange vows on the adjacent grounds of the Marin Art & Garden Center, intimate weddings can be accommodated here. However you decide to use the attractive facilities of Woodlands Garden Restaurant, you can be sure that its enchanting gardens will always be in view.

CEREMONY & EVENT/RECEPTION CAPACITY: Outdoors, the garden holds 150 seated or 250 standing. Indoors, the restaurant holds 75 seated guests.

MEETING CAPACITY: Indoors, 75 seated guests.

FEES & DEPOSITS: For special events, 50% of the $1,300 facility rental fee is required as a partially refundable deposit when you book the site. The remaining balance is due 7 days prior to the event.

Catering is provided by *Woodlands Catering:* luncheon buffets range $10–20/person, dinners range$18–40/person. Alcohol, tax and a 15% service charge are additional.

AVAILABILITY: Year-round, daily. Monday–Friday 7am–11am or 3pm–10pm; all day Saturday and Sunday until midnight.

SERVICES/AMENITIES:

Catering: provided by *Woodlands Catering*
Kitchen Facilities: n/a
Tables & Chairs: provided
Linens, Silver, etc.: provided
Restrooms: wheelchair accessible
Dance Floor: provided
Meeting Equipment: n/a
Other: event coordination, florals, wedding cakes, security

Parking: large lot, valet CBA
Accommodations: no guest rooms
Telephone: CBA
Outdoor Night Lighting: yes
Outdoor Cooking Facilities: CBA
Cleanup: provided
View: gardens, fountain & towering redwoods

RESTRICTIONS:

Alcohol: provided
Smoking: not allowed
Music: no amplified, acoustic OK w/volume limits

Wheelchair Access: yes
Insurance: not required

---

*This is important! Tell facilities you're reading **Here Comes The Guide** and ask if our information is still current.*

Dominican College

50 Acacia Avenue, San Rafael
(415) 485-3228, fax (415) 458-3727

monestere@dominican.edu

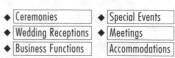

◆ Ceremonies   ◆ Special Events
◆ Wedding Receptions ◆ Meetings
◆ Business Functions   Accommodations

Set on 80 wooded and landscaped acres in the San Rafael hills, the Dominican College campus is lovely enough to entice anyone back to school. A wide variety of trees surrounds the older Spanish-style buildings as well as the more contemporary structures, and views of the encircling hills can be had from almost everywhere.

The campus feels more like a country retreat than a school, and the Shield Room, where most wedding receptions are held, puts you right in the middle of this harmonious combination of nature and architecture. This modern banquet facility is spacious and airy, with a cathedral ceiling and three walls of windows that overlook a sheltered patio and the redwoods, pines and eucalyptus just beyond. The interior is refreshingly simple: support pillars and the walls separating windows are covered with warm, fruitwood paneling, and the glossy tile floor is perfect for dancing. Wall sconces illuminate the wooden shields hung around the room—all annual gifts from graduating seniors to the freshman class, and the source of the room's name. In summer, if you have your reception indoors, you can open the windows and let the breezes flow in; if you prefer to dine al fresco, you can set up tables on the expansive patio.

The adjacent Creekside Room is a more intimate space for rehearsal dinners or small receptions. It has the same paneling and tile as the Shield Room, and its two walls of windows face patios, front and back. The semicircular rear patio is particularly inviting for an outdoor cocktail party or open-air dinner. Bordered by a small creek, and gently enclosed by pine, oak and bay trees, it's a totally private and serene spot.

If the woodsy setting and unpretentious decor haven't quite convinced you to come here, there are two more things: Dominican College has ample free parking, and is one of the most conveniently located facilities around—it's only twenty minutes from San Francisco or the East Bay.

CEREMONY CAPACITY: The grounds can accommodate up to 250, the Shield Room 250, the Creekside Room 60 and Guzman Hall up to 150 seated guests.

EVENT/RECEPTION CAPACITY, FEES & DEPOSITS: Half the rental fee is the non-refundable deposit required to secure your date. The balance is due 90 days prior to the event.

Area	Standing	Seated	Rental Fee
Shield Room	400	250	$950
Shield Room w/dance floor	—	200	950
Creekside Room	100	64	450
Guzman Lecture Hall	200	150	550

Catering costs range $5–8/person for breakfasts, $10–18/person for luncheons and $20–30/person for dinners; alcohol, tax and a 15% service charge are additional. 50% of the anticipated food and beverage total is payable 2 weeks prior to the event.

MEETING CAPACITY:

Area	Standing	Theater-style	Seated	Rental Fee
Meadowlands Assembly Hall	100	75	—	$275
Library 207/208	80	70	—	275
Creekside Room	11	—	70	350
Guzman Lecture Hall	200	200	—	400

AVAILABILITY: The Shield Room and grounds are available year-round, weekends only, 8am–11pm. All other meeting and reception rooms are available year-round, daily, 8am–11pm.

SERVICES/AMENITIES:

Catering: provided, no BYO
Kitchen Facilities: n/a
Tables & Chairs: some provided
Linens, Silver, etc.: provided
Restrooms: not wheelchair accessible
Dance Floor: yes
Bride's Dressing Area: CBA
Meeting Equipment: TV, VCR in most rms.

Parking: large lot, on-street
Accommodations: no guest rooms
Telephone: pay phones
Outdoor Night Lighting: CBA
Outdoor Cooking Facilities: BBQ CBA
Cleanup: provided
View: wooded grounds
Other: baby grand piano

RESTRICTIONS:

Alcohol: provided or corkage $5/bottle
Smoking: outdoors only
Music: amplified OK indoors only,
time & volume limits

Wheelchair Access: yes
Insurance: certificate required

The professionals in the back of the book are the best in the business! **How do we know? Read page 681.**

Embassy Suites Marin County

Hotel

101 McInnis Parkway, San Rafael
(415) 499-9222 ext. 4028, fax (415) 472-4746

www.embassysuites.com

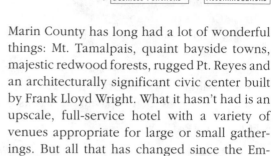

◆ Ceremonies ◆ Special Events
◆ Wedding Receptions ◆ Meetings
◆ Business Functions ◆ Accommodations

Marin County has long had a lot of wonderful things: Mt. Tamalpais, quaint bayside towns, majestic redwood forests, rugged Pt. Reyes and an architecturally significant civic center built by Frank Lloyd Wright. What it hasn't had is an upscale, full-service hotel with a variety of venues appropriate for large or small gatherings. But all that has changed since the Embassy Suites Marin Hotel threw open its doors for business.

When you pass through the lobby into the fabulous Atrium around which the hotel is built, you may think you've stepped onto the set of the movie "Jurassic Park." A forest of mature palm trees of every variety surrounds an immense natural rock waterfall, whose splashing cascades delight the ear as well as the eye. Plantings of tropical foliage throughout the Atrium add to the jungle-like atmosphere. The Atrium is a public area, so it isn't available for functions, but it's an understandably popular spot for photos. Beyond the Atrium, you'll find the enormous, 6,000 square-foot San Rafael Ballroom. White wainscotted walls, crystal chandeliers, and carpeting with an intricate Oriental-style design in shades of teal, sage, and dusty rose give the Ballroom a simple elegance, and a thirteen-foot ceiling keeps even the biggest party from feeling claustrophobic. If you're planning a function for less than 600 people, air walls allow the San Rafael Ballroom to be divided into smaller ballrooms. All have separate heating and cooling systems, dance floors, and risers for the head table. A state-of-the-art lighting and sound system, plus a knowledgeable staff, makes the Embassy Suites Marin a favorite with bands and DJs. When more than one event is scheduled in the ballrooms, the staff leaves an empty ballroom between the two functions as a "buffer," if possible. This means that your business presentation won't be interrupted by the rollicking sounds of the party next door!

Other event sites include the San Rafael Foyer, just outside the Ballroom. This area is perfect for a stand-up reception or prefunction cocktails. Potted plants, rattan chairs and deep green carpeting, give it a casual feel, and it also has its own private, sunny patio. The patio has tables and market umbrellas, and can be used in a variety of ways—one innovative group used it for their steel drum band. The private dining room off the hotel's restaurant is a favorite spot for rehearsal dinners and similar events. Partial brick walls, contemporary paintings, Oriental-style carpeting and white wrought-iron accents make this room cheerful and cozy. French doors allow access to the restaurant, while sheer curtains give you privacy, but let you feel like you're part of the "action." This room also has a private terra-cotta-walled patio, screened from afternoon breezes by a wisteria-covered lattice. For business functions, eight independent meeting rooms are available in addition to the San Rafael Ballroom. The Santa Rosa room has a large window, with views of Marin's tree-covered hills.

One of the best features about this hotel is its central location. It's just a few minutes from Highway 101 and the Marin Civic Center, making it easily accessible for your guests or colleagues, and if anyone wants to stay a few days to sightsee, a host of famous attractions are within easy reach: Muir Woods, beaches, Marine World Africa USA, the Napa and Sonoma Valleys and San Francisco, just to name a few. With its great location, well-appointed function areas, and knowledgeable, courteous staff, the Embassy Suites Marin is a full-service hotel in every sense of the word. Whether your event includes five or 500 of your closest friends, the Embassy Suites Marin will be happy to accommodate you.

CEREMONY CAPACITY: The San Rafael Ballroom holds 500, the Tiburon, Ross or Petaluma Rooms hold 50 seated each, or the Santa Rosa Room 80 seated guests.

EVENT/RECEPTION CAPACITY:

Room	Seated	Standing	Room	Seated	Standing
San Rafael Ballroom	485	650	Santa Rosa Room	65	75
Tiburon, Ross, Petaluma Rooms	40	60			

MEETING CAPACITY:

Room	Theater-style	Classroom-style	Room	Theater-style	Classroom-style
San Rafael Ballroom	500	280	Ross or Petalua Rms	50	28
Tiburon	40	20	Santa Rosa Room	80	40

FEES & DEPOSITS: 25% of the estimated event total is required to reserve the date. The balance is due 2 weeks prior to the event. For wedding packages, meals range $36–46/person and include passed hors d'eouvres, salad, entree, champagne toast, 2 bottles of wine per table of 10 and a suite for the bride and groom. Alcohol, tax and an 18.5% service charge are additional. A $1.50/person cake cutting fee is extra. For business meetings, continental breakfasts range $8–11/person, luncheons range $15–20/person, and dinners $25–35/person. Rental fees may apply depending on estimated food and beverage total and space rented.

AVAILABILITY: Year-round, daily; 6am–midnight.

SERVICES/AMENITIES:

Catering: provided, no BYO
Kitchen Facilities: n/a
Tables & Chairs: provided
Linens, Silver, etc.: provided
Restrooms: wheelchair accessible
Dance Floor: portable provided
Bride's & Groom's Dressing Area: yes
Meeting Equipment: podium, microphone, other equipment CBA

Parking: large lot
Accommodations: 238 guest rooms
Telephone: pay phones
Outdoor Night Lighting: access only
Outdoor Cooking Facilities: CBA
Cleanup: provided
View: no view
Other: table centerpieces, event coordination

RESTRICTIONS:

Alcohol: provided or corkage $10/bottle
Smoking: outdoors only
Music: amplified OK indoors

Wheelchair Access: yes
Insurance: not required

Falkirk Mansion

1408 Mission Avenue, San Rafael
(415) 485-3328, fax (415) 485-3404

www.falkirkculturalcenter.org

Historic Mansion

◆ Ceremonies ◆ Special Events
◆ Wedding Receptions ◆ Meetings
◆ Business Functions ☐ Accommodations

Magnificent oaks and magnolias frame the historic Falkirk Mansion, a lovely Queen Anne Victorian in the heart of San Rafael. Built in 1888, the house is the creation of the same architect who designed the Stanford University campus chapel and the now demolished City of Paris department store in San Francisco. In keeping with the style of the day, it has a complex and intriguing roof line of gables and chimneys, variously shaped bays and plenty of decorative details.

When the original owner died, the property was purchased by Captain Robert Dollar, a Scotsman who'd made his fortune in timber and shipping. He added many features to the house, including the brick steps and pond, rolling lawns, the greenhouse, carriage house and even a swimming pool that no longer exists. A civic-minded man, he donated generously to both San Rafael and his hometown of Falkirk, Scotland—hence the name of the Mansion.

Today, Falkirk Cultural Center serves as a historic site, contemporary art gallery, cultural and educational center, as well as a popular spot for weddings. You can have your ceremony on the sprawling lawns, in the parlor, or on the front steps with your guests seated below on the private driveway. The Mansions's interior is beautifully rendered in rich redwood paneling, and features ornate mantelpieces, hardwood floors and elegant wall coverings. The foyer has a huge decorative fireplace and floor-to-ceiling stained glass windows. Have your reception indoors or, during warmer months, dine and dance on the veranda. This secluded wooden porch is enclosed by camellia bushes and an ancient oak. When you reserve the Mansion, you can use the entire first floor any way you like. It doesn't matter how you orchestrate your wedding, Falkirk will imbue it with intimacy and a century's worth of Victorian charm.

CEREMONY CAPACITY: The Parlor holds 50 seated or 75 standing; outdoors the site can accommodate 125 seated guests.

EVENT/RECEPTION CAPACITY: October–April, standing capacity is 100; seated capacity 50–60 guests. April–October, the house and veranda hold up to 125 guests.

MEETING CAPACITY: Indoors, 60 theater style or 20 conference style; outdoors 80 seated theater style.

MEETING CAPACITY: Indoors, 60 theater style or 20 conference style; outdoors 80 seated theater style.

FEES & DEPOSITS: A non-refundable deposit of 50% of the rental fee is required to reserve your date. Weekend rates for a 6-hour minimum block are: $1,500 from April 15 to October 14, and $1,200 from October 15 to April 14. Additional charges will apply for overtime hours. A refundable $500 security deposit and any remaining balance are payable 45 days in advance of your event. Weekday rates vary; call for more information. Special rates for non-profits.

AVAILABILITY: Year-round. Saturdays from 1pm–11pm, Sundays all day. Weekdays 9am–11pm by arrangement.

SERVICES/AMENITIES:

Catering: select from approved list
Kitchen Facilities: minimal
Tables & Chairs: provided
Linens, Silver, etc.: BYO
Restrooms: wheelchair accessible
Dance Floor: yes
Bride's Dressing Area: yes
Meeting Equipment: limited

Parking: large lot
Accommodations: no guest rooms
Telephone: pay phone
Outdoor Night Lighting: CBA
Outdoor Cooking Facilities: no
Cleanup: caterer
View: wooded park & grounds

RESTRICTIONS:

Alcohol: BYO
Smoking: outside only
Music: amplified OK to 90 decibels

Wheelchair Access: yes
Insurance: extra liability required
Other: no candles, decorations restricted

---

*This is important! Tell facilities you're reading **Here Comes The Guide** and ask if our information is still current.*

Marin Civic Center Cafe & Patio

Civic Center & Gardens

3501 Civic Center Drive, San Rafael
(415) 499-6387, fax (415) 499-3795

- ◆ Ceremonies
- ◆ Wedding Receptions
- ◆ Business Functions
- ◆ Special Events
- ◆ Meetings
- Accommodations

Anyone who has driven along Highway 101 through San Rafael has seen Marin County's distinctive blue-and-beige civic center built along the crest of the hills. Completed in the 1960s, it's one of the last public facilities designed by Frank Lloyd Wright and is a National Historic Landmark. Wright was inspired by the setting, and designed this building to enhance its natural surroundings. It does. Just approaching the entrance from the parking lot provides a breathtaking view of the lush Marin landscape, framed by the arch of the building where it bridges the drive.

Wright believed that government workings should be accessible to public view, and the Center definitely reflects his philosophy. A long escalator takes you from the entrance upward through a vast, oblong atrium toward a domed glass ceiling. On the way you can see all three levels of offices, which are set off open corridors that ring the atrium. In addition to all this openness, architectural elements inside and out rely heavily on curves rather than traditional right angles, giving the structure a style that was way ahead of its time—in fact, two futuristic movies have been filmed here.

The *pièce de résistance* is a hilltop patio garden that seems to float above its lush, wooded surroundings. A low wall encloses and embraces the space, which is beautifully landscaped with a fountain as its centerpiece and a stream running through it. From here the view stretches all the way to the edge of the bay and beyond to the East Bay hills. Imagine a garden wedding on the lawn, followed by a sunny reception at umbrella-shaded tables on the patio. At night, the garden is well lit and makes a dramatic setting for gatherings under the stars.

The adjoining cafe is perfect for indoor events. Although it's large (it seats 250!), indirect light from enormous windows that run the length of the room gives it a warm, intimate feel. The windows also frame the outdoor landscape, and provide a close-up view of Wright's decorative rounded grillwork railings and semicircular openings along the edge of the building's roofline. You can adjust the size of the cafe by using drapes to close off portions of the room you don't want to use, and you can set up tables and chairs in whatever configuration is most suitable for your event. One of the cafe's interior walls is floor-to-ceiling glass, and through it you can see the lobby, a wide, skylit hall that's used for overflow guests or break-out sessions for training seminars and workshops.

Those of us who happen to be Frank Lloyd Wright fans feel fortunate to have one of his creations right here in the Bay Area. And truth be told, this remarkable building may still be way ahead of its time.

CEREMONY CAPACITY: The Patio Gardens hold 125 seated or 300 standing guests.

EVENT/RECEPTION CAPACITY: The Cafe and Patio Gardens, combined, can accommodate 250 seated or 600 for a cocktail reception.

MEETING CAPACITY: From 15, for a small meeting, to 300 guests seated theater-style.

FEES & DEPOSITS: The rental fee is required, in full, to secure your date. Rental fees range $100–1,200 depending on the space(s) selected. Catering prices range $15–100/person depending on menu selection and services requested.

AVAILABILITY: Year-round, weeknights, 4pm–11pm (2-hour min.); weekends, 6am–11pm (6-hour min.).

SERVICES/AMENITIES:

Catering: select from preferred list
Kitchen Facilities: fully equipped
Tables & Chairs: some provided
Linens, Silver, etc.: provided, extra fee
Restrooms: wheelchair accessible
Dance Floor: tile floor
Bride's & Groom's Dressing Area: yes
Meeting Equipment: PA system, stage risers

Parking: complimentary, ample
Accommodations: no guest rooms
Telephone: pay phones
Outdoor Night Lighting: yes
Outdoor Cooking Facilities: BBQ CBA
Cleanup: provided
View: of Marin hills & lagoon

RESTRICTIONS:

Alcohol: provided or BYO w/corkage fee
Smoking: outside only
Music: amplified OK inside w/volume limits

Wheelchair Access: yes
Insurance: certificate may be required
Other: no confetti, rice or birdseed

The professionals in the back of the book are the best in the business! **How do we know? Read page 681.**

McNears Beach

Beach & Garden

End of Point San Pedro Road at Cantera, San Rafael
(415) 383-9355, (800) 481-9255, fax (415) 383-9336

allseasons7@aol.com

◆ Ceremonies	◆ Special Events
◆ Wedding Receptions	Meetings
Business Functions	Accommodations

Here's a location that offers a unique trio of amenities: a secluded garden setting, a quiet, sandy beach and an experienced on-site caterer. If you've been dreaming of an outdoor, waterfront wedding but the logistics (private beach access, guest parking, hauling foodstuffs over sand) seem too overwhelming, McNears Beach is the answer.

Located at the end of Point San Pedro Road in San Rafael, McNears is a public, Marin County-owned beach, but the Beachside Group area at the end of the cove (at a nice remove from McNears' public swimming pool), can be reserved for private events. It's an idyllic spot with lush, level lawns shaded by towering oak and palm trees, and a stretch of sand that slopes down to the gentle, shallow waters of San Francisco Bay. The verdant hillside that rises steeply from the lawn creates the feeling of a hidden grove; here you won't see intrusive signs of civilization except, perhaps, for a few passing sailboats or a wayfaring beachgoer who has happened up the path.

This is a terrific locale for a casual beach party and barbecue, but a formal affair held here could be downright entrancing. Imagine a warm summer evening, the sky full of stars, your reception lit by candles and tiki torches and music provided by the soft, rhythmic sound of waves lapping on the beach. Add some superb cuisine, and it will be a celebration your guests will never forget.

CEREMONY CAPACITY:

Area	Seated	Standing	Area	Seated	Standing
Beachside	500	1,000	Vista Point	250	500
Arbor	50	80	*Other spots CBA for smaller ceremonies.*		

EVENT/RECEPTION CAPACITY: Virtually unlimited, from 20 to 2,000 guests.

FEES & DEPOSITS: Half the anticipated food and beverage total plus half the rental fee are the refundable deposits required to book the site. The rental fee is $75–500 depending on guest count and site selected. The final catering and rental fee balance are payable 10 days prior to the event. Catering is provided by *All Seasons Party Productions:* luncheons start at $15/person, BBQs at $12/person and dinners at $18/person. Alcohol, tax and a 15% service charge are additional.

AVAILABILITY: Daily, April–November 9am–sunset, weather permitting.

SERVICES/AMENITIES:

Catering: provided or BYO

Kitchen Facilities: n/a

Tables & Chairs: provided

Linens, Silver, etc.: provided

Restrooms: wheelchair accessible

Dance Floor: several paved areas

Bride's & Groom's Dressing Area: yes

Meeting Equipment: n/a

Parking: large lot

Accommodations: no guest rooms

Telephone: pay phone

Outdoor Night Lighting: no

Outdoor Cooking Facilities: BBQ

Cleanup: provided

View: San Francisco Bay and skyline

Other: event coordination

RESTRICTIONS:

Alcohol: provided, or corkage $3/bottle

Smoking: outdoors only

Music: amplified OK

Wheelchair Access: limited depending on area

Insurance: not required

Other: no pets, no helium balloons, no rice

This is important! Tell facilities you're reading **Here Comes The Guide** *and ask if our information is still current.*

233

The Alta Mira

Restaurant & Hotel

125 Bulkley Avenue, Sausalito
(415) 332-1350, fax (415) 331-3862

◆ Ceremonies
◆ Special Events
◆ Wedding Receptions
◆ Meetings
◆ Business Functions
◆ Accommodations

The Alta Mira is one of Marin's oldest and most renowned hotels. It was originally the residence of Thomas Jackson, who later converted it into a hotel; after the original structure was lost in a fire, Jackson's son rebuilt the Alta Mira as a Spanish-style villa. Today, it's a very popular spot for private gatherings.

A huge deck off the main dining room has one of the most spectacular panoramic views of the San Francisco skyline, Sausalito Harbor and Angel Island. Round tables shaded by bright umbrellas add to the festive, "French Riviera" ambiance.

The main dining area itself is relaxed but elegant, featuring leaded glass mirrors and floral arrangements. A private dining room called the Fiesta Room has high ceilings, chandeliers and a gorgeous fireplace with hand-painted tiles displaying a country garden. Large mirrors extend the open, sunny feeling of this beautiful room, and the adjoining deck has a lovely view of Sausalito Bay. Outdoors, the Garden Terrace, with its surrounding flowers and bay view, provides a romantic setting for ceremonies and receptions. Rooms at the hotel are available, including a suite in an adjacent Victorian house that has a sitting room, kitchenette and deck.

CEREMONY CAPACITY: The Fiesta Room holds 100 seated; the garden holds 150 seated or standing guests.

EVENT/RECEPTION CAPACITY: The Annex Dining Room and Deck can hold 200 standing guests and 150 seated. There is a food and beverage minimum requirement for this space. The Fiesta Room can accommodate 100 for a buffet and 90 seated guests, with a 35-guest minimum. The Outdoor Patio seats 150, and the Garden Terrace accommodates 150 seated and 200 standing.

MEETING CAPACITY: The Fiesta Room holds 80 standing or seated theater style, or 88 seated at round tables.

FEES & DEPOSITS: For special events, a $500 non-refundable deposit is required to reserve a date and is applied towards the food and beverage bill. For a luncheon or dinner, there's no rental fee. Half the anticipated total is due 30 days prior to your function; the balance is due the day of the event. Food service is provided. Hors d'oeuvres receptions average $35–45/person and seated meals $30–45/person, including bar service. Alcohol, tax and a 15% gratuity are additional.

For meetings in the Fiesta Room there is a $200 charge for a full day, or $150 for a half day.

AVAILABILITY: The Annex and Deck are available Saturdays, 2:30pm–6:30pm, and Sundays, 5pm–10pm. The Fiesta Room is available any time during the week, noon–5pm or 6:30pm–11pm Saturday, and 4pm–10pm Sunday. The Garden Terrace is available in conjunction with one of the other event spaces for a $300 fee.

SERVICES/AMENITIES:

Catering: provided, no BYO

Kitchen Facilities: n/a

Tables & Chairs: provided

Linens, Silver, etc.: provided

Restrooms: limited wheelchair access

Dance Floor: yes

Bride's Dressing Area: CBA

Meeting Equipment: CBA, extra fee

Parking: valet or on-street parking

Accommodations: 29 guest rooms

Telephone: pay phone

Outdoor Night Lighting: patio only

Outdoor Cooking Facilities: no

Cleanup: provided

View: SF skyline and bay

Other: event planning services

RESTRICTIONS:

Alcohol: provided, corkage $10/bottle

Smoking: allowed

Music: no amplified

Wheelchair Access: limited, entry CBA

Insurance: sometimes required

The professionals in the back of the book are the best in the business! **How do we know? Read page 681.**

235

Bay Area Discovery Museum

Fort Baker, 557 McReynolds Road, Sausalito
(415) 289-7288, fax (415) 332-9671
www.badm.org
mpressman@badm.org

Museum

◆ Ceremonies	◆ Special Events
◆ Wedding Receptions	◆ Meetings
◆ Business Functions	Accommodations

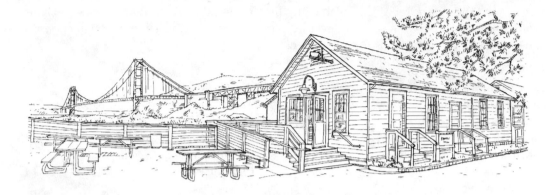

Located in historic Fort Baker just beneath the northern tower of the Golden Gate Bridge, the Discovery Museum offers a lovely natural setting, and a fun environment certain to bring out the kid in everyone. This children's museum features hands-on exploratory exhibits ranging from an undersea tunnel to a space maze, all housed in landmark, 1940s structures.

The museum's various buildings, exhibit rooms and outdoor spaces offer numerous options for celebrations. For a wedding ceremony with an unparalleled view of the Golden Gate, take your vows on the terrace next to the museum's cafe or atop a bluff just behind the Discovery Hall. For large, outdoor receptions, tent the area between the Discovery Hall and the Art Spot; smaller gatherings can celebrate in the charmingly renovated Tot Spot, once the Fort Baker stable. Most popular for private events is the Discovery Hall, a new building designed with the white, clapboard architecture of the existing structures. Its high, cathedral ceiling, picture windows and adjacent patio with bay and bridge view create a flexible space for buffets, seated dinners, cocktails and dancing—and your guests can go for an exhibit-filled stroll in the Exhibition Hall next door. If you have a sense of whimsy, host your party in the San Francisco Bay Hall. This exhibit recreates the total environment of San Francisco Bay and the ports of Berkeley and Oakland through the use of colorful children's murals and a child-size mock-up of Fisherman's Wharf.

Upon request, the museum's exhibits are kept open during your reception, meaning that children can be happily occupied while adults engage in their own kind of fun. Remarkably versatile, the Discovery Museum has hosted functions ranging from "basic picnic" to "black-tie," but they all have one thing in common—people just seem to enjoy themselves here, no matter what their age.

CEREMONY CAPACITY: The Bay Hall holds 60 seated or 150 standing; the picnic area 200 seated or 500 standing; and the Discovery Hall, 200 seated or 500 standing. The adjacent park has multiple ceremony spots which can accommodate more than 500 guests.

EVENT/RECEPTION & MEETING CAPACITY:

Area	*Seated*	*Standing*	*Theatre-style*	*Area*	*Seated*	*Standing*	*Theatre-style*
Bay Hall	30	150	70	Discovery Hall	130	300	150
Outdoor Areas	500	1,200	80				

FEES & DEPOSITS: A non-refundable deposit of 50% of the rental fee is payable when the contract is submitted; the balance and a refundable $500 security deposit are due 15 days prior to the event. The security deposit will be returned after the event pending the property's condition.

Area	*Rental Fee*	*Area*	*Rental Fee*
Entire Site	$2,500	Discovery Hall	$1,500
Bay Hall	700	Architecture Hall	700
Entry Pavilion	800	Art Spot	600

AVAILABILITY: Year-round, daily. On days that the Museum is open to the public, events take place after 6pm in 5-hour blocks. Overtime runs $150/hour. The Museum is available all day Monday and Tuesday with flexible times for events.

SERVICES/AMENITIES:

Catering: BYO with approval
Kitchen Facilities: fully equipped
Tables & Chairs: BYO
Linens, Silver, etc.: BYO
Restrooms: wheelchair accessible
Dance Floor: in Discovery Hall or BYO
Bride's Dressing Area: yes
Meeting Equipment: VCR & overhead projector

Parking: large lot
Accommodations: no guest rooms
Telephone: pay phones
Outdoor Night Lighting: access only
Outdoor Cooking Facilities: BYO
Cleanup: caterer or renter
View: SF Bay & skyline, Golden Gate Bridge
Other: tours or activities for children

RESTRICTIONS:

Alcohol: BYO
Smoking: designated areas outdoors
Music: amplified OK

Wheelchair Access: yes
Insurance: certificate required
Other: no open flames, rice, confetti or glitter

This is important! Tell facilities you're reading **Here Comes The Guide** *and ask if our information is still current.*

Bay & Delta Charters

Yacht Charter

Caruso's Sport Fishing Pier, Foot of Harbor Drive, Sausalito
(415) 332-3291, fax (415) 332-3295

www.bayanddelta.com

◆ Ceremonies	◆ Special Events
◆ Wedding Receptions	◆ Meetings
◆ Business Functions	◆ Accommodations

You and your guests will be reenergized and your spirits uplifted when cruising the waters of San Francisco Bay. While away an afternoon or evening, taking in the ever-changing skyline, the bridges, Angel and Alcatraz islands, and the vast expanse of the sea, dotted with sailboats. Being on the Bay holds a magical attraction for everyone—longtime Bay Area residents, tourists, party-throwers, and romantics alike.

"There's nothing like the look of anticipation on people's faces as they board a motor yacht for a sunset cruise," says an enthusiastic Captain Gerry Robertson, owner of Bay & Delta Charters. He holds a 100-ton Ships Master License and has been chartering boats on the Bay for the past twenty years. Gerry offers a small fleet for charter, including a 36-foot sailboat, three powerboats and the *Avalon,* a classic motor yacht. You can hire one of Gerry's vessels for a quick, breezy spin around the Bay, a more elaborate, formal seated affair, or a corporate cocktail party. Weekly Wednesday sunset cruises and monthly singles cruises are regular events that take place aboard the *Avalon,* Bay & Delta's premier vessel.

Avalon plied the San Diego coastal waters for ten years prior to its tenure in San Francisco Bay. Recently refitted both inside and out, this 70-foot yacht is specifically designed for entertaining. It features three comfortable viewing decks (fore, aft and bridge), a large salon, another salon for formal dining, fully-equipped galley and four well-appointed staterooms for overnight guests. The upper deck provides an escape from the world, with areas for quiet conversation, sipping cocktails or sunbathing; a royal blue canopy offer respite from the sun.

A quick survey of the *Avalon* and you can see that the vessel looks shipshape—decks shine, handrails have been revarnished, metal hardware has been buffed and new paint gleams. Fine mahogany and teak hardwood add warmth and richness to both the interior and exterior. They've even refurnished the salons and purchased new linens and tableware.

Bay & Delta Charters handles everything, from limousine service and specialty wines to overnight accommodations and entertainment. *Avalon's* sound system can accommodate CDs or cassettes and there's even room for a small band. An added benefit is that if you'd like to say "I do" onboard, you can either have the Captain or Rev. George McLaird, from the nearby Sausalito Presbyterian Church, perform your ceremony.

Making events run smoothly is something the crew has down pat—the bartender and the preferred caterer have been working with Bay & Delta Charters for seven years, and really know the ins and outs of having an event come off without a hitch. "I've been successful in chartering vessels for special events," Gerry says, "because I cater to each client's individual needs—putting in the extra little bit of energy to do whatever the client wants."

CEREMONY, EVENT/RECEPTION & MEETING CAPACITY: The *Avalon* holds 49 guests, the *Courageous* holds 6.

FEES & DEPOSITS: 50% of the anticipated event balance is required as a deposit to secure your date; the balance is payable 10 days prior to the charter date. For special events, charters run $350/hour with a 3-hour minimum. Remote pickups/dropoffs can be arranged for an additional cost. The captain performs ceremonies for $150, and charter staff cost $15/hour/staffperson.

AVAILABILITY: Year-round, daily, any time.

SERVICES/AMENITIES:

Catering: provided or select from preferred list

Kitchen Facilities: fully equipped

Tables & Chairs: some provided

Linens, Silver, etc.: provided

Restrooms: not wheelchair accessible

Dance Floor: on decks

Bride's & Groom's Dressing Area: yes

Meeting Equipment: CBA, extra charge

Parking: large lot

Accommodations: 3 state rooms

Telephone: cell phone CBA

Outdoor Night Lighting: some on decks

Outdoor Cooking Facilities: n/a

Cleanup: provided

View: SF Bay & skyline, Golden Gate Bridge

Other: captain perfoms ceremonies, event coordination

RESTRICTIONS:

Alcohol: provided, or corkage $5/bottle

Smoking: outside only

Music: amplified OK

Wheelchair Access: no

Insurance: not required

The professionals in the back of the book are the best in the business! **How do we know? Read page 681.**

Campbell Hall and Garden

Reception Hall

Corner of San Carlos & Santa Rosa Avenues, Sausalito
(415) 332-0858

◆ Ceremonies   ◆ Special Events
◆ Wedding Receptions   Meetings
◆ Business Functions   Accommodations

A well-preserved vintage structure hidden in the hills of Sausalito, Campbell Hall is designed to blend into its woodsy, residential neighborhood. Although it's a popular meeting space for community functions, it looks so much like the neighboring brown shingle homes you might not even notice it—but that would be a shame, since you'd be missing a lovely spot for weddings and receptions.

Most events are held in the Main Reception Room on the top floor, a large wood-paneled space with gleaming hardwood floors. Multiple windows and French doors on each side let in lots of sunlight, and the high, wood-beamed ceiling creates a lofty, open feeling. A raised hardwood stage provides plenty of space for either a head table or musicians, and the adjoining garden-view balcony terrace is a terrific spot for pre-dinner socializing.

On the floor beneath the Main Reception Room is the Garden Room, a cozy space with a white, wood-beam ceiling, enormous stone fireplace and overstuffed, floral-print furnishings. The Garden Room can be used for an intimate rehearsal dinner, as a bride's dressing room, or as an alternate reception site. It opens to a freeform patio nestled in a lush, forest-like grove, with a partial ocean view and blissful ambiance. Though Campbell Hall is located in the "banana belt," an area of Sausalito that receives daily sunshine, the patio garden is restful and cool even in summer. Pretty and unpretentious, Campbell Hall is a relaxed Sausalito wedding spot you shouldn't overlook.

CEREMONY CAPACITY: Ceremonies require advance approval. Call for details.

EVENT/RECEPTION CAPACITY: The Main Reception Room holds 140 seated or 250 standing guests. If the adjoining terrace is used, you can increase the seated capacity by 40 guests. The Garden Room holds 30–35 seated or 55 standing guests. The Main Reception Room and Garden Room, combined, hold 210 seated. The Outdoor Garden accommodates 200 standing guests.

FEES & DEPOSITS: A refundable cleaning/security deposit equal to two-thirds the rental fee is required to confirm a date. The rental fee itself is payable in full 10 days prior to the event.

Area	Rental Fee		Area	Rental Fee
Main Reception Room & Terrace	$900		Garden Room	$300
Garden Room used w/above	add $150		Garden Room w/	$450
Outdoor Garden used w/above	add $300		Kitchen Use	

AVAILABILITY: Year-round, daily. Monday–Thursday (except Tuesday evening) 8am–9pm, Friday and Saturday, 8am–11pm, Sunday 1pm–9pm. Music must stop at 10pm on Friday and Saturday evenings.

SERVICES/AMENITIES:

Catering. BYO

Kitchen Facilities: fully equipped

Tables & Chairs: some provided

Linens, Silver, etc.: BYO

Restrooms: not wheelchair accessible

Dance Floor: hardwood floor

Bride's Dressing Area: CBA

View: limited bay view

Parking: on street, shuttle or valet required for larger events

Accommodations: no guest rooms

Telephone: emergency use only

Outdoor Night Lighting: no

Outdoor Cooking Facilities: no

Cleanup: caterer or renter

Meeting Equipment: large screen, stage

RESTRICTIONS:

Alcohol: BYO

Smoking: permitted

Music: amplified OK indoors w/volume limits

Wheelchair Access: limited

Insurance: certificate required

---

*This is important! Tell facilities you're reading **Here Comes The Guide** and ask if our information is still current.*

Casa Madrona Hotel

and Mikayla Restaurant

801 Bridgeway, Sausalito
(415) 332-0502, fax (415) 332-2537

www.casamadrona.com
casa@casamadrona.com

Hotel & Restaurant

◆ Ceremonies	◆ Special Events
◆ Wedding Receptions	◆ Meetings
◆ Business Functions	◆ Accommodations

At the base of the Sausalito hills, a stone's throw from the Bay's edge, lies the Casa Madrona Hotel and Mikayla Restaurant—a haven of comfort and retreat. Built in 1885, the original Victorian mansion has been expanded to include three cottages and the New Casa—a collection of sixteen uniquely decorated rooms set into the hillside facing the water. The result is a grand establishment that offers a variety of services and settings.

Mikayla Restaurant has a dramatic, glass-enclosed terrace, with a retractable sliding glass roof and walls that create an open, outdoor feeling and allow for spectacular views. Below the Restaurant is a 1,300-square-foot outdoor tiled terrace where panoramas of Angel and Belvedere Islands, Sausalito Harbor, the Bay Bridge and San Francisco skyline are unsurpassed.

Villa Madrona Suite is perfect for smaller receptions. Its three verandas overlook the San Francisco Bay, and two private terraces and a fireplace add to the intimate atmosphere. This recently renovated room, like all the others, shows meticulous attention to detail.

CEREMONY CAPACITY: The Lower Terrace holds 80 guests (35 standing and 40 seated), or 100 standing guests.

EVENT/RECEPTION CAPACITY:

Area	Seated	Standing	Facility Fee
Mikayla Restaurant	110	150	$850
Villa Madrona Suite	50	65	330
Parlor	14	20	200

MEETING CAPACITY: The Hotel can accommodate 22 seated conference-style, and 35 seated theater-style in the Villa Madrona Suite.

FEES & DEPOSITS: An $850 non-refundable deposit is required when you make reservations. 80% of the anticipated event total is due 1 month prior to the event; the balance is payable on the day of the event. The average per person food cost including alcohol is $50; tax and a 17% service charge are additional. Reduced rates are offered November through February. A ceremony setup fee for the Lower Terrace runs $100.

AVAILABILITY: Year-round, daily. Mikayla Restaurant is available Saturdays 11:30am–4:30pm; Sundays 4:30pm–9:30pm. The Villa Madrona Suite is available evenings, 5pm–10pm.

SERVICES/AMENITIES:

Catering: wine & beer provided, no BYO
Kitchen Facilities: n/a
Tables & Chairs: provided
Linens, Silver, etc.: provided
Restrooms: not wheelchair accessible
Dance Floor: in Restaurant's Bistro
Bride's Dressing Area: no
Meeting Equipment: TV, VCR, flip chart

Parking: lot, valet for hotel guests only
Accommodations: 34 guest rooms
Telephone. pay phone, guest phones
Outdoor Night Lighting: access only
Outdoor Cooking Facilities: no
Cleanup: provided
View: of San Francisco Bay, SF & Sausalito skyline, bridges

RESTRICTIONS:

Alcohol: provided, no BYO
Smoking: in designated areas
Music: amplified OK indoors only

Wheelchair Access: no
Insurance: not required

The professionals in the back of the book are the best in the business! **How do we know? Read page 681.**

Chart House Sausalito

201 Bridgeway, Sausalito
(415) 332-0804, fax (415) 332-1425

Historic Restaurant

◆ Ceremonies ◆ Special Events
◆ Wedding Receptions ◆ Meetings
◆ Business Functions · Accommodations

If walls could talk, the Chart House's would have some interesting stories to tell. It first opened its doors in 1893 as a biergarten called Walhalla, serving food and libations to the local boat builders whose clipper ships sailed around the globe. It thrived even during Prohibition, and in 1946, Sally Stanford, the infamous San Francisco madame, purchased the building and gave it a whole new life. She renamed it Valhalla (which means "heavenly place" in Norwegian) and renovated it, extending its dining room and furnishing it with Victorian antiques. For the next 32 years, Ms. Stanford was a constant, regal presence in the bar, presiding over the restaurant's operations from her "throne"—a 19th-century dentist's chair. Thanks to her influence, Valhalla became a haven for local artists, writers and movie stars, with the likes of Jack London, Rita Hayworth and Orson Welles making frequent visits.

The restaurant's long and colorful past is revealed in the furnishings, vintage photos and memorabilia that decorate the lounge. Even Sally Stanford's renowned dentist's chair still remains and her portrait hangs over the bar. The two oceanfront dining rooms, the Trellis Room and the Stanford Room, have magnificent views of Angel Island, Tiburon, Alcatraz and the San Francisco skyline, and are available for special events. By day, the tropical color scheme of teal blue, rose and white, along with lots of sunlight streaming through the wraparound picture windows and planters of palms and ficus trees all create a cheery, upbeat ambiance. By moonlight, the mood is definitely more romantic.

Whether you're having a sales meeting, company awards dinner or wedding, your event here will be fun—the Chart House is a relaxed and unpretentious place with an emphasis on fresh food and great service. We imagine Sally Stanford would have wanted it that way.

CEREMONY CAPACITY: The Trellis Room holds 110 seated.

EVENT/RECEPTION CAPACITY: The Trellis Room holds 110 seated or 175 standing; the Stanford Room 150–220 seated or 400 standing. The Chart House is also available for exclusive daytime or evening use for private parties, luncheons, weddings or all-day meetings of 25–260. If you want to reserve the entire restaurant for an evening event, a buyout is required with some day/date restrictions.

MEETING CAPACITY: The Trellis Room holds 72 classroom style, 50 conference style and 110 theater style. The Stanford Room holds up to 150, depending on the seating configuration.

FEES & DEPOSITS: For events, a $200 non-refundable deposit, which is applied toward the food and beverage total, is required to confirm your date. There's a $600 rental fee for daytime weddings, with an additional $200 fee if the ceremony is also held here; for evening receptions there's no fee with a 70-guest minimum. Reception luncheons start at $22/person, dinners at $25/person. The event balance is due on completion of the party. Tax, alcohol and an 18% service charge are additional. The minimum buyout for exclusive evening use is $15,000 or 250 guests at $60/person food and beverage cost.

For meetings, the rental fee ranges $250–600.

AVAILABILITY: Year-round, daily, 8am–4pm or 5pm–1am.

SERVICES/AMENITIES:

Catering: provided, no BYO
Kitchen Facilities: n/a
Tables & Chairs: provided
Linens, Silver, etc.: provided
Restrooms: wheelchair accessible
Dance Floor: provided
Bride's Dressing Area: yes
Meeting Equipment: AV, VCR, podium
Other: event coordination

Parking: complimentary on-site
Accommodations: no guest rooms
Telephone: pay phone
Outdoor Night Lighting: access only
Outdoor Cooking Facilities: no
Cleanup: provided
View: San Francisco skyline and Bay, Alcatraz and Angel Island

RESTRICTIONS:

Alcohol: provided, corkage $5–10/bottle
Smoking: outside only
Music: amplified OK until 4pm

Wheelchair Access: yes
Insurance: not required

This is important! Tell facilities you're reading **Here Comes The Guide** *and ask if our information is still current.*

Discovery Yacht Charters

Yacht Charter

Berth 98, Marina Plaza Harbor, 2310 Marinship Way, Sausalito
Remote pickups from San Francisco or Berkeley
(415) 331-1333, fax (415) 789-9273

www.sfyacht.com
charter@sfyacht.com

◆ Ceremonies ◆ Special Events
◆ Wedding Receptions ◆ Meetings
◆ Business Functions Accommodations

There are few things more adventurous and romantic than a shipboard wedding, and anyone planning a wedding or similar festive event in the San Francisco Bay Area has a virtual flotilla of charter companies to choose from. But if you want to have a truly memorable affair aboard a first-class yacht, you'll be delighted with Discovery Yacht Charters' *Ka'iulani*. Built for a millionaire industrialist, no expense was spared in the construction of this classic 86-foot schooner, which logged almost 60,000 miles under her original owner. Though she's named after *Ka'iulani*, the last Hawaiian princess in line for the throne, this vessel's graceful lines, acres of teak and varnished trim, and luxurious appointments make her fit for a queen (or king).

For wedding ceremonies, the *Ka'iulani* sails to a sheltered spot in the lee of Angel Island. You exchange vows on the foredeck, where there's plenty of room for guests. Captain Robert Michaan (who is also an ordained minister), has a novel way of staging the ceremony: he stands with *his* back to the audience, so you and your intended can face your beaming family and friends. "After all," he says, "they aren't here to see me. The couple should be able to see their guests." An added benefit is a video camera attached to the mast and hooked up to a TV below decks, which gives a bird's-eye view of the proceedings. The camera can be controlled from inside the cabin, allowing guests to zoom in or select different camera angles. And you can keep the tape as a wedding memento, if you like.

Often, it's the little things that mean the difference between a ho-hum event facility and one that's really smashing, and the *Ka'iulani* has a host of details that put her clearly ahead of the competition. The benches you see on the decks are not only made of teak, but have been painstakingly constructed in a convex shape for extra comfort and stability. In the stern, the swiveling winch chairs are a feature you won't find on any other charter boat, power or sail. Below decks, the main cabin features fine hardwoods such as mahogany, teak, and meranti from Southeast Asia; comfy upholstered seating, and old-fashioned brass-and-glass hanging lamps. In the corner, a bronze-trimmed potbellied stove adds a quaint, homey touch. Even the bathrooms are like "real" bathrooms, and in the Captain's Cabin, which serves as the bride's dressing room, the fully equipped bathroom even has a shower. Attention to detail is also evident in the services the *Ka'iulani*'s staff provide. They work with five different caterers, offer vegetarian and custom menus, and can accommodate almost every price range.

Just in case all of the above hasn't convinced you that the *Ka'iulani* is a great value for your money, the owners encourage potential customers to check out the competition. In fact, so confident are they that you'll choose the *Ka'iulani* for your special event, that they offer a "Champagne guarantee." They'll give three cases of Mumm's Cuvee Napa champagne, and a free bay cruise for twenty-four to the first person who can find a better charter boat in the *Ka'iulani*'s size and class on the West Coast! With a guarantee like this, there's just no reason not to put the *Ka'iulani* at the top of your list when planning your ocean-going event.

CEREMONY, EVENT/RECEPTION & MEETING CAPACITY: The yacht holds 49 guests.

FEES & DEPOSITS: Half of the anticipated charter and catering cost is required to secure your date; the balance is payable 3 weeks prior to the event. On average, meals run $20–55/person depending on menu selection; beer, wine and tax are additional. There is also a 10% crew gratuity. Ceremonies can be performed by the captain for a $100 charge. Beverage packages can be arranged, starting at $15/person. Charters run $425/hour; a 4-hour minimum charter for weddings, or a 3-hour minimum for corporate or private functions. Holiday rates may be higher.

AVAILABILITY: Year-round, daily, any time, including holidays.

SERVICES/AMENITIES:

Catering: provided, no BYO
Kitchen Facilities: n/a
Tables & Chairs: provided
Linens, Silver, etc.: provided
Restrooms: not wheelchair accessible
Dance Floor: no
Meeting Equipment: VCR, TV
Other: event coordination, ceremonies performed by Captain, photography, entertainment, skycam, videotaping

Parking: ample, free parking
Accommodations: no guest rooms
Telephone: cellular, emergency only
Outdoor Night Lighting: yes
Outdoor Cooking Facilities: n/a
Cleanup: provided
View: SF Bay & skyline, landmarks vary with charter course

RESTRICTIONS:

Alcohol: BWC provided, no BYO
Smoking: on deck only
Music: amplified OK
Other: no red wine; no rice, glitter or confetti

Wheelchair Access: no wheelchair access, but other CBA
Insurance: not required

The professionals in the back of the book are the best in the business! **How do we know? Read page 681.**

Hawaiian Chieftain

Sailing Ship

Marina Plaza Harbor, 2310 Marinship Way, Sausalito
(415) 331-3214, fax (415) 331-9415

www.hawaiianchieftain.com
tallship@hawaiianchieftain.com

◆ Ceremonies ◆ Special Events
◆ Wedding Receptions ◆ Meetings
◆ Business Functions ◆ Accommodations

Imagine throwing a party or hosting a corporate retreat on board a majestic 103-foot square-rigged sailboat! The *Hawaiian Chieftain*, docked at Sausalito's Marina Plaza, can be rented for sunset sails around the Bay or custom charters, including overnight adventures. Her design conjures up images of Captain Hook—in fact, she has been host to pirate theme parties as well as weddings, hands-on sailing trips, and elegant private dinners. Food can be catered by the *Hawaiian Chieftain's* chef, or brought on board by an outside caterer, and is most often served on deck, buffet style. A group of ten can be served a sit-down meal below deck at a beautiful mahogany table.

After a meal, guests can relax on plushly appointed window seats or try out their sea legs on deck. Captain Ian McIntyre and his affable crew, intent on providing adventure, will teach you and your guests how to maneuver 100 different lines controlling ten separate sails. The *Hawaiian Chieftain's* magnificent network of rigging is a sight to behold and everything is hand operated—no push buttons or winches are used to control the sails. This kind of challenge is well suited to company team-building exercises.

An onboard sound system makes it possible to listen to music while taking in breathtaking views of the Golden Gate and San Francisco's waterfront or to crank up the dance tunes for an on-deck dance party out at sea! For extended voyages, the boat comes equipped with twelve bunks, built in what was once the cargo hold, topped by hand-hewn teak-framed skylights. If you picture an unusual setting for your event, this historically designed sailboat with state-of-the-art facilities fits the bill.

CEREMONY, EVENT/RECEPTION & MEETING CAPACITY: The ship holds 47 including catering and entertainment personnel.

FEES & DEPOSITS: Half the estimated total is required to reserve the ship; the balance is due 7 days prior to the event. Rates run $350/hour with a 3-hour minimum. Pickup points other than Marina Plaza can be arranged for $200.

AVAILABILITY: Year-round, daily April–October in San Francisco Bay, November–March in Southern California.

SERVICES/AMENITIES:

Catering: provided or BYO
Kitchen Facilities: no
Tables & Chairs: n/a
Linens, Silver, etc.: with in-house catering
Restrooms: not wheelchair accessible
Dance Floor: no
Meeting Equipment: VCR, TV
Other: environmental education

Parking: on-site parking
Accommodations: 12 berths on board
Telephone: cellular, emergency only
Outdoor Night Lighting: minimal
Outdoor Cooking Facilities: no
Cleanup: with in-house catering
View: SF Bay & skyline, landmarks (varies with charter course)

RESTRICTIONS:

Alcohol: BW provided or BYO
Smoking: deck only
Music: amplified OK

Wheelchair Access: on deck only
Insurance: not required

---

*This is important! Tell facilities you're reading **Here Comes The Guide** and ask if our information is still current.*

Sausalito Presbyterian Church

Historic Church

112 Bulkley, Sausalito
(415) 332-3790, fax (415) 332-5809

www.sausalitopresbyterian.com
office@sausalitopresbyterian.com

- ◆ Ceremonies
- ◆ Wedding Receptions
- ◆ Business Functions
- ◆ Special Events
- ◆ Meetings
- Accommodations

Nowadays, you can get married just about anywhere. People tie the knot jumping out of planes, at the bottom of the ocean, on the Golden Gate Bridge—you name it, someone's gotten married there. But let's face it: there is something elegantly classic, something comfortingly traditional about getting married in a church. And when the church is as beautiful as the Sausalito Presbyterian, well, there's simply no reason to look anywhere else.

Clinging to the steep, oak-clad hills of Sausalito, this century-old church is a warm, intimate place to exchange vows. Its redwood shingle exterior blends effortlessly with the surrounding oaks, dogwood trees and flourishing shrubs, while the building's Gothic-arched porch and series of peaked rooflines draw the eye skywards. The interior is paneled entirely in redwood, much of it intricately carved. One of the church's most unusual features is the dramatic pyramid-shaped vault in the ceiling, whose leaded glass windows serve as skylights. Other design elements include rich, red carpeting covering the aisle and altar; wood-and-glass chandeliers, and twenty-four glass wall sconces. For a truly magical effect at your wedding, these sconces can be outfitted with real candles. On the practical side, Sausalito Presbyterian has a state-of-the-art sound system and a brand-new organ that can duplicate any instrument from a delicate harp to a *fortissimo* trumpet.

Downstairs, Thomson Hall is available for receptions. It features hardwood floors, a grand piano, white walls with wide dark-wood trim and wainscotting, plus plenty of leaded-glass windows to showcase the beautiful views. A wood-decked, landscaped courtyard just off Thomson Hall allows your guests to enjoy the sunshine and sea breezes. If you'd like a larger venue for your reception, fine hotels such as the Alta Mira and Casa Madrona are just steps away from Sausalito Presbyterian.

When you choose to get married at Sausalito Presbyterian Church, you get not only an exquisite wedding site, but a host of other services such as a wedding coordinator, music director, private bride's room and scheduled rehearsal time. People of all faiths and nationalities can be married here. You can write your own vows or, if you're suffering from writer's block, Rev. George McLaird and his staff will inspire you with some sample ceremonies. And this isn't the kind of church where you're forgotten as soon as the birdseed is swept off the church steps! Sausalito Presbyterian has some of the most sophisticated, realistic pre-and post-wedding educational programs to be found anywhere, including an invitation to participate in the church's monthly "Committed Couples Gathering" and discounted registration for couples' education workshops. Rev. McLaird encourages couples to proceed on two tracks: "First, designing the wedding of your dreams. Second, creating the marriage of your dreams." So if your idea of marriage includes not only a storybook wedding, but a vision of "happily ever after," head for the hills of Sausalito and the Sausalito Presbyterian Church!

CEREMONY CAPACITY: The sanctuary holds 170 seated in pews.

EVENT/RECEPTION CAPACITY: Thomson Fellowship Hall holds 80 seated or up to 125 standing guests with use of the adjacent patio. The patio holds 25–30 for cocktail receptions.

MEETING CAPACITY: Thomson Fellowship Hall holds 90–100 seated theater-style or 50 seated conference-style. There are 3 small meeting rooms that hold 15–20 seated guests, each.

FEES & DEPOSITS: A $200 non-refundable deposit is required to reserve your date; the rental balance is payable 10 days prior to the event. The Church rental fee runs $875–925 for a 4-hour function. For weddings, a 1-hour rehearsal is included in the fee.

AVAILABILITY: Year-round, daily, 9am–9pm, except Easter Sunday and Christmas Day. Saturday ceremonies 9am–4:30pm, however the last ceremony must start no later 3:30pm; Sunday ceremonies can take place noon–midnight.

SERVICES/AMENITIES:

Catering: preferred list or BYO w/approval
Kitchen Facilities: fully equipped, extra charge
Tables & Chairs: provided, extra charge
Linens, Silver, etc.: linens CBA, silver extra charge
Restrooms: not wheelchair accessible
Dance Floor: hardwood floor or patio
Meeting Equipment: audio-visual and sound system
View: Sausalito hills

Parking: on street or CBA
Accommodations: no guest rooms
Telephone: house phone w/approval
Outdoor Night Lighting: yes on patio
Outdoor Cooking Facilities: through caterer with approval
Cleanup: caterer or CBA
Other: 2 baby grand pianos, candelabras, organist, wedding & event coordination, decor CBA

RESTRICTIONS:

Alcohol: caterer or BYO w/corkage fee
Smoking: outdoors only
Music: amplified OK indoors until 10pm w/volume restrictions

Wheelchair Access: limited but CBA
Insurance: not required
Other: no birdseed, rice, confetti or glitter

The professionals in the back of the book are the best in the business! **How do we know? Read page 681.**

Sausalito Woman's Club

Historic Landmark

120 Central Avenue, Sausalito
(415) 332-0354, fax (415) 332-0354

◆ Ceremonies   ◆ Special Events
◆ Wedding Receptions   ◆ Meetings
◆ Business Functions   Accommodations

This landmark is a craftsman-style Julia Morgan building, a bit hidden in a residential neighborhood in the Sausalito hills overlooking San Francisco Bay. Since its dedication as a woman's club in 1918, it's been one of Marin's preferred places for weddings and receptions. It not only has a very pretty, woodsy setting with filtered views of the Bay, it has both indoor and outdoor spaces that can be used for special events—and that's a real bonus.

The modest brown-shingle structure is designed with the simple and understated detailing typical of Arts and Crafts period structures. Indoors, the main room has an ample stage, original fixtures, hardwood floor and large windows that keep the space well lit during the day. Multiple French doors open onto a small brick patio sheltered by mature oaks, a lovely spot for mingling. The landscaping is well-maintained and although there's a canopy of trees surrounding the Woman's Club, you can still catch an incredible view of the Bay.

Unpretentious yet stately, the Woman's Club fits into the neighborhood perfectly—you'd hardly know it's there. Consequently, it's a bit hard to find, but when you do, you'll consider it—and the pleasant drive through the Sausalito hills—well worth the trip.

CEREMONY CAPACITY: The Club interior holds 125–150 seated guests; the patio holds up to 40–50 seated or standing guests.

EVENT/RECEPTION CAPACITY: The Club can accommodate 150 seated or standing guests.

MEETING CAPACITY: The Club holds 150 people in the auditorium.

FEES & DEPOSITS: For weekend events, a refundable $500 deposit is due when the rental contract is submitted. The rental fee for 48 hours' use is $950 on Friday, Saturday or Sunday. For weekday events a $300 deposit is required; the rental fee is $450 for 12 hours' use. The rental balance is due 4 weeks prior to the function.

AVAILABILITY: Year-round, daily until 9pm.

SERVICES/AMENITIES:

Catering: BYO
Kitchen Facilities: fully equipped
Tables & Chairs: provided
Linens, Silver, etc.: BYO
Restrooms: wheelchair accessible
Dance Floor: yes
Bride's Dressing Area: yes
Meeting Equipment: auditorium-size, pull-down screen

Parking: on-street, shuttle encouraged
Accommodations: no guest rooms
Telephone: house phone
Outdoor Night Lighting: no
Outdoor Cooking Facilities: no
Cleanup: caterer or renter
View: of San Francisco Bay & city skyline

RESTRICTIONS:

Alcohol: BYO
Smoking: outside only
Music: no amplified; acoustic OK until 9pm

Wheelchair Access: yes
Insurance: certificate required
Other: decorations restricted

---

*This is important! Tell facilities you're reading **Here Comes The Guide** and ask if our information is still current.*

Spinnaker Restaurant

100 Spinnaker Drive, Sausalito
(415) 332-1500, fax (415) 332-7062

www.thespinnaker.com

Waterfront Restaurant

◆ Ceremonies   ◆ Special Events
◆ Wedding Receptions   ◆ Meetings
◆ Business Functions   Accommodations

The Spinnaker Restaurant, on Sausalito's waterfront, has recently added a spacious new banquet facility to its list of delicious offerings. The new wing is adjacent to the Sausalito Yacht Harbor, and is completely separate from the main dining room. It even has its own kitchen area that caters solely to the new facility. Like the restaurant, the banquet room is partially built on piers over the water, and has floor-to-ceiling glass throughout, a warm interior in shades of cream and rose and the same distinctive wood-slat ceiling. From any spot in the room you have sweeping views that include Belvedere, Angel Island, the Bay Bridge and San Francisco's skyline. Sliding glass doors open onto an adjoining outdoor deck that offers an additional 1,000 square feet of bayside space. From here you can read the names of the boats as they glide past, their colorful spinnakers fluttering and white sails billowing in the breeze.

The banquet room can be set up any way you like. Audio/visual systems are available for business functions, and there is ample space for a band and portable dance floor for wedding receptions and holiday parties. It's also a great setting for a small private affair such as a bridal shower luncheon or an anniversary or birthday party. Quiet and tasteful, the Spinnaker is an inviting and welcome addition to waterfront dining.

CEREMONY & EVENT/RECEPTION CAPACITY: The deck holds 40 seated or 70 standing and the banquet room holds 160 seated or 220 standing.

MEETING CAPACITY: The Banquet Room holds 200 seated theater-style or 160 seated conference-style.

FEES & DEPOSITS: To reserve your date, a $500 non-refundable deposit is required (which is applied towards the event balance). The food and beverage balance is payable at the event's completion. Monday–Friday, the food and beverage minimum is $1,000, Saturday-Sunday, $1,500. In-house catering is provided. Buffets or seated meals run approximately $30/person; alcohol, tax and a 17% service charge are additional. A $250 room charge, $100 bartending fee and $150 dance floor fee may apply. For ceremonies, there's a $150 set up charge.

For business luncheons, dinners or for smaller groups, special rates can be arranged.

AVAILABILITY: Year-round, daily, 7am–1am, in 4-hour blocks.

SERVICES/AMENITIES:

Catering: provided, no BYO
Kitchen Facilities: n/a
Tables & Chairs: provided
Linens, Silver, etc.: provided
Restrooms: wheelchair accessible
Dance Floor: CBA, extra fee
Bride's Dressing Area: no
Meeting Equipment: PA, microphones

Parking: valet parking
Accommodations: no guest rooms
Telephone: pay phone
Outdoor Night Lighting: on deck
Outdoor Cooking Facilities: no
Cleanup: provided
View: of San Francisco Bay & bridges
Other: event coordination, cakes, music CBA

RESTRICTIONS:

Alcohol: provided, or corkage $10–12/bottle
Smoking: designated areas
Music: amplified OK

Wheelchair Access: yes
Insurance: not required

The professionals in the back of the book are the best in the business! ***How do we know? Read page 681.***

Stinson Beach "Creekside"
Community Center & Chapel

32 Belvedere Avenue, Stinson Beach
(415) 868-1444, fax (415) 868-1904

www.stinsonbeachonline.com
communitycenter@hotmail.com

Community Center & Chapel

◆ Ceremonies	◆ Special Events
◆ Wedding Receptions	◆ Meetings
◆ Business Functions	Accommodations

Looking for a special spot near the ocean? Here's one you'd never know about unless you went looking for it. Situated alongside a meandering creek and in front of coastal foothills are the Stinson Beach Community Center and Chapel. They sit next to each other on a quiet, residential side street away from the bustle of town activities.

The Community Center is a modest one-story building, with a sloping shake roof and a wide porch. In the spring, the oaks in front of the building are covered with long, delicate, white flowers, which hang in such profusion you can hardly see the Center's entry. Inside is a large open space with a vaulted wood-beam ceiling, hardwood floor, working stone fireplace and large windows overlooking a creekside patio.

For receptions, the outdoor area is very inviting. The patio borders a creek (actually the confluence of two bubbling creeks) and makes a delightful space for al fresco dining. An added feature is a huge maple tree, whose branches create a shady canopy overhead. For ceremonies, the Chapel is just a step away and a minister is also available. Both the Center and Chapel offer a casual, warm and friendly environment for weddings and receptions.

CEREMONY CAPACITY: The Community Chapel can accommodate 110 seated guests.

EVENT/RECEPTION CAPACITY:

Area	*Seated*	*Standing*
Community Center	150	300
Center with Patio Space	200	350

MEETING CAPACITY:

Area	*Seated*	*Standing*
Main Hall	200	300
Board Room	25	40

FEES & DEPOSITS: For special events, a partially refundable $200 security/cleaning deposit is required to secure your date. The rental fee is $850 for the Center and full use of the kitchen, payable 2 months prior to the event. The fee covers a block from 7am–midnight. The Chapel rents for $100/day.

The rate for business functions is $25/hr.; for non-profits it's $15/hr.

AVAILABILITY: For special events, year-round, daily, 7am–midnight. For business functions, available weekdays evenings; if group is larger than 25, weekends only.

SERVICES/AMENITIES:

Catering: BYO or CBA

Tables & Chairs: provided

Kitchen Facilities: new, fully equipped

Linens, Silver, etc.: BYO or some provided, extra charge

Restrooms: wheelchair accessible

Dance Floor: hardwood floor indoors

Bride's Dressing Area: CBA

Meeting Equipment: limited, ask for specifics

Parking: Center's pkg area & on street

Accommodations: no guest rooms

Telephone: emergency only

Outdoor Night Lighting: on porch & patio

Outdoor Cooking Facilities: no

Cleanup: caterer and renter

Other: some event coordination, grand piano, chapel minister and organ

View: of Stinson Beach hills, part of Mt. Tamalpais

RESTRICTIONS:

Alcohol: BYO

Smoking: outside only

Music: amplified OK

Wheelchair Access: yes

Insurance: certificate required

Corinthian Yacht Club

Historic Yacht Club

43 Main Street, Tiburon
(415) 435-4812, fax (415) 435-5498

www.cyc.org
catering@cyc.org

◆ Ceremonies   ◆ Special Events
◆ Wedding Receptions   ◆ Meetings
◆ Business Functions   Accommodations

One of California's oldest landmarks, the Corinthian Yacht Club sits right at the edge of the water and has a breathtaking panoramic view of San Francisco and the Bay. It was established in 1886 by disgruntled members of the San Francisco Yacht Club who felt their interests were not being represented. They created their own organization, called it the Corinthian Yacht Club ("gentlemen yachtsmen, sportsmen, men of fashion and pleasure") and erected their own clubhouse here on this spot. It was replaced in 1911 with the distinctive structure you see today.

Although the building looks largely as it did at the turn of the century, its foundation and pilings have been completely rebuilt, and of course the Club enjoys all the modern conveniences you would expect. Several spaces are available for receptions, corporate functions and private parties. The most popular is the Ballroom, a spacious room paneled entirely in California redwood, with a high ceiling, stage, hardwood dance floor and impressive stone fireplace.

The adjacent glass-enclosed Solarium has a fantastic vista of Tiburon Harbor and San Francisco Bay (including Angel Island, the Bay Bridge and Alcatraz). When you reserve the Ballroom, you have access to the Solarium, as well as a large bar and a deck right over the water. Most receptions take place indoors, but the deck is actually the best spot for appreciating the extraordinary view while enjoying champagne, hors d'oeuvres and the company of good friends.

The newly remodeled Main Dining Room, located on the first floor, is also available for parties on weekdays. Its deck overlooks the picturesque marina and has a similarly sensational vista of the Harbor and San Francisco. Twilight is a particularly enchanting time when the sky turns shades of sunset red, the water becomes jet black and the City's lights glitter in the distance.

All kinds of events have been hosted here, including Christmas and New Year's parities, a "Shore Dinner" (complete with Maine lobster, oysters and clams), and a Casino Night. The Club is near the center of town, and your guests arriving from San Francisco can make the most of their journey into Tiburon by taking the ferry—the ferry landing is just a short walk from the Yacht Club. That way they can have fun even before they get to the party, an unexpected asset not many facilities can claim.

CEREMONY CAPACITY: The Solarium accommodates 75 seated with additional room for 30 standing guests; the Deck holds 35 seated guests.

EVENT/RECEPTION CAPACITY: The Ballroom can hold 250 seated or up to 400 standing guests; the Main Dining Room up to 135.

MEETING CAPACITY: The Ballroom seats 300, the Solarium 50, the Library 20 and the Dining Room 135.

FEES & DEPOSITS: An $1,800 partially-refundable deposit is applied towards the total cost and is required at the time of booking. The rental fee Monday–Thursday is $1,100; Friday, Saturday and Sunday, $1,800. The Dining Room rental fee, Monday–Thursday, is $500. Fees cover a 5-hour block; extra hours can be negotiated. 80% of the estimated total is due 1 month prior to the event, and the balance is due the week of the event.

Catering is provided; menu prices range $30–55+/person. A $600 minimum for bar service is required; bar prices range $15–25/person, based on consumption. Tax and an 18% service charge are additional.

AVAILABILITY: The Ballroom is available daily 9am–midnight. The Dining Room, Monday–Thursday, 9am–midnight.

SERVICES/AMENITIES:

Catering: provided, no BYO
Kitchen Facilities: n/a
Tables & Chairs: provided
Linens, Silver, etc.: provided
Restrooms: limited wheelchair access downstairs
Dance Floor: yes
Meeting Equipment: limited

Parking: public lot nearby
Accommodations: no guest rooms
Telephone: pay phone
Outdoor Night Lighting: yes
Outdoor Cooking Facilities: no
Cleanup: provided
View: San Francisco Bay and skyline, Angel Island and Alcatraz

RESTRICTIONS:

Alcohol: provided, or BYO wine and champagne w/corkage fee
Smoking: on decks only
Music: amplified OK w/volume restrictions

Wheelchair Access: downstairs only
Insurance: not required
Other: security required

The professionals in the back of the book are the best in the business! **How do we know? Read page 681.**

Guaymas

Restaurant

#5 Main Street, Tiburon
(415) 435-6303, fax (415) 435-6802

www.citysearch.com
www.tiburon.com

	Ceremonies	◆	Special Events
◆	Wedding Receptions	◆	Meetings
◆	Business Functions		Accommodations

Guaymas features authentic regional Mexican cuisine in a truly spectacular location. Set at the edge of Tiburon Harbor, the restaurant has a sweeping view of the Marin hills and San Francisco, as well as the local boats docked a stone's throw from the dining room. The restaurant has a festive ambiance: vibrantly colored, hand-cut paper flags hang from wooden beams and flutter in the breeze; displays of tropical fruit and whimsical Mexican artwork decorate walls and counters. Rough hewn chairs and tables covered with sun gold tablecloths and pink napkins add zest. And in winter, a huge adobe fireplace warms the semiprivate area in the Main Dining Room.

The real attraction, however, is the Arriba Deck—a glorious place for a rehearsal dinner or reception. Bordered by sky and water, this upstairs patio is open to sun, stars and sea breezes. Geranium-filled planters provide color and greenery, and a wind shield and heaters keep guests comfortable. The Private Dining Room is perfect for smaller rehearsal dinners. It overlooks the deck and features a large decorative fireplace and glass doors with the same wonderful vistas shared by the rest of the restaurant. It's easy to understand why people come from all over to dine and celebrate at Guaymas.

CEREMONY CAPACITY: Ceremonies usually don't take place here.

EVENT/RECEPTION CAPACITY:

Area	*Seated*	*Standing*
Main Dining Room	65	80
Private Dining Room	25	40
Arriba Deck	170	220

MEETING CAPACITY: The Private Dining Room holds 25 seated conference style.

FEES & DEPOSITS: A deposit is required to confirm your reservation. Per-person food service costs are: $15–24 for luncheons, $18–30 for dinners and $15–25 for buffets. Alcohol, tax and an 18% service charge are additional. The balance is due at the event's conclusion.

AVAILABILITY: Year-round, daily except Christmas and Thanksgiving: Monday–Thursday 11:30am–10pm, Friday and Saturday 11:30am–11pm, and Sunday 10:30am–10pm.

SERVICES/AMENITIES:

Catering: provided, no BYO
Kitchen Facilities: n/a
Tables & Chairs: provided
Linens, Silver, etc.: provided
Restrooms: wheelchair accessible
Dance Floor: concrete and brick floor
Bride's Dressing Area: no
Meeting Equipment: CBA, extra fee

Parking: validated M–F, 11:30am–4pm
Accommodations: no guest rooms
Telephone: pay phone
Outdoor Night Lighting: deck only
Outdoor Cooking Facilities: no
Cleanup: provided
View: San Francisco, Alcatraz, Angel Island and San Francisco Bay

RESTRICTIONS:

Alcohol: provided, or WC corkage $10/bottle
Music: allowed with restrictions
Smoking: outdoors only

Wheelchair Access: main dining level only
Insurance: not required

---

*This is important! Tell facilities you're reading **Here Comes The Guide** and ask if our information is still current.*

Old St. Hilary's

Landmark Chapel

Esperanza Road via Beach Road, Tiburon
(415) 435-1853

◆ Ceremonies	◆ Special Events
Wedding Receptions	Meetings
Business Functions	Accommodations

If you'd like to have your ceremony in a very special place, reserve Old St. Hilary's in Tiburon. This is a simple deconsecrated chapel (built in 1888)—one of the few California examples of Carpenter's Gothic style to survive in its original condition. It's situated atop a knoll overlooking Belvedere, Angel Island and the Golden Gate—a site protected as a rare wildflower preserve. The small white clapboard building with high peaked roof has interior walls of natural redwood, a ceiling of Douglas fir, oak pews and is lit by replicas of the original oil-burning chandeliers. The only original stained-glass window, which is above the door, depicts St. Hilary, patron saint of scholars; the other windows are Gothic arches of amber glass. Take your vows in an uncluttered space that embraces you with a sense of peace and tranquility. Not only is the church a well-known place for weddings, it's also a popular photo site. And the auditorium, which has excellent acoustics, can accommodate meetings, musical programs and recordings.

CEREMONY OR OTHER EVENT CAPACITY: Total occupancy, 125. No standing room.

FEES & DEPOSITS: For weddings, a $100 deposit is required to reserve your date. The rental fee is $900, which includes rehearsal, setup and ceremony time. A refundable security deposit is $250. All fees are payable 45 days prior to the ceremony. Fees for other types of events and photo/movie shoots are negotiable.

AVAILABILITY: Year-round, any day or evening except Wednesday and Sunday afternoons April–October, 1pm–4pm.

SERVICES/AMENITIES:

Catering: not allowed
Kitchen Facilities: n/a
Tables & Chairs: stationary oak pews
Linens, Silver, etc.: n/a
Restrooms: wheelchair accessible
Dance Floor: no dancing

Parking: limited to 7 cars, shuttle required
Accommodations: no guest rooms
Telephone: house phone
Outdoor Night Lighting: access only
Outdoor Cooking Facilities: no
Cleanup: renter

Bride's Dressing Area: yes
Meeting Equipment: BYO

RESTRICTIONS:

Alcohol: not allowed
Smoking: not allowed
Music: acoustic inside only

View: SF Bay, Richardson Bay and Mt. Tam
Other: concert piano & wedding bell

Wheelchair Access: yes
Insurance: proof of personal liability coverage
Other: decorations restricted; no food/
beverages indoors or outdoors; no rice,
seeds, grains, petals or confetti

The professionals in the back of the book are the best in the business! **How do we know? Read page 681.**

Tiburon Peninsula Club

Private Club

1600 Mar West, off of Tiburon Boulevard, Tiburon
(415) 435-0968, (415) 459-6505, fax (415) 435-6629

www.jps.net/wtcal/anaffairto.html
aatrcaters@aol.com

◆ Ceremonies ◆ Special Events
◆ Wedding Receptions ◆ Meetings
◆ Business Functions Accommodations

Snuggled in a grassy hillside, the Tiburon Peninsula Club has a secluded and pastoral setting. This peaceful scene is enhanced by a view of Old St. Hilary's, a landmark Victorian chapel perched on a knoll just above the Club. It not only adds a touch of historic charm, but is frequently used for ceremonies by couples holding their reception at the Club.

The clubhouse is a casual, ranch-style building with large bays of sliding glass doors on both sides of the long room. It's spacious and light, with hardwood floors throughout and an open-beamed ceiling. On a cool evening, you can have a fire in the flagstone fireplace, and serve cocktails or hot drinks from a small built-in bar. The front of the building opens onto a large patio and garden area, with a nice-size lawn and beds of flowers, all of which are enclosed by a wooden, wisteria-draped fence. The clubhouse and gardens can easily be dressed up for any occasion, and the Club facilities—tennis courts and a lap pool (which are behind the building)—can be closed off from view by curtains. We don't normally talk about restrooms, but the Tiburon Peninsula Club's are an added treat. Beautifully faux-finished and hand painted, they're works of art: the women's features a rose-covered arbor, iridescent humming-birds, and butterflies; the men's sports a stag, a cougar, and a gnarled oak tree.

If you don't tie the knot at Old St. Hilary's, the Club has its own pleasant setting for an outdoor wedding around the side of the building—a grassy glade bordered by a stand of pine and oak trees. There are plenty of good outdoor photo opportunities, and the Club is a terrific place for kids, too. A large, fenced-in play area with swings and a climbing structure is set well apart from the building and garden, but within easy viewing distance for parents. Whether your event is down-home casual or more formal in style, having it here will make you feel like you're in a simpler place and time.

CEREMONY CAPACITY: Homan Hall holds 135 seated or 200 standing; the Garden Patio holds 125 seated or 250 standing guests.

EVENT/RECEPTION CAPACITY: Homan Hall holds 100 seated or 200 standing; the Garden Patio holds 125 seated or 250 standing guests.

MEETING CAPACITY: Homan Hall accommodates 125 people seated theater-style or 100 seated conference-style.

FEES & DEPOSITS: A $700 non-refundable rental deposit is required to secure your date. The fee varies depending on guest count, and includes cleaning and setup.

In-house catering is provided by *An Affair To Remember*. A 10% food and beverage deposit is required when you book the site; 65% is payable 30 days prior, the balance 10 days prior to the event. Luncheon meals range from $15–25/person and dinners from $25–50/person; alcohol, tax, staff, rentals and a 15% service charge are additional.

AVAILABILITY: Year-round, daily, 9am–midnight.

SERVICES/AMENITIES:

Catering: provided
Kitchen Facilities: n/a
Tables & Chairs: provided
Linens, Silver, etc.: through caterer, extra fee
Restrooms: not wheelchair accessible
Dance Floor: parquet
Bride's Dressing Area: no
Meeting Equipment: BYO

Parking: large lot and on street
Accommodations: no guest rooms
Telephone: pay phones
Outdoor Night Lighting: yes
Outdoor Cooking Facilities: through caterer
Cleanup: provided
View: of garden, Olympic-size pool
Other: event coordination

RESTRICTIONS:

Alcohol: BYO or caterer, corkage $2–3/bottle
Smoking: outdoors only
Music: amplified OK until midnight

Wheelchair Access: yes
Insurance: certificate required

---

*This is important! Tell facilities you're reading **Here Comes The Guide** and ask if our information is still current.*

Tutto Mare

Restaurant

#9 Main Street, Tiburon
(415) 435-6303, fax (415) 435-6802

www.tiburon.com

Ceremonies	◆ Special Events
◆ Wedding Receptions	◆ Meetings
◆ Business Functions	Accommodations

This upscale eatery specializing in Italian seafood is a terrific new addition to the quaint, waterfront village of Tiburon. Located next to the Angel Island ferry landing, Tutto Mare's driftwood-grey facade sports white trim and green awnings and faces the boutiques and restaurants of Tiburon's picturesque Main Street. An open-air, tree-shaded patio flanks both sides of the archway leading into the restaurant, providing an engaging, restful spot for al fresco lunches or evening cocktails.

Inside the main entrance, a wood-burning pizza oven and an oversize fireplace give a warm glow to the luscious yellow, olive, terra-cotta and sea mist-green Mediterranean color scheme used throughout the restaurant. In the lively, first-floor dining room, the custom concrete floor provides a rustic backdrop for the stand-up oyster bar, the Italian hardwood tables and chairs and the U-shaped banquettes lining one wall. On the opposite side, a wood, brass and stainless steel cocktail bar is backed by a wall of glass that overlooks the walkway leading to the ferry. At the far end of the dining room, large picture windows bring in views of boats and the glistening bay.

The upstairs dining room is more traditional, with a combination carpet and hardwood floor, a row of leather-upholstered booths along one wall and cloth-covered tables placed throughout the room. The twelve-foot-high, open-beam ceiling is decorated with oars purchased from the U.C. Berkeley crew team, creating an ambiance like that of an old Italian boathouse—clubby and cozy, yet spacious enough for sizable gatherings. Sliding glass doors open onto a small deck with spectacular views of downtown San Francisco and both Alcatraz and Angel Islands. Along with its waterfront location and delectable cuisine, Tutto Mare offers an understated yet elegant atmosphere that's just right for sophisticated celebrations.

CEREMONY CAPACITY: Ceremonies are not held here.

EVENT/RECEPTION CAPACITY: The Ristorante (upstairs) holds 150 seated or 200 standing guests; the outdoor deck holds 70 seated or 80 standing; combined, they hold 220 seated or 280 standing guests. The Taverna (downstairs) holds 70 seated or 120 standing guests. In addition, a semi-private area in the Main Dining Room is available for groups up to 35.

MEETING CAPACITY: The Taverna seats 40 theater style and 50 conference style.

FEES & DEPOSITS: A signed contract and a deposit for half the estimated food and beverage total are required when the event is confirmed; the balance is due the day of the event. Per-person food costs are $18–35 for luncheons or $25–45 for dinners. Alcohol, tax and a 20% service charge are additional. Food and beverage minimums will apply for private functions.

AVAILABILITY: Year-round except Christmas and Thanksgiving. Events take place Mon–Thurs, 11:30am–10pm; Fri & Sat 11:30am–11pm; Sunday 10:30am–10pm.

SERVICES/AMENITIES:

Catering: provided, no BYO

Kitchen Facilities: n/a

Tables & Chairs: provided

Linens, Silver, etc.: provided

Restrooms: wheelchair accessible

Dance Floor: portable CBA, extra fee

Bride's Dressing Area: no

Meeting Equipment: CBA, extra fee

Parking: validated M–F, 11:30am–4pm

Accommodations: no guest rooms

Telephone: pay phones

Outdoor Night Lighting: yes

Outdoor Cooking Facilities: no

Cleanup: provided

View: Alcatraz, Angel Island, SF skyline

Other: event coordination

RESTRICTIONS:

Alcohol: provided, CW $10–15/bottle corkage

Smoking: outdoors only

Music: allowed with restrictions

Wheelchair Access: yes, elevator

Insurance: not required

The professionals in the back of the book are the best in the business! **How do we know? Read page 681.**

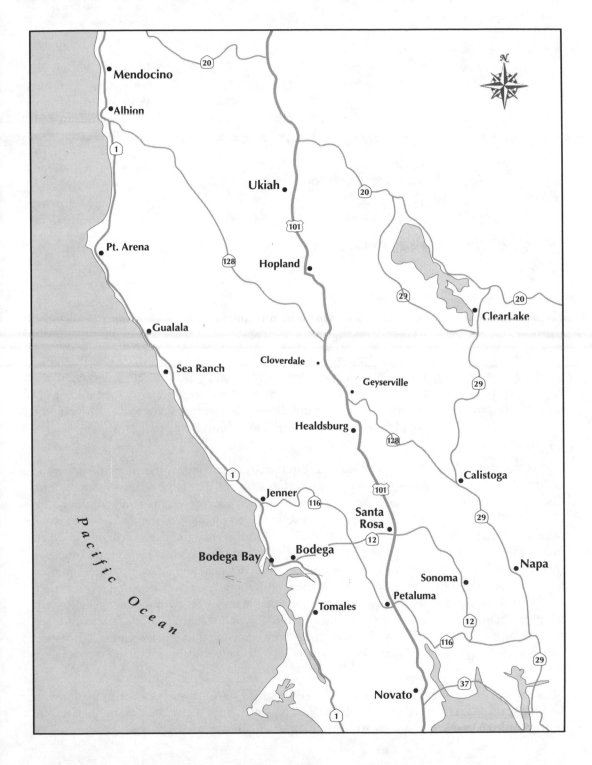

Albion River Inn

3790 North Highway One, Albion
(707) 937–1919, (800) 479–7944, fax (707) 937–2604

www.albionriverinn.com
ari@mcn.org

Inn & Restaurant

◆ Ceremonies   ◆ Special Events
◆ Wedding Receptions   Meetings
Business Functions   ◆ Accommodations

It's a glorious day for a wedding. You and your beloved are standing on an intimate bluff-top lawn ringed by an old-fashioned garden. White daisies, yellow hollyhocks and purple sprays of Mexican sage hug the edge of the grass, while a rough wooden fence holds back a riot of magenta roses. Waves crash on distant rocks, a fog horn sounds, and the sea air seems to purify you as you breathe it in. Exhilarated, you think to yourself, what an extraordinary place to get married!

The Albion River Inn has occupied this dramatic stretch of the North Coast since 1982. Set along ten acres of weathered bluffs, its restaurant and guest cottages overlook the inlet where the Albion River flows into the ocean. Designed in a simple, New England style, the buildings fit in well with the austere beauty of their surroundings. This setting alone would probably be enough to enchant any couple planning a wedding here, but it's only part of what makes the Inn so special.

The restaurant, which *Bon Appetit Magazine* referred to as "one of the finest to grace the Golden State shore," also has a lot to do with the Inn's appeal. The large picture windows look out over the bluff-top lawn, affording every table in the room a sweeping view of the ocean beyond. White linens and fresh flowers are a refined complement to the dark wood chairs, redwood ceiling and cozy brick fireplace. And the food? Although, alas, a scheduling glitch prevented us from staying for dinner and making our own assessment, we can report that the Inn's cuisine has received much critical acclaim. Executive Chef Stephen Smith, whose training included a stint at Stars in San Francisco and the California Culinary Academy, infuses a variety of meats, fowl, local seafood, fresh fruits and vegetables with his own unique style. Award-winning sommelier, Mark Bowery, has put together a wine list that *The Wine Spectator* called "one of the best in the world." Wedding luncheons are served in the restaurant and on the lawn, and you can select from a list of delectable options, or have the chef create a custom menu for you.

After experiencing one of the Inn's divine repasts, in the midst of such coastal splendor, you will not want to go home. You will, instead, be consumed with the desire to walk over to one of the cottages and settle in for a while—maybe even a few days. Each guest room is full of thoughtful touches: robes, binoculars (for whale watching), glassed-in wood-burning fireplaces, wine, and fresh coffee and teas. You can soak in the romance of a fiery sunset from your private deck or soak in a whirlpool tub for two. Feel like stretching your legs? The Inn is only minutes from Mendocino shops and galleries, state parks and beaches. Tennis, golf, canoeing and other sports are easily arranged. In fact, if you're planning a wedding at the Inn, your entire event can be easily arranged. In-house coordinator Sandy Frey will help you put the whole thing together, freeing you to enjoy the visual and spiritual bounty of this gorgeous region. Book early, though—the Albion River Inn has a large and loyal following who, like the swallows of Capistrano, come back year after year.

CEREMONY CAPACITY: The Cliffside Garden holds 75 seated or 100 standing guests.

EVENT/RECEPTION CAPACITY: The restaurant can hold up to 85 seated or 100 standing guests.

FEES & DEPOSITS: For special events, a $1,000 facility fee is required: a $500 non-refundable rental deposit is needed to reserve your date; the remaining $500 rental balance is due 3 months prior to the event. Buffets start at $30/person, which includes hors d'oeuvres, salad, entree, side dishes and a selection of nonalcoholic beverages. Alcohol, tax and an 18% service charge are additional.

AVAILABILITY: Year-round, daily, 11:30am–4pm.

SERVICES/AMENITIES:

Catering: provided, no BYO
Kitchen Facilities: n/a
Tables & Chairs: provided
Linens, Silver, etc.: provided
Restrooms: wheelchair accessible
Dance Floor: carpeted area or CBA, extra charge
Bride's Dressing Area: yes
Meeting Equipment: no

Parking: ample on site
Accommodations: 20 guest rooms
Telephone: house phones
Outdoor Night Lighting: access only
Outdoor Cooking Facilities: no
Cleanup: provided
View: Pacific Ocean
Other: event coordination

RESTRICTIONS:

Alcohol: provided, no BYO ($100 set up for full bar)
Smoking: outdoors only
Music: amplified OK

Wheelchair Access: yes
Insurance: not required
Other: no rice or birdseed, adult supervision required for children under 6

---

*This is important! Tell facilities you're reading **Here Comes The Guide** and ask if our information is still current.*

Sonoma Coast Villa

Country Inn & Restaurant

16702 Coast Highway One, Bodega
(707) 876-9818, fax (707) 876-9856

www.scvilla.com, www.villaweddings.com
reservations@scvilla.com

◆ Ceremonies ◆ Special Events
◆ Wedding Receptions ◆ Meetings
◆ Business Functions ◆ Accommodations

Want to stroll over 60 acres of secluded countryside, as the warm sunshine melts away your cares? Do you dream of being the *padrone* of an estate, entertaining your friends with good food and fine wines? Well stop fantasizing! You can do all these things, and more, at the Sonoma Coast Villa, only an hour's drive from San Francisco.

The California coast has often been compared to the Mediterranean in climate and landscape, so it's not surprising to find architectural similarities as well. With its glowing terra cotta walls and tiled roof, the Sonoma Coast Villa does indeed resemble a villa in Tuscany. And, it also happens to be a wonderful place for all kinds of events.

Large weddings or receptions take place in the Courtyard, where olive trees, corkscrew willows and oleanders sustain the Mediterranean feel. Separated from the Courtyard by a grove of cypress and pine trees is the Meadow area, which lends itself to everything from a garden wedding to corporate team-building programs. An unusual setting for executive board meetings or corporate retreats is the Carriage House. The Sonoma Coast Villa was originally an Arabian horse farm, and the Carriage House occupies what used to be the stables. With its double doors, wood paneling and ceiling fans, it retains a warm country ambiance. Once your meeting is over, you can unwind at the Courtyard Spa, play pool or ping-pong, or improve your golf game on their nine-hole putting green.

The casual elegance of the Sonoma Coast Villa Restaurant is ideal for a wedding reception, family reunion or corporate dinner. More Italian influences are evident in the green-slate-tiled floor, fireplace with marble mantel, and vaulted wood-beamed ceiling. On the straw-colored walls, decorative plates are interspersed with original paintings done by the owner's mother. Pewter vases, ceramic rabbits and fresh sunflowers from the Villa's garden add a bit of rustic charm to the room. The restaurant's windows overlook the pool and terrace area, where rosemary, azaleas, begonias and century plants thrive in the warm sun. Many guests enjoy themselves so much, they decide to stay over and reserve one of the twelve deluxe guest rooms. And though ultimately it may be difficult to leave the peaceful seclusion of this coastal getaway, it's so close to home you can come back as often as you like.

CEREMONY CAPACITY:

Space	Seated	Standing	Space	Seated	Standing
Upper Terrace	75	120	Carriage House Courtyard	120	160
Meadow	200	250			

EVENT/RECEPTION CAPACITY:

Space	Seated	Standing	Space	Seated	Standing
Carriage House Courtyard	140	160	Carriage House Interior	70	80
Restaurant	40	75			

MEETING CAPACITY: The Carriage House can accommodate 50 guests seated theater-style or 40 conference-style.

FEES & DEPOSITS: For weddings and receptions, there is a $4,000 facility rental fee. A $1,000 non-refundable deposit secures your date. A second $5,000 deposit is due 30 days prior to the event; the remainder is payable the day of the event.

If the Villa is rented for a wedding reception, all guest rooms must be reserved for 2 nights; overnight room rates vary seasonally from $185 to $295. No rental fee is charged for business meetings if overnight accommodations are made. Catering prices start at $32/person for buffets or $40–70/person for seated luncheons or dinners; tax, alcohol and a 20% service charge are additional.

AVAILABILITY: Year-round, daily, 8am–11pm

SERVICES/AMENITIES:

Catering: provided, no BYO
Kitchen Facilities: n/a
Tables & Chairs: provided
Linens, Silver, etc.: provided
Restrooms: wheelchair accessible
Dance Floor: carriage house floor or patio
Bride's & Groom's Dressing Area: yes
Meeting Equipment: flip charts, easels, VCR; other equipment CBA

Parking: 75-car lot
Accommodations: 12 guest rooms
Telephone: house phone, credit card calls
Outdoor Night Lighting: yes
Outdoor Cooking Facilities: n/a
Cleanup: provided
View: Sonoma's rolling hills
Other: event coordination

RESTRICTIONS:

Alcohol: provided
Smoking: outdoors only
Music: amplified OK

Wheelchair Access: yes
Insurance: not required

The professionals in the back of the book are the best in the business! **How do we know? Read page 681.**

Compass Rose Gardens

Private Garden

Corner East Shore & Bay Flat Roads, Bodega Bay
(707) 875-2343, fax (707) 875-3552

www.compassrosegardens.com
donna@compassrosegardens.com, donna@monitor.net

◆ Ceremonies   ◆ Special Events
◆ Wedding Receptions   ◆ Meetings
◆ Business Functions   Accommodations

When we passed through the Compass Rose Gardens' humble iron gate, we felt as if we had encountered Narnia—the magical, otherworldly kingdom that C.S. Lewis wrote of in his famed children's books. Entering the gardens, you're immersed in a world of unbridled beauty. In every direction the eye is delighted—here the abundant blooms of rhododendrons, iris, camellias, over there delicate Japanese maples, cherry trees, towering redwoods. A year-round running brook unspools the length of the gardens, pausing now and again to calm itself in one of several lovely ponds. It is truly an idyllic place to hold a celebration.

Donna Cook Freeman is the exuberant owner and green thumb responsible for coaxing such beauty from what was once three acres of tangled briars, willows and blackberries. She began work on the grounds in 1986; the foliage was so thick she had to crawl in on her hands and knees to reach the interior. There she sat for hours in contemplation, dreaming her garden into existence. A ten-year labor of love ensued, during which Donna and her family hauled, excavated, pruned and thinned. They built footbridges and cottages, planted flowers and trees, eventually wrangling a magnificent garden from a tenacious coastal jungle. Then in homage to Bodega Bay's long seafaring history, she christened the gardens "Compass Rose" (a compass rose is the starlike insignia found on mariners' maps and compasses).

A variety of scenic spots are available to tie the knot, however, most couples prefer to marry on an oval lawn overlooking the property's largest pond. Guests are seated on the opposite bank (still within earshot) where they are afforded a perfect view of the bride and groom as they exchange vows underneath a venerable willow. After the ceremony, folks can lose themselves along the gardens' meandering paths before joining the feasting and festivities on the handsome, expansive wood deck at the far side of the gardens. The newlyweds may want to slip away to share a quiet moment in the meditation garden. Nestled in a ring of redwoods and planted with hydrangeas, it's just the place to collect oneself after all the hubbub. Couples are also welcome to participate in what has now become a Compass Rose tradition—the planting of a "wedding" sapling or placing a personalized bird house in a nearby tree, serve as both living memory and future promise for their journey together as husband and wife.

Although the Compass Rose is an ideal spot for outdoor weddings, it is also an excellent gathering place for any number of events—seminars, retreats, bar mitzvahs and anniversaries. For those who desire lodging nearby, plans are now underway for an eight-room inn and garden conservatory to be built just up the hill, with an opening forecast for the end of 1999.

The Compass Rose Gardens are one of Bodega Bay's best kept secrets, but given their extraordinary beauty, word is bound to get out soon. So if your heart is set on a garden party, call sooner rather than later—this is one opportunity you won't want to miss!

CEREMONY CAPACITY: The pond area holds 250 seated; the creekside 100 seated; the secret garden, 10 seated; and the deck, 140 seated guests.

EVENT/RECEPTION CAPACITY: The deck can accommodate 150 seated or standing guests; the creekside, 100; the pond area, 300. The site's maximum capacity is 300 guests.

MEETING CAPACITY: Meetings are generally outdoor workshops held on the deck. It accommodates 150 guests theater-style or 120 guests conference-style.

FEES & DEPOSITS: The weekend rental fee is $2,400 for up to 300 guests for a 6-hour event. To reserve a Saturday or Sunday date, half the rental fee is required; the balance plus a $500 refundable security deposit are payable 3 weeks prior to the event. Midweek rates are lower; call for details.

AVAILABILITY: Daily, May 1st to the end of October.

SERVICES/AMENITIES:

Catering: preferred list or BYO, licensed & insured
Kitchen Facilities: no
Tables & Chairs: BYO
Linens, Silver, etc.: BYO
Restrooms: not wheelchair accessible
Dance Floor: deck
Bride's Dressing Area: yes, small
Meeting Equipment: BYO

Parking: ample on street
Accommodations: no guest rooms
Telephone: no
Outdoor Night Lighting: limited
Outdoor Cooking Facilities: provided or BYO
Cleanup: caterer or renter
View: of garden
Other: event coordination; flowers, music CBA

RESTRICTIONS:

Alcohol: through licensed caterer
Smoking: allowed outdoors
Music: amplified OK w/volume limits

Wheelchair Access: limited
Insurance: certificate required
Other: no animals or rice

---

*This is important! Tell facilities you're reading **Here Comes The Guide** and ask if our information is still current.*

Jenner Inn & Cottages

Inn & Cottages

10400 Coast Highway 1, Jenner
(800) 732-2377, (707) 865-2377, fax (707) 865-0829

www.jennerinn.com
innkeeper@jenner-inn.com

◆ Ceremonies ◆ Special Events
◆ Wedding Receptions ◆ Meetings
◆ Business Functions ◆ Accommodations

Set just off the gorgeous Coast Highway, Jenner Inn is bordered by sandy beaches, the Russian River estuary and thousands of acres of state park. With surroundings like this, the Inn's a natural choice for a romantic honeymoon, and its owners have made it a lovely place for a wedding, too. Sheldon Murphy has been coordinating weddings for twelve years, and can handle all the details of your celebration; her husband, Richard, is a minister who performs many of the ceremonies that take place here. In addition to the collective talents of the proprietors, Jenner Inn offers numerous guest rooms, cottages and private homes with amenities like hot tubs, fireplaces and ocean views.

The Inn itself has three areas for ceremonies or receptions. The Parlor is the most intimate setting, with Galleon windows, a fireplace, antiques, fresh flowers and Victorian coastal charm. The Solarium, a lush, fully landscaped 2,000-square-foot greenhouse with spectacular views of the coast, is available for ceremonies and workshops only. For outdoor events, the Grotto is a lovely site. Bordered by spreading alder trees and the Jenner Creek, this verdant two-acre meadow is a sunny, protected spot with views of the surrounding pristine hills. You can set it up for an informal barbecue, an elegant, tented reception with stage and dance floor, or anything in between. Note that if you want to get married near the ocean, you can tie the knot on a bluff overlooking the Pacific or on any number of beaches. Each wedding is tailored to your tastes, your budget and, of course, your fantasies.

The Parlor and Solarium are also unique settings for small conferences, retreats and workshops, as are four of the Inn's cottages. But the Inn's newest event space, Mystic Landing, has been specifically designed with group gatherings in mind. The Murphys have taken the cedar log boathouse on the property and completely renovated it. Along with its three "Lincoln log" guest rooms, it has a conference room with fireplace, kitchen and three additional sleeping rooms with private baths. "The setting," Richard says, "exerts a powerful force for energizing, inspiration and healing of the spirit." So, whatever event you hold here, you'll come away feeling refreshed and renewed.

CEREMONY & EVENT/RECEPTION CAPACITY:

Area	*Seated*	*Standing*		*Area*	*Seated*	*Standing*
Parlor	30	50		Solarium	75	90
Grotto	200	200				

MEETING CAPACITY: Same as above, plus 4 cottages which each provide informal meeting space for up to 15. The Mystic Landing complex conference room will hold 20 people.

FEES & DEPOSITS: A $500 non-refundable deposit is payable when reservations are confirmed; the balance is due the day of the event. Rental fees are as follows: the Parlor fee is $400; the Solarium $300–400, the Grotto $800–1,200; ranges depend on guest count. Catering runs approximately $20–40/person; alcohol, tax and a 15% service charge are additional. The wedding coordination fee is 10% of the reception cost plus $20/hour. Overnight accommodations run $85–215 for rooms and $175–295 for private homes.

Fees for business functions vary depending on units and number of days booked, guest count and services requested. Midweek corporate rates are available October–May, holiday periods excepted.

AVAILABILITY: Year-round, daily, any time; the Grotto June through October.

SERVICES/AMENITIES:

Catering: provided

Kitchen Facilities: ample

Tables & Chairs: some provided

Linens, Silver, etc.: some provided

Restrooms: not wheelchair accessible

Dance Floor: yes

Bride's Dressing Area: in Solarium

Meeting Equipment: VCR, other CBA extra fee

Other: event coordination, inter-denominational minister

Parking: on- and off-street

Accommodations: 20 guest rooms and cottages plus several rental homes

Telephone: lobby phone

Outdoor Night Lighting: CBA for fee

Outdoor Cooking Facilities: CBA for fee

Cleanup: caterer

View: meadow, hillsides, estuary & ocean

RESTRICTIONS:

Alcohol: provided or corkage $7.50/bottle

Smoking: outdoors only

Music: amplified OK outdoors, restricted after 7pm amplified OK indoors, restricted after 11pm

Wheelchair Access: limited

Insurance: not required

The professionals in the back of the book are the best in the business! **How do we know? Read page 681.**

Shambhala Ranch

21200 Orr Springs Road, Mendocino County
(707) 937-3341, (415) 389-8787, fax (707) 937-1577

www.shambhalaranch.com
info@shambahlaranch.com

◆ Ceremonies ◆ Special Events
◆ Wedding Receptions ◆ Meetings
◆ Business Functions ◆ Accommodations

The road to Shambhala has to be one of the loveliest in Northern California. It winds through cool, shady forests and over rocky hills, covered with fields of dry grass that glow in the sun like parched honey. Sometimes, when you round the curve at the top of one of those hills, there's a breathtaking vista of distant mountains, hazy valleys and endless sky.

Shambhala is halfway between Ukiah and the coastal town of Mendocino and, thanks to the beautiful drive, we were already in a pleasantly altered state by the time we got there. "There" is a custom-built retreat and workshop center, nestled in 140 acres of rolling hills. The land was originally settled by Germans and Finns in the late 1800s, and you can still see an old wood building used for drying fruit just below the main house.

Stepping into the house only increased our sense of well being. It's constructed of redwood (milled on the property), which lends warmth to walls, beamed ceilings and trim throughout. Arched brick fireplaces and entryways manage to be both rustic and elegant at the same time. Homey, personal touches abound: an eclectic assortment of masks on the stairwell walls, collectibles in niches, colorful area rugs and comfortable furnishings placed around the gleaming hardwood floors. And of course there are windows everywhere, letting in the sunlight and views of the surrounding hills. The spacious conference room, which can be used for meetings, yoga, indoor receptions or dancing, has its own sound system, and opens onto a large deck and lawn. Upstairs bedrooms are light and airy, and two of them share a deck with a view of the forested hills, and the glimmering pond. If you like, music of your choice can be played throughout the house and decks. And, as wonderful as all this looks during the day, nighttime at Shambhala is just as breathtaking: the house and grounds are subtly lit, and the clear sky may as well be a swath of black velvet, embedded with stars and the bright streaks of wayward meteors.

The grounds reveal more delightful surprises. There's a spring-fed pond that's excellent for swimming, and a private beach along a clear stream with its own little waterfall and rock formations. Nearby orchards supply a variety of fruits, while vegetables and herbs are grown in a backyard garden area (which also happens to have patio tables and market umbrellas—in case you want to have a casual brunch or small reception). Numerous hiking paths lead you through a redwood forest, and to upper elevations with fantastic views. There's a large, grassy knoll where Indians once lived (a great place for meditation), and a multi-purpose meadow for rituals, camping and outdoor parties. Your ever-thoughtful hosts have also provided a pondside hot tub with a massage table under the trees, for the ultimate relaxing experience.

Weddings, retreats, family reunions and private parties all find a serene and spiritually uplifting home here. Although the ranch is quite civilized, civilization as we generally know it intrudes very little—you won't even see any electrical or telephone lines, as the center is solar powered. The quiet beauty of the landscape has a healing effect, which is only fitting for a place called "Shambhala." The name comes from a legendary Himalayan kingdom, where an enlightened society lived by a set Tibetan Buddhist teachings. One of them is that there is some magic in everything, waiting for each individual to discover it. Shambhala Ranch's magic lies not so much in its obvious natural gifts, but in the way it can help you find your own.

CEREMONY CAPACITY: In cooler months, Shambhala can hold 30–60 seated indoors. In warmer months, an additional 80 can be seated on the adjoining deck and lawn. Outdoors, there are several meadows that can hold 150 seated guests, each.

EVENT/RECEPTION CAPACITY: The outdoor meadows, decks and gardens can accommodate up to 150 guests, each. Indoors, the retreat holds 30–60 seated guests.

MEETING CAPACITY: The Conference Room holds 30–60 seated guests, based on the seating configuration. Future expansion may include a larger conference room.

FEES & DEPOSITS: To reserve your date, a deposit is required; call for details. The per night rate for any special event or retreat ranges from $30–90/person with an $800/night minimum. A separate day use charge for weddings and receptions starts at $750/day, depending on the season, guest count and day of the week. Rates for longer stays are negotiable. Exclusive use includes: use of the ranch house, the surrounding 140 acres and spring-fed pond, hot tub, music system throughout the house and decks, and a fully equipped kitchen.

AVAILABILITY: Year-round, daily, any time, including holidays.

SERVICES/AMENITIES:
Catering: CBA or BYO w/approval
Kitchen Facilities: fully equipped, commercial
Tables & Chairs: provided for up to 50 guests
Linens, Silver, etc.: provided for up to 50 guests, more CBA through caterer or BYO
Restrooms: limited wheelchair accessibility
Dance Floor: in Conference Rm & adjoining deck
Bride's & Groom's Dressing Area: yes
Meeting Equipment: VCR, TV, sound system, multimedia system, satellite system

Parking: large lots
Accommodations: 6 guest rooms or 30 guests; future expansion may include more guest rooms
Telephone: credit card use only
Outdoor Night Lighting: yes
Outdoor Cooking Facilities: BBQ
Cleanup: renter or caterer
View: spring-fed pond, meadows, redwood forest, orchards, rolling hills and valley
Other: special breakfasts on request; flowers and photography CBA, extra fee

RESTRICTIONS:
Alcohol: BYO, licensed server required
Smoking: outside designated areas only
Music: amplified OK w/restrictions

Wheelchair Access: limited
Insurance: extra liability/certificate required
Other: no open flames, campfire with permission; children require adult supervision; decorations need approval; no pets; no rice or confetti; candles for ceremonies only

The Sea Ranch Lodge

Restaurant & Lodge

60 Seawalk Drive, The Sea Ranch
(800) 732-7262, (707) 785-2371, fax (707) 785-2917

www.searanchlodge.com
info@searanchlodge.com

◆ Ceremonies   ◆ Special Events
◆ Wedding Receptions ◆ Meetings
◆ Business Functions ◆ Accommodations

In the early morning, a light mist veils the coast. Weathered redwood buildings float into view, hugged by deep green stands of cypress tress. Far below, the sea crashes against the rocks, and the rugged, serpentine coastline fades away into the fog. You blink, half expecting that when you open your eyes it will all disappear. But it doesn't. And you begin to understand why so many people consider The Sea Ranch a magical place.

Perched high on a bluff, The Sea Ranch Lodge is part of a small community of individualists who cherish the soothing solitude of this North Coast haven. And for those who don't have the luxury of living here permanently, the Lodge provides a temporary getaway. It's also a coveted site for a wedding.

Getting married here is an exhilarating experience. Outdoor ceremonies often take place on a point overlooking the sculpted cliffs and frothy shoreline that extends for miles in both directions. The short path down from the lodge that brings you here cuts through a meadow of golden grass, bordered by wildflowers in purple, yellow and white. As you walk towards the point, you can hear the surf pounding so close by, and smell the ocean's scent on the air. For a spiritual touch as you say your vows, have a bagpiper or flutist play a haunting melody.

From the point looking back towards the lodge, you see a wonderful old barn, set on the bluff's edge to your left. Its weatherworn charm makes it an unusual site for a reception. Narrow beams of sunlight filter through the cracks between ceiling and wall planks, suffusing the interior with a lambent glow. The floor is covered with straw, and the rafters can be draped with beautiful fabric or entwined with flowers to create a festive ambiance. After sunset, hundreds of small globe lights strung across the rustic beams heighten the romance.

If you'd rather have your celebration indoors, the Lodge has three interconnecting rooms, all with redwood walls and ocean views. The Fireside Room is a cozy space for a small reception, rehearsal dinner or dancing. A large river rock fireplace dominates one wall, while art done by local artists covers the others. A huge picture window and a skylight let in natural light. Larger receptions are held in the Dining Room, whose facade of windows overlooks the bluff and sea. The adjacent Solarium is an intimate atrium used for cocktails, hors d'oeuvres and mingling. Completely enclosed by glass, this bright space affords a floor-to-ceiling view of the meadows, ocean and sky.

The beauty of The Sea Ranch, aside from its abundant natural gifts, is that you and your guests can stay here long enough to really relax and enjoy it. Guest rooms are uncluttered and comfortable; all but one have ocean views, most have fireplaces, and only a couple have televisions. Diversions include exploring the beaches, hiking and biking along miles of trails, kayaking and playing golf on The Sea Ranch's own course. The Dining Room serves all meals and, of course, the staff here is as accommodating as you could wish. Not getting married? Don't let that stop you from coming to The Sea Ranch. The setting is just as uplifting for a romantic weekend, corporate retreat, or family reunion. Let's face it, when the earth was created, some places ended up much more enchanting than others. This is one of them.

CEREMONY CAPACITY: Outdoors, the bluff top can accommodate 150 seated or standing. Indoors, the barn holds 150 seated or standing, the Fireside Room 50 seated, and the Solarium 14 seated guests. A nearby church holds 150–200 seated and the Sea Ranch Chapel, 20 seated guests.

EVENT/RECEPTION CAPACITY: The barn holds 150 seated or standing, the Fireside 25–40 seated and the restaurant 75 seated guests.

MEETING CAPACITY: The Fireside Room holds 40 seated theater-style, 26 seated conference or classroom-style. The barn is available for casual business functions, up to 150 people.

FEES & DEPOSITS: A $200–500 non-refundable deposit, depending on the type of event and space rented, is required to secure your date; the final balance is payable upon departure. Catering is provided: luncheons start at $15/person, dinners at $30/person; tax, a 20% service charge and alcohol are additional. Rental fees are as follows: the barn runs $1,500, the Fireside Room $200, and the Solarium $150. Exclusive use of the restaurant is an additional $150 charge. You can book the Lodge for an entire weekend, with rates running $140-205/night, double occupancy.

AVAILABILITY: Year-round, daily, any time.

SERVICES/AMENITIES:
Catering: provided, no BYO
Kitchen Facilities: n/a
Tables & Chairs: provided, extra fee
Linens, Silver, etc.: provided, linens extra fee
Restrooms: not wheelchair accessible
Dance Floor: CBA extra fee
Bride's & Groom's Dressing Area: CBA
Meeting Equipment: easels, projectors
Other: wedding cakes, event coordination, recreational activity planning

Parking: large lots
Accommodations: 20 guest rooms
Telephone: pay & guest phones
Outdoor Night Lighting: access only
Outdoor Cooking Facilities: no
Cleanup: provided
View: Pacific Ocean, coastline, meadows, cypress trees

RESTRICTIONS:
Alcohol: provided, no BYO
Smoking: outdoors only
Music: amplified OK
Other: no pets; no rice, confetti or glitter

Wheelchair Access: restaurant only, other areas limited access
Insurance: not required

peninsula

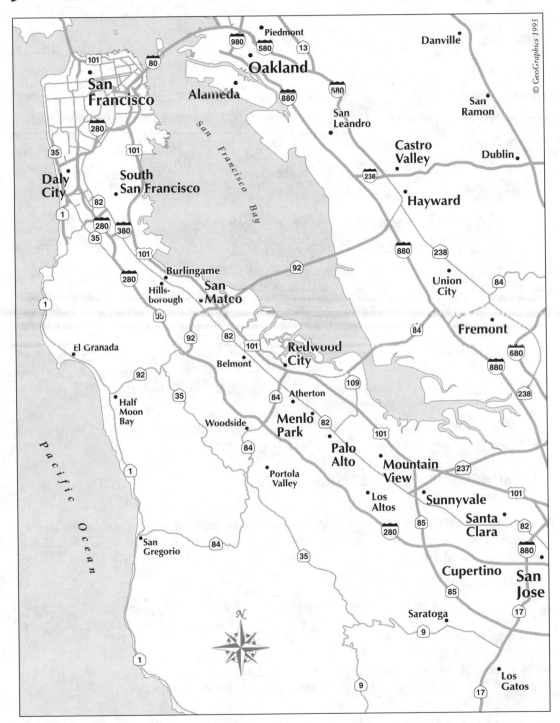

Holbrook Palmer Park

Historic Park

150 Watkins Avenue, Atherton
(650) 688-6534, fax (650) 688-6548

◆ Ceremonies   ◆ Special Events
◆ Wedding Receptions   ◆ Meetings
◆ Business Functions   Accommodations

Holbrook Palmer Park is what's left of an old estate, complete with historic buildings, mature oak trees and an 1870 water tower. Located on Watkins Avenue between El Camino and Middlefield Road, the park occupies twenty-two acres of open space in exclusive, residential Atherton.

The Main House rests in the center of the property and has wide, gracious steps that lead from the main reception room down to a spacious patio framed by large trees. The patio is perfect for an outdoor ceremony and has a lovely wedding arbor.

Nearby is the Jennings Pavilion, a modern structure which can accommodate large events and bands. Outside the Pavilion is another patio which is appropriate for outdoor seated functions. Additionally, the 1896 Carriage House is available for special parties and can be rented in conjunction with a large meadow area.

Although you might think that a facility in prestigious Atherton would require formality, just the opposite is true: the feeling here is relaxed and informal.

CEREMONY CAPACITY: The Main House holds 60 seated or 100 standing; the Main House Patio, 200 seated guests.

EVENT/RECEPTION CAPACITY: The Main House, with outdoor seating, can accommodate 100 guests; the Jennings Pavilion holds 200 guests including outside seating; the Carriage House seats 80 guests.

MEETING CAPACITY:

Area	Conf-style	Theater-style	Area	Conf-style	Theater-style
Pavilion	100	200	Main House	30	60
Carriage House	50	80			

FEES & DEPOSITS: For weddings, a $500 refundable security/damage deposit is required when reservations are made. Residents of Atherton pay a discounted rental fee.

Wedding Guests	Resident Fee	Non-Resident Fee
1–100	$1,800	$2,000
101–200	2,300	2,500

The use fee is required 1 month before the event. Fees are based on a 7-hour use period; 1–2 hours for setup, 4–5 hours for the event, 1 hour for cleanup. For events exceeding 7 hours, a charge of $100/hour will apply. Additional hours must be arranged in advance.

For meetings and business functions, the rates are as follows:

Area	No. Guests	Half Day	Full Day	Evenings
Main House	up to 75	$200	$300	+$25/hr.
Carriage House	up to 80	200	250	+$25/hr.
Jennings Pavilion	up to 100	300	400	+$25/hr.
	101–200	400	500	+$50/hr.

AVAILABILITY: Saturday weddings or special events, 10am–5pm or 5pm–midnight, including setup and cleanup. Sundays (only one event/day), 10am–9pm; cleanup must be completed by 10pm. Friday weddings and social events, 5pm–midnight, including cleanup.

Business functions, year-round, daily. Half-day events, 8am–noon or 1pm–5pm; full-day events 8am–5pm; evening events, 5pm–10pm. Additional hours can be arranged.

SERVICES/AMENITIES:

Catering: BYO or provided
Kitchen Facilities: yes
Tables & Chairs: provided
Linens, Silver, etc.: BYO
Restrooms: wheelchair access in Pavilion only
Dance Floor: CBA
Bride's & Groom's Dressing Areas: yes
Meeting Equipment: CBA

Parking: several lots
Accommodations: no guest rooms
Telephone: pay phones
Outdoor Night Lighting: yes
Outdoor Cooking Facilities: BYO
Cleanup: caterer
View: 22-acre landscaped park

RESTRICTIONS:

Alcohol: BYO
Smoking: outside only
Music: amplified OK inside only

Wheelchair Access: yes
Insurance: CBA or BYO

---

*This is important! Tell facilities you're reading **Here Comes The Guide** and ask if our information is still current.*

Sacred Heart Atherton

Address withheld to ensure privacy. Atherton
(650) 473-4087, fax (650) 322-7578

www.shschools.org
dmaclain@shschools.org

Historic, Private School & Grounds

◆ Ceremonies   ◆ Special Events
◆ Wedding Receptions   ◆ Meetings
◆ Business Functions   Accommodations

There are as many perceptions of beauty as there are eyes to perceive it, but we're sure most people will agree that the grounds and rooms of Sacred Heart School—63 acres in all, including gardens, playing fields, and buildings in styles from Romanesque to contemporary—are beautiful places to hold a wedding or corporate event. From the dramatic approach along the palm-lined drive to the intricate, painstakingly hand-stenciled doors and windows of the Main Building, elegance and fine detail abound.

Start with the Main Building, the recently restored south wing of the 1915 convent-school dormitory, and the building where most special events take place. This long, redbrick edifice, crowned by a bell-tower cupola, stretches symmetrically west and east of a columned porte-cochere facing landscaped gardens and lawns. It houses a two-story library with a book-filled wrought-iron balcony circling its perimeter; two elegant, high-ceilinged parlors decorated with Flemish tapestries and soft, pale drapes; a large, sunny conference room; and a multitude of second-floor schoolrooms ideal for small break-out meetings. Behind the building is one of its most impressive features—Palm Court, an enormous courtyard bordered by (not surprisingly) soaring palm trees; behind Palm Court is the Theatre, a charming older building with bleacher-style seating for 300 people.

The first floor of the Main Building can be rented in its entirety, or each room can be reserved separately. The conference room is just right for a small cocktail party, a business meeting, or as a generous changing room for a bride or groom. The two parlors on either side of the handsome central entry hall (no narrow corridor, but a beautiful, wood-detailed room itself) might be used in combination: cocktails in one, dinner in the other, back to the first for dessert and dancing on the polished hardwood floor. The library is in some ways the most interesting room: candlelight renders the dark-paneled space mysterious and romantic, while the balcony lends itself to luxuriant bridal draping. (The shady Redwood Grove, only a few short steps across the lawn from the library, is an ideal spot for an outdoor ceremony before dinner amongst the books; or, if your party is too large for the Grove, consider using the whole front lawn!) Palm Court looks lovely dressed with white tables and umbrellas for a large garden-style wedding, but it is equally well suited to grand tents, theatrical lighting, and guests in black tie.

Of course, the Main Building is only part of what Sacred Heart has to offer. Large corporate groups might conclude a day of intense meetings with a team-building softball game and relaxed cookout dinner on Keil Court. The gym is available for events from seated dinners to basketball playoffs. If you'd like to have a place to toss your bouquet, the McCanney Student Union's balcony is the perfect spot.

With such an enormous range of spaces, Sacred Heart can accommodate virtually any size or type of event—and can do it with grace and charm.

CEREMONY CAPACITY: Outdoors, Palm Court holds 450 seated or Keil Court 200 seated; there are a variety of other outdoor spaces to choose from. Indoors, the Piano Parlor holds 60 seated, the Board Parlor 40 seated and the Library 100 seated.

EVENT/RECEPTION CAPACITY: The Library holds 100 seated, the Piano Parlor holds 60 seated, and the Board Parlor 40 seated. Outdoors, the Palm Court holds 450 seated, Keil Court holds up to 200 seated or standing and the Pavilion, 300–400 seated or 750–900 standing guests.

MEETING CAPACITY: There are a variety of indoor spaces which can accommodate 5–90 seated depending on the seating configurations. There are 2 indoor theaters, which can hold 300 seated, each. Theater-style, the Gymnasium holds 500 seated or the Pavilion 900 seated.

FEES & DEPOSITS: For special events, the rental fee is $3,000 or more depending on guest count and spaces reserved. For business-related or smaller events, the rental fees range $200–400/hour depending on the rooms selected. Classrooms run less per hour.

To secure your date, 20% of the rental fee is required; the balance is payable 30 days prior to the event. A refundable $500 security/damage/cleaning deposit is due when the contract is submitted. With over 100 guests, additional security is required; call for current rates.

AVAILABILITY: Year-round, weekends, 8am–10pm or weekdays during holidays and summer months, 8am–10pm.

SERVICES/AMENITIES:

Catering: select from preferred list
Kitchen Facilities: 3 catering & 1 service kitchen
Tables & Chairs: BYO
Linens, Silver, etc.: BYO
Restrooms: wheelchair access
Dance Floor: in Parlors or BYO portables
Bride's & Groom's Dressing Areas: CBA
Meeting Equipment: BYO

Parking: several lots
Accommodations: no guest rooms
Telephone: pay phones
Outdoor Night Lighting: limited, extra CBA
Outdoor Cooking Facilities: through caterer
Cleanup: caterer
View: 63 landscaped acres, gardens
Other: grand piano & smaller pianos

RESTRICTIONS:

Alcohol: BYO or caterer, licensed server
Smoking: outside only
Music: amplified OK w/volume limits, curfew 10pm

Wheelchair Access: yes
Insurance: extra liability required
Other: no seeds, petals, rice, confetti, open flames or bubbles

Ralston Hall
at College of Notre Dame

Historic Mansion

1500 Ralston Avenue, Belmont
(650) 508-3501, fax (650) 508-3774

◆ Ceremonies	◆ Special Events
◆ Wedding Receptions	◆ Meetings
◆ Business Functions	Accommodations

This registered, national historic landmark is a stunning Victorian mansion, completed in 1867 by William Chap-man Ralston, founder of the Bank of California. Ralston purchased the land in 1864, and modified the original Italian villa with touches of Steamboat Gothic and Victorian details to create a lavish and opulent estate. The delicately etched-glass panes of the front doors, and windows dressed in striped awnings give you an indication of what you'll see inside.

The interior reflects the charm of a bygone era. The first floor consists of a large ballroom, several parlors, dining rooms and a sun porch. Each room is decorated with beautiful antiques, stunning crystal chandeliers and colorful Oriental rugs. The ballroom is particularly appealing. Its patterned hardwood floor is encircled by mirrored walls, and three delicate chandeliers hang gracefully from the huge skylight. At the far end of the room is a large bay window with a curving green moiré bench seat and regal, matching draperies. Musicians can set up in an alcove without interfering with the grandeur and flow of the ballroom floor. The spacious dining rooms were decorated with an attention to detail that is mindboggling by today's standards. Because of Ralston Hall's size and layout, you can choose from a variety of setups that include the entire first floor, the West or East wings, or the expansive lawn in front of the building. This facility is one of the Peninsula's few mansion locations and makes a terrific venue for a sophisticated and memorable wedding.

CEREMONY CAPACITY: The Ralston lawn holds 210 seated or standing; the Ballroom 210 seated or standing.

EVENT/RECEPTION CAPACITY: The facility can accommodate 210 seated guests or 300 standing guests. The East Wing, 210 seated guests (with dancing) and the West Wing, 100 guests with partial seating (without dancing).

MEETING CAPACITY:

Room	Seated	Room	Seated
Ballroom	150	Cipriani Parlor	40
Ballroom Annex	50	Sun Parlor	13
Ralston Parlor	40	Formal Dining Room	50

FEES & DEPOSITS: For weddings and large special events, a $500 refundable security deposit is required when you make reservations. For an 8-hour event, the rental fee ranges from $2,250 to $4,200 and is payable 6 months prior to the function. Fees include a security person and 2 hours for setup and 1 hour for cleanup. The security deposit is usually returned if the property is left in good condition.

For meetings and other special events, fees vary depending on day of week, time frame and guest count. Call for more information.

AVAILABILITY: Year-round, daily, 9am–1am, except Thanksgiving Day and December 24–25th.

SERVICES/AMENITIES:

Catering: BYO from approved list
Kitchen Facilities: moderate
Tables & Chairs: CBA
Linens, Silver, etc.: BYO
Restrooms: wheelchair accessible
Dance Floor: yes except for West Wing
Bride's Dressing Area: CBA
Meeting Equipment: BYO

Parking: ample
Accommodations: no guest rooms
Telephone: local calls only
Outdoor Night Lighting: no
Outdoor Cooking Facilities: BBQ
Cleanup: caterer
View: of lawn w/fountain
Other: security available

RESTRICTIONS:

Alcohol: BYO
Smoking: not permitted
Music: amplified OK

Wheelchair Access: yes
Insurance: extra liability required
Other: candles not permitted

The professionals in the back of the book are the best in the business! How do we know? Read page 681.

Kohl Mansion, "The Oaks"

2750 Adeline Drive, Burlingame
(650) 992-4668, fax (650) 342-1704

thekohl@ibm.net

Historic Mansion & Grounds

◆ Ceremonies   ◆ Special Events
◆ Wedding Receptions   ◆ Meetings
◆ Business Functions   Accommodations

Commissioned by Frederick Kohl and his wife in 1912, the Kohl Mansion was built on 40 acres of oak woodlands in Burlingame. Kohl, heir to a shipping fortune, loved to entertain and created this grand estate to include a manor house, pool, rose garden, tennis courts, greenhouses, and a large carriage house. Now, decades later, the elegant rosebrick Tudor mansion is again available for parties and has many inviting rooms for special events, business functions and picnics.

The wood-paneled Library features a large granite fireplace, bookcases and graceful French doors that open to a center courtyard. The room's Gothic bay window catches the light filtered through the oaks on the lawns just beyond. The sizable Great Hall, a copy of the Arlington Tudor Hall in Essex, England, was built for music and entertaining. Its very high ceiling, oak paneling and walnut floor create a fine acoustical setting for music. A lighter twin of the Library, the spacious and airy Dining Room, has delicate, pristine-white plaster relief on the walls and ceiling. This marvelous dining environment shares the Library's view of the oak-studded lawns through its own bay windows.

The Morning Room, with white lattice walls and black-and-white marble floors, adds a touch of formality to the East Wing. It overlooks the English Rose Garden and surrounding manicured grounds, where guests can stroll over the lawns or sample hors d'oeuvres on the large terrace. The Kohl Mansion is, indeed, a fabulous facility for anyone planning a stylish event.

CEREMONY CAPACITY:

Area	Seated	Standing	Area	Seated	Standing
Great Hall	200	400	Morning Room	25	50
Lawn	500	1,000	Patio	250	500
Library	100	200	Dining Room	100	200

EVENT/RECEPTION CAPACITY: Indoors, the Mansion can hold 300 seated or 600 standing guests. The indoor facilities plus outdoor tents can hold 500 seated or up to 1,000 standing guests.

MEETING ROOM CAPACITY:

Area	Theater-style		Area	Theater-style
Great Hall	225–250		Morning Room	50–65
Dining Room	125–150		Board Room	12–30

FEES & DEPOSITS: Rental fees are shown below; each event has an 8-hour minimum.

	January–November					December	
# of Guests	Saturdays	Sun & Holidays	Mon–Thurs	Fridays		Fri–Sat	Sun–Thurs
1–100	—	—	$2,400	$2,800		—	$4,000
101–200	$5,500	$4,500	3,200	3,600		$7,500	4,500
201–300	6,500	5,500	4,000	4,400		8,500	5,000
301–400	7,500	6,500	4,800	5,200		9,500	5,500

A $500 security deposit and half the rental fee are due when you reserve your date; the balance is due 60 days prior to the event. There is also a $250 setup charge, and a $100 fee for use of the baby grand piano. Valet parking is required for more than 200 guests.

AVAILABILITY: From September–June, parties and special events can be held after 3pm on weekdays and anytime on Saturday and Sunday. June through mid-August, every day, any time. Meetings can be held year-round, time frames subject to availability.

SERVICES/AMENITIES:

Catering: BYO, select from list
Kitchen Facilities: ample
Tables & Chairs: provided
Linens, Silver, etc.: BYO
Restrooms: wheelchair accessible
Dance Floor: yes
Brides & Groom's Dressing Areas: yes
Other: baby grand piano; swimming pool; tennis, basketball & volleyball courts

Parking: large lots
Accommodations: no guest rooms
Telephone: phone CBA
Outdoor Night Lighting: yes
Outdoor Cooking Facilities: BYO
Cleanup: caterer
Meeting Equipment: podium
View: San Francisco Bay and coastal hills

RESTRICTIONS:

Alcohol: BYO, bartender required
Smoking: outside only
Music: amplified OK inside until 11pm

Wheelchair Access: yes
Insurance: certificate required

---

*This is important! Tell facilities you're reading **Here Comes The Guide** and ask if our information is still current.*

Mill Rose Inn

615 Mill Street, Half Moon Bay (Tours by appt. only.)
(800) 900-ROSE, (650) 726-8750, fax (650) 726-3031

www.millroseinn.com
tb@millroseinn.com

Bed & Breakfast Inn

◆ Ceremonies   ◆ Special Events
◆ Wedding Receptions   ◆ Meetings
◆ Business Functions   ◆ Accommodations

When people drive past the Mill Rose Inn, they often come to a dead stop in front of it, overwhelmed by the beauty of the gardens they see before them. The flowers are so big, it's hard to believe they're real, and the gorgeous colors rival those in a painting by Monet. The Mill Rose Inn is the creation of owners Eve and Terry Baldwin, who clearly have a passion for flowers, not to mention degrees in horticulture. They've tended their gardens for twenty years, replanting monthly to make sure there's a year-round show, and the result is floral displays magnificent enough to appear in *Sunset Magazine* and many commercials.

With visual splendor like this, it's no wonder the Inn has been voted the best place to get married in Half Moon Bay. But you'll find that this romantic English country garden setting has far more to offer than flowers. A Four Diamond Award winner, its decor and service are equally noteworthy. The interior atmosphere is one of classic European elegance. The parlor is warm and welcoming, with rich colors and appointments that reflect attention to detail. The library, a small jewel of a room, features a beautifully painted fireplace, and a window alcove overlooking the colorful gardens. In the dining room, two walls of French doors open onto both gardens, allowing a comfortable flow outdoors.

Intimate weddings and receptions are held in the private flagstone courtyard, shaded by a large, handsome maple tree and a framed by a profusion of sensational floral displays. A rose-covered gazebo, arched arbor and cascading fountains add to the garden tapestry by day, and the space sparkles at night with thousands of tiny lights.

If you're planning an overnight stay (and of course you'll want to), the honeymoon suites have private entrances, and are filled with fine antiques, luxurious feather beds, and extravagant floral arrangements. You'll also find a hand-painted fireplace and double whirlpool tub in each one.

Even though the setting may make you feel as though you'd traveled abroad, the Mill Rose Inn is only 30 minutes south of San Francisco. While you're here, pay a visit to the shops, art galleries and restaurants of Half Moon Bay's historic business district, and enjoy the area's recreational activities, including horseback riding on the beach, hiking in redwood forests, wine tasting or a game of golf at one of the local golf courses overlooking the Pacific.

And if all this weren't enchanting enough, the Baldwins have put together an affordable wedding package that takes care of all your planning needs under one roof. It includes a honeymoon suite and guest rooms, catering, flowers and more. Eve will handle all the details, so that you can completely relax. She'll also assist with other local accommodations and activities for your out-of-town guests. Whether you're coming to the Inn for a wedding, retreat or conference, you'll appreciate the fact that only one event per day is allowed, so that the staff can provide plenty of personal attention and give you the first-rate experience you deserve.

CEREMONY CAPACITY: Outdoors, the garden holds up to 140 guests, indoors up to 60.

EVENT/RECEPTION CAPACITY: The Inn can accommodate 140 guests, which includes both gardens and interconnecting banquet room.

MEETING CAPACITY: The conference room holds 30 seated guests.

FEES & DEPOSITS: A $3,900 non-refundable deposit and a $500 refundable security deposit are required to reserve your date. Wedding packages using in-house catering are available. The $1,500 midweek package for 10–20 guests includes a minister, flowers, photography and honeymoon suite. A larger weekend package for 30–40 guests is available. Weddings and receptions for up to 100 guests start at $6,900, and can include rehearsal, cake, bar, music, corkage, floral arrangements, 3 overnight guest rooms and full event coordination. The food and beverage balance, sales tax and gratuity are payable 1 month prior to your event.

For business functions, memorial services and other special events call for quotes.

AVAILABILITY: Year-round, daily. Call for times.

SERVICES/AMENITIES:
Catering: provided or select from preferred list
Kitchen Facilities: ample
Tables & Chairs: provided
Linens, Silver, etc.: provided
Restrooms: not wheelchair accessible
Dance Floor: garden patio
Bride's Dressing Area: yes
Meeting Equipment: fax, VCR, flipcharts, screen, TV, white board

Parking: free off street
Accommodations: 6 guest rooms
Telephone: house & guest phones
Outdoor Night Lighting: yes
Outdoor Cooking Facilities: BBQs
Cleanup: provided
View: of gardens
Other: event coordination, floral arrangements, piano, sound system, children's playroom, outdoor heaters, tent

RESTRICTIONS:
Alcohol: provided or BYO
Smoking: outside only
Music: amplified OK

Wheelchair Access: limited
Insurance: certificate required
Other: no birdseed, rice or confetti

The Crocker Mansion

6565 Skyline Boulevard, Hillsborough
(650) 348-2272 ext. 301, fax (650) 344-9302

Historic Mansion & Grounds

◆ Ceremonies ◆ Special Events
◆ Wedding Receptions ◆ Meetings
◆ Business Functions Accommodations

The Crocker Mansion, a palatial estate designed by Arthur Brown, the architect of San Francisco's Opera House and City Hall, was built for W.W. Crocker in the 1930s. The large white facade and arches create an atmosphere of permanence and stability. Guests are ushered into the Mansion through impressive wood double doors, into a round foyer where a second set of double doors leads into the Ballroom. The Ballroom, complete with high arched glass doors, a grand piano and a fireplace with mantel, has an old-world sophistication—yet it's still a light and airy space. The room has a wide stone balcony with sensational views of the adjacent property, which is generously landscaped with orange and olive trees.

The building is bordered by impeccably kept gardens and a serene woodland extending 35 acres along Hillsborough's Skyline Ridge. Areas that are especially well-suited for outdoor weddings include the wide lawns, joined by a winding fieldstone stairway, and a cloistered courtyard. Both are graced with manicured hedges and bright flowers. This Italian Renaissance-style mansion, now a private school for children, is a beautiful and versatile event setting for large or small celebrations.

CEREMONY CAPACITY: Outdoors, the lawns can hold 275 seated; indoors, the Ballroom can accommodate 200 seated guests.

EVENT/RECEPTION CAPACITY: When the lawns are accessible (April 1–October 31), the Mansion can accommodate 275 guests outdoors. The Ballroom holds up to 120 seated, or combined with the courtyard, 200 seated guests.

DONATION: A $500 deposit is required to hold your date. The minimum donation is $3,000 and includes use of the Mansion for one 8-hour event. The donation, which is partially tax deductible, is paid in full usually 5–6 months prior to the event.

AVAILABILITY: Year-round, weekends only: Saturdays, 9am–10pm, Sundays 9am–8pm. Events take place in 8-hour blocks.

SERVICES/AMENITIES:

Catering: select from preferred list

Kitchen Facilities: moderate

Tables & Chairs: provided for 150 guests

Linens, Silver, etc.: through caterer

Restrooms: not wheelchair accessible

Dance Floor: in Ballroom

Bride's Dressing Area: yes

Meeting Equipment: n/a

Other: grand piano

Parking: large lots

Accommodations: no guest rooms

Telephone: pay phone

Outdoor Night Lighting: limited

Outdoor Cooking Facilities: CBA

Cleanup: caterer

View: long-distance views of SF Bay; Peninsula coastal hills

RESTRICTIONS:

Alcohol: BYO, licensed server

Smoking: outside only

Music: amplified OK inside, acoustic outside

Wheelchair Access: limited

Insurance: certificate required

Other: no seeds, rice, confetti or rose petals

The professionals in the back of the book are the best in the business! How do we know? Read page 681.

Fremont Hills Country Club

Private Country Club

12889 Viscaino Place, Los Altos Hills
(650) 948-1763, (650) 948-8261,
fax (650) 948-3271

www.fremonthills.com
office@fremonthills.com

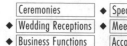

Ceremonies	◆ Special Events
◆ Wedding Receptions	◆ Meetings
◆ Business Functions	Accommodations

Fremont Hills Country Club is a handsome, relaxed, private facility which opens the doors of its airy clubhouse to both members and non-members for evening events. The spacious second-floor event room, combined with the country setting, immaculate grounds, and ample parking, make Fremont Hills a popular choice for all sorts of parties: weddings, anniversaries, bar mitzvahs, corporate fundraisers, and award ceremonies. Business clients may also use the club's small conference room (just off the main room) for small meetings; otherwise, the conference space is used as a changing area for a bride or a convenient spot for band.

Nestled in a valley of the Los Altos Hills, the club is ringed by slopes covered in pine and oak. In the flat of the valley lies its gigantic Olympic-plus-size swimming pool, a great stretch of turquoise framed by white cabanas and verdant lawns. Just up the rise above the pool is the clubhouse, a broad grey two-story building with white decks on all sides. Guests approach the clubhouse along a walk lined with vibrant gold and purple flowers, and enter a small marble-tiled foyer; from there, elevators take them to the second floor.

Upstairs, as you exit the elevator, a sky-lit atrium opens into the midpoint of the main event space, which stretches in both directions along the length of the clubhouse and curves back towards the hill at either end. The walls and soaring, angled ceiling of the room are painted a warm white which, together with the tan-and-beige carpet create a soft, neutral backdrop; complementary furnishings include natural wood chairs with white seats, and round tables of various sizes to suit your needs. French doors and many large picture windows open the room to wonderful views of the pool and surrounding hills; pots of tall bamboo and rubber plants bring greenery directly into the space. One has a sense of being in a vast, open tree house.

The right end of this long space is actually the Members' Lounge, which can be closed off from the rest of the room by sliding doors, creating an ideal pre-reception area. Cocktails can be served from the marble-topped, blond wood bar; green leather chairs and glass-topped cocktail tables are scattered around the area. At the far end of the room, between large plate glass windows, are an immense fireplace and a cozy gathering of soft, oversized tan-and-cream sofa and chairs.

Everyone at your event will appreciate the attributes of Fremont Hills. While guests are enjoying the main room's soaring second-floor views, caterers can pull their trucks up directly to the back of the building, on level with the second floor, and drop off food and other supplies at the fully equipped professional kitchen. It's just one more way in which Fremont Hills has created a successful event space, and provided the vital ingredients for a successful party.

CEREMONY CAPACITY: Ceremonies don't take place at this venue.

EVENT/RECEPTION CAPACITY: The Main Dining Room (which is connected to the Member's Lounge) holds 200 seated or standing with a dance floor.

MEETING CAPACITY: A small conference room holds 14 seated guests; the Main Dining Room, 200 seated conference-style or theater-style.

FEES & DEPOSITS: A $1,000 rental deposit is required to hold your date; the rental balance and a $600 cleaning/damage deposit are due 60 days prior to the event. Any remaining balance is payable at the event's conclusion. The Club rental fee is $2,300 January–November, or $2,500 in December. All beverages are provided by the Club; costs will vary depending on what beverages are selected. Bar service, hosted or not hosted bar setup and gratuities are extra.

AVAILABILITY: Year-round, daily, except major holidays, 5pm–midnight. Other time frames can be arranged; call for more information.

SERVICES/AMENITIES:

Catering: select from preferred list, or BYO licensed caterer
Kitchen Facilities: fully equipped, commercial
Tables & Chairs: provided
Linens, Silver, etc.: through caterer
Restrooms: wheelchair accessible
Dance Floor: CBA, extra charge
Bride's & Groom's Dressing Area: yes
Meeting Equipment: overhead projector, screen, microphone, slide projector, flip charts

Parking: large lots
Accommodations: no guest rooms
Telephone: pay or bar phone w/approval
Outdoor Night Lighting: access only
Outdoor Cooking Facilities: through caterer
Cleanup: caterer
View: Peninsula coastal hills and landscaped grounds

RESTRICTIONS:

Alcohol: provided, no BYO
Smoking: outside only
Music: amplified OK inside only until 11:30pm

Wheelchair Access: yes
Insurance: not required

---

*This is important! Tell facilities you're reading **Here Comes The Guide** and ask if our information is still current.*

Allied Arts Guild Restaurant

75 Arbor Road at Cambridge, Menlo Park
(650) 324-2588

www.alliedartsguild.org

Restaurant

◆ Ceremonies	◆ Special Events
◆ Wedding Receptions	◆ Meetings
◆ Business Functions	Accommodations

The Allied Arts Guild complex is tucked away in a quiet, residential neighborhood not far from the Stanford University campus. Built in 1929 as a crafts guild similar to those in Europe, Allied Arts sits on land that was once part of Rancho de las Pulgas, a Spanish land grant dating back to the 1700s.

The site holds a major place in California history and retains its original Spanish ambiance: white adobe walls, red tile roofs and well-planted patio courtyards. The meticulously maintained grounds are serene, and during spring and summer months a profusion of colorful and fragrant flowers makes a great background for wedding photos.

Surrounded by courtyard fountains and lush gardens, the Allied Arts Guild Restaurant has become a favorite site for wedding receptions. Spanish colonial in design, the restaurant has a large main dining room and terrace for indoor gatherings; outdoors, ceremonies take place in the garden courtyard, an intimate spot to tie the knot. This is one of the few facilities on the Peninsula that offers a relaxed and beautiful setting with both indoor and outdoor event spaces. Note that the restaurant is operated by the Palo Alto Auxiliary solely for the benefit of the Lucile Salter Packard Children's Hospital at Stanford, and that your gratuity is a tax deductible gift to the hospital.

CEREMONY CAPACITY: The main dining room and patio courtyard each hold 100 seated or 120 standing. The courtyard is available May 1–October 31.

EVENT/RECEPTION CAPACITY: A minimum of 100 guests is required for buffets and luncheon receptions. Between May 1 and October 31, the guest maximum is 175; from January through April, the maximum is 150. For hors d'oeuvres receptions, the maximum is 200 guests.

MEETING CAPACITY: The main dining room and enclosed terrace, combined, seat up to 175 guests; the outdoor courtyard seats 110.

FEES & DEPOSITS: The use fee is required as a deposit when reservations are confirmed. For wedding receptions, the fee is $1,250; for ceremonies and receptions the fee is $1,750. There will be additional charges for special rental requests. In-house catering is $30/person; tax is additional.

Fees for meetings and weekday events vary, and are based on space required and event duration. Food service is required.

AVAILABILITY: For weddings/receptions, Saturdays from January 2–October 31, 11am–4:30pm. Sundays and early evenings by special arrangement. For meetings or other special events, weekdays from January 2–October 31, 9:30am–4:30pm.

SERVICES/AMENITIES:

Catering: provided
Kitchen Facilities: n/a
Tables & Chairs: provided
Linens, Silver, etc.: provided
Restrooms: only one is wheelchair accessible
Dance Floor: yes
Bride's Dressing Area: yes
Meeting Equipment: CBA, extra fee

Parking: large lots, on street
Accommodations: no guest rooms
Telephone: pay phone
Outside Night Lighting: no
Outdoor Cooking Facilities: no
Cleanup: provided
View: of the garden and courtyard
Other: event coordination, flowers

RESTRICTIONS:

Alcohol: BYO CW only, corkage $8/bottle
Smoking: outside only
Music: amplified OK within reason

Wheelchair Access: yes
Insurance: required

The professionals in the back of the book are the best in the business! How do we know? Read page 681.

Stanford Park Hotel

Hotel

100 El Camino Real, Menlo Park
(650) 322-1234, fax (650) 322-0975
www.woodsidehotels.com

- ◆ Ceremonies
- ◆ Wedding Receptions
- ◆ Business Functions
- ◆ Special Events
- ◆ Meetings
- ◆ Accommodations

The Stanford Park Hotel, a Peninsula Mobil Four Star property, offers several choice spaces for your celebration. Inside the brass entry doors is a softly lit lobby with an immense brick fireplace and oak staircase. Just past the lobby is a beautiful inner courtyard with an old-world ambiance that we enthusiastically recommend for outdoor ceremonies and receptions. Although the Stanford Park is located on busy El Camino Real, its tranquil courtyard is completely insulated from the noise of traffic and urban bustle. It's beautifully landscaped, with multicolored flowers, good-sized trees and handsome stone benches. The upper courtyard is separated from the larger, lower courtyard by a vine-covered brick wall. Ceremonies are held in the upper level, next to which is a prefunction area where bridal processionals begin their walk down a lovely pathway bordered by blooming flowers. Permanently seated on a bench in the upper area is a full bronze statue of Benjamin Franklin, a guest at every wedding here. Freestanding white canvas umbrellas are available to shade wedding guests in the lower courtyard.

Inside the hotel, the Atherton and Menlo Rooms are popular for small indoor ceremonies, receptions and dinner parties. These pleasant spaces are designed in a classic style with a contemporary touch. They have high vaulted ceilings, soft muted colors and are furnished with pieces designed specifically for the Stanford Park. Another option is the Woodside Room which has a cathedral ceiling, bay windows and an adjacent foyer. And for honeymooners and their guests who'd like to stay overnight, we like the fact that very special room rates are offered to the wedding party.

CEREMONY & EVENT/RECEPTION CAPACITY, FEES & DEPOSITS:

Area	Seated	Standing	Room Fee	Setup Fee
Menlo Room	64	80	$400	$125
Atherton Room	64–80	80	300	125
Woodside Room	130	180	450	n/a
The Courtyard (Upper & Lower)	250	250	750	125

For weddings, a non-refundable $1,000 deposit is required when reservations are confirmed. 100% of the estimated event total is due 2 weeks prior to the event with any additional balance payable by the end of the function. For any time over 4-1/2 hours there is a $35/hour/waitperson charge. The ceremony setup fee is $750. Catering is provided. Buffets start at $38/person, dinners at $36/person. Alcohol, tax and an 18.5% service charge are additional.

For weekday business meetings and corporate events, call the catering department for additional information.

MEETING CAPACITY:

Area	Classroom style	Theater style	Conf style
Menlo Room	50	80	30
Atherton Room	35	80	30
Woodside Room	75	150	32
Los Altos Room	20	30	20
Board Room	—	—	8
Private Dining Room	10	12	15

AVAILABILITY: Year-round, daily, 9am–midnight. The Courtyard, May–September, 9am–9pm.

SERVICES/AMENITIES:

Catering: provided
Kitchen Facilities: n/a
Tables & Chairs: provided
Linens, Silver, etc.: provided
Restrooms: wheelchair accessible
Dance Floor: in Woodside Room & Courtyard
Bride's Dressing Area: yes
Meeting Equipment: CBA, extra fee

Parking: large lot
Accommodations: 163 guest rooms
Telephone: pay phones
Outdoor Night Lighting: yes
Outdoor Cooking Facilities: no
Cleanup: provided
View: courtyard
Other: event coordination

RESTRICTIONS:

Alcohol: provided
Smoking: designated areas
Music: amplified OK w/volume limits

Wheelchair Access: yes
Insurance: not required
Other: no birdseed or rice

---

*This is important! Tell facilities you're reading **Here Comes The Guide** and ask if our information is still current.*

Terrace Cafe at El Rancho Inn

Restaurant & Hotel

1100 El Camino Real, Millbrae
(650) 742-5588, fax (650) 742-5587

www.elranchoinn.com
terracecafe@msn.com

◆ Ceremonies ◆ Special Events
◆ Wedding Receptions ◆ Meetings
◆ Business Functions ◆ Accommodations

Bordered by four towering palms, a landscaped lawn and a shimmering aqua-blue pool, this hacienda-style restaurant is an urban oasis. Although it's right off El Camino Real at the El Rancho Inn, it's set far back from the street, removing it from the hustle and bustle of the city.

The Cafe invites you in with a sundrenched terrace, overlooking the pool. Terra cotta pots and planter boxes overflow with purple, pink and red flowers, while broad green umbrellas shade tables placed informally around the patio. This is a delightful spot for a small wedding ceremony or an hour of champagne and hors d'oeuvres, before going inside for your reception.

Large parties are held downstairs in the Palm Room, whose unique, serpentine bar was featured in the movie *The Right Stuff*. Curving along one side of the room, it faces a wall of arched windows, through which you can watch people swimming in the adjacent pool. At night, when the pool is lit, the Palm Room takes on a special glow, which only enhances its slightly sultry ambiance. Add a jazz pianist (there's a white baby grand piano at one end), or a fire in the fireplace (very cozy on chilly evenings), and you've got yourself quite the romantic place.

If you have a smaller celebration in mind, reserve the Veranda Room, upstairs off the main dining room. It's a private space with white walls inlaid with blue tile, wrought-iron chandeliers and a soft burgundy carpet. It opens out onto a lovely patio, enclosed by an adobe wall and sheltered from the sun by a latticework trellis overhead. You can also have small meetings in the Portola and Cortez Rooms, located a few steps away in the hotel.

When you have your event at the Cafe, you get a lot of personal attention. You deal directly with the manager and the chef, who never book more than one event at a time, and are incredibly easy to work with. They customize menus and packages, do menu tastings and help with referrals. They're also on site during your event, to make sure everything goes smoothly. The contemporary cuisine focuses primarily on steak, fresh seafood and pasta, but the four-star chef loves to be creative, and really enjoys it when a client requests something special.

In addition to weddings and corporate events, the Cafe has hosted showers, retirement parties and reunions. Out-of-town guests appreciate the convenience of staying in the hotel, and the fact that the San Francisco airport is just a few minutes away. Locations on the Peninsula are hard to come by, especially with the relaxed atmosphere and reasonable prices offered by the Terrace Cafe. So, stop in when you get a chance—you may be pleasantly surprised.

CEREMONY CAPACITY: The Patio holds 90 seated or 150 standing guests.

EVENT/RECEPTION CAPACITY: The Palm Room holds 150 seated or 175 standing; the Veranda Room 30 seated or 35 standing guests.

MEETING CAPACITY: The Portola Room holds 45 seated classroom-style; the Cortez Room holds 16 seated guests, conference-style.

FEES & DEPOSITS: When events are booked, a $500 refundable deposit is required for the Palm Room, a $100 deposit for the Veranda Room. 75% of the estimated event total is payable 2 weeks prior to the function; the balance is due at the event's conclusion. For wedding ceremonies, there is a $500 setup charge. Catering is provided in house; luncheons run $14–20/person, dinners $18–35/person; tax, a 17% service charge and alcohol are additional.

For an additional $5.50/person, a wedding package is available that includes dance floor, cake cutting, champagne toast, hors d'oeuvres and coffee service.

AVAILABILITY: Year-round, daily, 7am–1am. Closed Thanksgiving and Christmas Days.

SERVICES/AMENITIES:

Catering: provided, no BYO
Kitchen Facilities: n/a
Tables & Chairs: provided
Linens, Silver, etc.: provided
Restrooms: wheelchair accessible
Dance Floor: portable dance floor, extra fee
Bride's & Groom's Dressing Area: CBA
Meeting Equipment: CBA, extra charge
Other: event coordination

Parking: ample on-site
Accommodations: 307 guest rooms
Telephone: pay phones
Outdoor Night Lighting: yes
Outdoor Cooking Facilities: no
Cleanup: provided
View: underwater pool view & landscaped courtyard

RESTRICTIONS:

Alcohol: provided, or WC corkage $9/bottle
Smoking: outside only
Music: amplified OK w/volume limits

Wheelchair Access: yes
Insurance: not required
Other: no rice or confetti

The professionals in the back of the book are the best in the business! How do we know? Read page 681.

Westin San Francisco Airport

Hotel

1 Old Bayshore Highway, Millbrae
(650) 872-8147, fax (650) 872-8104

www.westin.com
dtorrano@westin.com

◆ Ceremonies   ◆ Special Events
◆ Wedding Receptions   ◆ Meetings
◆ Business Functions   ◆ Accommodations

According to the Westin's brochure, "a business hotel must run like a business hotel, but it doesn't have to feel like one." And this one doesn't. In fact, with its refined decor, warm ambiance and long list of amenities, you'd never know it *was* a business hotel. It's really more like an elegant resort, which explains why so many weddings, receptions and parties are held here.

Set on the cusp of a palm-lined drive near the edge of the bay, and just two minutes from the airport, the Westin is surprisingly quiet and peaceful. Even the lobby has a calming influence, with its rich mahogany paneling, custom carpet in vibrant autumn shades, and lush floral arrangement in the center.

From here, it's a short walk to the banquet rooms, and by the time you reach them, you're expecting something sophisticated and tasteful. You won't be disappointed. The Westin Ballroom, where most weddings, large meetings and special events take place, is a very lovely room. Brides are usually overjoyed with the decor, and have been known to exclaim, "Oh, this will match my dress perfectly!" That's because the walls are papered in a neutral champagne-and-taupe print that gives off a subtle gold sheen, the coffered ceiling is white, and ivory is a predominant color in the patterned carpet. One of the most striking features of this ballroom is the lighting. Instead of traditional chandeliers, there are fixtures fashioned from white globes, seemingly "scattered" behind a veil of pearl strands. When the lights are dimmed, you feel like you're gazing at clusters of stars, shining through golden clouds. Additional romantic lighting comes from alabaster and brass wall sconces. Although the Ballroom can be divided into four sections, only one event at a time is scheduled, so you can tailor the size of the space to fit your needs.

The expansive foyer area in front of the ballroom is not only refreshing to the eye, it's large enough to be set up with fountains, plants and an hors d'oeuvre buffet and have plenty of room left over for a crowd to mingle comfortably. And if you have kids at your event, you'll be ever-grateful to the Westin—they make a room with childcare available just off the foyer.

Smaller weddings and meetings are held in the Bayshore Ballroom, an intimate space with crystal chandeliers, alabaster wall sconces, and floor-to-ceiling windows overlooking the pool atrium. The atrium itself is popular for cocktail parties and more informal receptions. Huge potted ferns and rubber trees, as well as colorful flowers set around the pool, soak up the sunlight from the vaulted skylit "ceiling" and create a tropical ambiance.

Two dozen other rooms are available for functions, and award-winning chefs will create custom, culturally diverse menus. The combination of beautiful facilities, excellent food and personal service generates lots of repeat business for the hotel. Their "Letters To The Hotel" binder includes pages of laudatory comments such as, "The Westin is the *only* place to hold an event in San Mateo County! Period!" and "My daughter's dream of a perfect wedding day came true!" Read them all and you come away with a sense that guests feel quite welcomed here and very well taken care of. It's absolutely clear why they return to the Westin time after time—for many of them it's like coming home.

CEREMONY CAPACITY: The Bayshore Ballroom holds 200, the Westin Ballroom 600, and the Aspen Room 150 seated guests.

EVENT/RECEPTION CAPACITY:

Room	Seated	Standing	Room	Seated	Standing
Westin Ballroom	200–410	400–600	Bayshore Ballroom	130	200
Aspen	80	150	Poolside Atrium	48	125–150

MEETING CAPACITY: The Westin has over 22,000 square feet of function space, including 31 flexible rooms, from ballrooms and salons, to suites and boardrooms. Spaces can accommodate from 4 to 700 guests for business events.

FEES & DEPOSITS: For weddings, a non-refundable $1,000 deposit is required to secure your date; the event balance is due 1 week prior to the event. There are 3 wedding packages, ranging $58–80/person, that include centerpieces, champagne reception and toast, 5-course meal, hors d'oeuvres, wine with meal, overnight accommodations and breakfast for the bride and groom. If you don't want a package, all menus can be customized; luncheons range $25–40/person, dinners $35–50/person. Tax and a 19.5% service charge are additional. There is a $300 ceremony setup charge.

For other social events or business functions, prices will vary depending on the menu and services selected; call for specific rates. Meeting packages are also available.

AVAILABILITY: Year-round, daily until 1am, including holidays. For Saturday weddings, time frames are 11am–5pm or 6pm–1am.

SERVICES/AMENITIES:

Catering: provided, no BYO
Kitchen Facilities: n/a
Tables & Chairs: provided
Linens, Silver, etc.: provided
Restrooms: wheelchair accessible
Dance Floor: provided
Bride's & Groom's Dressing Area: guest room CBA
Meeting Equipment: full range & business center, in-room data port lines

Parking: ample, gated and secure lots
Accommodations: 400 guest rooms
Telephone: pay & guest phones
Outdoor Night Lighting: access only
Outdoor Cooking Facilities: no
Cleanup: provided
View: no
Other: event coordination, baby grand piano, ice sculpture, wedding cakes, limo service

RESTRICTIONS:

Alcohol: provided, or BYO, WC corkage $15/bottle
Smoking: outside only
Music: amplified OK

Wheelchair Access: yes
Insurance: not required
Other: no rice, birdseed, glitter or confetti

Montara Gardens

496 6th Street, Montara
(650) 728-7442

◆ Ceremonies ◆ Special Events
◆ Wedding Receptions Meetings
Business Functions Accommodations

For those of you who don't know where Montara is, it's a quiet and peaceful town right on the ocean, about eight miles north of Half Moon Bay. Montara Gardens, situated in the former Montara Grammar School, is now a designated historic landmark and is a handsome example of early 1900s Mission Revival architecture.

Although there is an oak-floored auditorium for indoor small- to medium-sized receptions, it's the outdoor spaces that make Montara Gardens such a delightful spot for weddings or special events. A redwood lath gazebo sits in a very pretty garden courtyard where you can smell the fresh air and occasionally feel ocean breezes. The gazebo is large enough to hold a sizable wedding party underneath its canopy, and the beautifully landscaped courtyard surrounding it is filled with annuals and perennials. Most of the garden is sheltered by enormous cypress trees, making it feel warm and comfortable even on chilly days. During the ceremony or reception, guests are treated to the natural beauty and serenity of the San Mateo coastside.

CEREMONY CAPACITY: The courtyard with gazebo holds 150 seated or standing; the auditorium 150 seated or standing.

EVENT/RECEPTION CAPACITY:

Area	Seated	Standing	Area	Seated	Standing
Auditorium	100	150	Courtyard	150	150
Entire Site	150	150			

FEES & DEPOSITS: To hold your date, 20% of the rental fee is required as a non-refundable deposit; the balance is due 2 weeks prior to the event. The $1,000–2,000 rental fee varies based on guest count.

For ceremonies only, the 2-hour rental fee varies from $500–750, depending on guest count.

AVAILABILITY: March–October, Saturdays only, noon–7pm.

SERVICES/AMENITIES:

Catering: BYO
Kitchen Facilities: moderate
Tables & Chairs: provided
Linens, Silver, etc.: BYO, or CBA, extra charge
Restrooms: wheelchair accessible
Dance Floor: yes
Bride's Dressing Area: yes
Meeting Equipment: n/a

Parking: medium-sized lot
Accommodations: no guest rooms
Telephone: no
Outdoor Night Lighting: access only
Outdoor Cooking Facilities: no
Cleanup: caterer, some provided
View: glimpses of ocean through foliage

RESTRICTIONS:

Alcohol: BYO, WBC only; no kegs
Smoking: outside only
Music: amplified OK inside only

Wheelchair Access: yes
Insurance: certificate required
Other: no rice, birdseed or pets; children must be supervised.

This is important! Tell facilities you're reading **Here Comes The Guide** *and ask if our information is still current.*

Crescent Park Grill

Restaurant

546 University Avenue, Palo Alto
(650) 326-0111, fax (650) 326-0878

cpgevents@aol.com

Ceremonies		◆	Special Events
◆ Wedding Receptions		◆	Meetings
◆ Business Functions			Accommodations

Crescent Park Grill has a number of terrific features, not least of which are these three: location, location, location. But in addition to being situated smack in the center of downtown Palo Alto with loads of free parking in the garage at back, Crescent Park offers sophisticated decor, a cosmopolitan menu of market-fresh organic ingredients, and a flexible space that can be alternately casual and airy or elegant and atmospheric. It depends entirely on which part (or parts) of the restaurant you use and at what time of day you host your wedding, rehearsal dinner, Christmas party, or business event.

In its purest form, Crescent Park is composed of just two rooms: the spacious main dining area and the smaller, private Crescent Room, reserved for special events. However, the main dining area is actually made up of several smaller sections that flow smoothly into one another, each with its own subtly different feel.

Dividing the room down the center is a long bar of burnished red-toned wood, which contrasts with the restaurant's cool white walls and ceiling. The same deep-colored wood shows up in strong, square pillars that further define the space, and in the seats and backs of the curved steel-framed chairs and barstools. To the right of the bar is a slender space lined with chocolate-brown leather banquettes and dark wood tables; a broad gas-burning fireplace completes the warm, intimate feel of this section. To the left of the bar is a wider and brighter area, with large plate-glass windows framing a grand wine rack (an indication of the breadth of Crescent Park's cellar). The front of the restaurant is very light and open, with tables next to French doors opening onto a tiled sidewalk patio; the patio itself, with its sun-dappled white linens and green bistro chairs, is bright and café-like, perfect for an al fresco engagement party or festive brunch. The private Crescent Room, at the back right of the restaurant, is quiet and secluded, separated from the main dining areas by heavy curtains and louvered wood doors; the doors can be thrown open, however, to extend seating for larger groups into the right-side banquette area (and beyond). The pale walls of the rectangular Crescent Room are accented with wood-framed mirrors and artwork in bright primary colors, and a second fireplace is centered in the rear wall.

The Crescent Room works equally well for corporate and festive events—as do all of the restaurant spaces. Set the room with round tables, top them with elegant centerpieces created by the in-house florist, and your anniversary party will shine; request conference-style seating, let Crescent Park take care of the AV equipment rental, and your lecture or awards presentation will unfold flawlessly. Hold a lively open-bar holiday event in the wide area left of the bar. Or rent the entire restaurant for your wedding—any time, any day—and let your guests dance the night away on the smooth wood floor in the front area. You'll feel entirely relaxed, knowing that the meal will be delicious, the staff solicitous, and the cake—well, it will be whatever you have directed Crescent Park's pastry chef to create. At the Crescent Park Grill, they make it easy for you to have exactly the kind of event you want.

CEREMONY CAPACITY: Ceremonies don't take place at this venue.

EVENT/RECEPTION CAPACITY: The entire restaurant can accommodate 200 seated or 275 standing guests. The Crescent Room holds 48 seated guests.

MEETING CAPACITY: The Crescent Room holds 48 guests seated conference-style.

FEES & DEPOSITS: A $500 deposit is required upon booking and is refundable up to 2 weeks prior to the function. The balance is due at the event's conclusion. Three-course luncheons run $20–25/person, dinners with hors d'oeuvres, $45–50/person; tax, alcohol and an 18% service charge are additional. There is a $2.50/person cake-cutting fee. For events in the Crescent Room with fewer than 20 guests, room rental fees will apply. To rent the entire restaurant on Saturday or Sunday, an $8,000 food and beverage minimum is required; on Sunday–Thursday evenings, $12,000 and on Friday or Saturday evenings, a $16,000 minimum.

AVAILABILITY: Year round, daily, 11:30am–midnight.

SERVICES/AMENITIES:

Catering: provided, no BYO
Kitchen Facilities: n/a
Tables & Chairs: provided
Linens, Silver, etc.: provided
Restrooms: wheelchair accessible
Dance Floor: yes
Bride's Dressing Area: no
Meeting Equipment: BYO or CBA, extra charge

Parking: free garage
Accommodations: no guest rooms
Telephone: pay phone
Outdoor Night Lighting: access only
Outdoor Cooking Facilities: no
Cleanup: provided
View: no
Other: flowers, wedding cakes

RESTRICTIONS:

Alcohol: provided, or BYO wine, corkage $10/bottle
Smoking: outside only
Music: amplified OK w/volume restrictions

Wheelchair Access: yes
Insurance: no
Other: no rice or birdseed

The professionals in the back of the book are the best in the business! How do we know? Read page 681.

The Elizabeth F. Gamble Garden Center

1431 Waverley Street, Palo Alto
(650) 329-1356, fax (650) 329-1688 Gabrielle Gross

Historic Home & Garden

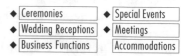

◆ Ceremonies ◆ Special Events
◆ Wedding Receptions ◆ Meetings
◆ Business Functions Accommodations

The Elizabeth F. Gamble Garden Center is one of the most perfect garden ceremony/reception sites we've seen. Miss Gamble willed the home and its grounds to the City of Palo Alto, which acquired the estate in 1985. The estate is now run by a community horticulture foundation.

The main house is a 1902 Colonial/Georgian Revival-style structure built in a lovely, older residential area of Palo Alto. Inside, a dining room, drawing room and library are available for receptions. Each room has been carefully restored using colorful, turn-of-the-century reproduction wallpapers. Dark, natural wood wainscotting has been returned to its original splendor and there are graceful, molded ceilings and nicely finished oak floors throughout. Each room has its own fireplace. A set of French doors in the Library opens onto a brick porch that leads down to the first of many beautifully landscaped spaces.

Behind the main house is the Tea House, constructed in 1948. Glass doors along the length of the house open onto a brick patio. Next to the Tea House is the Carriage House, which also has a separate kitchen adjacent to its large main room. Five French doors open out onto yet another brick patio.

As lovely as the buildings are, our favorite spots are the formal and informal gardens—the collective work of a full-time horticulturist and 300 volunteers. Each separately landscaped area feels like a private, secret garden: the rose garden (with its 100 species of roses), the wisteria garden, and the Victorian grotto—separately or combined—provide elegant settings for small wedding ceremonies and receptions. The Center has succeeded in creating a place of serenity and beauty. We recommend it highly.

CEREMONY CAPACITY: The Wisteria Garden, Rose Garden, Tea House Terrace and Carriage House each hold 75 seated or standing guests; the Drawing Room 40 seated or 75 standing guests.

EVENT/RECEPTION CAPACITY: The facility can host 2 functions per month for up to 75 guests, and an unlimited number of events for up to 50 guests.

MEETING CAPACITY: The Carriage House Main Room holds 30 seated conference-style, the dining room, 16 seated boardroom-style, and the Drawing Room, 30 seated conference-style.

FEES & DEPOSITS: For weddings, a $475 partially refundable deposit is required when reservations are confirmed. The rental fee on Saturdays and Sundays is $950 for an 8-hour block; Tuesdays–Thursdays, $50/hour with a 30-guest maximum; Friday evenings $75/hour with a 30-guest maximum. The rental balance and a $500 cleaning/damage deposit are due 120 days prior to the date reserved. The damage/cleaning deposit is generally refunded within 1 week following your event.

For meetings and business functions, fees vary based on rooms rented and rental time frames; call for more details.

AVAILABILITY: For weddings, Saturdays noon–10pm, Sundays 10am–9pm, Tuesday–Thursday 2pm–6pm, Fridays 6pm–10pm. For business functions, year-round, Tuesday–Thursday 9am–6pm.

SERVICES/AMENITIES:

Catering: BYO
Kitchen Facilities: fully equipped
Tables & Chairs: BYO
Linens, Silver, etc.: BYO
Restrooms: wheelchair accessible
Dance Floor: yes
Bride's Dressing Area: yes
Meeting Equipment: screen

Parking: lot
Accommodations: no guest rooms
Telephone: house phone
Outdoor Night Lighting: yes
Outdoor Cooking Facilities: no
Cleanup: renter or caterer
Views: Edwardian gardens
Other: piano available for $20 charge, event coordination

RESTRICTIONS:

Alcohol: BYO wine, beer or champagne; no beer kegs or red wine in main house
Smoking: not allowed
Music: no amplified or recorded music

Wheelchair Access: yes
Insurance: required
Other: all activities must end at 10pm; no rice, birdseed, confetti or glitter

---

Garden Court Hotel

Hotel

520 Cowper Street, Palo Alto
(800) 824-9028, (650) 323-1912, fax (650) 322-3440

www.gardencourt.com
ahotel@gardencourt.com

◆ Ceremonies ◆ Special Events
◆ Wedding Receptions ◆ Meetings
◆ Business Functions ◆ Accommodations

Designed as a re-creation of a European village square, this four-story hotel looks more like something you'd see in a Tuscan town than in bustling downtown Palo Alto. Yet it offers one of the few spots on the Peninsula where you can host your wedding and reception and house all your guests at the same location. The Garden Court Hotel provides a warm Mediterranean ambiance combined with modern facilities and top-notch service. The facility has a strong visual appeal: dark green and white trim contrast against terra cotta-colored walls, and potted planters are filled to the brim with colorful annuals and perennials. The Hotel encloses an inviting interior courtyard where guests can relax in the warm sun, sip champagne or sample hors d'oeuvres before heading off to the expansive Courtyard Ballroom for a seated meal. Just like in an Italian village, numerous balconies allow guests to watch and enjoy the activities from above.

Additional rooms on the Garden Court's second floor can accommodate receptions, and feature terraces and huge, arched windows. One of the benefits of having your celebration here is that the in-house caterer is Il Fornaio, a restaurant renowned for its Northern Italian cuisine. An added plus is that if you have a reception (with over 75 guests) at the Garden Court, you'll be offered a complimentary guest room for the wedding couple, complete with fireplace or jacuzzi, champagne and continental breakfast. What more could you ask for?

CEREMONY CAPACITY:

Space	*Seated*	*Standing*	*Space*	*Seated*	*Standing*
Grove Ballroom	100	120–170	Terrace Room	70	100
Courtyard Ballroom	120	175	Outdoor Courtyard	100	100

EVENT/RECEPTION & MEETING CAPACITY: Portable walls can also vary room size.

Space	*Seated*	*Standing*	*w/ Dancing*	*Conf-style*	*Theater-style*
Grove Ballroom	75–150	200	150	70	200
Terrace Room	30–50	80	—	25	70
Courtyard Ballroom	150–250	300	225	45	120

FEES & DEPOSITS: For weddings, a $1,500 non-refundable deposit, which is applied to the event balance, is due within 2 weeks of booking. The estimated total is due 2 weeks prior to the event, and any remaining balance is due 30 days after the event. The rental fee for the Grove Ballroom is $350 Sunday, $500 Saturday during the day, and $1,000 Saturday evening. The rental fee for the Courtyard Ballroom is $1,000. There is no rental fee for the Terrace Room, however there is a guaranteed 30-guest minimum. Meals start at $35/person; beverages, tax and a 18% service charge are additional. Optional security and coat room attendants can be arranged.

Fees for meetings or corporate events vary based on group size, room(s) selected, and catering needs. Call for more specifics.

AVAILABILITY: For meetings, Monday–Friday, 8am–5pm; weekday evening events, 6pm–11pm. For weekend special events or weddings, the following time frames apply:

Spaces	*Weekday*	*Saturday*	*Sunday*
Terrace Room (any 5 hours)	6pm–midnight	11:30am–4:30pm 6pm–midnight	10am–midnight
Grove Ballroom (any 5 hours)	6pm–midnight	11:30am–4:30pm 6pm–midnight	10am–midnight
Courtyard Ballroom (any 5 hours)	6pm–11pm	10am–11pm	10am–11pm

SERVICES/AMENITIES:

Catering: provided, no BYO

Kitchen Facilities: n/a

Tables & Chairs: provided

Linens, Silver, etc.: provided

Restrooms: wheelchair accessible

Dance Floor: yes

Bride's Dressing Area: CBA, extra fee

Meeting Equipment: full range CBA, extra fee

Parking: complimentary valet, large lot

Accommodations: 62 guest rooms & suites

Telephone: pay phones

Outdoor Night Lighting: access only

Outdoor Cooking Facilities: no

Cleanup: provided

View: of courtyard and downtown Palo Alto

RESTRICTIONS:

Alcohol: provided or WC corkage $15/bottle

Smoking: outside only

Music: amplified OK

Wheelchair Access: yes

Insurance: not required

Other: no birdseed or rice

The professionals in the back of the book are the best in the business! *How do we know? Read page 681.*

MacArthur Park

27 University Avenue, Palo Alto
(650) 321-9990, fax (650) 328-4066

◆ Ceremonies   ◆ Special Events
◆ Wedding Receptions   ◆ Meetings
◆ Business Functions   Accommodations

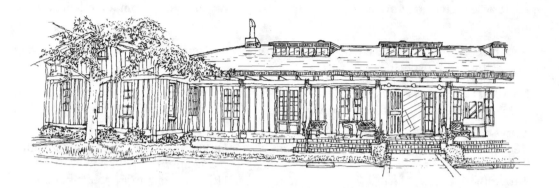

Although a popular restaurant, MacArthur Park's biggest secret is that it's also a great venue for special events: everything from business meetings to wedding receptions and intimate rehearsal dinners. The landmark building which houses MacArthur Park was designed in 1918 by renowned architect Julia Morgan, and originally served as a recreation facility for WWI troops. The structure's simple yet handsome design was dictated by a rock-bottom $1,800 YWCA budget, and is a fine example of Morgan's ability to combine craftsman style with utilitarian needs.

The main dining room has a vaulted ceiling with exposed wood trusses and beams. Details include several balconies and two large brick fireplaces situated at either end of the room. The decor is subdued: black chairs contrast against white linens; attractive framed artwork graces board and batten walls. Rooms are painted in rich, soothing café au lait colors. The very attractive private dining rooms feature the same warm tones and wall treatments as the main dining room and are well-suited for smaller rehearsal dinners and business meetings. Several sets of French windows are framed by long drapes, gathered and held back by brass knobs.

For outdoor functions, take a peek at the enclosed courtyard, an aggregate patio with white chairs and matching linen-covered tables. Striped fabric awnings shade guests from the sun, and heat lamps take the chill off during cooler months or during evening affairs.

CEREMONY CAPACITY: The patio can accommodate 200 seated or standing; the east or west dining room area can hold up to 300 seated guests, including lofts.

EVENT/RECEPTION & MEETING CAPACITY: The main dining room holds up to 240 seated guests; with balconies, the total indoor capacity rises to 300. The patio courtyard holds 120 seated guests or 180 for a standing reception. Lofts hold up to 26 guests, each. The Julia Morgan Room holds up to 60 seated and the Camp Fremont Room up to 36 seated guests.

FEES & DEPOSITS: To reserve the entire restaurant (up to 100 guests) the rental fee is $1,000. The rental fee serves as a partially refundable deposit, and is due when you book reservations. Food service is provided. Seated functions, including food, beverages, tax and service charge run $36–46/person.

For business functions and meetings please call for rates.

AVAILABILITY: For wedding receptions, the entire restaurant is available on Saturdays and Sundays from 9am–4pm. Private parties in separate banquet rooms are held Sunday–Friday 11:30am–1am or Saturday 5pm–1am.

SERVICES/AMENITIES:

Catering: provided, no BYO
Kitchen Facilities: n/a
Tables & Chairs: provided
Linens, Silver, etc.: provided
Restrooms: wheelchair accessible
Dance Floor: CBA
Bride's Dressing Area: yes
Meeting Equipment: CBA, extra fee

Parking: valet extra charge, large lot nearby
Accommodations: no guest rooms
Telephone: pay phone
Outdoor Night Lighting: yes
Outdoor Cooking Facilities: yes
Cleanup: provided
View: no
Other: floral arrangements, event coordinator

RESTRICTIONS:

Alcohol: provided or BYO, corkage $10/bottle
Smoking: not permitted
Music: amplified OK

Wheelchair Access: yes
Insurance: not required

This is important! Tell facilities you're reading **Here Comes The Guide** *and ask if our information is still current.*

Sheraton Palo Alto

Hotel

625 El Camino Real, Palo Alto
(650) 328-2800, fax (650) 324-9084

www.sheraton.com/paloalto

◆ Ceremonies   ◆ Special Events
◆ Wedding Receptions   ◆ Meetings
◆ Business Functions   ◆ Accommodations

Picture a clear, rocky stream running beneath foot bridges, past tall pines and bushy ferns. Sounds more like a combination of the Rocky Mountains and a tropical island than Palo Alto, but that's exactly where it is. At the Sheraton Palo Alto, you have a variety of event spaces, each with its own unique look, from the Spanish-tiled, glass-enclosed court, to the ballroom decorated with authentic Chinese antiques. The hotel's cluster of low buildings is located on a commercial boulevard, but because they're set back off the road and imaginatively landscaped, the Sheraton maintains an air of exclusivity.

A walk through the newly renovated, mostly glass lobby, suffused with light from windows and skylights, takes you to the large, rectangular swimming pool area. It's the perfect spot for a splashy cocktail hour: a brick-paved patio is bordered by trees and gardenias, and at night the pool is illuminated by underwater lights and the trees glow with twinkle lights.

The Reception Room is set in its own wing and the adjoining lawn and gazebo are equally suited for ceremonies or stargazing. A semicircular wall encloses the lawn, so only your group can access it, and tall poplar trees add to the sense of privacy. The room itself features two large crystal chandeliers, a dance floor and vaulted ceiling, and fold-out glass doors that open onto the lawn.

Justine's Area is highlighted by a beautiful glass-enclosed interior courtyard between spacious banquet rooms. It has Spanish tile, white stucco archways, arched mirrors and a glass ceiling shaded with rice paper blinds to minimize glare. The setting makes a picturesque backdrop for your ceremony, photographs and even the cake cutting. Use the banquet room that opens out onto a streamside patio for cocktails, then spread out into both dining rooms for dinner. Beneath Justine's Area is the Cypress Ballroom, an imperial room that features deep burgundy custom carpeting and royal white columns inset in the wall. Works of art from China are displayed in softly lit shadow boxes.

With its variety of event spaces, the Sheraton Palo Alto gives you plenty of options, and their creative and experienced staff guarantee to work wonders on your special day.

CEREMONY CAPACITY:

Area	Seated	Standing		Area	Seated	Standing
Reception Room	100	200		Cypress Ballroom	350	450
Piazza Courtyard	120	200				

EVENT/RECEPTION CAPACITY:

Area	Seated	Standing		Area	Seated	Standing
Reception Room	150	300		Cypress Ballroom	250	400
Justine's Area	350	500				

MEETING CAPACITY: Small meeting rooms and parlors are available in addition to the spaces below:

Area	Theater-style	Classroom-style		Area	Theater-style	Classroom-style
Cypress Ballroom	60–450	30–150		Sequoia & Oak Rm	100–300	30–100
Reception Room	150	85				

FEES & DEPOSITS: For weddings and special events, a $1,000 non-refundable deposit is required to secure your date. Seated luncheons and dinners start at $29/person, buffets at $34/person; alcohol, an 18% service charge and tax are extra. The anticipated food and beverage total is due 10 days prior to the event. Bride and groom receive a complimentary room with champagne and group rates can be arranged for overnight wedding guests. For meetings, room rental fees range $200–1,500.

AVAILABILITY: Year-round, daily, any time. Weddings can take place on Saturdays, April–September, 10–5pm or 6pm–11pm or in any 5-hour block, October–March.

SERVICES/AMENITIES:

Catering: provided, no BYO
Kitchen Facilities: n/a
Tables & Chairs: provided
Linens, Silver, etc.: provided
Restrooms: wheelchair accessible
Dance Floor: portable indoors or Piazza Courtyard
Bride's & Groom's Dressing Area: yes
Meeting Equipment: full range CBA

Parking: large lots
Accommodations: 350 guest rooms & suites
Telephone: pay phones
Outdoor Night Lighting: yes
Outdoor Cooking Facilities: BBQs
Cleanup: provided
View: of Stanford University, water gardens
Other: event coordination

RESTRICTIONS:

Alcohol: provided or BYO, corkage $12/bottle, no hard alcohol or beer
Smoking: outdoors only
Music: amplified OK

Wheelchair Access: yes
Insurance: not required
Other: no birdseed or rice

The professionals in the back of the book are the best in the business! How do we know? Read page 681.

Spago Palo Alto

265 Lytton Avenue, Palo Alto
(650) 833-1010, fax (650) 325-9586

◆ Ceremonies ◆ Special Events
◆ Wedding Receptions ◆ Meetings
◆ Business Functions Accommodations

Take a moment to observe what's outside Spago, and you gain surprising insight into what lies beyond its tranquil, vine-covered entrance. Your first hint of the restaurant's energy comes at the curb, where scarlet-vested valets nimbly negotiate the arrival of crowds of smartly attired diners. Then you notice the restaurant's name, which is scripted in intense primary colors and splashy letters, rushing forward along the length of the landmark building's simple white stucco wall. This mix of lively and calm, vibrant and cool, new and old extends throughout Spago's three spacious dining areas and its private room, where events ranging from intimate wedding ceremonies and rehearsal dinners to high-powered corporate banquets and fundraisers have unfolded.

Chef-owner Wolfgang Puck has garnered a deservedly high reputation for his European- and Asian-accented American cuisine, so food is a highlight of any event held at Spago; but architectural design is an equally important element. The main dining room, created by internationally-known designer Adam Tihany, is a wide, open, two-level space with forceful blocks of color—cobalt, brick, sunshine yellow, forest green—covering broad beams, posts, and ceiling-high window frames. Similarly saturated hues are showered over the carpet, the banquettes, the eccentric light sconces, and the large Robert Rauschenberg painting (commissioned for the space) that adorns one wall. Adding to the coursing energy of this room is the trademark open kitchen, which reveals not one—not two—but three lines of chefs working in heated concentration.

The adjacent terrace seems to quietly absorb guests who have spilled outside from the dining room's activity. Although the chatter from inside wafts onto the terrace through large French doors, the atmosphere remains serene. Slender white lamps provide evening illumination. Giant banana palms lean in, an old live oak arches overhead, and a new wood-beamed canopy provides shade and a visual connection to the third dining area, the Pavilion bar. This casual, airy space is decorated on two sides with lively murals of wine drinkers and diners; folding glass doors open the other two walls to the courtyard, creating a garden feel. The glass ceiling and overhead canvas canopies are retractable, bringing starry skies into your reception, while heat lamps keep you impervious to any evening chill.

Lastly, the private Oak Room, across from the Pavilion, is a self-contained cottage with a hacienda-style tile roof, a corner wood burning fireplace, and a small but significant collection of contemporary art. Gentle pin-spot lights and vivid carpet warm the curves and arches of the white space. But the Oak Room's most important attribute is this: it is very, very quiet. If you get married in this room (small, or standing room ceremonies only) while the dining room is in full swing, no unwanted sounds or interruptions will mar the event.

You can have Spago all to yourself, if you plan well in advance. Complete buy-outs are available on a limited basis. With the whole restaurant at your disposal, take advantage of the Pavilion bar for your cocktail reception, enjoy dinner in the main dining room, and return to the Pavilion for dancing on the smooth concrete floor. Or, if a buy-out isn't possible, consider holding your ceremony in the Oak Room and cocktails on the terrace, before dinner in the Pavilion. Indoors or out, celebrating at Spago's yields a sophisticated, zestful and delicious experience.

CEREMONY CAPACITY: The Oak Room holds 40–50 seated guests.

EVENT/RECEPTION CAPACITY: The Main Dining Room holds 150–200 seated or 300 for a cocktail reception; the Pavilion holds 60 seated and the Oak Room 40 seated guests.

MEETING CAPACITY: The Pavilion holds 75–80 seated theater-style; the Oak Room 40–50 theater-style or 25 seated conference style.

FEES & DEPOSITS: To book Spago, a deposit totaling 20–50% of the estimated event cost is required; the balance is payable at the event's conclusion. Luncheons (3-course plus hors d'oeuvres) start at $35/person, dinners (3-course plus hors d'oeuvres) at $65/person, tax, a 19% service charge and alcohol are additional. Food and beverage minimums may apply depending on day of week and type of event.

AVAILABILITY: Year-round, daily, including major holidays.

Room	*Time frame*
Entire Restaurant (buyout required)	Sat & Sun until 4pm or Sun–Wed 4pm–midnight
Pavilion & Oak Rooms	Daily until 4pm
Oak Room	Daily 4pm–midnight
Pavilion Room	Sun–Wed 4–midnight

SERVICES/AMENITIES:
Catering: provided, no BYO
Kitchen Facilities: n/a
Tables & Chairs: provided
Linens, Silver, etc.: provided
Restrooms: wheelchair accessible
Dance Floor: in Pavilion w/buyout
Bride's Dressing Area: no
Meeting Equipment: CBA, extra charge

Parking: valet or on-street
Accommodations: no guest rooms
Telephone: pay phone
Outdoor Night Lighting: yes
Outdoor Cooking Facilities: n/a
Cleanup: provided
View: garden courtyard

RESTRICTIONS:
Alcohol: provided, or wine corkage $16/bottle
Smoking: outside only
Music: amplified OK w/buyout until 4pm, acoustic OK until midnight

Wheelchair Access: yes
Insurance: not required

The Vintage Room and Courtyard
at Stanford Barn

Historic Banquet Facility

◆ Ceremonies ◆ Special Events
◆ Wedding Receptions ◆ Meetings
◆ Business Functions Accommodations

Corner of Welch and Quarry Roads, Palo Alto
(650) 325-4339, fax (650) 325-8068

www.calcafe.com
palo_alto.catering@calcafe.com

Built by Leland Stanford in 1888, this landmark building in the heart of the Peninsula has had a long and illustrious past as a working winery, dairy barn and cattlemen's association headquarters. A handsome, three-story brick structure shaded by mature palms and softened by ivy clinging to its walls, it now houses offices, the California Cafe and attractive retail shops. One of the last reminders of a time when Stanford was a farm, the Barn is a survivor of a bygone era. It stayed intact through the 1906 quake and luckily avoided the wrecking ball during the urban encroachments of the 40s, 50s and 60s. And even though the Stanford Shopping Center, Hospital and University have mushroomed around it, the Barn still stands, its exterior virtually unchanged since it was built.

The southwest portion of the ground floor and adjacent wind-protected courtyard are available for wedding events. The Vintage Room is brightened by French windows, several of which overlook the patio. Dark green shutters and window trim complement the terra-cotta color of old brick walls, and a fifteen-foot ceiling is supported by three wood posts which punctuate an otherwise open and uncluttered space. One set of doors opens onto a landscaped courtyard, perfect for seated ceremonies, outdoor receptions or champagne and hors d'oeuvres. Tenting can be arranged for the courtyard or the adjacent lawn to create another spacious "room." This combination of spaces is the answer for couples who beg us for the perfect Peninsula location: a garden spot with an interior space that can handle a large group—even when the weather proves uncooperative.

CEREMONY CAPACITY: The Courtyard holds 200 seated or 500 standing; the Vintage Room, 200 seated or 300 standing.

EVENT/RECEPTION CAPACITY: Inside, up to 160 seated or 300 standing guests. In combination with the Courtyard, up to 300 seated or 500 standing guests.

MEETING CAPACITY: The Vintage Room can accommodate 225 seated theater-style, 125 classroom-style.

FEES & DEPOSITS: For weddings and receptions, a non-refundable deposit in the amount of half the rental fee is required to secure your date. The rental fee balance plus a $750 refundable cleaning/security deposit are due 60 days prior to the event. The rental fee for 8-hours' use, including setup and cleanup, ranges from $1,000–2,000, depending on the day of the week and guest count. For weekday business functions and meetings, the rental fee ranges from $500–1,000 depending on the services selected and the event time frame.

Catering is provided by *California Cafe Catering*. Reception meals start at $35/person; 4 hour beverage packages start at $16/person. Alcohol, tax and service charges are additional.

AVAILABILITY: Year-round, daily from 8am–2am.

SERVICES/AMENITIES:
Catering: provided, no BYO
Kitchen Facilities: n/a
Tables & Chairs: most provided
Linens, Silver, etc.: provided
Dance Floor: CBA, $250 extra charge
Restrooms: wheelchair accessible
Bride's Dressing Area: minimal
Meeting Equipment: CBA, extra charge

Parking: large lot
Accommodations: no guest rooms
Telephone: pay phones
Outdoor Night Lighting: yes
Outdoor Cooking Facilities no
Cleanup: provided
View: of courtyard

RESTRICTIONS:
Alcohol: provided, no BYO
Smoking: outside only
Music: amplified OK indoors only

Wheelchair Access: yes
Insurance: not required

The professionals in the back of the book are the best in the business! How do we know? Read page 681.

Woman's Club of Palo Alto

475 Homer Avenue, Palo Alto
(650) 321-5821, fax (650) 325-1970

Historic Woman's Club

◆ Ceremonies ◆ Special Events
◆ Wedding Receptions ◆ Meetings
◆ Business Functions Accommodations

On June 20, 1894, 24 women gathered together to formally organize the Woman's Club of Palo Alto. Their goals were self-improvement, mutual help and community work, and they didn't waste any time fulfilling them. Within the first four years of the club's existence, they'd founded the city's first reading room and library as well as its first elementary school and high school.

Their dream of having their own clubhouse, however, was not realized until 1916. After twelve years of continuous fund-raising they'd managed to raise $5,300, and their Tudor-Craftsman-style "home" was built. At the time, they worried that it was too far removed from the center of town, but its location in a quiet, residential neighborhood has proved a felicitous one.

Weddings are held in the Ballroom, a simply designed space with grand proportions. On two sides, tall windows flood the room with light, which reflects off polished maple floors. Eight brass-and-glass fixtures suspended from the high ceiling and dark wood wainscotting and trim throughout add period character. Have your ceremony on the stage, which is framed by a red velvet curtain and illuminated by vaudeville lights along the front edge. There's even a pair of baby grand pianos for musical accompaniment.

Buffets are usually set up in the adjacent Fireside Room, aptly name for its tiled fireplace, and joined to the Ballroom by folding French doors. And for guests who want to sip champagne outside or children who need a place to play, there's a private, fenced-in area right next to the building. The founders of the Woman's Club of Palo Alto may not have envisioned their clubhouse being used for matrimonial celebrations, but its spacious, airy interior and ample kitchen facilities make it a popular spot for weddings. And besides, it's one of the few places we know of that has twice as many restrooms for women as for men. Good planning, ladies.

CEREMONY CAPACITY: The Ballroom and stage hold 225 seated guests.

EVENT/RECEPTION & MEETING CAPACITY: The Ballroom and stage can accommodate 225 seated; the Fireside Room 50 seated or 100 standing.

FEES & DEPOSITS: For weekend special events or weddings, the full day rental fee is $1,200 plus a $250 security deposit and a $50 janitorial fee. Half the rental fee and the security deposit are due with your signed contract; the balance is payable 2 weeks prior to the event.

For weekday meetings and multi-day bookings, the rental fee runs $75–125/hour depending on usage.

AVAILABILITY: Year-round, daily, any time.

SERVICES/AMENITIES:

Catering: BYO
Kitchen Facilities: fully equipped
Tables & Chairs: some provided
Linens, Silver, etc.: BYO
Restrooms: wheelchair accessible
Dance Floor: on stage, in Ballroom
Bride's Dressing Area: yes
Meeting Equipment: BYO

Parking: on-street parking and nearby lots
Accommodations: no guest rooms
Telephone: pay phone
Outdoor Night Lighting: access only
Outdoor Cooking Facilities: BYO BBQ
Cleanup: caterer or renter
View: of residential neighborhood

RESTRICTIONS:

Alcohol: BYO, CBW only
Smoking: outdoors only
Music: amplified OK indoors only until midnight; w/restrictions after 10pm

Wheelchair Access: yes
Insurance: not required

---

*This is important! Tell facilities you're reading **Here Comes The Guide** and ask if our information is still current.*

Ladera Oaks

3249 Alpine Road, Portola Valley
(650) 854-3101, fax (650) 854-5982

guia@laderaoaks.com

Swim Club and Clubhouse

- ◆ Ceremonies
- ◆ Wedding Receptions
- ◆ Business Functions
- ◆ Special Events
- ◆ Meetings
- Accommodations

Located off Alpine Road in Portola Valley, Ladera Oaks' shingled clubhouse and beautifully landscaped grounds provide a really pleasant spot for private parties and wedding receptions. The building's exterior is covered with vines and the courtyard garden between the clubhouse and pools has an extremely attractive interior garden, with two-tiered lawn areas surrounded by oak trees, flowering annuals and perennials.

The clubhouse Ballroom offers a sizable space for indoor dining, with hardwood floors and large picture windows overlooking the garden. An adjoining Lounge can be used in conjunction with the Ballroom or separately for smaller gatherings. Private and quiet, this is a great location for indoor/outdoor celebrations and company events.

CEREMONY CAPACITY: The Courtyard holds 50–250 depending on the season, the Ballroom up to 100 seated.

EVENT/RECEPTION CAPACITY: The Ballroom can seat 100–150 guests in the daytime, 180 in the evening and, in combination with the garden, 350. Alone, the Courtyard Garden can accommodate 200 seated guests. The Lounge can hold up to 35 seated. All spaces, in combination, can accommodate up to 500 for a cocktail reception.

MEETING CAPACITY: The Ballroom holds up to 200 seated.

FEES & DEPOSITS: A $500–1,000 partially refundable deposit and a signed contract are required to secure your date. For weddings, the rental fee runs $12/guest with minimums ranging from $1,200 to $3,000 depending on the season, day of week and time frame selected. The rental fee is payable 10 days prior to the event.

For weekday meetings and special events, the rental fee runs $6/guest with a $300 minimum for afternoon functions and a $600 minimum for evening events. The total fee will depend on the season, day of the week and time frame selected.

AVAILABILITY: For parties, weddings or receptions, Monday–Thursday 6pm–10pm, Fridays 6pm–1am or Saturdays 8am–1am. Sundays (October–March only) 8am–10pm.

For meetings or workshops, Monday–Thursday 7am–10pm, Fridays 7am–1am or Saturdays 8am–1am. Sundays (October–March only) 8am–10pm.

SERVICES/AMENITIES:

Catering: BYO

Kitchen Facilities: ample

Tables & Chairs: provided

Linens, Silver, etc.: BYO

Restrooms: wheelchair accessible

Dance Floor: yes

Bride's Dressing Area: yes

View: of garden and Peninsula coastal hills

Parking: large lots, limited weekdays

Accommodations: no guest rooms

Telephone: pay phone

Outdoor Night Lighting: yes

Outdoor Cooking Facilities: BBQ

Cleanup: caterer and club staff

Meeting Equipment: BYO

RESTRICTIONS:

Alcohol: BYO

Smoking: outdoors only

Music: amplified OK inside only

Wheelchair Access: yes

Insurance: not required

The professionals in the back of the book are the best in the business! How do we know? Read page 681.

Hotel Sofitel

At Redwood Shores

223 Twin Dolphin Drive, Redwood City
(650) 598-9000, fax (650) 598-0459

www.sofitel.com

Hotel

- ◆ Ceremonies
- ◆ Wedding Receptions
- ◆ Business Functions
- ◆ Special Events
- ◆ Meetings
- ◆ Accommodations

The Hotel Sofitel is special because, unlike most large hotels, it conveys a sense of warmth and intimacy. It's French owned, serves French cuisine prepared by French chefs, and has a California-style friendliness and an experienced staff that make you feel right at home.

The Hotel offers lots of reception choices—our favorite is Baccarat, a sophisticated restaurant on the premises which overlooks the water. With floor-to-ceiling bay windows, Baccarat is light and warm. This is a small, intimate space where you can eat at square tables instead of typical six foot rounds. Colors are soft and muted, in cream, pale pink and teal. At one end of the restaurant is the Crystal Room, named for the brilliant Baccarat chandelier suspended from the ceiling. When the etched glass doors are closed, this is a private dining room. Open them and voilà—another room for a buffet setup, bar or head table. The small marble-floored foyer leading into Baccarat is perfect for a gift table or guest book signing.

Adjacent to Baccarat is La Terrasse, an appealing two-tiered area with great views of the water and of the Hotel pool and patio. La Terrasse's floor is sensational—a woven geometric pattern in black, tan and rose colored rectangles of polished marble. You can elect to have your ceremony dockside on the waterfront, and then serve cocktails, champagne and hors d'oeuvres in La Terrasse before moving elsewhere for a seated meal. For the adventurous, the outdoor pool and patio can be tented for receptions.

If your guest list is large, don't worry. Hotel Sofitel's 6,200-square-foot Grand Ballroom can accommodate a sizable crowd. Guests will enter through the impressive marble-floored Hotel Lobby, and head to the Ballroom Foyer for prefunction champagne and hors d'oeuvres. Inside, the Grand Ballroom can be used in its entirety or divided in half, depending on the size of your party. The decor is done in traditionally elegant shades of deep burgundy, teal and cream, with translucent, golden domed chandeliers. For smaller receptions, wedding showers or rehearsal dinners, reserve the Grand Salon. To help you relax after the big event, Hotel Sofitel offers a complimentary suite for the bride and groom, and special group rates for out-of-town guests.

CEREMONY CAPACITY: Dockside (next to the lagoon) accommodates up to 140 seated; the Ballroom can hold 450 seated.

EVENT/RECEPTION CAPACITY:

Room	Seated	Standing	Room	Seated	Standing
Half Grand Ballroom	180	325	La Terrasse	—	300
Grand Ballroom	420	700	Grand Salon	80	100
Baccarat Dining Room	100	—	Pool & Patio	200	400

MEETING CAPACITY: 15 rooms are available including the Ballroom, the Executive Board Room, and a variety of hospitality suites. Seating capacity is as follows:

Classroom-style	Conference-style	U-shape	Theater-style
10–400	14–35	14–30	10–700

FEES & DEPOSITS: For events, a non-refundable $1,000 deposit is due 2 weeks after booking; the balance is due 2 weeks before the function, and a guaranteed guest count is required 72 hours in advance. Any remaining charges are payable at the conclusion of your event. Wedding packages range $60–100 per person; tax and a 17% service charge are additional. For meetings, room rental fees start at $275/day. The fee is reduced with a $30/person food and beverage minimum. Special billing arrangements can be made.

AVAILABILITY: Weddings in the Grand Ballroom are held 11am–4:30pm or 6pm–1am in 6-hour blocks. If no other receptions are scheduled on the day you have yours, the time frame is flexible. The Baccarat Dining Room is available Saturdays 11–4:30pm and on Sunday evenings from 4pm–midnight. Events elsewhere can be scheduled as available. For other types of events or meetings, hours are flexible. Call for details.

SERVICES/AMENITIES:

Catering: provided
Kitchen Facilities: n/a
Tables & Chairs: provided
Linens, Silver, etc.: provided
Restrooms: wheelchair accessible
Dance Floor: provided
Bride's Dressing Area: yes
Meeting Equipment: CBA, extra fee

Parking: large lot, valet
Accommodations: 419 guest rooms
Telephone: pay phones, private lines CBA
Outdoor Night Lighting: no
Outdoor Cooking Facilities: no
Cleanup: provided
View: lagoon or hills
Other: complete event coordination

RESTRICTIONS:

Alcohol: provided
Smoking: designated areas
Music: amplified OK

Wheelchair Access: yes
Insurance: not required
Other: no rice or birdseed indoors

---

*This is important! Tell facilities you're reading **Here Comes The Guide** and ask if our information is still current.*

Pacific Athletic Club at Redwood Shores

Athletic Club

200 Redwood Shores Parkway, Redwood City
(650) 593-1112, fax (650) 593-3106

www.5star-events.com
tdgpac@netwizards.net

◆ Ceremonies   ◆ Special Events
◆ Wedding Receptions   ◆ Meetings
◆ Business Functions   Accommodations

You know you're almost there once you see the distinctive, green copper pyramid-shaped roofs of this seven-acre complex of event spaces, restaurant, pools and athletic courts. Enter the foyer and step onto the tan mosaic flagstone floor. The space soars to thirty-five feet, with huge Douglas fir poles supporting an enormous skylight.

Wedding guests are led to the lounge and reception areas, the latter an octagon-shaped room with an unusual two-tone floor of Brazilian walnut and cherry hardwoods. There are several mirrored arches, one of which cleverly pushes back to provide a place for a band. Hors d'oeuvres and cocktails are served here before an event, and after a seated meal elsewhere, guests often return to dance. The adjacent Main Dining Room is a large, light-filled room with a sizable skylight and two walls of floor-to-ceiling glass. The other two walls feature pastel-colored landscapes. Four large Douglas fir poles that match those in the foyer support a very high, vaulted ceiling. Attached to these poles are multitiered pinpoint fixtures, making evening functions sparkle. Tables are dressed with crisp cream-colored linens overlapping chintz fabric prints.

Beyond the glass walls and doors is the garden courtyard, lushly planted and landscaped to accommodate outdoor ceremonies. Nearby is a large pergola, tennis court and croquet lawn. For outdoor events, you can also tent the adjacent lawns.

This is a must-see location for receptions. Be prepared to be impressed—we think that the Pacific Athletic Club is one of the better event sites on the Peninsula.

CEREMONY CAPACITY: The croquet lawn holds 400 seated; the garden courtyard, up to 100 seated guests.

EVENT/RECEPTION CAPACITY:

Area	Seated	Standing	Area	Seated	Standing
Dining Room	340	600	Outdoor Patio	60	200
Lounge & Reception	—	150	Lawn Area	600	1,000
Ceremony Courtyard	100	150			

MEETING CAPACITY: The Cypress and Sequoia Rooms each hold 12 guests conference style. Combined they accommodate 16 classroom style, 25 in a U-shape, 20 boardroom style and 50 theater style. The Dining Room holds 200 seated theater-style or 100 conference-style.

FEES & DEPOSITS: For special events, a $1,500 non-refundable deposit, which is applied to your event rental, is required to secure your date. The room rental fee is $1,100–2,000 depending on the day of the week reserved, and covers a 4-1/2-hour block of time. Half the anticipated food and beverage cost is payable 180 days in advance and the balance, along with a confirmed guest count, is due 10 working days prior to the function. Seated meals start at $24.50/person, not including hors d'oeuvres or beverages. Alcohol, tax and an 18% service charge are additional.

For meetings, room rentals are as follows: Cypress & Sequoia Rooms $200 each or $400 combined.

AVAILABILITY: Year-round. Saturday and Sunday weddings or special events take place in two time frames: 11:30am–4:pm or 6pm–10:30pm. Overtime is $100/half hour. Monday–Friday corporate or special events may begin after 3pm in the Dining Room. Meetings take place in the Cypress and Sequoia Rooms, and can be scheduled 7 days/week, anytime.

SERVICES/AMENITIES:

Catering: provided
Kitchen Facilities: n/a
Tables & Chairs: provided
Linens, Silver, etc.: provided
Restrooms: wheelchair accessible
Dance Floor: yes
Bride's Dressing Area: CBA
Meeting Equipment: CBA, extra fee
Other: event coordination

Parking: valet available, large lot
Accommodations: no guest rooms
Telephone: pay phones
Outdoor Night Lighting: yes
Outdoor Cooking Facilities: yes
Cleanup: provided
View: (from dining room) lawns, garden courtyard

RESTRICTIONS:

Alcohol: provided, corkage available
Smoking: designated areas
Music: amplified OK

Wheelchair Access: yes
Insurance: not required
Other: no birdseed, rice or helium balloons

---

*This is important! Tell facilities you're reading **Here Comes The Guide** and ask if our information is still current.*

Lark Creek San Mateo

50 East Third Avenue, San Mateo
(650) 344-9443, fax (415) 777-4411

Restaurant

◆ Ceremonies ◆ Special Events
◆ Wedding Receptions ◆ Meetings
◆ Business Functions Accommodations

Lark Creek's new event space is a room with a past—and a somewhat spicy one, at that. Although its recent remodeling has created a soft, understated, updated look, just ask about the room's history, and you'll turn up a tale or two.

Once upon a time—well, during the 1930s and 40s—the Peninsula Room was host to everyone from Betty Grable to the grande dames of neighboring Hillsborough and Atherton. As the ballroom of the Benjamin Franklin Hotel, one of the only fine lodging spots between San Francisco and San Carlos in those years, it was considered the premier event space in the area. It swelled with swells hosting society birthday and anniversary parties, swarmed with Stanford students and alums during post-game dinner dances and, as for Betty Grable—well, she threw herself a party in the Peninsula Room to celebrate a day's winnings at Bay Meadows Race Course.

But as commerce boomed throughout the area in later decades, other hotels sprang up, and the Peninsula Room's preeminence diminished. In 1980, the Ben Franklin was sold to a corporation for its own private use and the Peninsula Room was locked up tight. For the past ten years, only corporate guests saw even so much as its lobby entrance, with the looping peach-colored 1940s wrought-iron script "Peninsula Room" sign surmounting the double doors.

Lark Creek is changing all of that. Two years ago, they moved into what had once been the hotel coffee shop, to establish this third sibling in the Lark Creek family (sister to Walnut Creek's Lark Creek and Larkspur's The Lark Creek Inn). Extensive remodeling produced an open, airy dining space with warm natural wood details, whimsical hanging lamps with larks and forks fluttering after one another, and tall plate glass windows with views of the genteel antique stores, florists, and book shops of Third Avenue.

At the back of the restaurant, a glass door connects Lark Creek with the Peninsula Room, which has also been remodeled. The shape of the space is unchanged—a simple rectangle with four large structural columns—but the room's interior has been entirely updated. Wainscotting, doors, and trim have all been painted a deep peach color, offsetting cream-colored walls and plush new muted-green carpeting. Large hanging pendants and small wall sconces provide illumination, casting a warm glow into the vaulted center portion of the ceiling. Vibrant and whimsical art adorns the walls.

It's a rarity to find a space of this size attached to a restaurant with as fine a kitchen as Lark Creek. Good eating will be a prominent feature of any event held here. Since the kitchen is right next to the Peninsula Room, hot hors d'oeuvres can be whisked from the oven to your mouth in moments. Full-day meeting participants can feast on a Continental breakfast and three-course lunch; sit-down wedding banquets may include four courses or more.

In addition to wonderful food, guests will be grateful for evening valet service and nearby, daytime public parking. Parties and meetings will both benefit from the room's built-in sound system, and Lark Creek can provide services ranging from floral arranging to dance floor rental.

And of course, as you're dancing away the night, you can always contemplate the probability that Betty Grable took a celebratory spin in the exact same spot.

CEREMONY CAPACITY: The Peninsula Room holds 160 seated guests.

EVENT/RECEPTION CAPACITY: The Peninsula Room can accommodate 125 seated or 175 standing; the entire restaurant, 250 seated or 300 standing guests.

MEETING CAPACITY: The Peninsula Room holds 160 guests seated theater-style.

FEES & DEPOSITS: For wedding receptions and special events, a $500 non-refundable deposit is required to reserve your date. For private parties, there is a $100 room setup fee and a $1,000 food and beverage minimum for dinners, $500 minimum for luncheons. Tax and a 20% service charge are additional. For offsite wedding cakes, there is a $3/person cake cutting fee. Any menu can be customized: luncheons start at $19.50/person, dinners at $29/person.

For meetings, a $250 deposit is required, and there is a $250 room setup fee. The food and beverage minimum is $500; tax and a 20% service charge are extra.

AVAILABILITY: Year-round, daily 8am–midnight, except Christmas and New Year's Days.

SERVICES/AMENITIES:
Catering: provided, no BYO
Kitchen Facilities: n/a
Tables & Chairs: provided
Linens, Silver, etc.: provided
Restrooms: wheelchair accessible
Dance Floor: CBA, extra charge
Bride's Dressing Area: CBA
Meeting Equipment: CBA, extra charge
Other: wedding cakes, event coordination

Parking: valet CBA evenings; adjacent street & garage during the day
Accommodations: no guest rooms
Telephone: pay phones
Outdoor Night Lighting: access only
Outdoor Cooking Facilities: n/a
Cleanup: provided
View: outdoor patio and pool

RESTRICTIONS:
Alcohol: provided, no BYO
Smoking: outside only
Music: amplified OK w/restrictions

Wheelchair Access: yes
Insurance: not required
Other: no birdseed, rice or confetti; decorations require approval

The Historic Del Monte Building

100 South Murphy Avenue, Sunnyvale
(408) 735-7680, fax (408) 245-6693

Banquet & Event Facility

◆ Ceremonies ◆ Special Events
◆ Wedding Receptions ◆ Meetings
◆ Business Functions Accommodations

Built in 1904 as a seed plant, the three-story Del Monte Building had been long neglected when a local developer decided to save and restore it. The process wasn't easy. First they had to hire three trucks to carefully move the wooden structure from its location beside railroad tracks to a breezy corner across the street. Then they spent a year rebuilding it from the outside, in. Their hard work has paid off, and the beautifully refurbished Historic Del Monte Building is now a terrific place for weddings—right in the heart of the pre-1900 section of Sunnyvale's downtown.

The main entrance is on a lovely, tree-lined street. Take the wide, carpeted staircase (or the elevator at the rear entrance) to the second and third floors where the fully equipped banquet facilities are located. When you step into the Grand Ballroom, everything you see is brand new, from the golden Wilshire chandeliers set against a stark white ceiling, to the warm mahogany wainscotting. A gleaming hardwood dance floor dominates the room's center. During the day, light filters into the room through white-framed windows and French doors overlooking downtown on one side and a Mediterranean-style villa on the other. Set back into another wall is a handcrafted bar fashioned out of mahogany and beveled glass mirrors.

The third floor houses the Del Monte Room, a smaller space with a cathedral ceiling supported by ten white, fluted columns. At night, a dozen gold-plaited faux candle chandeliers glow overhead, while during the day natural light flows in through windows along two sides. Like the Ballroom, the Del Monte Room also has a built-in bar.

When you gaze up at the Del Monte Building, fronted by tall maple trees and illuminated by old-fashioned lamp posts, it's hard to believe that it was the first commercial structure erected in the city, that it led such a rugged prior existence and that it almost disappeared. By breathing new life into it, the developer not only preserved a little bit of Sunnyvale's past, but created a delightful place to celebrate.

CEREMONY & EVENT/RECEPTION CAPACITY: The Del Monte Room holds 250 seated, 350 standing; the Grand Ballroom, 400 seated or 700 standing guests.

MEETING CAPACITY: The Grand Ballroom holds 450 seated theater-style, 300 seated conference-style. The Del Monte Room holds 325 theater-style, 175 seated conference-style.

FEES & DEPOSITS: For weddings, 50% of the rental fee is required on booking; the balance is due 30 days prior to the event. Wedding packages vary, and can include meals, wedding cake, flowers, dj and service, starting at $22/person. Beverage packages and tax are additional. December pricing may vary; call for specific information. For other months, rental fees are as follows:

Grand Ballroom	Hours	Rental Fee	Del Monte Room	Hours	Rental Fee
Mon–Fri	8am–4pm	$1,000	Mon–Fri	8am–4pm	$600
Mon–Thurs	5pm–midnight	1,200	Mon–Thurs	5pm–midnight	800
Fri (5-hr block)	5pm–midnight	1,500	Fri (5-hr block)	5pm–midnight	1,000
Sat (5-hr block)	10am–5pm	2,500	Sat (5-hr block)	10am–5pm	1,500
	6pm–midnight	2,750		6pm–11:30pm	1,750
Sun (5-hr block)		1,500	Sunday (5-hr block)		1,000
Overtime per hour		400	Overtime per hour		250

AVAILABILITY: Year-round, daily, 8am–midnight. Weekend weddings are scheduled by choosing any 5-hour block between 10:00am–5pm or 6pm–midnight.

SERVICES/AMENITIES:

Catering: provided
Kitchen Facilities: n/a
Tables & Chairs: provided
Linens, Silver, etc.: caterer
Restrooms: wheelchair accessible
Dance Floor: provided
Bride's Dressing Area: yes
Meeting Equipment: full range

Parking: lots and on street
Accommodations: no guest rooms
Telephone: pay phone
Outdoor Night Lighting: deck only
Outdoor Cooking Facilities: no
Cleanup: caterer or renter
View: downtown Sunnyvale

RESTRICTIONS:

Alcohol: provided, no BYO
Smoking: deck only
Music: amplified OK indoors

Wheelchair Access: yes
Insurance: not required
Other: no open flames

The professionals in the back of the book are the best in the business! How do we know? Read page 681.

The Palace Restaurant & Event Center

Historic Theater

146 South Murphy Avenue, Sunnyvale
(800) PALACE-0, (408) 739-5179, fax (408) 739-5237

www.thepalacerestaurant.com

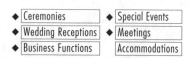

- ◆ Ceremonies
- ◆ Wedding Receptions
- ◆ Business Functions
- ◆ Special Events
- ◆ Meetings
- Accommodations

Restaurant, nightclub and special event venue—The Palace does it all. Located in the Murphy Avenue historical district of Sunnyvale, this 1930s movie theater has been splendidly restored, and transformed into an Art Nouveau paradise. Vivid imagination went into recreating every aspect of the original Palace. The exterior is a swirl of earthy orange tones that brings the building to life. Italian terraza graces the sidewalk, a hand-painted golden lion roars beneath the theater marquee and copper-and-bronze sculptures spruce up the door handles. The lobby is something to behold. Its walls are lined with Aegean gargoyle sconces, and pieces of slate, hand picked for their unusual shades of purple and mauve.

Inside, the theater is visually overwhelming. It's a fluid, multi-level space with deep-colored sculptured walls, a soaring ceiling, a beautiful stage, towering Gothic columns and arched mirrors. We especially appreciated the gleaming hardwood dance floor (refinished every few months to maintain its glow) and the handcrafted ironwork banisters. Couples—particularly those with large guest "audiences"—relish taking their vows on stage. The setting is absolutely opulent: layers of rich blue and greenish-gold velvet curtains spotlighted by dramatic stage lighting. For an especially dramatic ceremony, the staff can transform the interior with floral arrangements, velvet and votive candles.

The mezzanine, which overlooks the main floor, is a semi-private area with its own bar that can be used for smaller ceremonies or cocktails and hors d'oeuvres. The third level, once the projectionist's room, is an eclectic space with an expansive glass window that allows you to check out all the action below. Dominated by a plush blue sofa, this room can serve a multitude of purposes: rehearsal dinners, wedding photos, a bride's dressing room or a private suite for guests seeking a quiet hideaway.

Magnificent as the decor is, however, it's not the only thing that wows guests. The Palace's contemporary American cuisine is, according to the *San Francisco Chronicle,* "some of the most innovative cooking in the Bay Area." Seasonal menus range from tapas and pastas to wild game and creative seafood—all utilizing locally grown organic produce. So here's the big picture: The Palace is a posh place for anyone who appreciates a glamorous atmosphere, delectable cuisine and a sense of history. Stage your "show" in this historic gem and you can't go wrong.

CEREMONY, EVENT/RECEPTION & MEETING CAPACITY:

Area	*Seated*	*Standing*	*Area*	*Seated*	*Standing*
Stage and Main Floor	215–240	600	Private Suite	50	75
Mezzanine	60	100	Entire Facility	325	775

The facility holds up to 400 people seated theater-style

FEES & DEPOSITS: The rental fee is a non-refundable deposit required when you reserve the facility. Half the catering fee is due 60 days prior to the event; the balance is due the day of the wedding. Rental fees are: entire Palace $2,500, main floor only $1,500, mezzanine $500 and private suite $500. Per person food costs start at $20 for hors d'oeuvres receptions, $30 for buffets and $25 for seated meals; alcohol, tax and a 20% service charge are additional.

AVAILABILITY: Year-round, Sunday–Monday, any time. Tuesday–Saturday, 10am–7pm. Additional hours can be negotiated. Closed Christmas and Thanksgiving.

SERVICES/AMENITIES:

Catering: provided
Kitchen Facilities: n/a
Tables & Chairs: provided for 150
Linens, Silver, etc.: provided for 300
Restrooms: wheelchair accessible
Dance Floor: yes
Bride's Dressing Area: private suite
Meeting Equipment: full range CBA, extra fee

Parking: on street, city lots or valet CBA
Accommodations: no guest rooms
Telephone: pay phone
Outdoor Night Lighting: no
Outdoor Cooking Facilities: n/a
Cleanup: provided
View: no
Other: event coordination and DJ/entertainment coordination

RESTRICTIONS:

Alcohol: provided, or corkage $10/bottle
Smoking: not permitted indoors, outdoors only
Music: amplified OK

Wheelchair Access: main floor only
Insurance: certificate required

This is important! Tell facilities you're reading **Here Comes The Guide** and ask if our information is still current.

Thomas Fogarty Winery and Vineyards

Hilltop Winery

19501 Skyline Boulevard, Woodside
(650) 851-6772, fax (650)851-5840

www.fogartywinery.com
tfwinery@aol.com

◆ Ceremonies	◆ Special Events
◆ Wedding Receptions	◆ Meetings
◆ Business Functions	Accommodations

If we were to rate facilities on a scale from 1 to 10, the Fogarty Winery would be a 10! Located off Skyline Boulevard, this has got to be one of the best places we've seen not only for weddings, but for private parties and corporate functions, too.

Commanding an extraordinary panorama of the Bay and Peninsula, the Winery sits high on a ridge in a quiet, vineyard setting. As you drive in, vineyards and a lovely pond with circling swans come into view. At the top of the ridge is a large lawn, beautifully landscaped around the perimeter—a perfect spot for an outdoor ceremony.

Receptions and special events are held in the Hill House or the brand new Pavilion. True to its name, the former steps down the hill, and is designed with incredible attention to detail, featuring a stone fireplace, fine woodwork, skylights, a wine bar and professional kitchen. From comfortable seating indoors, as well as from the semi glass-enclosed terrace, you can see for miles—past the neighboring vineyard all the way to the distant Bay.

Adjacent to the Hill House is the Pavilion, a covered redwood deck suspended over the hillside. Calling it a "covered deck" may be something of an understatement: this 4,000-square-foot architectural treat is constructed of teal-painted columns and beams which support a peaked cedar roof inset with skylights. You have a 270-degree view of the surrounding oak-dotted hills and the Chardonnay vineyards below. The Pavilion is truly the perfect spot for cocktails and hors d'oeuvres or an open-air seated reception—no matter how hot the day is, there's always a breeze blowing here. You can reserve the House or Pavilion individually or use them in combination—they're connected by a deck, so there's a wonderful flow between them.

For small private dinners the Redwood Room is light and airy, arranged with custom-built 'barrel' tables, handcrafted leather chairs, a wood burning stove and full kitchen. Even the restroom is unique, with a blue-green slate and stone bathtub! And if you'd like to have a meeting in this glorious setting, hold it in the Board Room or the Hill house. A recent landscaping project has covered the hillside with ferns, manzanita and native plantings, not to mention tons of river rock. The improvements only add to the sense you get that the Winery has been designed with taste and sophistication to blend in with its surroundings. We can't recommend this facility highly enough.

CEREMONY CAPACITY: The garden holds 220 seated or standing.

EVENT/RECEPTION CAPACITY: The Hill House can accommodate 220 seated guests, maximum.

MEETING CAPACITY:

Area	Conference-style	Theater-style	Area	Conference-style	Theater-style
Board Room	20	—	Hill House	50	110
Pavilion	—	110			

FEES & DEPOSITS: For weddings, a non-refundable deposit of 50% of the rental fee is due when reservations are confirmed; the balance is payable 4 months prior to your function. The rental fee includes use of the lawn area, Hill House and Pavilion for 8 hours. The rental fee for the entire facility is $5,600 April 15–November 15; $3,500 November 16–April 14.

For other special events and business functions, fees vary depending on spaces selected, event duration, day of week and season. Call for rates.

AVAILABILITY: Year-round, daily. For weddings and receptions, weekends 8am–9pm. For corporate events, any day 7am–11pm. Closed Thanksgiving, Christmas and New Year's days and eves.

SERVICES/AMENITIES:

Catering: select from preferred list
Kitchen Facilities: fully equipped
Tables & Chairs: some provided
Linens, Silver, etc.: BYO
Restrooms: wheelchair accessible
Dance Floor: inside Hill House
Bride's Dressing Area: yes
Meeting Equipment: full range
Other: event coordination, wine tasting

Parking: for weddings, valet included in fee
Accommodations: no guest rooms
Telephone: pay phone
Outdoor Night Lighting: yes
Outdoor Cooking Facilities: CBA
Cleanup: caterer
View: panoramic vistas of SF Bay, and entire coastal region, including all major mtn peaks

RESTRICTIONS:

Alcohol: WC provided, no BYO
Smoking: outside only
Music: must select band from preferred list, DJs not permitted; acoustic only outdoors

Wheelchair Access: yes
Insurance: certificate recommended

The professionals in the back of the book are the best in the business! How do we know? Read page 681.

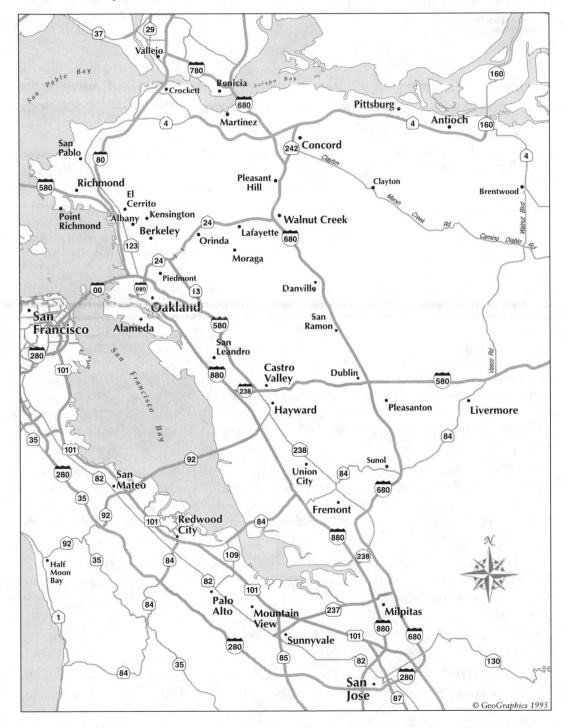

east bay

Camelot and Voyager

Compass Rose Yacht Charters

Marina Village Yacht Harbor, Alameda
(510) 523-9500, fax (510) 523-9200

www.compassrosecharters.com
cmpsrse@best.com

◆ Ceremonies   ◆ Special Events
◆ Wedding Receptions   ◆ Meetings
◆ Business Functions   ◆ Accommodations

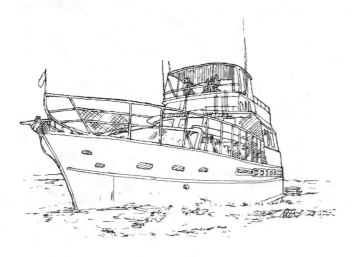

Invite your guests aboard one of Compass Rose's two luxury yachts for a wedding everyone will remember. The 65-foot motoryacht *Camelot* features exquisite interior detailing that is certain to meet anyone's standards. Highly polished exotic hardwoods, chandeliers, European tapestries, sterling silver tea sets, crystal vases and fine wool carpeting will make your guests feel like they've entered a prestigious home.

Owner Brad Agler, a long-time boating enthusiast, purchased the vessel to entertain his clients and friends. After they expressed an interest in chartering the yacht for their own functions, Brad decided to charter *Camelot* commercially to fill a market niche that wasn't being served. Now Coast Guard certified, *Camelot* supplies personalized, affordable elegance, from the large main salon and formal dining salon, each with rich mahogany paneling, to Italian marble vanities and tile floors in each of the two full-size bathrooms. Below, there are three staterooms decorated in antique ivory and jewel tones. A state-of-the-art sound system provides music throughout. Stay overnight in luxurious quarters featuring a master stateroom, master suite and bedroom sitting room.

The 75-foot *Voyager* is the perfect complement to *Camelot*. She's more spacious, with formal seated dining for 60 or a buffet for 80, and also features a full length bar, a hardwood dance floor, and a professional sound system. The flybridge (upper deck) is a popular setting for *al fresco* dining. Fully covered, the deck can be left open to sea breezes or enclosed to ensure the comfort of your guests.

Full bar service is available on each yacht and the chef will customize your menu to meet your individual needs. Operated out of Marina Village in Alameda, the yachts will greet and deliver guests around the Bay.

CEREMONY, EVENT/RECEPTION & MEETING CAPACITY: Maximum capacity including wedding staff is 48 for *Camelot* and 80 for *Voyager*.

FEES & DEPOSITS: Half the estimated event total is the deposit required to reserve your date; the balance is due 5 days prior to the event. The charter rate Friday evening, Saturday and

Sunday is $400/hour for *Camelot* and $525/hour for *Voyager;* weekdays including Sunday evenings it's $325/hour for *Camelot* and $450/hour for *Voyager.* Food and beverages are provided on board; menus are customized for each function. The average cost is $30/person including hors d'oeuvres, entrée and dessert. The captain's fee for performing a ceremony is $100.

AVAILABILITY: Year-round, daily, any time.

SERVICES/AMENITIES:

Catering: provided, or BYO licensed & insured

Kitchen Facilities: fully equipped

Tables & Chairs: some provided

Linens, Silver, etc.: provided

Restrooms: not wheelchair accessible

Dance Floor: yes

Bride's Dressing Area: provided

Meeting Equipment: AV, flipcharts, cordless microphone, overheads, etc.

Parking: several lots in Marina Village

Accommodations: 3 guest rooms

Telephone: onboard radio and cellular phones

Outdoor Night Lighting: yes

Outdoor Cooking Facilities: n/a

Cleanup: provided

View: of the entire San Francisco Bay

Other: wedding cakes, florals, referrals

RESTRICTIONS:

Alcohol: provided, corkage $7/bottle

Smoking: restricted to back deck

Music: sound system provided or BYO, amplified OK

Wheelchair Access: no

Insurance: not required

This is important! Tell facilities you're reading **Here Comes The Guide** and ask if our information is still current.

Commodore Dining Events

& the Commodore's Waterfront Cafe

Docked at Mariner Square, Alameda
Serving 12 ports around SF Bay
(510) 256-4000, fax (510) 256-4113

www.commodoredining.com
events@commodoredining.com

Dining Yachts & Cafe

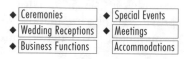

◆ Ceremonies	◆ Special Events
◆ Wedding Receptions	◆ Meetings
◆ Business Functions	Accommodations

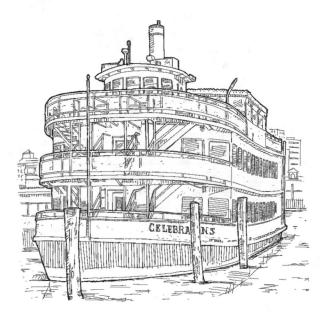

Whether you'd like to have your event on the water or right next to it, Commodore Dining Events (CDE) can offer you the best of both worlds. Their fleet of large white yachts—which serves twelve ports around San Francisco Bay—is docked at the foot of Mariner Square Drive in Alameda. Just steps away is their Waterfront Cafe, a relaxed, warm space with wraparound windows and views of the water no matter where you sit. If you decide to host your wedding and reception here, you can have your ceremony in the adjacent gazebo.

But most people prefer to celebrate on one of Commodore's six yachts. The *Celebrations Commodore*, built in 1991, is a three-deck replica of a Hudson River steamboat of yesteryear. It boasts two 30-foot dance floors with 50-inch screens for corporate, personal or music videos. The *Treasure Island Commodore* is San Francisco's Bay's largest 150-passenger yacht, with 3,600 square feet on its two decks. It, too, has a large dance floor and a 45-inch television for videos. The *TIC* is virtually a floating glass restaurant, with floor-to-ceiling windows, and it has a large outside area ideal for wedding ceremonies or kite flying (kids have a blast!). The *Chardonnay Commodore*, built in 1991, has an extended pilothouse, which is available as a changing room for brides, or as a gathering place for immediate family during the event. The *Cabernet Commodore* and *Zinfandel Commodore* are two 90-foot, million-dollar yachts that will carry you and your guests in stylish comfort. The *Champagne Commodore* may be the Bay's fastest dining yacht in its class, and is ideal for those wishing to circumnavigate the Bay.

In addition to weddings, corporate events and family reunions, CDE specializes in student parties. They have a special manager who coordinates these events, making sure that high school and college coeds have a sensational and safe time. Each vessel is well equipped and designed for entertaining on San Francisco Bay, with parquet dance floors, full galleys and bars on board. During their cruise, guests have unobstructed views of San Francisco and the bridges while dining or dancing. CDE has more than 25 years of experience in hosting events, and if their collection of thank-you letters is any indication—they received more than sixteen in one month!—they must be doing something right. So take a deep breath, relax, and let them take care of everything. Nothing beats a reception on the water.

CEREMONY, EVENT/RECEPTION & MEETING CAPACITY:

Space	*Seated*	*Standing*	*Space*	*Seated*	*Standing*
Celebrations Commodore	405	450	*Champagne Commodore*	72	75
Treasure Island Commodore	150	150	*Chardonnay Commodore*	80	111
Cabernet Commodore	150	150	*Zinfandel Commodore*	150	150
Commodore's Waterfront Cafe	125	200			

FEES & DEPOSITS: A refundable deposit in the amount of 25% of the event total is required to secure your date; the balance is payable 10 days prior to the event. For the vessels, fees run approximately $26–75/person, including 4-hour yacht charter and meals. Alcohol, tax and service charge are additional. The rental fee for the Waterfront Cafe runs $200/hour.

For daytime business meetings, fees will vary; call for specifics. If you need darkened space to run an overhead projector, note that windows can be curtained.

AVAILABILITY: Year-round, daily, any time day or night.

SERVICES/AMENITIES:

Catering: provided, BYO by arrangement
Kitchen Facilities: fully equipped
Tables & Chairs: provided
Linens, Silver, etc.: provided
Restrooms: not wheelchair accessible
Dance Floor: provided
Bride's Dressing Area: yes
Meeting Equipment: microphones, screens, slide & overhead projectors

Parking: large lot
Accommodations: no guest rooms
Telephone: ship-to-shore and cellular
Outdoor Night Lighting: yes
Outdoor Cooking Facilities: portable BBQs
Cleanup: provided
View: SF Bay & skyline, Alcatraz and bridges
Other: coordination, decorations, homing doves, nondenominational ceremonies

RESTRICTIONS:

Alcohol: provided, BYO by arrangement
Smoking: some restrictions
Music: amplified OK

Wheelchair Access: yes
Insurance: not required

The professionals in the back of the book are the best in the business! How do we know? Read page 681.

O'Club & Conference Center

641 West Red Line, Alameda
(510) 483-5210, fax (510) 483-6855

Historic Officer's Club

◆ Ceremonies	◆ Special Events
◆ Wedding Receptions	◆ Meetings
◆ Business Functions	Accommodations

The "O" in "O'Club" stands for "Officers," and the officers who frequented this club certainly lived like gentlemen. It was built at the Alameda Naval Air Station in 1941, when America was entering World War II, and Uncle Sam didn't stint on the luxuries. Even the entrance is imposing: a 40-foot-long canopy shelters the walkway from the street to the massive front doors. Walking under it makes you feel like a VIP, and it's no stretch of the imagination to picture the glamorous arrival of famous military, political and entertainment figures during the Club's heyday. John F. Kennedy, for example, attended a gala in his honor here, and Lucille Ball, Henry Fonda and Van Johnson were feted at a wrap party for Yours, Mine and Ours, a film shot on the base.

Once inside, you get the impression that nothing was too good for the Navy's elite. There are tables handcrafted from solid oak, chairs covered with the highest grade calfskin leather, and chandeliers made of leaded crystal; the O'Club was built and furnished in an era when people really cared about quality. And then there's the palpable sense of history, which practically oozes from behind every dark redwood panel. In the cozy Squadron Room, where Naval aviators gathered for a last drink before flying off to battle, their squadron insignia stare down in mute testimony to their heroics. You couldn't ask for a more intimate setting for a small wedding, or a better changing room for the bride at a large one.

Events that shaped history were conceived in the Trident Room next door. Officers planned military strategy from the comfort of the same leather wingback chairs you see here. The stately fireplace, plush carpets, dark oak paneling and antique crystal chandeliers give the Trident Room a rich, warm, comfortable feel—acoustically as well as visually. It's the ideal room for drinks and hors d'oeuvres before the wedding ceremony.

You might even be tempted to use the Trident Room for the ceremony itself—that is, until you see the Main Ballroom, which echoes the Trident Room's sumptuous decor, and has some innovative touches of its own. Along one wall, separated from the parquet dance floor by a gleaming brass railing, is a two-foot elevated platform with overstuffed leather booths. Above each booth is a crystal sconce that matches the chandeliers in every detail. It's the perfect place for the wedding party, family and guests of honor. To the right of the platform is a stage for the band, with a superb sound system and a large, pull-down movie screen, in case you want to show slides, movies or videos.

If you're planning a smaller wedding and don't need the space of the Main Ballroom or the Trident Room, the Garden Room, with its hand-painted floral motifs and green lattice work, provides a serene atmosphere. Or, on sunny days, you can move outdoors into the lovely Terrace Garden for a ceremony al fresco.

The O'Club was built to provide rest and relaxation for America's fighting men and women. But now that times have changed, it's proving to be a much better place for love than it ever was for war.

CEREMONY CAPACITY: Outdoors, the Main Patio holds 300 or the Terrace Garden 200 seated; indoors, the Trident Room holds 200 seated. A nearby, non-denominational chapel can accommodate up to 300 seated guests.

EVENT/RECEPTION & MEETING CAPACITY:

Room	Seated	Standing	Room	Seated	Standing
Terrace	100	130	Terrace Garden	250	300
Squadron	30	50	Trident	180	225
Main Ballroom	250	360	Main Patio	200	300
Gold Room	20	20	Caravan Room	50	20
Entire Facility	700	1,100			

FEES & DEPOSITS: To reserve your date, half of the rental fee is required as a deposit; the rental balance is payable 30 days prior to the event. A $500 food and beverage deposit is also payable when your booking is confirmed; the remaining 75% of the food total is due 5 weeks prior, and the balance is billed after the event. Luncheons start at $15/person, dinners at $25/person, and hors d'oeuvres at $20/person; tax, a 15% service charge and alcohol are additional. For an outdoor ceremony, the setup fee is $100. To rent specific rooms (6-hour minimum), rental fees run $50–100/hour depending on the room; for the entire Club, $2,500 for an 8-hour function; hourly rates will be charged for each additional hour.

AVAILABILITY: Year-round, daily, except major holidays, 6am–midnight. Saturday weddings take place 10am–4pm or 6am–midnight.

SERVICES/AMENITIES:

Catering: provided, no BYO
Kitchen Facilities: n/a
Tables & Chairs: provided
Linens, Silver, etc.: provided
Restrooms: wheelchair accessible
Dance Floor: parquet floor, portable & patio
Bride's & Groom's Dressing Area: yes
Meeting Equipment: CBA, extra charge

Parking: large lots
Accommodations: no guest rooms, CBA
Telephone: pay phones
Outdoor Night Lighting: yes
Outdoor Cooking Facilities: BBQs
Cleanup: provided
View: landscaped garden
Other: event coordination, San Francisco ferry access CBA

RESTRICTIONS:

Alcohol: provided; if BYO, service fee extra
Smoking: outside only
Music: amplified OK w/volume limits; curfew 11pm weekdays, midnight Fri & Sat

Wheelchair Access: yes
Insurance: extra liability may be required
Other: no rice or confetti; decorations require approval

Bancroft Hotel

2680 Bancroft Way, Berkeley
(510) 549-1000, fax (510) 549-1070

www.bancrofthotel.com
reservations@bancrofthotel.com

◆ Ceremonies ◆ Special Events
◆ Wedding Receptions ◆ Meetings
◆ Business Functions ◆ Accommodations

The Bancroft Hotel, located across the street from the University of California and next door to the University Art Museum, has become one of the premiere hotels in the area since it was built in 1928. Originally the home of the College Women's Club, it was designed by Walter T. Steilberg (an associate of Julia Morgan, the architect who designed San Simeon) and is currently a National Register landmark building. Julia Morgan-inspired furniture and period reproductions grace public spaces; furnishings in the Hotel's guest rooms were reproduced from Walter Steilberg's original drawings.

An absolute must-see is the Hotel's one-of-a-kind 4,000-square-foot event space. It's a large room with three sections, featuring floor-to-ceiling woodwork, Arts and Crafts period detailing, stained glass windows, hardwood floors and two large fireplaces. The raised stage at one end is suitable for musicians while the recessed middle section can be transformed into an intimate dance floor or dining space. The other end can be set up for wining and dining. The room is spacious and extremely flexible—you could probably arrange your party in a variety of ways and still have it work beautifully. The property has recently undergone an extensive restoration and it's now perfect for a warm, comfortable reception. This is a small boutique hotel, ideal for housing out-of-town relatives and friends—a real find in the East Bay. If you are looking for a distinctive indoor wedding site that imparts a sense of history, the Bancroft Hotel is a wonderful choice.

CEREMONY CAPACITY: Indoors, up to 200 seated guests.

EVENT/RECEPTION CAPACITY: The facility holds 175–225 seated guests (depending on whether or not a dance floor is required) or 300 for a standing reception.

MEETING CAPACITY: The Hotel can accommodate 250 seated theater-style.

FEES & DEPOSITS: To secure your date, the entire rental fee is required as a deposit when you sign your contract. The rental fee averages $300–900 and varies depending on season and day of week.

AVAILABILITY: Year-round, daily, any time.

SERVICES/AMENITIES:

Catering: select from preferred list
Kitchen Facilities: fully equipped
Tables & Chairs: CBA, extra charge
Linens, Silver, etc.: CBA, extra charge
Restrooms: wheelchair accessible
Dance Floor: CBA, extra charge
Bride's Dressing Area: CBA
Meeting Equipment: banquet tables, flip charts

Parking: adjacent lot or valet CBA
Accommodations: 22 guest rooms
Telephone: pay phones
Outdoor Night Lighting: CBA
Outdoor Cooking Facilities: no
Cleanup: provided
View: SF Bay & Oakland hills
Other: event coordinator CBA

RESTRICTIONS:

Alcohol: provided by caterer, no red wine
Smoking: not allowed
Music: amplified restricted

Wheelchair Access: yes
Insurance: not required
Other: decorations restricted; no rice, petals or confetti

*This is important! Tell facilities you're reading **Here Comes The Guide** and ask if our information is still current.*

347

Berkeley City Club

2315 Durant Avenue, Berkeley
(510) 848-7800, fax (510) 848-5900

bccevents@aol.com
berkctyclb@aol.com

Historic Social Club

♦ Ceremonies ♦ Special Events
♦ Wedding Receptions ♦ Meetings
♦ Business Functions ♦ Accommodations

The Berkeley City Club is a sensational landmark building, located just one block from the U.C. Berkeley campus. It's a private social club, designed in 1927 by Julia Morgan in a Venetian-Mediterranean style with landscaped inner courtyards and fountains. The Club includes a 75-foot swimming pool, dining room and bar lounges, along with conference and reception rooms, all of which are available for celebrations.

The detailing and craftsmanship are impressive throughout. The Drawing Room and Member's Lounge are large and gracious, with beamed ceilings, pianos, fireplaces, wall tapestries, tile floors, Oriental carpets and sizable leaded glass windows. The Ballroom is a theater-like space with a stage, parquet floor, concert grand piano and its own leaded glass windows. For an outdoor reception, the canopied Terrace is a wonderful outdoor spot on a warm day.

One of the nicest things about having an event at the Berkeley City Club is that many of the rooms adjoin and can serve double duty for both ceremonies and receptions. Campus and downtown life bustles all around the City Club, yet it remains a quiet, old-world oasis in the middle of town.

CEREMONY, EVENT/RECEPTION CAPACITY, FEES & DEPOSITS: A $750 non-refundable rental deposit is required when the reservations are confirmed; the balance and a final guest count are due 10 days prior to the function.

Room	*Ceremony*	*Standing*	*Seated*	*Fees*
Drawing Room	130	100	70	$400
Drawing Room & Courtyard	—	125 total	—	600
Courtyard	25	60	25	200
Loggia Court	—	—	12	60–150
Room	*Ceremony*	*Standing*	*Seated*	*Fees*
Venetian Ballroom	300	500	325	$950
Venetian Room	—	50	—	200
Member's Lounge	100	80	60	500
The Terrace	150	120	100	450
Julia Morgan Room *(for rehearsal dinners)*	—	—	40	250

All fees cover a 4-hour rental period. An additional flat fee of $500 is applied to Sunday and holiday-weekend events. For a separate bar setup, there's a $100 bartender fee. Luncheons range from $15–17/person, dinners or buffets, $24.50–29/person. Menus and event details can be arranged with the event coordinator. If your group would like to stay overnight, bed and breakfast rates will apply. Call for more information.

Fees for meetings range $15–75/hour, Monday–Friday, with a 4-hour minimum.

MEETING CAPACITY: The Berkeley City Club has 5 meeting rooms that can accommodate up to 300 seated theater-style, 180 seated conference-style or 125 seated classroom-style.

AVAILABILITY: Year-round, daily, 6am–10pm; extra hours can be arranged. Closed Thanksgiving, Christmas and New Years.

SERVICES/AMENITIES:

Catering: provided, no BYO
Kitchen Facilities: n/a
Tables & Chairs: provided
Linens, Silver, etc.: provided
Restrooms: wheelchair accessible
Dance Floor: yes
Bride's Dressing Area: yes
Meeting Equipment: full range CBA

Parking: City Club lot CBA, valet or prepaid
Accommodations: 20 guest rooms
Telephone: pay and guest phones
Outdoor Night Lighting: yes
Outdoor Cooking Facilities: no
Cleanup: provided
View: indoor courtyards
Other: event coordinator, candelabras

RESTRICTIONS:

Alcohol: provided, no BYO
Smoking: designated areas
Music: amplified OK

Wheelchair Access: yes
Insurance: sometimes required
Other: security sometimes required

DARY

The professionals in the back of the book are the best in the business! How do we know? Read page 681.

349

Brazilian Room

Tilden Park, Berkeley
(510) 540-0220, fax (510) 845-3614

www.ebparks.org
brazil@ebparks.org

Historic Banquet Facility

◆ Ceremonies ◆ Special Events
◆ Wedding Receptions ◆ Meetings
◆ Business Functions Accommodations

Once a part of the 1939 Golden Gate Exposition on Treasure Island, the Brazilian Room was presented as a gift to the East Bay Regional Park District by the country of Brazil. The original interior hardwood paneling was kept intact, while a new exterior of local rock and timber was constructed to permanently house the room. Natural light flows through the floor-to-ceiling leaded glass windows that run the length of the room on both sides, and parquet wood flooring and a huge stone fireplace give the space an added charm and warmth.

Outside, the large flagstone patio overlooks a sloping lawn and the adjacent botanical garden. Located in Tilden Park, nestled high in the Berkeley Hills above UC Berkeley, the serene, pastoral surroundings offer an environment free from noise and distraction. It's no surprise that the Brazilian Room has become one of the most popular wedding sites in Northern California.

CEREMONY CAPACITY: The patio holds up to 180 seated; the main room, up to 150 seated or 225 standing guests.

EVENT/RECEPTION CAPACITY: The main room holds 225 standing guests or 150 seated.

MEETING CAPACITY: The main room can accommodate 150 seated conference-style or 225 seated theater-style.

FEES, DEPOSITS & AVAILABILITY: A $350 non-refundable deposit is required to secure your date. The fee balance is due 120 days prior to the event. Optional services are available at an extra charge. For non-residents of Alameda and Contra Costa counties, add $200 on weekends and holidays only.

Weekend Rates (min. 5 hours)	Fee	Time Frames
Saturday, Sunday & holidays	$1,100	9am–4pm or 5pm–midnight
Friday evening	950	6pm–midnight
	1,225	3pm–midnight

Weekday Rates (min. 3 hours)

Monday, Wednesday, Thursday	$275	8am–midnight
Friday day, any 3-hour block	225*	
each additional weekday hour	$50	
special all day rate	300	8am–4pm
	225*	

Seasonal Sunday Rates (min. 6 hours)

November through March,		
any 6-hour block	$950	9am–midnight
each additional hour	150	

* *rates apply to business meetings, retreats and trainings*

SERVICES/AMENITIES:

Catering: select from approved list
Kitchen Facilities: ample
Tables & Chairs: provided
Linens, Silver, etc.: BYO
Restrooms: wheelchair accessible
Dance Floor: yes
Bride's Dressing Area: yes
Meeting Equipment: PA, projector & screen

Parking: large lot, no fees
Accommodations: no guest rooms
Telephone: pay phone
Outdoor Night Lighting: yes
Outdoor Cooking Facilities: yes
Cleanup: caterer
View: great views of Tilden Park with lots of trees and relative privacy

RESTRICTIONS:

Alcohol: BYO; WCB only, kegs of beer restricted to patio and kitchen
Smoking: outside only
Music: amplified OK inside only

Wheelchair Access: yes
Insurance: extra liability required
Other: decorations restricted

This is important! Tell facilities you're reading **Here Comes The Guide** *and ask if our information is still current.*

The Claremont Resort & Spa

41 Tunnel Road, Berkeley
(510) 843-3000, fax (510) 843-6239

www.claremontresort.com

Landmark Hotel

◆ Ceremonies ◆ Special Events
◆ Wedding Receptions ◆ Meetings
◆ Business Functions ◆ Accommodations

The brilliantly white, castle-like Claremont Resort has been a Bay Area landmark since 1915, when owner Frank Havens (who won the resort's 22 acres of land in a high-stakes game of checkers) opened the hostelry for groups of tourists attending San Francisco's Pan-Pacific Exposition. Snug against the hills on the border between Berkeley and Oakland, the sprawling resort commands one of the best views in the Bay Area, and that— along with its old-fashioned, Victorian appearance and luxurious amenities—has made it a perennial favorite with well-heeled travelers. Included among the hotel's devotées was the architect Frank Lloyd Wright, who proclaimed the Claremont "one of the few hotels in the world with warmth, character and charm." We tend to agree. After all, could the esteemed Mr. Wright be wrong?

Seated receptions take place in one of the Claremont's many ballrooms, and each has a distinct, individual style. Intimate gatherings will be delighted with the lobby-level Horizon Room; its rose, green and blue color scheme, faux marble pillars and vintage crystal chandeliers create a delicate, timeless elegance—and the panoramic view from the wall of west-facing windows encompasses both bridges and the San Francisco skyline. The adjacent Lanai Room, with matching decor, offers one of the nicest indoor ceremony spaces we've seen, and comes complete with an outdoor balcony for great photo opportunities.

An added bonus is the resort's $6-million spa facility with salon, specializing in wedding packages that include facials, hairstyling, manicures, pedicures and makeup applications—all of which will ensure that you'll be picture perfect on your wedding day. And if you'd like to calm those pre-wedding jitters, try the spa's herbal body treatment or the "Ultimate-80 Massage." If the planning alone has you stressed, just remember that the Claremont has an on-site florist and a phalanx of event coordinators and caterers who'll take care of all the details for you.

CEREMONY CAPACITY: The Lanai Room holds 50–100 seated; the Napa Ballroom 180 seated guests.

EVENT/RECEPTION CAPACITY: The largest ballroom can accommodate 325 seated with dancing, 430 seated without, or 550 standing for a cocktail reception. Capacities for the 20 other rooms range from 30–360 seated guests.

MEETING CAPACITY: There are 20 rooms that can accommodate 20–450 seated theater-style, 30–275 classroom-style, or 8–60 conference-style.

FEES & DEPOSITS: For special events and weddings, a $1,000 non-refundable deposit is required to hold your date. Half of the total estimated bill is due 4 months prior to the event; the balance is due at its conclusion.

Wedding packages are available starting at $72/person, and include dinner, wedding cake, floral arrangements for the tables, room rental fee, tax and service charges. Any menu can be customized. Seated meals start at $42/person; alcohol, tax and service charges are additional. The rental fee for any ballroom is $700. For ceremonies, there is a $600 setup charge in the Ballrooms, $300 for smaller rooms.

Fees for business functions and meetings vary depending on room(s) and services selected. Corporate day meeting packages are available; call for specific pricing.

AVAILABILITY: Year-round, daily, 6am–midnight.

SERVICES/AMENITIES:

Catering: provided, no BYO
Kitchen Facilities: n/a
Tables & Chairs: provided
Linens, Silver, etc.: provided
Restrooms: wheelchair accessible
Dance Floor: provided
Bride's & Groom's Dressing Area: CBA
Meeting Equipment: full range AV
Other: event coordination, spa

Parking: self parking and valet
Accommodations: 279 guest rooms
Telephone: pay phone
Outdoor Night Lighting: access only
Outdoor Cooking Facilities: no
Cleanup: provided
View: entire East Bay and San Francisco Bay plus San Francisco skyline

RESTRICTIONS:

Alcohol: provided, or corkage $15/bottle
Smoking: outdoors only
Music: amplified OK indoors only

Wheelchair Access: yes
Insurance: not required

The professionals in the back of the book are the best in the business! *How do we know? Read page 681.*

The Faculty Club

University of California at Berkeley, Berkeley
(510) 643-0834, fax (510) 540-6204

http://amber.berkeley.edu:5035
theclub@uclink.berkeley.edu

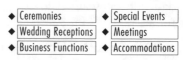

Historic Campus Club

◆ Ceremonies   ◆ Special Events
◆ Wedding Receptions   ◆ Meetings
◆ Business Functions   ◆ Accommodations

Nestled in a redwood grove along Strawberry Creek is the Faculty Club at the University of California at Berkeley, built in 1902 by the renowned architect Bernard Maybeck. Designed to recreate the feel of an English country manor, every inch of the Faculty Club oozes tradition. But its crowning glory is Maybeck's masterpiece, the Great Hall. Picture a Gothic cathedral, made of redwood instead of stone. Picture a three-story vaulted ceiling, a massive stone fireplace, and stained glass windows featuring heraldic crests of the great universities of the world. And everything is covered with rich, dark redwood paneling. This could sound gloomy; but it isn't, because Maybeck also included huge, floor-to-ceiling windows that suffuse the Great Hall with a warm golden glow. Instead of being intimidating, this monumental hall feels intimate. The smaller Seaborg and Heyns rooms (named after a chancellor and a distinguished University Nobel Laureate) echo the Great Hall's ambiance, and offer a few extra touches, including a priceless collection of William Morris chairs and imported English carpeting featuring Morris' designs.

The Faculty Club has long been a favorite spot for Bar and Bat Mitzvahs, anniversary parties, retirement dinners and, of course, class reunions. But it really comes into its own during weddings. Many couples like to have the ceremony right outside on the rolling green of Faculty Glade, then move into the Great Hall for the wedding feast. (The Heyns and Seaborg rooms also have private terraces for al fresco ceremonies.) And if the weather suddenly turns rainy, club staffers can move the whole shebang indoors in a matter of minutes. These experienced staffers are the Faculty Club's greatest asset. Sales & Marketing Director Janet Lukehart has been arranging events at the Club for sixteen years, and she and her crew are old hands at anticipating problems and making sure they don't happen. Do any of your guests have special dietary needs? The Faculty Club can provide wheatless, dairyless, nonfat, vegetarian, vegan or Kosher meals. For the ultimate in convenience, your guests can stay overnight in the upstairs bedrooms (which are otherwise reserved for visiting scholars) and walk down the stairs to the ceremony. If the bride needs a room to change in, or the florist needs a room to stash the flowers in, the Club will provide one at no cost. And there's no such thing as double booking. "If you reserve the Great Hall or any of our rooms, you're the only one who will have it all day," says Lukehart. "I just can't picture myself telling a bride she has to get married at 10 am because someone else needs the room at four o'clock."

The Faculty Club has a full catering service ("Everything but the wedding cake," says Lukehart) offering menus for every event, from a brunch buffet to a formal sit-down dinner, with afternoon tea thrown in for good measure. "But we're not rigid about it," says Lukehart. "If you want to combine something from one menu with something from another menu, no problem. We'll do whatever it takes to make it a special day." How serious is this commitment? Well, there are only two reserved parking spaces outside the Faculty Club. One is for the bride and groom. The other is for winners of the Nobel Prize.

CEREMONY CAPACITY: The Faculty Glade can seat 250 guests; indoors, up to 200 seated.

EVENT/RECEPTION CAPACITY: The Faculty Club holds 225 seated guests or 325 standing.

MEETING CAPACITY: The Club can accommodate 2–225 guests, seated theater-style.

FEES & DEPOSITS: For social events, a $750 refundable deposit is required to secure your date; the event balance is due 15 days prior to the event. For business functions, a $30–800 room rental fee acts as the deposit, due upon reservation; the balance is due at the end of the event. Catering is provided; meals run $15–50/person; tax, alcohol and a 15% service charge are additional. A $1/person cake-cutting fee is extra and for ceremonies, there's a $1/chair fee.

AVAILABILITY: Year-round, daily, any time.

SERVICES/AMENITIES:

Catering: provided, no BYO
Kitchen Facilities: n/a
Tables & Chairs: provided
Linens, Silver, etc.: provided
Restrooms: wheelchair accessible
Dance Floor: yes
Bride's & Groom's Dressing Area: yes
Meeting Equipment: BYO or CBA, extra charge
Other: event coordination

Parking: on-campus, pay parking available evenings and weekends
Accommodations: 23 guest rooms
Telephone: pay and house phones
Outdoor Night Lighting: yes
Outdoor Cooking Facilities: no
Cleanup: provided
View: lawn, creek and garden
Other: baby grand piano

RESTRICTIONS:

Alcohol: provided or BYO, corkage $9/bottle
Smoking: outside only
Music: amplified OK

Wheelchair Access: except to Seaborg Room
Insurance: not required
Other: no rice or glitter; decorations restricted

---

*This is important! Tell facilities you're reading **Here Comes The Guide** and ask if our information is still current.*

First Church of Christ, Scientist, Berkeley

Landmark Church

2619 Dwight Way, Berkeley
(510) 869-5105, fax (925) 284-9552

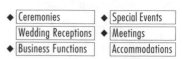

◆ Ceremonies   ◆ Special Events
Wedding Receptions   ◆ Meetings
◆ Business Functions   Accommodations

It's impossible. You can't walk into the auditorium of the First Church of Christ, Scientist, for the first time and not stagger for a moment, your mouth agape in awe-struck admiration. And that's exactly what the architect, Bernard Maybeck, intended.

When Maybeck built it in 1910, he wanted to create "a church that would satisfy the joyous, holy feelings of an early Christian." And he succeeded beyond our wildest dreams (if not his). Over the years, art historians have vied with each other for superlatives to describe its breathtaking grandeur. One early expert called it "a gilded, painted, gray and golden, blue and silver glory of Byzantine and Gothic elements that makes the heart sing to look at it."

Berkeley has many beautiful buildings, but The First Church of Christ, Scientist, is the only one to be declared a National Historic Landmark. A few years ago, the American Institute of Architects chose it as the third most beautiful church in the country, surpassed only by H.H. Richardson's Trinity Church in Boston and Frank Lloyd Wright's Unity Temple in Chicago.

With typical modesty, the Christian Scientists call the main room an "auditorium," but it's really a symphony of wood and glass—a blend of Gothic cathedral and California bungalow styles. Looking up, you see dark, massive wooden trusses soaring in front of exquisite wooden Gothic tracery. Imported Belgian glass catches light streaming in from below, transforming the area with a heavenly glow of aurora-like reflections. Medieval cathedral builders used stained glass to achieve this effect, but Maybeck was able to accomplish the same thing with translucent glass, artfully utilizing the flowers and trees outside and the fanciful painted ornamentation inside to filter the light into dazzling reds, blues, yellows and greens. More "light magic" comes from twenty pew lamps suspended from the ceiling—light cast through their internal cut-outs creates a sea of delicate starlights.

The auditorium is also acoustically perfect, which means you can have anything from a solo soprano sweetly singing "Amazing Grace" to the church's mighty pipe organ thundering the strains of Mendelssohn's Wedding March, and it will all sound great.

For smaller wedding parties, the jewelbox-like chapel—with its flying buttresses and handpainted tracery—and the inviting, appropriately-named Fireplace Room echo the themes and motifs of the auditorium on a smaller scale. If you prefer an outdoor ceremony, the exquisite, Japanese-influenced courtyard, with wisteria vines delicately dangling from trellises designed by Maybeck himself, provides a serene, almost Zen-like setting on warm, clear days.

It takes a genius to combine so many diverse elements and make it all work, but that's what Maybeck was. He created one of the most dramatic interiors in the world. And yet, for all its grandeur, it's also intimate. We can't imagine a more glorious setting for a bride and groom to start their lives together.

CEREMONY CAPACITY: The Main Auditorium holds over 500 seated, the Sunday School Chapel 150 seated, the Fireplace Room 75 seated and Garden Court 25–30 seated guests.

EVENT/RECEPTION CAPACITY: Wedding receptions do not take place at this venue.

EVENT/MEETING CAPACITY:

Room	Theater-style	Room	Theater-style
Main Auditorium	500	Fireplace Room	75
Sunday School Chapel	150	Garden Court	25–30

FEES & DEPOSITS: 20% of the rental fee is required as a non-refundable deposit to secure your date. A refundable $800 cleaning/damage/security deposit and the rental balance are due 30 days prior to the event. Rental fees are as follows: the Main Auditorium $1,200, the Sunday School Chapel $800, the Fireplace Room $500, and the Garden Court $300. Clergy is not provided. Ceremonies must be religious in nature and performed by a licensed officiant.

AVAILABILITY: Year-round, daily, except Sunday mornings and Wednesdays.

SERVICES/AMENITIES:

Catering: food not allowed
Kitchen Facilities: no
Tables & Chairs: some provided or BYO
Linens, Silver, etc.: n/a
Restrooms: not wheelchair accessible
Dance Floor: no dancing
Bride's & Groom's Dressing Area: yes
Meeting Equipment: microphone, podium, screen

Parking: small lot, on street & nearby lot
Accommodations: no guest rooms
Telephone: use with approval
Outdoor Night Lighting: access only
Outdoor Cooking Facilities: n/a
Cleanup: renter
View: no
Other: organist, wedding coordinator

RESTRICTIONS:

Alcohol: not allowed
Smoking: not permitted
Music: amplified OK w/volume limits

Wheelchair Access: yes
Insurance: not required
Other: no candles or thrown objects

The professionals in the back of the book are the best in the business! How do we know? Read page 681.

Hillside Club

Historic Club

2286 Cedar Street, Berkeley
(510) 848-3227

◆ Ceremonies ◆ Special Events
◆ Wedding Receptions ◆ Meetings
◆ Business Functions Accommodations

The Hillside Club was founded by a group of Berkeley citizens who wished to protect the hills of their town from "unsightly grading and the building of unsuitable and disfiguring houses." The original 1906 Club building was designed by architect Bernard Maybeck. Destroyed in the great fire of 1923, it was redesigned by Maybeck's partner, John White, and rebuilt that year.

Its style is that of an English Tudor hall, featuring a high wood-beamed ceiling and massive fireplace. Afternoon light traverses the tall, multi-paned windows, warming the dark wood interior. Recitals often make use of the stage, piano and newly improved lighting system. The hardwood floor is perfect for dancing. An integral part of Berkeley's history, the Hillside Club is a warm, friendly place to host your event.

CEREMONY, EVENT/RECEPTION CAPACITY: The Great Hall accommodates 200 standing or 125 seated for a reception.

MEETING CAPACITY: The Great Hall holds 150–200 seated theater-style.

FEES & DEPOSITS: $150 or 50% of the rental fee, whichever is larger, is due when reservations are confirmed. The facility rental fee weekdays and evenings (except Friday evening) is $200 for a 4-hour block and $40/hour for additional hours. On Friday evening, Saturday or Sunday, the fee is $400 for a 4-hour block and $80/hour for additional hours. The rental balance is payable 1 week before the event. Use fees for various items are: kitchen, $25:, fireplace, $15; or piano, $25.

AVAILABILITY: Year-round, daily until 11pm.

SERVICES/AMENITIES:

Catering: BYO
Kitchen Facilities: fully equipped
Tables & Chairs: provided
Linens, Silver, etc.: BYO
Restrooms: not wheelchair accessible
Dance Floor: yes

Parking: on street
Accommodations: no guest rooms
Telephone: no
Outdoor Night Lighting: access only
Outdoor Cooking Facilities: no
Cleanup: caterer or renter

Bride's Dressing Area: yes
Meeting Equipment: lectern

RESTRICTIONS:
Alcohol: BYO, BWC only
Smoking: not allowed
Music: amplified OK

View: no
Other: sound system, movie screen, piano

Wheelchair Access: yes
Insurance: not required
Other: no confetti or rice

This is important! *Tell facilities you're reading* **Here Comes The Guide** *and ask if our information is still current.*

International House Berkeley

Historic Residential & Conference Center

◆ Ceremonies ◆ Special Events
◆ Wedding Receptions ◆ Meetings
◆ Business Functions ◆ Accommodations

2299 Piedmont Avenue, Berkeley
(510) 642-0589, fax (510) 643-8314
www-ihouse.berkeley.edu/ih

For more than 65 years, the International House has played an important role in Berkeley's multicultural life by bringing together students and scholars from virtually every country in the world. Located adjacent to the UC Berkeley campus, this architecturally significant housing complex has been called home by students who went on to become prominent politicians (including Jerry Brown, Jr. and Pete Wilson), ambas-

sadors and Nobel Laureates. And what a home it is: built in 1930, the Spanish Mission Revival-style structure not only houses 600 students at a time, but has some exceptionally handsome spaces available for weddings, corporate functions and special events.

Enclosed by stone walls softened by lacy palms, the brick-paved Clarence E. Heller Patio offers a peaceful, olive tree-shaded outdoor setting for ceremonies or informal receptions. For large banquets or awards ceremonies, the splendid Chevron Auditorium showcases the building's Spanish/Moorish influences. Multiple wrought-iron chandeliers hang from an ornately hand-painted ceiling, softly illuminating the hardwood floor below. Dark wood wainscotting, arched windows, and walls defined with Moorish arches and rust, beige and black banners are additional elements. A raised theatrical stage at one end provides ample room for musicians or a head table; the spacious hardwood floor can accommodate both diners and dancers. The stage is also equipped with a sound system, stage lighting and movie screen for performances or symposiums. The adjacent Slusser Room, with its intimate proportions, wood wainscotting and long, mahogany banquet table, is eminently suitable for pre-party gatherings, rehearsal dinners or company conferences.

For small gatherings, workshops or meetings, the Golub Home Room features antique furnishings, a grand piano, a large decorative fireplace, a Bay-and-bridge-view balcony and a painted ceiling adapted from the Chapel in the Cathedral at Toledo, Spain. The Home Room reminds us of an inviting, elegant living room, just right for afternoon buffets or intimate, candlelit dinners. And should you desire a menu more exotic than the usual roast beef or chicken, the in-house catering department just happens to specialize in international cuisines—after all, it regularly satisfies the appetites of students so diverse that the International House has been dubbed "a mini-U.N." For a company event or personal celebration with a sophisticated, multicultural flair, the International House provides just the right setting.

CEREMONY CAPACITY: The Auditorium holds up to 475 seated or 490 standing, Heller Patio 70 seated or 125 standing, and the Home Room, 70 seated or 100 standing.

EVENT/RECEPTION & MEETING CAPACITY:

Area	Seated	Standing	Meeting	Area	Seated	Standing	Meeting
Auditorium	250–400	490	—	Slusser Room	30	50	30–40
Great Hall	200	300	—	Ida Sproul	30–45	45	30–45
Rbt. Sproul Rm	30–45	45	30–45	Ida/Rbt Sproul	70	100	90–100
Home Room	70	100	30–45				

FEES & DEPOSITS: Half the rental fee is the refundable deposit required to book your space; the rental balance and the estimated food and beverage total are payable 30 days prior to the event. Any other incurred costs are payable the day of the event. AV equipment (including podium and microphone) are provided at an extra charge. In-house catering is provided. Luncheons start at $15/person, dinners at $23/person or buffets at $20/person. Alcohol and tax are additional. If you don't use the in-house caterer, a catering buyout is available; call for details. Any outside caterer must be licensed and insured. Rental fees are as follows:

Area	Half Day	Full Day	Area	Half Day	Full Day
Auditorium	$585–700	$710–790	Great Hall	$500	$700
Heller Patio	$400		Smaller Rooms	$75–175	$110–275

AVAILABILITY: Year-round, daily, 8am–midnight, except December 21–January 3, when the facility is closed.

SERVICES/AMENITIES:

Catering: provided or BYO w/buyout
Kitchen Facilities: prep area only
Tables & Chairs: provided
Linens, Silver, etc.: provided
Restrooms: wheelchair accessible
Dance Floor: in auditorium
Bride's & Groom's Dressing Area: yes
Meeting Equipment: full range CBA

Parking: on street, pay lots nearby
Accommodations: 2 guest rooms
Telephone: pay phones
Outdoor Night Lighting: access only
Outdoor Cooking Facilities: BBQs CBA
Cleanup: provided, extra charge
View: of UC Campus and SF Bay
Other: event planning, grand pianos

RESTRICTIONS:

Alcohol: BWC provided, no BYO
Smoking: not allowed
Music: amplified OK indoors only

Wheelchair Access: yes, except Heller Patio
Insurance: sometimes required

The professionals in the back of the book are the best in the business! How do we know? Read page 681.

Valley Oak Nursery

7021 Lone Tree Way, Brentwood
(925) 516-7868, fax (925) 516-7370

Nursery & Garden

◆ Ceremonies   ◆ Special Events
◆ Wedding Receptions   Meetings
   Business Functions   Accommodations

Designed and planted by the horticultural experts at the Valley Oak Nursery, this flower-filled wedding and reception site in Brentwood is home to more than 2,000 carefully tended plants, trees, blossoming vines and rose bushes, not to mention perfectly manicured lawns, winding brick pathways and a koi-filled pond.

The entrance is through the rose garden, where varieties of rose bushes flourish in raised beds. Walk under a white wood pergola and along a brick path and you'll enter the amphitheater, a lush, shell-shaped expanse of emerald-green lawn surrounding a large, decagonal (ten-sided) white gazebo. Steps leading up to the gazebo provide a stage for the ceremony, and just outside the amphitheater, there's a lovely, secluded walkway where the bride and bridesmaids can relax before the wedding march begins.

You can also take your vows on an arched bridge that spans the garden's free-form pond, as guests look on from the adjacent paths and lawns. The constant care lavished on the plants guarantees that flowers will be blooming year round. If you're a garden gourmet, Valley Oak Nursery will definitely satisfy your horticultural tastes.

CEREMONY CAPACITY: The amphitheater holds 400 seated; the bridge and pond area can hold 400 seated and standing; the rose garden, 100 seated or standing.

EVENT/RECEPTION CAPACITY: The facility can accommodate 200–500 seated guests.

FEES & DEPOSITS: Half the rental fee is the deposit required to hold your date; the balance and a $100–500 security deposit are payable 30 days prior to the event. The rental fee, depending on services provided, starts at $350 for a 2-hour function.

AVAILABILITY: Outdoor functions occur March–November, weather permitting, 8:30am–9:30pm.

SERVICES/AMENITIES:

Catering: BYO

Kitchen Facilities: no

Tables & Chairs: provided

Linens, Silver, etc.: BYO

Restrooms: not wheelchair accessible

Dance Floor: provided

Bride's Dressing Area: CBA

Meeting Equipment: n/a

Parking: large lot

Accommodations: no guest rooms

Telephone: emergency use only

Outdoor Night Lighting: CBA

Outdoor Cooking Facilities: BYO BBQ

Cleanup: caterer or renter

View: lush gardens

RESTRICTIONS:

Alcohol: BYO, WBC only

Smoking: outdoors only

Music: amplified OK, w/volume limits

Wheelchair Access: yes

Insurance: certificate required

Other: no rice, birdseed, glitter, or confetti

This is important! Tell facilities you're reading **Here Comes The Guide** and ask if our information is still current.

Crockett Community Center

850 Pomona, Crockett
(510) 787-2414, fax (510) 787-3049

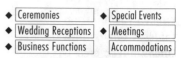

◆ Ceremonies ◆ Special Events
◆ Wedding Receptions ◆ Meetings
◆ Business Functions Accommodations

After looking at the rustic wooden exterior of the Crockett Community Center, one is surprised by the spacious vaulted auditorium inside, which can accommodate a large reception. Designed by San Francisco architect William Crim for the C&H Sugar Company, the building is constructed on a grand scale, featuring a post-and-beam style ceiling, hardwood floor, an enormous (and functional) stone fireplace, a monumental bar, commercial kitchen and a stage. In addition to the main hall, there is one smaller room with kitchenette that can be rented separately. A park area is also available for outdoor activities.

CEREMONY CAPACITY: The park near the Center holds 200–300; the Main Hall holds 350 seated guests.

EVENT/RECEPTION CAPACITY: The Main Hall accommodates 350 seated; another room can handle 50 people, maximum.

MEETING CAPACITY: The Main Hall holds 400 seated theater-style.

FEES & DEPOSITS: A $300 cleaning and damage deposit is required for all rentals.

Main Hall including park area (10-hour rental): $315 residents, $565 non-residents. For rentals over 10 hours, add $65/hour for overtime.

Kitchen Facilities: Add $50 to above rates for use of the kitchen.

Multipurpose Room (8-hour rental): Room and kitchenette rental is $50. Add $50 for use of large kitchen. *Park and Restroom facilities:* $50

AVAILABILITY: Year-round, daily, until 1am.

SERVICES/AMENITIES:

Catering: BYO
Kitchen Facilities: commercial
Tables & Chairs: provided
Linens, Silver, etc.: BYO
Restrooms: wheelchair accessible

Parking: on street
Accommodations: no guest rooms
Telephone: pay phone
Outdoor Night Lighting: access only
Outdoor Cooking Facilities: BBQs

Dance Floor: yes
Bride's Dressing Area: yes
Meeting Equipment: lectern, sound system

Cleanup: caterer or renter, CBA for a fee
View: no

RESTRICTIONS:

Alcohol: BYO
Smoking: not allowed
Music: amplified OK

Wheelchair Access: yes
Insurance: may be required
Other: decorations restricted

The professionals in the back of the book are the best in the business! *How do we know? Read page 681.*

Blackhawk Automotive Museum

Auto Museum

3700 Blackhawk Plaza Circle, Danville
(925) 736-2280, fax (925) 736-4818

www.blackhawkauto.org
museum@blackhawkauto.org

◆ Ceremonies   ◆ Special Events
◆ Wedding Receptions   ◆ Meetings
◆ Business Functions   Accommodations

The Blackhawk Automotive Museum is an exciting place for private events. Overlooking Blackhawk Plaza, the building is a study in glass, granite and stainless steel—a multi-million-dollar facility that showcases rare, classic automobiles and automotive fine art and artifacts in elegant, sumptuous surroundings. The foyer is awesome with its soaring skylights and dusty rose Italian granite floors and walls.

The juxtaposition of metal and stone with soft rich colors creates a vivid impression. As the sun sets through the tinted glass facade, the entire space is bathed in a warm glow.

The dining area presents a striking contrast—black from its granite floor to unadorned ceiling. Vintage cars border the dining area and can be illuminated or rendered invisible by a network of computerized lights. Here guests are dazzled by colorful fender curves, gleaming surfaces and sparkling brass and chrome.

And what's particularly nice about this 100,000-square-foot facility is that you have so many options from which to choose. The facility's numerous event spaces, including the automobile and automotive-art galleries, lobbies, mezzanine, terraces, classrooms, executive room, outdoor plaza with fountain, and more. So even if you're not an antique car buff, if you're seeking a smashing venue in the East Bay for a personal celebration or a company soirée, this is the place to have an unforgettable event.

CEREMONY CAPACITY:

Area	*Seated*	*Standing*	*Area*	*Seated*	*Standing*
Automobile Galleries	450+	1,000	Mezzanine	60	200
Automotive Art Wing	60	100	Terraces	40 ea.	70 ea.
Lobby	120	250	Outdoor Plaza	400	600

EVENT/RECEPTION CAPACITY:

Area	*Seated*	*Standing*	*Area*	*Seated*	*Standing*
Automobile Galleries	450+	1,000	Mezzanine	40	75
Automotive Art Wing	60	100	Terraces	40 ea.	70 ea.
Lobby	120	250	Outdoor Plaza	400	600

MEETING CAPACITY:

Area	*Theater-style*	*Conference-style*	*Classroom-style*
Automobile Dining Area	600	300	300
Executive Room	40	22	n/a
Classroom	120	60	80

FEES & DEPOSITS: The Museum rents space only; all food and beverage services are provided by *Scott's Catering* of Walnut Creek. 30% of the total anticipated fee is due when reservations are confirmed; the balance is payable 2 months prior to the event, with the exception of December bookings. A $1,000 refundable security deposit is due prior to the event; additional fees may be required for special dining area setups, equipment, maintenance and security.

Rental rates range $750–17,500 depending on the space(s) selected, type of event, day of week, date and time of day. Catering costs are additional; menus run $25–55/person; alcohol, tax and an 18% service charge are extra.

AVAILABILITY: Year-round, except Thanksgiving, Christmas and New Year's Days. During operating hours (Wed–Sun, 10am–5pm), functions with catered meals may be scheduled in the event areas 7:30am–5pm. The entire facility is available 5pm–11:30pm and all day Monday and Tuesday, when the museum is closed to the public.

SERVICES/AMENITIES:

Catering: provided, no BYO
Kitchen Facilities: n/a
Tables & Chairs: most provided
Linens, Silver, etc.: most provided
Restrooms: wheelchair accessible
Dance Floor: provided
Bride's Dressing Area: yes
Meeting Equipment: AV, podium, TV, riser, VCR, overhead/slide projectors, screen

Parking: large lots
Accommodations: no guest rooms
Telephone: pay phone
Outdoor Night Lighting: access only
Outdoor Cooking Facilities: no
Cleanup: provided
View: East Bay hills; Blackhawk Plaza's ponds, fountains and waterfalls
Other: piano

RESTRICTIONS:

Alcohol: provided, service until 11:30pm
Smoking: outside only
Music: amplified limited, must end by 11:30pm

Wheelchair Access: yes
Insurance: required

---

*This is important! Tell facilities you're reading **Here Comes The Guide** and ask if our information is still current.*

The Blackhawk Grille

Restaurant

3540 Blackhawk Plaza Circle, Danville
(925) 736-8261, fax (925) 736-1062

www.calcafe.com/danville/

Ceremonies	◆ Special Events
◆ Wedding Receptions	◆ Meetings
◆ Business Functions	Accommodations

"Water, water, every-where..." is a phrase you don't usually hear in drought-conscious California, but chances are it will spring to mind when you visit the Blackhawk Grille. Situated among the trendy shops in Blackhawk Plaza, the restaurant uses the waterfalls, cascades and lagoons that meander through the Plaza as stunning focal points for most of their entertainment areas, indoors and out.

One of Blackhawk Grille's most desirable event spaces is the terraced patio outside the main entrance. As the crystal-clear waters from the Plaza's tranquil lagoon lap at the patio's edge and flow over rock cascades on either side, you feel as though you've discovered your own private island. In the spring and summer, feathery mimosa trees flutter in the warm breeze scented by star jasmine flowers, and white-canvas market umbrellas shade you as you gaze out over the shimmering expanse of water. During fall and winter, heat lamps keep you warm while a brilliant sunset is reflected in the lagoon. The patio would be suitable for virtually any event, from a casual office get-together to a more formal luncheon. Your guests won't have to traipse in and out of the restaurant for their food and drinks, either, since everything, including a buffet, cake table, and music can be set up on the patio. You can reserve all or part of the patio and, if you take over the entire space, you can close the small iron gates in the fence surrounding the patio to ensure privacy.

Indoors, the decor is stylish and sophisticated. Large picture windows allow views of the lagoon and red-brick roofed Plaza buildings from almost everywhere in the restaurant. Three individual dining areas have unique characteristics suggested by their names: the Piano Terrace, a raised area in the middle of the restaurant, has a grand piano which dominates the space; the Fishbowl is a small but sought-after niche where water laps against a floor-to-ceiling bay window; the Vintners' Room boasts a 3,000-bottle glass-enclosed wine cellar, displaying jeroboams of fine wines. Although this room is private, guests can observe the exhibition kitchen and all the hustle and bustle of the main dining room through the glass doors that separate the two rooms. Oversized picture windows take advantage of the waterpark view, and walls painted in delicate, mottled shades of aqua and green blur the line where the windows stop and the water begins. Though decorated in cool colors, the overall ambiance of the Vintners' Room is one of cozy intimacy, like being in a secluded grotto.

If you're searching for a first-class venue for a social or business event, you owe it to yourself to check out the Blackhawk Grille. It's like finding an oasis in the desert!

CEREMONY CAPACITY: Ceremonies don't take place at this site.

EVENT/RECEPTION CAPACITY: The Patio holds 75 seated or 125 standing guests; the Vintners' Room holds 48 seated or standing.

MEETING CAPACITY: The Vintners' Room holds up to 48 guests seated theater or conference style.

FEES & DEPOSITS: For weddings and special events, a $300 refundable deposit is required to secure your date; the food and beverage balance is payable the day of the event. For business meetings, a $300 refundable deposit is required, with the food and beverage balance payable the day of the meeting. Per-person catering runs $10–23 for breakfasts, $18–25 for luncheons, or $33–56 for dinners or buffets. Tax and a 17% service charge are additional. There are no room rental fees.

AVAILABILITY: Year-round, daily, 7am–1:30am.

SERVICES/AMENITIES:

Catering: provided, no BYO

Kitchen Facilities: n/a

Tables & Chairs: provided

Linens, Silver, etc.: provided

Restrooms: wheelchair accessible

Dance Floor: patio

Bride's Dressing Area: no

Meeting Equipment: CBA, extra fee

Parking: ample lot, or valet CBA

Accommodations: no guest rooms

Telephone: pay phone

Outdoor Night Lighting: yes

Outdoor Cooking Facilities: no

Cleanup: provided

View: fountains, pools & Las Trampas Hills

RESTRICTIONS:

Alcohol: provided, or corkage $10/bottle

Smoking: outside only

Music: amplified with volume limits

Wheelchair Access: yes

Insurance: not required

The professionals in the back of the book are the best in the business! How do we know? Read page 681.

Crow Canyon Country Club

Country Club

711 Silver Lake Drive, Danville
(925) 735-5700, fax (925) 735-6516

◆ Ceremonies ◆ Special Events
◆ Wedding Receptions ◆ Meetings
◆ Business Functions Accommodations

Crow Canyon Country Club is a private club which has private dining rooms for rehearsal dinners, weddings and receptions. All activities take place in the Clubhouse, a versatile group of rooms surrounded by a championship eighteen-hole golf course, swimming pool and tennis courts. Large parties can be accommodated in the Mark Twain Room, the Country Club's main dining area. The windowed east side of this room overlooks the golf course and offers a spectacular view of Mt. Diablo. For added flexibility, a stage and hardwood dance floor are located in the center of the room.

Smaller groups are comfortably accommodated in the Jack London Lounge, a section of the Mark Twain Room. And for more intimate functions, such as a bridal shower or a rehearsal dinner, the Eugene O'Neill Room—which also has a dramatic view of the Diablo Valley—provides a private and sophisticated retreat.

Among Danville's handful of special event venues, the Crow Canyon Country Club stands out because it offers a wide range of services. Whether you have an informal affair or a sophisticated soirée in mind, this is one facility that can handle it from start to finish.

CEREMONY CAPACITY: The Jack London Lounge holds 150 seated and 200 standing. There is a $300 setup fee.

EVENT/RECEPTION & MEETING CAPACITY, FEES & DEPOSITS:

Room	*Seated*	*Standing*	*Guest Fee*	*Food & Bev. Min.*
Jack London Lounge	112	150	$400	$1,500
Mark Twain Room	280	400	750	2,500
Eugene O'Neill Room	80	100	400	1,000
Grill Room	80	100	300	1,000
John Steinbeck Room	10	15	50	100
Bret Harte Room	40	50	150	300
Zane Grey Room	32	40	150	300

For 50 or more guests, a $1,000 deposit is required. To open the clubhouse for private parties during non-member hours, a 75-person minimum is required. Saturdays, for large events, a $5,000 (daytime events) or $7,000 (evening events) minimum food and beverage total is required. The total estimated cost is due 2 weeks prior to the event. Food service is provided; catered events require 48-hour advance confirmation of guest count. Approximate per person rates for in-house service: breakfasts $9–14, luncheons $15–20, dinners $24–34, and buffet stations, $32. Customized menus are available. Alcohol, tax and an 18% service charge are additional.

AVAILABILITY: Year-round, daily, 7am–11pm.

SERVICES/AMENITIES:

Catering: provided
Kitchen Facilities: n/a
Tables & Chairs: provided
Linens, Silver, etc.: provided
Restrooms: wheelchair accessible
Dance Floor: yes
Bride's Dressing Room: yes
Meeting Equipment: overhead screen, VCR & monitor, flip charts, slide projector, phone lines

Parking: parking lot, valet available
Accommodations: no guest rooms
Telephone: pay phones
Outdoor Night Lighting: yes
Outdoor Cooking Facilities: BBQ CBA
Cleanup: provided
View: Mt. Diablo and golf course
Other: baby grand piano, upright piano

RESTRICTIONS:

Alcohol: provided, or corkage $10/bottle
Smoking: designated areas
Music: amplified OK indoors

Wheelchair Access: yes
Insurance: not required

---

*This is important! Tell facilities you're reading **Here Comes The Guide** and ask if our information is still current.*

Danville Station

Clubhouse

End of Mikado Place, Danville
(925) 837-4290, fax (925) 837-4503

◆ Ceremonies ◆ Special Events
◆ Wedding Receptions ◆ Meetings
◆ Business Functions ◆ Accommodations

With its shake roof, dormer windows and wide veranda, Danville Station could almost be mistaken for one of this community's spacious ranch homes. And while it's not an actual residence, it serves as the Danville Station Homeowners' Association clubhouse. The entrance is framed by tall birch and pine trees, and the building is surrounded by acres of well-tended lawn along with a pool and four tennis courts. You reach the facility via a concrete and wood footbridge, which spans a narrow creek whose banks are thick with cattails. A variety of birds pass their time at the creek, and it's not at all surprising to see powder-white egrets strolling on the grassy slope just above it.

If you decide to get married here, there's a lovely expanse of lawn beyond the pool that's practically custom made for an outdoor ceremony. You can seat your guests in front of a majestic oak, then exchange vows beneath its branches. A stand of smaller oaks forms a natural screen just behind you, and the rolling hills which ring the valley are visible through the trees.

Special events and business functions take place in the clubhouse and on the veranda. The interior has a high, beamed ceiling and light gray walls and carpet. For weddings, a fireplace area at one end of the main floor is often set up for the cake display and gift tables; the rest of the room can be used for dancing or dining. Two loft areas upstairs are softly lit by the light from the dormer windows, and are well-suited for dining. On a warm, sunny day however, most people prefer an al fresco repast on the veranda. No matter where you sit, this wraparound porch overlooks a lawn, and when the front porch is outfitted with wicker furniture, it has the feeling of a southern plantation. Danville Station has long been popular with local residents, and now this fresh, relaxed setting is available to the rest of us, too.

CEREMONY CAPACITY: The lawn accommodates up to 150 seated or standing.

EVENT/RECEPTION CAPACITY: Indoors, the Clubhouse holds 60–100 seated and up to 150 standing or seated using the veranda.

MEETING CAPACITY: One large and three smaller areas accommodate 25–75 seated.

FEES & DEPOSITS: A $100 non-refundable deposit (which applies toward the rental fee) and a signed agreement are required to reserve your date. The rental fee balance and a $250–500 security deposit are due 60 days prior to the event. Rental fees run $75–700/day, depending on the type of event and guest count. You can also reserve the facility the day before and/or the day after for set-up or take-down for $100/day. Note that Danville Station Homeowners Association members receive a discount.

AVAILABILITY: Year-round, daily, 8am–midnight, subject to availability.

SERVICES/AMENITIES:

Catering: BYO
Kitchen Facilities: moderate
Tables & Chairs: provided for 100 guests
Linens, Silver, etc.: BYO
Restrooms: not wheelchair accessible
Dance Floor: area provided
Bride's Dressing Room: bathroom or loft
Meeting Equipment: BYO

Parking: parking lot and on street
Accommodations: no guest rooms
Telephone: pay phone
Outdoor Night Lighting: access only
Outdoor Cooking Facilities: BYO BBQ grills
Cleanup: caterer or renter
View: Mt. Diablo & Las Trampas hills

RESTRICTIONS:

Alcohol: BYO
Smoking: outside only
Music: amplified OK indoors til 11pm

Wheelchair Access: no
Insurance: certificate of liability required

The professionals in the back of the book are the best in the business! How do we know? Read page 681.

Ardenwood Historic Preserve

34600 Ardenwood Boulevard, Fremont
(925) 462-1400, fax (925) 426-3075
www.ardenwoodaffairs.com
www.picnicpeople.com

Historic Farm & Preserve

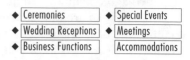

◆ Ceremonies ◆ Special Events
◆ Wedding Receptions ◆ Meetings
◆ Business Functions Accommodations

In 1849, George Patterson left the Midwest for California's gold fields. He tried mining for a year, but failed miserably. So, broke and sick, he decided to turn to something he knew how to do well: farming. By 1877, he had transformed himself into one of the wealthiest and most respected men in the area, and was able to acquire 6,000 acres of prime land. At last he had struck gold—not in the mines, but in the fertile plains of the East Bay.

Today, his home is still a working farm. Named after a forest described in Shakespeare's *As You Like It,* Ardenwood is a place where you travel back in time—draft horses still pull wagons, ladies wear Victorian dresses and the land still grows the kinds of crops it did 100 years ago. Guests can stroll through the beautiful gardens that surround the Patterson Mansion, the impressive focal point of Ardenwood. An expansive lawn, complete with a white, Victorian-style gazebo, provides a wonderful area for weddings and receptions. Evening receptions are especially magical, with old-fashioned oil lanterns glowing on each table. If you like, you can arrange a special tour of the house, which has been restored to its 19th-century elegance, or treat your guests to a trip around the property in a gleaming Victorian horse-drawn carriage.

Lovely as it is for weddings, Ardenwood is just as wonderful for picnics. Reserve one of the Deer Park Picnic Areas for your company party or family reunion, and you'll have exclusive use of it for the day. And your guests will not be bored: the impressive list of activities here includes softball, volleyball, horseshoes, ping pong and lawn bowling. You can even rent a dunk tank or play bingo (with prizes!). Kids have their own fun in the form of face painting, sand castle building and crafts. The farm offers other special features, too, such as country kitchen demonstrations, antique farm displays and a blacksmith shop.

Ardenwood is open to the public during the day, so while your actual event site is private, you may see public visitors strolling about outside your area. Note that to maintain the farm's authentic character, vehicles and music are restricted. These efforts to preserve a turn-of-the-century environment are worth it: the setting envelops you in the peace and quiet of the country, and modern civilization seems a million miles away.

CEREMONY CAPACITY: The gazebo area lawn can accommodate 225 seated during the day or up to 700 seated guests after 4:30pm.

EVENT/RECEPTION CAPACITY: The poolside area accommodates up to 225 seated or 300 standing guests; the gazebo area lawn, up to 700 seated or 1,000 standing guests. For picnics, the Deer Park Picnic Area holds groups from 50–1,200 guests.

FEES & DEPOSITS: For ceremonies only, the $675–800 non-refundable facility use fee is payable when the site is booked. The fee covers a 2-hour ceremony. For ceremonies with receptions, the non-refundable facility use fee ranges $800–1,000 for a 5-hour daytime event between 9am–3:30pm or $1,150–1,275 for a 5 1/2-hour evening event between 4:30pm–11pm. Half of the use fee is payable upon booking prior to February 1st; if the site is booked after February 1st, the entire use fee is payable upon booking. Menus run $16–37/person for food, and $5.25–7.25/person for beverage packages. The event balance is due 2 weeks before the event.

For picnics, the facility use fee ranges $400–4,000 depending on group size. Half of the use fee is payable upon booking prior to January 1st; if the site is booked after January 1st, the entire use fee is payable upon booking. A guest count guarantee is due 1 week before, and the balance is payable the day of the event. Picnic menus run $13–23/person, including a barbecue entree, assorted salads, and a beverage package (wine, beer and soft drinks).

AVAILABILITY: Ardenwood is available from 8am–11pm Tuesday–Sunday, April 1st to November 1st.

SERVICES/AMENITIES:

Catering: provided
Kitchen Facilities: n/a
Tables & Chairs: provided or picnic tables
Linens, Silver, etc.: provided for weddings; other tableware for picnics
Restrooms: wheelchair accessible
Dance Floor: yes, for weddings
Bride's Dressing Area: yes
Other: horse-drawn carriage CBA, complete event services

Parking: ample lots, lighted at night
Accommodations: no guest rooms
Telephone: pay phone, day hours only
Outdoor Night Lighting: yes
Outdoor Cooking Facilities: BBQs
Cleanup: caterer
View: gardens & Victorian Mansion
Meeting Equipment: full range CBA

RESTRICTIONS:

Alcohol: WBC provided
Smoking: allowed
Music: amplified OK after 4:30pm only, (and select Saturdays) w/volume restrictions

Wheelchair Access: yes
Insurance: not required
Other: open to public 10am–4:30pm

This is important! Tell facilities you're reading **Here Comes The Guide** *and ask if our information is still current.*

Palmdale Estates

159 Washington Boulevard, Fremont
(925) 462-1783, fax (925) 462-7522

Historic Estate

◆ Ceremonies   ◆ Special Events
◆ Wedding Receptions   ◆ Meetings
◆ Business Functions   Accommodations

Originally part of the Old Mission San Jose garden, Palmdale Estates is a beautifully landscaped site, featuring dozens of stately palms and native California trees, verdant lawns, gardens and even a pond. In the midst of this lovely setting is Best House, a Tudor-style mansion whose delightful interior and grounds create a storybook backdrop for weddings any time of year.

Built in 1915, the house reflects much of the elegant and ornate detailing of the period: graceful arched doorways, bas-relief ceiling moldings, crystal chandeliers, hand-painted murals and gleaming hardwood floors. Lace, velvet and moiré silk draperies add a rich, old-fashioned quality to the decor. The Ballroom, though the largest space in the house, still has an intimate feeling with its cream-colored walls, oversize decorative marble fireplace and a huge leaded glass window overlooking the garden. At one end of the Ballroom, a few steps take you up to the Music Room, a glitzy alcove with gold leaf walls and a colorful stained glass window. At the other end are the formal Dining Room and Solarium, two light and airy rooms with an abundance of leaded glass windows and views of the "backyard."

When you get married here, you have exclusive use of the main floor of the house as well as the adjacent lawns, and can orchestrate your wedding any way you like. During warm months, most couples tie the knot in the white gazebo on the rear lawn, which is bordered by pines and redwoods and dotted with palms and fruit trees. They have their reception outdoors as well, setting up tables on the grassy expanse next to the gazebo. Afterwards, guests are invited inside for dancing and cake cutting. In winter, receptions are generally held in the Ballroom with the other spaces used according to the couple's preferences; a fluid floor plan offers plenty of flexibility. (Note that the Starr Gardens, behind the adjacent Peach Mansion, is also available for ceremonies and receptions.) Whether you celebrate under the magnificent palms or in the gracious surroundings of Best House, you can't help but enjoy the quiet beauty of Palmdale Estates.

CEREMONY CAPACITY: The Best House Garden with gazebo can accommodate 300 seated; Starr Garden 200 seated guests.

EVENT/RECEPTION CAPACITY: Best House can hold 200 seated indoors and, combined with outdoor spaces, up to 500 guests. Starr Gardens can hold 200 seated guests.

MEETING CAPACITY: The Ballroom holds 100 conference-style or 75 theater-style.

FEES & DEPOSITS: To rent the mansion and garden, a $500 security deposit is due when the rental agreement is submitted. The rental balance is payable 6 months prior to the event. For Saturday and Sunday functions April–December, the facility provides catering. During other time periods, you can make arrangements for your own caterer.

Area	_Fees_	_Hours_	
Best House and Gardens			
Weekend	$2,000/8 hours	9am–11pm	(1999)
	$2,000–2,500/8 hours	9am–11pm	(2000)
Weekday (corporate rate)	$500/8 hours	9am–5pm	
Weekday Evenings	$200/hour	5pm–midnight	
Starr Gardens			
Weekend	$125/hour	10am–6pm	

AVAILABILITY: Year-round, daily except Thanksgiving and Christmas. On Saturdays, April–October, time periods for receptions are 9am–5pm or 3pm–11pm; ceremonies take place at 11am or 5:30pm.

SERVICES/AMENITIES:

Catering: provided on Saturdays or Sundays, April–Dec, or BYO other days/months
Kitchen Facilities: minimal
Tables & Chairs: provided for 200 guests
Linens, Silver, etc.: provided w/catering
Restrooms: wheelchair accessible
Dance Floor: Ballroom or Solarium
Bride's Dressing Area: yes
Meeting Equipment: PA system, flip charts, VCR, and overhead projector

Parking: large lot
Accommodations: no guest rooms
Telephone: lounge phone
Outdoor Night Lighting: CBA
Outdoor Cooking Facilities: BBQ
Cleanup: caterer or CBA
View: East Bay hills
Other: event coordination

RESTRICTIONS:

Alcohol: BYO WCB only, hard alcohol restricted
Smoking: outside only
Music: amplified OK within limits

Wheelchair Access: yes
Insurance: not required

The professionals in the back of the book are the best in the business! How do we know? Read page 681.

Centennial Banquet Hall & Conference Center

Banquet Hall

22292 Foothill Boulevard, Hayward
(510) 483-5210, fax (510) 483-6855

◆ Ceremonies ◆ Special Events
◆ Wedding Receptions ◆ Meetings
◆ Business Functions Accommodations

It was bound to happen. Sooner or later, someone would design a building that could handle a maximum number of people with a minimum of muss and fuss. That building is Centennial Hall, a traditional town hall with 21st Century technology.

Located at the geographic center of the Bay Area, at the intersection of four main highways, Centennial Hall is within 25 miles of every major regional attraction, including Oakland, San Francisco and San Jose airports. And with two enormous parking areas, it's easily able to house hundreds of automobiles. If you're a bride with guests coming from all over, or a business with several branch offices, or a convention or trade show, nothing could be more convenient.

And once you get here, you'll find that the convenience has only just begun. The centerpiece of the Hall is the 14,000-square-foot auditorium, which can accommodate 1,000 people or more with no problem. (For smaller parties, it can be separated into sections.) For presentations, lectures, or wedding music, the auditorium provides a professional quality stage, proven lighting system, excellent acoustics, state-of-the-art sound equipment, and backstage dressing rooms.

Ringing the auditorium are eight smaller meeting rooms, which can be used individually or in combination with the auditorium. Many corporate meetings at the Hall use the auditorium for the general sessions, then break for smaller conferences in the meeting rooms. Other groups use the Hall for trade shows or conventions. In addition, there's a luxurious executive conference room, skylit lobby, two spacious mezzanine areas—even a fully equipped barbecue patio.

Centennial Hall is completely air-conditioned, and its paging system brings crystal-clear voice communication to all corners of the facility. The comprehensive banquet kitchen can handle all food preparation on site, even for the largest of parties. Ample coat check and restroom facilities strategically located around the perimeter of the Hall mean no waiting lines for your guests. And uniformed security personnel, as well as closed circuit surveillance, provide unobtrusive but effective protection.

Whether it's a trade show, a convention, a corporate meeting or a traditional wedding, Centennial Hall can accommodate them all. And while the hall is large, its versatile design never makes guests feel dwarfed. There aren't many facilities in the Bay Area that offer so much space, comfort and convenience. Centennial Hall is an example of how to do it right.

CEREMONY CAPACITY: Indoors, the facility can accommodate 1,000 seated, the outdoor patio, 100 seated.

EVENT/RECEPTION CAPACITY: There are a variety of spaces which can accommodate 40–1,000 seated guests. Here's a list of some of the larger areas:

Room	Seated	Standing	Room	Seated	Standing
Hall A&B	700–1,000	1,700	Room 3	60	135
Hall A or B	350–430	850	Room 4	180–200	400
Room 1	60	135	Room 6	100–120	275
Patio	40	220	Room 7	70–100	190

MEETING CAPACITY:

Room	Theater-style	Room	Theater-style	Room	Theater-style	Classroom-style
Hall A&B	1,200	Room 2	60	Room 6	150	128
Hall A or B	500	Room 3	65	Room 7	132	60
Room 1	60	Room 4	250	Room 8	60	24
				Mezz A&B	100	64
				Mezz A or B	50	32

FEES & DEPOSITS: To reserve your date, $200 or half of the rental fee is required as a cleaning/damage deposit; the rental balance is payable 30 days prior to the event. A $500 food and beverage deposit is also payable when your booking is confirmed; the remaining 75% is due 5 weeks prior, and the balance is billed after the event. Luncheons start at $15/person, dinners at $20/person, and hors d'oeuvres at $15/person; tax, a 15% service charge and alcohol are additional. Rental fees run $110–1,945 depending on which room(s) you book; holiday rates may be higher. Room rentals for rehearsals run $50/hour.

AVAILABILITY: Year-round, daily, except major holidays, 8am–midnight.

SERVICES/AMENITIES:

Catering: provided or select from preferred list
Kitchen Facilities: n/a
Tables & Chairs: provided
Linens, Silver, etc.: provided
Restrooms: wheelchair accessible
Dance Floor: parquet floor, or portable, extra fee
Bride's & Groom's Dressing Area: yes, extra fee
Meeting Equipment: some provided, extra charge

Parking: 3-story garage and large lot
Accommodations: no guest rooms
Telephone: pay phones
Outdoor Night Lighting: yes
Outdoor Cooking Facilities: BBQs
Cleanup: provided
View: no
Other: event coordination

RESTRICTIONS:

Alcohol: provided; if BYO, service fee extra
Smoking: outside only
Music: amplified OK

Wheelchair Access: yes
Insurance: extra liability is required
Other: no rice or birdseed

Unitarian Universalist Church of Berkeley

Unitarian Church

1 Lawson Road, Kensington
(510) 525-0391, fax (510) 525-9631

bettyweb@aol.com

◆ Ceremonies ◆ Special Events
◆ Wedding Receptions ◆ Meetings
◆ Business Functions Accommodations

Although the First Unitarian Church of Berkeley is not actually in Berkeley, it's right next door in neighboring Kensington, high in the hills overlooking a good portion of Berkeley, El Cerrito, Kensington and beyond. Several elements make this 1960s church popular for weddings: a large central atrium, an adjacent sanctuary with a magnificent Aeolian-Skinner pipe organ, and an outdoor brick terrace with sweeping views of San Francisco Bay.

Ceremonies usually take place in the sanctuary, whose one-of-a-kind, 2,752-pipe organ will make your walk down the aisle a memorable one. Nineteen rows of wooden pews face a large altar flanked by cast iron candelabras and a wooden pulpit decorated with fiery orange ceramic tiles.

When the ceremony's over, the Atrium can be used for the reception or for champagne and hors d'oeuvres. Four towering rubber trees create a leafy canopy, and light from skylights filters in through the branches. In the room's center, a black marble fountain lined with azure tiles bubbles softly while guests mingle. If you need more space or you'd like an outdoor reception, tables can also be set up on the Terrace. It's one of the few places in the East Bay where you can dine while admiring vistas of the Golden Gate and Bay bridges or a divine sunset on a clear day.

Two additional reception options are the Social Hall, which has room for more guests and a stage for a band, and the Fireside Room, which has a working fireplace and is suitable for smaller gatherings. You don't have to be a Unitarian, or a member of the congregation to be married here and you may bring in your own officiant for a small fee.

CEREMONY CAPACITY: The Sanctuary holds 400 seated, the Atrium and Terrace, combined, 200 seated, and the Fireside Room up to 80 seated.

EVENT/RECEPTION CAPACITY:

Area	Seated	Standing	Area	Seated	Standing
Atrium and Terrace	125	200	Fireside Room	80	100
Social Hall	250	300	Sanctuary	400	—

MEETING CAPACITY: Only nonprofit organizations may hold business functions here.

Area	Theatre-style	Conf-style	Area	Theatre-style	Conf-style
Atrium and Terrace	125	125	Fireside Room	80	80
Social Hall	250	250	Sanctuary	400	—
Safir Room	40	25	Meditation Room	40	25

FEES & DEPOSITS: A $100 non-refundable booking deposit is required to secure your date. Half of the total fees are due when the room reservation agreement is signed, approximately 1 month after booking; the event balance is payable 1 month prior to the event.

Room rental fees for ceremonies range from $375–900; fees for ceremonies with receptions range from $1,000–2,400. There is a $200 refundable cleaning deposit; minister and organist charges are additional.

AVAILABILITY: Year-round, daily. Events are scheduled around the Church's programmed functions. Events on Saturdays take place 10am–midnight, on Sundays 4pm–midnight. Fees increase sharply after 10pm.

SERVICES/AMENITIES:

Catering: BYO, must be approved
Kitchen Facilities: fully equipped, no utensils
Tables & Chairs: provided
Linens, Silver, etc.: BYO
Restrooms: wheelchair accessible
Dance Floor: in Social Hall, Atrium or Terrace
Bride's & Groom's Dressing Area: yes
Meeting Equipment: PA, VCR & screen

Parking: large lot, 200 spaces
Accommodations: no guest rooms
Telephone: pay phone
Outdoor Night Lighting: access only
Outdoor Cooking Facilities: no
Cleanup: caterer or renter
View: panoramic view of SF Bay & region

RESTRICTIONS:

Alcohol: BYO BWC only
Smoking: outside only
Music: amplified OK indoors only

Wheelchair Access: yes
Insurance: not required
Other: no hard alcohol, rice, birdseed or confetti; no open flames

---

*This is important! Tell facilities you're reading **Here Comes The Guide** and ask if our information is still current.*

Lafayette Park Hotel

Boutique Hotel

3287 Mount Diablo Boulevard, Lafayette
(925) 283-3700, (800) 368-2468, fax (925) 284-3937

www.woodsidehotels.com
lph@woodsidehotels.com

◆ Ceremonies   ◆ Special Events
◆ Wedding Receptions   ◆ Meetings
◆ Business Functions   ◆ Accommodations

The Lafayette Park maintains a standard of comfort, ambiance and service rarely found in hotel environments nowadays, and treats brides and grooms like royalty. It's no wonder they've received the Mobil Four Star Award—the only hotel in the East Bay with that claim to fame.

The Hotel is easy to find—its distinctive Norman French architecture, with dormers, French windows, green shutters and peaked roofline, makes it a Lafayette landmark. Designed around three European-style courtyards, it offers a variety of spaces for ceremonies and receptions.

If you're interested in an outdoor ceremony or party, the interior Fountain Courtyard is especially lovely. Here you'll find ivy-trellised urns which support flowering trees and overflow with multicolored flowers. Umbrella-shaded tables encircle a hand-carved Italian limestone fountain, which provides a wonderful background for wedding photos. If you'd like the option of an indoor/outdoor reception, tall French doors lead to interior rooms. For more private, intimate gatherings, try the second-floor Wishing Well Courtyard, which has an imported stone wishing well as its centerpiece. With an 18th-century imported marble mantel, wood-burning fireplace, oak floors and tasteful furnishings, the Diderot Library makes a perfect venue for rehearsal dinners or bridal showers. All meals in the Library, created by the hotel's award-winning chef, are served on china and crystal. And if this weren't enough, the Hotel offers a complimentary fireplace room for the honeymoon couple and special overnight rates for your wedding guests.

CEREMONY CAPACITY:

Room	*Seated*	*Room*	*Seated*
Fountain Courtyard	200	Wishing Well Courtyard	64
George Washington Room	130		

EVENT/RECEPTION CAPACITY:

Room	Seated	Standing	Room	Seated	Standing
Independence Hall	175	220	Fountain Courtyard	150	300
George Washington Room	100	130	Independence Hall		
Mandarin Room	67	80	with Courtyard	280	500
Diderot Library	20	30	Wishing Well Courtyard	50–60	100

MEETING CAPACITY:

Room	Theater-style	Conf-style	Room	Theater-style	Conf-style
Independence Hall	220	45	Conference Suite	—	8
G. Washington Room	130	30	Mandarin Room	67	25
Diderot Library	30	25	Board Room	—	14

FEES & DEPOSITS: A $1,000 non-refundable deposit is required to reserve your date. The Hotel's wedding package includes butler service champagne and hors d'oeuvres, beverages, linens, centerpieces and guest room with fireplace. The rental fee for Independence Hall and the Fountain Courtyard is $995. Special wedding menus range from $34–45/person. Tax and service charges are additional.

Fees for business functions vary depending on overnight rooms, services and menus selected.

AVAILABILITY: Year-round, daily. Business functions 8am–5pm or 6pm–11pm; weddings 11:30am–4:30pm or 6pm–11pm.

SERVICES/AMENITIES:

Catering: provided
Kitchen Facilities: n/a
Tables & Chairs: provided
Linens, Silver, etc.: provided
Restrooms: wheelchair accessible
Dance Floor: yes
Bride's Dressing Area: complimentary
Meeting Equipment: full range, AV company

Parking: lot and valet
Accommodations: 139 guest rooms
Telephone: pay phones
Outdoor Night Lighting: yes
Outdoor Cooking Facilities: CBA
Cleanup: provided
View: of courtyard & fountain
Other: event coordination

RESTRICTIONS:

Alcohol: provided, corkage $12.50/bottle
Smoking: outdoors only
Music: amplified OK within limits

Wheelchair Access: yes
Insurance: not required

The professionals in the back of the book are the best in the business! How do we know? Read page 681.

Postino

Italian Restaurant

3565 Mount Diablo Boulevard, Lafayette
(925) 299-2434, fax (925) 299-2433

◆ Ceremonies	◆ Special Events
◆ Wedding Receptions	◆ Meetings
◆ Business Functions	Accommodations

Postino Restaurant was originally designed in 1937 as a post office, but you'd never know to look at it. Recently updated by architect Steven Samuelson (who also designed San Fran-cisco's Loongbar) its unique cottage exterior has been preserved, while the interior has been transformed into a warm, rustic, and sometimes whimsical atmosphere evocative of the Italian countryside.

The building and its setting are story-book perfection. A tidy hedge dotted with white flowers shelters Postino from the street. Its ivy-covered brick facade rises to a pointed, double-layered turret with an iron pennant jutting out at a permanent, jaunty flutter. The sharp top of the grey slate roof gives way to a gentle outward curve as it slopes down over the terrace along the building's left side. A small black gate in the hedge swings open to welcome visitors up the walk, along the lush lawn (just right for photos), and past the neat border garden with a gently trailing birch tree.

Inside, the delicious aromas of fresh-made pasta and meats and vegetables roasting *al forno* will pull you straight from the front door into the Atrium, the main dining area. The entire back of the room is open to the kitchen; a high, rustic wood counter separates chefs from diners, and serves as a buffet for private events. Tables and chairs can be removed altogether to free space for dancers to take a spin on the slate floor. The Atrium is open and full of light; the sun's rays spill through a glass-paned ceiling and a diaphanous canopy of parachute silks, illuminating the frescoes of Tuscan countryside scenes that decorate the brick walls.

Peek into some of the smaller, more contained dining areas that open off of the Atrium. There's the Family Room on the right, with its giant wood-framed fireplace and cockleshell lanterns floating overhead. Adjacent to the Family Room is the Alcove, a semi-private space just right for a gathering of intimates. The Tavollazza, in the left wing, features a single long country-style table; the atmospherically subdued Library, also on the left, houses the Capo table, a massive oval nearly enclosed by a soft banquette.

At the far end of the left wing, past the 30-foot copper bar, is Postino's completely private dining room, the Buca. (All of the other rooms are semi-private, partly open to either the Atrium or the bar area.) Here, the brick walls have been white-washed and decorated with painted olive-leaf vines. Mullioned doors on the left side open directly onto the terrace, where white canvas umbrellas shade guests sipping cocktails before a reception. The Buca's ceiling rises to a sharp point accentuated by unpainted wood beams. With furniture removed, the effect of the room is chapel-like, making the Buca as well-suited for a small wedding ceremony as it is for a private dinner.

For a rehearsal or corporate dinner, a well-heeled bachelor/ bachelorette party, or an afternoon wedding with a distinctly Italian flavor, Postino is the place. Event options here are plentiful, and atmosphere is unlimited. *Buona fortuna!*

CEREMONY CAPACITY: The Restaurant can accommodate up to 50 seated guests.

EVENT/RECEPTION CAPACITY: The Buca Room holds 30 seated and the Alcove 14 seated. The entire restaurant can seat up to 150 guests.

MEETING CAPACITY: The Buca Room holds 30 seated and the Alcove 14 seated.

FEES & DEPOSITS: For weddings, there is a $5,500 food and beverage minimum. Half of the anticipated food and beverage total is payable as a partially refundable deposit to reserve your date. The balance is due 3 days prior to the event. Menus can be customized: 3-course meals start at $32/person, 4-course meals at $40/person, and reception buffets at $40/person; alcohol, tax and an 18% service charge are additional. There is a $50 setup charge for less than 30 guests, a $100 charge for 30 guests or more. For other special events and business functions, there's no food and beverage minimum or rental fee.

AVAILABILITY: Year-round, daily, 5:30pm–10pm, except for major holidays. Wedding receptions take place any day of the week, 10am–3pm only.

SERVICES/AMENITIES:

Catering: provided, no BYO
Kitchen Facilities: n/a
Tables & Chairs: provided
Linens, Silver, etc.: provided
Restrooms: wheelchair accessible
Dance Floor: in Atrium
Bride's Dressing Area: CBA
Meeting Equipment: BYO or CBA

Parking: large lot or on street
Accommodations: no guest rooms
Telephone: pay phone
Outdoor Night Lighting: yes
Outdoor Cooking Facilities: no
Cleanup: provided
View: garden courtyard
Other: event coordination

RESTRICTIONS:

Alcohol: provided, or BYO corkage $10/bottle
Smoking: outdoors only
Music: amplified OK w/volume limits

Wheelchair Access: yes
Insurance: not required
Other: furnishings are not moveable

This is important! Tell facilities you're reading **Here Comes The Guide** *and ask if our information is still current.*

Wildwood Acres

1055 Hunsaker Canyon Road, Lafayette
(925) 283-2600, fax (925) 283-2608

www.wildwoodacres.com
wildwood@slip.net

◆ Ceremonies   ◆ Special Events
◆ Wedding Receptions   ◆ Meetings
◆ Business Functions   Accommodations

It's hard to believe, as you drive through the suburban sprawl that makes up most of Contra Costa County, that a rustic jewel like Wildwood Acres could exist here. Nestled in a wooded canyon only five miles from downtown Lafayette, it's suitable for a wide variety of events. Whether you're planning a country-style reception, family reunion, or frothy Victorian wedding with picture hats and parasols, Wildwood Acres can magically transform itself into the ideal venue.

The indoor facility is a large clubhouse that looks like a cross between a hunting lodge and your Great Aunt Clara's parlor. Trophy heads of deer and boar line the walls, amid festoons of greenery; Oriental rugs, bookshelves, and a fireplace with benches on either side make the room cozy. There's even a pool table and bar. This would be especially nice for a Christmas party or other winter event.

The outdoor facilities, however, are what make Wildwood Acres so special. If you're getting married here there's a lovely ceremony site up on a hill in a fern grotto, deep in a grove of towering bay trees and bigleaf maples. Exchange vows on a stone platform in one corner while your guests, seated in the adjacent open area, savor their surroundings. Afterwards, have your reception on two terraces, shaded by a natural canopy of alder and maple trees. A redwood gazebo houses the band, and there's plenty of room to kick up your heels on the sunken dance floor. All around, pottery urns overflowing with impatiens and ferns add spots of color, and winding paths lead to shady nooks containing wrought-iron or wooden benches.

CEREMONY, EVENT/RECEPTION & MEETING CAPACITY:

Area	Seated	Standing	Area	Seated	Standing
Clubhouse	120	150	Terrace Area	275	275
Fern Grotto *(ceremonies only)*	275	275			

FEES & DEPOSITS: The site rental fee is $900, May–October; $600, November–April. To reserve your date, a non-refundable $450 deposit is required. For weddings, ceremony and reception charges include the rental fee and ceremony setup fee, plus in-house catering, starting at $33/person, with champagne, beer, wine and soft drinks.

Mid-week business functions start at $30/person, including rental fee, continental breakfast, lunch and nonalcoholic beverages.

For all events, a 15% tax/service charge is additional.

AVAILABILITY: Year-round, daily, 7:30am–2am.

SERVICES/AMENITIES:

Catering: provided, no BYO
Kitchen Facilities: n/a
Tables & Chairs: provided
Linens, Silver, etc.: provided
Restrooms: limited wheelchair access
Dance Floor: indoor and outdoor provided
Bride's & Groom's Dressing Area: yes
Meeting Equipment: full range

Parking: ample
Accommodations: no guest rooms
Telephone: calling cards OK
Outdoor Night Lighting: yes
Outdoor Cooking Facilities: provided
Cleanup: provided
View: of canyon
Other: event coordination

RESTRICTIONS:

Alcohol: provided, no BYO
Smoking: outdoors only
Music: amplified OK

Wheelchair Access: yes
Insurance: not required
Other: no rice or glitter

The professionals in the back of the book are the best in the business! How do we know? Read page 681.

Murrieta's Well

3005 Mines Road, Livermore
(925) 456-2425, fax (925) 456-2401

www.wentevineyards.com

Historic Winery

◆ Ceremonies ◆ Special Events
◆ Wedding Receptions ◆ Meetings
◆ Business Functions Accommodations

Tucked away in Livermore's wine country is Murrieta's Well, an historic winery that is blessed with something you seldom find: appealing spaces for both indoor and outdoor weddings and receptions. A drive across a small bridge leads you to the winery, surrounded by a pastoral scene of vineyards, sycamores and olive trees. The main building, a handsome, two-story structure built in 1885 by the original owner, Louis Mel, is a delightful blend of old and new.

Upstairs, century-old concrete walls (with some of the original metal rebar peeping through), contrast with more contemporary crisp, white walls and gleaming oak floors. The ceiling is gloriously high with hefty, exposed natural wood beams. And along the sides of the entryway, a few pieces of antique wine-making equipment and historic photos taken during the 1890s harken back to the winery's past. The entryway's long foyer can easily be set up for a receiving line or a bar, and at the end of the foyer, a large attractive room designed in muted earth tones is perfect for cocktails and hors d'oeuvres. Windows overlooking the vineyards and the twenty-foot ceiling make this comfortable room light and airy, and leather couches and chairs can be arranged to suit your needs. A small balcony with French doors can be used for indoor ceremonies, or as a place to throw the bouquet to awaiting hands below.

Downstairs is the fragrant Barrel Room. Wine casks line the concrete walls of this cellar, and huge double doors open to a patio adjacent to grapevines. When it's warm outside, the cellar remains cool and comfortable and the aroma of aging wine permeates the air. The patio can be used for additional seating, a band, DJ or dancing. Planning an event in the East Bay? Murrieta's Well is a special place you shouldn't miss.

CEREMONY CAPACITY: The Balcony Room holds 125 seated; the Vineyard Patio 140 seated guests.

EVENT/RECEPTION CAPACITY: The Balcony Room holds 60 seated or 140 standing; the Barrel Room holds 140 seated or 150 standing guests.

MEETING CAPACITY: The Balcony Room holds 10–70 guests depending on a variety of seating configurations.

FEES & DEPOSITS: For weddings, a $1,500 non-refundable facility deposit is required to reserve your date. Half of the anticipated event total is payable 30 days prior and the event balance is payable 10 days prior to the event. The facility fee is $1,500. Catering is provided by *Wente Vineyards Catering*; luncheons start at $29/person, dinners at $38/person. Tax, a 19% service charge and beverages are additional. Wedding packages are available, however any menu can be customized.

For other social functions, a $500 facility fee is required to reserve your date. The menu pricing is the same as above. For meetings and business-related events, conference packages start at $32.50/person. Fees will vary depending on menus and services; call for more specific information.

AVAILABILITY: Year-round, daily, including holidays until 11pm. Saturday weddings take place either 10am–3pm or 6pm–11pm in 5-hour blocks.

SERVICES/AMENITIES:

Catering: provided by *Wente Vineyards Catering*, no BYO

Kitchen Facilities: n/a

Tables & Chairs: provided

Linens, Silver, etc.: provided

Restrooms: not wheelchair accessible

Dance Floor: patio or in Barrel Room

Bride's Dressing Area: yes

Other: event coordination

Parking: ample, large lots

Accommodations: no guest rooms

Telephone: emergency use only

Outdoor Night Lighting: yes

Outdoor Cooking Facilities: CBA

Cleanup: provided

View: vineyards and Livermore hills

Meeting Equipment: CBA, extra charge

RESTRICTIONS:

Alcohol: provided, BWC corkage $10/bottle

Smoking: outside only

Music: amplified OK until 10pm

Wheelchair Access: yes

Insurance: not required

Other: no rice, birdseed, glitter or confetti

This is important! Tell facilities you're reading **Here Comes The Guide** and ask if our information is still current.

Purple Orchid Inn

Country Inn & Spa

Address withheld to ensure privacy. Livermore
(415) 456-8806, fax (415) 382-2056

◆ Ceremonies   ◆ Special Events
◆ Wedding Receptions   ◆ Meetings
◆ Business Functions   ◆ Accommodations

Consider this wedding scenario: the groom's parents, who have a horror of anonymous hotels, are traveling across the country for the big event. They'd like to stay in a quiet B&B, cozy but stylish, with a pool and a garden surrounded by neat rows of new olive trees (if it's not too much to ask). The bridesmaids insist on treating the nervous bride to an indulgent set of spa treatments—facial, manicure, massage, hot oil rub, salt glow—on the morning of the wedding. The bride's mother is obsessed with the idea of a sit-down dinner of elegant grilled food—salmon, chicken, loads of Tuscan-style vegetables—followed by dancing under the stars in a garden a-twinkle with tiny white lights. The bride dreams of making her entrance to the ceremony down a staircase with a harpist playing on a balcony behind her, the groom wants to be married outside in the country, and all in all, the busy couple wish someone would just take over the planning for them.

Can all of these people have their wishes? Yes, indeed. Each of these things—and more—is possible at the Purple Orchid Inn. As proprietor Karen Hughes says, "Guests can have whatever they want here. The answer is always Yes."

Ringed by low hills and surrounded by vineyards and ranches, the Inn is a perfect hideaway for a family-centered wedding weekend or an executive retreat. You'll have a strong sense of privacy here; the Inn can be entirely yours for either bridal or corporate events. The setting is casual country (the entrance drive, for instance, is smoothly graded dirt) but the building and grounds are carefully groomed. Attention to detail is evident everywhere—in the carved wooden guest room doors, the fountain and waterfall, the smooth contours of the swimming pool, and in the abundance of flowers and plants. Ivy and ferns spill from pockets in the stone entryway wall, dried flower wreaths adorn almost every room, painted vines twine through the dining hall, fire-red rose bushes lean along the front fence—and, of course, there are orchids, too.

Wedding ceremonies can take place in the dining room, with the French doors thrown open at back to the pool and fountain just beyond, or in the garden, under a white wooden arch that frames the young olive trees that surround the property. Either way, the bride has a staircase on which to make her dramatic descent. Catering is done exclusively by Michael Goldstein, who shares Karen's belief that anything is possible. Meals he's prepared at the Purple Orchid range from white-glove, 70-person, sit-down dinners of beef tenderloin to 400-person buffets with pasta stations and Latin-influenced fare.

So if, in fact, you really are feeling utterly overwhelmed, and wish somebody would take charge for you—don't hesitate to call. "We can do everything or nothing at all," says Karen. "It's up to you."

CEREMONY & EVENT/RECEPTION CAPACITY: Indoors, the dining area can seat 50 guests; outdoors, the Pavilion holds 450 seated and lawn area up to 700 seated. There are a variety of other areas for ceremonies, including lawns, gardens and an area around the pool.

MEETING CAPACITY: The Boardroom holds 15 seated, the Dining Room 50 seated, and the Spa building up to 45 seated guests. The Pavilion holds up to 600–700 seated theater-style.

FEES & DEPOSITS: A $900 non-refundable rental minimum or 50% of the anticipated event total (the facility fee and lodging) is required to as a deposit to reserve your date. The facility fee ranges $1,500–5,200 depending on number of accommodations. There is a 2-night minimum if the event includes a Saturday night. The rental balance is due 120 days prior to the event. Catering is provided by *Michael Goldstein Catering*. All menus are customized; luncheons or dinners start at $20/person.

Spa services can be arranged, and include massages, facials and other body care services.

AVAILABILITY: Year-round, daily, any time.

SERVICES/AMENITIES:

Catering: provided, no BYO
Kitchen Facilities: n/a
Tables & Chairs: through caterer
Linens, Silver, etc.: through caterer
Restrooms: wheelchair accessible CBA
Dance Floor: CBA, extra charge
Bride's & Groom's Dressing Area: guest room CBA
Meeting Equipment: TV, VCR, dry erase board; other CBA

Parking: ample on site
Accommodations: 8 guest rooms
Telephone: guest & house phones CBA
Outdoor Night Lighting: yes
Outdoor Cooking Facilities: through caterer
Cleanup: provided
View: olive groves, hills, wildflowers, vineyards
Other: full range of spa services

RESTRICTIONS:

Alcohol: provided or BYO, corkage $7.50/bottle
Smoking: outside only
Music: amplified OK

Wheelchair Access: yes
Insurance: extra liability required
Other: no rice or birdseed indoors; children require adult supervision

---

The professionals in the back of the book are the best in the business! How do we know? Read page 681.

Shrine Event Center

Banquet Facility

170 Lindbergh Avenue, Livermore
(925) 294-8667, fax (925) 294-8666

www.beetscater.com
beets@beetscater.com

◆ Ceremonies   ◆ Special Events
◆ Wedding Receptions   ◆ Meetings
◆ Business Functions   Accommodations

This relatively new facility has two things going for it. The first is that it can hold a really large crowd for a wedding reception—up to 450 seated guests! We know of no other site in the Tri Valley area that offers this square footage indoors. The second is that *Beets Catering* is the exclusive caterer/coordinator.

Although the Center is an unpretentious auditorium with a stage, vaulted ceiling and an expansive linoleum floor, *Beets* can transform it into something special. If you'd like to get married inside, they'll place a large, white lath gazebo in the middle of the room so you can have your ceremony underneath it. They're more than happy to add festive touches by decorating the space with balloon arches or greenery from a plant rental outfit. Whatever you want, whether it's budget-minded or sky's-the-limit, *Beets* can probably do it. We'd also like to point out that *Beets* does a fine job in the catering department, too. From fancy, gourmet finger foods to modest but tasty morsels for a gathering of six hundred, this caterer does a professional job. So if you've got a sizable guest list, and Livermore is geographically well-suited to your needs, call and ask for a tour.

CEREMONY CAPACITY: The main room holds up to 250 seated in rows.

EVENT/RECEPTION CAPACITY: The facility accommodates 450 seated guests; 1,000 for a standing reception.

MEETING CAPACITY: The main auditorium holds 1,000 guests seated theater-style.

FEES & DEPOSITS: For weddings, a non-refundable deposit is required to hold your event date. The rental fee for Friday, Saturday or Sunday is $725. Rental covers a 5-hour event plus 2 hours for setup. The full rental fee and 50% of the estimated food total are due 60 days prior to the event. The balance is due 1 week prior to the function, with any remainder due the day of the event. Additional event staff are available.

Fees for meetings vary based on services and menus selected; call for specifics.

AVAILABILITY: Year-round, daily. Meetings Monday–Friday, 8am-midnight; weddings Fridays and weekends 8am–midnight.

SERVICES/AMENITIES:

Catering: provided, no BYO

Kitchen Facilities: n/a

Tables & Chairs: provided

Linens, Silver, etc.: CBA

Restrooms: wheelchair accessible

Dance Floor: yes

Bride's Dressing Area: CBA

Meeting Equipment: PA system, large screen

Parking: large lot

Accommodations: no guest rooms

Telephone: pay phone

Outdoor Night Lighting: CBA

Outdoor Cooking Facilities: CBA

Cleanup: provided

View: East Bay foothills

Other: event coordination

RESTRICTIONS:

Alcohol: BYO

Smoking: outside only

Music: amplified OK

Wheelchair Access: yes

Insurance: certificate required

This is important! Tell facilities you're reading **Here Comes The Guide** *and ask if our information is still current.*

Wente Vineyards Restaurant
and Visitors Center

5050 Arroyo Road, Livermore
(925) 456-2425, fax (925) 456-2401
www.wentevineyards.com

Winery

◆ Ceremonies ◆ Special Events
◆ Wedding Receptions ◆ Meetings
◆ Business Functions Accommodations

Situated in a picturesque canyon at the southern end of the Livermore Valley, Wente Vineyards Restaurant and Visitors Center is surrounded by vineyards, sycamore groves and rolling hills. The site offers your guests unparalleled vistas and an appealing, natural environment for all kinds of special events, from weddings and receptions to conferences and business retreats.

The grounds also include a Visitor's Center, Conference Center and an award-winning, casually elegant restaurant serving North American cuisine. The white, Spanish-style stucco buildings are accented with tile roofs and floors, terra cotta pots full of flowering plants and acres of vineyards, which all convey a strong Mediterranean feeling. Shimmering white and green in the bright afternoon sun, this winery is an oasis in the midst of our dry California hills.

CEREMONY CAPACITY: The Lawn and Garden can accommodate 500 seated; the Vineyard Veranda, 100 seated; the Museum Room, 70 seated guests.

EVENT/RECEPTION CAPACITY:

Area	*Seated*	*Area*	*Seated*
Lawn & Garden	500	Restaurant	15–200
Visitor's Center	180		

MEETING CAPACITY:

Area	*Theater-style*	*Classroom-style*	*U-Shape*	*Hollow Square*
Charles Wetmore Room	120	50	32	48
Cresta Blanca	30	16	18	20
Vineyard Room	30	16	18	20

FEES & DEPOSITS: For weddings, a $1,500 facility rental fee deposit plus 20% of the anticipated event total is required to confirm a reservation. Catering is provided: buffets and seated meals, including wedding cake, range $28–45/person. The anticipated catering balance is payable 2 weeks prior to the event; all incurred expenses are due the day of the event.

For business functions and meetings, the rental fees are as follows: Charles Wetmore Room, $250/day (9-hour maximum) plus $125/day to use the additional Cresta Blanca breakout room; the cost for the Vineyard Room is $200/day (9-hour maximum). Food is provided; prices will vary depending on menus and services selected; call for specific rates.

AVAILABILITY: Year-round, daily, 10am–11pm.

SERVICES/AMENITIES:

Catering: provided
Kitchen Facilities: n/a
Tables & Chairs: provided
Linens, Silver, etc.: provided
Restrooms: wheelchair accessible
Dance Floor: on patio
Bride's Dressing Area: yes
Meeting Equipment: full range, extra charge

Parking: large lot w/parking attendants
Accommodations: no guest rooms
Outdoor Night Lighting: yes
Outdoor Cooking Facilities: no
Telephone: pay phones
Cleanup: provided
View: vineyards surrounded by rolling hills
Other: event coordination

RESTRICTIONS:

Alcohol: provided, BWC only, WC $10/bottle
Smoking: outside only
Music: amplified OK

Wheelchair Access: yes
Insurance: not required
Other: no birdseed, rice or petals

The professionals in the back of the book are the best in the business! How do we know? Read page 681.

Montclair Women's Cultural Arts Club

Historic Women's Club

1650 Mountain Boulevard, Montclair
(510) 339-1832, fax (510) 339-1851

mwcaclub@aol.com

◆ Ceremonies   ◆ Special Events
◆ Wedding Receptions   ◆ Meetings
◆ Business Functions   Accommodations

Anyone familiar with the circa 1925 Mediterranean-style Montclair Woman's Club will be delighted to learn of its new lease on life. After 70 years in existence, the Club has been leased to music and cultural events producer Barbara Price, who recently closed it down for a complete facelift. In three short months, with much volunteer help, she transformed the Club, giving it an entirely new look and purpose. Now, in addition to being a special event space, it houses a nonprofit women's cultural arts center, hosting everything from art exhibits, concerts, and theater productions to classes and workshops. It's also home to the Montclair Women's Big Band, a 17-piece all-women dance band that can play for your swing-era parties.

The interiors have been spruced-up with deep, rich colors painted on the walls, new flooring (the same type used at the Louvre Museum), and recessed spot lights. The gallery, artistically updated in cranberry with contrasting trim in teal and gold, displays a hint of old-world elegance. It can be used for small art exhibits, and makes a dramatic setting for an intimate formal sit-down dinner. It also serves as a lush backdrop for buffet tables, while the adjoining ballroom is set up for a large sit-down dinner and dancing. Painted a pearly blue with teal ceiling and beams, the ballroom retains its original hardwood floors and comes complete with a stage and newly reclaimed projection booth and sound system. The grand piano, which can easily be moved, was the very instrument on which conductor Antonia Brico (noted for being the first female conductor) practiced as a child. The ballroom's four large double doors open to the wooded courtyard, which is used for receptions, buffets and ceremonies.

The Fireside Salon, off the main entry hall, glows with a whimsical interpretation of the Garden of Eden painted on persimmon-red sponged walls. Trees laden with golden fruit and a mermaid disappearing into the sea are just some of the delightful details you'll encounter here. Deep green moldings, a gleaming mahogany-topped bar and foot rail, a large Arts and Crafts ceramic tile fireplace, and an Oriental area rug all add warmth to the salon. Traditionally used as a spot for passed hors d'oeuvres and cocktails, business seminars, and luncheons, we think this new incarnation also begs for a ladies' tea, poetry reading, or a 1920s theme party, where guests glide about in silk smoking jackets, knotted ascots, and feather boas.

Much of the year, the private corner garden and lawn create a pleasant spot for a small outdoor ceremony or a natural backdrop for formal photographs. The Club's other neat features—a real coat check room, a ticket booth, and a will-call window—add many creative use options to this spirited and newly inspired space.

CEREMONY CAPACITY:

Area	Seated	Standing	Area	Seated	Standing
Garden	80	80	Courtyard	200	300
Fireside Salon	—	50	Ballroom	200	300

EVENT/RECEPTION & MEETING CAPACITY: The Ballroom holds 200 seated or 300 standing, the Gallery 24 seated or 50 standing, and the Salon 24 seated or 50 standing guests.

FEES & DEPOSITS: To reserve your date, a refundable $500 security/cleaning deposit and half of the rental fee (as a non-refundable deposit) are required. The rental balance is payable 45 days prior to the event. For use of the courtyard, grand piano and/or sound and light system, additional fees will apply. Preference is given for entire-facility rentals on weekends and holidays, which have a 6-hour minimum.

Space	Wkdays	Wkends, Holidays	Space	Wkdays	Wkends, Holidays
Facility Interior	$200/hr	$300/hr	Salon & Gallery	$100/hr	$150/hr
Facility & Courtyard	250/hr	350/hr	Salon	50/hr	100/hr
Ballroom	100/hr	200/hr	Kitchen	$50 flat fee	$100 flat fee

AVAILABILITY: Year-round, daily until 11pm.

SERVICES/AMENITIES:

Catering: BYO or CBA
Kitchen Facilities: fully equipped
Tables & Chairs: provided
Linens, Silver, etc.: BYO or CBA, extra fee
Restrooms: wheelchair accessible
Dance Floor: in Ballroom, Gallery & Salon
Bride's Dressing Area: yes
Meeting Equipment: CBA, extra fee

Parking: off street and lot
Accommodations: no guest rooms
Telephone: limited use
Outdoor Night Lighting: yes
Outdoor Cooking Facilities: BYO
Cleanup: caterer or renter
View: wooded landscape
Other: grand piano & console piano, coordination/entertainment services

RESTRICTIONS:

Alcohol: BYO, WCB only; controlled bar required
Smoking: outside only
Music: amplified OK indoors until 11pm

Wheelchair Access: yes
Insurance: may be required
Other: no tape or thumbtacks

This is important! Tell facilities you're reading **Here Comes The Guide** *and ask if our information is still current.*

Hacienda de las Flores

2100 Donald Drive, Moraga
(925) 376-2521, fax (925) 376-2034

www.ci.moraga.ca.us
rent@moraga.ca.us

Historic Home & Garden

◆ Ceremonies ◆ Special Events
◆ Wedding Receptions ◆ Meetings
◆ Business Functions Accommodations

An authentic Spanish-style mansion, the Hacienda de las Flores sits on land that was once the hunting ground for Miwok Indians. The historic, city-owned structure is painted white with blue trim, and is surrounded by well-maintained park grounds. Inside the Hacienda, hardwood floors, beamed ceilings, a fireplace and red leather furniture create a warm and inviting setting. Outdoors, a large lawn spreads out behind the building, enhanced by blue spruce trees, weeping willows, palms and flowers. A circular flower bed and fountain in the middle of the patio serve as the focal point for large parties or wedding receptions.

From the upper Hacienda lawn, flagstone stairs lead down to the Pavilion, a semicircular building with huge Corinthian columns overlooking a walled garden with lawn and patio. A set of large wrought-iron gates leads guests into the enclosure, where small seated functions or ceremonies can take place. Tranquil and secluded, the Hacienda offers one of the prettiest garden environments for special events in the East Bay.

CEREMONY CAPACITY:

Area	Seated	Standing	Area	Seated	Standing
Hacienda	—	75	Pavilion	40	50
Hacienda lawn	200	200	Pavilion Lawn	100	100

EVENT/RECEPTION CAPACITY: The Hacienda accommodates 200 guests outdoors or 100 for a seated meal indoors. The Pavilion seats 40 inside and has an outdoor capacity of 100.

MEETING CAPACITY: There are 7 rooms which can accommodate 24–40 seated guests.

FEES & DEPOSITS: For special events, a $500 security deposit plus half the rental fee are due when the facility is booked. The security deposit will be refunded within 30 days after the event provided all conditions have been met. A completed rental packet and remaining fees are due 6 months before the event.

Friday Night (3pm–10pm)	*Nov–Apr*	*May–Oct*
Hacienda	$1,210	$1,435
Pavilion	1,040	1,265
Hacienda & Pavilion	1,945	2,170
Saturday/Sunday (8 consecutive hours)		
Hacienda	$1,450	$1,750
Pavilion	1,250	1,550
Hacienda & Pavilion	2,350	2,600

For weekday business meetings, the fees vary depending on room(s) selected, and include room setup. There is an additional fee for use of the Hacienda kitchen.

AVAILABILITY: For special events, Friday, Saturday and Sunday (8 consecutive hours); additional hours are not available. For weekday business meetings, the facility is available 8am–5pm. Site previews take place 1pm–5pm, Monday–Friday.

SERVICES/AMENITIES:

Catering: select from preferred list
Kitchen Facilities: ample
Tables & Chairs: provided
Linens, Silver, etc.: BYO
Restrooms: wheelchair accessible
Dance Floor: yes
Bride's Dressing Area: yes
Meeting Equipment: projector, screen, flip chart, VCR

Parking: on street and lot
Accommodations: no guest rooms
Telephone: pay phone
Outdoor Night Lighting: access only
Outdoor Cooking Facilities: no
Cleanup: provided
View: fountain, lawns, flowerbeds & trees

RESTRICTIONS:

Alcohol: BYO, WCB only
Smoking: outside only
Music: no amplified music outdoors

Wheelchair Access: yes
Insurance: included in fees
Other: decorations restricted, no birdseed, rice or mylar balloons

---

The professionals in the back of the book are the best in the business! How do we know? Read page 681.

Holy Trinity Cultural Center

Cultural Center

1700 School Street, Moraga
(925) 376-5982, (925) 939-4337, fax (925) 906-9636

◆ Ceremonies   ◆ Special Events
◆ Wedding Receptions   ◆ Meetings
◆ Business Functions   Accommodations

Many couples are looking for a tranquil setting for their wedding reception, and at the Holy Trinity Cultural Center, you'll have that and more: The entire reach of the curving Moraga hills will sweep into your reception hall, framed by a full wall of floor-to-ceiling windows set in alternating arched and rectangular black-framed panels. Outside, you'll also have a lawn surrounded by yellow-flowering shrubs (perhaps the right backdrop for your photos), a small cement courtyard with a redwood arbor (a good area for cocktails), and the sweet sounds of birdsong to accompany your guests' conversation. The Cultural Center is located on an exceptionally quiet street, and only an occasional passing car will interrupt the quiet sounds of the natural world surrounding you.

Inside, the Cultural Center is a unusually capacious space. Composed of two main rooms, the Fireside Room and the large main hall, it also offers a series of small rooms for changing, private time, or entertaining children—one of the rooms is a dedicated kids' playroom equipped with toys, a large-screen TV, and video.

The Fireside Room, like the hall, has large plate-glass windows (in this case behind the full-length mahogany bar), framing the lawn and the oak- and pine-covered hills beyond. The wall opposite the bar is adorned with a brightly colored mural of Belgrade, created by a visiting Yugoslavian artist; a third wall is taken up with a slate-covered fireplace, which brings a warm glow to winter events.

After cocktails in the Fireside Room or on the patio, invite your guests into the main hall for dinner. If you wanted to, you'd have enough space to seat everyone at tables around the circumference of the hall, leaving room for dancing in the center; but more likely, you'll take advantage of the built-in hardwood dance floor at the far end of the room. Included in the rental of the hall are all of the china, silver, and glassware you'll need to set your tables (also included) and make the room sparkle; follow the example of one couple who added ficus trees embedded with tiny white lights, and your reception will shine.

And one more advantage to the Holy Trinity Cultural Center—your caterer will thank you. The full commercial-style kitchen is stocked with everything from top-of-the-line cooking equipment to a professional dishwasher, making cleanup a breeze, and there's easy access to and from the kitchen and the bar, hall, and exterior of the building.

CEREMONY CAPACITY: The lawn holds 450 seated; the Main Hall holds 450 seated guests.

EVENT/RECEPTION CAPACITY: The Main Hall (which includes use of the garden and patio) holds 350 seated guests.

MEETING CAPACITY: The Fireside Room holds 70 seated. There are 2 additional breakout rooms which hold 10–20 seated guests each. The Main Hall holds over 450 seated guests, theater-style.

FEES & DEPOSITS: For events, a $300 deposit is required to secure your date; the rental fee and $150 cleaning deposit are payable 10 days prior to the event. The Main Hall rental fee runs $900–1,100, the Main Hall with Fireside Room runs $1,200–1,500. Use of the lawn and patio are included with rental of either room. If you use an outside caterer, use of the kitchen runs $300.

AVAILABILITY: Year-round, daily, 7am–midnight.

SERVICES/AMENITIES:

Catering: provided or BYO w/approval
Kitchen Facilities: fully equipped, commercial
Tables & Chairs: provided
Linens, Silver, etc.: BYO or through caterer
Restrooms: wheelchair accessible
Dance Floor: hardwood floor
Bride's Dressing Area: CBA
Meeting Equipment: sound system, podium, portable microphone

Parking: large, private lot
Accommodations: no guest rooms
Telephone: use with approval
Outdoor Night Lighting: access only
Outdoor Cooking Facilities: no
Cleanup: caterer or provided
View: Moraga hills & garden courtyard

RESTRICTIONS:

Alcohol: BYO, service provided
Smoking: outside only
Music: amplified OK indoors only until midnight

Wheelchair Access: yes
Insurance: extra liability required
Other: decorations require approval, no rice, birdseed or glitter

---

This is important! Tell facilities you're reading **Here Comes The Guide** and ask if our information is still current.

Camron-Stanford House

1418 Lakeside Drive, Oakland
(510) 836-1976, fax (510) 874-7803

Lakeside Victorian Mansion

◆ Ceremonies ◆ Special Events
◆ Wedding Receptions ◆ Meetings
◆ Business Functions Accommodations

Gracing the shore of Lake Merritt, the Camron-Stanford House is the last of the grand Victorian homes that once ringed the lake. Constructed in 1876, it derives its name from the Camrons who built it and the Stanfords who occupied it for the longest period. When the building was scheduled for demolition in the late 1960s, concerned citizens formed the Camron-Stanford House Preservation Association and spent the intervening years raising funds to return the home to its former splendor.

Elaborate molding, and authentic-looking wallpaper and fabrics have all been recreated to match the originals as closely as possible. Rooms filled with period artifacts, antiques and photos take you back to the late 1800s. The only operational gas chandelier in Northern California is located here. Outside, an enormous rear veranda overlooks Lake Merritt. Receptions can take place in the house, on the veranda or on the expansive lawn that extends to the lake. An iron fence enclosing the site ensures privacy while allowing guests to appreciate the colorful tapestry of boats, birds and joggers that surrounds them.

CEREMONY CAPACITY: The lawn, facing the lake, and the Veranda hold up to 450 seated; the Veranda alone, up to 100 seated guests.

EVENT/RECEPTION & MEETING CAPACITY: The facility accommodates 125 guests inside; 250 outside. The maximum in one room is 75 seated.

FEES & DEPOSITS: Half the rental fee and a refundable $50 cleaning deposit are due when the facility is booked.

Area	*Fee*
Garden, Veranda, Hall, Dining Room, Kitchen (2 hours)	$375–575
Garden, Veranda, Hall, Dining Room, Kitchen (4 hours)	$575
Additional time	$100/hour
Period Rooms (maximum 2 hours)	$50/hour

AVAILABILITY: Year-round, weekdays until 10pm; Saturdays until 11pm.

SERVICES/AMENITIES:

Catering: BYO licensed
Kitchen Facilities: moderate
Tables & Chairs: BYO
Linens, Silver, etc.: BYO
Restroom: wheelchair accessible
Dance Floor: CBA
Bride's Dressing Area: CBA
Meeting Equipment: screen, slide projector

Parking: on street, lot
Accommodations: no guest rooms
Telephone: emergencies only
Outdoor Night Lighting: BYO
Outdoor Cooking Facilities: BYO
Cleanup: caterer
View: of Lake Merritt & Oakland city skyline

RESTRICTIONS:

Alcohol: BYO
Smoking: outside on lawn only
Music: amplified OK outside only

Wheelchair Access: limited
Insurance: proof required
Other: no tacks or tape; no candles,
flame-heated chafing dishes, confetti or rice

The professionals in the back of the book are the best in the business! How do we know? Read page 681.

Clarion Suites Lake Merritt Hotel

1800 Madison Street at Lakeside, Oakland
(510) 832-2300, fax (510) 832-7150

Hotel & Conference Facility

◆ Ceremonies	◆ Special Events
◆ Wedding Receptions	◆ Meetings
◆ Business Functions	◆ Accommodations

Totally enclosed in twenty-foot floor-to-ceiling windows, this hotel's Terrace Room presents an enchanting panorama of Lake Merritt, Lakeside Park and the Oakland hills. At night, the view is of the glittering lake, its surface reflecting the Necklace of Lights gracing its perimeter. Over $1 million was spent to turn the Hotel and restaurant into one of Oakland's premier entertainment sites. This classic, 1927 Art Deco landmark has been restored with new furnishings, carpeting and attention to detail throughout.

During the day, the multilevel Terrace Room is bathed in light. In the evening, it has an intimate, almost cabaret feeling. Here you'll find a semicircular hardwood dance floor, lush potted plants and a sizable mural along one wall (circa 1956) depicting Lake Merritt forty some odd years ago. Fresh flowers, a shiny, black grand piano and Art Deco fixtures are nice finishing touches. In addition to having a great location along the perimeter of Lake Merritt, the hotel offers an in-house restaurant and highly personalized services, many of which can be specifically tailored to your special event.

CEREMONY CAPACITY: The Terrace Room holds 50–200 standing and/or seated guests.

EVENT/RECEPTION CAPACITY: The Terrace Room accommodates 275 standing or seated guests.

MEETING CAPACITY:

Room	Conference-style	Theater-style	Classroom-style
Deluxe Suite	12	20	10
Paramount Room	40	100	50
Mural Room	25	60	30
Terrace Room	60	400	200

FEES & DEPOSITS: A $500–750 non-refundable security deposit is required to reserve your date. An estimated 50% payment is required 2 months prior and the balance is due 1 month prior to your event. For events, room rental fees vary from $250–1,000 depending on room selection. In-house food and beverage service is provided. For full seated service including food and beverage, rates run $19–35/person; buffets run $15–42/person; tax and an 18% service charge are additional. Any menu can be customized.

AVAILABILITY: Year-round, daily, weekends 11am–5pm or 6:30pm–12:30am. Weekday time frames are more flexible.

SERVICES/AMENITIES:

Catering: provided, no BYO

Kitchen Facilities: n/a

Tables & Chairs: provided

Linens, Silver, etc.: provided

Restrooms: wheelchair accessible

Dance Floor: yes

Bride's Dressing Area: CBA

Meeting Equipment: full service, extensive AV

Parking: valet CBA

Accommodations: suites & packages CBA

Telephone: pay phone & dedicated lines

Outdoor Night Lighting: access only

Outdoor Cooking Facilities: no

Cleanup: provided

View: Lake Merritt & Oakland hills

Other: event coordinator on site

RESTRICTIONS:

Alcohol: provided, corkage CBA

Smoking: outdoors only

Music: amplified OK w/volume limits

Wheelchair Access: yes

Insurance: not required

Other: no food or beverages in lobby

This is important! Tell facilities you're reading **Here Comes The Guide** and ask if our information is still current.

Dunsmuir House and Gardens

Historic Mansion & Grounds

2960 Peralta Oaks Court, Oakland
(510) 615-5555, fax (510) 562-8294

www.dunsmuir.org

◆ Ceremonies ◆ Special Events
◆ Wedding Receptions ◆ Meetings
◆ Business Functions Accommodations

Nestled in the East Bay hills, the historic Dunsmuir House and Gardens offers a lovely and secluded setting featuring a turn-of-the-century white mansion and a 40-acre expanse of lawn and trees, evoking the serenity of a bygone era. The mansion was a romantic wedding gift from Alexander Dunsmuir to his bride on the occasion of their marriage in 1899. Its foyer offers a formal, softly lit space for ceremonies. The bride can make an impressive entrance as she descends the staircase, and a baby grand piano is always available to provide musical accompaniment.

The Pond Area near the mansion, with its weeping elms and delicate white gazebo, is the most popular site for ceremonies. Receptions are often held on its beautiful lawn with vistas of the historic mansion and landscape.

The Carriage House is a unique, rustic setting for indoor receptions. Its quaint seating nooks and mahogany paneling add an old-fashioned feel. In 1999, a temporary hillside pavilion will be available to accommodate both casual or formal receptions, and in the year 2000, the brand new, spacious Garden Pavilion will be finished, featuring an open terrace with a view of the pond. The grounds here are private, peaceful and beautiful throughout the year.

Although this is one of the most exceptional sites in the Bay Area for a wedding celebration, Dunsmuir House and Gardens is great for other special events, picnics and business functions, too.

CEREMONY CAPACITY:

Area	Standing	Seated	Area	Standing	Seated
Mansion	75	20	North Pond	75–400	300
Carriage House	150	100	South Pond	75–400	300
Pavilion	299	299	Meadow	4,500	4,500
Mansion Lawn	200	200			

EVENT/RECEPTION CAPACITY:

Area	Standing	Seated		Area	Standing	Seated
Carriage House	200	100		Meadow *(partial use)*	200–500	200–500
Pavilion	299	299		Meadow *(full use)*	4,500	4,500
Pond Area	400	300				

MEETING CAPACITY: The Carriage House holds 150 theater-style, and the Pavilion holds 299 seated theater-style. There is a meeting room that accommodates up to 35 seated.

FEES & DEPOSITS: For weddings, a non-refundable $500 deposit reserves your date. Half of the rental balance is payable 6 months prior, the other half is due 30 days prior to the event. There's also a $50/hour wedding rehearsal charge. Use fees below are for a 7-hour time block and include a choice of 2 separate sites for the wedding or reception, use of some tables and chairs as well as setup and breakdown. Any additional equipment must be rented through Dunsmuir House.

75 Guests	100 Guests	150 Guests	200 Guests
$1,900	$2,100	$2,500	$2,900

Fees for business functions and meetings vary depending on group size, room setup and equipment; call for specific rates.

AVAILABILITY: For weddings and special events, daily, February–October 9am–4pm or 5pm–midnight. For business functions and meetings, February–October, Tuesday–Friday, 8am–5pm.

SERVICES/AMENITIES:

Catering: select from exclusive list
Kitchen Facilities: no
Tables & Chairs: provided
Linens, Silver, etc.: through caterer
Restrooms: wheelchair accessible
Dance Floor: CBA, extra fee
Meeting Equipment: CBA
Bride's Dressing Area: yes

Parking: on street, or $50/parking lot
Accommodations: no guest rooms
Telephone: pay phone
Outdoor Night Lighting: access only
Outdoor Cooking Facilities: CBA
Cleanup: provided
View: mansion & grounds, pond
Other: mansion photos, $200/hour

RESTRICTIONS:

Alcohol: BWC, through caterer only
Smoking: outside only
Music: amplified OK

Wheelchair Access: yes
Insurance: may be required
Other: decorations limited; no rice; no food or drink in the mansion

---

The professionals in the back of the book are the best in the business! How do we know? Read page 681.

Highlands Country Club

Country Club

110 Hiller Drive, Oakland
(510) 849-0743, fax (510) 849-1104

◆ Ceremonies   ◆ Special Events
◆ Wedding Receptions   ◆ Meetings
◆ Business Functions   Accommodations

Suppose you wanted a place for your event that had a genuine "country club" ambiance, but you only had a limited budget. Where could you go? Well, you might want to take a little drive over to the Highlands Country Club.

Embraced by a sloping green sweep of lawn, and overlooking tennis courts and crystal-blue swimming pools, this architectural phoenix has literally risen from its ashes (the original club was destroyed in the 1991 Berkeley-Oakland Hills fire). The community surrounding the club has also been rebuilt, and few, if any, traces of the previous devastation are visible from the club itself.

What is visible from the club's Fireside Room is a panoramic view of the San Francisco Bay and adjacent communities that is so spectacular it almost makes additional decoration redundant. Hardwood floors, a neutral color scheme and large windows showcase the magnificent vista, while the soaring stone fireplace and antique brass chandeliers add a touch of friendly rusticity. There's even a small balcony that affords you the luxury of watching the sun set over the Golden Gate or the fog pour over the Berkeley hills as you sip champagne and enjoy the breeze. In front of the clubhouse, a sunny patio surrounded by verdant lawns and small trees is available for outdoor receptions. Although it's high up on a hill, this country club is fresh, unpretentious and quite down-to-earth.

CEREMONY CAPACITY: The Fireside Room or the Patio accommodate 100 seated guests.

EVENT/RECEPTION CAPACITY: The Fireside Room and Patio combined hold up to 130 seated or standing guests.

MEETING CAPACITY: The Club holds up to 100 seated theatre-style or conference-style.

FEES & DEPOSITS: The rental fee is $750, and includes use of the Fireside Room, deck and patio areas for 4 hours; extra hours can be arranged. To secure your date, half of the non-refundable rental fee plus a refundable $750 security deposit are required. The rental balance is payable 60 days before the event.

AVAILABILITY: Year-round, daily, 8am–11pm, however other hours may be arranged. Use of the deck and patio is seasonal. Only one event is booked per day.

SERVICES/AMENITIES:

Catering: BYO

Kitchen Facilities: moderately equipped

Tables & Chairs: provided

Linens, Silver, etc.: CBA or BYO

Restrooms: wheelchair accessible

Dance Floor: dining room or patio

Bride's Dressing Area: no

Meeting Equipment: microphones, screen

Parking: on street

Accommodations: no guest rooms

Telephone: pay phones

Outdoor Night Lighting: access only

Outdoor Cooking Facilities: BBQ

Cleanup: caterer or renter

View: East Bay hills & San Francisco Bay

Other: piano, bar

RESTRICTIONS:

Alcohol: BYO

Smoking: outdoors only

Music: amplified OK w/volume limits

Wheelchair Access: yes

Insurance: certificate required

Other: no rice, birdseed, petals or glitter

This is important! *Tell facilities you're reading* **Here Comes The Guide** *and ask if our information is still current.*

Joaquin Miller Community Center

Community Center

3594 Sanborn Drive, Oakland
(510) 848-3542, fax (510) 848-0724

◆ Ceremonies ◆ Special Events
◆ Wedding Receptions ◆ Meetings
◆ Business Functions   Accommodations

Hidden in the redwoods of Joaquin Miller Park is the Joaquin Miller Community Center, a beautiful wood-framed structure whose rustic design belies the state-of-the-art facility within, including sophisticated lighting and a commercial-quality kitchen.

True to the legacy of the great nature poet Joaquin Miller, the center looks like it has lived in harmony with its natural surroundings since time immemorial. In fact, it's only three years old. And the builders did it right. All the rooms are modular; that is, they can be used alone or in seamless conjunction with each other. The two large assembly rooms and three smaller conference rooms (plus outdoor decks and an indoor fireplace alcove) give you a lot of flexibility.

The two assembly rooms feature hardwood floors, wooden wainscoting and what seems like an endless row of picture windows, affording an incomparable vista of Joaquin Miller Park and the Bay beyond. The windows also let in plenty of natural light, imparting a cheery, wide-open feeling during the day. As the sun goes down, the atmosphere changes, and the the natural light combines with the browns and tans of the floor and wainscoting to bathe the assembly rooms in an amber glow.

The assembly rooms come with a microphone, podium and twin pull-down movie screens making them excellent spaces for the most serious business meeting. Dimmable lighting and hardwood floors also make them equally appropriate for the most lighthearted party. The smaller conference rooms are useful for breakout sessions and seminars or, if you need a place to entertain kids during a party, convert one into a playroom.

But it's weddings that seem to bring out the most creative uses of this versatile facility. Many couples get married out on the deck that hugs one half of the building, and then move inside for the reception. Others eschew the indoors altogether, exchanging their vows nearby in Joaquin Miller Park, in front of a fountain, a reflecting pool or a natural waterfall, and then having their reception on the deck. (And for really, really big weddings, the nearby Woodminster Amphitheater seats up to 5,000.) Either way, guests enjoy strolling around the outdoor deck, taking in the lovely view.

There isn't room here to dwell at length on some of the Center's other attractions, such as the alcove, with its fanciful, almost cartoon-like ceramic fireplace and benches, and the reception area, with its beautiful stained glass doors. Suffice it to say that the Joaquin Miller Community Center is as refreshing as it is versatile.

CEREMONY CAPACITY: The Deck accommodates 50–75 seated; Assembly Rooms 1 and 2, combined, up to 200 seated guests.

EVENT/RECEPTION CAPACITY: Assembly Rooms 1 and 2 each hold 80 seated or 150 standing; combined, 150 seated or 200 standing. The outdoor deck holds 50–75 seated guests.

MEETING CAPACITY: Conference Rooms A, B and C each hold 24 seated theater-style or 16 seated classroom-style; combined, 72 seated theater-style or 48 seated classroom-style.

FEES & DEPOSITS: A non-refundable $200–500 deposit reserves your date; the rental balance is payable 1 month prior to the event. The setup/teardown fee is $150; the fee for serving alcoholic beverages is $50. Rental fees are as follows:

Room	*Fee*	*Room*	*Fee*
Assembly Room 1 or 2 *(4-hr min)*	$80–90/hour	Entire Building	$225–250/hour
Assembly Room 1 & 2 *(4-hr min)*	$160–170/hour	Kitchen	$100+
Conf. Rooms A, B or C *(2-hr min)*	$30–40/hour	Holiday Surcharge	+$15/hour
Conf. Rooms A, B & C *(2-hr min)*	$75–85/hour		

Catering is provided by *Glass Onion Catering*. Luncheons start at $15/person, buffets at $18/person and seated dinners at $25/person. Miscellaneous rentals, alcohol, tax and staff service charges are additonal.

AVAILABILITY: Year-round, daily, 7am–1am.

SERVICES/AMENITIES:

Catering: by *Glass Onion Catering,* or BYO
Kitchen Facilities: fully equipped, commercial
Tables & Chairs: provided
Linens, Silver, etc.: through caterer
Restrooms: wheelchair accessible
Dance Floor: oak floor provided
Bride's & Groom's Dressing Area: yes
Meeting Equipment: microphone, podium, pull-down screens

Parking: large lot, additional parking nearby
Accommodations: no guest rooms
Telephone: pay phones
Outdoor Night Lighting: yes
Outdoor Cooking Facilities: through caterer
Cleanup: provided
View: panoramic views of Bay & coastline
Other: mansion photos, $200/hour

RESTRICTIONS:

Alcohol: BYO or CBA
Smoking: designated areas
Music: amplified OK w/volume limits

Wheelchair Access: yes
Insurance: may be required
Other: decorations restricted

The professionals in the back of the book are the best in the business! How do we know? Read page 681.

The Lakeview Club

300 Lakeside Drive, 28th Floor, Oakland
(510) 271-4115, fax (510) 271-4127

Private Club

- ◆ Ceremonies
- ◆ Wedding Receptions
- ◆ Business Functions
- ◆ Special Events
- ◆ Meetings
- Accommodations

High up on the 28th floor of the Kaiser Center Building, you'll find one of Oakland's best views. It belongs to the Lakeview Club, whose sweeping vistas of Lake Merritt, the Oakland hills and the San Francisco Bay provide a dramatic backdrop for wedding receptions. The Club has nine private dining rooms that are primarily for members only, but nonmembers can also use them with member sponsorship.

Once guests arrive at the 28th floor via a swift elevator, they're personally greeted by staff at a marble reception desk who'll take gifts and coats and direct them to the right room. Every space has floor-to-ceiling picture windows and most have rich cherry mahogany detailing. The warm texture of the wood, accented by a hunter green and mauve color scheme, complements the panoramic views and gives the Club an understated tone. Tasteful contemporary paintings hang throughout, and colorful Oriental carpets cover marble tile hallways. The lounge area, which can be used for hors d'oeuvres and conversation, has a built-in bar, a piano, large floral arrangements and sliding French doors that can be closed to create more privacy. The two main dining rooms accommodate cocktail receptions or seated meals; each has a grand piano, floral arrangements and a wall of windows affording an outstanding vista of the East Bay.

Depending on the size of your wedding, you can rent a single room, a combination of rooms or the entire Club. No matter which you choose, you can't go wrong: the Lakeview Club is known for its attention to detail and personal service. Robert Romero, the Club's experienced event coordinator, provides plenty of hand-holding. He's quick to emphasize the chef's award-winning culinary talents and willingness to customize any menu. Robert, himself, has helped hundreds of couples with referrals to great services and has created many specialized wedding feasts, such as African, Persian and Chinese, to name but a few. If you haven't reviewed the Lakeview Club yet, we recommend you schedule a walk-through to see for yourself.

CEREMONY CAPACITY:

Room	Seated	Standing	Room	Seated	Standing
De Anza Room	170	200	Lounge	30	120
Kaiser or Trefethen Rooms	30	50	Peralta Room	120	200

EVENT/RECEPTION & MEETING CAPACITY:

Room	Seated	Standing	Room	Seated	Standing
Peralta Room (incl. Lounge)	320	500	De Anza Room	90	200
Kaiser or Trefethen Rooms	40	50			

FEES & DEPOSITS: A $1,000 deposit is due within 30 days of reserving your date. The estimated balance is due 3 days prior to the event. Room rental fees range $50–300. Luncheons start at $20/person and dinners at $30/person; tax, alcohol and a 20% service charge are additional. All-inclusive packages are available. For meetings with no food or beverage consumption, a larger room rental will apply.

AVAILABILITY: Year-round, daily. Meetings can be scheduled any time depending on room availability. Weddings are scheduled noon–4:30pm or 6:30pm–midnight. Other times are negotiable; closed major holidays. There is an extra charge for use on Sunday.

SERVICES/AMENITIES:

Catering: provided
Kitchen Facilities: n/a
Tables & Chairs: provided
Linens, Silver, etc.: provided
Restrooms: wheelchair accessible
Dance Floor: marble floor
Bride's & Groom's Dressing Rooms: yes
Meeting Equipment: flipcharts, TV, VCR
Other: event coordination, piano

Parking: Kaiser Center garage, validated parking is available
Accommodations: no guest rooms
Telephone: house phones
Outdoor Night Lighting: n/a
Outdoor Cooking Facilities: n/a
Cleanup: provided
Views: panoramic view of entire Bay Area

RESTRICTIONS:

Alcohol: provided
Smoking: Lounge only
Music: amplified OK

Wheelchair Access: yes
Insurance: not required
Other: no open flames, rice or birdseed

---

*This is important! Tell facilities you're reading **Here Comes The Guide** and ask if our information is still current.*

Mills College Chapel

College Chapel

5000 MacArthur Boulevard, Oakland
(510) 430-2145, fax (510) 430-2312

www.millsedu/admin_info/vpft/hmds/conf/conf.chapel.html
tommiett@mills.edu

◆ Ceremonies | Special Events
Wedding Receptions | Meetings
Business Functions | Accommodations

Is it possible to get married in the city, but avoid the crowds and the hectic pace? The answer is a resounding yes if you choose to say your vows at the Mills College Chapel. Located on a peaceful, arbor lined street on the campus of Oakland's Mills College, this graceful chapel is an oasis of tranquility.

Built in the round and designed by California architects Callister and Payne, the chapel is inspired by Shinto temples Callister encountered while visiting Japan. The Japanese influence is evident as you walk under the arched, beamed entrance, through the heavy cedar doors and into the warm wood sanctuary of the chapel. Here guests will find themselves encircled by low glass walls which open out onto patios. Overhead, fourteen enormous cedar panels vault up into a glass cupola skylight. Outside, the view is of redwoods and oaks, and the blend of light and leaf shadows that spills through the windows heightens the spare beauty of the interior. The effect is dazzling and adds natural drama to any ceremony.

Known for its exceptional sound quality (a detail couples often overlook when scouting wedding sites), the chapel was designed for enhanced acoustics by an organist, the architects and an acoustician. Also taking advantage of the unique acoustics is the statuesque wood and brushed steel pipe organ which rises almost to the ceiling. No matter how full the chapel is, you can pledge your vows confident that your guests can hear each tender word and nervous stammer.

Another distinguishing feature is the chapel's unconventional seating arrangement—four curved rows of redwood pews which face each other on either side of a rough cut granite altar which allows for an intimacy between guests and the wedding couple not usually found in larger, more traditional settings.

Indeed, if intimacy, serenity and natural beauty are what you envision for your wedding, then the evocative setting of Mills College Chapel is the place for you.

CEREMONY CAPACITY: The Chapel accommodates 175 seated guests.

FEES & DEPOSITS: The $450 deposit is the rental fee, due when reservations are confirmed.

AVAILABILITY: Year-round, daily 8am–10pm.

SERVICES/AMENITIES:

Tables & Chairs: no

Restrooms: wheelchair accessible

Bride's Dressing Area: yes

View: of trees and patio

Parking: on street

Telephone: no

Cleanup: renter

RESTRICTIONS:

Alcohol: not allowed

Smoking: not allowed

Music: acoustic only

Wheelchair Access: yes

Insurance: not required

Other: no rice or birdseed, only tie-on decorations

The professionals in the back of the book are the best in the business! *How do we know? Read page 681.*

Oakland Hills Tennis Club

Tennis Club

5475 Redwood Road, Oakland
(510) 531-3300, fax (510) 531-8353
www.oaklandhills.com

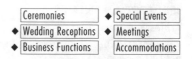

Ceremonies	◆ Special Events
◆ Wedding Receptions	◆ Meetings
◆ Business Functions	Accommodations

Set on six acres high in the Oakland Hills, this facility not only hosts wedding receptions, but has a killer view of the Bay. Don't be deterred by the front door which says "members only." If you reserve the Club for functions after regular hours, you'll be more than welcome. The entry walk to the front door is shaded by old oaks and new landscaping. The swimming pool is on your right and the multiple tennis courts are below, on your left. Although you'll find the usual paraphernalia of a tennis club inside (sports clothing, equipment, lockers and the like), the building is new and nicely designed. For receptions, you'd use the west part of the building. The aerobics room, a large, uncluttered space with a shiny, oak hardwood floor, a vaulted wood-beamed ceiling, a wall of mirrors and wall-to-wall windows has a remarkable, unobstructed view of the Bay Area.

For outdoor entertaining, the long deck running the length of the room can be arranged with tables, chairs and umbrellas. The Club's cafe next door is connected to the aerobics room by way of double doors, and both spaces can be used simultaneously for larger receptions. If you're looking for a pleasant, contemporary space for a prenuptial dinner or reception, we think the Club is an excellent choice.

CEREMONY CAPACITY: Ceremonies do not take place at this facility.

EVENT/RECEPTION & MEETING CAPACITY: The Club holds 90 seated guests or 150 for a standing reception.

FEES & DEPOSITS: The rental fee plus a $250 non-refundable security deposit reserves your date. An extra $75/hour will be charged for any use of the facility after 10pm. Rental fees are as follows:

Guest Count	*Rental Fee*	*Guest Count*	*Rental Fee*
up to 50	$500	66–75	$600
51–65	550	76–90	650
		90–150	*inquire for rate*

AVAILABILITY: Year-round, Friday, Saturday and Sunday after 4pm. Rentals prior to 4pm will only be considered during the Club's non-peak times.

SERVICES/AMENITIES:

Catering: preferred list
Kitchen Facilities: fully equipped
Tables & Chairs: provided
Linens, Silver, etc.: BYO or provided, extra charge
Restrooms: wheelchair accessible
Dance Floor: yes
Bride's Dressing Area: CBA
Meeting Equipment: CBA
Other: some event coordination provided

Parking: large parking lot, 86 spaces on site
Accommodations: no guest rooms
Telephone: pay phone
Outdoor Night Lighting: yes
Outdoor Cooking Facilities: CBA
Cleanup: caterer
View: panoramic vistas of San Francisco Bay & skyline, parts of Marin and San Mateo

RESTRICTIONS:

Alcohol: BYO, some restrictions
Smoking: outside only
Music: amplified OK w/volume restrictions

Wheelchair Access: yes
Insurance: required

---

*This is important! Tell facilities you're reading **Here Comes The Guide** and ask if our information is still current.*

Oakland Museum of California

Art, History & Natural Science Museum

1000 Oak Street, Oakland
(510) 238-2920, fax (510) 238-2258

www.museumca.org
jocelyn_ferguson@museumca.org

◆ Ceremonies	◆ Special Events
◆ Wedding Receptions	◆ Meetings
◆ Business Functions	Accommodations

Since it opened in 1969, the Oakland Museum has been one of the city's most distinctive landmarks. Its dramatic, tiered architecture and exhibits highlighting the rich diversity of California's geography and culture make it obvious that this is no stuffy, antiquated museum fit only for elementary school field trips.

The Oakland Museum is built on three levels, with stairs and walkways leading the visitor through the building's intriguing maze of courtyards, terraces, and gardens. A koi pond, full of well-fed fish, water lilies and papyrus plants, graces the first level. Sculptures and artifacts, such as a statue of a Greek youth holding a sundial, giant contemporary metal artworks, and a replica of an Early California wagon dot the grounds. The Gardens, a spacious lawn shaded by deodar cedars, sweet gum and alder trees, would be lovely for a wedding, reception, corporate picnic or similar event. Just beyond the Gardens is Rishell Court, an intimate space suggesting an ancient temple. Concrete pillars topped by planters form two sides of the courtyard; creeping-fig-covered walls form the other two sides. The air is perfumed by swags of Japanese honeysuckle, interspersed with mounds of blue cape plumbago and purple lantana. Sunlight pours through the open roof, and a stately blue Atlas cedar provides shade. Other outdoor venues include the Terrace, which overlooks the koi pond, and the Patio, a sunny space enclosed by plantings of red and yellow lantana. Another terrace has a view of Lake Merritt and the Oakland hills. If you happen to be wandering around the Museum grounds and see a perfect spot, but don't find it listed for rent, ask about it. The Oakland Museum will let you reserve almost any of its exterior spaces.

For indoor functions, consider the Museum's restaurant, which forms a "bridge" over one of the Museums's main stairways. Two floor-to-ceiling windows allow you to view the koi pond from one side, or the bustling Museum patrons from the other. At the restaurant's entrance, a beautiful free-standing stained glass window depicting herons, peach trees and other Asian art motifs captures the eye, and children's art adds a homey touch to the walls. The James Moore Theatre and the Lecture Hall are suitable for business meetings and seminars. The theater is often used for musical events because of its sound system and large stage, but dancing is not allowed.

The Oakland Museum was the site of what has to be one of the most unusual weddings we've heard of so far. A regulation ring had been set up for a boxing-related exhibit, and one creative couple decided that this would be the perfect place to tie the knot. The bride and groom wore authentic boxing shorts, shoes, and gloves. Instead of walking down the aisle, they came out of their corners and were advised to "fight fair" as they touched gloves. Now most folks probably wouldn't want to incorporate pugilism into their ceremony, but as you can see, the Oakland Museum can accommodate all sorts of possibilities.

CEREMONY CAPACITY: The Museum Gardens can accommodate 600 seated guests or 1,000 standing. The Terrace and Patio area combined can hold 200 seated or 300 standing guests.

EVENT/RECEPTION CAPACITY: For the Gardens, Terrace and Patio areas, see figures above. The museum restaurant holds 150 seated guests or 250 standing. The Upper Level Terraces can accommodate 1,500 seated or standing guests.

MEETING CAPACITY: The James Moore Theatre holds 290 seated, auditorium-style. The Lecture Hall holds 115 seated theater-style; the Terrace and Patio hold 200 seated theater-style.

FEES & DEPOSITS: To reserve your date, a non-refundable deposit in the amount of half the estimated event total plus a $250 refundable cleaning/damage deposit are required; within 30 days of the event, the entire amount is payable. In-house catering is provided by *Grace Street Catering*; cocktail parties run $30–45/person, buffets $40–60/person, and seated meals, $60–80/person. Alcohol, tax and an 18% service charge are additional. A $20/hour per staff person charge, with a 4 hour minimum, may apply. If an outside caterer is used, a $500 surcharge applies. For large events and when the Museum is closed to the public, security guards are required at $23/hour per guard with a 2-hour minimum.

AVAILABILITY: Year-round, daily, 6:30am–2am. The museum restaurant is available Monday–Thursday and Saturday before 10am or after 5pm; Sunday before noon or after 5pm.

SERVICES/AMENITIES:

Catering: provided or select from preferred list
Kitchen Facilities: fully equipped
Tables & Chairs: provided
Linens, Silver, etc.: provided or BYO
Restrooms: wheelchair accessible
Dance Floor: provided or BYO
Bride's Dressing Area: CBA
Meeting Equipment: full range

Parking: museum garage rental $175/hour
Accommodations: no guest rooms
Telephone: pay phones
Outdoor Night Lighting: CBA or BYO in gardens
Outdoor Cooking Facilities: provided
Cleanup: provided or caterer
View: Lake Merritt from upper level
Other: some event coordination provided

RESTRICTIONS:

Alcohol: provided, no BYO
Smoking: outside only
Music: amplified OK

Wheelchair Access: yes
Insurance: not required
Other: no rice

Preservation Park

660 & 668 13th St. at Martin Luther King Jr. Way, Oakland
(510) 874-7580, fax (510) 268-1961
www.oaklandnet.com/features/preser.html
prespark@california.com

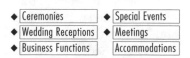

◆ Ceremonies   ◆ Special Events
◆ Wedding Receptions   ◆ Meetings
◆ Business Functions   Accommodations

Occupying two blocks just a heartbeat away from Oakland's City Center, Preservation Park is an eye-catching re-creation of a Victorian neighborhood. Sixteen Victorian homes have been beautifully restored and colorfully painted. The setting has been further enhanced with period park benches, ornate wrought-iron fences, old fashioned street lamps and a bronze fountain from Paris.

The Park's social center is the Pavilion, a graceful bandstand where ceremonies usually take place. While the bride and groom exchange vows on stage, their guests, seated on the lawn just below them, can appreciate the lovely landscaping and vintage architecture that surrounds them. Outdoor receptions are held in the adjacent Fountain Circle, a circular plaza with a large, two-tiered fountain topped by the moon goddess Diana at its center. There's plenty of room for a band, or you could have an outdoor buffet on either side of the Pavilion.

If you're planning an indoor reception, two houses just off the Fountain Circle are available. The Ginn House, circa 1890, features two delightful light and airy parlors reminiscent of those in an English country home. Nile Hall, circa 1911, is a craftsman-style building with a sensational space for a grand and elegant party. It has a 30-foot-high ceiling, skylights, multiple windows, a stage and a theatrical lighting and sound system. This room is well designed, with soft colors, nice detailing and attractive appointments—and enough space to accommodate an extensive guest list. You can reserve one or both houses, as they're connected by a spacious interior hallway.

The Park is not only popular for weddings, it's hosted a wide range of events: trade shows, luncheons, awards dinners—even a World Figure Skating reception! When you reserve the outdoor spaces, you can have the run of the entire park. The entrance gates are closed to cars, so you and your guests can savor the feeling of having this charming "town" all to yourselves. For a remarkable glimpse of old-time Oakland, pay a visit to Preservation Park—it's well worth the trip.

CEREMONY CAPACITY: Ginn House holds 50 seated; Nile Hall holds 150 seated guests; the Pavilion Area holds 150–300 seated or 300–1,000 standing.

RECEPTION & MEETING CAPACITY:

Area	Seated	Standing	Area	Seated	Standing
Ginn House	50	125	Nile Hall	150	200
Large Parlor	50	105	Ginn & Nile	150	200
Small Parlor	15	20	Pavilion Area	300	1,000

FEES & DEPOSITS: A $250 deposit is required to secure your date. The rental fee is payable 60 days prior to the event. The fee for Nile Hall is $750; for Nile Hall plus the Ginn House, $1,175. The rental fee for the outdoor stage is $475 without setup. If you rent the stage in conjunction with Ginn House and Nile Hall, the fee is $275 without setup. For functions during the Christmas season, a $500 non-refundable rental deposit is required.

AVAILABILITY: Year-round, daily, 8am–midnight.

SERVICES/AMENITIES:

Catering: provided; if BYO caterer, extra charge

Kitchen Facilities: setup only

Tables & Chairs: provided, extra fee outdoors

Linens, Silver, etc.: provided by caterer

Restrooms: wheelchair accessible

Dance Floor: CBA

Bride's Dressing Area: CBA

Meeting Equipment: sound equipment, VCR, slide projector, microphones, flip charts, overhead

Parking: on street or City lot nearby

Accommodations: no guest rooms

Telephone: pay phones

Outdoor Night Lighting: yes

Outdoor Cooking Facilities: no

Cleanup: caterer

View: gardens and fountain

RESTRICTIONS:

Alcohol: provided, no BYO

Smoking: outside only

Music: amplified OK

Wheelchair Access: yes

Insurance: may be required

The professionals in the back of the book are the best in the business! How do we know? Read page 681.

421

Scott's Seafood Restaurant

#2 Broadway at Jack London Square, Oakland
(510) 444-5969, fax (510) 444-6917

www.scottseastbay.com

Waterfront Restaurant

◆ Ceremonies   ◆ Special Events
◆ Wedding Receptions   ◆ Meetings
◆ Business Functions   Accommodations

Waterfront event sites in Oakland are few and far between, making Scott's Seafood Restaurant a much sought-after location. It's conveniently situated in Jack London Square at the edge of the Oakland estuary, with great views of Alameda, San Francisco and the ships passing by.

With five banquet rooms and a waterfront pavilion, Scott's can handle just about any type of event. Ceremonies are often held on the pier right next to the restaurant, or in the Public Pavilion, a freestanding, covered structure with removable walls that can be left off for a full, open-air effect or put up for privacy. Even with the walls in place, you can leave open the waterfront side and still enjoy a view of the estuary. During the day, sunlight filters in through the translucent ceiling, and at night white globe fixtures suspended from the support beams cast a warm glow. The space can be easily decorated with flowers, balloons or props to complement the theme of your celebration.

If you have a large party but the Pavilion is rented, fear not! Host it in the three Harbor View Rooms (each can be reserved individually). They all have a view of the harbor, and when they're used together, the French doors that separate them are opened. All three have deep dusty rose ceilings, brass-and-glass chandeliers and soft blue-grey carpeting. While Harbor View Room "A" has a wall of windows overlooking the water, the other two rooms have mirrored walls that make them feel larger and add extra sparkle.

Smaller dinners, meetings and private parties take place in the Bay View and Terrace Rooms, which are often reserved together. The Bay View Room has a more formal ambiance, with its neutral color scheme, carpeting and alabaster-and-brass chandeliers. Step into the Terrace Room, however, and you're surrounded by color: a bright slate-blue wall, red Oriental carpet and taupe wrought-iron chairs. And perhaps best of all, this room has a bank of floor-to-ceiling windows that overlook the water.

Scott's also offers amenities you won't find in a standard banquet room: elegant china in black, gold and white, marble-topped counters, and very comfortable upholstered chairs. They can almost always find a way to work within your budget, and they're happy to customize a menu for you. With a terrific setting and service to match, Scott's is one East Bay facility you'll definitely want to consider for your next event.

CEREMONY CAPACITY: The Jack London Pier holds 350 seated or standing; the Public Pavilion 350 seated or 800 standing; the Harbor View Rooms 250 seated or 450 standing.

EVENT/RECEPTION CAPACITY:

Room	Seated	Standing	Room	Seated	Standing	Room	Seated	Standing
Harbor View A	80	120	Bay View	60	80	Combined ABC	250	450
Harbor View B	50	80	Public Pavilion	350	800	Bay View/Terrace	80	120
Harbor View C	60	80	Terrace	30	50			

MEETING CAPACITY:

Room	Theater-style	Conf.-style	Room	Theater-style	Conf.-style
Harbor View A	150	60	Combined ABC	300	150
Harbor View B	60	30	Bay View/Terrace	60	35
Harbor View C	60	35	Public Pavilion	600	250

FEES & DEPOSITS: A $500/room non-refundable deposit is required to secure your date. The food and beverage balance is payable 72 hours prior, with the remaining balance due the day of the event. Per-person prices: seated meals and buffets $30–40, hors d'oeuvres $15–25. Alcohol, tax and an 18% service charge are additional. A $50/hour room rental fee is charged for meetings.

AVAILABILITY: Year-round, daily. For weddings and other special events, 7am–midnight except for Christmas day. Saturday receptions are usually held 11am–4pm or 6pm–midnight. For meetings and business functions, 7am–midnight.

SERVICES/AMENITIES:

Catering: provided
Kitchen Facilities: n/a
Tables & Chairs: provided
Linens, Silver, etc.: provided
Restrooms: wheelchair accessible
Dance Floor: yes, extra charge
Bride's Dressing Area: no
Meeting Equipment: full range

Parking: valet or parking lot
Accommodations: no guest rooms
Telephone: pay phone
Outdoor Night Lighting: yes
Outdoor Cooking Facilities: BBQs
Cleanup: provided
View: SF skyline & Bay, Alameda Harbor
Other: event coordination, floral arrangements

RESTRICTIONS:

Alcohol: provided
Smoking: designated areas
Music: amplified OK

Wheelchair Access: yes
Insurance: not required

This is important! Tell facilities you're reading **Here Comes The Guide** and ask if our information is still current.

Sequoia Lodge

2666 Mountain Boulevard, Oakland
(510) 848-3542, fax (510) 848-0724

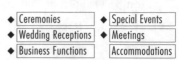

There's nothing fancy about Sequoia Lodge, and that's part of its charm. This rustic, one-story California bungalow, nestled in a quiet sequoia grove on the edge of Oakland's Joaquin Miller Park, is versatile enough to accommodate many different kinds of events, but it really shines as a site for family gatherings.

Its center is a large atrium with walls and ceiling paneled in unfinished redwood—a nice contrast to the elaborate geometrical design of the inlaid parquet floor. A large skylight above and picture windows along the walls keep the interior light and airy, as well as affording a lovely view of the surrounding redwoods and sequoias. Just off the atrium is a sunken alcove boasting a stone fireplace, which makes an excellent backdrop for an intimate wedding ceremony.

Couples often hold their entire wedding inside, but many prefer to use the wide wooden deck for either the ceremony or reception. The deck, which runs completely around the lodge, overlooks the natural beauty of Joaquin Miller Park. And there's yet another option to throw into your mix: a large outdoor picnic area with wooden picnic tables, just a stone's throw from the lodge itself.

But for people seeking the perfect family site, the thing that makes the Sequoia Lodge so special is the children's playground. It has everything: slides, swings, teeter-totters, playhouses and climbing trees—a veritable child's paradise that will keep the youngsters happily occupied for hours.

CEREMONY CAPACITY: The Lodge holds 100 seated guests indoors or 75 seated on the outdoor deck.

EVENT/RECEPTION CAPACITY: The Lodge holds 80 seated or 150 standing guests indoors or 75–85 standing guests on the outdoor deck for cocktail receptions.

MEETING CAPACITY: The Lodge holds 100 seated theater-style.

FEES & DEPOSITS: A $200 rental deposit is required to secure your date. Rental fees (4-hour minimum required) are $65/hour for Oakland residents or $75/hour for non-residents. A $50/hour room rental is charged for meetings. Catering is provided by *Glass Onion Catering*. Buffets start at $15/person, hors d'oeuvres at $18/person and seated meals at $25/person. Service staff, miscellaneous rentals, beverage service and service charges are additional. The food and beverage balance is payable 72 hours prior, with the remaining balance due the day of the event.

AVAILABILITY: Year-round, daily. For weddings and other special events, 7am–midnight except for Christmas Day. Saturday receptions are usually held 11am–4pm or 6pm–midnight. For meetings and business functions, 7am–midnight.

SERVICES/AMENITIES:

Catering: by *Glass Onion Catering,* or BYO
Kitchen Facilities: prep only
Tables & Chairs: provided
Linens, Silver, etc.: provided by caterer
Restrooms: wheelchair accessible
Dance Floor: yes, extra charge
Bride's Dressing Area: no
Other: full event coordination, floral arrangements

Parking: valet or parking lot
Accommodations: no guest rooms
Telephone: pay phone
Outdoor Night Lighting: yes
Outdoor Cooking Facilities: BBQs
Cleanup: provided
View: San Francisco skyline, San Francisco Bay & Alameda Harbor
Meeting Equipment: full range

RESTRICTIONS:

Alcohol: provided; alcohol fee $50
Smoking: designated areas
Music: amplified OK

Wheelchair Access: yes
Insurance: not required

The professionals in the back of the book are the best in the business! How do we know? Read page 681.

Waterfront Plaza Hotel

10 Washington Street, Oakland
(510) 836-3800, fax (510) 832-5695

www.waterfrontplaza.com
wfph@ix.netcom

Waterfront Hotel

- Ceremonies   ◆ Special Events
- Wedding Receptions   ◆ Meetings
- Business Functions   ◆ Accommodations

Its dockside location and Bay views may lure you to the Waterfront Plaza, but this hotel's appeal goes far beyond the scenery. They take the hassle out of planning a wedding by providing coordination, food, drink, cake, flowers and a honeymoon suite, not to mention Sunday brunch and lodging for your guests.

The hotel occupies a quiet spot at one end of lively Jack London Square, and when you enter the modern, high-ceilinged lobby, you leave the bustle behind. Many brides make their entrance across the lobby on a white runner, which takes them out through the double glass doors (with their brass ship's-cleat handles), and directly onto the pool deck, where expectant guests are basking in the sun or watching a yacht tie up at the boat dock. White iron rails topped with burnished wood encircle this area, setting it apart from the public boardwalk just beyond. A white wooden gazebo is set up poolside for the ceremony, and afterwards, guests stroll down the boardwalk to the Spinnaker Room for the reception. It opens out onto the boardwalk and overlooks the water.

The Spinnaker Room and several other event spaces are designed to hold business meetings as well as weddings, rehearsal dinners, and other finctions. As such, they are neutral and understated in decor. However, a number of them offer lovely waterfront views, and the hotel is extremely flexible in adapting to your design ideas and special requests. For a pair who became engaged in Hawaii, the pool was strewn with tropical flowers, buffets bristled with pineapple ice sculptures, and a palm tree was installed for the evening. A couple as much in love with their motorcycles as each other were able to ride their "hogs" directly into their Spinnaker Room ceremony.

For a snazzy change of pace, hold your rehearsal dinner in Jack's Bistro, the hotel's bright and airy restaurant. Accented with light-hearted murals and multi-colored stools, it's a fun spot for a party. Guests might gather around the grand piano at one end of the room, or under the bright red umbrellas in the outdoor dining area. And by the way, if you happen to pay the hotel a visit during the day, stop into the elegant bakery at the front of the restaurant—the heady fragrance may persuade you to order your cake on the spot.

At the end of your big day you can collapse into bed in one of the hotel's comfortable suites. Of course, this is contingent on your not sailing away on a yacht in a dramatic farewell. Anything's possible at the Waterfront Plaza.

CEREMONY CAPACITY:

Area	Seated		Area	Seated
Spinnaker Room	275		Regatta Room	200
Poolside Area	120		Chart Room	60
Compass Room	50			

RECEPTION CAPACITY:

Area	Seated	Standing		Area	Seated	Standing
Spinnaker Room	200	300		Regatta Room	140	200
Poolside Area	140	150		Chart Room	50	70
Compass Room	40	65				

MEETING CAPACITY:

Area	Classroom-style	Theater-style		Area	Classroom-style	Theater-style
Spinnaker Room	170	275		Regatta Room	120	200
Chart Room	30	60		Compass Room	30	50
Portside Room	30	70		Starboard Room	30	70

There are five other rooms that can accommodate 12 guests seated conference-style.

FEES & DEPOSITS: For weddings, a $1,000 non-refundable deposit is required 2 weeks after receipt of the signed contract. The balance is due 72–hours prior to the event. A $300 ceremony set up fee is additional. Meals run $45–65/person. This price includes a suite for the bride and groom, a bartender for 4 hours and a 3-course sit-down or buffet meal. Alcohol is additional. Some packages include champagne, hors d'oeuvres and dinner wines. Honeymoon packages are available.

For other social or business functions, a $500 non-refundable deposit is due 2 weeks after receipt of the signed contract. Meals run $21–30/person. Tax, alcohol and a 17.5% service charge are additional.

AVAILABILITY: Year-round, daily, anytime.

SERVICES/AMENITIES:

Catering: provided by Jack's Bistro, no BYO
Kitchen Facilities: n/a
Tables & Chairs: provided
Linens, Silver, etc.: provided
Restrooms: wheelchair accessible
Dance Floor: yes
Bride's & Groom's Dressing Area: yes
Meeting Equipment: AV equipment or CBA, extra fee

Parking: valet CBA, parking facilities CBA
Accommodations: 144 guest rooms
Telephone: pay phones
Outdoor Night Lighting: yes
Outdoor Cooking Facilities: no
Cleanup: provided
View: San Francisco Bay
Other: ice sculpture, wedding cakes, arch with poolside ceremonies

RESTRICTIONS:

Alcohol: provided or BYO, WC corkage $10/bottle
Smoking: outside only
Music: amplified OK indoors until midnight, outdoors until 11pm

Wheelchair Access: yes
Insurance: not required

Piedmont Community Hall

Community Park Building

711 Highland Avenue, Piedmont
(510) 420-3081, (510) 420-3075, fax (510) 420-3027

◆ Ceremonies   ◆ Special Events
◆ Wedding Receptions   ◆ Meetings
◆ Business Functions   Accommodations

This facility is one of the most popular event venues in Northern California—and for good reason. The building is not only very attractive, inside and out, but it has the added benefit of being situated in a lovely park setting.

Azaleas and camellias provide splashes of color near the round, landscaped plaza in front of the Hall. Redwoods and flowering cherry trees shade portions of the plaza, and behind the building a stream and more trees complete the circle of greenery.

The garden is home to another structure, a mini-sized Japanese Tea House which was relocated here after it was donated to the City of Piedmont. Couples can have a small ceremony in the Tea House, or brides can spend some quiet time here before the wedding or use it as a private place to dress and get ready for the big event. Two side walls of the Tea House are removable, so when the weather is mild, it's a terrific spot for an extra bar or hors d'oeuvres station.

Receptions take place in the Piedmont Community Hall, a splendid structure, Mediterranean in style with light taupe walls and terra-cotta tile roof. The Hall's interior was renovated in 1994, and looks better than ever—in fact, it looks so chic, you'd never believe this is a city-owned facility. The main event space is a great party room, with a high beamed ceiling, shining herringbone hardwood floors and chandeliers. Floor-to-ceiling windows allow lots of natural light and ensure that the feeling of the adjacent park carries over to your reception. This is a refined, nicely designed space, suitable for an elegant wedding, company party or corporate retreat. As we said, it's a popular spot, so remember to reserve early.

CEREMONY CAPACITY:

Area	Seated	Standing	Area	Seated	Standing
Indoors	200	223	Patio	300	300
Tea House & Deck	90	120	Amphitheater	50	100

EVENT/RECEPTION & MEETING CAPACITY: The Hall accommodates 223 standing or 104 seated guests. The patio area holds 300 standing or 200 seated guests.

FEES & DEPOSITS: For events on Friday, Saturday, Sunday or holidays, a $400 security deposit is due 2 weeks after booking and is refundable 4 weeks after the event. The facility is rented in 6-hour blocks. For residents, the fee is $950; and non-residents, the fee is $1,800. Payment is due 30 days prior to the event. For Monday–Thursday rates, please call for specifics.

Weekday rates for business functions vary depending on guest count and event duration; call for specifics.

AVAILABILITY: Year-round, daily, 8am–midnight (one event per day). The summer months are booked quickly.

SERVICES/AMENITIES:

Catering: BYO
Kitchen Facilities: fully equipped
Tables & Chairs: provided
Linens, Silver, etc.: BYO
Restrooms: wheelchair accessible
Dance Floor: hardwood floor
Bride's Dressing Area: yes, on lower level
Meeting Equipment: overhead projector, screen, TV, VCR, microphones, PA system

Parking: on and off street
Accommodations: no guest rooms
Telephone: pay phone
Outdoor Night Lighting: yes
Outdoor Cooking Facilities: BYO
Cleanup: caterer or renter
View: park setting

RESTRICTIONS:

Alcohol: BYO, must have controlled bar
Smoking: not allowed
Music: amplified OK

Wheelchair Access: yes
Insurance: included in weekend rates; for weekday use, BYO or purchase from Hall

---

*This is important! Tell facilities you're reading **Here Comes The Guide** and ask if our information is still current.*

Pleasant Hill Community Center

320 Civic Drive, Pleasant Hill
(925) 676-5200, fax (925) 676-5630

◆ Ceremonies   ◆ Special Events
◆ Wedding Receptions   ◆ Meetings
◆ Business Functions   Accommodations

Tucked away in the heart of Contra Costa County, the Pleasant Hill Community Center used to be known only to local residents. But now the secret's out, and you, too, can take advantage of this large, versatile event space that has a lot more going for it than just a great location.

One of the things we liked about this facility is that it's surrounded by a lovely park. Understated landscaping uses graceful deodar cedars, sugar pines, and Japanese maples to soften the gray expanse of the building; an Oriental stone lantern, lacy Japanese maples and bright azaleas add color and interest. Further out, the sweeping green lawn planted with majestic oaks and bisected by a winding path is home to playful squirrels. Viewed from this perspective, the building seems like a natural, organic part of the landscape, a subtle backdrop to all the burgeoning greenery.

The main venue for weddings and special events is a combination of the Parkside Room, Dance Studio and patio. The Parkside Room features a raised stage and floor-to-ceiling windows that bring the outdoors inside. Two walls of sliding glass doors open to the nicely landscaped patio, perfect for ceremonies or for extending dining outdoors. The Dance Studio, which is immediately adjacent to the Parkside Room, has large windows, a grand piano, and a hardwood dance floor. For smaller, more business-oriented functions, there's the Lower Club Room.

Outdoor weddings and receptions are held on the patio just outside the Parkside Room. The wedding party can approach this patio by way of a path that meanders over a lawn and through shady oaks. In spring and summer, you'd be hard put to find a prettier spot. For a nominal fee, you can announce your intentions to the world on the reader board out front. Also available for smaller events is the Winslow Center, which is a few blocks away from the Pleasant Hill Community Center proper. We didn't see it, but we hear that it has a great view of Mt. Diablo.

So don't think of the Pleasant Hill Community Center as a glorified neighborhood rec center. Think of it as a huge blank canvas on which to paint the celebration of your dreams.

CEREMONY CAPACITY: The Patio holds 40–75 seated, 200 standing; the Courtyard, 50–75 seated or 150 standing; the Parkside Room, 194 seated or 210 standing guests.

EVENT/RECEPTION CAPACITY: The Parkside Room holds 194 seated or 250 standing; the Upper Club Room, 60 seated or 75 standing; the Winslow Center, 100 seated or 150 standing.

MEETING CAPACITY: Seated capacities: Parkside Room, 275; Winslow Center, 100–150; Lower Club Room, 40–90; Upper Club Room, 60; and Conference Room, 20.

FEES & DEPOSITS: For the Community Center only, a $300–500 refundable security deposit is required to reserve your date. The Parkside Room rental fee for parties of 200 or fewer runs $525–1,620 depending on residency, day of week and event duration. Additional hours are $100/hour; all fees are due 30 days prior to event. The rate for the Upper Club Room/ Conference Room and Patio (May–Oct), for small weddings, parties and meetings is $40–45/ hour. The weekday rate for non-banquet facilities runs $18–60/hour.

AVAILABILITY: Year-round, daily, Monday–Thursday, 9am–10pm; Friday and Saturday, 9am–1am; Sunday, 2pm–11pm. Closed Thanksgiving and Christmas.

SERVICES/AMENITIES:

Catering: BYO

Kitchen Facilities: commercially equipped

Tables & Chairs: provided w/setup

Linens, Silver, etc.: BYO or some available

Restrooms: wheelchair accessible

Dance Floor: provided

Bride's & Groom's Dressing Area: CBA

Meeting Equipment: PA, overhead projector, TVs w/VCR, slide projector

Parking: ample lot

Accommodations: no guest rooms

Telephone: pay phone

Outdoor Night Lighting: access only

Outdoor Cooking Facilities: BYO or caterer

Cleanup: renter

View: of park setting

RESTRICTIONS:

Alcohol: BYO

Smoking: outside only

Music: amplified OK

Wheelchair Access: yes, except Winslow Center

Insurance: not required

The professionals in the back of the book are the best in the business! How do we know? Read page 681.

The Pleasanton Hotel

Historic Hotel

855 Main Street, Pleasanton
(925) 846-8112, (925) 846-8106, fax (925) 846-9758

◆ Ceremonies   ◆ Special Events
◆ Wedding Receptions   ◆ Meetings
◆ Business Functions   Accommodations

The Pleasanton Hotel, ensconced in the center of Pleasanton's historic downtown, is a 130-year-old Victorian, flanked by stately magnolia and palm trees. The building is vintage 1860s, with "gingerbread" detailing on the exterior, and period furnishings and decor inside.

Recently redecorated, the interior boasts two large dining rooms and several adjacent smaller rooms, all of which can be connected via folding doors to accommodate large parties. Shades of ivory, burgundy and forest green predominate, and there are numerous chandeliers, Tiffany lamps and Victorian appointments. The magnolia-shaded patio outdoors has a raised area that's great for wedding ceremonies, DJs or bands. A brick BBQ and outdoor bar are modern amenities, while a bubbling fountain brings a bit of the Hotel's vintage ambiance outside.

CEREMONY CAPACITY: The garden courtyard can accommodate 150 seated or 200 standing guests.

EVENT/RECEPTION CAPACITY: The Hotel can seat 200 guests inside, 100 on the patio.

MEETING CAPACITY:

Room	*Classroom-style*	*Theater-style*
Victorian Room	70	145
Garden Room	25	48

The Victorian Room and Garden Room can be combined to accommodate larger groups.

FEES & DEPOSITS: For weddings and special events, a $650 non-refundable deposit is required to secure your date. Full meal service is provided. Luncheons range $16–20/person or dinners $23–27/person. Alcohol, tax and a 17.5% service charge are additional. The event balance is payable 14 days prior to the event.

Fees for meetings vary depending on room(s) and services selected; call for specifics.

AVAILABILITY: Year-round, daily. Business functions Monday–Friday, 6am–11pm. Weddings on Saturdays 11am–4pm or 6pm–11pm; Sundays 5:30pm–11pm.

SERVICES/AMENITIES:

Catering: provided, no BYO

Kitchen Facilities: n/a

Tables & Chairs: provided

Linens, Silver, etc.: provided

Restrooms: wheelchair accessible

Dance Floor: yes

Bride's Dressing Area: yes

Meeting Equipment: CBA

Parking: lot

Accommodations: no guest rooms

Telephone: pay phone

Outdoor Night Lighting: yes

Outdoor Cooking Facilities: BBQ

Cleanup: provided

View: garden patio

Other: event coordination

RESTRICTIONS:

Alcohol: provided, no BYO

Smoking: not allowed

Music: amplified OK

Wheelchair Access: yes

Insurance: not required

Other: no rice or birdseed

This is important! Tell facilities you're reading **Here Comes The Guide** and ask if our information is still current.

Ruby Hill Golf Club

Private Golf Club

3400 West Ruby Hill Drive, Pleasanton
(925) 417-5840, fax (925) 417-5845

czwieg@sigprop.com

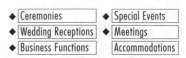

◆ Ceremonies ◆ Special Events
◆ Wedding Receptions ◆ Meetings
◆ Business Functions Accommodations

Judging by its beautiful entrance, with a Tuscan-style gatehouse, trellised driveway and meticulous landscaping, Ruby Hill is no ordinary golf club. In fact, what lies beyond the impressive gates is not just a golf course, but an exclusive, private community surrounded by vineyards and spread over acres of open land. So exclusive, in order to take a peek at this lovely facility, you have to make an appointment prior to viewing.

The Clubhouse and fairways are a short drive up the hill, and as you make your way slowly to the top, you pass dozens of spectacular homes, whose graceful architecture defines the development. Most of these houses are reminiscent of Italian villas, and when you finally reach the Clubhouse, you're hardly surprised to find that it's the largest and most striking "villa" of them all.

Step through the arched front door and you're more than a little awestruck by the grand scale and inviting ambiance of the foyer. The vast marble floor gleams softly, bathed in natural light from a stunning domed skylight overhead. Elegant conversational seating is arranged beneath the skylight, and in front of a large stone fireplace. You can't help but notice rich details, like the crown molding, wall sconces and window trim, all seemingly fashioned from stone, and the eclectic antiques and art, which add a personal touch.

From the foyer, walk down the regal staircase into the Main Dining Room, where indoor ceremonies, receptions and special events are held. (Brides, take note: the staircase could very well have been designed with your show-stopping entrance in mind.) The sheer grandeur of the space makes you want to sit down to fully appreciate the soaring 40-foot ceiling, giant potted palms and abundant light, streaming in through a multitude of high windows and glass doors. Walls are painted a warm Tuscan wheat, accented with creamy white trim, and the Florentine motif in the custom carpet swirls beneath your feet in muted earth tones.

To one side of the Main Dining Room is a similarly appointed small private dining room, for rehearsal dinners or meetings. On the other side is the Lounge, a clubby space with dark maple woodwork, a marble fireplace and granite-topped bar that's well-suited for cocktails. All three rooms open out onto an expansive arcaded patio that overlooks a formal garden and emerald lawn, as well as views of the golf course, the Livermore hills and Mt. Diablo.

It also overlooks a stunning oval terrace, that's custom-made for *al fresco* ceremonies and receptions. Paved with smooth Napa Valley stone and enclosed by two wisteria-covered trellises, the terrace feels intimate, despite the fact that it's completely open to the sky, the breeze and panoramic vistas.

The effort that has gone into making Ruby Hill a showplace is evident in unexpected places, too. The women's lounge and carpeted "locker room" is practically palatial, not only in size, but in amenities such as elaborately tiled bathrooms with gorgeous granite counters, plush seating and mirrors everywhere. Even the telephone booths are refined private nooks with their own doors, granite counters and art on the wall!

This is a glorious spot for any upscale affair or holiday party. And if you're interested in a corporate golf tournament, Ruby Hill has the first Jack Nicklaus-designed golf course in Northern California. The Clubhouse was built to exacting standards so that when Ruby Hill residents come up here they'll feel right at home. Given the splendid surroundings, we're quite sure they do.

CEREMONY CAPACITY: The Dining Room can seat 250. The Terrace can seat 250.

EVENT/RECEPTION CAPACITY: The Dining Room can accommodate 300 seated guests or 350 standing. The Terrace can hold 250 seated or 300 standing.

MEETING CAPACITY:

Space	Theater-style	Conference-style	Classroom-style
Private Dining Room	10–50	8–20	16
Conference Room	10–30	8–20	12
Small Conference Room	—	10	—

FEES & DEPOSITS: A $2,000 non-refundable deposit is required to reserve your date. The estimated food and beverage total is due 1 month prior to the event. Meals range $29–39/person; tax, alcohol and an 18% service charge are additional. A $2/slice cake-cutting fee is extra. Please call for details regarding fees for events occurring Monday–Friday and Sunday.

AVAILABILITY: For weddings, Ruby Hill is available January–November. The facility is available year-round for other events. Daily, 10am–11pm.

SERVICES/AMENITIES:

Catering: provided, no BYO
Kitchen Facilities: n/a
Tables & Chairs: provided
Linens, Silver, etc.: provided
Restrooms: wheelchair accessible
Dance Floor: CBA, extra charge
Bride's Dressing Area: yes
Meeting Equipment: CBA, extra charge

Parking: large lot and valet
Accommodations: no guest rooms
Telephone: pay phones
Outdoor Night Lighting: yes
Outdoor Cooking Facilities: yes
Cleanup: provided
View: vineyards, Jack Nicklaus golf course
Other: event coordination, cakes

RESTRICTIONS:

Alcohol: provided or BYO corkage $15/bottle
Smoking: outside only
Music: amplified OK w/restrictions

Wheelchair Access: yes
Insurance: not required
Other: no rice, birdseed or glitter

Linsley Hall and Chapel

235 Washington Avenue, Point Richmond
(510) 235-7338, fax (510) 412-9044

Historic Chapel & Event Facility

◆ Ceremonies ◆ Special Events
◆ Wedding Receptions ◆ Meetings
◆ Business Functions Accommodations

Linsley Hall, designed by Julia Morgan and built in 1904 as a church, is now a distinctive, multiuse facility located in historic Point Richmond. With its vaulted ceiling, wood paneling and lovely original stained glass windows, the Chapel offers its guests turn-of-the-century warmth and dignity. The sanctuary's acoustics are so outstanding that it's rented quite often for concerts and recitals.

Downstairs, the Reception Room has a custom-built oak bar and guests can flow out into the attractive flower garden which has shade trees, brickwork, a gazebo and lawn. Evening weddings in the church are enhanced by candlelight, and daytime ceremonies are often performed in the gazebo outdoors.

CEREMONY CAPACITY: The Chapel seats 80 guests with room for an additional 30 standing guests. The total capacity is 110 guests.

EVENT/RECEPTION & MEETING CAPACITY: The Hall can hold up to 110 guests; the Reception Room 10–60 seated and the Garden 50 seated guests.

FEES & DEPOSITS: A non-refundable deposit (25% of the rental fee) is due when reservations are made. For weddings, the rental fee is $900.

For weekday meetings, the fee is $25/hour, with a 2-hour minimum.

AVAILABILITY: Year-round, daily, 9am–7pm.

SERVICES/AMENITIES:

Catering: BYO
Kitchen Facilities: moderate
Tables & Chairs: most provided
Linens, Silver, etc.: BYO
Restrooms: not wheelchair accessible
Dance Floor: yes
Bride's Dressing Area: yes
Meeting Equipment: tables & chairs

Parking: on street
Accommodations: no guest rooms
Telephone: local calls only
Outdoor Night Lighting: access only
Outdoor Cooking Facilities: yes
Cleanup: caterer
View: no

RESTRICTIONS:

Alcohol: BYO, WCB only

Smoking: outside only

Music: no amplified music outdoors

Wheelchair Access: limited

Insurance: not required

This is important! *Tell facilities you're reading* **Here Comes The Guide** *and ask if our information is still current.*

437

Rockefeller Lodge

Address withheld to ensure privacy. San Pablo
(510) 235-7344, fax (510) 237-3163

Historic Lodge

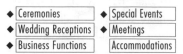

◆ Ceremonies ◆ Special Events
◆ Wedding Receptions ◆ Meetings
◆ Business Functions Accommodations

Have you always wanted to do something a bit different? Maybe have a Victorian theme in one room and French lace and balloons in another? Or maybe treat your guests to milk and cookies baked on the spot? Whatever your fantasy, the owner and staff of the Rockefeller Lodge love the challenge of making your special event a reality. And with its variety of rooms and outdoor areas, the Lodge can accommodate a wide range of creativity.

Once a Japanese Buddhist temple, the Rockefeller Lodge still offers a fragrant, woodsy serenity. The brown-shingled building derives its secluded feeling from the surrounding trees and quiet neighborhood. Winding brick paths and wisteria-covered arbors invite leisurely, relaxed strolls through the grounds. Outdoor ceremonies are often held in the gazebo area. You can have your reception or company party in the spacious, interior rooms, featuring hardwood floors, hand-hewn ceiling beams and a noteworthy fireplace constructed from burnt bricks from the 1906 earthquake.

CEREMONY & EVENT/RECEPTION CAPACITY: The Lodge and grounds accommodate 300 seated guests; the Lodge alone holds 150 seated. The entire site holds 500 for a reception.

MEETING CAPACITY:

Room	Seated	Room	Seated
Rockefeller Room	38	Garden Room	60
Lady Irene Room	23	Front Garden	100
Back Garden Court	100		

FEES & DEPOSITS: A $300–600 deposit (depending on day of week) plus a $75 refundable security deposit are required to secure your date. The facility rents for $300 on Friday (day or evening); $600 on Saturday and Sunday (day or evening). Monday–Thursday there is no rental fee for use of Rockefeller Lodge; charges are for food and beverages only. A 1-hour rehearsal can be arranged on Wednesday or Thursday evenings for $50.

Buffets for over 100 guests range $9–16.50/person. Catering for 50 people, minimum, starts at $13.50/person. Tax, alcohol and a 15% service charge are additional. Full payment is required

14 days prior to the event. There is a $2.50–3/person beverage service charge which includes labor, glasses, and non-alcoholic beverages. Any menu can be customized for your party.

AVAILABILITY: Year-round, daily, 10am–5pm or 6pm–11pm.

SERVICES/AMENITIES:

Catering: provided, no BYO

Kitchen Facilities: n/a

Tables & Chairs: provided

Linens, Silver, etc.: provided

Restrooms: wheelchair accessible

Dance Floor: yes

Bride's Dressing Area: yes

Meeting Equipment: BYO

Parking: 2 lots

Accommodations: no guest rooms

Telephone: pay phone

Outdoor Night Lighting: yes

Outdoor Cooking Facilities: no

Cleanup: provided

View: landscaped grounds & waterfalls

Other: full event planning, silk flowers

RESTRICTIONS:

Alcohol: BYO, service fee required

Smoking: not allowed

Music: amplified OK inside only, 4-piece band limit

Wheelchair Access: yes

Insurance: not required

Other: no rice or birdseed

The professionals in the back of the book are the best in the business! How do we know? Read page 681.

Mudd's Restaurant

Restaurant & Gardens

10 Boardwalk, San Ramon
(925) 837-9387, fax (925) 820-3663

www.mudds.com
banquets@mudds.com

◆ Ceremonies   ◆ Special Events
◆ Wedding Receptions   ◆ Meetings
◆ Business Functions   Accommodations

Surrounded by ten acres of open space and situated next to a two-acre organic garden, Mudd's Restaurant feels like it's in the Wine Country rather than simply a mile from I-680. Virginia Mudd, the restaurant's founder and namesake, had a vision: she wanted to create a beautifully appointed restaurant in a bucolic setting. Luckily for us, she was most successful.

Stroll among the acres of organic flowers, herbs and fruit trees. Gaze up at the towering oaks, elms and bay trees, and explore the creek canyons below. While much attention has been paid to the grounds here, Mudd's banquet facilities deserve their share of accolades too. The Fireside Room adjacent to the main restaurant is the larger of the two private event spaces. It features a beamed ceiling, split levels (including a dance floor) and an old-fashioned brick fireplace. Windows overlook the canyon and garden areas, and two sets of double French doors lead out onto a secluded deck, bordered by cobblestone paths and lush lawns. From here, the view of the garden seems endless, making the deck an ideal spot for your ceremony.

For larger Saturday weddings (over 100 guests), Mudd's entire main restaurant may be reserved. Built in the shape of a Greek cross, its architecture is unique. Although the dining area is made up of three separate rooms, a head table placed in the center of the "cross" is visible from everywhere in the restaurant. The acoustics are also exceptional—even if the band is playing in one room, you can still have a normal conversation in another one. Maximum visual access to the outdoors is achieved through dozens of windows in all sorts of shapes and sizes, each one overlooking a garden tapestry of vivid colors and subtle shades of green. The interior design is as appealing as the landscaping: a harmonious blend of natural wood, subtle green carpeting and dusty rose tile is complemented by imported Danish teak seating and white cotton linens. Numerous French doors open to patios screened by overhead trellises, where you may dine al fresco.

If you're planning a smaller reception, rehearsal dinner or meeting, host it in the Board Room. It has its own deck, and like Mudd's other rooms, it has a view of the lovely surroundings— this time overlooking a native oak grove. And for those of you who worry about everything going smoothly, you can rest easy. The on-site wedding planner and the chef have almost two decades of experience at Mudd's between them.

All in all, Mudd's is a rare find. If you're looking for the optimum garden setting with all the benefits of a full service restaurant, we suggest that you start your search here.

CEREMONY CAPACITY: The Fireside Deck and lawn can seat up to 175 guests.

EVENT/RECEPTION CAPACITY: Board Room, 20 seated; Fireside Room, 70 seated; Fireside Room & Deck, 75–100 for a standing reception; the Main Dining Room, 125 seated guests.

MEETING CAPACITY: The Board Room holds 16 people seated around one table, 20 seated around 2 tables, and 35 seated theater-style. The Fireside Room holds 70 seated at rounds or 135 seated theater-style.

FEES & DEPOSITS: A $500 non-refundable deposit is required to secure your date; any remaining balance is due the day of the event. There's a $1,000 fee to reserve the entire restaurant or a $500 fee to reserve the Fireside Room and $200 for the Board Room. Luncheons range $15–25/person, dinners $25–50/person and wedding buffets $25–35/person. Alcohol, tax and an 18% service charge are additional.

AVAILABILITY: The entire restaurant and grounds can be reserved only on Saturday 11:30am– 4:30pm. The Board Room and Fireside Room can be reserved any time.

SERVICES/AMENITIES:
Catering: provided
Kitchen Facilities: n/a
Tables & Chairs: provided
Linens, Silver, etc.: provided
Restrooms: wheelchair accessible
Dance Floor: yes
Bride's Dressing Area: yes
Meeting Equipment: full range

Parking: large lot
Accommodations: no guest rooms
Telephone: pay phone
Outdoor Night Lighting: no
Outdoor Cooking Facilities: no
Cleanup: provided
View: garden, hills and canyons
Other: event coordination

RESTRICTIONS:
Alcohol: provided, corkage $10/bottle
Smoking: outside only
Music: amplified OK indoors only

Wheelchair Access: yes
Insurance: not required
Other: no birdseed, rice or confetti

---

*This is important! Tell facilities you're reading **Here Comes The Guide** and ask if our information is still current.*

San Ramon Community Center

12501 Alcosta Boulevard, San Ramon
(925) 275-2300, fax (925) 830-5162

www.ci.san-ramon.ca.us
srparks@ci.san-ramon.ca.us

Community Center

◆ Ceremonies   ◆ Special Events
◆ Wedding Receptions   ◆ Meetings
◆ Business Functions   Accommodations

925-
973-
3200

We'd like to introduce you to a sophisticated facility whose spaces can compete with those of the best event sites. There's even a rose garden for ceremonies! Would you believe that this beautifully designed venue is a community center?

Built in 1989, this outstanding rose-colored granite and glass structure features pools, fountains and lush landscaping. Inside, the Fountain Room is the most popular area for receptions. Curved, laminated beams radiate from a center point, creating a domed ceiling 40 feet high. This sizable room, decorated in subtle plums and lavenders, is equally suitable for black tie affairs, casual parties and large meetings.

For smaller events, we like the Terrace Room and Gallery, which are rented as a duo. The cool, gray Terrace Room can be used for intimate dinners, while the semicircular Gallery is ideal for hors d'oeuvres and champagne receptions. The Gallery interior, which features different works of art each month, is warmed by light filtering through a 40-foot wall of windows that overlook a fountain courtyard. If you're interested in a site in this area, come take a look. We think that the San Ramon Community Center is a real find—the price and the ambiance are both sure to please.

CEREMONY CAPACITY: Outdoors, the Rose Garden can hold 160 seated. Indoors, the Fountain Room holds 450 seated, the Terrace Room 150 seated and the Gallery 50 standing guests.

EVENT/RECEPTION CAPACITY: The Fountain Room holds 250 seated guests, 500 for a cocktail reception. The Terrace Room, which comes with the Gallery, can accommodate 80 seated or 150 for a standing reception. Outdoors, the Rose Garden holds 60 seated or 200 standing guests.

MEETING CAPACITY: The Center has 2 small conference rooms which can each accommodate 35 theater-style, 20 seated conference-style or 12 seated classroom-style. A larger room can hold 60 seated theater-style, 30 seated conference-style or 20 seated classroom-style. The Fountain Room holds 350 seated theater-style.

FEES & DEPOSITS: A $100–200 security deposit is due when you book the facility and a second $100–200 deposit is due 90 days prior to the event. The rental fee is payable 30 days prior to the event (or when you book the site) and ranges $50–85/hour weekdays and $60–140/hour weekends depending on spaces rented and San Ramon residency (residents are charged a discounted rate). A 2-hour minimum is required. Weekend rates apply to holiday bookings.

AVAILABILITY: Year-round, daily. Sunday–Thursday and holidays, 7am–11pm; Friday and Saturday 7am–1am.

SERVICES/AMENITIES:

Catering: preferred list, BYO w/approval
Kitchen Facilities: fully equipped, extra fee
Tables & Chairs: provided
Linens, Silver, etc.: some available, extra fee
Restrooms: wheelchair accessible
Dance Floor: yes
Bride's Dressing Area: CBA, extra fee
Meeting Equipment: full range, extra charge
Other: baby grand piano, extra fee

Parking: ample lot
Accommodations: no guest rooms
Telephone: pay phone
Outdoor Night Lighting: yes
Outdoor Cooking Facilities: no
Cleanup: renter or caterer
View: San Ramon Valley hills, landscaped gardens, fountains

RESTRICTIONS:

Alcohol: BYO
Smoking: outside only
Music: amplified OK inside only

Wheelchair Access: yes
Insurance: sometimes required
Other: decorating restrictions; no birdseed, confetti, glitter, rice, petals or bubbles; red wine & punch discouraged

---

The professionals in the back of the book are the best in the business! How do we know? Read page 681.

San Ramon Senior Center

Senior Center

9300 Alcosta Boulevard, San Ramon
(925) 275-2316, fax (925) 275-2363

www.ci.san-ramon.ca.us
srparks@ci.san-ramon.ca.us

◆ Ceremonies ◆ Special Events
◆ Wedding Receptions ◆ Meetings
◆ Business Functions   Accommodations

While senior activities take priority, this contemporary building (completed in 1992) has something for everyone. We particularly like the Vista Grande Room—an upscale event space, well suited for wedding receptions. The walls are painted a pleasant dusky peach, and the light oak floor is great for dancing. A high, vaulted ceiling, recessed lighting and windows with views of rolling hills add to its charm. The room's terrace, accessible through multiple doors, and the adjacent fully equipped commercial kitchen are additional attractions.

Outdoors, the East Terrace is a peaceful courtyard, surrounded by a terraced, landscaped hillside, abloom with wild lilac and purple Mexican sage. You can arrange tables with umbrellas in this wind-protected area for luncheons, or just set up buffet tables for champagne and hors d'oeuvres. We think the San Ramon Senior Center is very attractive and, for those on a budget, very easy on the pocketbook.

CEREMONY CAPACITY: The Vista Grande Room holds 115 seated or 200 standing; the East Terrace, 100 seated or standing.

EVENT/RECEPTION CAPACITY:

Area	Seated	Standing	Assembly
Vista Grande Room & Terrace	115	200	150
Half Vista Grande	60	125	75
East Terrace	40	100	100

MEETING CAPACITY: The Center has 2 conference rooms which can accommodate 30 and 50 seated for assembly, 12 and 15 seated classroom-style, or 15 and 20 seated conference-style. There is also one large meeting room which can seat 150 for assembly.

FEES & DEPOSITS: A $100 security deposit is due when you book the facility and a $100 cleaning deposit is due 90 days prior to the event. The rental fee, averaging $45–90/hour on weekends and $30–55/hour on weekdays (with a two-hour minimum rental charge), is payable

30 days prior to the event. San Ramon residents are charged a discounted rate. The Vista Grande Room can be partitioned in half, and may be rented as a half space. There is an additional fee to reserve the East Terrace. Weekend rates apply to holiday bookings.

AVAILABILITY: Year-round, Monday–Thursday 5pm–11pm, Friday 5pm–1am, Saturday 7am–1am, and Sunday 7am–11pm.

SERVICES/AMENITIES:

Catering: preferred list, BYO w/approval
Kitchen Facilities: fully equipped, extra fee
Tables & Chairs: provided
Linens, Silver, etc.: BYO
Restrooms: wheelchair accessible
Dance Floor: yes
Bride's Dressing Area: CBA, extra fee
Meeting Equipment: easel, slide & overhead projector, screen; all are extra charge

Parking: ample lot
Accommodations: no guest rooms
Telephone: pay phone
Outdoor Night Lighting: yes
Outdoor Cooking Facilities: BBQ, extra fee
Cleanup: renter or caterer
View: Las Trampas regional park hills, landscaped surroundings
Other: piano, extra fee

RESTRICTIONS:

Alcohol: BYO, insurance required
Smoking: outside only
Music: amplified OK inside only

Wheelchair Access: yes
Insurance: sometimes required
Other: decorating restrictions; no birdseed, confetti, rice, glitter, petals or bubbles; red wine & punch discouraged

---

This is important! Tell facilities you're reading **Here Comes The Guide** *and ask if our information is still current.*

Elliston Vineyards

463 Kilkare Road, Sunol
(925) 862-2377, fax (925) 862-0316

www.elliston.com
elliston@elliston.com

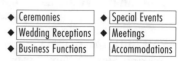

◆ Ceremonies   ◆ Special Events
◆ Wedding Receptions ◆ Meetings
◆ Business Functions   Accommodations

When gold rush pioneer Henry Ellis carved out an estate for himself in 1890, he picked a prime setting: a sheltered canyon tucked between two tree-covered ridges. Here he set up house in a three-story mansion, constructed of thick sandstone from nearby Niles Canyon, and went about enjoying life in the country. Today his lovely homestead, now surrounded by acres of vineyards, has become a prime setting for making wine, and for hosting weddings, receptions and private parties.

Ceremonies are held outdoors next to the mansion, in a picture-perfect rose garden with a lawn and arbor. Stage your photos here, and you'll have some striking options for a backdrop—the century-old stone house, a 100-year-old bay tree, and vibrant displays of azaleas and camellias. But if you'd like to search for more photographic possibilities, go right ahead. When you have your event at Elliston, you have exclusive use of the event area for the day.

A short walkway takes you from the garden to the Terrace Room, a secluded 2,000-square-foot banquet room set into the hillside. Its vaulted ceiling and glass walls add to the feeling of spaciousness, while the surrounding deck gives guests a chance to dine al fresco at umbrella-shaded tables. A Victorian gazebo next to the deck is large enough for a bridal table of sixteen. The entire site is sheltered by oak, eucalyptus and olive trees, and fortunately for us, the folks at Elliston have used a judicious hand when it comes to landscaping. They've blended new plantings with the native flora, preserving much of the hillside's untamed quality.

The mansion's rooms are available for small private parties. Furnished with antiques—including a square grand Steinway piano, and Ellis' original carved walnut bedroom set shipped round the Horn—they lend a bit of historic atmosphere to an intimate dinner. And if you'd like to have dinner here but don't want to host an actual event, Elliston offers its own Winetaster Dinners at the mansion. Held Friday and Saturday evenings by reservation, they feature four-course meals, each course paired with a selected wine.

Whether you're a bride planning your wedding or a wine aficionado treating yourself to a special dinner, Elliston Vineyards is the place to go. Although you're close to civilization, you'd never know it—the quiet country atmosphere will give you the delicious feeling of being a million miles away.

CEREMONY CAPACITY: Outdoors, the rose garden lawn can accommodate 250 seated; indoors the Terrace Room can accommodate 100 seated guests.

EVENT/RECEPTION CAPACITY: The Terrace Room and adjoining deck seat 250 guests. The historic Ellis Mansion may be reserved for rehearsal or private dinner parties for up to 38 guests.

MEETING CAPACITY: The facility can accommodate up to 60 seated guests.

FEES & DEPOSITS: For weddings, a non-refundable $500 deposit is required when reservations are confirmed. Functions Monday–Friday start at $2,000, on Saturday at $8,000 and on Sunday $5,000. The actual cost will depend on the menu selected and guest count. The total cost includes meals, rental fees and beverages. Half the estimated cost is due 3 months prior to your function, an additional 25% 2 months prior and the balance, with a confirmed guest count, 2 weeks prior to the event.

For other special events, the Terrace Room has a 40-guest minimum. Any menu can be customized; luncheons and dinners start at $30/person, buffets at $33/person; alcohol, tax and an 18% service charge are additional.

For meetings and conferences, a non-refundable $100 deposit is required when reservations are confirmed. Room fees run $300/day. Continental breakfast, full lunch and afternoon snack cost $29.50/person.

AVAILABILITY: Year-round, daily. Monday–Saturday until 9pm, Sunday until 6pm.

SERVICES/AMENITIES:

Catering: provided, no BYO
Kitchen Facilities: n/a
Tables & Chairs: provided
Linens, Silver, etc.: provided
Restrooms: wheelchair accessible
Dance Floor: yes
Bride's Dressing Area: yes
View: vineyards & hills
Other: event planning

Parking: large lot, parking attendants
Accommodations: no guest rooms
Telephone: office phone
Outdoor Night Lighting: yes
Outdoor Cooking Facilities: no
Cleanup: provided
Meeting Equipment: AV, overhead projector, screen, flip charts, podium, VCR & monitor

RESTRICTIONS:

Alcohol: WC provided, no BYO
Smoking: outside only
Music: amplified OK inside only

Wheelchair Access: yes
Insurance: not required
Other: no rice, birdseed or confetti

The professionals in the back of the book are the best in the business! *How do we know? Read page 681.*

Admiral's Mansions at Mare Island
and St. Peter's Chapel

Walnut Avenue, Mare Island, Vallejo
(707) 557-1538, fax (707) 552-3266

www.foothold.com/~mihp
kenz@crl.com

[handwritten: Space only]

[handwritten: 649-8029 (crossed out)]

[handwritten: GARDEN AVAIL. DOROTHY 649-8024]

Mansions, Historic Chapel & Park

◆ Ceremonies	◆ Special Events
◆ Wedding Receptions	◆ Meetings
◆ Business Functions	Accommodations

With the 1996 closure of Mare Island Naval Installation, three landmark buildings are now available for special events. These venues are operated by the Mare Island Historic Park Foundation—so you no longer need military connections. And since they're located in the island's quaint historic district (which dates back to the mid 1800s) you feel like you have an entire small town all to yourself.

Set in its own grassy park with a eucalyptus grove, St. Peter's is a picturesque interdenominational chapel. Built in 1901, it's the oldest naval chapel in the United States. A classic example of Victorian Gothic architecture, this tidy brown shingle, with cream-colored trim, steep pitched roof and a soaring octagonal spire, has as much charm and history inside as out. The largest collection of Tiffany glass under one roof is displayed in the chapel's 29 exquisite stained glass windows, and they fill the intimate interior with a soft, rosy light. One window depicts Sir Galahad who, when illuminated by sunlight, becomes the ultimate knight in shining armor. Rich wood paneling complements the creamy plaster walls, and open beams accentuate the vaulted ceiling. The chapel also displays a collection of memorial plaques. Some are set into the ceiling and others (one dates back to the Civil War), hung on the walls, make intriguing reading.

Naturally there's a pipe organ (it's the original one from 1928!) to fill the sanctuary with strains of *Here Comes The Bride*. After the ceremony, take advantage of the lovely setting for formal photos while your guests make the short trip back down Walnut Avenue to Officer's Row.

Receptions and business retreats are held in the Admiral's and the Captain's former quarters, two of the sixteen white Colonial Revival mansions lining Officer's Row. As you enter the Admiral's Quarters, it's easy to imagine the social galas of a century ago. The brass nautical lamps that lit the entryway then still hang on either side of the massive oak front door; the wide front veranda graced with Corinthian columns still invites guests to stroll outside for a leisurely chat. The gracious feel of the place continues inside in the vestibule, a large U-shaped entry hall complete with an inviting fireplace and built-in seating. Your guests can enjoy cocktails and hors d'oeuvres in here and as they explore the first- and second-floor rooms, all furnished in period pieces. The Captain's Quarters, similar in style to the Admiral's, is often reserved for smaller functions.

For an alfresco treat, set up a buffet and umbrella-shaded tables in the Victorian gardens adjacent to both of these mansions: it's an acre of lawns interspersed with low hedges, flower beds, and a variety of trees brought back from the far corners of the world by sea captains.

If you really want to make a splash, depart via ferry or yacht—the ferry terminal and marina are just a short distance from the island. But no matter which mode of transportation you choose, an event here is a trip back in time and a chance to relive a little of the grace and gentility of another era.

CEREMONY CAPACITY: The Chapel holds 200 seated guests. Each Mansion holds up to 80 seated guests on the first floor; additional space is available on the second floor.

EVENT/RECEPTION CAPACITY:

Space	Seated	Standing	Space	Seated	Standing
Chapel Park	1,000	2,000	Admiral's Mansion	80	150
Admiral's Garden	1,000	2,000	Captain's Mansion	60	125
Captain's Garden	1,000	2,000			

MEETING CAPACITY: In addition to those below, there are smaller rooms for meetings.

Space	Theater-style	Conf-style	Space	Theater-style	Conf-style
Admiral's Dining Rm	—	40	Admiral's Parlor	35	25
Captain's Dining Rm	—	40	Admiral's Living Room	40	30
2nd Floor Rooms	—	10–30 ea.			

FEES & DEPOSITS: For weddings, a non-refundable rental deposit plus a $500 refundable security deposit are required to secure your date. Organ and organist are available for $150, use of the piano is $25/event. Catering is provided by *Alex's Catering, Beyond Imagination* and *Catered With Care.* Fees for business meetings vary; call for more information.

Space	Donation	Deposit
Chapel	$500	$250
Chapel Park	$600 min. or $2.50/person	50%
Admiral's Mansion & Garden	$1,000 min. or $5/person	50%
Captain's Mansion & Garden	$750 min. or $5/person	50%

AVAILABILITY: Year-round, daily, 8am–10pm.

SERVICES/AMENITIES:

Catering: select from preferred list
Kitchen Facilities: moderately equipped
Tables & Chairs: BYO

Parking: large lot and private street parking
Accommodations: guest rooms for 16 guests
Telephone: emergency use only

Linens, Silver, etc.: caterer
Restrooms: wheelchair access CBA
Dance Floor: patio, or CBA, extra charge
Bride's & Groom's Dressing Area: yes
Other: grand piano, event coordination, tours of Mare Island's historic locations

Outdoor Night Lighting: CBA
Outdoor Cooking Facilities: through caterer
Cleanup: caterer, renter or CBA, extra fee
Meeting Equipment: video player
View: Historic Alden Park

RESTRICTIONS:

Alcohol: CBA or BYO, licensed & insured server
Smoking: designated outdoor areas
Music: amplified OK w/volume limits
Other: no rice, food or alcohol in Chapel

Wheelchair Access: Chapel has limited access, Mansions have ramps; Gardens have full access
Insurance: certificate required

The Gardens at Heather Farm

Garden Education Center

1540 Marchbanks Drive, Walnut Creek
(925) 947-1678, fax (925) 947-1726

◆ Ceremonies	◆ Special Events
◆ Wedding Receptions	◆ Meetings
◆ Business Functions	Accommodations

Something is always in bloom at this nonprofit garden education center which was originally part of a horse ranch. Now covering five landscaped acres, it features a series of concrete footpaths that wind their way through a colorful variety of flower beds, herb and rock gardens. Off in the distance, there's a well-stocked duck pond (belonging to the city park next door) and a view of Mt. Diablo.

During warm-weather months, hold your entire event outdoors. Anyone who equates romance with roses will want to tie the knot beneath the fragrant, rose-covered gazebo, surrounded by rose bushes that bloom continuously from spring through fall. Afterwards you and your guests can stroll through the gardens, admiring the wide range of floral and herbal displays—all meticulously labeled—on your way to the reception terrace. This large patio, like the rest of the garden center, offers an abundance of olfactory and visual treats. Concrete-and-tile planters border the space and are filled with a horticultural riot of textures, scents and hues. One section, aptly named the Sensory Garden, was developed for the blind and is meant to be touched and smelled. A large lawn serves as another outdoor reception option, and a caterer-friendly pavilion—complete with sink, electrical outlets, lighting and four easy-access tiled counters—is great for a buffet setup or as a serving station for a patio cocktail party.

Indoor receptions are usually held upstairs in the Camellia Pavilion Room, a light and airy space with a high, beamed ceiling and large picture windows with a panoramic view of Mt. Diablo, the gardens and the deck. Guests who want to explore the gardens simply take the ramp or stairs from the deck to the patio and pavilion below. The smaller Rotary Rose Room on the ground floor has direct access to the patio area, and a wall of windows overlooking it. With their neutral walls and linoleum floors, both rooms are pleasant and easy to decorate. But if you can swing it, we recommend an outdoor celebration, where you can take full advantage of this location's delightful (and educational!) garden setting.

CEREMONY CAPACITY:

Area	Seated	Standing	Area	Seated	Standing
Gazebo	150	150	Rose Garden	150	150
Patio Area	100	100			

RECEPTION & MEETING CAPACITY:

Area	Seated	Standing	Area	Seated	Standing
Camellia Room	150	150	Rotary Room	25	30
Patio	100	100			

FEES & DEPOSITS: A $250 security deposit is required to hold your date; the event balance is due 12 weeks prior to the event. A garden ceremony setup is an additional $100–250 charge. Weekday rental fees, Monday–Friday 3pm, range $30–80/hour with a 2-hour minimum. Rental fees Friday 3pm–Sunday and holidays are as follows:

Timeframe	May1–Sept 30 Camellia Rm or Rotary Rm & Patio	Oct 1–April 30 Camellia Room
Friday	$110/hour	$110/hour
Saturday	$1,100–1,800/event	$875–1,500/event
Saturday extra hours	$150/hour	
Sunday	$875/event	$875/event
Sunday extra hours	$125/hour	
	Garden Areas	**Rotary Room**
	w/room rental $100–250	$50/hour

AVAILABILITY: Year-round, daily. Weekday and Sunday hours are flexible. On Saturdays, events take place 9am–3:30pm or 5:30pm–midnight. For Saturday daytime functions that go past 3:30pm, or an evening function that begins before 5:30pm, there is a 10-hour minimum.

SERVICES/AMENITIES:

Catering: BYO
Kitchen Facilities: commercial
Tables & Chairs: provided
Dishes, Silver, etc.: provided, extra fee
Restrooms: wheelchair accessible
Dance Floor: yes
Bride's Dressing Area: yes
View: gardens, Mt. Diablo & pond

Parking: lot and on street
Accommodations: no guest rooms
Telephone: pay phone
Outdoor Night Lighting: yes
Outdoor Cooking Facilities: BYO BBQ
Cleanup: caterer or renter
Meeting Equipment: podium, PA, overhead projector

RESTRICTIONS:

Alcohol: BYO
Smoking: outside only
Music: amplified OK indoors only

Wheelchair Access: yes
Insurance: proof of insurance required
Other: no confetti, rice, birdseed, flower petals or balloon releases

---

The professionals in the back of the book are the best in the business! How do we know? Read page 681.

Lindsay Wildlife Museum

Museum

1931 First Avenue, Walnut Creek
(925) 935-1978, fax (925) 9935-8015

www.wildlife-museum.org

◆ Ceremonies ◆ Special Events
◆ Wedding Receptions ◆ Meetings
◆ Business Functions Accommodations

Located in a pleasantly shaded suburban park, the Lindsay Wildlife Museum is a one-of-a-kind setting for all types of corporate and private celebrations. More formal events are held in the Exhibit Hall on the upper level of the Museum. A striking example of modern architecture, it features high ceilings, interesting angles and unconventional wall arrangements. Lots of natural light flows in through skylights, making the space bright and airy. During an event, you're surrounded by live native wildlife, an experience you probably wouldn't get anywhere else. Eagles, bobcats, foxes and often a mountain lion or coyote provide beautiful and fascinating viewing while you're dining or strolling through the Hall. The charismatic combination of eye-catching architecture and wildlife theme make the Exhibit Hall a dramatic setting for corporate cocktail receptions, dinners and weddings.

The Community Room, situated on the lower level of the facility, has an unusual focal point: a life-size model of Mt. Diablo's Balancing Rock. The sculpture rises two stories through an opening in the ceiling into the museum's lobby, and it's covered with native flora and fauna. A circular walkway leads to the far side of the rock and to a high, semicircular wall of windows overlooking the park. The room itself is a comfortable, convenient space for parties of all kinds, including bar mitzvahs, and graduation or reunion parties. Crisp white walls are lined with art, and the patterned grey-and-red concrete floors are excellent for dancing. If you're having a business meeting or training session, the room can be easily configured to meet your particular needs.

Another unique feature of the Lindsay Museum is its very popular live animal presentation. You can arrange a "meet and greet" program to introduce your guests to the museum's most exotic wildlife. So while you and your nearest and dearest may not be "party animals," you can still have animals at your party.

CEREMONY CAPACITY: Larkey Park, a public park adjacent to the Museum, holds 100–300 guests. The park is booked through the City of Walnut Creek (925/934-5859) and use requires a permit.

EVENT/RECEPTION CAPACITY: The Exhibit Hall holds 150 seated, or 200 standing. The Community Room holds 150 seated or 175 standing.

MEETING CAPACITY: The Community Room holds up to 175 guests. Smaller rooms are also available.

FEES & DEPOSITS: A $50–100 non-refundable rental deposit secures your date. A signed contract plus the rental fee balance and a $400–500 refundable cleaning/security deposit are due 2 months prior to the event. If alcohol is served, a $45 alcohol beverage service fee is charged. The Museum's "meet and greet" live animal presentation can be arranged. A list of preferred caterers is available on request. The rental fee for the Exhibit Hall is $2,000/evening, 5pm–10pm. Other spaces are available; rental fees are as follows:

	Residents	*Non-residents*
Friday–Sunday	$80/hour	$100/hour
Weekdays	$50/hour	$75/hour

AVAILABILITY: Year-round, weekends 10am–10pm. Call for weekday availability.

SERVICES/AMENITIES:

Catering: BYO w/approval
Kitchen Facilities: fully equipped
Tables & Chairs: provided
Linens, Silver, etc.: BYO
Restrooms: wheelchair accessible
Dance Floor: concrete floor
Bride's Dressing Area: CBA
Meeting Equipment: overhead projector, VCR

Parking: ample on-site
Accommodations: no guest rooms
Telephone: pay phone
Outdoor Night Lighting: access only
Outdoor Cooking Facilities: no
Cleanup: caterer
View: landscaped grounds
Other: wedding coordination

RESTRICTIONS:

Alcohol: BYO, licensed server
Smoking: outdoors only
Music: amplified OK w/volume restrictions

Wheelchair Access: yes
Insurance: may be required
Other: no rice, birdseed, helium balloons, glitter, or confetti; decorations must be free-standing

---

Scott's Gardens

1333 North California Boulevard, Walnut Creek
(925) 934-0598, fax (925) 934-5619

www.scottseastbay.com

- ◆ Ceremonies
- ◆ Wedding Receptions
- ◆ Business Functions
- ◆ Special Events
- ◆ Meetings
- Accommodations

Take note! If you're looking for an exceptional East Bay outdoor wedding spot, you must see this facility. Scott's Gardens is a site that could be aptly described as an urban oasis. Situated in the heart of Walnut Creek's retail district, Scott's has spared no expense to transform a small hillside into a brick-walled, multi-terraced courtyard garden with a conservatory cover. If you're worried about the weather, don't fret—during Novem

ber through April, the garden is totally glass enclosed and heated to keep your guests comfortable.

Under the broad canopy of a four-hundred-year-old oak tree (the site's centerpiece) you'll find handsome amenities such as designer wood benches, large heat lamps and sizable, free-standing umbrellas, in addition to lush landscaping. Of special interest are a green lattice aviary, several fountains and an antique water wheel. Observe the details here. All of the terraces are paved with slate and even the outdoor bar and indoor dressing room feature marble counters. The latter is absolutely the best bride's dressing room we've ever seen—with floor to ceiling mirrors and well-lit makeup area. At the topmost terrace, you'll find a back stairway leading to Scott's restaurant, where there's another outdoor patio for evening rehearsal dinners and small weekend receptions. Inside the restaurant, additional private and semi-private rooms are available for parties.

CEREMONY CAPACITY: The Oak Terrace holds 130 seated or 140 standing guests.

EVENT/RECEPTION CAPACITY: The Garden can accommodate a maximum of 200 seated guests, 300 for a standing reception.

MEETING CAPACITY:

Room	Theater-style	Conf-style	Room	Theater-style	Conf-style
Shell Ridge	40	16	Shell Ridge/Diablo	100	—
Diablo	50	22	John Muir	75	22

FEES & DEPOSITS: A non-refundable deposit of $1,000 is due when the event date is booked. The rental fee on Saturday is $1,000, Sunday–Friday, $500. Rental includes tables, chairs, linens, silverware, setup and cleanup. Hors d'oeuvre receptions start at $20/person, buffets at $30/person, seated luncheons or dinners at $25/person. Alcohol, tax and an 18% service fee are additional. The estimated food and beverage total is due 7 days prior to the event; the remaining portion is payable at the event's conclusion. Coffee and cake cutting runs $2.50/person. The ceremony setup fee is $150.

For Monday–Friday business functions, the fee for use of the meeting rooms runs $25 with meal service, $100 without.

AVAILABILITY: Year-round, daily, 8am–4pm or 6pm–midnight.

SERVICES/AMENITIES:

Catering: provided, no BYO
Kitchen Facilities: n/a
Tables & Chairs: provided
Linens, Silver, etc.: provided
Restrooms: wheelchair accessible
Dance Floor: yes
Bride's Dressing Area: yes
Meeting Equipment: full range audio-visual

Parking: complimentary valet
Accommodations: no guest rooms
Telephone: pay phone
Outdoor Night Lighting: yes
Outdoor Cooking Facilities: CBA
Cleanup: provided
View: of landscaped garden
Other: event coordination, flowers, wedding cakes, invitations, music, transportation, favors

RESTRICTIONS:

Alcohol: provided, no BYO
Smoking: outside only
Music: DJ or small combos only

Wheelchair Access: yes
Insurance: not required

The professionals in the back of the book are the best in the business! How do we know? Read page 681.

Shadelands Art Center

111 North Wiget Lane, Walnut Creek
(925) 943-5846, fax (925) 937-2787

Arts & Education Center

◆ Ceremonies   ◆ Special Events
◆ Wedding Receptions   ◆ Meetings
◆ Business Functions   Accommodations

The Shadelands Arts Center is an oak-shaded, spacious and comfortable hall, owned by the city of Walnut Creek. Its convenient location, just off of Ygnacio Valley Road, makes it a great choice for weddings, receptions, meetings or just about any kind of special event where guests are coming from around the Bay Area.

The building's design and decor are easy to work with: the high-ceilinged interior is a cool white, amenable to virtually any kind of decorating, and a large parquet floor is available for dancing. The room rental also includes the use of banquet tables and chairs, further simplifying your event planning. For corporate functions, Shadelands supplies most of the equipment required for standard presentations: an overhead video projector, automatic screen, slide projectors, sound equipment—even a complimentary phone hook-up for Internet use.

The Center's staff are also very accommodating, and go out of their way to help you create the event you want, while staying within your budget. One of the terrific perks they offer is the use of the fully equipped professional kitchen, with the option of bringing in your own caterer. If you like, you can even head into the kitchen yourself, and whip up a spectacular feast for anywhere from 30 to 300 guests. This is a real benefit for couples planning a casual wedding or rehearsal dinner.

Shadelands Art Center's flexibility, easy access, ample parking and reasonable prices have made it a local favorite. So if you want to host a wedding, private party or corporate event that's very much your own, this is definitely an alternative worth considering.

CEREMONY CAPACITY: The Banquet Room holds 450 seated.

EVENT/RECEPTION CAPACITY: The Banquet Room can accommodate 300 seated guests.

MEETING CAPACITY: The Banquet Room holds 450 seated theater-style or 300 guests seated conference-style.

FEES & DEPOSITS: A $300 non-refundable deposit and a $200–500 security deposit are required to secure your date; the event balance is due 90 days prior to the function. An additional $45 fee is charged if alcohol is served. Rental fees include tables, chairs, microphone, use of the kitchen and security attendant, and are as follows:

Time Frame		Hourly Rate
Weekdays until 3pm Friday	Non-profits	$55
	Other Renters	75
	Commercial	85
3pm Friday–Sunday 1am	Non-profits	90
	Other Renters	100
	Commercial	110

AVAILABILITY: Year-round, daily until 1am. Later time frames can be negotiated.

SERVICES/AMENITIES:

Catering: BYO

Kitchen Facilities: fully equipped, commercial

Tables & Chairs: provided

Linens, Silver, etc.: BYO or caterer

Restrooms: wheelchair accessible

Dance Floor: provided

Bride's & Groom's Dressing Area: yes

Meeting Equipment: full range

Parking: large lots, ample parking

Accommodations: no guest rooms

Telephone: pay phones

Outdoor Night Lighting: access only

Outdoor Cooking Facilities: BYO

Cleanup: renter or caterer

View: no

RESTRICTIONS:

Alcohol: BYO

Smoking: outside only

Music: amplified OK, indoors only

Wheelchair Access: yes

Insurance: not required

Other: no rice, birdseed or confetti

This is important! Tell facilities you're reading **Here Comes The Guide** and ask if our information is still current.

Shadelands Ranch
and Historical Museum

2660 Ygnacio Valley Road, Walnut Creek
(925) 935-7871, fax (925) 935-7885

Historic Ranch Home

◆ Ceremonies   ◆ Special Events
◆ Wedding Receptions   Meetings
◆ Business Functions   Accommodations

Shadelands is a 1903 Colonial Revival-style home that exists today in virtually its turn-of-the-century state, with the original owner's furnishings and memorabilia intact. Hiram Penniman, an early Walnut Creek pioneer, acquired portions of a Mexican land grant in the early 1850s. Here he planted 320 acres in fruit and nut trees. It's believed that Hiram built the homestead for his eldest, unmarried daughter who died, unfortunately, six years after the house was completed. The house and two and a half acres were passed down through family members, and in 1948, a foundation was set up to administer the estate. Donated to the City of Walnut Creek in 1970, it is now listed on the National Register of Historic Places.

Shadelands is an exceptional spot to have a wedding or reception. Repainted in its original soft burgundy with cream trim, the house is really inviting, with broad steps leading to a veranda that sweeps around one side of the building. The grounds have been nicely landscaped, with shade trees, roses and flowering annuals. In the back, a new gazebo designed in keeping with the house, awaits the bridal party. Red roses cling to the posts, and the shady interior is perfect for sunny days. Expansive emerald lawns, beautifully maintained, surround the gazebo. For receptions, you can set up tables with umbrellas either on the lawns or on a medium-sized patio adjacent to the house. If you'd like to get married in a pretty and pleasant outdoor environment with an old-world appeal, Shadelands is worth a visit.

CEREMONY & EVENT/RECEPTION CAPACITY: The outdoor gazebo area, lawn and patio hold up to 250 seated or standing guests.

FEES & DEPOSITS: A $100 non-refundable rental deposit plus a refundable $250 cleaning/security fee secures your date. Both are payable when reservations are confirmed. The rental fee for outdoor functions is $125/hour; use of the kitchen is an additional $50/event.

AVAILABILITY: Year-round, daily, 8am–10pm.

SERVICES/AMENITIES:
Catering: BYO
Kitchen Facilities: minimal

Parking: large lots
Accommodations: no guest rooms

Tables & Chairs: 200 chairs provided
Linens, Silver, etc.: BYO
Restrooms: wheelchair accessible
Dance Floor: on patio
Bride's Dressing Area: no
Meeting Equipment: n/a

Telephone: house phone
Outdoor Night Lighting: yes
Outdoor Cooking Facilities: CBA
Cleanup: renter or caterer
View: of garden & surrounding hills

RESTRICTIONS:

Alcohol: BYO
Smoking: outside only
Music: amplified OK within reason

Wheelchair Access: yes
Insurance: not required
Other: no candles indoors, no rice

The professionals in the back of the book are the best in the business! How do we know? Read page 681.

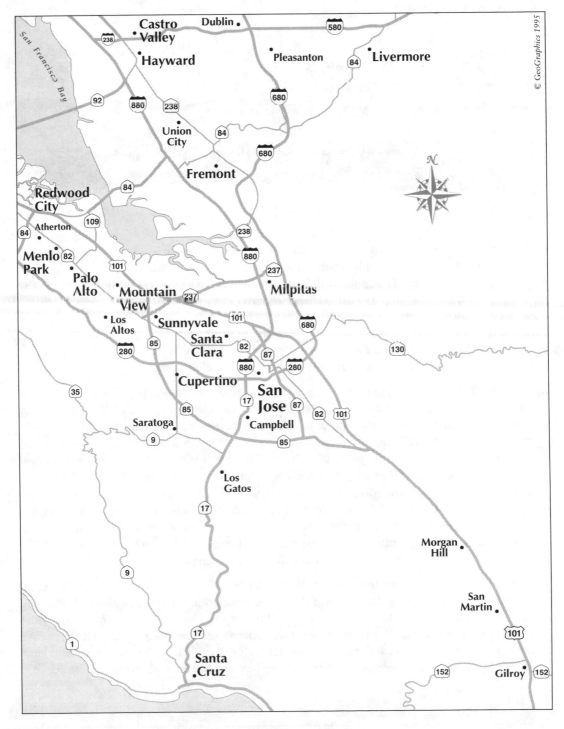

south bay

Ainsley House and Gardens

300 Grant Avenue, Campbell
**(408) 866-2119, catering (408) 972-0830,
fax (408) 379-6349**
http://web.nvcom.com/chm/

Historic House & Gardens

◆ Ceremonies ◆ Special Events
◆ Wedding Receptions ◆ Meetings
◆ Business Functions Accommodations

In 1925, in the twilight of a highly successful life as the founder of a local fruit cannery and export company, expatriate Englishman John Colpitts Ainsley built for himself and his wife Alcinda a lovely English Tudor Revival home. With fifteen rooms (including a terrifically modern kitchen with an icebox, a six-burner two-oven stove, and adjoining maid's quarters), large bay windows, a swooping, curved, mock thatch roof, and blooming English-style gardens, the Ainsley's home was one of the finest in the Santa Clara Valley. Today, caterer Julie Spear of San Jose-based *Special Events by Julie* uses the Ainsley House lawn and gardens as the setting for some of the area's prettiest weddings and celebrations.

In the years following JC Ainsley's death in 1937, his home was unoccupied, used only by far-flung family members for occasional Christmas parties or other reunions. In 1989, the family donated the historic house to the city of Campbell, which moved the building to its present location (in the midst of a small, immaculate public park, with ample parking nearby) and immediately set about restoring its original luster. The result is a living museum with period furniture (most of it original to the house), walls covered in delicate silk fabric, glowing oak-paneled hallways, closets that display period gowns and tiny flapper-era shoes, and a kitchen stocked with cans of JC's fruit! Because of the fragile nature of these antiques and artifacts, the interior of the house is not available for parties. It is, however, extremely popular with wedding couples as a backdrop for photos, and you may use the interior for pictures whether you're holding your ceremony and reception at the site or elsewhere.

The gardens that now surround Ainsley House are scaled-down versions of the original gardens on Bascom Avenue. Blossoming crabapples, rhododendrons, irises, and bridal veil encircle the house and back lawn; several rose bushes were transplanted straight from the Ainsley's 1925 flowerbeds. The front of the house opens onto the Orchard City Green, a lush public lawn used in summer for the local concert series; the back opens onto a private lawn bordered by flowers and evergreens, and enclosed by an attractive redwood lattice fence.

One ceremony possibility is to screen the front lawn for privacy and seat guests with a view of the picturesque house and front garden. The back yard can then be saved for your reception, with table seating on the lawn and dancing on the shaded patio just outside the graceful French doors at the back of the house. If, however, you prefer to hold both your ceremony and reception in the more private back area, Julie Spear's crack catering crew will arrange this for you. Preset tables are tucked behind screens along the sides of the lawn. For the ceremony, the bridal party enters the yard through the French doors and proceeds across the lawn to the wisteria-shaded redwood arbor at the far end. Afterwards, tables are moved into place for dining. As evening falls, tiny white lights in the arbor cast a shimmer over your celebration.

However you use the Ainsley House grounds, Julie and her staff will work with you to ensure that your affair runs smoothly. The *Special Events* team can coordinate everything from choreography to flowers to food, and they will customize a menu to suit your tastes. With a beautiful garden setting, delicious cuisine and a cooperative, professional catering team, your event at the Ainsley House will be a memorable one.

CEREMONY CAPACITY: The garden holds 200 seated guests. Indoors, the Parlor holds up to 15 seated and standing guests.

EVENT/RECEPTION & MEETING CAPACITY: The garden holds 200 seated or 300 standing for a cocktail reception.

FEES & DEPOSITS: For special events, a $275 refundable security deposit and the rental fee is required to secure your date. For ceremonies and rehearsals, the rental fee is $300–500 for a 2-hour minimum; for a reception, the fee is $500–000 for a 4 hour minimum. For each additional hour, there is a $100–125/hour charge. Catering is provided by *Special Events by Julie* (408) 972-0830.

AVAILABILITY: Year-round, depending on weather conditions, typically April through October. Very small events can take place indoors; call for more information.

SERVICES/AMENITIES:

Catering: *Special Events by Julie* or BYO
Kitchen Facilities: no
Tables & Chairs: BYO or caterer
Linens, Silver, etc.: BYO or caterer
Restrooms: wheelchair accessible
Dance Floor: cement area
Bride's Dressing Area: yes
Meeting Equipment: BYO

Parking: adjacent lot
Accommodations: no guest rooms
Telephone: emergency use only
Outdoor Night Lighting: yes
Outdoor Cooking Facilities: BYO
Cleanup: renter or caterer
View: English cottage garden
Other: event coordination

RESTRICTIONS:

Alcohol: BYO, CWB only
Smoking: not restricted
Music: amplified OK w/volume limits

Wheelchair Access: yes
Insurance: not required
Other: no rice, birdseed or confetti

This is important! Tell facilities you're reading **Here Comes The Guide** *and ask if our information is still current.*

Byington Winery

Winery

21850 Bear Creek Road, Los Gatos
(408) 354-1111 ext. 212, fax (408) 354-2782
www.byington.com
events@byington

◆ Ceremonies
◆ Wedding Receptions
◆ Business Functions
◆ Special Events
◆ Meetings
Accommodations

The Byington Winery and Vineyards are located up above Los Gatos, in one of the oldest grape growing regions in the U.S. Although a relative newcomer, Byington is already reserved well in advance for weddings and special events because of its great location and wonderful amenities. For ceremonies, follow the brick path up to the "wedding hill." The path is bordered by vineyards and at the very top, guests are treated to a sensational panorama. You couldn't ask for more incredible views of the mountains and distant Monterey Bay.

After taking your vows, descend to the winery. It's constructed of gray stone, with a terra cotta roof, and has several balconies dotted with blue umbrellas. Before the reception, greet guests in the VIP Room which features an oak hardwood floor, black baby grand piano, mahogany bar, stone fireplace, overstuffed sofas and wingbacked chairs. For formal, seated functions, the VIP dining area with its overhead chandelier sets an elegant tone. For larger functions, both the Private Tasting Room and the Barrel Room are available. They overlook the wine cellar, which is filled with French oak barrels and large fermentation tanks. A real plus is the well-designed bride's changing room, which has a four-poster bed, full length mirror and its own bath. Byington is extremely service oriented: only one wedding per day is scheduled so that staff can provide brides and grooms or corporate clients with lots of personal attention.

CEREMONY CAPACITY: The Wedding Hill holds up to 250 seated; the VIP Suite holds 100 standing and seated, combined. The Barrel Room seats 150 guests.

EVENT/RECEPTION CAPACITY: The facility holds 150 for winter functions; 250 for summer events.

MEETING CAPACITY: The VIP Room holds up to 30 seated; the Barrel Room, 150 seated classroom-style or 200 seated theater-style.

FEES & DEPOSITS: For weddings, 50% of the rental fee is a non-refundable deposit, due when the contract is signed. Rental fees are as follows: Friday and winter months, $1,750–3,350, Saturday or Sunday, May 1st–October 30th, $2,350–4,350 depending on group size. Overtime is $350/hour. The remaining 50% is payable 6 months prior to the wedding. A $500 refundable security deposit is also required.

For weekday meetings, the fee is $300–750; for weekend business functions, $1,550; rates vary depending on guest count and services required.

AVAILABILITY: Year-round. Monday–Friday, 8am–5pm for meetings and business functions. Weddings take place Friday–Sunday, 9am–11pm in 8-hour blocks. Overtime hours are available upon request. Ceremonies for up to 250 people (without receptions) can take place weekends, 9am–3pm, depending on availability.

SERVICES/AMENITIES:

Catering: select from preferred list

Kitchen Facilities: ample

Tables & Chairs: provided

Linens, Silver, etc.: BYO

Restrooms: limited wheelchair access

Dance Floor: CBA

Bride's Dressing Area: yes

Meeting Equipment: AV CBA

Other: picnic area, baby grand piano some event coordination

Parking: 100 spaces, carpooling recommended

Accommodations: no guest rooms

Telephone: pay phone

Outdoor Night Lighting: yes

Outdoor Cooking Facilities: BBQ

Cleanup: caterer

View: panoramic view of mountains, forest, vineyards and distant views of Monterey Bay

RESTRICTIONS:

Alcohol: provided, no BYO

Smoking: outside only

Music: amplified OK indoors only

Wheelchair Access: yes

Insurance: proof of insurance required

Other: no confetti, rice or birdseed

The professionals in the back of the book are the best in the business! How do we know? Read page 681.

California Cafe

Restaurant

50 University Avenue, Los Gatos
(408) 354-8118, fax (408)354-1400
www.calcafe.com

◆ Ceremonies   ◆ Special Events
◆ Wedding Receptions   ◆ Meetings
◆ Business Functions   Accommodations

If you like pleasant surprises, take a look at the brand new California Cafe Los Gatos. It's one of those places where the simple exterior makes you think you're in for a tame experience, but what you get when you cross the threshold is a visual and gustatory joyride.

From the front door, a red and purple slate walkway angles back into the Main Dining Room. You immediately notice the purple wall on your right, separating you from the Lounge and Bar areas, as well as the impressive wine display. Everywhere your gaze falls, there are exciting colors and textures: round columns made from striped African Tiger wood; banquettes and booths covered in gold-and-purple fabric, woven in striped or geometric patterns; undulating railings made from blackened steel and copper; a black granite bar; and a purple ceiling with orange, red and green soffits. In the rear of the room, tables are set in a yellow ocher arcade, facing a brick-red wall of windows overlooking the Los Gatos hills. Now, before you start thinking that this rainbow of hues may verge on the garish, let us assure you that it doesn't: the colors have been muted to appear rich and vivid, but never too bright; the overall effect is not just inviting—it's scintillating.

For a very small get-together, you can take over one of the seating areas in the Main Dining Room. But most events are held in the adjacent Monte Bello and Mount Eden Rooms. Set side by side, they can be reserved individually or together. Both have textured plaster walls, a deep-green ceiling, and olive carpeting, sprinkled with purple and red accents. Sheer purple and orange curtains filter the afternoon sunlight, as it flows in through tall arched windows. A double-sided fireplace enclosed in a floor-to-ceiling orange "box" marks the centerpoint between the two rooms; the open space on either side of the fireplace can be closed off by bifold doors on one side, and bifold windows on the other.

The Monte Bello Room is dominated by a striking, 27-foot abstract mural in vibrant shades of green, terra cotta, yellow and red. Wedge-shaped sections of mirror are scattered over the rear wall like pieces of pie, reflecting a kaleidoscope view of the trees and adjacent patio through the front windows. The slightly smaller Mount Eden Room also overlooks the wood-and brick patio, which is shaded by oaks and bordered by large terra cotta pots, brimming with flowers.

Serve cocktails outdoors and dinner inside, or set tables in both areas for an indoor/outdoor dining experience

The California Cafe is in demand for weddings, receptions, meetings (some companies stay all day!) and lots of private parties. And it's not just the dazzling decor that wins people over. As luck would have it, what the Cafe offers your taste buds may be even more intriguing than what it offers your eyes. The chef, trained in Southern France, has developed his own version of California Cuisine: a fusion of fresh local ingredients with Country French, Pacific Rim and American Southwest influences. Oenophiles will also rejoice in the restaurant's outstanding wine list. A French restaurateur with distinguished culinary credentials dined here recently and was duly impressed saying, "You've created a beautiful marriage of what the best restaurants of the world have to offer." Ahhh, it's nice to know you don't have to travel the globe to enjoy world-class cuisine—it's right here in your own backyard.

CEREMONY CAPACITY: The Patio holds 40 seated, the Mount Eden Room 50 seated and the Monte Bello Room 70 seated guests.

EVENT/RECEPTION CAPACITY:

Space	*Seated*	*Standing*	*Space*	*Seated*	*Standing*
Entire Restaurant	300	400	Patio	30	40
Mount Eden Room	30	40	Monte Bello Room	50	60

MEETING CAPACITY: The Patio holds 30 seated, the Mount Eden Room 30 seated, and the Monte Bello Room 50 seated guests.

FEES & DEPOSITS: For daytime events, a $200 refundable deposit is required; for evening events, a $400 deposit. The total event cost is payable at event's conclusion. The are no room rental fees. A 2-course brunch runs $20/person, luncheon packages are $23 or $28/person, and dinner packages $30, $45, or $55/person. Alcohol, tax and an 18% service charge are additional. If you bring in your own wedding cake, a $3/person cake cutting fee will apply.

AVAILABILITY: Year-round, daily except Christmas Day, 8am–11pm.

SERVICES/AMENITIES:

Catering: provided, no BYO
Kitchen Facilities: n/a
Tables & Chairs: provided
Linens, Silver, etc.: provided
Restrooms: wheelchair accessible
Dance Floor: in Lounge
Bride's & Groom's Dressing Area: CBA
Meeting Equipment: CBA, extra charge
Other: baby grand piano, event coordination

Parking: ample on-site
Accommodations: no guest rooms
Telephone: pay phones
Outdoor Night Lighting: yes
Outdoor Cooking Facilities: no
Cleanup: provided
View: garden patio with heritage oak trees, Santa Cruz foothills and mountains

RESTRICTIONS:

Alcohol: provided, or corkage $10/bottle
Smoking: not allowed
Music: amplified OK w/volume limits

Wheelchair Access: yes
Insurance: not required
Other: decorations require approval; no rice confetti or glitter

Los Gatos Lodge

50 Los Gatos-Saratoga Road, Los Gatos
(408) 354-3300 ext. 100, fax (408) 354-9978

◆ Ceremonies   ◆ Special Events
◆ Wedding Receptions   ◆ Meetings
◆ Business Functions   ◆ Accommodations

Los Gatos Lodge is an oasis of serenity, just minutes away from the center of picturesque Los Gatos. Nestled on ten green acres in the Santa Cruz Mountains, it's an honest-to-goodness lodge with touches of classic '50s ranch-style architecture (cool stone walls and hefty wood beam ceilings in some areas), an attractive garden setting and a warm, unpretentious atmosphere. Its accessible location—close to the junction of two major highways and several airports—makes it very convenient both for business travelers and out-of-town wedding guests.

The two-story lodge offers 128 guest rooms and over 5,000 square feet of banquet facilities, including five meeting rooms of varying sizes (equipped with pull-down screens and white boards) for seminars, retreats, conferences, weddings, and receptions. There are a number of outdoor event spaces, including the Wedding Garden (designed exclusively for ceremonies), a large pool and patio (with ample space for a band or DJ), and emerald-green lawns (great for wedding photos, cocktail receptions, or just a quiet stroll).

The Wedding Garden is a private, covered arbor set slightly outside of the circle formed by the lodge's main buildings. It's available for rental whether you're holding your reception at the Lodge or elsewhere, and it nicely combines both natural and decorative elements. Guests are seated on white garden chairs, while the wedding party makes its entrance through a frame of cypress trees and along a green aisle runner, taking their places under a wooden arch festooned with silk ivy and tulle.

After the ceremony, the tree-shaded pool patio provides a pleasant outdoor option for your reception. You can dance poolside until 10pm (when outside music must end), then move your party to the indoor lounge, with its massive fireplace and full bar, and boogie 'til dawn. If you decide to hold your entire affair indoors, the large El Gato Room is a good choice. With its soft carpet and lights that resemble large hanging bowls, the space has a sophisticated feel. It can be outfitted with a dance floor, and there will still be plenty of room left for tables.

The guestrooms and additional facilities at Los Gatos Lodge offer many advantages. If you're planning a large wedding with a lot of out-of-town guests, you can reserve a block of rooms.

The Lodge provides brides with a room for use as a changing area close to the Wedding Garden so that you can make a dramatic entrance. Wedding and business guests alike will appreciate the spa, putting green, bocce ball court, and full-service restaurant. You might consider organizing a morning-after-the-wedding brunch in the restaurant dining room—hungry guests will be grateful to discover that the restaurant opens at 7 am on Saturday and 8am on Sunday.

However you decide to utilize this flexible facility, you'll find the management extremely accommodating. "We would be honored to help you plan the most important day of your life," says manager Connie Schneider. And she means it.

CEREMONY CAPACITY: The Wedding Garden seats 200 guests.

EVENT/RECEPTION CAPACITY: Wedding receptions take place in the El Gato Room, which holds 110 seated guests, and the outdoor patio and pool area, which holds 200 seated guests. For other events, the Vasona Room holds 30, the DeAnza Room 80 and the Saratoga Room 40 seated guests.

MEETING CAPACITY:

Room	Classroom-style	Theater-style	Room	Classroom-style	Theater-style
Vasona Room	15	30	Saratoga Room	18	48
DeAnza Room	40	100	El Gato Room	60	150

FEES & DEPOSITS: For social events, deposits range $250–750 depending on the space reserved, due within 7 days of making reservations. The event balance is due 72 hours prior to the event. Room rental fees run $150–550, and meals run $19–28/person; tax, alcohol and an 18% service charge are additional. A $30–75 cake-cutting fee applies depending on number of guests.

For business functions, a deposit may be required. The event balance is due at the end of the function. Meeting rooms run $125–350 and meals run $18–26/person; tax, alcohol and 18% service charge are additional.

AVAILABILITY: Indoor spaces are available year-round, daily, including holidays, 7am–midnight. The Wedding Garden and patio area are available May 1–October 15 10am–10pm.

SERVICES/AMENITIES:

Catering: provided, no BYO
Kitchen Facilities: n/a
Tables & Chairs: provided
Linens, Silver, etc.: provided
Restrooms: wheelchair accessible
Dance Floor: CBA, $200 extra charge
Bride's Dressing Area: yes
Meeting Equipment: CBA, extra charge

Parking: ample on-site
Accommodations: 128 guest rooms
Telephone: pay phones
Outdoor Night Lighting: yes
Outdoor Cooking Facilities: no
Cleanup: provided
View: garden courtyard

RESTRICTIONS:

Alcohol: provided, no BYO
Smoking: outside only
Music: amplified OK outdoors until 10pm

Wheelchair Access: yes
Insurance: not required
Other: no confetti, rice or birdseed; no staples, tacks or tape

Maison du Lac & Gardens
and Terrace Hill House & Cottage Garden

Private Gardens

Address withheld to ensure privacy. Los Gatos Mountains
(408) 353-2083, (408) 353-3189, fax (408) 353-2083

◆ Ceremonies	◆ Special Events
◆ Wedding Receptions	Meetings
◆ Business Functions	Accommodations

Way up in the Santa Cruz Mountains, but just minutes from Highway 17, you'll find a very attractive garden that comes with an equally appealing duo of caterers who handle each event: Sandra and Bev. They offer extraordinarily personalized, creative wedding receptions at a site that would "wow" even the most jaded bride-to-be.

A narrow gravel road flanked by meadows and oaks leads to a wide opening where an idyllic setting, complete with large duck ponds ringed by rocks, lawn and multi-colored blossoms, unfolds before your eyes. The gardens are well tended but informal: large slabs of rock, encircled by flowers and trees, are "benches" tucked discreetly into the landscape. Most ceremonies take place under towering redwoods which form a natural and serene outdoor cathedral—perfect for taking vows. And as a backdrop to this pastoral setting, a rambling house with stone fireplace resides at the far end of the largest pond.

You can also rent Terrace Hill House, an English, cottage-style garden which is situated not too far away. The garden, filled with a profusion of multicolored flowers, is an intimate, charming oasis suitable for smaller functions. It has a wonderful feel, with stone walls, and a flagstone patio and lawn area with fantastic views of the Santa Cruz Mountains. A rose arbor makes a great spot for a ceremony. Guests seated facing the arbor can see the distant hills.

No matter which site you choose, Sandra and Bev serve their delectable edibles from tables laden with flowers and colorful glass and dinnerware. Everything is a visual delight. Note that much of what you see or eat comes directly from the owners' multilevel vegetable and flower terraces. Although a bit off the beaten path, we think the Maison du Lac and Terrace Hill House are worth a visit if you're looking for a private, "backyard" wedding in a truly unique and intimate place.

CEREMONY CAPACITY: Maison du Lac's redwood cathedral area, and the pond's edge can each hold 300 guests. Terrace Hill House can accommodate up to 75 seated guests outdoors.

EVENT/RECEPTION CAPACITY: Maison du Lac's outdoor areas hold up to 120–300 seated guests. Terrace Hill holds up to 75 guests outdoors. Non-wedding events take place at Terrace Hill House only.

FEES & DEPOSITS: Maison du Lac: a $400 non-refundable deposit is required to hold your date. The rental fee is $3,800. The buffet wedding package starts at $65/person and includes food, flowers, service, nonalcoholic beverages and all table setup and cleanup. Special menus can be arranged. Half of the estimated total is payable 1 month prior to the event; the balance is due 1 week in advance.

Terrace Hill House: a $400 non-refundable deposit is required. The rental fee is $1,300. The food and beverage package is the same as above.

AVAILABILITY: May–October 15th, daily, 10am–sunset.

SERVICES/AMENITIES:

Catering: provided, no BYO
Kitchen Facilities: n/a
Tables & Chairs: provided
Linens, Silver, etc.: provided
Restrooms: wheelchair accessible
Dance Floor: outdoor patio & lawns or portable CBA
Bride's Dressing Area: yes
Other: event coordination

Parking: ample on-site
Accommodations: no guest rooms
Telephone: emergency only
Outdoor Night Lighting: no
Outdoor Cooking Facilities: BBQs
Cleanup: provided
Meeting Equipment: n/a
View: Santa Cruz Mountains

RESTRICTIONS:

Alcohol: BYO or CBA
Smoking: designated areas only
Music: amplified limited

Wheelchair Access: limited
Insurance: not required

Mirassou Champagne Cellars

Historic Winery

300 College Avenue, Los Gatos
(408) 395-3790, fax (408) 395-5830
www.mirassou.com

◆ Ceremonies ◆ Special Events
◆ Wedding Receptions ◆ Meetings
◆ Business Functions ☐ Accommodations

This is one lovely spot. Mirassou Champagne Cellars is housed on the grounds of the Sacred Heart Novitiate, an old Jesuit seminary with stone walls, a large winery, huge shade trees and lots of privacy. The road leading up to this site is through a pleasant residential neighborhood, but once you go through the Novitiate's stone and wrought-iron gates, you leave the world behind.

It was on top of this knoll that Jesuits began missionary work in California in the late 1860s. The first seminary was built here in 1888, giving way to a more permanent winery building in 1893. The latter is a fine example of a 19th-century gravity-flow winery, with the top floor built for receiving and crushing harvested grapes. The Jesuits stopped making Novitiate wines in 1985 and have leased the winery to Mirassou. The original winery building still stands, forming the core of the present-day Champagne Cellars.

Both indoor and outdoor spaces are available for weddings, special events and business functions. Outdoors there's a sunny, quiet courtyard patio, with an ivy-planted bank on one side and trees on the other. On either side of the terrace, recessed into the bank, are two stepped, wooden platforms, perfect for musicians or ceremonies.

Indoors, the Tasting Room and Blanc de Noirs room hold small parties and receptions. However, it's the entry, La Cave, that's unique. It actually resembles a cave, with a vaulted, stone ceiling and champagne bottles stacked on end for riddling along one wall. Photos depicting the history of the Novitiate Winery are on the other side of La Cave. It's dimly lit, cool and very old world. A gentle slope with a wide runner of red carpet leads the bride and groom to the doorway arch, under which they can take their vows. You couldn't ask for a more tranquil and beautiful environment for any kind of event.

CEREMONY CAPACITY: The Patio holds 150 seated; La Cave 75 seated guests.

EVENT/RECEPTION CAPACITY: The Tasting Room can be combined with the Terrace for evening receptions and special events.

Space	*Seated*	*Standing*	*Space*	*Seated*	*Standing*
Patio	150	200	Tasting Room	50	75
Blanc de Noirs Room	120	150			

MEETING CAPACITY:

Space	Conf-style	Theater-style	Space	Conf-style	Theater-style
Blanc de Noirs Room	30	80	Tasting Room	20	50

FEES & DEPOSITS: For weddings, 50% of the estimated facility fee is payable as a non-refundable deposit to hold your date. The balance and a refundable $300 security deposit are payable 1 month prior to the event. Use fees (not including meals) run $10/person (with a $600 minimum) for a 2-hour ceremony/champagne reception, or $20/person (with a $900 minimum) for a 5-hour function that includes ceremony, reception, wine and champagne. The final guest count is due 48 hours prior to the event. A rehearsal and 2 meetings with the hospitality coordinator are included in the facility use fee and can be scheduled 9am–5pm, weekdays only.

For meetings, the rental fee is $12/person with a $180 minimum; for other special events, the fee is $10/person with a $180 minimum. Meetings include 8am–5pm use, tour and tasting (optional), continental breakfast, coffee service and wine with lunch.

AVAILABILITY: Year-round, daily in 4-hour blocks. Business meetings, 9am–5pm; special events, indoors after 5pm and outdoors 9am–9:30pm. Tours and tastings can be arranged; wines can be paired with all meals. Weddings on weekends, 9am–9:30pm. For a ceremony and/or champagne reception, 2 hours are allowed; for receptions with seated meals, 5 hours.

SERVICES/AMENITIES:

Catering: preferred list
Kitchen Facilities: no
Tables & Chairs: provided up to 200 guests
Linens, Silver, etc.: through caterer
Restrooms: wheelchair accessible
Dance Floor: outdoor patio or tasting room
Bride's Dressing Area: yes
Meeting Equipment: CBA

Parking: 2 lots
Accommodations: no guest rooms
Telephone: pay phone
Outdoor Night Lighting: yes
Outdoor Cooking Facilities: no
Cleanup: caterer
View: Los Gatos hills
Other: event coordination; custom wine labels for weddings or corporate events

RESTRICTIONS:

Alcohol: WC provided by Mirassou
Smoking: outside only
Music: amplified OK

Wheelchair Access: yes
Insurance: certificate required
Other: no rice, birdseed or confetti; no hard alcohol or beer

---

The professionals in the back of the book are the best in the business! How do we know? Read page 681.

Opera House

140 West Main Street, Los Gatos
(408) 354-1218, fax (408) 354-2759

www.operahousebanquets.com

Landmark Building

◆ Ceremonies   ◆ Special Events
◆ Wedding Receptions   ◆ Meetings
◆ Business Functions   Accommodations

For large weddings, The Opera House is now the only game in town. Occupying a 1904 landmark brick building with crisp, white trim, its 8,000 square feet can seat up to 500 guests!

Enter the downstairs foyer and wind your way up the formal, sweeping staircase to the main event floor. Award-winning Bradbury & Bradbury wallpaper in blues, creams and golds adorns the stairwell. Walls and ceilings are covered with original pressed tin in fifteen different Victorian motifs, and antique light fixtures abound. The Grand Ballroom has a 24-foot ceiling, with a rectangular skylight in the center that brings in natural light. From the Balcony up above, you can toss your bouquet or watch the dancing below.

The lower portion of the room, called the Mezzanine, has a wall of windows facing north. Soft pastels, creams and taupes predominate, and a large mural on an upper wall facing the Ballroom depicts the Opera House's original theater curtain.

Because of the way this facility is configured, groups of 100 or fewer won't feel dwarfed in this space. Additional enhancements are a movable dance floor and a beautiful turn-of-the-century-style mahogany bar. And if you haven't been able to whittle down your invitation list, we think the Opera House is a must-see.

CEREMONY CAPACITY: The Mezzanine holds 160 seated; the main room up to 350 seated.

EVENT/RECEPTION CAPACITY:

Space	*Seated*	*Standing*	*Space*	*Seated*	*Standing*
Entire Facility	450	750	Balcony	90	150
Mezzanine	40	150	Main Event Floor	320	450

MEETING CAPACITY: The facility holds 39–300 seated conference-style or theater-style.

FEES & DEPOSITS: For weddings, a non-refundable $1,000 deposit is required within 1 week of confirming reservations. A second deposit, the amount dependent on size and type of event, is due 120 days prior to the event. The balance for the entire event, including a $500 refundable damage deposit, is due 1 week prior to your function. An optional wedding package for 250 guests or more includes food service, a 5-hour hosted bar with champagne toast, wedding cake, wedding coordinator and valet parking. Depending on the day of week, packages start at $58/person including tax and service charge. Customized wedding receptions are also available.

For meetings and business functions, the rental fee starts at $1,000. Food and beverage service is provided; rates will vary depending on guest count and services desired.

AVAILABILITY: Year-round. Mon–Fri 7am–1am; Sat 9am–1am, and Sunday any time in a 5-hour block. All-day functions can be negotiated.

SERVICES/AMENITIES:
Catering: provided or select from preferred list
Kitchen Facilities: prep only
Tables & Chairs: provided for 350 guests
Linens, Silver, etc.: provided
Restrooms: wheelchair accessible
Dance Floor: yes
Bride's Dressing Area: yes
Meeting Equipment: CBA

Parking: valet and attendant parking
Accommodations: no guest rooms
Telephone: pay phone
Outdoor Night Lighting: access only
Outdoor Cooking Facilities: no
Cleanup: provided
View: Santa Cruz Mtns. & Old Town Los Gatos
Other: event coordination

RESTRICTIONS:
Alcohol: provided, no BYO
Smoking: allowed
Music: amplified OK

Wheelchair Access: yes, elevator
Insurance: not required
Other: decorations restricted

*This is important! Tell facilities you're reading **Here Comes The Guide** and ask if our information is still current.*

475

The Toll House Hotel

Boutique Hotel

140 South Santa Cruz Avenue, Los Gatos
(408) 395-7070, fax (408) 395-5906

◆ Ceremonies ◆ Special Events
◆ Wedding Receptions ◆ Meetings
◆ Business Functions ◆ Accommodations

Nestled at the base of the Santa Cruz Mountains, the Toll House Hotel in Los Gatos offers a friendly, unpretentious atmosphere and quaint charm. Its gray-shingled walls, cheerful balconies and mansard-roofed clock tower give it an old-fashioned feel. And those planning a special event appreciate its convenient location—it's within easy walking distance of shops and restaurants, and Santa Cruz and Monterey Bay are a short drive away via nearby Highway 17.

The hotel has both indoor and outdoor event spaces. Inside, the aptly named Board Room is tailor-made for corporate functions. The Cabernet and Chardonnay rooms are used for weddings and receptions, and have plenty of room for dancing. Pre-reception events are held in the adjacent Lower Lobby, whose overstuffed green damask chairs and loveseats tempt you to relax and contemplate the classical paintings hung on the walls. There's also a meeting room off the Clocktower Bar & Grill. This room is popular for business-oriented events, and meetings sometimes continue informally in the bar itself.

In the center of the Toll House Hotel, the sunny courtyard is a favorite place for weddings and receptions. Potted plants trail from the hotel balconies that rise above the patio. A splashing lion-head fountain and small trees add refreshing coolness. On the second floor, a small deck overlooks the courtyard. This is also a nice spot for weddings and related events, and rehearsal dinners are frequently held here. The five adjoining rooms that open onto this deck are often rented by the wedding party or close friends. No need for a designated driver when the party is right outside your room!

The hotel's relaxed atmosphere makes it a favorite spot for children's parties as well. Events popular with the cake-and-ice-cream crowd are bar- and bat-mitzvahs, some with Hawaiian luau or outer space themes. The Toll House is the kind of place that's posh enough to make adults feel really pampered, but casual enough to make children feel at home, too.

CEREMONY CAPACITY: The Courtyard holds 250 seated; the Ballroom 140 seated.

EVENT/RECEPTION CAPACITY: The Courtyard accommodates 200 seated, the Ballroom 130 seated with dance floor, up to 170 without. The Dining Room, only available prior to 5pm, holds up to 120 seated guests.

MEETING CAPACITY:

Space	Theater-style	Conf-style	Space	Theater-style	Conf-style
Board Room	40	24	Chardonnay	70	—
Cabernet	100	—	Ballroom	180	—
Zinfandel	40	24	Burgundy	50	30

FEES & DEPOSITS: A $750 non-refundable deposit is required to reserve your date; the balance is payable 1 week prior to the event. A $450 ceremony fee covers setup and breakdown. With fewer than 100 guests, a $250 rental fee for the Dining Room, Courtyard or Ballroom may apply. For meetings and business functions, the room rental fee ranges from $150–950 depending on guest count and catering costs.

Meal prices run $25–35/person, alcohol $10–12/person. Tax and an 18% service charge are additional. A $75/bartender charge for each 4-hour block may apply.

AVAILABILITY: Year-round, daily, 7am–midnight.

SERVICES/AMENITIES:

Catering: provided, no BYO
Kitchen Facilities: n/a
Tables & Chairs: provided
Linens, Silver, etc.: provided
Restrooms: wheelchair accessible
Dance Floor: in Courtyard & Ballroom
Bride's Dressing Area: no
Meeting Equipment: CBA

Parking: garage, complimentary
Accommodations: 97 guest rooms
Telephone: pay phones
Outdoor Night Lighting: yes
Outdoor Cooking Facilities: CBA
Cleanup: provided
View: Santa Cruz Mtns. & Old Town Los Gatos
Other: event & wedding coordination

RESTRICTIONS:

Alcohol: provided, no BYO
Smoking: designated areas
Music: amplified OK w/volume limits

Wheelchair Access: yes
Insurance: not required
Other: no confetti or glitter

The professionals in the back of the book are the best in the business! How do we know? Read page 681.

Village Lane

Restaurant

320 Village Lane, Los Gatos
(408) 354-1040, fax (408) 354-1041

www.villagelane.com

◆ Ceremonies ◆ Special Events
◆ Wedding Receptions ◆ Meetings
◆ Business Functions Accommodations

Village Lane is a little bit of southern France, smack dab in the middle of Los Gatos. Formerly known as the Village House & Garden, it has been completely remodeled into a sparkling Mediterranean Villa. The new Village Lane is its own little world—light, airy and serene.

You'll notice the difference as soon as you enter the courtyard. The former white picket fence has been enlarged into a wall, lined with terra cotta planters and topped by warm, copper gas lamps. The wall forms an effective buffer between the outside world and the utter tranquility inside. You hear birds, soft music (of your own choosing) and the soothing sound of the courtyard fountains. It feels like you're in a leisurely Provençal cafe (albeit a very upscale one), with washed wooden shutters and sun-shading umbrellas.

Inside the restaurant (which seems more like a house), the entry hall is separated from the two main rooms by a half-wall, with shutters on the upper half that open up to further increase the feeling of space. The main rooms reveal a comforting mix of contemporary and old-fashioned elements: textured stucco walls, fireplaces (one with a copper hood, echoing the copper light fixtures and the gleaming copper gutters outside), distressed wood ceilings, and soft cloth-covered banquettes along the walls. Skylights above, plus two sets of French doors opening onto the courtyard, maximize window space and suffuse the whole interior with natural light.

The folks at Village Lane have designed a courtyard that is more cozy and private than many interior sites, and interior rooms that are lighter and airier than many outdoor sites. This creates quite a few options for orchestrating your event: You could have the wedding ceremony in the sunlit courtyard, then move inside for hors d'oeuvres in one room and dinner and dancing in the other. Or you could just as easily reverse the order, with equally delightful effect.

And the best thing is that all these possibilities are open to you, because when you reserve Village Lane, the whole place is yours, indoors and out, for the duration. No other parties are allowed to impinge on your day—or distract the attention of Village Lane staff from you and your guests.

If a wedding where you can take time to savor your special day like a fine French wine is what you have in mind, then Village Lane could be the perfect place for you.

CEREMONY CAPACITY: The Courtyard holds 75 seated, restaurant indoors, 120 seated.

EVENT/RECEPTION & MEETING CAPACITY: The entire restaurant, including the Courtyard, holds 120 guests, seated or standing.

FEES & DEPOSITS: For special events, a non-refundable $1,000 rental deposit is required when confirming reservations. 50% of the anticipated food and beverage total is due 45 days prior to the event, the balance is payable 5 working days prior to event. Any remaining balance is due at the event's conclusion. All menus are customized; luncheons run $20–35/person, dinners $35–75/person; alcohol, tax and a 17% service charge are additional.

The rental fee for the entire restaurant is $1,000, and may be waived depending on food and beverage minimums.

AVAILABILITY: Year-round, daily until 5pm, Sundays 10am–11pm.

SERVICES/AMENITIES:

Catering: provided, no BYO
Kitchen Facilities: n/a
Tables & Chairs: provided
Linens, Silver, etc.: provided
Restrooms: wheelchair accessible
Dance Floor: indoors
Bride's & Groom's Dressing Area: yes
Meeting Equipment: BYO or CBA

Parking: nearby parking lot
Accommodations: no guest rooms
Telephone: pay phone
Outdoor Night Lighting: yes
Outdoor Cooking Facilities: CBA
Cleanup: provided
View: partial view of Santa Cruz Mountains
Other: event coordination

RESTRICTIONS:

Alcohol: BW provided, or BYO corkage $15/bottle
Smoking: not allowed
Music: amplified OK indoors; outdoors w/volume limits

Wheelchair Access: yes
Insurance: not required

---

*This is important! Tell facilities you're reading **Here Comes The Guide** and ask if our information is still current.*

Bella Mia Restaurant

58 South First Street, San Jose
(408) 280-5108, fax (408) 280-5624
www.bellamia.com

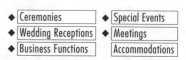

Restaurant

◆ Ceremonies   ◆ Special Events
◆ Wedding Receptions   ◆ Meetings
◆ Business Functions   Accommodations

It's hard to imagine a more congenial site for a wedding than the Bella Mia Restaurant in San Jose. Owners Bill and Julie Carlson founded the Bella Mia in Saratoga in 1985, and it was a hit with the locals from the moment it opened its doors. In 1993 the Bella Mia moved to its present location—and a lot of their old customers followed.

Downstairs is a restaurant straight out of the Victorian era, with brass light fixtures, green banquettes, wooden wainscoting, a massive Victorian bar, and dark blue carpet with green diamond patterns. And that's just the part the general public sees. The Bella Mia's most beautiful rooms are upstairs, where private events are held: two Fireside Club Rooms, the Garden Room, and the Skylight Grand Ballroom.

The Fireside Club Rooms are in the style of a 19th-century gentleman's club. Roaring fireplaces, high ceilings, mahogany wainscoting and large windows overlooking a tree-lined street make the Club Rooms a favorite place for business meetings. These rooms could be used for theme parties, too. If you'd like to pretend to be Sherlock Holmes for a night, here's a perfect setting to stage a murder mystery party,

Next door, the Garden Room is just the opposite: light, airy and spacious—almost as if you were dining outdoors on a perfect summer day. Technically, the Garden Room isn't a room at all. It's the upstairs foyer, which has been ingeniously converted into a dining/reception space. A lovely, handpainted mural of a Tuscany hillside adds to the al fresco feeling.

Then there's the Skylight Grand Ballroom. A soaring space featuring chandeliers, arched panels with pastoral murals and, yes, a gorgeous skylight. If you need a stage for your band or DJ, a portable one is available that can expand or contract to accommodate whatever size group or equipment is necessary for your event. At the far end of the room, you can exit onto a small balcony area overlooking the garden patio.

The private rooms can be used individually, or in combination. For instance, have your wedding ceremony in the Garden Room, hors d'oeuvres in the Club Rooms, and dinner and dancing in the Skylight Grand Ballroom.

But the Bella Mia's greatest calling card is the people who run it. Owners Bill and Julie Carlson are, quite simply, two of the nicest people around, and their staff takes its cue from them. The

Carlsons treat the staff like family, and the staff, from top to bottom, treats the customers the same way. Bill Carlson's favorite saying is "There are no strangers here, only friends you haven't met." The folks at Bella Mia take that saying to heart, and go to great lengths to make all their guests comfortable. They're an experienced group, and will do whatever it takes to make your event a happy memory for you.

CEREMONY CAPACITY: Indoors, the restaurant seats 120 guests; outdoors it seats 80 with extra room for standing guests.

EVENT/RECEPTION & MEETING CAPACITY:

Area	Seated	Area	Seated	Area	Seated
Grand Ballroom	120	Balcony	30	Small Clubroom	24
Large Clubroom	50	Garden Room	22		

FEES & DEPOSITS: For weddings, a $500 refundable deposit is payable when you make your reservations. The Ballroom's Saturday evening rental fee is $1,000. For wedding ceremonies, there is a $450 setup charge for use of the Garden Patio. Wedding luncheons and dinners start at $30/person, depending on the menu; tax, a 17% service charge and alcohol are additional. Full payment is due 2 weeks prior to the event.

For other special events and business functions, meals run $26–50, depending on the menu selection. A $100 deposit is required, and the event balance is payable at the event's conclusion.

AVAILABILITY: Year-round, daily, any time, closed major holidays. Weddings usually occur 10am–4pm or 6pm–11:30pm, but different times can be arranged.

SERVICES/AMENITIES:

Catering: provided, no BYO
Kitchen Facilities: n/a
Tables & Chairs: provided
Linens, Silver, etc.: provided
Restrooms: wheelchair accessible
Dance Floor: provided, extra fee
Bride's & Groom's Dressing Area: CBA
Meeting Equipment: BYO or CBA, extra fee

Parking: adjacent city parking lots or CBA
Accommodations: no guest rooms
Telephone: pay phone
Outdoor Night Lighting: yes
Outdoor Cooking Facilities: no
Cleanup: provided
View: garden patio from balcony
Other: wedding cakes

RESTRICTIONS:

Alcohol: provided, no BYO
Smoking: balcony only
Music: amplified OK w/volume limits

Wheelchair Access: yes
Insurance: not required
Other: decorations need approval; no glitter or confetti

Briar Rose Bed & Breakfast Inn

Bed & Breakfast

897 East Jackson Street, San Jose
(408) 279-5999, fax (408) 279-4534

www.briar-rose.com
worthy@briar-rose.com

◆ Ceremonies ◆ Special Events
◆ Wedding Receptions ◆ Meetings
◆ Business Functions ◆ Accommodations

Important message to prospective brides and grooms: If you ever, as a child, imagined your future mate as a courtly Victorian gentleman or lady; if you pictured your wedding unfolding under a flowering bower of pale-pink roses; if you dreamt of a wedding night spent in a tidy cottage dripping with fragrant trumpet vines—or even if you're just looking for a garden wedding site with unusual charm—then you must not, under any circumstances, miss the Briar Rose Inn. Carefully restored and run as a Victorian B&B, this 123-year-old home is a unique setting for weddings and special events, such as anniversary celebrations, afternoon teas, holiday parties and small corporate retreats.

In 1875, prominent businessman Cornelius Harrison built the Briar Rose as his home in the center of 100 acres of walnut orchards. Today, the Inn is surrounded by small houses in a corner of a quiet residential neighborhood, just a few blocks away from San Jose's Japantown. It's encircled on all sides by lawns and gardens, heady with floral scent and riotous with color from roses, impatiens, poppies, columbine, foxglove, star jasmine, and hydrangeas—to name just a few.

The gardens provide several options for ceremony sites. The front lawn, separated from the sidewalk by an ornate white iron fence and a broad border of rose bushes, offers a white period gazebo in the shade of a stately elm tree. The western end of the back garden holds a heart-shaped arbor covered in climbing roses; add some trailing ivy and additional flowers, and this spot is almost impossible to beat for romantic atmosphere. Our favorite site, however, is the west-side garden. Its rectangular lawn is bordered by gorgeous flowers and a white picket fence. Say your vows in front of a small, intricately detailed arch cut into the fence, and flanked by shy, stone Cupids, while your guests sit in neat rows on the green grass. If you like, sprinkle the lawn with rose petals, and this area takes on the feeling of a flower-strewn open-air chapel.

Wedding receptions and other large events take place in the rear garden, where there is space to seat up to 150 people with room left for dancing on the bougainvillea-covered brick patio. (Very large weddings can expand into the front and side yards for more seating; very small weddings or other parties can take place inside the Inn, as long as the six guestrooms are also booked for the event.) Hors d'oeuvres are served outside on the lawn, while a dinner buffet is set up in the breakfast room just inside; cake cutting is usually done on the back veranda, which also provides a great spot for the bride to toss her bouquet.

For the past three years, the Briar Rose has been owned and run by the Worthy family, who staff all events themselves. This includes doing everything from decorating the ceremony and reception areas to catering the meal (from hors d'oeuvres to dessert), tending the bar, and cleaning up afterwards—not to mention preparing and serving a full country breakfast for guests the next morning. Wedding packages include all of these services and more: Battenburg lace tablecloths, customized menus, and—yes, it's what you've dreamt of—use of the two-story Garden Cottage as both a bride's changing room, and a wedding night getaway.

Although the Worthys stop short of finding your wedding vestments for you, their Inn and packages provide almost everything you need. And when it comes to Victorian charm and period details, the Briar Rose is unmatched.

CEREMONY CAPACITY: The garden holds up to 150 seated guests.

EVENT/RECEPTION CAPACITY: The garden holds up to 150 seated or 200 standing guests.

MEETING CAPACITY: The Inn's parlors each hold 15 seated; the garden holds up to 100 seated guests, theater-style.

FEES & DEPOSITS: For weddings, a $500 non-refundable deposit is required to secure your date. The anticipated event balance is payable 2 weeks prior to the event. The facility use fee is $2,000, which covers use of the site, tables, chairs, linens, flowers, setup, cleanup, and use of the Inn's cottage during the event, and an overnight stay for the bride and groom. Catering is provided; hors d'oeuvres start at $15/person, brunch receptions at $25.50/person, and dinners at $22.50/person. Tax and a 15% service charge are additional. There is no corkage or cake-cutting fee.

For other social or business-related events, the facility use fee is $50/hour. Food service is customized, and prices will vary depending on the menu and services selected; call for more information. Higher rates may apply for holiday parties.

AVAILABILITY: Year-round, daily until 9pm if outdoors, or until 11pm if indoors.

SERVICES/AMENITIES:

Catering: provided, no BYO
Kitchen Facilities: n/a
Tables & Chairs: provided
Linens, Silver, etc.: provided
Restrooms: not wheelchair accessible
Dance Floor: covered brick patio
Bride's Dressing Area: guest room
Meeting Equipment: CBA, extra charge

Parking: on street
Accommodations: 6 guest rooms
Telephone: emergency use only
Outdoor Night Lighting: limited
Outdoor Cooking Facilities: no
Cleanup: provided
View: landscaped garden
Other: floral arrangements

RESTRICTIONS:

Alcohol: BYO, WB only
Smoking: outside only
Music: no bands; DJs only w/volume limits

Wheelchair Access: limited, but CBA
Insurance: extra liability required
Other: no rice, birdseed or confetti

Capital Club Athletics

196 North Third Street, San Jose
(408) 292-1281, fax (408) 292-7260

leightonallen@ourclub.com

◆ Ceremonies   ◆ Special Events
◆ Wedding Receptions   ◆ Meetings
◆ Business Functions   Accommodations

Located in the heart of historic downtown San Jose, this 1924 landmark building is no ordinary athletic club. As you walk up the broad granite steps, past the enormous urns and soaring columns, you can't help but be impressed by the stately elegance of its Neoclassic design.

That impression carries through to the interior spaces as well. The Corinthian Room is the Club's main ballroom, and it has all the elements of a *true* ballroom. You enter through a foyer, regally outfitted with a crystal chandelier and a hand-painted wood-beam ceiling. Once inside the Corinthian Room, you're struck by its grand proportions and majestic features. The 60-foot ceiling has massive wood beams, and is inset with alternating panes of blue glass and intricately detailed panels of gold leaf grillwork. Eight extraordinary wrought-iron-and-glass lanterns hang from the ceiling like giant luminous earrings, while five 30-foot palm trees embedded with twinkle lights add sparkle. At one end of the room is a stage with a carved stone proscenium arch framing red velvet curtains; at the other end is a carved granite balcony, where just-married couples often dance their first dance. Banquettes along the sides of the room make cozy seating areas, and there's a raised section that's ideal for the head table. The hardwood dance floor is permanently ensconced in front of the stage.

Smaller functions take place in the Silver, Gold and Bronze Rooms. All have crystal chandeliers, cream walls, red carpeting and ceilings baffled for sound. You can reserve these rooms individually, or combine them to make one long room—the perfect space for a wedding ceremony. And all three rooms have access to the Bar/Lounge, a more casual space with faux-candle chandeliers, and a mix of antiques and contemporary furnishings. The Olympia Room, a large private room with white walls and pastel detailing, is available for small meetings and as a bride's dressing area. Note that when you have your wedding and reception at the Club, you have exclusive use of all the rooms.

Given its refined event spaces, it's easy to forget that the Capital Club also has full athletic facilities. Corporations can use the pool, gym, cardio and yoga rooms for a variety of team-building exercises and games. Whether you're getting married or planning a company meeting or party, the Club's staff will help you orchestrate it, and, if you like, the executive chef will design a special menu for you. And if you're inviting out-of-town guests, they'll appreciate being close to many of San Jose's best hotels and cultural activities.

CEREMONY CAPACITY: The Gold, Silver and Bronze Rooms, combined, hold up to 150 seated guests; the Olympia Room holds up to 80 seated guests, and the Corinthian Room up to 300 seated.

EVENT/RECEPTION CAPACITY:

Room	Standing	Seated	Room	Standing	Seated
Columns Lounge	250	100	Corinthian Room	400	100–300
Olympia Room	100	80	Gold, Silver, Bronze Rms	200	150

MEETING CAPACITY:

Room	Conf-style	Theater-style	Room	Conf-style	Theater-style
Corinthian Room	—	350	Olympia Room	32	60
Gold, Silver, Bronze	26 ea.	30 ea.	Gold, Silver, Bronze (combined)		200

FEES & DEPOSITS: For special events and weddings, a $1,000 non-refundable deposit secures your date and is due when reservations are made. For 5 hours' use, the rental fee for the Corinthian Room is $1,000, for the Olympia Room, $200, and for the Gold, Silver and Bronze Rooms, $150 each. There is a $500 ceremony setup charge. In-house catering is provided; meals run $23.50–34/person; alcohol, tax and an 18% service charge are additional. Full payment is due 3 days prior to your event. Note that there is a $10,500 minimum for functions held on Saturday evenings in the Corinthian Room.

For business functions, weekday morning and afternoon rental rates run $150–500 depending on the room(s) selected. Food prices will vary depending on the type of function, guest count and event duration.

AVAILABILITY: Year-round, daily, 6am–1am. Weddings are in 5-hour blocks; extra hours may be available for an additional $100/half hour charge.

SERVICES/AMENITIES:

Catering: provided, no BYO
Kitchen Facilities: n/a
Tables & Chairs: provided
Linens, Silver, etc.: provided
Restrooms: wheelchair accessible
Dance Floor: yes
Bride's Dressing Area: CBA
Meeting Equipment: AV, other CBA, extra fee
Other: event coordination, poolside parties

Parking: street or nearby garage, free on weekends & weekdays after 6pm
Accommodations: no guest rooms
Telephone: pay phone
Outdoor Night Lighting: yes
Outdoor Cooking Facilities: BBQ
Cleanup: provided
View: no

RESTRICTIONS:

Alcohol: provided
Smoking: outside only
Music: amplified OK indoors

Wheelchair Access: yes
Insurance: not required
Other: no helium balloons in Corinthian Room; no confetti, birdseed or rice indoors

The Hayes Mansion
and Conference Center

200 Edenvale Avenue, San Jose
(408) 226-3200, fax (408) 362-2388

www.hayesconferencecenter.com
dmarks@ntwkcco.com

Historic Mansion & Grounds

- ◆ Ceremonies
- ◆ Wedding Receptions
- ◆ Business Functions
- ◆ Special Events
- ◆ Meetings
- ◆ Accommodations

Completed in 1905, the Hayes Mansion is one of the South Bay's most distinctive and historic structures. Mary Hayes Chynoweth built the 65-room Mediterranean Revival-style mansion to replace an earlier Victorian home destroyed in a fire. Although she died before the mansion was finished, her two sons—politicians and publishers of the *San Jose Mercury* and the *San Jose Herald*_and their families lived in the house for four decades. Known as Edenvale Estate, it was a center of social and political activity for the Santa Clara Valley until 1952, when it was sold to the city of San Jose.

Sadly, the mansion stood empty for many years. No one was sure what to do with it until 1991, when the Network Conference Company proposed that it be turned into a high-tech meeting facility. The subsequent $12-million renovation transformed the Hayes Mansion into a luxurious special events site while keeping its turn-of-the-century character. A wide, circular drive leads to the front entrance, a four-story tower topped by a red-tile roof. Wedding ceremonies and receptions can be held on the lush lawns surrounding the house, or on a separate, circular lawn in the center of the drive. Bordered by beds of marigolds and dotted with towering palm trees, the emerald-green lawns create an inviting, manicured setting. With the stately mansion in the background, a garden party is very appropriate here.

Indoor celebrations are equally delightful. The rooms adjoining the main lobby, the Folsom Library, the Everis Anson Parlor and the Jay Orley Parlor, are consummate examples of early 1900s artistry. The library's coffered, mahogany ceiling and glass-fronted bookcases create just the right cozy-yet-formal ambiance for post-ceremony champagne toasts. The two parlors across the hall feature a mahogany-mantled fireplace, brass and glass Victorian chandeliers, mahogany molding and wainscotting and a bay windowed alcove. If you have a small reception, host a seated dinner in one of the parlors and reserve the other for music and dancing. This combination is just one of the options you'll have at the Hayes Mansion; should you choose another, you'll find that every room has been meticulously restored and furnished with fine, period details. If you're a lover of Victorian style, you'll be thoroughly entranced by this new venue for special events, corporate functions and weddings.

CEREMONY CAPACITY: The San Jose Room and Guadalupe Room each seat 80 guests; the Edenvale Room holds 300 seated and the East Lawn up to 1,000 seated or standing.

EVENT/RECEPTION CAPACITY:

Space	Seated	Standing	Space	Seated	Standing
Edenvale Room	230	395	Silver Creek Dining Room	150	208
Willow Glen Room	48	49	Jay Orley Parlor, Everis Anson		
Silver Creek Patio	100	150	Parlor & Folsom Library *(combined)*	72	100
Orlo's Restaurant	80	100	Eagle Rock & Westwood Patios ea.	48	49
Entire Mansion	—	1,500	East Lawn	500	1,000

MEETING CAPACITY: There are 14 rooms (15,000 square feet of meeting space) which can each accommodate 12–56 seated classroom-style or 25–75 seated theater-style. Exclusive use of the 14 rooms requires a 1,000-guest minimum (maximum 1,500 guests).

FEES & DEPOSITS: For weddings, half the estimated event total is the deposit required to book any portion of the facility; the balance is due 7 days prior to the event. The rental fee is $3,000 for evening use, $1,500 for afternoon use. Customized wedding packages run $80–85/person, and include champagne & hors d'oeuvres greeting, champagne toast, wine, meal, wedding cake, taxes, gratuities and overnight accommodations for bride and groom. For a 1-hour ceremony, the $1,000 fee includes 200 chairs, rehearsal, setup and coordination. For other special events and business functions, 50% of the estimated total is required to confirm reservations; the event balance is payable 30 days prior to the event. Rental fees range $350–1,500 depending on guest count and space(s) selected. Dinner entrees start at $30/person, station menus at $80/person. Alcohol, tax and an 18% service charge are additional.

AVAILABILITY: Year-round, daily, any time. Weddings take place on Saturdays; other time frames may be negotiated.

SERVICES/AMENITIES:
Catering: provided, no BYO
Kitchen Facilities: n/a
Tables & Chairs: provided
Linens, Silver, etc.: provided
Restrooms: wheelchair accessible
Dance Floor: provided, extra fee
Bride's & Groom's Dressing Area: CBA
Meeting Equipment: computer networking capabilities, video conferencing equipment, etc.

Parking: complimentary valet; large lots
Accommodations: 135 guest rooms & suites
Telephone: pay phones
Outdoor Night Lighting: yes
Outdoor Cooking Facilities: CBA
Cleanup: provided
View: Santa Cruz Mtns.
Other: event coordination, grand piano, outdoor pool, tennis, volleyball

RESTRICTIONS:
Alcohol: provided, no BYO
Smoking: designated areas
Music: amplified OK, indoors only

Wheelchair Access: yes
Insurance: not required
Other: no birdseed, rice or confetti

Hotel De Anza

and La Pastaia

Hotel & Restaurant

233 West Santa Clara Street, San Jose
(800) 843-3700, (408) 286-1000, fax (408) 286-2087

www.hoteldeanza.com
getinfo@hoteldeanza.com

◆ Ceremonies ◆ Special Events
◆ Wedding Receptions ◆ Meetings
◆ Business Functions ◆ Accommodations

The Hotel De Anza is not only an historic hotel, it's one of San Jose's most beautiful event facilities. A recent infusion of $10 million has brought back its original Art Deco splendor: gold accents, etched glass and distinctive fixtures are everywhere. Serve pre-party cocktails in the Hedley Club, the De Anza's classic lounge. This extraordinary space has a highly detailed ceiling, painted in golds, raspberries and blues. An enormous stone fireplace glows in winter, illuminating the room's large paintings, eclectic furnishings and glass-backed bar. French doors lead to the adjacent Palm Court Terrace, an outdoor courtyard enclosed by terra-cotta colored walls covered with ivy. Three fountains are set into the limestone floor and sunlight filters through the white, draped awning that shades the entire space. Palms, ferns and flowers around the perimeter add the freshness and color of a garden.

For an indoor event, have a dazzling reception in the De Anza Room, a magnificent space with warm gold walls, hand-stenciled with gold-leaf leaves. The ceiling's concrete beams are intricately painted in shades of gold, burgundy, blue and green, and a beautiful mural on a freestanding screen adds more color.

The hotel's restaurant, La Pastaia (which means "pasta maker" in Italian), is a feast for the senses. Designed in a Northern Italian style, it showcases an abundance of slate tile in banquettes, booths and softly curving arches. Lemony yellow walls are hand painted in a faux marble pattern and the stone floor is a melange of subdued earth tones. The exhibition kitchen area is tantalizing: a long marble counter is laden with delectable desserts and fresh-baked bread, and a wood burning oven glows continuously at one end. Small alcoves with a combination of banquettes and tables are cozy, intimate spaces. Create your own menu—no matter what you select, your guests will appreciate the genuine Italian cuisine, professionally served in a Tuscan-chic atmosphere.

And when the festivities are over, you can honeymoon in the hotel's luxurious Penthouse, whose sumptuous bathroom beckons with black marble floors, marble counters and a whirlpool bathtub large enough for four. We can't say enough about the Hotel De Anza and La Pastaia; take your time when visiting, so that you can fully savor this one-of-a kind place.

CEREMONY CAPACITY: The San Jose Room holds 55 seated or 60 standing, the Palm Court Terrace, 130 seated or 150 standing, and the De Anza Room, 70 seated or 80 standing guests.

EVENT/RECEPTION CAPACITY:

Room	*Seated*	*Standing*	*Room*	*Seated*	*Standing*
Boardroom	14	n/a	Palm Court Terrace	130	150
De Anza	64	100	La Pastaia Restaurant	160	160
San Jose	40	60			

MEETING CAPACITY: There are 5 meeting rooms which can accommodate 8–75 seated guests; the Palm Terrace holds up to 130 seated for business functions.

FEES & DEPOSITS: For business functions, a $100–625 room rental fee may apply, depending on room selected and event duration. For weddings, the rental fee is $1,300–1,500.

The entire rental fee and a $10/person food and beverage deposit are due when the facility is booked; the balance is payable 1 week prior to the event. Catering is provided by La Pastaia, with prices ranging $25–50/person for a seated meal. Menus can be customized. Alcohol, tax and a 19% service charge are additional.

AVAILABILITY: Year-round, daily, 7am–midnight.

SERVICES/AMENITIES:

Catering: provided, no BYO
Tables & Chairs: provided
Kitchen Facilities: n/a
Linens, Silver, etc.: provided
Restrooms: wheelchair accessible
Dance Floor: CBA, extra fee
Bride's Dressing Area: CBA
Meeting Equipment: AV, other CBA

Parking: nearby lots and valet
Accommodations: 100 rooms & Penthouse
Telephone: pay phone
Outdoor Night Lighting: yes
Outdoor Cooking Facilities: no
Cleanup: provided
View: San Jose skyline from upper floors
Other: event coordination, cakes

RESTRICTIONS:

Alcohol: provided
Smoking: outside only
Music: amplified OK

Wheelchair Access: yes
Insurance: not required

The professionals in the back of the book are the best in the business! How do we know? Read page 681.

Il Fornaio at the Hyatt Sainte Claire

Historic Hotel

302 South Market Street, San Jose
(408) 271-3350, fax (408) 286-6632

www.ilfornaio.com or www.hyattsainteclaire.com

◆ Ceremonies ◆ Special Events
◆ Wedding Receptions ◆ Meetings
◆ Business Functions ◆ Accommodations

In 1992, when the stately old Hotel Sainte Claire was undergoing a major refurbishing, workmen broke through a false wall and stumbled on something that had been completely forgotten for years: an exquisite little Spanish courtyard, with graceful arches, hanging terra cotta planters and intricate, jewel-like, geometric tile work that a Spanish grandee would envy. It was the crowning touch to a multi-million-dollar project that lovingly restored the beautiful 1926 hotel—a registered National Historic Landmark—to its former glory.

Today, the hotel is called the Hyatt Sainte Claire, and the dining and event rooms are operated by Il Fornaio. Together, they have resurrected not just the Courtyard, but other historic rooms. Among them: the Grande Ballroom, a luxurious space featuring antique wrought iron chandeliers; the Sala Del Vino, an elegant private dining room framed in glass, with a long captain's table; the Sala Del Fornaio, the chef's personal room, with a large butcher block table in the middle; the Courtyard Room, mirroring the style of the Grande Ballroom, which connects the Ballroom with the Courtyard; and the Palm Bar adjoining the Courtyard, has a sweeping curved bar, carved mahogany ceiling, and a wrought-iron balcony just above on the second floor, overlooking the courtyard (more about that later).

Wedding choreography possibilities are mind boggling. Here's one scenario: Have your ceremony in the Courtyard, cocktails in the Courtyard Room, and dinner and dancing in the Grande Ballroom. Throw in the rehearsal dinner in the Sala Del Vino or the Sala Del Fornaio for good measure. (Whichever one you don't choose, you can use for a bridal shower.) And at the end of the day, you're back to the courtyard, where the two of you emerge onto the second floor balcony, toss the bridal bouquet to the onlookers below, and wave goodbye. But, of course, you can mix and match the spaces in any other combination, and it would work just as well.

Flexibility and understated elegance are also in evidence when Il Fornaio hosts business events in the conference rooms on the second floor. At first glance, they look like standard meeting rooms found in any hotel. But then you start to notice the subtle little touches: curved hardwood chairs with upholstered seats, plush rugs, delicate Spanish decoration around the molding, large windows that bathe the conference rooms in natural light, and dark wood wainscoting.

The conference rooms, which each have a wet bar, private bathroom and audio-visual equipment, can be used singly or in tandem with each other. They can also be used as satellites of the Sainte Claire Room, a smaller-scale version of the Grande Ballroom. Its stylish decor, excellent acoustics and comfortable seating capacity—plus the availability of state-of-the-art audio-visual equipment—makes the Sainte Claire Room an excellent site for a large group presentation before breaking up for seminars or workshops in the conference rooms.

Il Fornaio is a full-service restaurant/caterer, offering food and beverage packages at price levels for every kind of event, business or pleasure. And, of course, the Hyatt Sainte Claire can put up all your out-of-town guests. If you're looking for an all-in-one facility that can handle everything with a touch of class, Il Fornaio at the Hyatt Sainte Claire could be the place for you.

CEREMONY CAPACITY: The outdoor courtyard can accommodate up to 180 seated guests plus extra standing room; other indoor arrangements can be made to accommodate up to 300 seated guests.

EVENT/RECEPTION CAPACITY:

Area	Seated	w/dance floor	Area	Seated	w/dance floor
Grande Ballroom	270	250	Sainte Claire Room	100	80
Grande Ballroom &			Outdoor Courtyard	100	—
Courtyard combined	350	330			

MEETING CAPACITY:

Room	Theater-style	Classroom-style	Room	Theater-style	Classroom-style
Grande Ballroom	350	165	Courtyard Room	100	50
Sainte Claire Room	160	70	Ballroom	235	120
Santa Vesta Room	72	36	Saratoga Room	55	24
Santa Cruz Room	55	24			

The Boardroom can seat 12 people conference-style.

FEES & DEPOSITS: For weddings, a $1,000 non-refundable deposit is required 2 weeks after making reservations. The estimated event balance is payable 2–4 weeks prior to the event; any remaining balance is due at the event's conclusion. The Courtyard rental fee is $500. All-inclusive wedding packages (3) include hors d'oeuvres, champagne toast, wine with served meals, cake cutting, tax and service charges. The package prices run $60–90/person depending on the menu selected. You can also customize any reception menu; luncheons or dinners start at $20/person; an 18% service charge, tax and alcohol are additional.

For other special events, deposits range $250–1,000 depending on the room and services selected. Meals and cocktail/hors d'oeuvres parties vary in price. For business functions, meeting packages are available including a continental breakfast, lunch and 2 mid-meeting breaks and room rental; call for more detailed information.

AVAILABILITY: Year-round, daily, any time until 1am. Saturday weddings in the Grande Ballroom usually take place 10am–4:30pm or 6pm–1am.

SERVICES/AMENITIES:

Catering: provided by Il Fornaio, no BYO

Kitchen Facilities: n/a

Parking: nearby lots or valet

Accommodations: 170 guest rooms

Tables & Chairs: provided
Linens, Silver, etc.: provided
Restrooms: wheelchair accessible
Dance Floor: provided
Bride's & Groom's Dressing Area: CBA
Meeting Equipment: full range including AV

Telephone: pay phones
Outdoor Night Lighting: in courtyard
Outdoor Cooking Facilities: n/a
Cleanup: provided
View: no
Other: full event coordination

RESTRICTIONS:

Alcohol: provided, or wine & champagne corkage CBA
Smoking: outdoors only
Music: amplified OK indoors only

Wheelchair Access: yes

Insurance: not required
Other: decorations must be approved

This is important! Tell facilities you're reading **Here Comes The Guide** and ask if our information is still current.

492

San Jose Woman's Club

75 South Eleventh Street, San Jose
(408) 294-6919, fax (408) 985-9888

Historic Woman's Club

◆ Ceremonies ◆ Special Events
◆ Wedding Receptions ◆ Meetings
◆ Business Functions Accommodations

With its facade of tall, arched windows and imposing entryway, the San Jose Woman's Club building makes a graceful impression. Completed in 1929, the Spanish-style structure has hosted a wide variety of events over the years, and many locals continue to get married here.

The foyer, with its fireplace niche and tiled stairway, is often used for small ceremonies; the stairs serve as both an entrance for the bride and a convenient spot for photos. It's also a relaxed space for sipping champagne and mingling

The Ballroom, however, is the building's *pièce de résistance*. A high, slightly vaulted ceiling spans the enormous room, and light from a wall of tall arched windows brings out the shine on the oak floor. The floor itself is unusual in that it has a special "spring" construction to enhance dancing. Up above, the beams crisscrossing the ceiling are all hand-stenciled, and the ornate parchment-and-wrought-iron chandeliers glow amber when lit. You can exchange vows on the curtained stage, while your favorite tune is played on the Steinway baby grand piano.

The Ballroom has plenty of space for a large reception, but if you need additional seating, the adjacent Tea Room comes in very handy. Separated from the Ballroom by a huge, sliding glass pocket door, it has easy access to the kitchen via a pass-through counter at one end. Like the Ballroom, its pastel, unadorned walls make a neutral backdrop for potted plants and flowers. The Club offers a great deal of flexibility not only for weddings, but for private parties, seminars, concerts or lectures—and its fees won't break the bank.

CEREMONY CAPACITY: The Club holds 400 seated.

EVENT/RECEPTION CAPACITY: The Ballroom holds 300 seated; the Tea Room holds 50 seated guests.

MEETING CAPACITY: The Ballroom holds 400 seated theater-style; the Tea Room holds 100 seated theater-style.

FEES & DEPOSITS: A $300 refundable cleaning/security deposit is required to hold your date, and is returned 10 days after the event if the site is in good condition. For weddings and special events, the $1,200 rental fee covers a 6-hour function and is payable 60 days prior to the event.

Each additional hour runs $100. Security personnel is required; 1 off-duty police officer for up to 150 guests, 2 for over 150 guests at $28–30/hour per officer.

For weekday business functions or meetings, the rental rate varies depending on guest count and event duration. Call for specifics.

AVAILABILITY: Year-round, daily, 9am–midnight.

SERVICES/AMENITIES:

Catering: BYO

Kitchen Facilities: fully equipped

Tables & Chairs: provided

Linens, Silver, etc.: BYO

Restrooms: wheelchair accessible

Dance Floor: in Ballroom

Bride's Dressing Area: yes

Meeting Equipment: lighted podium, stage w/lights

Parking: adjacent lot, on street

Accommodations: no guest rooms

Telephone: pay phone

Outdoor Night Lighting: yes

Outdoor Cooking Facilities: BYO

Cleanup: renter and caretaker

View: no

RESTRICTIONS:

Alcohol: BYO BWC only

Smoking: outside only

Music: amplified OK

Wheelchair Access: yes

Insurance: not required

Other: no rice, birdseed or confetti; no tacks or tape on walls

---

The professionals in the back of the book are the best in the business! How do we know? Read page 681.

Silicon Valley Capital Club

50 West San Fernando, 17th Floor, San Jose
(408) 971-9300, fax (408) 283-4149

www.silcapclub.com
scottknoblach@ourclub.com

◆ Ceremonies	◆ Special Events
◆ Wedding Receptions	◆ Meetings
◆ Business Functions	Accommodations

Located on the penthouse floor of the Fairmont Plaza in the heart of downtown San Jose, this private club offers a genteel ambiance, fine dining and sensational views. The overstuffed furnishings, coffered ceiling, marble floors and picture windows of the Capital Club's lobby seem just right for a post-ceremony reception area. Its mauve, coral and slate blue color scheme is carried throughout the club, along with an abundance of ash-colored oak paneling and millwork. A grand piano and the adjacent Buena Vista cocktail bar also make the lobby a pleasant place to gather before moving on to one of the club's dining rooms for a seated reception.

The formal main dining room features walls of windows, Neoclassic chandeliers, hardwood tables and tapestry-upholstered chairs. On the south side of the room, doors open onto a wide terrace, where the 17th floor's sweeping views of downtown San Jose and the Silicon Valley are impressive. If you're hosting an intimate affair, you might want to celebrate in one of the Capital Club's four private dining rooms; each comes with panoramic vistas, and all have private balconies.

If you're planning a soirée, we can't think of a more fitting location. At night, when the sun goes down and the sunset begins to fade, you'll feel like you're on top of the world. A glittering carpet of twinkling lights spreads beneath you, creating a dramatic ambiance for a wedding reception or any kind of event.

CEREMONY CAPACITY: The North Terrace holds 150 seated or standing, the indoor Lounge 150 seated or standing.

EVENT/RECEPTION CAPACITY: The Club can accommodate 150 seated guests indoors, 250 with indoor and outdoor seating.

MEETING CAPACITY:

Room	*Conf-style*	*Theater-style*	*Room*	*Conf-style*	*Theater-style*
Alum Rock	14	—	Quicksilver	24	65
Mount Hamilton	14	—	Pacific Rim	70	200
Venture Library	20	40			

FEES & DEPOSITS: A $1,000 non-refundable deposit is required to book the Club. Food and beverage service is provided; meals run $25–45/person. A $500 non-member guest fee is added to the estimated total, which is paid in 2 installments. Half of the estimated catering total is due 30 days prior to event, the balance 24 hours prior. Alcohol, tax and a 20% service charge are additional, as is a $300 ceremony fee.

AVAILABILITY: Year-round, daily, Monday 7am–7pm, Tuesday–Friday 7am–midnight, and Saturday 6pm–midnight. For events starting before 6pm on Saturday or any time on Sunday, there's a $500 facility opening fee. Closed most major holidays.

SERVICES/AMENITIES:

Catering: provided, no BYO
Kitchen Facilities: n/a
Tables & Chairs: provided
Linens, Silver, etc.: provided
Restrooms: wheelchair accessible
Dance Floor: portable, extra fee
Bride & Groom's Dressing Area: yes
Meeting Equipment: AV equipment

Parking: garage w/validation after 5pm
Accommodations: no guest rooms
Telephone: house phones
Outdoor Night Lighting: yes
Outdoor Cooking Facilities: n/a
Cleanup: provided
View: panoramic view of Silicon Valley
Other: coordination, piano

RESTRICTIONS:

Alcohol: provided, no BYO
Smoking: outside only
Music: amplified OK

Wheelchair Access: yes, elevator
Insurance: not required
Other: no rice or birdseed

This is important! Tell facilities you're reading **Here Comes The Guide** and ask if our information is still current.

496

The Tech Museum of Innovation

Museum

201 South Market Street, San Jose
(408) 795-6221, fax (408) 279-7167
www.thetech.org
maureenl@thetech.org

Ceremonies	◆ Special Events
◆ Wedding Receptions	◆ Meetings
◆ Business Functions	Accommodations

All you people who yawn at the prospect of going to a museum listen up: The Tech is not just a museum, it's an adventure. In fact, The Tech may be the most exciting thing to happen to the South Bay in years.

Located in downtown San Jose, facing Plaza de Cesar Chavez and just across from the Fairmont Hotel, this bright mango building houses 300 high tech, interactive exhibits that will energize the most jaded visitor. And wonder of wonders!—if you host an event here, the exhibits are available for your guests' enjoyment.

Events are held in the museum lobby, the four major exhibit galleries, and the Hackworth IMAX Dome Theater. You can reserve any combination of spaces or rent the entire museum. The lobby is a fantastic place for a large party. It's a three-level atrium with a 45-foot cylindrical tower rising up through it and, when used in conjunction with the adjacent New Venture Hall, it can accommodate 500 for a sit-down dinner.

The galleries lend themselves to standing receptions. They're thoroughly modern, displaying a mix of steel, glass and plastic, with walls and ceilings painted in jewel shades of purple, yellow and blue. Each gallery has a different theme. *Innovation: Silicon Valley and Beyond* focuses on the story of Silicon Valley, and the people and inventions that made it famous. Have you ever wanted to know how they make silicon chips? In here you can take an air shower, put on a bunnysuit and watch grains of sand become polished silicon wafers. *Life Tech : The Human Machine* shows us how technologies save lives and enhance human performance. Take a tour of a virtual hospital operating room or ultrasound yourself and watch an image of your bones wiggling on a monitor. *Exploration: New Frontiers* gives you the opportunity to go places you've only been able to imagine. Here you can shake in an earthquake, explore under the sea and fly over the surface of Mars. And in *Communication: Global Connections,* you'll learn how communication technologies have made our world very small indeed.

In addition to these extraordinary galleries, The Tech has one more cutting-edge gem that will dazzle you and your guests: the Hackworth IMAX Dome Theater. The only one of its kind in Northern California, it features a giant hemispherical screen whose image dwarfs that of a conventional theater, and puts the audience in the center of the action. Outfitted with state-of-the-art audio/visual equipment, the theater can be reserved exclusively for a performance or presentation, but we recommend you also use it for viewing an IMAX film. Initially, the museum will be showing *Everest,* a movie that chronicles the IMAX film crew's spellbinding climb up sheer vertical walls and over bottomless crevasses to the summit of Everest.

The Tech aims to inspire the innovator in everyone, yet even if you don't come away wanting to be a scientist when you grow up, you'll have to admit that this place makes traditional meeting rooms and party themes feel obsolete. Part of the next generation of museums, The Tech triumphs at making science, math and technology not only accessible, but positively fun.

CEREMONY CAPACITY: Ceremonies don't take place at this venue.

EVENT/RECEPTION CAPACITY: The Tech can accommodate 500 seated guests and 2,500 standing.

MEETING CAPACITY: The Small Meeting Room can hold 35, the Large Meeting Room, 65 and the New Venture Hall, 300.

FEES & DEPOSITS: A deposit of 50% of the rental fee is required to secure your date. The rental fee ranges from $500–10,000 depending on the space(s) used. Exclusive use of the Hackworth IMAX Dome Theater can be arranged at an additional cost. Fees are based on a 4-hour time period. An additional 30% per hour will be charged after the first 4 hours.

AVAILABILITY: Year-round, daily, 6pm–midnight. Closed Thanksgiving Day, Christmas Eve and Day, New Year's Eve.

SERVICES/AMENITIES:

Catering: provided, or select from list
Kitchen Facilities: prep only
Tables & Chairs: BYO or through caterer
Linens, Silver, etc.: through caterer
Restrooms: wheelchair accessible
Dance Floor: CBA
Meeting Equipment: CBA, extra charge
Other: on-site coordinator

Parking: Convention Center garage, nearby lots
Accommodations: no guest rooms
Telephone: pay phone
Outdoor Night Lighting: no
Outdoor Cooking Facilities: no
Cleanup: through caterer
View: no

RESTRICTIONS:

Alcohol: through caterer
Smoking: outdoors only
Music: amplified OK

Wheelchair Access: yes
Insurance: certificate required

Arboleda

Private, Creekside Home

3600 San Juan Canyon Road, San Juan Bautista
(831) 623-1066, fax (831) 623-2066

www.arboleda.com
arboleda@hollinet.com

◆ Ceremonies   ◆ Special Events
◆ Wedding Receptions   ◆ Meetings
◆ Business Functions   ◆ Accommodations

Do you ever want to throw off your hectic life like a scratchy wool suit and "slip into something more comfortable"? Then pay a visit to Arboleda, whose rustic beauty and country ambiance will make you feel as relaxed and care-free as putting on your favorite pair of jeans!

Tucked in a woodsy, se-cluded canyon near the historic town of San Juan Bautista, Arboleda (just saying this mellifluous word relaxes you) is the private home of Kim Cox, whose whimsical and artistic sensibilities are reflected in every inch of the place. Indoors, a harmonious combination of stone, concrete and rough wood, plus a fireplace with half-log mantel, lends a certain rusticity. These elements are softened and perfectly complemented, however, by gauzy curtains, rich fabrics draped over furniture, and a vast collection of antique treasures. When you sit down at the long dining room table, you can't help but admire the 20-foot ceiling and purple faux-candle chandeliers overhead, as well as the chairs all around, elegantly dressed in tied-back canvas. When the French doors are open, the fragrance of lavender (which is planted near the entry) wafts in, and the overall feeling is one of being in a charming house in Provence.

One of the advantages of reserving Arboleda for the entire weekend is you get to fully experience the guest rooms, whose original and often fanciful decor will put a smile on your face. One has an incredible view, antique trunks and whimsical bunkbeds; another sports a large fish painting on the wall, a fish-print bedspread and pillows made from old fur coats. The fetching sleeping porch has a western theme, based on the novel "Even Cowgirls Get the Blues." Each of the fence-post beds in this rough-walled bedroom is named after a cowgirl, and all of them are clad in rodeo-print bedspreads and more fur-coat pillows (where *did* she get all those coats?). Naturally, there are matching rodeo-print drapes, horseshoes and framed Gene Autry puzzles, too. Why not have a pre-wedding slumber party here with your bridesmaids? What a fabulous way to spend your last night as a single woman!

Delightful as the house is, the grounds are just as wonderful. Out back, the grove of sprawling native sycamores for which the property is named (*arboleda* is Spanish for "grove of trees") shelters a ceremony site with a small amphitheater, barbecue pit and campfire area. A creek runs below the grove, bordering the property and adding its voice to those of numerous birds. A path leads down to a small pond, where you can float candles to illumine your ceremony. In front of the house, beyond the grape arbor, lavender field and another creek, is a spacious lawn which makes a pleasant, sunny area for ceremonies, receptions, picnics and lawn croquet.

On the more practical side, Arboleda has a host of features guaranteed to make your event run smoothly. A fully equipped, commercial kitchen makes food preparation a breeze; an on-site parking lot and shuttle service to a nearby lot eases transportation problems. For stressed-out brides, grooms, businesspeople, (or anyone needing to decompress) massages can be arranged. Best of all, Kim Cox is a fun, creative host, who will move heaven and earth to make your special event a success. Kim herself admits that she hates to leave Arboleda, even for a vacation, and after a weekend spent at this fabulous facility, we're sure you'll feel the same way.

CEREMONY, EVENT/RECEPTION & MEETING CAPACITY: Outdoors, the lawn area holds 250 seated; the Terrace holds 60 seated. Indoors, Arboleda can accommodate 24 seated or 50 standing guests. The site maximum is 250 guests.

FEES & DEPOSITS: For weekend exclusive use May–October, the site fee is $3,000 for up to 75 guests or $4,000 for up to 150 guests. November–April the fee is $2,700, with a 50-guest maximum. The site fee includes weekend use of Arboleda, Friday and Saturday night accommodations for 15 guests, and breakfast for all guests on Saturday and Sunday morning. A non-refundable $1,000 security deposit is required to secure your date; half the rental fee is payable 90 days prior to the event and the remaining balance 2 weeks prior. Massage, additional overnight stays, meals and tenting can be arranged for an extra charge.

AVAILABILITY: Year-round, weekends only.

SERVICES/AMENITIES:

Catering: select from preferred list
Kitchen Facilities: fully equipped, commercial
Tables & Chairs: some provided
Linens, Silver, etc.: some provided, or caterer
Restrooms: wheelchair accessible
Dance Floor: small indoors, outdoors CBA
Bride's & Groom's Dressing Area: yes
Meeting Equipment: BYO

Parking: on-site lot & shuttle to nearby lot
Accommodations: up to 15 guests
Telephone: house phone CBA
Outdoor Night Lighting: limited
Outdoor Cooking Facilities: BBQ
Cleanup: caterer
View: wooded canyon, ponds, gardens
Other: massage CBA, lawn croquet

RESTRICTIONS:

Alcohol: BYO, licensed server required
Smoking: outside only
Music: amplified OK w/volume limits

Wheelchair Access: main floor only
Insurance: certificate required
Other: no rice, glitter or birdseed

The professionals in the back of the book are the best in the business! *How do we know? Read page 681.*

Adobe Lodge

University Club

Santa Clara University, Santa Clara
(408) 554-4059, fax (408) 554-7848

www.scu.edu/adobelodge
psalazar@mailer.scu.edu

Ceremonies	◆ Special Events
◆ Wedding Receptions	◆ Meetings
◆ Business Functions	Accommodations

The Adobe Lodge is the only structure to have survived the 1926 fire on the grounds and remains the single structural remnant of the original 1822 Mission Santa Clara. It has been remodeled extensively, but still has a Mission-era flavor. To reach the Club, you stroll through the Old Mission Gardens, and under an ancient, wisteria laden pergola. This particular vine deserves mention because it's breathtaking, with 150-year-old trunks the size of small trees. In the spring, the pergola overflows with color. In fact, all of the landscaping flanking the entry path is delightful. Everything from the palms dotting the lawns to the multi-hued roses and pansies is perfectly maintained. There is no traffic noise in this interior garden, only the sounds of the birds.

The Spanish-tiled Adobe Lodge building is surrounded by a vine-covered porch, and inside there's a main dining room which is formally resplendent in creams and golds. The Club's outdoor patio is inviting and intimate, with Chinese elms providing dappled shade overhead. These indoor and outdoor spaces create one of the most attractive reception sites we've ever seen—it's one of our favorite places in the Santa Clara Valley.

CEREMONY CAPACITY: Ceremonies do not take place at this venue.

EVENT/RECEPTION CAPACITY: The main dining room holds 100 seated guests, 75 with a dance floor or 200 standing; the adjacent porch seats 22; the patio holds 60 seated or 90 standing. The Mission's gardens can accommodate 150–600 seated guests during warmer months.

MEETING CAPACITY: The main dining room can accommodate 80 seated theater-style; the Private Dining Rooms 12–16 seated classroom-style.

FEES & DEPOSITS: For weddings, a $650–850 rental fee, which includes use of the facility for 4 hours, is due when the rental contract is submitted. A final guest count is due 10 days prior to the wedding. Food services are provided. Special wedding menus for served or buffet-style meals, including passed hors d'oeuvres, range $22–55/person. Customized menus are also available. Alcohol, tax and a 17% service charge are additional. The food and beverage balance is payable 5 days prior to the event. Extra hours may be arranged at $300/hour.

For other special events and business functions, the rental fee ranges $15–350 depending on room(s) selected. Fees are based on a 3-hour rental period; additional time can be arranged for an extra fee. Prices for breakfast meetings and luncheons vary depending on services requested.

AVAILABILITY: Year-round, daily, 7:30am–midnight.

SERVICES/AMENITIES:
Catering: provided, no BYO
Kitchen Facilities: n/a
Tables & Chairs: provided
Linens, Silver, etc.: provided
Restrooms: wheelchair accessible
Dance Floor: yes
Bride's Dressing Area: no
Meeting Equipment: full range CBA, extra fee

Parking: large lot
Accommodations: no guest rooms
Telephone: pay phone
Outdoor Night Lighting: CBA
Outdoor Cooking Facilities: CBA
Cleanup: provided
View: Mission Gardens

RESTRICTIONS:
Alcohol: provided, corkage $8.50/bottle
Smoking: outside only
Music: amplified OK indoors, outdoors w/volume limits

Wheelchair Access: yes
Insurance: certificate required
Other: no rice or birdseed; decorations restricted

This is important! Tell facilities you're reading **Here Comes The Guide** and ask if our information is still current.

502

Decathlon Club

Private Club

3250 Central Expressway, Santa Clara
(408) 736-3237, fax (408) 738-0320

www.decathlon-club.com
catering@decathlon-club.com

◆ Ceremonies	◆ Special Events
◆ Wedding Receptions	◆ Meetings
◆ Business Functions	Accommodations

One of Silicon Valley's finest athletic clubs, the Decathlon Club is ingeniously designed to accommodate private parties, business meetings and weddings without disturbing its membership. As you enter, there is a shaded atrium setting with a bubbling stream that flows through the building, beautifully separating the social-function spaces from the Club's athletic areas. Ficus trees glow with white twinkle lights at night, and abundant greenery creates a lush indoor garden.

For special events, guests are invited into their private area without having to mingle with Club members. The large, skylit dining area is filled with natural light during the day, and on a clear night you can see stars sparkling overhead. There is a lot more sparkle inside, however, and it comes from the chairs. *Chaivari* chairs to be more precise. Ornate and gilded, these special seats add elegance and a bit of glamour to your dining experience. After enjoying your meal, take a turn on the raised, hardwood dance floor, or step out onto the redwood deck. Sundrenched by day, it overlooks a manicured lawn that slopes down to the tennis court below.

A nine-acre complex, the Decathlon Club is extremely well-suited for corporate functions. Using the deck, lawn and tennis court in combination, you can design your own, private tournament for fundraising, corporate fun or a tennis match. For team building, company picnics and other group activities, all the Club's sports facilities are available for rental. Corporate challenges or inter-office games can be played here, all supported by a helpful and experienced staff.

In fact, no matter what kind of event you have here, the staff is committed to making it a total success. The executive chef and professional event planners will coordinate everything for you, including entertainment, flowers, photography and overnight accommodations. That's great news for brides who feel overwhelmed. "They can stop worrying when they come through our door," says the Catering Director. "We will handle all the details, with one exception—we won't shop for the wedding dress."

CEREMONY CAPACITY: The garden terrace holds 200 seated or 250 standing guests.

EVENT/RECEPTION CAPACITY: Indoors, the Club can accommodate 600 guests for receptions; the outdoor stadium tennis court and outside deck areas hold 500 guests.

MEETING CAPACITY: The Monterey Room accommodates 12 seated conference-style, the Peninsula Room holds 25 seated conference-style, 40 seated theater-style or 30 seated classroom-style. Meeting rooms come with screen and white board.

FEES & DEPOSITS: For weddings, a $1,000 rental fee covers a 5-hour period; overtime is available at $200/hour. A non-refundable $1,000 deposit is due when your reservation is confirmed; 75% of the estimated food and beverage total is due 45 days prior to the event and the balance is due 72 hours prior to the event. Per-person rates: luncheons and dinners $24–30, buffets $28–33; hors d'oeuvres start at $5 and BBQs $13–25. Beverage packages start at $12/person. Tax and an 18% service charge are additional. A $500 wedding ceremony fee includes setup, cleanup, coordinator and rehearsal. Dollar minimums may be required for functions taking place during prime dates and times.

For other events or business functions, rates vary depending on rooms and services selected. Conference rooms run $300/event.

AVAILABILITY: Special events and business functions, year-round, daily until 1am. Wedding receptions take place in 5-hour blocks; on Saturdays the blocks are 11am–4pm or 6pm–11pm. Discounts are available for weddings on Sundays; call for more information.

SERVICES/AMENITIES:

Catering: provided, BYO w/approval
Kitchen Facilities: prep only
Tables & Chairs: provided
Linens, Silver, etc.: provided
Restrooms: wheelchair accessible
Dance Floor: yes
Bride's Dressing Area: yes
Meeting Equipment: full range

Parking: large lots
Accommodations: no guest rooms
Telephone: pay phone
Outdoor Night Lighting: yes
Outdoor Cooking Facilities: BBQ
Cleanup: provided
View: indoor garden, outdoor coastal hills
Other: event coordination

RESTRICTIONS:

Alcohol: provided, WC corkage $10/bottle
Smoking: outside deck only
Music: amplified OK indoors

Wheelchair Access: yes
Insurance: not required
Other: no birdseed, rice or mylar balloons

The professionals in the back of the book are the best in the business! *How do we know? Read page 681.*

Triton Museum of Art

1505 Warburton Avenue, Santa Clara
(408) 277-0661, fax (408) 277-0678

Art Museum

◆ Ceremonies	◆ Special Events
◆ Wedding Receptions	◆ Meetings
◆ Business Functions	Accommodations

An art museum may not be the first place that comes to mind when planning your event, but maybe it should be, especially if it's Santa Clara's Triton Museum of Art. This community-oriented museum offers a variety of venues, both indoors and out, that make a refreshing change from more traditional sites.

Outside, the museum is visually stunning. With its angled white stucco walls, pyramidal skylights, and columned entrance flanked by palm trees, the building is reminiscent of Egypt or Morocco. Go through the revolving door, and you're in the Rotunda. Coolly elegant, with marble floors, concrete pillars, and sinuous floor-to-ceiling windows that bring the outdoors inside, the Rotunda is suitable for cocktail parties, seated or standing receptions, or dancing. This room overlooks a seven-acre park, also available for events, with rolling lawns, majestic redwoods, and statues and sculptures of every description. Everything from traditional sit-down dinners to innovative corporate parties has been held in this park. For example, the creative folks at Sierra Semiconductor constructed a clear-sided wraparound tent with different themes and games inside sections of the tent, while in front of the museum, a mural of a ship was erected, complete with a gangplank for guests to climb.

Other options include the Cowell Room, an octagonal space with pale gray carpeting and walls, used for community-oriented art shows, college art exhibits, and ArtReach, a program that provides art instruction for school children. When not being used for these programs, the Cowell Room is available on a limited basis for business or social events. The Museum's two galleries are available as well, though rental is subject to the type and fragility of art being shown, and there may be restrictions on the food and beverage service. However, if your event is approved, you'll be able to enjoy the fine art exhibits, tasteful ambiance, and stunning pyramidal skylights which can be opened in sunny weather. One unique feature of the Triton Museum is that with their lighting system and skylights, they can give the effect of natural sunlight 24 hours a day.

The Triton Museum has other amenities to make your event trouble-free. There's lots of parking, all event spaces are wheelchair accessible, and it's in a central location easily reached by major freeways. So, when you plan your next party or business meeting, consider the Triton Museum of Art. Your "critics" will rave, and wonder where you came up with such a clever idea.

CEREMONY CAPACITY: The outdoor Sculpture Garden holds 50–500 seated or 1,000 standing guests.

EVENT/RECEPTION CAPACITY: The Rotunda accommodates 50–150 seated or 250 standing guests. The Warburton Gallery holds 220 seated; the Museum's indoor spaces hold a total of 400 seated or 600 or more for standing functions.

MEETING CAPACITY: The Cowell Room holds 100 guests and can accommodate a variety of seating arrangements.

FEES & DEPOSITS: A $1,500 rental fee is required as a deposit to reserve your date, along with a $500 deposit to the in-house caterer. The rental balance is due 2 weeks prior to event. The fee for the entire Museum, including outdoor areas, is $3,750; for use of the outside area only, the fee is $1,750.

The estimated food and beverage balance is due 5 working days prior to the event. Per person meal costs are as follows: breakfasts $8.50–18, luncheons $12.50–20 and dinners $20–40; alcohol, tax and a 15% gratuity are additional.

AVAILABILITY: Business functions, year-round, Monday 7am–10pm; Tuesday–Friday, 5pm–10pm. Special events and weddings, Friday–Sunday, indoors 5pm–midnight; Friday–Sunday outdoors 8am–10pm. The Museum is closed on major holidays.

SERVICES/AMENITIES:
Catering: provided, no BYO
Kitchen Facilities: n/a
Tables & Chairs: provided for 100, additional CBA, extra fee
Linens, Silver, etc.: caterer or BYO
Restrooms: wheelchair accessible
Dance Floor: concrete floor in Rotunda
Bride's & Groom's Dressing Area: yes

Parking: ample lot
Accommodations: no guest rooms
Telephone: pay phones
Outdoor Night Lighting: yes
Outdoor Cooking Facilities: BBQ CBA
Cleanup: caterer
View: Sculpture Garden
Meeting Equipment: slide projector, screen

RESTRICTIONS:
Alcohol: provided or BYO
Smoking: outside only
Music: amplified OK outside until 10pm; indoors until midnight

Wheelchair Access: yes
Insurance: may be required

This is important! Tell facilities you're reading **Here Comes The Guide** *and ask if our information is still current.*

506

Chateau la Cresta at the Mountain Winery

Mountaintop Winery

14831 Pierce Road, Saratoga
(408) 741-0763, fax (408) 741-0733

www.chateaulacresta.com
events@chateaulacresta.com

◆ Ceremonies   ◆ Special Events
◆ Wedding Receptions   ◆ Meetings
◆ Business Functions   Accommodations

Set high up in the Santa Cruz Mountains, this historic winery has a view of the entire Santa Clara Valley far below, and on a clear day, you can even see the sun glinting off buildings in distant cities. Amazingly, a fifteen-minute drive from the valley gets you here, and once you arrive, you'll be delighted with everything you see on the mountaintop as well.

The two main buildings on the property, the Winery and Chateau La Cresta, were constructed in 1905 by French winemaker Paul Masson. Both are fashioned out of stone masonry, and represent fine examples of French country architecture. Masson lived in the Chateau, where he often entertained guests like John Steinbeck and Charlie Chaplin (who had a fondness for pressing grapes himself). Host your own event here, and you'll understand why Chaplin was such a frequent visitor.

Most parties in the Chateau are held in the Vista Room and Sun Porch. Together, they form a large L-shaped space with stone walls, French antiques and spectacular valley views through almost floor-to-ceiling windows. A heavy wooden door opens out onto a brick patio where guests can mingle and dance. Small celebrations and executive board meetings take place upstairs, in the Bordeaux Room, whose gleaming mahogany table seats twelve. Brides often use this room too—as a dressing area. They love its seclusion, and its private deck, which offers another opportunity to sample the fabulous vistas.

If you're planning a large indoor event, like a casino night or fundraising gala, reserve the ivy-covered Winery building. Its stone walls and fragrant oak casks give the space a delicious, old-world ambiance. Intimate outdoor ceremonies, champagne receptions and wine tastings are held in the Wishing Well area, a tranquil flagstone patio and ivy-covered wishing well bordered by a grove of redwoods.

Expecting a large crowd? Fête them on the Deck, an expansive wooden terrace at the edge of the crest. Flanked by landscaped gardens and oak trees, it provides a view of the valley that will take your breath away. And if you need a theater setting for your event, the Concert Bowl is seasonally available. Used for summer concerts, it has a stage with a striking backdrop: the entire stone facade of a San Jose cathedral that crumbled in the 1906 quake.

This site is so versatile, you're bound to find an area that suits you. In addition, corporations looking for team building programs will appreciate the innovative packages offered, including gourmet cooking, wellness and stress management and creative art. Chateau La Cresta has expanded its scope since its early days as a family winery, but it still offers the same beauty and serenity that enchanted Paul Masson when he first came here almost a century ago.

CEREMONY CAPACITY:

Area	Seated	Standing	Area	Seated	Standing
Deck	280	550	Concert Bowl	1,700	2,000
Picnic Area	200	300	Wishing Well (Redwood Grove)	280	350

EVENT/RECEPTION CAPACITY:

Area	Seated	Standing	Area	Seated	Standing
Chateau	100	140	Deck	300	400
Winery	250	300	Wishing Well	180	220
Plaza	500	650			

MEETING CAPACITY: There are 5 different indoor meeting rooms that can accommodate 10–300 seated, and multiple outdoor areas that can hold up to 1,700 people.

FEES & DEPOSITS: The rental fee, contract and estimated guest count are required when the facility is reserved. For weddings, rehearsals are allowed Mon–Fri, 9am–3pm. Meals run $16–25/person, plus tax and a 17% service charge. Unlimited wine, beer and champagne starts at $12.50/person. The final balance is due 1 week prior to the event. Rental fees are as follows:

# of Guests	Rental Fee	# of Guests	Rental Fee	# of Guests	Rental Fee
50	$2,500	101–125	$3,250	176–200	$4,000
51–75	2,750	126–150	3,500	201–225	4,250
76–100	3,000	151–175	3,750	226–250	4,500
				251–275+	4,750

For other special events and business functions, the following rates apply. The 8-hour prices are for all-day meetings.

Area	4 hours	8 hours	Area	4 hours	8 hours
Winery Bldg	$1,000	$1,000	Entire Chateau	$1,200	$1,200
Vista Room	400	500	Sun Porch Rm	250	350
Board Room	200	400	Vintage Room	400	500
Bordeaux Room	200	300	Pool Area	500	500
Redwood Area	250	350	Concert Bowl	1,500	2,500

The rental fee includes use of the site, linens, glassware, china, silver, chairs, tables, setup, cleanup and staff. For business functions, it also includes meeting equipment.

AVAILABILITY: Year-round with some restrictions for the Villa Montalvo Presents Summer Series which runs June–September. Weddings take place weekends, 10am–3:30pm or 5:30–11:30pm. Special events or meetings year-round, daily 8am–midnight in either 4-hour or 8-hour blocks.

SERVICES/AMENITIES:

Catering: provided
Kitchen Facilities: n/a
Tables & Chairs: provided
Linens, Silver, etc.: provided
Restrooms: limited wheelchair accessibility
Dance Floor: CBA
Bride's Dressing Area: yes
View: of the entire South Bay & coastal hills

Parking: large lot
Accommodations: no guest rooms
Telephone: pay phone
Outdoor Night Lighting: yes
Outdoor Cooking Facilities: BBQ
Cleanup: provided
Meeting Equipment: flipcharts, overhead projector, screen

RESTRICTIONS:

Alcohol: provided, WC only,
corkage $10/bottle
Smoking: outside only
Music: amplified OK w/volume limits

Wheelchair Access: limited
Insurance: not required
Other: no rice, confetti

The professionals in the back of the book are the best in the business! How do we know? Read page 681.

Manhattans of Saratoga

12378 Saratoga-Sunnyvale Road, Saratoga
(408) 257-2131, fax (408) 257-5548

www.manhattans-saratoga.com

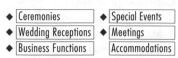

Restaurant & Banquet Facility

◆ Ceremonies   ◆ Special Events
◆ Wedding Receptions ◆ Meetings
◆ Business Functions Accommodations

Your dream wedding: a quiet ceremony site with a private reception room attached; row upon row of tables draped in cream linens with matching napkins and cream-colored chairs; shimmering chandeliers reflected in gilded mirrors; decorative silk trees twinkling with white lights. Your reality: a finite budget.

Your solution: Manhattan's, a family-owned restaurant/event facility that provides cost-conscious catering and planning packages for all types of events, including business breakfasts, engagement luncheons, and holiday parties.

Manhattan's is also uniquely suited for wedding celebrations. The physical space, shaped like a backwards 'L', is perfectly configured for seamless movement from ceremony to reception. Guests enter directly into the ceremony area (the shorter part of the 'L') at the front of the building. Following the marriage service, heavy damask curtains at the back of the space are opened to reveal a set of wide arches leading into the main dining room, a large rectangular space (the longer part of the 'L') decorated with Renaissance prints, urns full of tumbling ivy and Greco-Roman statues. At the back of the dining room is a full bar with a faux-marble top; just past the bar is a foyer with a large round beveled-glass table, useful for holding gifts or a guest book. The enclosed patio area at the front of the building can be set with cocktail tables and is a popular haven for celebratory cigar smokers, while the small courtyard at back is often used for photos.

Manhattan's offers a great selection of service packages, from simple rental of the facility to complete wedding planning and coordination (including creating custom menus, scheduling limousine service, and arranging for your band). Even the basic rental package comes with an unusual array of wedding-oriented design and decorating options. Interior designer that you are, you may prefer Manhattan's' white brocade chairs to the Corinth-patterned chairs. Pair either sort with brightly colored tablecloths and napkins—numerous color choices are available—to create a less traditional, more light-hearted look for your reception. There are multiple options for table decoration, too: Will you use the hurricane lanterns, the bud vases, the gold cherubs or the round mirror centerpieces? It may be difficult to choose one, because they all coordinate so well with Manhattan's' gold-rimmed china (and with the gilded picture-frames adorning the walls, too).

In addition, Manhattan's can supply many of the practical elements that go into the making of a great party. There's no need to rent a dance floor here, as both the ceremony and reception areas have smooth faux-marble floors well-suited to fancy footwork. You'll want music, of course: Take advantage of the CD sound system or use the digital synthesized piano for live ceremony accompaniment. Guests will also be grateful for the ample parking and convenient location.

Food is an essential at any party, and Manhattan's offers American Continental menus ranging from casual buffets to four-course banquets. The staff will happily work with you to customize your meal, and can arrange for one of several providers to create the perfect wedding cake. At Manhattan's, the wealth of possibilities gives you the opportunity to put together exactly the wedding you'd like to have.

CEREMONY CAPACITY: Manhattans can accommodate up to 115 seated guests.

EVENT/RECEPTION CAPACITY: The entire restaurant can accommodate 250 seated with a dance floor, 300 seated without a dance floor, or up to 500 standing. The Main Ballroom holds 160 guests with dance floor, or 200 seated without; the Apollo Room holds 75–100 seated guests.

MEETING CAPACITY: Theater-style, the Ballroom seats 280 guests, the Apollo Room 130.

FEES & DEPOSITS: For social events, a non-refundable deposit of 25% of the estimated event total is required to secure your date; the event balance is due 2 weeks prior to the function, along with a final guest count. Wedding packages run $29–49/person and include champagne toast, hors d'oeuvres, salad, entree, wine and cake. Buffets are also available. Tax, an 18% service charge and alcohol are additional. Events on Sunday–Friday or Saturday afternoon are discounted 10–15%.

For business functions, a non-refundable deposit is required to secure your date, the event balance and final guest count are due 1 week prior to the function. Banquets run $15–28/person; holiday packages run $34–54/person. Tax, alcohol and an 18% service charge are additional. If using an off-site caterer, $500–2,500 room rental fees will apply.

AVAILABILITY: Year-round, daily; social events 10am–2am including holidays, business-related events from 6am. Friday evening events may require a buyout.

SERVICES/AMENITIES:

Catering: provided or BYO w/approval
Kitchen Facilities: fully equipped; extra charge if BYO off-site caterer
Tables & Chairs: provided
Linens, Silver, etc.: provided except if BYO caterer
Restrooms: wheelchair accessible
Dance Floor: yes
Bride's Dressing Area: yes
Other: special linens and table decor

Parking: large lot
Accommodations: no guest rooms
Telephone: pay phone
Outdoor Night Lighting: yes
Outdoor Cooking Facilities: n/a
Cleanup: provided
View: courtyard and patio
Meeting Equipment: BYO

RESTRICTIONS:

Alcohol: provided or BYO, WC corkage $10/bottle
Smoking: patio area only
Music: amplified OK

Wheelchair Access: yes
Insurance: not required
Other: no rice or birdseed; no nails or tacks on walls

The Plumed Horse

14555 Big Basin Way, Saratoga
(408) 867-4711, fax (408) 867-6919

www.plumedhorse.com
plumed@plumedhorse.com

◆ Ceremonies ◆ Special Events
◆ Wedding Receptions ◆ Meetings
◆ Business Functions Accommodations

"Old world charm" is a phrase that's so overused it has ceased to be meaningful. But the Plumed Horse Restaurant in Saratoga is one spot that truly exhibits what these three words were meant to convey: it's old-fashioned but not outdated, elegant but not stodgy, and it offers a sense of history and relevance to its surroundings.

With a name like "The Plumed Horse," you'd expect the place to have a story behind it, and it does. In the mid-1800s, a local tinker boarded his horse in a livery stable that occupied part of the land the restaurant now occupies. During the summer, the tinker's cherished steed was plagued by heat and flies. The resourceful tinker found an old straw hat and stuck a large, bobbing ostrich feather on it, and voila! the problems were solved. The tinker, with his plumed horse, was a familiar sight around Saratoga, and became something of a local celebrity. Eventually, the stable burned down, and was rebuilt as "The Plumed Horse Junk Shop." After that, it became a tea room, then in 1952 it opened as a restaurant. Although the site has had many incarnations, the name "The Plumed Horse" has lived on.

From the hoof prints in the cement of the restaurant's awning-covered entranceway, to the etched glass rose windows in the Rose Room, the Plumed Horse is full of delightful details. In the Green Room, you'll find a wonderful country feel, thanks to the whitewashed-board paneling, exposed beams, and stone fireplace. In the center of the room, a five-foot-tall jardinière painted with Oriental designs and brimming with flowers is a dramatic focal point. The restaurant's namesake is well represented in this room, first in the form of a large carved wooden horse, then in a stained-glass window featuring the well-dressed steed, and finally in a fanciful wrought-iron gate that takes the shape of an abstract rendering of the animal. Next to the Green Room is the Red Room, which features Honduran mahogany paneling, red silk fabric on walls decorated with antique china plates, brass wall sconces, mirrors, and stuffed pheasants perched on an iron étagère. There are three smaller rooms: the Gold Room, which has stained-glass windows and an ornate black marble-topped buffet, lavishly carved and gilded; the French Room, an intimate space with charming French Provincial printed fabric on the walls and a delicate chandelier made of enamel and gold-leaf roses; and the Rose Room, with rose-etched windows and shaded sconces hung with crystals. The largest facility, the Oak

Room, is fully self-contained, with its own bar and restrooms. Among its other amenities are a sunny garden patio, ficus trees hung with twinkle lights, oak paneling and brass-and-etched-glass sconces. Elegant enough for the most sophisticated soirée, these rooms can easily be converted to quiet, private spaces for business meetings, seminars, and conferences. In addition to its aesthetic attributes, the restaurant is renowned for its seasonal French country cuisine. The Plumed Horse has received numerous awards including the DiRona Award, Distinguished Restaurants of North America Award and, since 1987, *The Wine Spectator* Grand Award for having "one of the greatest wine lists in the world." So the next time you hear a place described as having old world charm and great food compare it to the Plumed Horse. Chances are, it won't measure up.

CEREMONY CAPACITY: The Green Room holds 80 seated or 100 standing guests, the Oak Room, 140 seated or standing guests. Weddings can also take place in an adjacent public park.

EVENT/RECEPTION CAPACITY: The Lounge holds 150 standing, the Red Room 60 seated or standing, the Green Room 100 seated or standing, and the Green & Red Rooms combined, 160 seated or 175 standing. The Oak Room holds 100 seated or 150 standing guests.

MEETING CAPACITY: Oak Room, 140 seated; Gold Room, 36; Rose Room, 32; French Room, 20; The Cellar, 30.

FEES & DEPOSITS: To reserve your date, a $500 deposit is required. The anticipated balance is payable at the event's conclusion. There is a $300 wedding ceremony setup fee; for other functions, a $50 setup fee is charged for smaller rooms, $100 for larger rooms. For Sunday events, there is a $750 facility fee which includes setup. Events run $40–80/person, including hors d'oeuvres, seated meals, music, flowers, wedding cake, and alcohol/beverages. Tax and an 18% service charge are additional.

AVAILABILITY: Year-round, Monday–Saturday, except major holidays. Saturday wedding receptions, 9am–2am. The facility is available on Sundays for events with over 100 people. Evening and Sunday hours are relatively flexible.

SERVICES/AMENITIES:

Catering: provided, no BYO
Kitchen Facilities: n/a
Tables & Chairs: provided
Linens, Silver, etc.: provided
Restrooms: wheelchair accessible
Dance Floor: lounge area
Bride's Dressing Area: yes
Meeting Equipment: fully equipped

Parking: free public parking; valet available
Accommodations: no guest rooms
Telephone: pay phones
Outdoor Night Lighting: patio
Outdoor Cooking Facilities: no
Cleanup: provided
View: Santa Cruz foothills
Other: wedding & event coordination

RESTRICTIONS:

Alcohol: provided, corkage $15/bottle
Smoking: outdoors only
Music: provided, $100 charge if BYO

Wheelchair Access: yes
Insurance: not required
Other: no rice, confetti, or glitter; decorations w/approval

Saratoga Foothill Club

20399 Park Place, Saratoga
(408) 867-3428

♦ Ceremonies   ♦ Special Events
♦ Wedding Receptions   ♦ Meetings
♦ Business Functions   Accommodations

In a spot you'd never expect, on a quiet residential street near the crossroads of Big Basin and Sunnyvale/Saratoga Roads, lies the Foothill Club. This decorative 1915 Arts-and-Crafts-style building was designed by Julia Morgan as a women's club, and houses the oldest social organization in Saratoga. This structure ranks among the distinguished small redwood buildings of California, and in 1978, the Clubhouse received the distinction of being listed in the National Register of Historic Landmarks.

The old-fashioned brown-shingled facade has a wood trellis framing unusually shaped windows. An adjoining paved courtyard is dotted with Japanese maples. It's small but very pretty and private.

The Club's formal redwood entry ushers you into a room that's perfect for a buffet arrangement. It has a 30-foot-high ceiling, a raised platform stage, hardwood floor and an elaborate window that filters in glorious sunlight, setting the room aglow. A buffet table can be situated in front of the window, creating a special and highlighted place for the wedding cake and cutting ceremony. With its overall feeling of old-world comfort and warmth, the Saratoga Foothill Club provides a pleasant and intimate environment for reception celebrations.

CEREMONY CAPACITY: The outdoor patio holds 100–130 seated; the Club's interior can hold 175 seated.

EVENT/RECEPTION CAPACITY: From November–May, the Club's indoor and outdoor combined maximum capacity is 150 guests. From June–October the combined capacity is 185. The indoor maximum seated capacity is 126 guests.

MEETING CAPACITY: The Main Room holds 175 seated guests theater-style.

FEES & DEPOSITS: A $200 refundable security deposit is required when reservations are made. For weddings, the rental fee is $800 for a 5-hour block. For business meetings, the rental fee is $500.

AVAILABILITY: Tuesday through Sunday, 9:30am–9pm.

SERVICES/AMENITIES:

Catering: BYO

Kitchen Facilities: moderate

Tables & Chairs: provided

Linens, Silver, etc.: BYO

Restrooms: wheelchair accessible

Dance Floor: yes

Bride's Dressing Area: yes

Meeting Equipment: BYO

Parking: adjacent church lot, $50 donation

Accommodations: no guest rooms

Telephone: house phone

Outdoor Night Lighting: access only

Outdoor Cooking Facilities: no

Cleanup: caterer

View: of coastal hills & courtyard

Other: baby grand available

RESTRICTIONS:

Alcohol: BYO, WC only

Smoking: outside only

Music: amplified OK w/volume limits

Wheelchair Access: no

Insurance: certificate required

---

*This is **important!** Tell facilities you're reading **Here Comes The Guide** and ask if our information is still current.*

Savannah-Chanel Vineyards

Winery & Vineyards

23600 Congress Springs Road, Saratoga
(408) 741-2930, fax (408) 867-4824

www.savannahchanel.com
cshepard@savannahchanel.com

◆ Ceremonies   ◆ Special Events
◆ Wedding Receptions   ◆ Meetings
◆ Business Functions   Accommodations

Take Congress Springs Road about three miles west from Saratoga Village, make a sharp left at the Savannah-Chanel Vineyards sign, and soon you'll see some of the loveliest scenery upon this earth. Encircled by the cool, deep valleys and tree-covered ridges of the Santa Cruz mountains, the winery's 58 acres are so gorgeous they could easily be mistaken for the mythical Shangri-la. This perennially green and peaceful enclave contains two sites for weddings and special events, each with its own splendid, natural setting.

On a plateau at the vineyard's hilltop, the circa-1923 Villa de Monmartre and its adjacent lawn and garden make up the winery's main reception site. The emerald-green lawn traverses the length of the villa, a Mediterranean-style structure with a second-story, wraparound arcade. Bordered by walnut, apple, pear and willow trees on one side and a colorful flower bed on the other, the lawn also features a round, rock-rimmed fountain and a bevy of rose bushes. Next to the lawn is a large, canopied area overlooking Silicon Valley that can also be used for receptions. The white canopy is normally open on all sides, but can be converted into a tent in inclement weather.

A wide staircase from the second floor of the villa descends to a patio near the fountain, a perfect spot for ceremonies. If you place a white lattice arch here, it frames a spectacular view of the vineyards and mountains. The winery's second ceremony site is the Redwood Grove, nestled in a valley of towering trees a few hundred yards down the hill from the villa. Its cool, sheltering shade makes the Redwood Grove most popular in the warm summer months. Four giant redwoods form a fabulous natural grotto that seems custom-made for tying the knot. Add some acoustic music, or let the sound of the gently burbling stream nearby accompany your ceremony. If you've been looking for an outdoor paradise in the South Bay, Savannah-Chanel Vineyards is it.

CEREMONY CAPACITY: Redwood Grove holds 200 seated or 201–300 seated and standing; the patio area holds 200 seated guests.

EVENT/RECEPTION CAPACITY: The lawn and garden area can accommodate 200 seated or 201–300 seated with restrictions.

MEETING CAPACITY: The first floor of the Villa can accommodate 15 seated conference-style.

FEES & DEPOSITS: For weddings and receptions, half the rental fee and a refundable $250 security deposit are required to reserve your date; the rental balance is payable 60 days prior to the event. For ceremonies in the Redwood Grove, add $250 to the rental fee. Rental fees vary depending on day of week and guest count: a 6-hour Lawn and Canopy reception of up to 200 guests ranges from $3,000–4,000. An 8-hour ceremony and reception of up to 200 guests ranges from $3,500–4,500. Packages include wedding coordinator, tables, umbrellas, chairs, canopies, lattice arch, bridal changing room and parking attendants. Wine and champagne must be purchased through Savannah-Chanel Vineyards. Events of 201–300 guests have restrictions, call for details.

For corporate meetings and private functions other than weddings, the fees range $20–35/person depending on day of week.

AVAILABILITY: Year-round for special events and business functions. For weddings, April through October, daily, 8am–dusk.

SERVICES/AMENITIES:

Catering: select from preferred list
Kitchen Facilities: prep only
Tables & Chairs: most provided
Linens, Silver, etc.: caterer
Restrooms: wheelchair accessible
Dance Floor: on patio
Bride's Dressing Area: yes
Meeting Equipment: flipcharts, screen, overhead projector

Parking: several lots
Accommodations: no guest rooms
Telephone: emergency use only
Outdoor Night Lighting: access only
Outdoor Cooking Facilities: through caterer
Cleanup: caterer and renter
View: Santa Cruz Mtns., redwood forest, Santa Clara Valley
Other: event coordination, wine consultation

RESTRICTIONS:

Alcohol: WC provided, no BYO
Smoking: outside only
Music: amplified OK w/volume limits
Other: no rice, birdseed or glitter

Wheelchair Access: outdoors and first floor of Villa only
Insurance: certificate required

The professionals in the back of the book are the best in the business! How do we know? Read page 681.

Villa Montalvo

15400 Montalvo Road, Saratoga
(408) 961-5814, fax (408) 961-5850

www.villamontalvo.org
kprescott@villamontalvo.org

◆ Ceremonies   ◆ Special Events
◆ Wedding Receptions   ◆ Meetings
◆ Business Functions   Accommodations

Nestled against a wooded slope in the private and secluded Saratoga hills is Villa Montalvo, a beautiful Mediterranean-style mansion. Originally developed in 1912 as the private residence of Senator James Duval Phelan, the property is now home to an arboretum and a nonprofit center for the arts.

A narrow, one-way road leads up to the Villa. As you round the last turn, you get your first glimpse of the estate's expansive, manicured lawns and colorful gardens, as well as the mansion's terra cotta tile roof, light stucco walls and wide veranda. To your left, you'll also see the Love Temple, one of two ceremony sites on the grounds. Recently renovated, it's an open-air, white-columned pavilion, set at the end of a wide brick path. Couples get married on its steps, with a view of the surrounding Mediterranean garden, and the Villa and woods in the background.

Directly behind the Villa, the Oval Garden offers a rose garden setting complete with classical statues and wisteria-covered pergolas. This open-air courtyard is an intimate and delightful place for a ceremony; a brick pathway serves as your center aisle and a column-supported arcade is the backdrop for taking vows.

The Villa's first floor and some of its outdoor patios are available for receptions. Guests can mingle on the veranda, sipping champagne and sampling hors d'oeuvres while enjoying splendid views of the estate's lawns and gardens. Reserve well in advance. Villa Montalvo is an extraordinary site for an elegant and sophisticated wedding.

CEREMONY CAPACITY: The Oval Garden accommodates 200 seated or standing. The Side Veranda seats 135 in case of inclement weather. Capacity for the Love Temple is 150 seated or standing.

EVENT/RECEPTION CAPACITY: The Villa's indoor capacity is 175 seated, 200 standing; outdoors, it's 200 seated or standing. The Love Temple accommodates 150 seated or standing. Events in the Villa with over 200 guests incur an additional cost, and require special arrangements with the Wedding Manager.

MEETING CAPACITY: The Phelan Suite holds 15 seated; the Villa's lower floor 200. Conference seating can be arranged for up to 300 people in the newly renovated carriage house.

FEES & DEPOSITS: For weddings, the Montalvo Circle reception rental fee is $6,700 for 6 hours use. For a ceremony and reception, the rental fee is $7,500 for 8 hours. Any amount over $3,200 is tax deductible. Half the total fee is required as a non-refundable deposit when the site is booked; the balance is payable 30 days prior to the event along with a refundable $1,000 security deposit and a certificate of insurance. The rental fees for ceremonies only for both the Oval Garden and the Love Temple range $1,400–1,950. A champagne celebration option is available at the Oval Garden or Love Temple. During the four-hour block from 9am to 1pm, you may have a ceremony followed by a champagne celebration for $2,600–3,200.

Changes to the final guest count must be delivered, in writing, to the event coordinator 1 week prior to the event. The final balance is due, together with any other additional fees, 30 days prior to the wedding. Rehearsals (45 minutes maximum) must be scheduled 1 month in advance of the event and are held 9am–4pm the Thursday or Friday afternoon preceding the ceremony.

For other special events and business functions, the rental fee Sunday–Thursday is $2,600, Friday–Saturday it's $3,200. Weekday functions 9am–5pm run $1,500 for groups up to 200, or $300 for the Phelan Suite. Fundraisers require board approval.

AVAILABILITY: Ceremonies are held between March and October, and take place between 9am and 2pm in 2-hour blocks. Receptions can be held year-round, daily, from 9am to 10pm in 6- or 8-hour blocks. For other special and business functions, year-round, daily, 8am–10pm.

SERVICES/AMENITIES:

Catering: select from preferred list
Kitchen Facilities: ample
Tables & Chairs: provided
Linens, Silver, etc.: caterer
Restrooms: wheelchair accessible
Dance Floor: Main Gallery
Bride's Dressing Area: yes
View: manicured lawns, formal gardens and views of Santa Clara Valley

Parking: valet required for over 200 guests; carpooling encouraged, lot for 125 cars
Accommodations: no guest rooms
Telephone: pay phone
Outdoor Night Lighting: yes
Outdoor Cooking Facilities: no
Cleanup: caterer
Meeting Equipment: full range CBA, extra fee

RESTRICTIONS:

Alcohol: BYO or CBA
Smoking: outdoors only
Music: amplified OK w/restrictions until 10pm

Wheelchair Access: yes
Insurance: certificate required

This is important! Tell facilities you're reading *Here Comes The Guide* and ask if our information is still current.

wine country

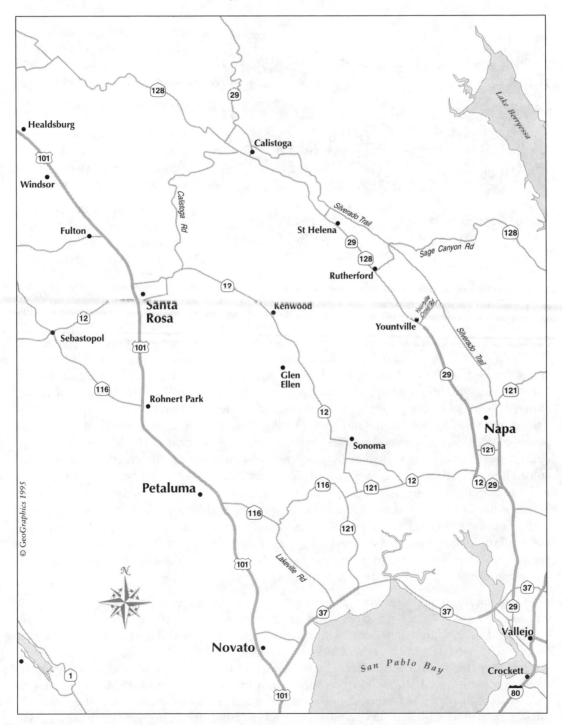

Hans Fahden Vineyards

Winery

4855 Petrified Forest Road, Calistoga
(888) A1-cater, (707) 256-2900, fax (707) 256-2906

www.hansfahden.com

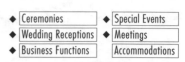

- ◆ Ceremonies
- ◆ Wedding Receptions
- ◆ Business Functions
- ◆ Special Events
- ◆ Meetings
- Accommodations

High in the mountains between Santa Rosa and Calistoga, the Hans Fahden family has created an incredible place with outdoor sites elegant enough for satin gowns and tuxedos, and a marvelous indoor facility with some of the most extraordinary features we've ever seen.

Even at first glance, the winery's gardens and event facilities are quite lovely, but like a Fabergé egg, their outward beauty is only a prelude to a wealth of creativity, craftsmanship and aesthetic richness within. Your special event may start in the Teahouse, a quaint wooden structure covered with wisteria, grapevines, and red climbing roses. Small gatherings can use the Teahouse for ceremonies or receptions, but larger groups mingle there before descending into the gardens below. The gardens are an exquisite combination of French country style and wildlife habitat, and if they remind you of an Impressionist painting, it's no coincidence. Winery owners and landscapers Antone and Lyall Fahden relied heavily on Monet's paintings of the gardens at Giverny when they designed their own. As you travel the path down to the pond, your senses are tantalized by the sights and smells of roses, iris, petunias, pansies, cornflowers, poppies, ornamental grasses and native shrubs. The garden has been cleverly planted so that something different blooms each month, creating one wave of color after another. In late spring, roses take center stage; other floral "coming attractions" include matilija poppies, oleander, zinnias, sunflowers, and blue pitcher sage. Midway between the Teahouse and pond, a terraced lawn bordered by a volcanic-ash rock wall and beds of pink evening primroses, lavender, roses, and California poppies, serves as a ceremony site for large weddings. The covered bridge spanning the lily pond can also be used for weddings, brings you close to a variety of wildlife—thanks to the ducks, egrets, quail and mourning doves that call the gardens home.

After exchanging vows, join your guests in the winery building, a long, graceful structure whose mellow wood exterior and peaked, sage-green roof blend with the rugged mountainside behind it. Inside, a gray slate floor, high, beamed ceiling of grooved pine and redwood, and cream walls give the room a simple beauty that complements the glory of the gardens viewed through French doors. In one corner, a grand piano provides background music as your guests nibble appetizers and sip champagne. Just when everyone thinks that their eyes simply couldn't take in any more beauty, the 400-pound Douglas fir doors at one end of the room are thrown open to reveal a wine cave containing candlelit tables set for dinner. This amazing cave is like the jewel within a Fabergé egg: gorgeous, surprising, and utterly unique. Formed of volcanic ash rock, the T-shaped cave's walls are lined with wine barrels; metal fixtures with grape-leaf cut-outs and twinkle-light-wrapped poles provide subtle lighting. At the T's apex, two wine barrels support a massive arrangement of fresh flowers; above, gold candle sconces in floral designs await lighting. When these sconces are lit, along with the candelabras on the tables and the twinkle lights, Ali Baba's cave itself could not be more enchanting. Magical doesn't even begin to describe an event here—as you sit down to dinner, surrounded by flowers, flickering shadows and the piquant smell of aging wine, you'll feel as if you're part of a breathtaking fairy tale. And, unlike limestone caves, this cave's volcanic-ash rock adjusts to body temperature when occupied, so you can wear the most daring *décolleté* gown and never have to throw a jacket over your shoulders.

If you're thinking that Hans Fahden sounds like a wonderful place, but you're not planning to get married any time soon, keep in mind that the winery can accommodate all types of events, from a gala celebration to a business seminar. But we can't help feeling that the site's stunning visual appeal may be most appreciated at a wedding. So, brides, if your fantasy includes a vision of you in a magnificent Vera Wang gown against a backdrop of pristine natural beauty, you owe yourself a visit to Hans Fahden Winery. They can make your dream wedding a beautiful reality!

CEREMONY CAPACITY: The Teahouse can accommodate up to 50 seated guests; the Ampitheater 120 guests.

EVENT/RECEPTION CAPACITY: The Main Hall can accommodate 85 seated or 120 standing guests; the Wine Cave, 60 seated guests. The facility can accommodate up to 85 guests November–April or 120 guests outdoors, May–October.

MEETING CAPACITY: The Main Hall holds 60 seated theater-style; the Wine Cave 60 guests.

FEES & DEPOSITS: For events, a $1,000 deposit is required to reserve your date; the balance is due 10 days prior to the event. The rental fee is as follows:

Day	*Fee*	*Day*	*Fee*
Friday	$1,500	Saturday	$2,500
Sunday	$2,000	Weekday	$1,500

AVAILABILITY: Year-round, daily, 10am–10pm.

SERVICES/AMENITIES:

Catering: provided by *Wine Valley Catering*
Kitchen Facilities: prep only
Tables & Chairs: provided
Linens, Silver, etc.: BYO
Restrooms: wheelchair accessible
Dance Floor: cement floor
Bride's Dressing Area: yes
Meeting Equipment: BYO

Parking: on-site lot
Accommodations: no guest rooms
Telephone: pay phones
Outdoor Night Lighting: yes
Outdoor Cooking Facilities: BBQ
Cleanup: caterer
View: vineyards, valley hills
Other: baby grand piano

RESTRICTIONS:

Alcohol: WCB provided or BYO
Smoking: outdoors only
Music: amplified OK until 10pm

Wheelchair Access: limited
Insurance: certificate required
Other: no rice, birdseed or confetti

Mountain House Winery & Lodge

Winery & Lodge

33710 Highway 128, Cloverdale
(707) 894-5683, fax (707) 894-5684

www.mtnhousewinery-lodge.com
mtnhouse@sonic.net

◆ Ceremonies ◆ Special Events
◆ Wedding Receptions ◆ Meetings
◆ Business Functions ◆ Accommodations

You're driving along Highway 128 outside Cloverdale, a twisting, turning stretch of road that traverses countryside so unspoiled it seems virtually untouched by human hands. The roads dips into shady oak woodlands, and rises again to reveal vistas of rolling golden hills and dark redwood forests. You begin to feel as if you're the last person on earth as your car crests yet another hill, when suddenly your eyes are dazzled by a grand building whose white clapboard gables, cobblestone facade and splashing fountain are all doubled in a mirror-still pond. Blinking your eyes, you wonder if this welcoming sight could be a mirage, but we're happy to tell you that the Mountain House Winery & Lodge is indeed real. Better still, this lovely facility is available for a wide variety of functions, from weddings to business retreats, and everything in between.

For over one hundred years, travelers have found refuge at the junction of Highway 128 and Mountain House Road, the spot where the Mountain House Winery & Lodge now stands. Originally a stage stop and inn run by pioneer Alexander McDonald to provide lodging for the growing traffic between Mendocino County, Ukiah and San Francisco, the Mountain House Inn was put out of business by the advent of the railroad. The inn was given new life when it was restored in 1996 by the Page family, who also built the new winery just up the road to serve as a special event facility.

The winery itself has three function areas, all included in the rental price. In the Tasting Room, design elements such as a high, wooden-barrel ceiling, arched windows and display areas, echo the curves of the distant hills. Both the long light-wood bar topped with tiles, and the cozy chairs in the spacious bay window are great places to relax with a prefunction drink. You could even arrange to have your own wine tasting party here, sampling the Chardonnay and Pinot Noir for which the region is justly famous. Across the foyer from the Tasting Room, the Banquet Room is spacious and airy, thanks to its off-white walls, white molding, high, peaked ceiling and plenty of large windows. In the center of the room is a hardwood dance floor, and the nearby bay window would be the perfect spot for a small band or DJ. The simple decor of this room gives you unlimited decorating possibilities, and its neutral tone will harmonize with virtually any color scheme. The building's second floor contains a lovely bride's dressing room, as well as rooms for overnight guests.

Just off the Banquet Room, the sun-splashed terrace has everything you need for a felicitous wedding or party. At one end, a white-lattice gazebo is the preferred spot for exchanging vows; at the other, a generous redwood arbor provides shade on warm days. Flowerbeds glow with color from roses, geraniums, coreopsis, evening primroses and foxgloves. Beyond the flowerbeds, the oak-clad hills provide yet more visual delights.

Take a short drive down the road to view the Inn, once the McDonald family's ranch house. The Inn does not have any indoor event spaces, but very small gatherings may wish to use either of the Inn's terraces, set among tall oaks and furnished with wrought-iron tables and chairs. A stone's throw up the hill, country cottages surround a pond complete with cattails, red-winged blackbirds and a resident bullfrog. A rustic wooden bridge spans the pond's far edge, making a romantic spot for tying the knot or taking wedding photos. Though the Mountain House Winery and Lodge may not be a mirage, it's a dream come true for anyone seeking a charming all-purpose event facility in a breathtaking woodland setting.

CEREMONY CAPACITY: Outdoors, the patio holds 200 seated; indoors, the winery holds up to 100 seated; some additional standing guests can be accommodated. A grassy meadow, which will hold 200 seated, is planned for spring of 1999; call for updates.

EVENT/RECEPTION CAPACITY: The Tasting Room holds 50 seated or 90 standing guests for a cocktail reception, the Banquet Room holds 86 seated or 150 standing, and the patio holds 100 seated or 150 standing guests.

MEETING CAPACITY: The Tasting Room holds 60 seated theater-style or 50 seated conference or classroom-style; the Banquet Room holds 150 seated theater-style or 86 seated conference or classroom-style.

FEES & DEPOSITS: For weddings, a partially refundable deposit of half the site fee is required when you book the winery. The site fee balance is payable 4 months prior to the event.

Guest Count	Site Fee Saturday	Site Fee Sunday
100	$2,000	$1,500
150	2,500	2,000
200	3,000	2,500

The site fee covers a 5-hour function; for any time over 5 hours, a $300/hour fee will apply. For Sunday events on major holidays, the higher fee site fee will apply.

For business functions and other social events, the site fee varies depending on services required; call for more information.

AVAILABILITY: Year-round, daily. Special events take place Monday–Thursday 9am–9pm or Friday–Sunday 9am–11pm, in 5-hour blocks.

SERVICES/AMENITIES:

Catering: select from preferred list or BYO with approval

Kitchen Facilities: limited

Tables & Chairs: provided for up to 100 guests

Parking: ample on site

Accommodations: 6 guest rooms and 15 cottages

Telephone: emergency use only

Linens, Silver, etc.: through caterer or BYO
Restrooms: wheelchair accessible
Dance Floor: provided
Bride's & Groom's Dressing Area: yes
Meeting Equipment: CBA, extra charge

RESTRICTIONS:

Alcohol: wine provided or corkage $7/bottle
Smoking: outdoors only
Music: amplified OK w/volume restrictions until 10pm

Outdoor Night Lighting: yes
Outdoor Cooking Facilities: no
Cleanup: provided, extra fee
View: mountains
Other: limited coordination

Wheelchair Access: yes
Insurance: certificate required
Other: no rice, birdseed, glitter or confetti; children must have adult supervision

---

This is important! *Tell facilities you're reading* **Here Comes The Guide** *and ask if our information is still current.*

Trentadue Winery

Winery

19170 Geyserville Avenue, Geyserville
(707) 433-3104, (707) 542-1235, fax (707) 433-5825

www.trentadue.com
info@trentadue.com

◆ Ceremonies ◆ Special Events
◆ Wedding Receptions ◆ Meetings
◆ Business Functions Accommodations

Italians are famous for their warm hospitality and zest for living. They may not have invented *la dolce vita* ("the sweet life"), but they perfected the recipe for it: good friends, good food and good wine, plus a generous splash of lively music. If this sounds like your idea of a good time, you'll be happy to know that Trentadue Winery can provide all the ingredients for a really smashing special event.

The winery entrance is marked by stone pillars topped with crouching lions; from here it's a short drive through the vineyards to the tasting room and event facilities. A bubbling lion-head fountain marks the entrance to the Garden Area, which consists of a quaint lattice arbor with stage, dance floor, room for tables, and a sunny lawn area. At one end of the lawn, a smaller arbor, almost smothered by a flourishing white-flowered vine, makes a romantic spot for exchanging vows. Along the west side of the entire space, a windbreak of sweet gum and redwood trees casts a shade as cool and refreshing as a drink of spring water on a hot afternoon. The vine that covers the wedding arbor also clambers up into the redwoods, over the lattice arbor, and along the fences, encircling this enchanting space like a floral drawstring (and we've been assured that this vine blooms year round). Standing here in the sun, it's hard to imagine anything lovelier, but at night, with twinkle lights covering fences, trees, and both arbors, everything sparkles like a miniature Milky Way. Additional lighting, thoughtfully equipped with dimmers, means your guests will be able to see the festivities without being blinded.

But what if your event is planned for the cooler months? Never fear—the Trentadue family has built an indoor facility, the *Sala del Leone* ("Hall of the Lion"). This expansive space has a white, peaked beamed ceiling, hand-sponged golden walls, and intriguing glass and wrought-iron light fixtures and sconces. Plenty of arched French doors all around the building allow your guests to feel connected to the natural beauty that surrounds them, yet protected from the elements. Potted olive trees (yes, they can be strung with twinkle lights) and white wooden columns can be brought in to create a "Mediterranean" look, but this versatile room blends with any decor. Recently, a corporate event featured a Morrocan theme, draping the walls to resemble a Bedouin tent. Should your guests wish to wander over to the arbor area, they are free to do so, because when you host your event at Trentadue, all the facilities are included in the rental price. And though the panoramic views of spreading vineyards and distant wooded mountains may make you think you're far from the madding crowd, the bustling town of Santa Rosa is a mere twenty minutes away!

So if you like to party "Italian style," the folks at Trentadue Winery would be happy to help you out. They can provide everything from award-winning Sangiovese wines to top-notch coordination services. All you need to do is add friends and stir!

CEREMONY, EVENT/RECEPTION & MEETING CAPACITY: The Sala del Leone Events Center holds 250 seated. The lawn can accommodate up to 300 guests, seated or standing.

FEES & DEPOSITS: A $1,000 non-refundable rental deposit and signed contract are required to reserve your date. The rental fee balance, plus a $750 refundable security deposit are required 30 days before the event. Events are held in 5-hour time blocks; overtime is available at $300/hour. There is a $150 ceremony fee.

Guests	*Fee*		*Guests*	*Fee*
0–100	$3,000		151–200	$4,000
101–150	$3,600		201–250	$4,400

AVAILABILITY: Year-round, daily, 11am–11pm.

SERVICES/AMENITIES:

Catering: select from preferred list
Kitchen Facilities: ample
Tables & Chairs: provided
Linens, Silver, etc.: through caterer and winery
Restrooms: wheelchair accessible
Dance Floor: indoor and outdoor provided
Bride's & Groom's Dressing Area: yes
Meeting Equipment: BYO

Parking: ample on-site
Accommodations: guest house; 2 bedrooms
Telephone: pay phone
Outdoor Night Lighting: yes, lawn area
Outdoor Cooking Facilities: no
Cleanup: provided
View: mountains and vineyards
Other: event coordination, wine service

RESTRICTIONS:

Alcohol: provided, or BYO w/corkage
Smoking: outdoors only
Music: amplified OK w/volume restrictions, music until 10pm

Wheelchair Access: yes
Insurance: extra liability required
Other: no confetti, rice, birdseed or glitter; no tacks or nails; children must be supervised

---

The professionals in the back of the book are the best in the business! How do we know? Read page 681.

B.R. Cohn Winery

Winery

15140 Sonoma Highway, Glen Ellen
(707) 938-4064, (800) 330-4064, fax (707) 938-4585

www.brcohn.com
bruce@brcohn.com

◆ Ceremonies   ◆ Special Events
◆ Wedding Receptions   Meetings
◆ Business Functions   Accommodations

Located 45 minutes north of the Golden Gate Bridge in the heart of Sonoma Valley, the 100 pastoral acres of B.R. Cohn Winery have a romantic, turn-of-the-century atmosphere. A winding, gravel road leads to the bluff-top tasting room; from there, a short walk down a west-facing slope leads you to the Theater in the Vines, a spectacular site for ceremonies. The Theater's outdoor platform stage comes with a stunning natural backdrop: an enormous oak shades the stage with its gnarled, leafy branches; beyond are acres of vineyards and valley, and the tree-covered peaks of the Sonoma Mountains. Guests are seated in a grassy amphitheater with an unobstructed view of the stage and the lovely panorama behind it. After tying the knot, serve champagne and hors d'oeuvres on the Theater stage or the Tasting Room Terrace so that everyone can savor the view for a while, before heading uphill to the Olive Grove for a seated dinner. Semi-enclosed by a white, split-rail fence, the Olive Grove's lush, level lawn and numerous hundred-year-old olive trees create a superb spot for al fresco receptions.

At this winery, you'll have plenty of opportunities to give your wedding a creative twist. The first bride ever married here made her entrance in a covered, horse-drawn carriage. After the ceremony, the newlyweds enjoyed a leisurely drive around the grounds, and then the carriage took groups of guests for festive rides through the countryside. Last year a horse-drawn, flatbed wagon took guests into the vineyard where a couple got married beneath the canopy of a large tree. Afterwards, everyone headed towards the Olive Grove for a Tuscan-style reception. With its numerous possibilities, peaceful setting, fine wines, and friendly, experienced event coordinator, B.R. Cohn Winery is definitely a superior spot for special events.

CEREMONY CAPACITY: The Theater in the Vines holds 160 seated or 225 standing on the stage; the Olive Grove holds 300 seated. Other options are available.

EVENT/RECEPTION CAPACITY: The Olive Grove accommodates 300 seated or standing; the Amphitheater, 150–300 seated. Other options are available.

FEES & DEPOSITS: 25% of the rental fee is the non-refundable deposit required to secure your date; another 25% is due March 1st, and the balance is due 1 month before the event. The rental fee ranges $2,500–3,000 depending on guest count, and includes use of the entire facility and the services of an event coordinator.

AVAILABILITY: May through early November, every day, flexible hours.

SERVICES/AMENITIES:

Catering: select from list or BYO w/approval
Kitchen Facilities: prep area only
Tables & Chairs: BYO or through caterer
Linens, Silver, etc.: BYO
Restrooms: wheelchair accessible
Dance Floor: CBA
Bride's Dressing Area: yes
Meeting Equipment: n/a

Parking: large lot
Accommodations: no guest rooms
Telephone: office phone
Outdoor Night Lighting: yes
Outdoor Cooking Facilities: BBQ
Cleanup: caterer or renter
View: of vineyards and Sonoma Mountains
Other: event coordination

RESTRICTIONS:

Alcohol: wine provided, can BYO beer
Smoking: designated areas
Music: amplified OK until 10pm

Wheelchair Access: yes
Insurance: certificate of liability required

Jack London Lodge
and Calabazas Creek Cafe

13740 Arnold Drive, Glen Ellen
(707) 938-8510, fax (707) 939-9642
www.jacklondonlodge.com

Lodge, Restaurant & Historic Tavern

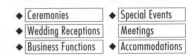

◆ Ceremonies	◆ Special Events
◆ Wedding Receptions	Meetings
◆ Business Functions	◆ Accommodations

Located in the lush hamlet of Glen Ellen, the Jack London Lodge is a new option for wine-country celebrations. Named for the famous writer who lived nearby until his death, the lodge includes the historic 1905 building that houses the saloon, and a newer, adjacent structure containing the Calabazas Creek Cafe, a brasserie-style restaurant. Its chic, yet homey interior features hunter green walls and a rustic brick fireplace. Add to that a sophisticated menu and a lovely setting on the banks of Sonoma Creek, and you've got a premiere spot for receptions and rehearsal dinners. And, if you'd like to have a ceremony nearby, there are several lovely churches just minutes away, including an historic church within walking distance from the Lodge.

You can host a special event on the Creekside Patio, which is shaded by the branches of towering trees and overlooks Sonoma Creek. With its bubbling stone fountain and outdoor serving bar, it's an al fresco setting adaptable for all types of gatherings, from casual barbecues to candlelit suppers.

If you'd prefer to celebrate indoors, the entire restaurant can be reserved. Its warm, intimate ambiance is perfect in cooler months, and a small, split-level patio just off the dining room provides a place to mingle outside. The saloon next door is also a great place for socializing. Your guests can wander over for a change of scene during or after your event, and its period decor, Jack London memorabilia, Tiffany lamps and antique oak bar will give them a taste of another era. With its cozy combination of garden setting and historic atmosphere, the Jack London Lodge is a welcome wedding venue.

CEREMONY CAPACITY: Informal ceremonies can be arranged on the patio or lawn for 100–150 guests, standing and seated.

EVENT/RECEPTION CAPACITY: The Creekside Patio holds 175 seated or 200 seated and standing, Calabazas Creek Cafe 75 seated or 175 seated and standing.

FEES & DEPOSITS: For weddings or special events, a refundable $600 deposit is required when you book the facility; the estimated event balance is payable 2 weeks prior to the event. A confirmed guest count is due 5 days prior. The rental fee for the Creekside Patio is $500 or the Creekside Dining Room is $300–400. In-house catering is provided by *Calabazas Creek Cafe.* Hors d'oeuvres start at $8/person, buffet dinners at $22/person and buffet luncheons at $16/person; alcohol, tax and a 17% service charge are additional. Any menu can be customized as well as beverage/bar packages. Ceremony setup fees range $100–400 depending on guest count.

AVAILABILITY: Daily 11am–10pm. Indoor events year-round; outdoor functions May–October.

SERVICES/AMENITIES:

Catering: provided

Kitchen Facilities: n/a

Tables & Chairs: most provided

Linens, Silver, etc.: provided

Restrooms: not wheelchair accessible

Dance Floor: deck, patio or dining room floor

Bride's Dressing Area: guest room CBA

Meeting Equipment: n/a

Parking: on street and lot

Accommodations: 22 guest rooms

Telephone: pay phone

Outdoor Night Lighting: yes

Outdoor Cooking Facilities: CBA

Cleanup: provided

View: tree-lined Sonoma Creek

Other: table decorations

RESTRICTIONS:

Alcohol: provided, WC corkage $10/bottle

Smoking: outdoors only

Music: no live amplified; DJ OK

Wheelchair Access: mostly accessible

Insurance: not required

Other: no rice, birdseed, confetti, tape or staples

The professionals in the back of the book are the best in the business! How do we know? Read page 681.

Terra Cielo

Address withheld to ensure privacy. Glen Ellen
(707) 935-0344, fax (707) 935-0255

◆ Ceremonies   ◆ Special Events
Wedding Receptions   ◆ Meetings
Business Functions   Accommodations

Terra Cielo means "heaven and earth" in Italian, and seldom have we seen a spot more appropriately named. Located high on a wooded hill above the Valley of the Moon, heaven seems only an arm's length away, while all around you, the bird-filled woods, flower-sprinkled meadows and sweeping valley views present earthly delights. Since 1953, Terra Cielo has been "heaven on earth" for the Kirk family, and now they've opened it to the public as a special event facility.

At Terra Cielo you won't find manicured lawns, formal flowerbeds or carefully clipped topiaries. Instead, the Kirks have wisely left the grounds of their home virtually untouched. The Mediterranean-style residence, sandstone-colored, flagstone-bordered swimming pool and golden quartz paths are the only "improvements" that have been made to the property, and these features enhance, rather than detract from, the natural beauty of the surrounding oaks, madrones and moss-covered boulders.

Ceremonies usually take place on a large packed golden quartz patio next to the pool. Here, the gnarled oaks have graciously withdrawn their branches, allowing you to enjoy magnificent views of the Sonoma Valley. In the near distance, wooded slopes, vineyards and a ridge topped with sharply pointed firs are reminiscent of a Tuscan countryside. Towns and farms can be seen beyond, and finally, a distant sliver of silver marks the northernmost end of the San Francisco Bay. Though this spot is quite lovely on its own, you can also dress it up with a bridal arch, either in front of the view or where the path from the bride's dressing room enters the patio area. For receptions or other festive events, tables can be set up here, or under a canopy of oak trees just beyond the pool.

Except for a dressing room for the bride and bathroom facilities, the interior of the Kirk residence is not accessible to you and your guests; however, you can take advantage of all exterior spaces, including the home's attached terrace and the pool area. A short flight of wide stairs, flanked by rock-walled flowerbeds containing lavender, star jasmine and Santa Barbara daisies, leads from the pool to the terrace. This sunny, sandstone-flagged spot is perfect for a band; dancing takes place around the pool. At one end of the terrace, a green-roofed ramada shelters a stone fireplace that can be lit if a sunset breeze chills the air.

If you're seeking an event site that combines unspoiled natural beauty, Wine Country ambiance and rustic Mediterranean charm, Terra Cielo is just what you're looking for. One glance at these tranquil grounds, and you'll be convinced it's "heaven on earth," too.

CEREMONY CAPACITY: The Terrace can seat 60 guests. The Grove can hold 120 seated or 150 standing guests.

EVENT/RECEPTION CAPACITY: The Grove can accommodate 150 seated or standing.

MEETING CAPACITY: The Grove can hold 150 seated theater-style.

FEES & DEPOSITS: A $1,500 facility fee is required to book this site. The facility fee is $1,500 for up to 100 guests, and $15 for each additional guest. A $500 refundable cleaning/damage deposit is due 30 days prior to the event.

AVAILABILITY: May–October, 9am–10pm.

SERVICES/AMENITIES:

Catering: by *The Best of Everything*
Kitchen Facilities: n/a
Tables & Chairs: BYO
Linens, Silver, etc.: BYO
Restrooms: wheelchair accessible
Dance Floor: CBA, extra charge
Bride's Dressing Area: yes
Meeting Equipment: BYO

Parking: shuttle service, extra charge
Accommodations: no guest rooms
Telephone: for emergency use
Outdoor Night Lighting: access only
Outdoor Cooking Facilities: through caterer
Cleanup: caterer
View: Sonoma Valley, Valley of the Moon, panoramic vistas

RESTRICTIONS:

Alcohol: WCB provided by *The Best of Everything*, no hard alcohol
Smoking: outside only
Music: amplified OK w/some restrictions, curfew 10pm

Wheelchair Access: yes
Insurance: liability required
Other: no rice, birdseed or confetti

This is important! *Tell facilities you're reading* **Here Comes The Guide** *and ask if our information is still current.*

Hanna Winery

Winery

9280 Highway 128, Healdsburg
(707) 431-4310, fax (707) 575-3977

www.flavorweb.com/hanna

◆ Ceremonies ◆ Special Events
◆ Wedding Receptions ◆ Meetings
◆ Business Functions Accommodations

As you drive down the entrance road to Hanna Winery, past oak trees dripping with Spanish moss and acres of vineyards, the beauty and peacefulness of the Alexander Valley become palpably apparent. The newly built tasting room, where events are held, is the perfect place from which to savor this halcyon scene. A simple, square structure with a graceful series of tall, arched window/doors on each side, the room has a 360-degree view of the surrounding landscape. In spring, when patches of lupine carpet the rolling hills, the landscape is especially breathtaking.

The tasting room is nicely designed for a wide variety of functions. It's spacious, and extremely light, thanks to a multitude of windows—including a dozen skylight panels just below the ceiling. Mustard and white walls complement the blue-gray tile floor, imported from Italy. Thick pine beams and woodwork high overhead and mahogany trim throughout add warmth. There's an enormous fireplace if you've got a yen for a crackling blaze, and you can serve your guests the fruit of the local vines from the elegant copper-topped mahogany bar.

On warm days or evenings, open all the doors and expand your party or meeting onto the wrap-around, tiled veranda, or host an entire dinner on the semi-circular deck and lawn in front of the tasting room. Constructed beneath a gigantic heritage oak, the deck is partially shaded by the tree's branches, and both the deck and garden courtyard overlook the vineyards. Whether you're planning a corporate seminar, formal dinner or casual get-together, Hanna Winery provides a very private and lovely setting.

CEREMONY CAPACITY: The Garden Courtyard holds 30–40 seated guests; the deck that overlooks the courtyard holds an additional 70 standing. Indoors, the winery can accommodate 100 seated or 200 standing guests.

EVENT/RECEPTION & MEETING CAPACITY: Indoors, the winery can accommodate 100 seated or 200 standing guests; outdoors 30–40 seated and/or 70 standing guests on the decks.

FEES & DEPOSITS: For special events, half of the rental fee is required as a non-refundable deposit to secure your date; the rental balance and a $500 refundable security/damage deposit are payable 2 months prior to the event. The rental fee for weddings is $1,500 for up to 60 guests, $2,000 for 61–100 guests. For over 100 guests, call for rates. The rental fee for meetings or other special events runs $200/hour. The ceremony setup fee is $200. Hanna wine is purchased by the case; a 3-case minimum is required.

AVAILABILITY: Year-round, daily, until midnight. Weddings and receptions take place 4pm–midnight.

SERVICES/AMENITIES:

Catering: preferred list or BYO w/approval

Kitchen Facilities: fully equipped, commercial

Tables & Chairs: caterer or renter

Linens, Silver, etc.: caterer or renter

Restrooms: wheelchair accessible

Dance Floor: tile floor

Bride's & Groom's Dressing Area: yes

Meeting Equipment: CBA, extra charge

Parking: 2 lots, ample parking

Accommodations: no guest rooms

Telephone: office phone w/approval

Outdoor Night Lighting: yes

Outdoor Cooking Facilities: BYO or caterer

Cleanup: caterer or renter

View: rolling hills & vineyards

RESTRICTIONS:

Alcohol: wine provided (no BYO); can BYO champagne & beer

Smoking: outdoors only

Music: amplified OK indoors only, until 11:30pm

Wheelchair Access: yes

Insurance: certificate required

Other: no hard alcohol; children require adult supervision

The professionals in the back of the book are the best in the business! How do we know? Read page 681.

Healdsburg Country Gardens

Address withheld to ensure privacy. Healdsburg
(707) 431-8630, fax (707) 431-8639

gogrube@ap.net

Private Country Farm & Vacation Rentals

◆ Ceremonies	◆ Special Events
◆ Wedding Receptions	Meetings
◆ Business Functions	◆ Accommodations

Walt and Barbara Gruber's wine country farm is not only a gorgeous place to live, it's an idyllic spot for a garden wedding, private party, or other special event. Sweeping views of nearby vineyards catch your eye the moment you enter the gardens, which are dotted with flowers, ancient oaks and towering redwoods. And although Mother Nature has created her own work of art here, the Grubers have

enhanced the site's natural beauty with rose-covered arches, rose and fragrance gardens, and old-fashioned picket fences. Walkways wind through lawns bordered by beds of brightly colored lavender, lilacs, roses and wisteria, past a bubbling fountain and two aviaries filled with cockatiels and singing canaries.

The site's showcase event space is the historic redwood barn. Built in 1902, it's been renovated without losing its rustic appeal. Walls are decorated with bouquets of dried flowers, and the barn doors open to a grape arbor-covered terrace. The view is lovely, from the enormous oak at the garden's edge to the sweeping panorama of the vineyards beyond. At night, tiny white lights in the arbor and soft lighting inside the barn and throughout the gardens add a romantic glow while dining, dancing or just strolling through the grounds.

Couples usually get married under the oak tree, next to two spacious lawns that provide plenty of room for ceremony seating and the reception afterwards. Two nearby guest houses are an added bonus: the wood-paneled Cottage is often used as a dressing room for the bridal party, as well as a honeymoon hideaway for the newlyweds; the Country Home can accommodate a half dozen overnight guests. Its wraparound redwood deck offers ample space for al fresco luncheons or dinners, and there's a hot tub for soaking beneath the oaks and redwoods. The Grubers have put a lot of effort into making their wine country farm not only a haven for themselves, but one that they can share with others. Come and enjoy their hospitality.

CEREMONY CAPACITY: The large lawn with the oak tree can accommodate 150 seated guests.

EVENT/RECEPTION CAPACITY: The terrace, lawns and garden can accommodate 150 seated.

FEES & DEPOSITS: For weddings, half the rental fee is the refundable deposit that holds your date. The rental fee is $3,600. The rental balance and a $400 refundable cleaning/security deposit are payable 90 days prior to the event. The fee covers a 6-hour block plus setup and cleanup time. Rehearsal dinners can be arranged; prices will vary depending on guest count and location selected.

Fees for other special events and business functions will vary based on the requirements of each event; call for specifics.

AVAILABILITY: May–October, 11am–9pm.

SERVICES/AMENITIES:

Catering: BYO, licensed & insured

Kitchen Facilities: prep only

Tables & Chairs: provided; market umbrellas provided

Linens, Silver, etc.: BYO

Restrooms: not wheelchair accessible

Dance Floor: on terrace, or barn's cement floor

Bride's & Groom's Dressing Area: yes

Other: horse-drawn carriage & rehearsal dinners CBA

Parking: ample lot, attendant provided

Accommodations: 3 guest rooms

Telephone: guest phone CBA

Outdoor Night Lighting: yes

Outdoor Cooking Facilities: CBA

Cleanup: caterer and renter

Meeting Equipment: CBA

View: panoramic view of vineyards, rolling hills and Fitch Mountain

RESTRICTIONS:

Alcohol: caterer or BYO

Smoking: outdoors only

Music: amplified OK until 9pm with restrictions

Wheelchair Access: yes

Insurance: certificate required

Other: no pets, rice or birdseed; children must be supervised; decorations are restricted

---

This is important! Tell facilities you're reading **Here Comes The Guide** and ask if our information is still current.

538

Villa Chanticleer

1248 North Fitch Mountain Road, Healdsburg
(707) 431-3301, fax (707) 431-2852
www.ci.healdsburg.ca.us

◆ Ceremonies	◆ Special Events
◆ Wedding Receptions	◆ Meetings
◆ Business Functions	Accommodations

Atop a gentle slope, within a seventeen-acre park at the edge of Healdsburg, you'll find Villa Chanticleer, a casual, no-frills facility owned by the City of Healdsburg, which has undergone a $1.4 million renovation. The redwood tree setting is pleasant, quiet and cool. Built in 1910 as a lodge resort for San Franciscans, this one-story structure is surrounded on three sides by a wide veranda, shaded by a substantial wisteria-covered trellis.

The entryway leads directly into a room containing a large, U-shaped bar with a southwest-style mural painted on the back wall. On either side of the bar are two more rooms: the Ballroom and the Dining Room, 3,000 square feet each. Both have light-toned hardwood floors, redwood paneled walls and white ceilings. The Ballroom has a large stone fireplace at its center; the Dining Room has a more open, lighter ambiance and views of the adjacent hillside. These spacious rooms can accommodate a relaxed, down home party, or be dressed up for a formal affair. What's nice about this facility is that it can handle a large crowd, the spaces are flexible and the price is quite attractive. No wonder Villa Chanticleer is a natural favorite among brides and grooms as well as local companies.

CEREMONY CAPACITY: The Ballroom or Dining Room can each accommodate 300 seated guests, each; the outdoor area holds up to 300 guests.

EVENT/RECEPTION CAPACITY: The Dining Room and Ballroom each hold 300 seated or standing guests. The Annex accommodates 150 seated guests or 200 for a standing reception. Outdoor picnic facilities can accommodate up to 300 people. The bar area can hold up to 100 guests.

MEETING CAPACITY: For corporate functions, the entire building can hold up to 632.

FEES & DEPOSITS: The 8-hour rental fee for the Villa is $1,959 on Saturday ($1,175 for Healdsburg residents), $1,306 on Fridays and Sundays ($980 for residents) or $653 Monday–Thursday ($490 for residents). The rental fee for the Villa Annex is approximately half that of the Villa. An hourly rate is also available for both buildings; call for details. Rental fees are due when reservations are confirmed. A $400 cleaning deposit is required for the Villa; $200 for the Annex. These are due 60 days prior to your event and will be refunded 30 days after the event. There is a $300 rental fee for use of the picnic area; no cleaning deposit is required. The American Legion is the single server of alcohol, arrangements must be made through them.

AVAILABILITY: Year-round, daily, including holidays.

SERVICES/AMENITIES:

Catering: BYO

Kitchen Facilities: ample

Tables & Chairs: most provided

Linens, Silver, etc.: most provided, BYO linens

Restrooms: wheelchair accessible

Dance Floor: yes

Bride's Dressing Area: CBA

Meeting Equipment: PA, flipcharts, blackboard, screen

Parking: large lot, 175 spaces

Accommodations: no guest rooms

Telephone: pay phone

Outdoor Night Lighting: yes

Outdoor Cooking Facilities: BBQ

Cleanup: caterer

View: nearby mountain range

RESTRICTIONS:

Alcohol: BYO, service only through American Legion

Smoking: outdoors only

Music: amplified OK

Wheelchair Access: yes

Insurance: extra required

Other: no rice, birdseed, metallic balloons, streamers or confetti

The professionals in the back of the book are the best in the business! How do we know? Read page 681.

540

Annadel Winery and Gardens

Private Estate & Winery

Address withheld to ensure privacy. Kenwood
(800) 446-7832, fax (510) 548-2463

www.instead-of-you.com
maxine@instead-of-you.com

◆ Ceremonies ◆ Special Events
◆ Wedding Receptions ◆ Meetings
◆ Business Functions Accommodations

Visit Annadel Winery and Gardens late on a summer's afternoon and you'll undoubtedly experience the sublime perfume of thousands of roses pulsing on a gentle wind. It's just one of many uncommon pleasures this private estate has to offer.

Located in the heart of the Valley of the Moon, at the crest of a narrow country road flanked by walnut trees, Annadel occupies 114 acres of Sonoma Valley woodlands, vineyards and rose fields. A versatile event location, it easily accommodates a wide variety of functions, from weddings to seminars to corporate events, and is equally well-suited for small and large-scale celebrations.

Annadel's main event space is the Courtyard, a striking open-air ruin, which is all that remains of the original winery that burned down in the late 1800s. With rough stone walls several feet thick and over twelve feet high, the Courtyard provides a timeless setting for ceremonies and dinners; it's especially magical when burnished by the day's last light or softly lit by hundreds of candles beneath a star-filled sky. Ancient oak trees provide shade, and a wide border of rose bushes and other flowering plants scent the air. In addition to being open to the sky, the Courtyard opens on two sides to the surrounding terrace, an excellent area for receiving guests as well as dancing the night away.

Just below the Courtyard and Terrace is an expansive lawn sheltered by tall shade trees on one side and bordered by fields of blooming roses on the other. If you're worried about a long guest list, relax—the lawn is spacious enough to handle a multitude of well-wishers and any type of seating arrangement, whether it's for a theater-style conference or a tented, seated dinner.

A few yards from the Courtyard is the century-old, green-and-white gabled Barn. With vaulted ceilings, exposed beams and original horse stalls, it's a fantastic setting for a private dinner party or rehearsal dinner, as well as an alternative area for dancing, dessert or cake-cutting activities.

The romantic allure of Annadel is perhaps most strongly felt at night, when custom copper lights softly illuminate tables, and artful lighting dramatically outlines the Courtyard walls and surrounding trees. For a few charmed hours, you're convinced you're in a stone villa in the Italian countryside, and there's no place you'd rather be.

CEREMONY CAPACITY: The Courtyard holds 225 seated.

EVENT/RECEPTION CAPACITY:

Area	Seated	Standing	Area	Seated	Standing
Courtyard	150	250	Barn	60	130
Lawn	350	500	Terrace	—	150

FEES & DEPOSITS: To reserve Annadel, a $2,500 non-refundable rental deposit is required; the rental balance and a $1,000 refundable security deposit are payable 3 months prior to the event. The rental fee is $5,000.

AVAILABILITY: Year-round, daily until 10:30pm; additional hours can be arranged.

SERVICES/AMENITIES:

Catering: preferred list, BYO w/approval
Kitchen Facilities: minimal
Tables & Chairs: CBA
Linens, Silver, etc.: CBA
Restrooms: not wheelchair accessible
Dance Floor: CBA or in barn
Bride's & Groom's Dressing Area: yes
Meeting Equipment: CBA or BYO
Other: event coordination

Parking: limited, shuttle service required
Accommodations: no guest rooms
Telephone: emergency use only
Outdoor Night Lighting: CBA
Outdoor Cooking Facilities: CBA
Cleanup: caterer
View: of rose garden, Victorian farmhouse, barn, creek & Mt. Hood

RESTRICTIONS:

Alcohol: caterer or BYO, licensed & insured server
Smoking: designated areas
Music: amplified OK w/volume restrictions

Wheelchair Access: mostly accessible
Insurance: extra required
Other: no rice; decorations require approval

*This is important! Tell facilities you're reading **Here Comes The Guide** and ask if our information is still current.*

542

Landmark Vineyards

Winery

101 Adobe Canyon Road, Kenwood
(707) 833-0053 ext. 21, fax (707) 833-1164

www.landmarkwine.com
hospitality@landmarkwine.com

◆ Ceremonies ◆ Special Events
◆ Wedding Receptions ◆ Meetings
◆ Business Functions ◆ Accommodations

In the heart of the serene Valley of the Moon, at the junction of Adobe Canyon and Highway 12, you'll find Landmark Vineyards' relatively new facility. Constructed in an Early California style with shake roof and post-and-beam supports, the building encloses a very attractive patio courtyard accented with terra cotta pots and pavers, and featuring a large, tiled fountain. Your guests will savor the setting and award-winning Landmark wines while dining at tables or mingling in the courtyard. From this vantage, the views of the adjacent vineyards and the hills beyond are magnificent.

Indoors, Landmark has plenty of room for special events, too. The structure houses a large tasting room with a high beamed ceiling, terra cotta paved floors and windows overlooking the outdoor courtyard. Of note is an interesting and colorful mural over the tasting room bar, depicting a lush, vineyard scene. For smaller, more intimate parties, take a look at the private dining room that comes with its own courtyard, accessible through multiple French doors.

It doesn't matter which space you choose—this is one facility that's not only designed for special events, but has a staff that bends over backwards to make your event run smoothly.

CEREMONY CAPACITY:

Outdoors	*Seated*	*Standing*	*Indoors*	*Seated*	*Standing*
Courtyard	140	140	Dining Room	50	75
Dining Room Patio	25	50	Tasting Room	80	100
Lawn	140	140			

EVENT/RECEPTION & MEETING CAPACITY: Landmark can accommodate 130 seated or 100–140 for a standing reception indoors. The Dining Room holds 40–50 seated; the Tasting Room, after hours, can seat up to 80 guests. The Courtyard holds up to 140 seated or standing guests. The site's maximum capacity for weddings is 140.

FEES & DEPOSITS: For weddings and special events, half the facility use fee, which is applied toward the event, is required when reservations are confirmed. The remaining use fee, food and beverage balance and a guaranteed guest count are due 7 days prior to the function. The facility use fee ranges from $300 for a ceremony to $3,400 for a large reception. In-house catering is provided: casual hors d'oeuvres receptions start at $15/person, seated luncheons at $22/person and dinners at $30/person. Alcohol, tax and a 17.5% service charge are additional.

Rental fees for weekday business functions vary depending on group size and length of the event. Call for additional information.

AVAILABILITY: Year-round, daily, 8am–11pm. Outdoor use is seasonal.

SERVICES/AMENITIES:

Catering: provided, no BYO
Kitchen Facilities: n/a
Tables & Chairs: provided
Linens, Silver, etc.: provided, extra charge
Restrooms: wheelchair accessible
Dance Floor: CBA, extra charge
Bride's Dressing Area: yes
Meeting Equipment: CBA

Parking: lot provided
Accommodations: cottage & suite
Telephone: pay phone
Outdoor Night Lighting: yes
Outdoor Cooking Facilities: no
Cleanup: provided
View: of vineyards & Sugarloaf Ridge
Other: event coordination

RESTRICTIONS:

Alcohol: WCB provided
Smoking: outside only
Music: amplified OK w/some restrictions

Wheelchair Access: yes
Insurance: not required
Other: decorations restricted

The professionals in the back of the book are the best in the business! How do we know? Read page 681.

Churchill Manor

Historic Bed & Breakfast

485 Brown Street, Napa
(707) 253-7733, fax (707) 253-8836

◆ Ceremonies   ◆ Special Events
◆ Wedding Receptions   Meetings
◆ Business Functions   ◆ Accommodations

Hidden from the street by tall privot hedges and century-old cedar trees, and surrounded by an acre of rose gardens and manicured lawns, Churchill Manor presents a very pretty picture. Guests get their first glimpse of the Manor as they enter through a trellis covered with pink Queen Elizabeth roses, and step into an area graced by a formal fountain whose base is dotted with colorful annuals. Built in 1889 in the heart of historic residential Napa, the Manor has been hosting weddings for 100 years. Now a Victorian bed and breakfast inn, it features an antique-appointed interior, wide verandas and lovely landscaped grounds.

The main entry doors—notable for their detailed leaded glass panels—lead into several parlors, each with a grand fireplace, period furnishings, fine woodwork, original brass and crystal fixtures and ornate ceilings. The airy white-painted solarium adjacent to the main buffet room is very inviting, with large leaded glass windows overlooking the garden, a mosaic marble tile floor and white furniture. Churchill Manor's interior spaces all combine to make you feel like you've stepped back in time to a slower, more gracious period. The Manor's innkeepers, Brian and Joanna, take great pains to assist with every detail, from Joanna's event coordination to Brian's in-house catering expertise. You can reserve all 10 guest rooms and have exclusive use of the Manor for your friends and family!

CEREMONY CAPACITY: The lawns can hold up to 150 seated; the rotunda area holds up to 125 seated. The parlor can hold up to 50 seated guests or 70 standing.

EVENT/RECEPTION CAPACITY: In winter, the Manor accommodates a maximum of 70 guests indoors. In spring and fall, including the veranda, 125 guests. During summer months, including the garden and veranda, 150 guests.

FEES & DEPOSITS: A $1,000 refundable damage deposit is required and will be returned if no damages are incurred. For a full-service wedding on Saturday, the wedding fee is $2,750, and includes event coordination, tables, chairs, linens, glassware and corkage. For Sunday–Friday events the fees vary: $1,750 for up to 25 guests, $20/guest for 26–75 guests, and $2,750 for over 75 guests. Food service is provided; any menu can be customized. A buffet reception costs approximately $22.50–27.50/person including an extensive hors d'oeuvres table and seated buffet dinner. Tax and a 15% service charge are additional. The total balance, with a final guest count, is due 10 days prior to the wedding date.

Special events are required to reserve the Inn's 10 guest rooms. The total guest room fee is $1,600/night plus tax, including a full breakfast. Note that if the event occurs on a Saturday, guest rooms must be booked for a minimum of 2 nights.

AVAILABILITY: March–November, daily, noon–9pm in any 6-hour block.

SERVICES/AMENITIES:

Catering: provided, no BYO

Kitchen Facilities: n/a

Tables & Chairs: provided

Linens, Silver, etc.: provided

Restrooms: wheelchair accessible

Dance Floor: yes, inside only

Bride's Dressing Area: CBA

Meeting Equipment: n/a

Parking: small lot or on street

Accommodations: 10 guest rooms

Telephone: house phone, guest room phones

Outdoor Night Lighting: yes

Outdoor Cooking Facilities: CBA

Cleanup: provided

View: parklike grounds; rose gardens

Other: piano, event coordination

RESTRICTIONS:

Alcohol: BYO, WCB only

Smoking: outside only

Music: acoustic outside until 7pm, amplified indoors until 9pm

Wheelchair Access: limited

Insurance: not required

Other: children discouraged, must be supervised

This is important! Tell facilities you're reading **Here Comes The Guide** *and ask if our information is still current.*

546

Embassy Suites Napa Valley

Hotel

1075 California Boulevard, Napa
(707) 253-9540 ext. 1031, fax (707) 224-7708

www.embassynapa.com
suitenapa@aol.com

◆ Ceremonies ◆ Special Events
◆ Wedding Receptions ◆ Meetings
◆ Business Functions ◆ Accommodations

With its brick arches, awnings, and broad circular front drive lined with towering palms, the Embassy Suites Napa Valley welcomes you with a warmth reminiscent of the Mediterranean.

Wedding ceremonies are held in the Atrium, a vibrant three-story enclosed courtyard with stone pavers. The open-air feeling is enhanced by potted trees bedecked with twinkle lights and a lush array of plants and vines cascading from the balconies around the Atrium's perimeter. There's even an indoor stream with a bridge and a waterfall that runs behind the quaint white gazebo where you'll say your vows. While this is a public area, the profusion of greenery creates a sense of privacy.

Just outside the Atrium, built over a large stone-banked pool, is a little surprise—a rustic mill house, complete with working water wheel, swans and ducks. It's a beautiful spot for photos, and while you're having your pictures taken, guests can gather for champagne in a large terra cotta-tiled, indoor courtyard with a central stone fountain.

Receptions are held in the ballrooms at either end of this area. Spacious and neutral in color scheme, they're easy to decorate. For more intimate gatherings, treat your guests to a cozy fireside meal in one of two smaller rooms that feature stone fireplaces topped with wooden mantles. And for a rehearsal dinner or private party, reserve the private dining area in Rings, the hotel's lovely indoor garden restaurant. Part of the Atrium, it has a verdant, tropical interior. The cuisine is a blend of "California Freestyle" and seasonal specialties.

The Embassy Suites is well designed for conferences too. Each ballroom can be divided with air walls, creating up to three smaller meeting areas. And of course what better reason to hold your event in a hotel than for the convenience of being able to stay over. The facility boasts indoor and outdoor swimming pools, as well as a sauna and Jacuzzi to ensure a relaxed conclusion to your festivities. So, for a sunny sojourn in the heart of the wine country, you've come to the right place.

CEREMONY CAPACITY: The Atrium (which has an indoor gazebo) holds 150 indoors.

EVENT/RECEPTION CAPACITY:

Room	Seated		Room	Seated
Chardonnay A,B,C	200		Pinot Noir A,B,C	180
Atrium	150		Cabernet Fireplace Room	60
Sauvignon Fireplace Room	60			

MEETING CAPACITY:

Room	Classroom-style	Theater-style		Room	Classroom-style	Theater-style
Chardonnay A,B,C	40–45 ea.	75–80 ea.		Sauvignon	45	80
Chardonnay A,B,C	150	225		Cabernet	45	80
Pinot Noir A,B,C	36–45 ea.	50–80 ea.		Board Room	14	—
Pinot Noir A,B,C	120	180				

FEES & DEPOSITS: For weddings, a $1,000 non-refundable deposit is required to secure your date and is payable 2 weeks after making a tentative booking. For ceremonies using the indoor gazebo and Atrium, the rental fee is $1,000; the fee for the ballroom is $1,200. Fees may be waived with a $40/person food and beverage minimum. Entrees range from $34–42/person; alcohol, tax and an 18% service charge are additional. A wedding package is available that includes centerpieces, wine with dinner, champagne toast and cake cutting.

For business functions or meetings, room rental fees run $200–1,200 depending on food and beverage minimums. Call for additional information.

AVAILABILITY: Year-round, daily, 6am–midnight. Wedding ceremonies are held 1–3pm Saturday and Sunday.

SERVICES/AMENITIES:

Catering: provided, no BYO
Kitchen Facilities: n/a
Tables & Chairs: provided
Linens, Silver, etc.: provided
Restrooms: wheelchair accessible
Dance Floor: provided
Bride's & Groom's Dressing Area: yes
Meeting Equipment: full range audio visual

Parking: large lots
Accommodations: 205 suites
Telephone: pay phones
Outdoor Night Lighting: limited, more CBA
Outdoor Cooking Facilities: no
Cleanup: provided
View: surrounding Napa hills
Other: grand piano, event planning

RESTRICTIONS:

Alcohol: provided, CW only, corkage $10/bottle
Smoking: outdoors only
Music: amplified OK indoors

Wheelchair Access: yes
Insurance: not required

The professionals in the back of the book are the best in the business! How do we know? Read page 681.

548

Garden Valley Ranch

Rose Ranch

498 Pepper Road, Petaluma
(707) 795-0919, fax (707) 792-0349

www.gardenvalley.com
gvr@gardenvalley.com

- ◆ Ceremonies
- ◆ Wedding Receptions
- ◆ Business Functions
- ◆ Special Events
- ◆ Meetings
- Accommodations

If you're a rose lover, or a gardening or horticulture buff, this eight-acre ranch, located three miles north of Petaluma, is the perfect location for an outdoor celebration. It's one of the few wedding sites where you can hold both your ceremony and reception amongst thousands of rose bushes—some 8,000 to be exact. The roses are cultivated for the sale of their blooms, and there's also a one acre garden where fragrant plants are grown for potpourri blends.

Several Victorian-style structures, a large lawn and adjacent gardens are available for large functions. Tents, canopies and tables with umbrellas can be set up on lush lawns, creating a comfortable environment for the ultimate garden wedding. Note that this is a privately owned facility, and that appointments are required to preview the site.

CEREMONY CAPACITY: The Victorian Belvedere area holds 200 seated or standing.

EVENT/RECEPTION CAPACITY: The facility can accommodate up to 200 guests for outdoor functions.

MEETING CAPACITY: The site has only outdoor facilities for meetings, and can accommodate 200 seated theater-style, maximum.

FEES & DEPOSITS: A non-refundable deposit totaling 30% of the rental fee is payable when reservations are confirmed. A $500 refundable security deposit and the 70% rental balance are due 4 weeks prior to the function. The rental fee runs $30/adult or $12.50/child (12 years and under), and includes use of the site for 5 hours, setup, cleanup and all rental equipment. Extra time is available for an additional fee.

AVAILABILITY: May–October, Wednesday–Sunday 10am–8pm; only one event per day.

SERVICES/AMENITIES:

Catering: select from preferred list
Kitchen Facilities: n/a
Tables & Chairs: provided

Parking: large lots, attendants provided
Accommodations: no guest rooms
Telephone: emergency only

Linens, Silver, etc.: provided, linens extra charge
Restrooms: wheelchair accessible
Dance Floor: brick patio
Bride's Dressing Area: yes
Meeting Equipment: no

RESTRICTIONS:
Alcohol: BYO
Smoking: allowed
Music: amplified OK

Outdoor Night Lighting: minimal
Outdoor Cooking Facilities: BBQ
Cleanup: provided
View: acres of roses
Other: event coordination, cakes, florals; tents CBA extra fee; CD player provided

Wheelchair Access: yes
Insurance: extra required
Other: children must be supervised; decorations restricted

*This is important! Tell facilities you're reading **Here Comes The Guide** and ask if our information is still current.*

550

Auberge du Soleil

Luxury Inn & Restaurant

180 Rutherford Hill Road, Rutherford
(707) 963-1211, fax (707) 963-0283

www.aubergedusoleil.com
aubdusoleil@aol.com

◆ Ceremonies ◆ Special Events
◆ Wedding Receptions ◆ Meetings
◆ Business Functions ◆ Accommodations

On a Napa hillside, near the Silverado Trail, you'll find the lovely and highly acclaimed Auberge du Soleil. The Mediterranean-style building welcomes guests through a simple yet refined garden court-yard, shaded by a canopy of gray olive trees. The beautifully appointed, understated lobby, is refreshing in light pastels, and gives you a sense of what's to come.

The inn's private dining rooms are at the base of a curved staircase that descends from the lobby. The Cedar Room is the smaller of the two. It's circular, and right in its center, seemingly supporting the ceiling, is a cedar tree trunk which acts as the room's focal point. Light, sand-colored walls frame the many French doors and windows which overlook the valley below; original artwork and cozy, multicolored upholstered furnishings lend a fresh, contemporary flavor to the room. The wood ceiling and floor plus a large stone fireplace make this a very comfortable spot, one where guests can chat or just curl up in front of the fire. The Cedar Room is terrific for smaller gatherings and dinners, and also serves as a cocktail area, expanded dinner seating or as a place for a band and dancing.

The adjacent Vista Rooms are two connected dining rooms which can accommodate larger groups. Everything here is designed to be soothing to the eye: an olive-hued carpet inscribed with an olive branch pattern, stone wall sconces, natural cedar ceiling and soft, sand-colored walls combine to make an inviting environment. No matter where you sit, you'll be able to take in glorious, panoramic views of the Napa Valley. One mirrored wall is strategically placed to reflect acres of vineyards into the room, and multiple French doors invite diners to amble outside onto the adjacent decks. The Terrace and ceremony deck have unparalleled vistas, and on warm days or evenings can be set up for outdoor dining with tables and white umbrellas. A stone-sculpted fountain is set off to one side of the Terrace, and terra cotta pots filled with brilliantly colored annuals are placed around its periphery. A wisteria-entwined trellis at one end of the Terrace offers guests a sheltered spot where they can enjoy hors d'oeuvres, watch a sunset or wedding ceremony. The ceremony deck, a small, circular area that extends out from the Terrace, offers the bride and groom a special spot to take their vows while their lucky guests get to see them, framed by the panorama beyond.

The ambiance here is both warm and *trés chic*. For an upscale, California-style wedding, the Auberge has few peers.

CEREMONY CAPACITY: The Terrace and ceremony deck hold 30 seated or 160 standing.

EVENT/RECEPTION CAPACITY: The Cedar Room holds up to 75 standing or 40 seated guests; the Vista Room I and II, combined hold 160 seated or 225 standing.

MEETING CAPACITY:

Room	Theater-style	Conf-style	Room	Theater-style	Conf-style
Cedar Room	—	14	Vista I	100	30
Vista II	60	25			

FEES & DEPOSITS: A deposit is due 2 weeks after the date has been tentatively booked. Half the estimated event total is due 60 days prior to the event; the balance is payable upon departure. The rental charge is $300–1,200, depending on guest count and room selected. In-house catered luncheons run $30–45, dinners $49–69. Alcohol, tax and a 20% service charge are additional.

For business meetings or conferences, a $12/person conference fee applies which includes coffee and tea service.

AVAILABILITY: Year-round, daily, 6am–1am. Weddings take place 11am–4pm or 6pm–1am.

SERVICES/AMENITIES:

Catering: provided, no BYO
Kitchen Facilities: n/a
Tables & Chairs: provided
Linens, Silver, etc.: provided
Restrooms: wheelchair accessible
Dance Floor: yes
Bride's & Groom's Dressing Area: CBA
Meeting Equipment: CBA

Parking: valet, $3/person
Accommodations: 50 guest rooms & suites
Telephone: pay phone
Outdoor Night Lighting: yes
Outdoor Cooking Facilities: no
Cleanup: provided
View: panoramic view of Napa Valley

RESTRICTIONS:

Alcohol: provided, no BYO
Smoking: outdoors only
Music: amplified OK with approval, no DJs

Wheelchair Access: elevator
Insurance: not required

The professionals in the back of the book are the best in the business! How do we know? Read page 681.

Luther Burbank Center for the Arts

Center for the Arts

50 Mark West Springs Road, Santa Rosa
(707) 527-7006, fax (707) 545-0518

www.lbc.net

◆ Ceremonies   ◆ Special Events
◆ Wedding Receptions   ◆ Meetings
◆ Business Functions   Accommodations

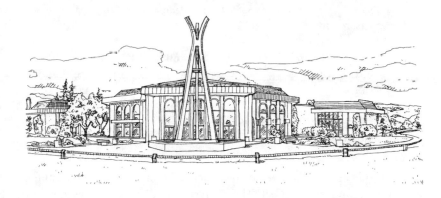

With three acres of facilities—all under one roof! and a 53-acre setting, the Luther Burbank Center for the Arts takes the prize for the largest event venue we've ever seen. Constructed in 1969 as a Pentacostal church, it enjoyed a brief period of prosperity before closing its doors. Shortly thereafter, a few Santa Rosa business leaders purchased the property and converted it into a successful non-profit center for the arts. The Santa Rosa Symphony, the Actor's Theater, and the California Museum for the Arts are just a few of the organizations which now call the Center home.

As you might imagine, given its enormity, the Center offers an assortment of event spaces as well as an array of theatrical and technical equipment. Whatever your pleasure—a lovely garden wedding or the pomp and parade of an antique auto show—the Center will gladly accommodate you.

Traditional weddings usually take place in the Center's chapel, a capacious sanctuary whose white brick walls, wrought-iron chandeliers and high ceilings braced by wood beams are reminiscent of California mission architecture. Displayed on the west wall is the chapel's most striking feature—a huge stained glass window through which light bathes the interior in colored hues. If your guest list is long, consider the main theater, an extraordinary performance space with a seating capacity of 1,550. With a thrust stage, and a concert sound and lighting system at your fingertips, a ceremony here can be a truly dramatic affair! For outdoor celebrations, there's the Courtyard, a pretty garden and patio where couples can tie the knot on a cool green swath of lawn bordered by a bed of multicolored flowers.

Lectures, seminars and receptions can also take place in a number of other rooms and halls, the most notable being the Lobby. An enormous horseshoe-shaped promenade with floor-to-ceiling windows, the Lobby commands a view of the Center's signature tower and fountain. Awash in light and painted in warm peach hues, this setting has an elegance and glamour certain to impress your guests.

Lastly there's the South Lawn, an expansive green veldt that garners rave reviews and is often the place for such colossal affairs as car shows, festivals and grand receptions. A mammoth three-spired tent is also available, allowing your outdoor soirée to be a smashing good time, rain or shine. With such a panoply of sites and staging possibilities, what more could you ask for? And don't worry about the price tag: the Luther Burbank Center for the Arts is one of the most reasonably priced venues we've ever encountered—a very sweet deal indeed!

CEREMONY CAPACITY: The Chapel holds 325 seated; the main theater, 1,550 seated; the Courtyard, 250 seated or 600 standing; and the South Lawn, 800 seated or 1,000 standing guests.

EVENT/RECEPTION & MEETING CAPACITY:

Space	*Seated*	*Standing*	*Classroom-style*	*Theater-style*
Classrooms	75	100	20–80	100
E. Auditorium	—	—	425	425
Courtyard	250	600	—	—
Gold Room	150	200	85	150
Lobby	400	800	400	600
Mall	500	800	—	—
South Lawn	800	1,000	800	1,000
Theater	—	—	—	1,550

FEES & DEPOSITS: To reserve any space, 25% of the room's rental fee ($100 min.) is required as a non-refundable deposit. The event balance is payable 60 days prior to the event. A $200 refundable cleaning/breakage deposit for use of the kitchen is also required. For weddings, 2-hour ceremonies are allowed plus a 1-hour rehearsal. Rental fees for ceremonies and receptions run $325–1,200; other social and business functions, $75–1,000.

AVAILABILITY: Year-round, daily, 7am–midnight. The outdoor lawn is available June 1–Oct 30.

SERVICES/AMENITIES:

Catering: provided or BYO
Kitchen Facilities: moderately equipped
Tables & Chairs: provided
Linens, Silver, etc.: linens provided,
BYO other tableware
Restrooms: wheelchair accessible
Dance Floor: CBA
Bride's Dressing Area: yes

Parking: ample on site
Accommodations: no guest rooms
Telephone: pay phones
Outdoor Night Lighting: limited
Outdoor Cooking Facilities: BBQs CBA
Cleanup: caterer or renter
View: surrounding hills
Meeting Equipment: full range

RESTRICTIONS:

Alcohol: licensed bartender required
Smoking: outdoors only
Music: amplified OK indoors,
outdoors w/volume limits

Wheelchair Access: yes
Insurance: certificate required
Other: no rice or birdseed

Paradise Ridge Winery

Winery

4545 Thomas Lake Harris Drive, Santa Rosa
(707) 528-9463, fax (707) 528-9481

www.paradiseridge.com
paradise@netdex.com

◆ Ceremonies	◆ Special Events
◆ Wedding Receptions	◆ Meetings
◆ Business Functions	Accommodations

Eighteen years ago, Walter and Marijke Byck discovered "paradise" atop a ridge overlooking the Russian River Valley, and soon after, a dream was born. Within the first year of purchasing the 156-acre ranch, the Bycks planted a few acres of vineyards, and by 1986, eighteen acres of premium Sauvignon Blanc and Chardonnay vines were flourishing on their land. It wasn't long before a tasting room was in the planning stages.

It took another five years to bring the winery and hospitality center to fruition, and in May 1994, both were opened to the public. The winery is constructed in what the Bycks call "California style," an architectural mix reflecting the state's diverse cultural heritage. Rooflines and exterior walls display a Japanese influence; the lower level's loggia is purely Spanish. Designed to be unpretentious, the winery fits into the surrounding countryside like a hand in a glove, and its ridgeline location commands a spectacular view of the Russian River Valley.

Once past the ancient oaks shading the front entrance, you'll be in the Vine Room, a lofty, light-filled space with large picture windows all along its west side. An arched ceiling with mahogany wood-beam accents, burgundy carpeting patterned with grape vines, a hand-painted tile fireplace and walls showcasing contemporary art create a fresh, colorful environment. The Vine Room's wraparound, covered mahogany deck overlooking the valley is a great place for sunset dining or for sipping wine served at the winery's unique tasting bar, which is handcrafted from eight different exotic woods.

From the deck, a staircase leads to an expansive terra cotta terrace bordered on one side by a sculpted, white stucco wall. Water spills forth from openings in the wall into sparkling tile fountains at its base. A heritage oak spreads its branches over a raised, six-sided redwood platform at the far end of the terrace, creating an intimate site for ceremonies. We can't help but admire the paradise the Bycks have created, and we think you will, too.

CEREMONY CAPACITY: The Poetry Terrace holds 250 seated and the Barrel Room 175 seated.

EVENT/RECEPTION CAPACITY:

Area	Seated	Standing	Area	Seated	Standing
Vine Room	150	250	Poetry Terrace	250	250
Barrel Room	125	250	Deck	110	—

MEETING CAPACITY:

Area	Theater-style	Classroom-style	Area	Theater-style	Classroom-style
Vine Room	200	80	Poetry Terrace	250	—
Barrel Room	200	80			

FEES & DEPOSITS: Half the rental fee is required to confirm your date. The rental balance is due 4 months prior to the event; a beverage deposit and a refundable $300 security deposit are due 30 days prior. The rental fee on Saturdays starts at $3,200, which covers the first 150 guests, tables, chairs, linens, champagne, wine and beer glasses, use of facility, setup and cleanup. For over 150 guests, the following per person fees apply: 151–199 guests, $12; 200–250 guests, $10. There is a $200 (minimum) ceremony setup fee. A 6-hour block is allowed for ceremonies and receptions; overtime runs $300/hour. Wine, champagne and beer are charged by consumption, with the estimated total payable 30 days in advance. Note that on Friday and Sunday, and January–March, the facility offers lower pricing.

For business meetings or seminars, the rental fee varies depending on guest count, day of week and time of day. Weekday minimums are $400; weekday evenings, $500 minimum.

AVAILABILITY: Year-round, daily. Special events and business functions, 8am–midnight.

SERVICES/AMENITIES:

Catering: provided
Kitchen Facilities: n/a
Tables & Chairs: provided
Linens, Silver, etc.: provided
Restrooms: wheelchair accessible
Dance Floor: tiled floor
Bride's Dressing Area: yes
Meeting Equipment: podium, microphone, full audio system

Parking: ample on-site
Accommodations: no guest rooms
Telephone: courtesy phone
Outdoor Night Lighting: yes
Outdoor Cooking Facilities: no
Cleanup: caterer & facility
View: of vineyards & Russian River Valley

RESTRICTIONS:

Alcohol: WBC provided
Smoking: designated area outdoors
Music: amplified OK with volume limits

Wheelchair Access: yes
Insurance: certificate required
Other: no confetti, glitter, rice or birdseed

The professionals in the back of the book are the best in the business! How do we know? Read page 681.

Cline Cellars

Winery

24737 Arnold Drive (Highway 121), Sonoma
(707) 935-4310, fax (707) 935-4319

www.clinecellars.com
epcline@sonic.net

◆ Ceremonies ◆ Special Events
◆ Wedding Receptions ◆ Meetings
◆ Business Functions ☐ Accommodations

Fred and Matt Cline spent their childhood summers in Oakley, California, learning farming and winemaking from their grandfather, Valeriano Jacuzzi (inventor of the Jacuzzi spa). Obviously the teacher and his lessons had a profound influence. The Cline brothers' Rhone-style wines, created from some of the oldest and rarest grapevines in California, recall an earlier era of winemaking. Even their Sonoma Valley winery has an old-fashioned, country charm, one as eternally appealing as Mom's apple pie.

Thousands of rose bushes line the drive to the winery's tasting room, an authentic 1850s farmhouse with Old Glory flying from the wide, wraparound veranda. Expansive lawns on either side of the farmhouse contain rock-walled, fresh water koi ponds, a remainder from the winery's past, when it was the first North American carp farm. To get to the perfect spot for taking vows, walk over an arched stone bridge spanning a stream, and you'll find yourself on a shady flagstone patio rimmed by a lotus pond with a stone fountain. The true-to-period reconstructed Adobe Mission is a charming nod to this site's history—it's where the original Mission San Francisco Solano was founded in 1823.

Ceremonies or receptions can be held in several locations: in the Adobe Mission or the Adobe's flagstone patio. Another popular site is the expansive great lawn bordered by roses and mature trees. Here you have the option of using Cline Cellars' white, 40'x40' white festival tent to create an intimate environment for dining and dancing, giving guests the option of mingling inside or outside on the landscaped grounds. A relaxed, serene environment and vintage ambiance make Cline Cellars a good choice for special celebrations.

CEREMONY CAPACITY: The front lawn can hold 125–1,000 guests. For smaller ceremonies, the Mission, the area under the willow tree, and several other locations are available.

EVENT/RECEPTION CAPACITY: The lawn to the right of the farmhouse can accommodate 125–1,000, the Barrel Room 200–500 or more. The 40' by 40' tent can handle 140 seated guests.

MEETING CAPACITY: Depending on the seating configuration, the Barrel Room can hold 500 plus guests, the Railcar Deck up to 150, the Railcar or Mission up to 30 seated guests. Outdoor locations have unlimited seating.

FEES & DEPOSITS: A $500 deposit is required to secure your date. The basic site fee is $30/person (guest minimums may apply) and includes tables, chairs, wineglasses and wine bar with servers for 5 hours. 50% of the basic fee is due 90 days prior to the event; the balance is payable 30 days prior. Overtime is $400/hour.

AVAILABILITY: Year-round, daily, any time.

SERVICES/AMENITIES:

Catering: select from preferred list
Kitchen Facilities: setup only
Tables & Chairs: provided
Linens, Silver, etc.: through caterer
Restrooms: wheelchair accessible
Dance Floor: deck or portable CBA, extra fee
Bride's Dressing Area: CBA
Meeting Equipment: no
Other: special event personnel

Parking: ample
Accommodations: no guest rooms
Telephone: pay phone
Outdoor Night Lighting: limited
Outdoor Cooking Facilities: CBA
Cleanup: caterer
View: panoramic views of landscaped property and vineyards

RESTRICTIONS:

Alcohol: WB provided, no BYO
Smoking: outdoors only
Music: amplified OK until 9pm

Wheelchair Access: yes
Insurance: certificate required
Other: no rice, glitter or confetti

This is important! Tell facilities you're reading **Here Comes The Guide** and ask if our information is still current.

The Depot Hotel, Cucina Rústica

241 First Street West, Sonoma
(707) 938-2980, fax (707) 938-5103
www.depotel.com
depotel@interx.net

Restaurant

◆ Ceremonies ◆ Special Events
◆ Wedding Receptions ◆ Meetings
◆ Business Functions ☐ Accommodations

Originally a private home, the Depot Hotel has played an active role in Sonoma's past as a restaurant and hotel. It is currently located in an historic plumstone building near the Plaza in downtown Sonoma.

Enter through the Fireplace Parlor, comfortably furnished with overstuffed chairs and couches. The soft rose walls, luxurious burgundy upholstery and an Italian tapestry give the feel of an Italian country inn. Glass doors lead out onto a covered terrace encircling the formal garden. The garden is serene and secluded, landscaped with flowers, hedges and a large reflecting pool. A comfortable dining area decorated with antique Italian china is enlarged by a glass-enclosed garden room. Here you can have the benefits of indoor dining while feeling that you're outdoors. The Depot also offers an additional benefit: the services of Chef Ghilarducci, who received the prestigious national award, Grand Master Chef of America.

CEREMONY CAPACITY: The Fireplace Parlor holds 12–40; the Garden Arbor Area 12–150 guests.

EVENT/RECEPTION CAPACITY: The Depot can accommodate up to 150 guests: indoors 100 seated or 150 standing; outdoors 120 seated or 150 standing guests.

MEETING CAPACITY: Conference-style, the Garden Room holds 26, the Main Dining Room 40, and the Garden 80.

FEES & DEPOSITS: A $200–400 deposit is required when you make your reservation and is applied towards the food and beverage cost. There is no rental fee. Food service is provided, and prices range from an hors d'oeuvres reception at $15–22/person to seated meals at $12–22/person. All event costs are payable the day of the event.

AVAILABILITY: Smaller functions, anytime; larger parties (over 30 guests) on weekends noon–4pm, or anytime on Monday or Tuesday.

SERVICES/AMENITIES:

Catering: provided, no BYO
Kitchen Facilities: n/a
Tables & Chairs: provided
Linens, Silver, etc.: provided

Parking: large lots
Accommodations: no guest rooms
Telephone: pay phone
Outdoor Night Lighting: yes

Restrooms: wheelchair accessible
Dance Floor: outside terrace
Bride's Dressing Area: CBA
Meeting Equipment: BYO

RESTRICTIONS:

Alcohol: provided or corkage $8/bottle or $6/person
Smoking: allowed for private parties

Outdoor Cooking Facilities: BBQ
Cleanup: provided
View: Italian garden w/reflection pool and Roman fountain

Wheelchair Access: yes
Insurance: not required
Music: amplified OK

The professionals in the back of the book are the best in the business! How do we know? Read page 681.

Garden Pavilion

23450 Arnold Drive, Sonoma
(707) 935-1273, fax (707) 938-0627

Private Garden

◆ Ceremonies ◆ Special Events
◆ Wedding Receptions ◆ Meetings
◆ Business Functions ◆ Accommodations

Sometimes we visit an event facility that is so lovely, that has so many outstanding features, we don't know where to begin in describing them all. Garden Pavilion, located in the town of Sonoma, is just such a place. Its old-fashioned ambiance, breathtaking gardens and eclectic design elements make it a real stand-out in a region that boasts a wealth of fabulous event venues.

The Garden Pavilion grounds consist of a large, square lawn, flanked on three sides by the various function areas. The Pavilion itself, patterned after the Garden Room at the Metropolitan Museum, was only built two years ago, but it looks as if it has occupied this spot since the Gilded Age. Constructed of green wooden latticework that supports a profusion of climbing roses, this graceful structure makes a splendid spot for dining and dancing. At one end, an enclosed half-round stage, backed by a series of green wooden arches, is perfect for a small band or DJ. And no matter how warm it is outside, the Pavilion itself stays cool, thanks to a green shade cloth roof that can lower the inside temperature by fifteen degrees. During receptions and similar social functions, the Pavilion is dressed up with awnings and fluttering ribbons; in the evening, Tivoli lights give it a festive air.

The pool area is separated from the lawn by white Chinese Chippendale fences, fronted by roses and oleander trees covered with frothy, bridal-white blooms. Here, a sparkling azure swimming pool stretches in front of an elegant Palladian poolhouse, which sleeps two, and can be used as a bridal dressing room or honeymoon cottage. Just beyond the poolhouse, couples tie the knot in the Chinese Gazebo. This captivating green-and-gold wooden structure supports a host of pale-pink roses; surrounding flowerbeds are bright with lilies, Iceland poppies, evening primrose, nasturtiums, and so many other blooms you'd need famous horticulturist Luther Burbank to name them all. Between the gazebo and pool, a lawn, partly shaded by palm trees, provides room for guest seating.

Of special interest is the Greek Revival Victorian home that sits directly across the lawn from the pool. Once the home of the property's original owners, this historic landmark is not available for events, but its rooms can be rented overnight by the couple or their family members. You can, however, use the shady, wisteria-draped veranda for your ceremony. In fact, just about every square foot of this enchanting garden environment is lovely enough for exchanging vows.

Though we've described the Garden Pavilion mostly in terms of weddings, the entertainment possibilities here are almost limitless. An afternoon tea dance would make you feel like someone out of "The Great Gatsby." Or, how about a Gay Nineties-themed party, with a band playing Scott Joplin ragtime tunes in the Pavilion? If you're stumped for ideas, plan a visit to this fabulous facility. One glimpse of the Garden Pavilion, and your imagination will burst into bloom!

CEREMONY, EVENT/RECEPTION & MEETING CAPACITY: The Pavilion can accommodate up to 190 seated or 250 standing.

FEES & DEPOSITS: A $150 non-refundable deposit is due upon reservation; the rental balance is due 2 weeks prior to the event. The site rental fee is $1,650 for 100 guests and $10 for each additional guest, and includes one guest room for two nights. If children under 6 are attending, a lifeguard must be hired for an extra $50.

AVAILABILITY: May to October, daily, 7am–11:30pm

SERVICES/AMENITIES:

Catering: select from preferred list
Kitchen Facilities: no
Tables & Chairs: BYO or through caterer
Linens, Silver, etc.: BYO or through caterer
Restrooms: not wheelchair accessible
Dance Floor: yes, cement floor
Bride's Dressing Area: yes
Meeting Equipment: BYO

Parking: lot for 85 cars & shuttle service
Accommodations: 1 guest room
Telephone: pool house phone
Outdoor Night Lighting: yes
Outdoor Cooking Facilities: BBQs
Cleanup: caterer
View: garden and vineyards

RESTRICTIONS:

Alcohol: BYO
Smoking: allowed
Music: amplified OK until 10pm w/volume restrictions

Wheelchair Access: limited
Insurance: extra insurance required

This is important! Tell facilities you're reading **Here Comes The Guide** *and ask if our information is still current.*

Gloria Ferrer Champagne Caves

Winery

23555 Highway 121, Sonoma
(707) 996-7256 ext. 231, fax (707) 996-0720

www.gloriaferrer.com
tomsco01@sprynet.com

◆ Ceremonies	◆ Special Events
◆ Wedding Receptions	Meetings
◆ Business Functions	Accommodations

You can find this winery atop a gentle slope in the Sonoma Carneros area by driving up the long, private entry road, through picturesque rolling hills dotted with vineyards. At the crest, you'll spy Gloria Ferrer Champagne Caves, a Spanish-style hacienda with old-world hospitality. The main building is large and impressive, with a red tile roof and wide entry steps. Inside, the tasting room—called the Sala de Catadores—is a warm and inviting space highlighted by an attractive mahogany bar and fireplace of matching wood and stone. Adjoining the Sala is a terrace that takes full advantage of the panoramic view of Sonoma Valley and the Ferrer vineyards below. On a warm, windless day, this is a great place for wine tasting and mingling with friends. It also makes a lovely ceremony spot.

For corporate parties or small receptions, the Executive Dining Room is intimate and elegant, with mahogany wood accents. It has windows that look out onto a colorfully landscaped promenade. This winery is an off-the-beaten-path, very private getaway for any event.

CEREMONY CAPACITY: The Vista Terrace or Tasting Room can accommodate up to 150 seated or standing guests.

EVENT/RECEPTION CAPACITY: The Sala de Catadores holds up to 120 seated or 150 for a standing reception. The Executive Dining Room seats 40.

FEES & DEPOSITS: Half the rental fee is required as a non-refundable deposit to book the facility; the balance is payable the day of the event.

# of Guests	Rental Fee		# of Guests	Rental Fee
1–25	$1,500		76–100	$2,900
26–49	1,900		101–150	3,200
50–75	2,500			

The sparkling wine fee is a required 2-case minimum purchase of Gloria Ferrer Brut for up to 75 guests, a 3-case minimum for 75–100, and a 4-case minimum for 101–150 guests. Additional wine may be purchased by the bottle; call for current prices. Tax is additional.

AVAILABILITY: Year-round, daily 6:30pm–11pm, except Thanksgiving, Christmas and New Year's days.

SERVICES/AMENITIES:

Catering: select from preferred list

Kitchen Facilities: ample

Tables & Chairs: some provided

Linens, Silver, etc.: BYO

Restrooms: wheelchair accessible

Dance Floor: provided

Bride's Dressing Area: yes

Other: event coordinator

Parking: large lot

Accommodations: no guest rooms

Telephone: house phone

Outdoor Night Lighting: minimal

Outdoor Cooking Facilities: no

Cleanup: caterer

View: of vineyards and surrounding foothills

RESTRICTIONS:

Alcohol: wine & champagne provided

Smoking: outside only

Music: amplified OK inside only

Wheelchair Access: yes

Insurance: not required

The professionals in the back of the book are the best in the business! How do we know? Read page 681.

Sonoma Mission Inn and Spa

Resort & Spa

Highway 12 and Boyes Boulevard, Sonoma
(707) 938-9000, fax (707) 996-5358

www.sonomamissioninn.com
sales@smispa.com

◆ Ceremonies ◆ Special Events
◆ Wedding Receptions ◆ Meetings
◆ Business Functions ◆ Accommodations

Amidst eight acres of eucalyptus trees, manicured lawns and colorful gardens, the Sonoma Mission Inn & Spa is a most attractive oasis for special celebrations or business functions. The Inn offers a variety of reception and meeting rooms, most with high ceilings, muted colors and natural sunlight. The largest, the Sonoma Valley Room, has an inviting fireplace for cold winter evenings, and French doors that open onto terraces during warm weather.

Banquet menus range from simple hors d'oeuvres to elegant, seated dinners and theme buffets. To help with your event, the Inn provides a professional, efficient and courteous staff. They will oversee all aspects of your event, from initial party setup to overnight accommodations for your guests. With the Spa's full range of beauty services helping your guests to look and feel their best, it's no wonder that this spot is so popular.

CEREMONY CAPACITY: Outdoors, the center lawn can accommodate up to 400 seated, the small fountain area up to 45 seated and the South Lawn 200 seated. Indoors, the Sonoma Valley Room holds up to 200 seated guests.

EVENT/RECEPTION CAPACITY, FEES & DEPOSITS: The rental fee is used as a non-refundable deposit to reserve a date. The anticipated food and beverage total is payable 60 days prior to the event. Food service is provided by the Inn, with meals starting at $34/person; bar service and bartender, alcohol, tax and a 20% service charge are additional. Rental fees and capacities are:

Room	Standing	Seated	Rental Fee
Sonoma Valley Room	250	150	$20/person
Kenwood Room	—	32	$20/person
Tent	—	350	$20/person plus a $750 tent rental fee

On Saturdays, there's a 100-guest minimum. On Sundays, the Inn offers a special wedding package which includes a round of champagne for the first toast, overnight room for the bride and groom (Sunday only) and group rates for overnight guests (Sunday only, must have a minimum 60 guests). Call for more information and rates.

MEETING CAPACITY:

Room	Conf-style	Classroom-style	Theater-style
Wine Room	10	—	—
Vineyard Room	12	—	20
Glen Ellen	18	24	30
Kenwood Room	24	30	45
Sonoma Valley Room	60	110	200
Carneros Room	12	—	—
Harvest Room	24	—	—

AVAILABILITY: Year-round, daily, anytime.

SERVICES/AMENITIES:

Catering: provided, no BYO
Kitchen Facilities: n/a
Tables & Chairs: provided
Linens, Silver, etc.: provided
Restrooms: wheelchair accessible
Dance Floor: provided
Bride's Dressing Area: yes
Meeting Equipment: full range AV

Parking: large lot, complimentary valet
Accommodations: 198 guest rooms
Telephone: pay phone
Outdoor Night Lighting: yes
Outdoor Cooking Facilities: yes
Cleanup: provided
View: grounds and gardens
Other: event coordination, wedding cakes

RESTRICTIONS:

Alcohol: provided, or corkage $10/bottle
Smoking: restricted
Music: amplified OK until 11pm

Wheelchair Access: yes
Insurance: not required

---

*This is important! Tell facilities you're reading **Here Comes The Guide** and ask if our information is still current.*

Bella Costa Sorrento

Bed & Breakfast

Address withheld to ensure privacy. St. Helena
(707) 942-5432, fax (707) 942-9029

www.piperjohnsoncatering.com
pjcater@napanet.net

◆ Ceremonies   ◆ Special Events
◆ Wedding Receptions   Meetings
◆ Business Functions   ◆ Accommodations

If you've always wanted to have an event in Napa Valley, but are put off by the tourists, traffic jams and theme-park approach encountered at some of the region's larger wineries, you'll appreciate the complete lack of fanfare at the Bella Costa Sorrento. Nestled in a wooded hollow and overlooking a vineyard, this outstanding facility offers a very private version of the classic wine country setting.

The minute you turn into the driveway, you're enveloped in an atmosphere of peaceful serenity. Drive past the gnarled trees of an old walnut orchard and park your car, then wander over to a brick cottage, partially screened by shrubs and vines. This charming old structure, with its tall, arched doorways and white-shuttered windows, is the Carriage House, part of the original Pratt estate. Mr. Pratt owned a brick kiln, and when he built the Carriage House in 1864 it was the first brick building in the upper Napa Valley. Though it's not used for events, it is included in the rental price, and is available to you and your guests for a two night stay. Tastefully appointed in a European-country style, it features elegant metal furniture, hand-crafted by the owner. Although there really isn't any other way to describe his work, calling it "metal furniture" is like calling caviar "fish eggs."

Right next to the Carriage House is a little, white, brick-and-wood structure that was once a blacksmith's shed. There's also a small lawn and gravel area surrounded by plum trees, privet shrubs, and a massive Douglas fir, which collectively provide a shady spot for prefunction mingling, as does the Carriage Houses's brick patio. From here it's a short stroll along leafy pathways to the main function area, a split-level lawn shaded by graceful oaks and an impressive black walnut tree. The property sits forty feet above the valley floor, affording sweeping views of the vineyard below and the hazy mountains in the distance. Exchange vows on the lower lawn, under an ethereal wire gazebo sitting on a raised wooden platform. This white filigree confection looks about as substantial as thistledown, but its delicate-looking frame can support flower garlands, ribbons, frothy tulle draperies, or whatever you fancy. Guests congregate on the upper lawn, connected to the lower one by steps set in a rose-flanked retaining wall. A late-morning wedding is breathtaking here, as the sun pours through the leaves, casting gold-and-green shadows on the grass. Feel free to wander about the grounds, lingering in shady grottoes decorated with statues and urns.

The estate was given the name "Bella Costa Sorrento" ("beautiful coast of Sorrento") by its original owners, an Italian family who thought the property's fog-shrouded valley floor looked like the ocean near the Italian seaside town of Sorrento. You might envision something different as you gaze across the valley floor, but whatever you see will definitely be beautiful!

CEREMONY& EVENT/RECEPTION CAPACITY: The site holds 100 guests, maximum.

FEES & DEPOSITS: For special events, half of the $3,000 site fee (treated as a non-refundable deposit) and a $1,000 refundable cleaning/damage deposit are required to secure your date; the rental balance is payable 2 months prior to the event. The rental fee includes accommodations for 2 nights in the 2-bedroom, 2-bath Carriage House, which can sleep 4 guests. For a 6-hour rehearsal dinner scheduled the night before a wedding, the B&B is available for an additional $1,000.

Catering is provided by *Piper Johnson Catering*. Menus are customized; seated luncheons, dinners or buffets start at $28/person; tax, a 16% service charge, event supervision and alcohol are additional.

AVAILABILITY: Events take place outdoors, April–November, 10am–10pm.

SERVICES/AMENITIES:

Catering: provided, no BYO
Kitchen Facilities: n/a
Tables & Chairs: rented through caterer
Linens, Silver, etc.: through caterer
Restrooms: wheelchair accessible
Dance Floor: portable CBA
Bride's & Groom's Dressing Area: carriage house
Meeting Equipment: n/a

Parking: large lots or in orchard
Accommodations: 2-bedroom carriage house
Telephone: emergency use only
Outdoor Night Lighting: limited
Outdoor Cooking Facilities: through caterer
Cleanup: caterer
View: vineyards, rolling hills, orchard

RESTRICTIONS:

Alcohol: BYO, licensed server required
Smoking: designated areas only
Music: acoustic only, volume limits

Wheelchair Access: yes
Insurance: extra liability required
Other: no rice, birdseed, confetti or glitter; no bubbles

The professionals in the back of the book are the best in the business! How do we know? Read page 681.

Meadowood Napa Valley

Resort

900 Meadowood Lane, St. Helena
(707) 963-3646, fax (707) 963-4139

www.meadowood.com

◆ Ceremonies	◆ Special Events
◆ Wedding Receptions	◆ Meetings
◆ Business Functions	◆ Accommodations

Driving into the exclusive Meadowood Resort is indeed a pleasure. You follow a narrow, tree-shaded lane, flanked by immaculately tended vineyards and forested hillsides, to the sophisticated resort complex, which includes a wine school, executive conference center and first-rate recreational facilities. The superbly designed buildings are reminiscent of New England during the early 1900s, with white balconies, gabled roofs and gray clapboard siding. All is secluded on 250 acres of densely wooded Napa Valley countryside.

The sprawling, multi-tiered Clubhouse accommodates private parties. It's set high, overlooking lush, green fairways and manicured lawns. The large Vintners' Room and Woodside Room are available for indoor meetings or receptions. The Vintners' Room is fabulous, with high ceilings and a stone fireplace, decks with umbrella-shaded tables and outstanding views. The nearby lawn slopes down to steps adjacent to a dry creek bed planted with willows, leading to a footbridge which crosses over to golf fairways. For outdoor celebrations, Meadowood arranges tables and tents on the lawns next to the Vintners' Room. There is something very special about this facility. It provides award-winning cuisine, deluxe accommodations and an environment to match. It ranks high on our list of special event locations.

CEREMONY CAPACITY:

Area	Seated	Standing	Area	Seated	Standing
Vintners' Glen	250–300	300–400	Croquet Glen	100	150
Woodside Lawn	60–80	80–100			

EVENT/RECEPTION CAPACITY: The Vintners' Room seats 120 guests indoors, with the lawn area, up to 300 seated guests. The Woodside Room seats 60 guests, 80 if in conjunction with an adjacent lawn area.

MEETING CAPACITY:

Area	Theater-style	Classroom-style	Conference-style
Vintners' Rm	140	80	50
Woodside	80	60	30
Madrone	40	25	20

Area	*Theater-style*	*Schoolroom-style*	*Conference-style*
Courthouse	30	25	20
Board Room	—	—	20
Wine Library	24	20	12

FEES & DEPOSITS: For weddings, a $1,000–3,000 deposit is required to secure your date. The facility fee ranges from $1,000–3,000, and includes ceremony coordination, rehearsal and set up, and white aisle runner. Also included are china, glassware and floor-length white table linens with overlays and napkins. Votive candles and Japanese lanterns are provided for evening events. Catering services are provided: buffets and barbecues at start at $65/person, 3-course luncheons start at $36/person, and 3-course dinners range $49–64/person. Tax and an 18% gratuity are applied to the final total.

For business functions or other events, fees vary depending on room(s) selected and services required; call for more specific information.

AVAILABILITY: For special events and business functions, year-round, daily, any time. Weddings take place Sunday–Thursday, 11am–4pm or 6pm–10pm; Friday–Saturday 11am–4pm or 6pm–11pm.

SERVICES/AMENITIES:

Catering: provided, no BYO

Kitchen Facilities: n/a

Tables & Chairs: provided

Linens, Silver, etc.: provided

Restrooms: wheelchair accessible

Dance Floor: Vintners' & Woodside Rooms CBA

Bride's Dressing Area: CBA

Meeting Equipment: full range CBA

Parking: multiple lots; valet CBA

Accommodations: 99 guest rooms and suites

Telephone: pay phones

Outdoor Cooking Facilities: provided

Outdoor Night Lighting: yes

Cleanup: provided

View: golf course and Napa hills

Other: spa & fitness center, business center

RESTRICTIONS:

Alcohol: provided, no BYO

Smoking: allowed

Music: amplified OK indoors only

Wheelchair Access: yes

Insurance: not required

This is important! Tell facilities you're reading **Here Comes The Guide** *and ask if our information is still current.*

V. Sattui Winery

1111 White Lane, St. Helena
(707) 963-7741, fax (707) 963-7536

www.vsattui.com
angela@vsattui.com

Winery

◆ Ceremonies   ◆ Special Events
◆ Wedding Receptions   ◆ Meetings
◆ Business Functions   Accommodations

V. Sattui Winery, located in the heart of Napa Valley, is a small, family winery founded in 1885. It occupies a massive stone building in the classic manner of California's early wineries, and is surrounded by lush lawns, giant oak trees, two acres of tree-shaded picnic grounds, and 35 acres of vineyards. The setting is really lovely, with vistas of the Napa Valley hills beyond.

Wedding guests can dine in a castle-like cellar lined with oak barrels and filled with the pungent aromas of aging wines. Through a stone archway are four caves where wines are aged behind heavy wrought-iron gates. A second cellar provides a more intimate spot for smaller gatherings. Hand-hewn stone walls, heavy ceiling timbers and wine barrels create an old-world atmosphere suitable for either elaborate formal dinners or casual buffets. In front of the winery, there's a small patio with steps leading down to a lawn—a great site for an outdoor ceremony. Services can be performed on the top step using the building as a colorful, picturesque backdrop.

CEREMONY CAPACITY: The lawn in front of the tower holds 200 seated or 250 standing, the cellar holds 200 seated or 350 standing, and the lower cellar patio 120 seated or 200 standing.

EVENT/RECEPTION CAPACITY: The Barrel Cellar holds 200 seated guests, the tri-level stone courtyard holds 160 seated and the outdoor lawn and grounds can accommodate 350 or more seated guests.

MEETING CAPACITY: The Barrel Cellar holds 300 seated theater-style or classroom-style and 200 seated guests conference-style.

FEES & DEPOSITS: Half of the site rental fee is a non-refundable deposit required to secure your date. For Saturday evenings, the rental fee is $3,000 for the first 100 guests, and $15/person for each additional guest. The fee for any other day is $2,250 for the first 100 guests, and $15/person for each additional guest. Rental fees plus a final guest count are due 2 weeks prior to the event. All weddings require a professional wedding coordinator.

AVAILABILITY: Year-round, daily 6pm–11:30pm.

SERVICES/AMENITIES:

Catering: select from preferred list
Kitchen Facilities: fully equipped
Tables & Chairs: provided for up to 250
Linens, Silver, etc.: glassware provided, other rentals through caterer
Restrooms: wheelchair accessible
Dance Floor: portable CBA, extra fee
Bride's Dressing Area: yes
Meeting Equipment: CBA, extra fee

Parking: large lot
Accommodations: no guest rooms
Telephone: pay phone
Outdoor Night Lighting: yes
Outdoor Cooking Facilities: BBQ
Cleanup: caterer
View: vineyards, landscaped grounds, valley hills
Other: event coordinator, winetender

RESTRICTIONS:

Alcohol: V. Sattui wine only, BYO beer w/corkage
Music: amplified OK indoors only
Smoking: outside only

Wheelchair Access: ramp and lift
Insurance: certificate required
Other: no hard liquor

The professionals in the back of the book are the best in the business! How do we know? Read page 681.

Napa Valley Grille

Restaurant

6795 Washington Street
Highway 29 at Madison Street, Yountville
(707) 944-8506, fax (707) 944-2870

www.calcafe.com

◆ Ceremonies ◆ Special Events
◆ Wedding Receptions ◆ Meetings
◆ Business Functions Accommodations

Located in the quaint town of Yountville, the Napa Valley Grille is conveniently situated right on Highway 29, but a convenient location is just the beginning of this restaurant's amenities. From its striking multi-level fieldstone facade to its four charming, versatile banquet rooms, the Napa Valley Grille is one of those wonderful establishments that has made this region as famous for its fine dining as its wines. Whether you're planning a gala wedding, sophisticated cocktail party or business seminar, the Napa Valley Grille can accommodate you in style.

The Estate Room is a sophisticated blend of classical Mediterranean and French Empire influences, with inlaid tile floors, textured off-white walls, gray molding, and generous windows swagged with twinkle-light-twined white fabric. Seating is provided by a long gray-and-green-striped banquette along one wall, and simple wrought-iron chairs upholstered in green. Chandeliers and sconces, consisting of cones of frosted glass set in swirls of wrought-iron and accented by metal leaves, make a stunning visual statement while adding a soft glow to your affair. A Corinthian-pillared pedestal and stone bench give the room a classical touch, while gold-framed pictures, some depicting Parisian scenes, add color to the walls. Though the subtle white-and-gray color scheme is quite striking on its own, the addition of some bright floral displays and coordinating tablecloths would really make this room sing!

The California or Private Reserve Rooms are perfect for smaller events. Both have subtly patterned brown carpeting, cream walls with beige molding, and wooden chairs upholstered in richly colored tapestry fabric with a grapevine pattern. Contemporary paintings of wine-country scenes enliven the walls, and large windows overlook the Napa Valley Grille's courtyard. The California Room also has French doors leading to a small terrace, where guests can mingle and sip wine or champagne. If you're seeking a small venue for a business-oriented function, you can't go wrong with the Vintner's Room. This intimate space (seating 16) is similar to the California and Private Reserve Rooms, but with its own unique features, such as a patterned, sponged wall in shades of terra cotta and cream, potted plants, wrought-iron candelabras and paintings. Large windows add light and a sense of spaciousness.

The Napa Valley Grille's brochure states, "You provide the occasion and the guests, and Napa Valley Grille will arrange the rest," and that's no idle boast. They can provide everything from a string quartet to audio-visual equipment, custom-tailor a menu to suit the most discriminating palate, and help you create an event that reflects your unique style. Add a beautiful wine-country setting, and *voila!* You have everything you need for an affair that you and your guests will remember for years to come.

CEREMONY CAPACITY: The Courtyard at Washington Square holds 120 seated; the Estate Room holds 90 seated guests.

EVENT/RECEPTION CAPACITY: The Estate Room accommodates 90 seated or 130 standing; the entire restaurant (with buyout) holds 120 seated or 175 standing guests.

MEETING CAPACITY:

Room	Conference-style	Room	Conference-style
Vintners Room	16	California Room	48
Private Reserve Room	32	Estate Room	90

FEES & DEPOSITS: For special events, a $500 refundable deposit is required; the event balance is payable at the event's conclusion. Luncheons run $20–50/person, dinners $35–100/person; tax, beverages, alcohol and an 18% service charge are additional. To reserve the entire restaurant, a $4,000–12,000 food and beverage minimum may apply depending on day of week and time frame.

For luncheons in the Estate Room, there's a $100 room rental fee and a $1,200 food and beverage minimum; for dinners, there's a $200 room rental fee and a $2,400 minimum.

AVAILABILITY: Year-round, daily 8am–midnight, except Christmas Day.

SERVICES/AMENITIES:

Catering: provided, no BYO
Kitchen Facilities: n/a
Tables & Chairs: provided
Linens, Silver, etc.: provided
Restrooms: wheelchair accessible
Dance Floor: yes
Bride's & Groom's Dressing Area: CBA
Meeting Equipment: BYO; or CBA, extra charge

Parking: ample on-site
Accommodations: no guest rooms
Telephone: pay phones
Outdoor Night Lighting: yes
Outdoor Cooking Facilities: no
Cleanup: provided
View: vineyards and landscaped courtyard
Other: event coordination, wedding cakes

RESTRICTIONS:

Alcohol: provided, or BYO wine corkage $10/bottle
Smoking: outside only
Music: amplified OK

Wheelchair Access: yes
Insurance: not required

This is important! Tell facilities you're reading **Here Comes The Guide** and ask if our information is still current.

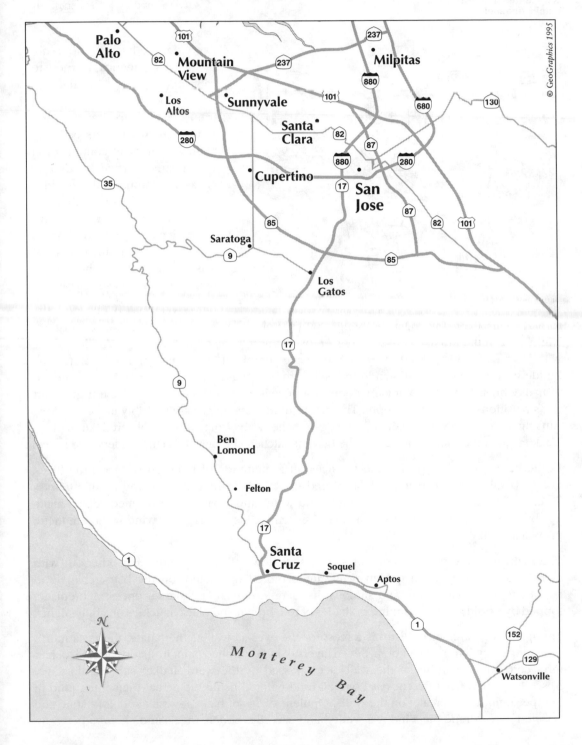

santa cruz area

© GeoGraphics 1995

Palo Alto

Mountain View

101

82

Los Altos

Sunnyvale

237

237

Milpitas

880

101

680

130

Santa Clara

82

87

280

35

Cupertino

880

280

San Jose

17

87

85

82

101

Saratoga

9

85

Los Gatos

17

9

Ben Lomond

Felton

17

Santa Cruz

Soquel

Aptos

1

152

129

Watsonville

1

N

Monterey Bay

575

Bittersweet Bistro

787 Rio del Mar Boulevard, Aptos
(831) 662-9799, fax (831) 662-9779

www.bittersweetbistro.com
vinolus@got.net

- ◆ Ceremonies
- ◆ Wedding Receptions
- ◆ Business Functions
- ◆ Special Events
- ◆ Meetings
- Accommodations

Every decade has its food trend: in the 70s, America learned to call noodles "pasta;" in the 80s, fusion cooking ran the gamut from delicious to dreadful, and in the 90s, restaurants claiming to serve American comfort food with a Paris-bistro *je ne sais quoi* are as ubiquitous as McDonald's. That's why Bittersweet Bistro is such a delightful find: its outstanding cuisine, award-winning wine list and stunning decor put it as far ahead of the other restaurants that call themselves bistros.

Bittersweet Bistro occupies the former Deer Park Tavern, a rambling, 100-year-old, gray-brick structure located just off Highway 1 in the Rio del Mar section of Aptos. Owners Thomas and Elizabeth Vinolus, along with his parents, Marge and Stacy Vinolus, have completely renovated and redecorated the building from the ground up, and the results are breathtaking. As you enter through the 50-year-old, brass-trimmed mahogany doors, your eye is immediately drawn to the intriguing art glass partitions in the Chef's Room. The panes' undulating edges are invisibly lit from below, causing them to glow like chain lightning. Soft ocher walls, colorfully upholstered banquettes, black lacquered chairs and a view of the bustling kitchen complete this chic, understated space.

In the bar area, light sparkles and bounces off a multitude of polished surfaces: the black granite bar, back-bar mirror, black lacquered stools, glistening glassware and gleaming brass accents. Slate floors, hand-textured goldenrod walls, and a pale, open-beamed ceiling make a subtle counterpoint to all the brilliance. Nestled against the big bay window, a banquette provides a cozy space to drink and chat.

The main dining area is a series of spaces that flow effortlessly into each other, all with meticulously faux painted golden walls, multicolored upholstery on the black chairs and banquettes, blue carpeting, and sinuous, handcrafted metal-and-glass sconces. A fireplace, topped by a bold abstract painting in shades of red, brown and black, crackles on chilly nights.

Though all of Bittersweet Bistro is a feast for the eyes as well as the palate, the restaurant's crowning glory is the Angel Room. Seven layers of hand-applied paint in shades of gold, ocher, terra cotta and cream make the walls seem kissed by the warm Italian sun. Subtle angel frescoes, copied from frescoes at Pompeii (and painted using the actual pigments found in Pompeii), flutter ethereally on the walls. Opulent swags of black raw silk and gold lamé and tasseled cords drape the windows while hand-carved wooden angels and cherubs perch on the windowsills. Sometimes on the tables, single pink lily flowers float in large glass bowls placed on mirrors and surrounded by votive candles. Two fireplaces add another dimension of mellow warmth to this elegant, romantic room.

Small parties and rehearsal dinners can be held outside in the courtyard, a heated patio enlivened by hanging flowers, plants and potted blooms. But by early 1999, Bittersweet will have a brand new area available for larger outdoor events: the Tuscan Garden. Enclosed by a six-foot wall, this private oasis will feature a stone fireplace, fountain and plenty of umbrella-shaded tables.

Award-winning food and wine, chic yet comfortable decor and superb, personalized service make Bittersweet Bistro the perfect spot for receptions, birthday or anniversary parties, and business luncheons. And despite the dual nature of its name, this restaurant will leave your guests with nothing but sweet memories!

CEREMONY CAPACITY: The Main Dining Room and Angel Room each hold 100–125 seated.

EVENT/RECEPTION & MEETING CAPACITY: The Angel Room holds 20–125 seated or 260 standing guests; with a dance floor, it can accommodate up to 100 seated. The outdoor patio holds 20 seated; the indoor Patio Room, 25 seated. With an mid-day buyout, the entire restaurant holds 285 seated guests.

FEES & DEPOSITS: For weddings, a $1,000 non-refundable deposit is required to secure your date. Two thirds of the estimated cost is due 30 days in advance; the remainder is payable the day of the event. Wedding meals start at $40/person; tax, an 18% service charge and alcohol are additional. The Angel Room rental fee is $700; the entire restaurant is $3,000. There's an extra charge for ceremony setups. For events with more than 50 guests, security may be required. For other social functions, luncheons start at $25/person, dinners at $35/person. The Angel Room rental fee runs $100–300. Rates for business functions vary depending on the menu and services selected; call for more specific information.

AVAILABILITY: Year-round, daily (except Monday), including holidays. The entire restaurant is available for a buyout 10am–3pm; the Angel Room and other smaller rooms, 10am–midnight. Events take place in 5-hour blocks.

SERVICES/AMENITIES:
Catering: provided, no BYO
Kitchen Facilities: n/a
Tables & Chairs: provided
Linens, Silver, etc.: provided
Restrooms: wheelchair accessible
Dance Floor: CBA, extra fee
Bride's & Groom's Dressing Area: CBA
Meeting Equipment: PA system, microphone; other equipment CBA

Parking: ample, large lot
Accommodations: no guest rooms
Telephone: pay phone
Outdoor Night Lighting: yes
Outdoor Cooking Facilities: CBA
Cleanup: provided
View: walled, Tuscan garden
Other: event coordination

RESTRICTIONS:
Alcohol: provided, no BYO
Smoking: outside only
Music: amplified OK w/volume limits

Wheelchair Access: yes
Insurance: not required
Other: no rice, birdseed, glitter or confetti; no open flames; decorations require approval

Seascape Resort

1 Seascape Resort Drive, Aptos
(831) 688-6800, fax (831) 685-3059

www.seascaperesort.com
weddings@seascaperesort.com

Oceanfront Resort

◆ Ceremonies ◆ Special Events
◆ Wedding Receptions ◆ Meetings
◆ Business Functions ◆ Accommodations

Spread out along the bluffs overlooking Monterey Bay, this resort definitely lives up to its name. From almost any vantage point, inside or out, you have sweeping ocean vistas, and if you're one of those people who comes alive in the sea air (and who isn't?), you'll find the surroundings here quite rejuvenating.

Take the ceremony spot, for example: it's an expanse of lawn on top of a bluff, set against a postcard-beautiful backdrop of cypress trees and shimmering sea. The mini-forest at the edge of the property is a favorite place for the bride and groom to have their pictures taken, and a short path leads down to the beach for a walk along the sand.

Receptions are held indoors in one of five contemporary rooms. The largest, the Seascape Room, is in pleasant shades of teal and grey and has a view of the sea. Smaller weddings take place in the Riviera Room, which has one wall of windows that face the bay, and another that overlooks the tree tops. A skylight adds to the natural light in the space. Probably the most popular room for intimate gatherings is the Bayview Room. It not only faces the ocean, but has its own terrace, which can be used just for cocktails and "scenery appreciation," or set up for al fresco dining. For a very small party or rehearsal dinner, reserve the Peninsula Room. It, too, benefits from an abundance of windows and views of the bay and the tree-studded bluff.

All of these spaces, along with three smaller rooms, are also available for meetings. Each one has state-of-the-art audio, video, computer and modem hookups, and in-house professional meeting planners will help you plan your function.

Whether you're getting married or hosting a meeting, conference or retreat here, Seascape is a great place to bring your guests for an extended stay. All of the accommodations (from studios to 2-bedroom suites) have decks or patios, kitchenettes and fireplaces, and many have views. You can go for a dip in one of three pools and relax in the spa, or take advantage of the tennis courts, gym and Olympic-size pool at the Seascape Sports Club. There's a restaurant on site, a golf course nearby, and of course the Santa Cruz/Monterey/Carmel coastline is one of the most spectacular stretches of coast in the country. So if you're tempted to turn your event into a vacation, go ahead—Seascape makes it easy.

CEREMONY CAPACITY: The Wedding Bluff can accommodate 270 seated guests.

EVENT/RECEPTION & MEETING CAPACITY:

Spaces	Seated	Standing	Spaces	Seated	Standing
Seascape Room	270	350	Riviera Room	110	110
Pacific Room	70	70	Bayview Room	50	50
Rio Room	120–140	—	Island	100–150	—

Eight rooms, accommodating 35–400 guests, are available for meetings.

FEES & DEPOSITS: For weddings or special events, a non-refundable $1,000–2,000 deposit is required to reserve your date. Half the estimated balance is due 60 days before the event, with the remainder due 6 days before the event. Wedding prices start at $70/person including catering and room rental. Seated meals for non-wedding special events or business functions start at $41/person; alcohol, tax and an 18% service charge are additional.

For meetings with overnight accommodations, room rental fees range $300–800/day; without overnight accommodations, the fee is $80/person per day. Catering can be à la carte or as part of a package. Seasonal rates may apply. Large events may require security at an extra charge.

AVAILABILITY: Year-round, daily, 7am–11pm. Wedding receptions are held on Saturdays in the Seascape Room 4pm–9pm or in the Riviera, Pacific or Bayview Rooms 1pm–6pm. Sunday hours are flexible for all 4 rooms. For meetings or conferences, please call the sales department.

SERVICES/AMENITIES:

Catering: provided, no BYO
Kitchen Facilities: n/a
Tables & Chairs: provided
Linens, Silver, etc.: provided
Restrooms: wheelchair accessible
Dance Floor: provided
Bride's & Groom's Dressing Area: rentable suites
Meeting Equipment: fully equipped

Parking: on-site for 500 guests
Accommodations: 284 guest suites
Telephone: pay phones
Outdoor Night Lighting: yes
Outdoor Cooking Facilities: provided
Cleanup: provided
View: expansive lawn & Monterey Bay
Other: coordination, theme & beach events

RESTRICTIONS:

Alcohol: provided, no BYO
Smoking: outdoors only
Music: amplified OK with limits

Wheelchair Access: yes
Insurance: not required
Other: no rice, confetti, birdseed or uncontained candles

The professionals in the back of the book are the best in the business! How do we know? Read page 681.

Sesnon House at Cabrillo College

Historic Estate & Grounds

6500 Soquel Drive, Aptos
(831) 479-6229, fax (831) 479-5743

www.cabrillo.cc.ca.us
casumma@cabrillo.cc.ca.us

◆ Ceremonies   ◆ Special Events
◆ Wedding Receptions   ◆ Meetings
◆ Business Functions   Accommodations

You know just the kind of place you want for your event: beautiful, dignified, and historic, but not a painstakingly preserved "museum" where your guests will be afraid to walk on the fragile Aubusson carpet or put their glass down on the polished Louis XIV rosewood console. You'd like it to look like a mansion, and have a sophisticated feel, yet be spacious enough to allow plenty of room to dance and mingle, but not so huge your guests feel like they're partying in a warehouse. Of course you want well-landscaped outdoor spaces, to take advantage of sunny Santa Cruz weather while having a luncheon under umbrella-shaded tables or a quiet ceremony. And you have to find all these things while staying within your less-than-lavish budget. Sound impossible? Not at Sesnon House!

It was built in 1911 by Mary and William Sesnon, and now occupies a quiet section of the Cabrillo College campus. Originally named "Pino Alto" after a large pine tree on the property, the house combines Moorish, Mission and American elements in a style known as "Californian." At the entrance, graceful columns frame the leaded-glass and polished-wood double doors opening onto the Foyer. This space has hardwood floors, a sweeping staircase, open-beamed ceiling, and brass-and-glass chandeliers and sconces. Two large rooms open off the Foyer. In the McPherson Room, creamy peach walls and white molding make a pleasant contrast to the dark-beamed ceiling and mantelpiece. On either side of the terra-cotta tiled fireplace, large windows topped by leaded-glass arches overlook the pine-fringed lawn surrounding Sesnon House. A raised hardwood stage with a baby grand piano is the perfect spot for a band, DJ, or toasting the newlyweds. The Pino Alto is similar to the McPherson Room, with French doors, a fireplace, high wainscoting and three glass-and-brass chandeliers.

Beyond the Foyer, the Simpkins Terrace is a charming spot for outdoor functions. Set up tables with umbrellas out here, or use the Terrace in conjunction with one of the indoor spaces. A short path leads from the Terrace across a velvety lawn to a diminutive Japanese pavilion, installed 70 years ago by the former owner who had an avid interest in Asian artifacts. Shaded by pines and cedars, and painted in cheerful shades of red, gold and green, this historical structure makes an intriguing ceremony spot.

The grand Sesnon House is nothing if not versatile, and a sound system, VCRs, TVs, easels, overhead projectors and Internet access make this the perfect place for combining business and pleasure. Its easy-to-find location (just off Highway 1) and abundant parking add to the facility's popularity. So if you're fretting over a list of party-planning requirements that seem insurmountable, check out Sesnon House. They may not be able to solve all your problems (like how to keep your brother-in-law from eating all the shrimp, or how to stop Aunt Edna from dancing the Macarena), but at least your surroundings will be just what you had envisioned.

CEREMONY CAPACITY: The outdoor area, including the Alan and Phyllis Simpkins Terrace and lawn, can accommodate 200 seated guests.

EVENT/RECEPTION CAPACITY: The Sesnon House can hold up to 128 seated, maximum, or 200 standing guests.

MEETING CAPACITY:

Room	Classroom-style	Room	Theater-style	Classroom-style	Boardroom
Monterey Bay	18	Piño Alto	50	30	40
Foyer	20	Mcpherson Room	75	60	50
Room 1824	16				

FEES & DEPOSITS: For weddings, a $500 refundable security/damage deposit plus half of the $1,800 site use fee are payable within 5 working days of making tentative reservations. The use fee balance is due 30 days prior to the event. The use fee covers a 10 hour event. For business-related events and other social special events, use fees will vary depending on the day of week, time frame and guest count; call for more information.

In-house catering can be provided; luncheons start at $8/person, dinners at $18/person. Tax, gratuities and alcohol are additional.

AVAILABILITY: Year-round, daily, 8am–10pm except on Cabrillo College holidays. Weddings take place Friday 11am–10pm, Saturday 11am–10pm, and Sunday 11am-10pm.

SERVICES/AMENITIES:

Catering: provided or select from preferred list
Kitchen Facilities: n/a
Tables & Chairs: provided indoors; BYO outdoors
Linens, Silver, etc.: through caterer
Restrooms: wheelchair accessible
Dance Floor: hardwood floor in foyer
Bride's & Groom's Dressing Area: yes
Meeting Equipment: VCR, TV, easel, overhead projector, screen, microphone, internet access

Parking: large lots
Accommodations: no guest rooms
Telephone: pay phones or local calls CBA
Outdoor Night Lighting: yes
Outdoor Cooking Facilities: through caterer
Cleanup: caterer
View: lawn and terrace
Other: baby grand piano, sound system

RESTRICTIONS:

Alcohol: BYO beer & wine only, approved server required
Smoking: parking lot only
Music: amplified OK

Wheelchair Access: yes
Insurance: extra liability required
Other: decorations require approval; no rice, seeds or petals; no open flames

White Magnolia Restaurant

Restaurant

8041 Soquel Drive, Aptos
(831) 662-1890, fax (831) 662-1893

chefmjr@aol.com

◆ Ceremonies   ◆ Special Events
◆ Wedding Receptions   ◆ Meetings
◆ Business Functions   ◆ Accommodations

People are always waxing nostalgic about the "good old days," when architecture, furniture, and other cultural artifacts had a dignified beauty and attention to detail that we simply don't see today. But to re-experience the aesthetic pleasures of yesteryear, how many of us would be willing to do without the technology that makes modern life such a breeze? Not many. How nice, then, to know there is one place that allows you to enjoy the best of both worlds—the White Magnolia Restaurant, a beguiling combination of the old and new.

The White Magnolia Restaurant is located in Aptos' historic Bayview Hotel, a classic example of Late Victorian Italianate architecture. The hotel opened for business in 1878, and is the oldest continually operating hotel on Monterey Bay. The original owner, Jose Arano, ordered handmade furniture from Spain and marble fireplaces from France for his establishment, and personally inspected every board that went into its construction. Though the hotel has changed hands over the years, it looks much as it did when it first opened, and is still shaded by the venerable magnolia tree that gives the restaurant its name.

In the restaurant's bar area, elements from the past form a striking backdrop for modern appointments. Here, the sleek, black-and-gray granite floor and understated, light wood-and-metal chairs harmonize effortlessly with the carved, columned washed-wood bar. On the ceiling, an elaborate round plaster molding shares space with suspended, conical white light fixtures. Above the bar, a bountiful garland of dried magnolia flowers, hydrangea blossoms and silk greenery adds a soft, feminine element. The Main Dining Room is painted magnolia-blossom white, with teal-upholstered chairs and gray carpeting. An airy chandelier, consisting of fluted, frosted glass and filigree wire, hangs from an ornate plaster molding. Touches of green are provided by a dried-flower-and-leaf wreath over the carved marble fireplace (one of those installed by Jose Arano), and feathery potted palms. The Vintage Room, with brass-and-glass light fixtures and a bay window, is perfect for small gatherings. Also available are two enclosed porches, whose decor resembles that of the Main Dining Room. Tall, wraparound windows give you the feeling of being outdoors, yet protect you from the elements.

Behind the hotel, a concrete and brick patio makes a pleasant, sunny spot for outdoor weddings, receptions, or champagne and hors d'oeuvres. Raised beds, planted with flowers, vegetables and herbs, act as a visual *aperitif*, since much of what you see growing here ends up on the restaurant's menu. A white tent and market umbrellas provide shade during hot weather, and heat lamps warm things up when the fog creeps in. Of special interest is a 100-year-old "Belle of Portugal" rose, trained as a small tree, whose pointed, pink blooms release a heady fragrance into the surrounding air. Wedding photos taken with this gorgeous rose as a backdrop are *très romantique!*

Though the White Magnolia's decor and ambiance evoke the days of picture hats and high-button shoes, you'll be happy to know that the restaurant's efficient service and up-to-date amenities are firmly rooted in the present. So, if you appreciate the stately beauty of yesteryear *and* today's modern conveniences, you owe yourself a visit to the White Magnolia Restaurant.

CEREMONY CAPACITY: During the summer months, the garden can accommodate 50 seated guests or 100 standing. The Main Dining Room can hold 30 seated or 50 standing guests.

EVENT/RECEPTION CAPACITY: The garden can hold 80 seated guests or 100 standing. The restaurant can accommodate 75 seated guests.

MEETING CAPACITY: The Vintage Room can seat 16 people conference-style.

FEES & DEPOSITS: For weddings, a $400 non-refundable rental deposit is required to secure your date; the event balance is payable at the event's conclusion. Luncheons start at $15/person, dinners at $22/person; tax, alcohol and an 18% service charge are additional. For other special events, the rental fee runs $100–400/event depending on the space(s) selected and the event duration.

AVAILABILITY: Year-round, Tuesday–Sunday, 11:30am–10pm. Saturday weddings take place 11:30am–4:30pm; on Sundays, 2:30pm–7:30pm.

SERVICES/AMENITIES:

Catering: provided, no BYO
Kitchen Facilities: n/a
Tables & Chairs: provided
Linens, Silver, etc.: provided
Restrooms: wheelchair accessible
Dance Floor: outdoor patio
Bride's Dressing Area: CBA
Meeting Equipment: BYO

Parking: on-site lots
Accommodations: 11 rooms in Bayview Hotel
Telephone: house phones for local calls
Outdoor Night Lighting: yes
Outdoor Cooking Facilities: no
Cleanup: provided
View: garden

RESTRICTIONS:

Alcohol: provided, no BYO
Smoking: patio only
Music: amplified OK w/volume limits

Wheelchair Access: yes
Insurance: not required
Other: no rice, birdseed or confetti

This is important! Tell facilities you're reading **Here Comes The Guide** *and ask if our information is still current.*

Highlands House & Park

Historic House & Park

8500 Highway 9, Ben Lomond
(831) 454-7956, fax (831) 454-7950

www.co.santa-cruz.ca.us/parks

◆ Ceremonies ◆ Special Events
◆ Wedding Receptions ◆ Meetings
◆ Business Functions Accommodations

In the early 1900s, Lord and Lady Anderson of England managed to make their way to this beautiful area just outside Felton, whereupon they bought the 43 acres which now make up Highlands Park. Naturally, they built themselves an English-style mansion on the property and named it "The Highlands" in honor of Lord Anderson's Scottish heritage. In the '30s, the Nasser family bought the estate, tore down the aging mansion and built the home which you see today, Highlands House. Santa Cruz County purchased the property and then opened it as a park in 1977, and the site has been a favorite of the public ever since.

The park's grounds have been used for a wide variety of events, and the vast lawn next to the house is where many of them take place. Spread out under the sun and ringed by towering oaks, pines and elms, it's custom made for a summer wedding. There's plenty of room for couples to get married in front of a white gazebo at one end of the lawn, and then walk over to tables set up on the other end for their reception. It's also an ideal spot for a corporate picnic or family reunion, whether you plan to bring in picnic tables, spread blankets right on the grass for a genuine lawn party, or stage a formal affair with linens, silver, and market umbrellas. The lawn is actually big enough to have several activities going at once!

The Highlands House is also available for group events. Surrounded by trees and flowers (the camellia bushes and the magnolia tree are gorgeous in bloom), it has several rooms on the first floor which can be used in a multitude of ways. For weddings, set up a buffet in the living room and have your reception in the much larger Lorenzo Room, a pleasant space with a hardwood floor (great for dancing) and multipaned windows overlooking the garden. Decorate the foyer with flowers and use it for a small ceremony or a gift room. The adjacent Garden Room is the coolest in the house, and is considered the best place for the cake and for overheated relatives. During the week, these same rooms work just as well for meetings or other business functions.

You'll be pleased to note that if you're a bride, there's a sizable changing room upstairs, and a second-floor balcony from which you can toss your bouquet. Another park perk is the swimming pool right next to the house. During the warm months, you and your guests are invited to take a dip, but keep in mind that you might be sharing the cool blue water with members of the public. The same goes for the tennis courts, kids' play area and the nature trail, just a short walk from the house. Highlands House & Park spent almost half a century as a family retreat and getaway, and it continues to provide a natural and relaxing environment for everyone who's lucky enough to spend some time here.

CEREMONY & EVENT/RECEPTION CAPACITY: The Lorenzo Room holds 50 seated or 90 for standing receptions; the lawn area seats 200. The Highlands House has a 200-guest limit. Company picnics or family reunions for over 200 people can be arranged in conjunction with the ballfields and group picnic areas next to Highlands House.

MEETING CAPACITY: Highlands House holds 75 seated theater-style; 50 conference-style.

FEES & DEPOSITS: The rental fee plus a security deposit are due when the site is booked. For Santa Cruz County residents, the fee (which covers use of House and lawn) is $650–700 for 8 hours of use and $85–90 for each additional hour. For non-residents, the fee is $750–800 for 8 hours and $95–100 for each additional hour. The security deposit is $200 if alcohol is served, $100 if not. There is a 25% discount from November 1 to March 31.

Ballfields and group picnic areas can be reserved for $110–125/day, each, with a 10% surcharge for nonresidents.

AVAILABILITY: Year-round, daily except Thanksgiving and Christmas days. Hours are 10am–midnight on Fridays and Saturdays, 10am–10pm, Sunday–Thursday. There's an 8-hour minimum on weekends, 2 hour minimum on weekdays.

SERVICES/AMENITIES:

Catering: BYO
Kitchen Facilities: moderately equipped
Tables & Chairs: 125 chairs, 15 tables provided
Linens, Silver, etc.: BYO
Restrooms: not wheelchair accessible
Dance Floor: in Lorenzo Room
Bride's Dressing Area: yes
Meeting Equipment: BYO

Parking: ample, $2/car in summer months
Accommodations: no guest rooms
Telephone: pay phone
Outdoor Night Lighting: yes, limited
Outdoor Cooking Facilities: BYO
Cleanup: mostly renter, some provided
View: of park grounds

RESTRICTIONS:

Alcohol: BYO BWC, no hard liquor
Smoking: outside only
Music: amplified restricted

Wheelchair Access: limited
Insurance: usually not required

The professionals in the back of the book are the best in the business! How do we know? Read page 681.

The River House

Address withheld to ensure privacy. Ben Lomond
(831) 688-0355, fax (831) 688-0527

◆ Ceremonies   ◆ Special Events
◆ Wedding Receptions   ◆ Meetings
◆ Business Functions   Accommodations

Nestled in the Santa Cruz mountains just minutes from the tiny enclave of Ben Lomond, River House strikes the perfect balance between a rustic wooded hide-away and a gracious country estate. This two-story California ranch-style home, built entirely of wood and river rock, is set in a large, level clear-ing ringed by oaks and redwoods. Lots of picture windows overlook the sprawling grounds and the San Lorenzo River. Adding to the natural woodland setting, manicured lawns curve around groves of oak and are bordered by flower beds planted with dogwood, rhododendrons, azaleas, and lots of annuals for color. A large, aggregate stone patio between the house and lawns has sweeping contoured lines, while a flower-lined path encircles the property. An adjacent county park adds yet more acres of woods.

With 14,000 square feet of lawns alone, the facility is a haven for outdoor events, especially weddings. The bridal procession makes a striking entrance from the back deck, dressed up with flowers for the occasion. The bride and her entourage then cross the lawn to the wood gazebo, where the couple will say their vows. Set at the foot of an oak, it's a dreamy sun-dappled spot, not only for the ceremony, but for displaying the wedding cake, too. If you're hosting a formal garden wedding, white umbrella-shaded tables laid with white linens add the right touch of elegance. Or, if you're like the couple who opted for a country and western theme, square tables with checked table cloths fit in perfectly with the woodsy setting. A few bales of hay placed here and there were all that was needed to turn River House into a mountain ranch. But even if you're not planning to wear cowboy boots to dance in, the patio is the place to kick up your heels while the band or DJ plays music on the back deck. And for a memorable final touch, brides love to toss their bouquet from the second-story balcony, which overlooks the patio and gardens.

With its close proximity to Silicon Valley, River House is a great place for corporate functions and private parties, too. Give your staff or coworkers a relaxing break from their daily rigors with a barbecue or company mixer. Or invite your family and friends here for a reunion, anniversary or birthday party. A huge fire pit set off the patio by the side of the house offers a warm and intimate gathering spot—it'll take the chill off early spring or late fall events. You can also use the expansive covered porch that wraps around the front and side of the house to seat extra guests or as a place to set up a buffet. No matter what kind of event you have in mind, River House offers a setting that's hard to resist: peaceful, secluded and downright beautiful.

CEREMONY, EVENT/RECEPTION & MEETING CAPACITY: The site holds 250 guests, maximum.

FEES & DEPOSITS: A $500 non-refundable rental deposit is required to secure your date; the balance plus a $500 refundable cleaning/damage deposit are payable 1 month prior to the event. The total rental fee is $1,500. Event coordination is available for $55/hour.

AVAILABILITY: May through October, 10am–6pm.

SERVICES/AMENITIES:

Catering: select from preferred list
Kitchen Facilities: prep only
Tables & Chairs: through caterer
Linens, Silver, etc.: through caterer
Restrooms: not wheelchair accessible
Dance Floor: on patio
Bride's Dressing Area: yes
Meeting Equipment: BYO or CBA

Parking: on site private lot
Accommodations: no guest rooms
Telephone: emergency use only
Outdoor Night Lighting: access only
Outdoor Cooking Facilities: BYO or CBA
Cleanup: caterer
View: San Lorenzo River, redwoods & oak trees
Other: event coordination

RESTRICTIONS:

Alcohol: BYO BWC only, licensed server
Smoking: outside only
Music: amplified OK w/volume restrictions

Wheelchair Access: yes
Insurance: certificate required
Other: no birdseed

This is important! Tell facilities you're reading **Here Comes The Guide** and ask if our information is still current.

Shadowbrook

Restaurant & Gardens

1750 Wharf Road, Capitola
(831) 475-1222, fax (831) 475-7664

www.shadowbrook-capitola.com
office@shadowbrook-capitola.com

◆ Ceremonies	◆ Special Events
◆ Wedding Receptions	◆ Meetings
◆ Business Functions	Accommodations

Shadowbrook is unlike any place we've ever seen and, truth be told, you can't really see it until you're actually in it. Almost completely hidden at the base of a steep, beautifully land-scaped hillside, the site has a tantalizing aura of mystery. We were intrigued. Instead of taking the cable car to the bottom, we walked down the winding path through a riot of palm trees, ferns, brightly colored flowers and rushing waterfalls.

When we finally reached the restaurant, it proved to be quite remarkable. The building—which was originally built in the 1920s as a log cabin summer home—now consists of six distinctly different rooms and two patios that flow down the hill in tiers, toward Soquel Creek. Shadowbrook has been named "Most Romantic Restaurant" by several publications, and it's easy to see why. The garden theme, so meticulously executed outside, is carried throughout the interior. Greenery is visible everywhere, from the potted palms and hanging flower pots in the Greenhouse Room to the vines clinging to the ceilings in the main dining room. And then there's your choice of views: gardens, woods, the quietly flowing creek or all of the above.

The rooms themselves have their own individual charms. The Fireside Room, which dates back to 1947 and has never been remodeled, has a rustic feel, with a large stone fireplace, redwood walls, and craftsman-style lighting fixture. Wedding ceremonies can be held here, either in front of the fireplace, or in a stairway alcove in front of a beveled-glass mirror. Another favorite spot for indoor weddings is the Atrium Area in the newly remodeled entry lounge. Small weddings or parties often take place in the Redwood Room. Warmed by the afternoon sun as well as the richness of redwood beams, window trim and wainscotting, this space also has its own private deck, bordered by an herb garden. The Owner's Private Reserve is an ideal space for a meeting or rehearsal dinner, providing diners with an imposing river rock fireplace and a wall of windows overlooking the upper patio. Larger groups who still want a sense of seclusion will feel right at home in the Wine Cellar, a redwood and brick room with a brick fireplace at one end, and storage for hundreds of wine bottles. If you like the idea of a tree growing through the middle of your dining room, you'll love the Garden Room—it's built around a thriving redwood tree in its center.

Although each of Shadowbrook's dining rooms is unique, our favorite one is the Greenhouse Room. Filled with plants and light, it delights the senses. Windows, which run along the entire length of the room, overlook the creek and open to let in soft breezes. Even the ceiling can be opened to the sky. The Greenhouse Room and the Wine Cellar are often combined for receptions, and the adjacent River Patio at the edge of the creek is the preferred spot for outdoor ceremonies. We didn't have a chance to sample the award-winning food, but if it's half as good as the setting, you're in for a treat. Few places combine nature, architecture and dining in a way that's as satisfying as Shadowbrook's, so we heartily suggest you stop by for a peek.

CEREMONY CAPACITY: The patio holds 15 seated and 150 standing, the Main Dining Room 10 seated and 120 standing, the Wine Cellar 20 standing, or the Herb Garden 25 standing.

EVENT/RECEPTION & MEETING CAPACITY: For large events or wedding receptions, you can reserve the entire restaurant, which accommodates up to 225 seated guests. Several floors may be rented separately. For smaller social or business functions: the Greenhouse Room holds 54 guests, the Wine Cellar 46, the Redwood Room 26, and the Owner's Private Reserve Room 18.

FEES & DEPOSITS: For weddings, a deposit equal to the food and beverage minimum is required; the event balance is payable the day of the event. The rental fee is $600 on Saturday and $200 Sunday–Friday. There is an extra $500 ceremony fee which includes a coordinator and rehearsal. A 2-course meal runs $17–19/person; hors d'oeuvres $4–6/person. Tax, alcohol and an 18% service charge are additional. A $2,500 food and beverage minimum applies to wedding events. The average price including food, alcohol and fees runs $45–65/person. For smaller social or business events with food service, there is no rental fee, but a $300 deposit is required to reserve space.

AVAILABILITY: Daily, 9am–1am. Earlier hours for business meetings can be arranged.

SERVICES/AMENITIES:

Catering: provided, no BYO

Kitchen Facilities: n/a

Tables & Chairs: provided

Linens, Silver, etc.: provided

Restrooms: wheelchair accessible

Dance Floor: in lounge area

Bride's & Groom's Dressing Area: yes

Meeting Equipment: PA, microphones, other CBA

Parking: ample lots

Accommodations: no guest rooms

Telephone: pay phones

Outdoor Night Lighting: on patio

Outdoor Cooking Facilities: no

Cleanup: provided

View: of Soquel Creek & gardens

Other: event coordination

RESTRICTIONS:

Alcohol: provided, no BYO

Smoking: patio only

Music: amplified OK w/volume limits

Wheelchair Access: yes

Insurance: not required

Other: no rice or birdseed

The professionals in the back of the book are the best in the business! How do we know? Read page 681.

Quail Hollow Ranch

800 Quail Hollow Road, Felton
(831) 454-7956, fax (831)454-7950
www.co.santa-cruz.ca.us/parks

Ranch & Ranch House

◆ Ceremonies ◆ Special Events
◆ Wedding Receptions ◆ Meetings
◆ Business Functions Accommodations

Most of us who live in California are familiar with *Sunset* magazine, also known as "the Magazine of Western Living." Nowhere was this lifestyle more enthusiastically embraced than at Quail Hollow Ranch, where *Sunset* publisher Laurence Lane and his family lived the robust outdoor life celebrated in the magazine for over 100 years. Once part of an 1833 Spanish land grant known as Rancho Zayante, the land was purchased in 1866 by Joseph and America Kenville. They built the ranch house and outbuildings that still stand today, and farmed the land successfully for 35 years. In 1937, the Lane family purchased the property, where many of the ideas and philosophies found in the magazine took shape amid the glorious California scenery.

A narrow, winding road leads you to Quail Hollow Ranch, where you are first greeted by a circle of gargantuan eucalyptus trees, said to be 300 feet tall! Just beyond, an immense lawn, dotted with picnic tables and shaded by a spreading live oak, separates the rambling white ranch house from the stables. Look past the white fence that encloses the compound, and see verdant meadows, woodlands, and tree-shrouded hills rising in the distance. A short walk from the house, a still pond almost hidden by willows beckons to you. Though it's mostly used as a backdrop for photographs, you can have a pond-side ceremony during warm, dry weather.

The ranch house is a handy and homey complement to the outdoor spaces. Flower-sprinkled wall paper, rag rugs and comfy furnishings constitute the simple and rustic decor; the collection of memorabilia and family photos make it seem as if the Lane family still lives here. On hot summer days, the house provides a cool, quiet retreat for Gram and Gramps, or an out-of-the-way play spot for the kids. At night or during the winter, if it gets too chilly to dance outside, move the band indoors and feel free to light a fire in the fireplace for extra warmth.

Quail Hollow Ranch is not only historically significant, it's also ecologically notable. The surrounding county park provides miles of trails that allow your guests to view the park's diverse habitats (such as riparian, maritime chaparral and mixed evergreen), as well as an occasional endangered species like the golden eagle, western pond turtle, and Rattans monkeyflower.

So if you're looking for a secluded, unspoiled spot for your event that's chock-full of natural beauty, at a price that will make you think it's 1937, take a stroll around Quail Hollow Ranch. Who knows, you may be inspired to start your own magazine!

CEREMONY CAPACITY: The lawn under the oak tree holds 100 seated; the area at the pond's edge holds 100 seated guests. Trailside ceremonies can be arranged; call for more details.

EVENT/RECEPTION CAPACITY: The patio and lawn, combined, hold 100 seated. The Ranch House interior can accommodate up to 50 seated guests.

MEETING CAPACITY: The Ranch House interior can accommodate up to 50 seated guests.

FEES & DEPOSITS: Site use fees are required to secure your date and are payable when reservations are confirmed. Use fees are as follows: for Santa Cruz County residents, $400–500, for non-County residents, $450–600. A refundable $100–200 security/damage deposit is also required when reservations are made. For rentals taking place Nov 1–March 31, a 25% rental discount will apply.

AVAILABILITY: Year-round, daily, except Thanksgiving and Christmas. Events on Friday and Saturdays, 10am–midnight; Sunday through Thursday, 10am–10pm.

SERVICES/AMENITIES:

Catering: BYO
Kitchen Facilities: moderately equipped
Tables & Chairs: some provided
Linens, Silver, etc.: renter or caterer
Restrooms: not wheelchair accessible
Dance Floor: patio
Bride's & Groom's Dressing Area: yes
Meeting Equipment: BYO

Parking: large lot
Accommodations: no guest rooms
Telephone: pay phone
Outdoor Night Lighting: BYO
Outdoor Cooking Facilities: BBQ
Cleanup: renter or caterer
View: meadow, ponds, wooded hillsides

RESTRICTIONS:

Alcohol: BYO, WCB only
Smoking: designated areas
Music: amplified OK w/volume limits

Wheelchair Access: limited, but CBA
Insurance: not required
Other: no rice

---

*This is important! Tell facilities you're reading **Here Comes The Guide** and ask if our information is still current.*

Roaring Camp & Big Trees Railroad

Roaring Camp & Graham Hill Roads, Felton
(831) 335-4484, fax (831) 335-3509

www.roaringcamprr.com
rcamp448@aol.com

Outdoor Events Facility

◆ Ceremonies	◆ Special Events
◆ Wedding Receptions	◆ Meetings
◆ Business Functions	Accommodations

The high, lonesome sound of a train whistle echoes in the forest stillness, followed by the determined chug-chug of the engine. White clouds of steam billow through the redwoods, and bluejays fly up, scolding, as the train rounds the bend. Suddenly, shots ring out, and masked desperadoes leap from the underbrush and board the slow-moving train, waving guns and forcing the engineer, at gunpoint, to bring the train to a halt. But just as the bandits are relieving the terrified passengers of their valuables, the valiant sheriff of Roaring Camp and his men gallop up to save the day! Sound like a page out of yesteryear? No, it's just your average day at Roaring Camp & Big Trees Narrow-Gauge Railroad!

Of course, this isn't a real train robbery, but one staged for the patrons of Roaring Camp on special occasions. And although this may seem the stuff of a modern-day theme park, Roaring Camp actually dates back to the 1830s, when California was under Mexican rule. It was one of the West's first American communities, and in 1845, it was here that the Bear Flag Revolt—which led to California's independence from Mexico—was planned. The railroad, too, has an illustrious history, and has been carrying passengers to the Big Trees for over a century.

Roaring Camp is nothing if not versatile, and can accommodate everything from a country wedding to a Wild West corporate event. And speaking of weddings, if you and your intended are train aficionados, why not have your ceremony in Cathedral Grove? The train will transport you and your wedding party to this stand of virgin redwoods (some over 2,000 years old) to exchange vows, then take you back to Roaring Camp for a barbecue reception and country-western dancing. (A mischievous groom can even arrange to have the bride "kidnapped" en route—but he'd better make sure she shares his sense of humor!) If you choose the Covered Bridge/Willow Pond option, you'll be transported by horse-and-buggy to the ceremony site, where you'll exchange vows overlooking a willow-fringed pond and quaint covered bridge. If you'd like more privacy, the Deer Creek Grove is a serene, magical spot, with 200-foot redwoods, bay trees, and a natural amphitheater, all bordered by a burbling stream.

For receptions, corporate events, family reunions and other large gatherings, Roaring Camp offers the perfect setting. The main picnic area has a large lawn, that can be tented for privacy and shade. Nearby, a rustic wooden theater hosts old-fashioned melodramas, complete with dancing girls and mustachioed villains (on Sundays only). An adjacent concrete pad makes a great dance floor, and you can even arrange for a square-dance caller. For real old-time fun, give your guests "Tom Sawyer" hats and let them fish their dinner out of the well-stocked trout pond, then toss it on the barbecue! The enormous main barbecue area has three barbecue pits and numerous picnic areas, separated by lattices and shaded by awnings. If you prefer a more secluded spot for your event, the Deer Creek Picnic Areas are tucked away in the redwoods.

Roaring Camp also offers: Moonlight Steam Train parties, which include the Camp's Chuckwagon Barbecue, music, dancing, and plenty of romance; a variety of "living history" days for school field trips; train rides through the redwoods to Bear Mountain or the Santa Cruz Boardwalk and, of course, gunfights and train robberies. Best of all, the staff here will take care of every detail, leaving you free to enjoy the day. And hey, maybe the engineer will even let you blow the whistle!

CEREMONY CAPACITY: The Cathedral Grove holds 200 standing guests; Deer Creek Grove, 200 standing guests. The Covered Bridge/Willow Pond area accommodates 150 standing.

EVENT/RECEPTION CAPACITY: The Main Barbeque Area holds up to 2,000 seated guests or 2,500 standing. Deer Creek Right can accommodate 75 seated or 100 standing; Deer Creek Left, 200 seated or 250 standing. Upper Deer Creek can hold up to 250 seated or 300 standing guests.

MEETING CAPACITY: Any of the above spaces may be rented for meetings. The following spaces may also be used for business functions:

Area	Conference-style	Area	Conference-style
Caboose	10	Schoolhouse	20
Frontier Tent	200	Multiple Train Cars	40–50
Barn	200	Main BBQ Area	500

FEES & DEPOSITS: 25% of the total event cost is payable 90 days prior to the event; the balance is due 10 days prior to the event with final guest count. For weddings, a $500 site fee applies. Rental fees range from $200–700, depending on which space(s) are selected. Prices run $25–40/person, and include a meal and train ride; a 10% service charge is additional. Parking is $5/vehicle. If an outside caterer is used, a $3/person fee is additional. A $175/hour fee applies for events after 6pm.

AVAILABILITY: Year-round, daily, including major holidays (except Memorial Day), 6am–midnight.

SERVICES/AMENITIES:

Catering: provided or BYO
Kitchen Facilities: no
Tables & Chairs: provided
Linens, Silver, etc.: only tablecloths provided
Restrooms: wheelchair accessible
Dance Floor: cement pad and hard-packed dirt
Bride's Dressing Area: yes, groom's CBA
Meeting Equipment: BYO or CBA, extra charge

Parking: large lot
Accommodations: no guest rooms
Telephone: pay phone
Outdoor Night Lighting: yes
Outdoor Cooking Facilities: BBQs
Cleanup: provided
View: meadows, redwoods
Other: train rides

RESTRICTIONS:

Alcohol: BYO
Music: amplified OK w/restrictions
Smoking: allowed, must pick up cigarette butts

Wheelchair Access: limited
Insurance: not required
Other: no rice or candles

Chaminade at Santa Cruz

Resort Hotel & Conference Center

1 Chaminade Lane, Santa Cruz
(800) 283-6569, (831) 475-5600, fax (831) 476-4798
www.chaminade.com
kimcraw@chaminade.com

◆ Ceremonies ◆ Special Events
◆ Wedding Receptions ◆ Meetings
◆ Business Functions ◆ Accommodations

Chaminade is a lovely Mediterranean-style resort and conference center retreat set high on a mountain bluff overlooking rolling wooded hills, with a panoramic view of Monterey Bay and the Santa Cruz Mountains.

Constructed in the 1930s as a boys' school, the original Mission-style buildings have been expanded and remodeled into a well-designed complex that includes a fine dining restaurant, a 14,000-square-foot Executive Fitness Center, and twelve banquet/conference rooms, all on 300 acres of forestland.

Spectacular surroundings make Chaminade a prime spot for any event, and weddings are no exception. Ceremonies usually take place on an expansive manicured lawn at the top of a hill, with a sweeping vista of native woodland and the brilliant blue bay in the distance. Guests are seated in white chairs, while the couple recites their vows beneath a lattice arch. Songbirds often add their voices to the celebration, and curious, tame deer have been known to make guest appearances. For small groups, a redwood deck with a valley view is also available.

On sunny days (and there are 300 of them per year on average), you may want to have your reception outdoors, too. This is easily accomplished on the red tile patio, which also has a sweeping view of the sea. Surrounded by gardens of lavender and blooming perennials, it provides a fragrant garden party atmosphere. Soft harp, violin or cello music provides an elegant touch. Larger receptions are held in the Santa Cruz Ballroom. A high, soffited ceiling arches overhead, while windows on three sides overlook views of the wooded valley and the ocean. The Ballroom has a generous dance floor, and opens onto its own private patio.

Although weddings here are a specialty, Chaminade is equally in demand for corporate retreats and conferences. To start with, you get your own conference planning manager, whose only assignment is to know you, your group and your goals, and make sure all of your needs are met. Meeting rooms are actually designed for meetings, with ergonomic chairs and state-of-the-art audiovisual setups. Organized group recreational and team-building activities, including a ropes course, scavenger hunt and a variety of sports tournaments, can be incorporated into your plan. Even the guest rooms offer amenities business travelers expect, such as work areas equipped with digital phones, and modem and analog lines.

After a day of meetings (or prior to your wedding ceremony) sink into a whirlpool spa, indulge in a massage or get a little exercise—there's the pool, fitness center, tennis courts and, of course, plenty of hiking trails. And let's not forget dinner at the Sunset Dining Room, the resort's award-winning restaurant, specializing in local fresh produce and seafood, seasoned with herbs from their own garden. Off property you can stroll on a beach, go wine tasting, rock climb, or board a yacht for a sunset sail on the bay.

At Chaminade, they have one mission: the absolute success of your wedding, business function or special event. And, given the attentive staff, outstanding facilities and gorgeous surroundings all contributing to that end, success is virtually guaranteed.

CEREMONY CAPACITY: The ocean view lawn holds 250 seated, the redwood deck 15–100 seated guests.

EVENT/RECEPTION CAPACITY: The site holds 25–250 guests, with dance floor, 240 seated.

MEETING CAPACITY:

Room	Theater-style	Classroom-style	Room	Theater-style	Classroom-style
Santa Cruz	220–224	153–170	Seascape	100–120	70–80
Natural Bridges	100–120	70–80	Cowell	72–80	45–55
New Brighton	72–80	45–55	Capitola	72–80	45–55
Rio Del Mar	58	30–37	La Selva	58	30–37

Other rooms are available.

FEES & DEPOSITS: For weddings, a $500–6,000 non-refundable deposit is required (based on guest count); the balance is due the day of the event. Ceremony and rental fees are as follows:

Area	Ceremony Fee	Rental Fee	Area	Ceremony Fee	Rental Fee
Ocean View Lawn	$1,000	—	Redwood Deck	$600	—
Santa Cruz Ballroom	—	$1,000	Ocean View Sunset Patio	—	$800
Library	—	600	& Greenhouse		
Seascape Room	—	600			

For Saturday evening Ballroom events, there is a 150-guest minimum. Catering is provided: luncheons run $60–70/person, dinners $70–90/person; tax and service charges are additional. For meetings, conferences or retreats, fees and deposits vary depending on group size and scope of event. Call the corporate sales department for more details.

AVAILABILITY: Year-round, daily. Wedding reception luncheons 11am–4:30pm; dinners 5pm–midnight. For business meetings, conferences and retreats contact the sales department.

SERVICES/AMENITIES:

Catering: provided, no BYO
Kitchen Facilities: n/a
Tables & Chairs: provided
Linens, Silver, etc.: provided
Restrooms: wheelchair accessible
Dance Floor: provided
Bride's Dressing Area: complimentary w/ceremony
Meeting Equipment: full range, state-of-the-art audio-visual

Parking: complimentary valet
Accommodations: 152 guest rooms
Telephone: pay phone
Outdoor Night Lighting: limited
Outdoor Cooking Facilities: no
Cleanup: provided
View: rolling wooded hills & Pacific ocean
Other: personal wedding coordination

RESTRICTIONS:

Alcohol: provided, no BYO
Smoking: outdoors only
Music: amplified OK outdoors w/restrictions

Wheelchair Access: yes
Insurance: not required
Other: no rice, birdseed

Hollins House at Pasatiempo

Banquet Facility

20 Clubhouse Road, Santa Cruz
(831) 459-9177, fax (831) 459-9198

www.hollinshouse.com
ray@pasatiempo.com

◆ Ceremonies   ◆ Special Events
◆ Wedding Receptions   ◆ Meetings
◆ Business Functions   Accommodations

The Hollins House, built in 1929 by championship golfer Marion Hollins, is located above the Pasatiempo Golf Club in the Santa Cruz Mountains, not far from Highway 17. Approached through acres of green fairways, the house is situated atop a knoll and offers panoramic views of Monterey Bay. You can reserve either the entire facility or just the Hollins Room and patio.

The main dining room is very long, with high ceilings, big mirrors and picture windows with views of the garden and ocean beyond. There's also a fireplace and hardwood parquet dance floor. The Tap Room is a more informal space, a cocktail lounge with a long wood bar, fireplace and windows overlooking garden and ocean. The adjacent garden is narrow, with a lawn bordered by profusely blooming impatiens. A medium-sized patio surrounded by wisteria and situated next to the Hollins Room is a picturesque place for an outdoor reception. The Hollins Room is an intimate private dining room with a big mirror over the fireplace, chandelier, rounded bay windows with bench seat and a vista of the Pacific Ocean framed by nearby oak trees. The banquet coordinator will assist you with all of your event arrangements, from flowers to specialized menus.

CEREMONY CAPACITY: The garden with gazebo can hold 80 seated or 200 standing guests.

EVENT/RECEPTION CAPACITY: The entire facility can accommodate 80–250 seated or standing guests in the summer and fall, 175 guests during cooler months. The Hollins Room and patio combined can accommodate 45 seated guests.

MEETING CAPACITY: The Hollins Room accommodates 6–25 conference style; the Dining Room holds 50 conference or theater style.

FEES & DEPOSITS: A non-refundable $1,000 deposit for the entire Hollins House or $500 deposit for the Hollins Room is required to secure your date. The facility fee for the entire Hollins House ranges $1,000–1,250. For the Hollins Room and patio it's $2 per person. The ceremony setup fee is $500. Per person food service rates: hors d'oeuvres/buffets are approximately $27 and seated meals for up to 45 seated guests vary from $18–28. Alcohol, tax and an 18% service charge are additional. You may customize your menu with help from the chef and in-house event coordinator. There's also a $50 per 100 guests cake cutting charge. The total balance is due in full by the end of your event.

For meetings, Hollins House offers a $50/person package which includes continental breakfast, full lunch, afternoon snack and some meeting equipment.

AVAILABILITY: For weddings, the entire Hollins House is available Monday–Saturday 11am–4pm or Sunday 4pm–9pm. For the Hollins Room and patio; 6pm–midnight Saturday and 10am–2pm Sunday. Meeting availability is 8am–4pm Monday–Friday, and evenings Wednesday–Saturday.

SERVICES/AMENITIES:

Catering: provided, no BYO
Kitchen Facilities: n/a
Tables & Chairs: provided
Linens, Silver, etc.: provided
Restrooms: wheelchair accessible
Dance Floor: yes
Bride's Dressing Area: yes
Meeting Equipment: AV, extra charge
Other: meetings with golf

Parking: large lots
Accommodations: no guest rooms
Telephone: pay phone
Outdoor Night Lighting: yes
Outdoor Cooking Facilities: BBQ CBA
Cleanup: provided
View: Monterey Bay & Pasatiempo Golf Course

RESTRICTIONS:

Alcohol: provided or corkage $10/bottle
Smoking: allowed
Music: amplified OK if entire facility rented

Wheelchair Access: yes, ramp
Insurance: not required

The professionals in the back of the book are the best in the business! How do we know? Read page 681.

597

The Wood Duck

Address withheld to ensure privacy. Santa Cruz
(831) 688-0355, fax (831) 688-0527

www.darkwater.com/woodduck
don@darkwater.com

◆ Ceremonies ◆ Special Events
◆ Wedding Receptions ◆ Meetings
◆ Business Functions ◆ Accommodations

A fortuitous turn of fate led Don McArthur to this magical retreat, four miles north of Santa Cruz. One Father's Day weekend, while he and his son were out driving along a stretch of country road, they just happened to come across a "property for sale" sign and couldn't resist a look-see. Don was immediately smitten with the Wood Duck and wanted to buy it. Unfortunately, there was one minor problem: it had already been sold. Luckily for Don, that sale fell through and he was next in line. The rest is history, and as Don says, finding this place was one of those things that just seemed meant to be.

Don's good fortune can be yours too. If you're planing a wedding, you can celebrate the day in an enchanted secret garden so serene and beautiful, you might just think you're in heaven. Set among gently rolling wooded hills, two creeks, and three redwood groves, the Wood Duck was designed and built by the previous owners, a craftsman master builder and his landscape architect wife. Their reverence for nature is apparent in every inch of this sprawling property: lush lawns are bordered by cedar hedges, and flower beds brim with colorful blooms. The garden's centerpiece is a picturesque 65-foot pond, dotted with lily pads. It's stocked with koi and has its own island. Don's home and a separate guest house, built entirely by hand from rich woods and river rock, add an informal rustic warmth to the setting.

Your bridal procession begins by crossing the creek on a carved footbridge and continues across the lawn to a Japanese-style pergola, draped with fragrant jasmine, where you'll say your vows. After the ceremony, gather on the patio by the pond for refreshments while tables, set with bright white linens and fresh flowers, are readied on the lawn back by the pergola. Your guests will enjoy exploring the meandering paths, discovering statuary and benches nestled among the greenery, and strolling down to the beach by the creek. Children love the ivy-covered fairytale treehouse; its arched door leads into the hollow trunk and up to the turret, where even a few wedding couples have been known to savor a quiet moment.

While this location is a sublime spot for weddings, it's just as wonderful for other types of events. Corporations love to have their seminars, barbecues and mixers here, and you couldn't find a more delightful place for a garden party.

You won't want to leave these magnificent grounds at the end of the day, and you don't have to—begin your honeymoon or weekend getaway in the guest house. Here you'll be surrounded by satiny hand-finished woods, from the floor to the cathedral ceiling. Before bedding down for the night, however, snuggle up by the wood burning stove or take a soak in the nearby hot tub, set in a redwood cathedral. Then climb into the loft bed, where you can view the starry heavens through skylights, and marvel at your good fortune at having found paradise.

CEREMONY CAPACITY: The site can accommodate 150 guests outdoors. There are no indoor facilities.

Space	Seated	Standing	Space	Seated	Standing
Main Lawn	150	150	Waterfall Area	—	15
Lily Pond	30	50			

EVENT/RECEPTION & MEETING CAPACITY: The Main Lawn accommodates 150 seated guests.

FEES & DEPOSITS: A $500 non-refundable rental deposit is required to secure your date. The rental fee balance plus a refundable $200 security deposit are payable 1 month prior to the event. Event coordination services are available for a fee of $55/hour.

The rental fee for ceremonies only is $1,000–2,000 depending on guest count; for ceremonies plus receptions, $1,500–2,500 depending on guest count. The wedding reception/ceremony fee includes a 1-hour rehearsal the previous day and use of the Guest Cottage during the event. The Guest Cottage is also available the night of the event until 1pm the next day. The $150 Cottage rental fee includes a continental breakfast the following morning. Additional days are available at $125/day. Catering prices range $20–60/person for buffets or seated meals. Tax, alcohol and a 15% service charge are additional.

AVAILABILITY: May–October, weather permitting, 10am–5pm. Other time frames can be arranged. Ceremonies are allowed a 2-1/2 hour block; receptions an 8-hour block. Additional time can be arranged for an extra fee.

SERVICES/AMENITIES:

Catering: preferred list
Kitchen Facilities: n/a
Tables & Chairs: through caterer
Linens, Silver, etc.: through caterer
Restrooms: not wheelchair accessible, portable CBA
Dance Floor: CBA
Bride's Dressing Area: guest cottage
Meeting Equipment: CBA

Parking: on site, shuttle provided to nearby lot
Accommodations: guest cottage, sleeps 4
Telephone: emergency use only
Outdoor Night Lighting: yes
Outdoor Cooking Facilities: river rock BBQ
Cleanup: caterer
View: gardens, ponds, redwood groves, streams & waterfalls, country hillsides
Other: event coordination, tenting CBA

RESTRICTIONS:

Alcohol: BYO WC only, licensed server
Smoking: not permitted
Music: no amplified, DJ OK w/volume limits
Other: children must be supervised; no birdseed or rice

Wheelchair Access: grounds accessible, cottage has step
Insurance: certificate required

Kennolyn Conference Center

Hilltop Hacienda & Logging Town

Address withheld to ensure privacy. Soquel
(831) 479-6700, fax (831) 479-6730

www.kennolyn.com
kennolyncc@aol.com

Special Event & Retreat Center

- Ceremonies
- Wedding Receptions
- Business Functions
- Special Events
- Meetings
- Accommodations

Kennolyn Conference Center has some unique facilities for special events, but the newest, and in our estimation the most striking, is the Hilltop Hacienda. Set literally on top of one of the Santa Cruz mountains, and overlooking redwood forests and Monterey Bay, it not only has a fabulous view, but it's so quiet up here you can truly hear yourself think (or not think, as the case may be).

You enter this Spanish-style building through a sun-drenched courtyard, with a four-tiered fountain bubbling in its center and pots of vibrant flowers all around. The interior is as cool as the outside is warm. Spacious and simple in design, it has an open-beamed ceiling, wrought-iron chandeliers, and sets of French doors along two sides that open onto either the courtyard or a heavenly patio that faces the bay. Walls are painted white, doors are trimmed in teal, and the ends of all of the ceiling beams are tipped in rich red. When the sun goes down, you can extend the day's warmth by lighting a fire in the fireplace. As you might imagine, weddings here are delightful, and for corporate seminars or retreats, you'd be hard pressed to find a more restful spot.

Located in another part of this 300-acre, redwood paradise is the Logging Town, named for its quaint row of old-west buildings. It contains a terrific dining hall, a variety of meeting spaces, sports facilities and the Center's overnight accommodations. While this area is most often used for meetings and seminar retreats, it also makes an unusual wedding site. One couple and their guests started off the wedding day with a ropes course, then had their ceremony on the patio next to the pool, followed by the reception on the dining hall deck, and finally a group swim and a few games of tennis. (By the way, the ropes course is a popular, corporate team-building activity.)

The old-fashioned dining hall, with its great river rock fireplace, is the Logging Town's main space, and is used for dining, meeting or both. Smaller meeting rooms nearby have knotty pine ceilings, skylights, and brick walls. You can even have your meeting in a replica of an old schoolhouse, complete with chalkboard and teacher's desk. Your guests can stay in quaint and comfortable log cabins appointed with antiques, and if you have extra company, some come with day beds. There are also completely modern private guest rooms with full bathrooms, skylights and ceiling fans.

Although the words "Conference Center" figure predominantly in this facility's name, Kennolyn is the antithesis of your standard conference locale. Its gorgeous surroundings will take the stiffness out of business functions, and bring beauty and serenity to any event.

CEREMONY CAPACITY: The site holds up to 50 seated indoors or 300 seated outdoors.

EVENT/RECEPTION CAPACITY: Indoors, up to 150 seated or standing; outdoors 300 seated or standing guests.

MEETING CAPACITY: There are 9 meeting rooms which can hold 8–150 seated guests.

FEES & DEPOSITS: Saturday rental fees start at $2,500 for a 5-hour period; Sunday rental fees start at $1,500/5-hour period. For events Monday–Friday, the fee is $1,000 for a 5-hour block. There is a $500 ceremony fee (which includes an extra 1/2 hour of facility use, chairs, changing rooms, ceremony coordinator, setup and breakdown). To reserve your date, 25% of your anticipated event total is required as a non-refundable deposit. The balance plus a refundable $500 damage deposit are payable 3 days prior to the event. In-house catering is provided, starting at $30/person; alcohol, tax and an 18% service charge are additional.

AVAILABILITY: Year-round, daily, 8am–10pm in any 5-hour block.

SERVICES/AMENITIES:

Catering: provided, no BYO
Kitchen Facilities: n/a
Tables & Chairs: provided
Linens, Silver, etc.: provided
Restrooms: wheelchair accessible
Dance Floor: courtyard or CBA, extra fee
Bride's & Groom's Dressing Area: yes
Meeting Equipment: full range

Parking: ample, several lots
Accommodations: 26 log cabins
Telephone: pay phones
Outdoor Night Lighting: yes
Outdoor Cooking Facilities: BBQ
Cleanup: provided, renter cleans decorations
View: vistas of Monterey Bay and Santa Cruz
Other: event coordination, carriage rides, full range of sports activities

RESTRICTIONS:

Alcohol: through preferred bartender
Smoking: courtyard or patio only
Music: amplified OK until 10pm

Wheelchair Access: most areas, not all
Insurance: certificate required
Other: no pets, glitter, rice or birdseed; decorations with approval

The Millpond

Pond & Meadow

Address withheld to ensure privacy. Soquel
(831) 462-1866, fax (831) 475-8321

www.themillpond.com
marlin@themillpond.com

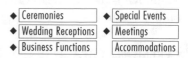

◆ Ceremonies   ◆ Special Events
◆ Wedding Receptions   ◆ Meetings
◆ Business Functions   Accommodations

The Millpond is not just "pretty as a picture," it's evocative of an 18th-century tableau, where the dream-like landscape glows with an ethereal light. The entrance is shaded by a tall stand of redwoods, so it's quite a surprise when you suddenly come upon a vast meadow and two ponds, bathed in sunlight. Acres of grass are ringed by hills, densely covered with madrone, oak, and bay trees and, except for the owner's home, there are no signs of civilization anywhere.

Given this halcyon scene, it's hard to imagine that in the late 1800s this site was a lumber mill and that in 1927, all the surrounding trees were clearcut. It later became an angling club, and rumor has it that Shirley Temple signed on as a life member and had her own special angling spot.

Over time, the land rejuvenated itself, and the current owners have decided to host weddings and special events on the property. Couples almost always get married in front of the small pond, whose still waters reflect the encircling trees. Reeds and cattails sprout along its edge, and resident ducks are often seen gliding over its surface.

Just beyond the meadow, there's a grove of redwoods, where receptions are held. As you dine in dappled shade, and gaze up at the sun-limned tracery of branches high overhead, you can't help but experience the peace and tranquility of this natural cathedral. The grounds are wonderful for corporate picnics, team building exercises (you can set up your own ropes course!) and family reunions, too. Ride ponies, swim in the lake or stock it with trout for fishing. Feel free to be creative and design your own activities.

Hidden away in the Santa Cruz Mountains, the Millpond fills the eye with beauty and expands the spirit. And while it may look like a painting, fortunately for us it's very real.

CEREMONY CAPACITY: The area under the sycamore tree, by the pond, can seat 200; the redwood grove holds 200 seated guests.

EVENT/RECEPTION CAPACITY: The site can hold 200 seated or standing guests; if offsite parking can be arranged, more than 200 guests can be accommodated. Note that on-site parking is restricted to 100 vehicles.

FEES & DEPOSITS: A $250 rental deposit is required to book the site. An additional $300 deposit is payable 3 months prior, with the rental balance and a $200 refundable cleaning/security deposit due 10 days prior to the event. The rental fee is $1,000, which covers use of the site for the day.

AVAILABILITY: May 1st through October 31st, 9am–6pm, weather permitting.

SERVICES/AMENITIES:
Catering: BYO or CBA
Kitchen Facilities: no
Tables & Chairs: CBA, extra fee
Linens, Silver, etc.: BYO
Restrooms: wheelchair accessible
Dance Floor: CBA
Bride's Dressing Area: CBA
Meeting Equipment: BYO

Parking: up to 100 cars, attendant provided
Accommodations: no guest rooms
Telephone: emergency use only
Outdoor Night Lighting: access only
Outdoor Cooking Facilities: large BBQ grill
Cleanup: caterer or renter
View: ponds, redwood forest, Santa Cruz Mountains

RESTRICTIONS:
Alcohol: BYO BWC only, licensed server
Smoking: outdoors only
Music: amplified OK w/volume restrictions

Wheelchair Access: yes
Insurance: certificate required
Other: no rice

Theo's Restaurant

Restaurant

3101 North Main Street, Soquel
(831) 462-3657, fax (831) 462-9459

www.theosrestaurant.net

◆ Ceremonies	◆ Special Events
◆ Wedding Receptions	◆ Meetings
◆ Business Functions	Accommodations

When chef Etan Hamm and his wife Greta decided to open a restaurant in Soquel, their goal was to create a small, family-owned restaurant like the ones they had enjoyed so much when they lived in France. Eighteen years later, the continued success of Theo's testifies to the fact that they have accomplished this goal. And when the Hamms say "family-owned," that's exactly what they mean: while Etan, who was educated at the Ecole Hotelier de Thonon les Bains in France, prepares savory gourmet meals using the produce grown in the restaurant's gardens, the rest of the family takes care of every other detail, from selecting the wines to arranging the flowers.

Located on a quiet street near Soquel's main shopping district, Theo's even looks like a comfortable private home. In front, the small brick-rimmed patio has a jasmine-twined trellis and wrought-iron tables and chairs. A low stucco wall, with a gargoyle-headed fountain, allows guests to view the passing parade as they sip pre-function champagne. In the Main Dining Room, pale peach walls, burgundy-upholstered cane-back chairs, and soft mauve carpeting glow in the firelight from the stone fireplace in winter, or sunlight pouring through generous windows during the summer months. Contemporary art and floral displays add visual interest to this relaxed, understated room. A popular spot for business functions is the Wine Cellar, an intimate, private room with a floor-to-ceiling wine rack on one side and an antique mirror-backed sideboard on the other.

Though weddings and other festive events can be accommodated in the restaurant, they're more often held in Theo's expansive "backyard." Here, an aggregate patio, partially shaded by a green wood pergola, overlooks a large lawn and organic garden. Heat lamps enable this refreshing area to be used at night or in cool weather. Next to the patio, a quaint wood-burning oven bakes pizza, bread and chicken to a smoky perfection. In the garden, plum, fig, citrus and nectarine trees mingle with over 100 rose bushes, whose flowers grace the restaurant's tables. Raised beds containing a cornucopia of thriving flowers, vegetables and herbs line the lawn area, and don't be surprised if the succulent tomatoes you admire in the garden show up minutes later on your plate! At the back of the lawn area an arbor has been erected for ceremonies.

Theo's Restaurant is a family restaurant in the best sense of the word: intimate, relaxed and friendly, with gracious service accompanying the world-class cuisine. Spend a little time here, and the Hamms will undoubtedly make you feel like you're part of their family.

CEREMONY CAPACITY: The outdoor garden holds 125 seated guests.

EVENT/RECEPTION CAPACITY: Indoors, the restaurant holds 65 seated or 100 standing; the Wine Cellar can accommodate up to 18 seated guests. Outdoors, the garden holds 125 seated guests. The site maximum is 125 seated.

MEETING CAPACITY: The Wine Cellar can accommodate 18 seated conference-style, the Main Dining Room 55 seated, conference-style.

FEES & DEPOSITS: For weddings, a non-refundable $250 minimum site deposit is required to book the restaurant; the balance is payable at the event's conclusion. A refundable $250 security deposit is due 1 week prior to the event. Wedding luncheons run $20–35/person, dinners $25–40/person; tax, a 17% service charge and beverages are additional.

For other special events and business functions, prices will vary depending on menus and services selected; call for more specific information.

AVAILABILITY: Year-round, daily, until midnight. Weddings usually take place on weekends, noon–5pm.

SERVICES/AMENITIES:
Catering: provided, no BYO
Kitchen Facilities: n/a
Tables & Chairs: provided
Linens, Silver, etc.: provided
Restrooms: wheelchair accessible
Dance Floor: patio
Bride's & Groom's Dressing Area: Wine Cellar
Meeting Equipment: BYO
Other: wedding cakes, event coordination, wood-burning pizza oven

Parking: on-street & adjacent large lots
Accommodations: no guest rooms
Telephone: emergency use only
Outdoor Night Lighting: yes
Outdoor Cooking Facilities: wood-burning oven & BBQ
Cleanup: provided
View: colorful, landscaped garden

RESTRICTIONS:
Alcohol: provided, or BYO, corkage $10/bottle
Smoking: outdoors only
Music: amplified OK w/volume restrictions

Wheelchair Access: yes
Insurance: not required

---

*This is important! Tell facilities you're reading **Here Comes The Guide** and ask if our information is still current.*

monterey peninsula

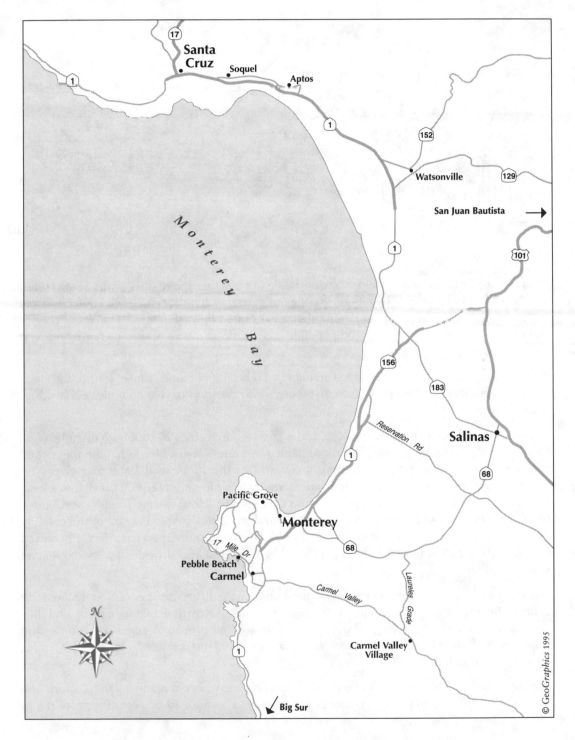

Stone House

Private, Oceanfront Home

Address withheld to ensure privacy. *Big Sur Coast*
(831) 626-3868, fax (831) 626-5838

stonehouse@redshift.com

◆ Ceremonies ◆ Special Events
◆ Wedding Receptions ◆ Meetings
◆ Business Functions ◆ Accommodations

Built of native granite and nestled in a rock saddle just 100 feet above the Pacific, Stone House overlooks the unsurpassed beauty of the Big Sur Coast. A wide sandy beach stretches away to the north. The Santa Lucia Mountains, their peaks often draped in a soft blanket of clouds, meet the ocean from the east. No other building is visible as the view sweeps north and west to the horizon.

William Wurster, the world-renowned architect who designed Stone House, said of the site... "it's so magnificent and huge in scale that there is no reason to have a complicated structure to compete with it."

Hence the simplicity of the house's design. The great room, with its 20-foot-high open-beamed ceiling, fir plank floors and huge fireplace framed by granite slabs, blends in with the natural surroundings. A wall of floor-to-ceiling windows fills the room with light, and gives you unobstructed coastal views. At one end of the room, four wide steps take you down into a large kitchen. Colonial in style, it has three-foot-thick rock walls, a low, beamed ceiling and a brick floor. Your guests will feel quite cozy sitting around the antique table in front of the cooking fireplace. The kitchen opens onto a walled brick courtyard, landscaped with flower beds and potted trees. It's most often used as an informal bar area, but also provides additional seating space for dining.

Attached to the main house are extensive guest quarters, built around a pool/solarium in their center. The guest rooms are all interconnected, allowing an easy flow between them, and they can serve as meeting, dancing or dining areas, as well as overnight accommodations. The solarium, with its inverted gable glass ceiling and exotic plants, makes an intriguing spot for cocktails and mingling.

For larger gatherings or outdoor ceremonies, the imaginative event planner can transform the driveway by bringing in flowers, laying down a carpet or lawn, or adding creative props. From here, the view of the coast is spectacular—you can watch mile-long waves crash along the shore. Another dramatic spot for ceremonies and photos is the rocky point above the house. Identified as a Native American sacred site, it affords a 360-degree view of the Big Sur Coastline. One couple, not content to admire the Pacific from afar, led their guests in a bagpipe procession down to the beach, a short walk along the bluff through seasonal wildflowers.

Bordered by the Pacific, State Park lands and a year round creek, Stone House is completely private, and pervaded by a sense of majesty and peace. But just in case you feel the urge to do a little shopping or sightseeing while you're here, downtown Carmel is only 12 miles away. The entire facility is available by the day or week by special arrangement with the owner.

CEREMONY CAPACITY: The Great Room holds 80–100 seated, the Pool Room 50 seated; the Courtyard 50 seated, the rock peak 50 seated or standing, or the driveway, 150 seated guests.

EVENT/RECEPTION & MEETING CAPACITY:

Area	Seated	Standing	Area	Seated	Standing
Great Room	60	100	Courtyard	30	50
Outdoor Spaces	—	150			

FEES & DEPOSITS: For weddings, the rental fee is $3,500–4,500/day depending on guest count. If you'd like to have exclusive use of Stone House for a week, the rate is $7,000–10,000 depending on services required. Half of the rental fee and a non-refundable $1,000 rental deposit are required to confirm your date. The rental balance and a refundable $1,500 damage/security deposit are payable 2 weeks prior to the event.

AVAILABILITY: Year-round, by special arrangement.

SERVICES/AMENITIES:

Catering: preferred list or BYO w/approval
Kitchen Facilities: fully equipped
Tables & Chairs: through caterer
Linens, Silver, etc.: through caterer
Restrooms: not wheelchair accessible
Dance Floor: wood plank floor or brick floor
Bride's & Groom's Dressing Area: yes
Meeting Equipment: BYO
View: Pacific Ocean & Santa Lucia Mountains, Big Sur beaches

Parking: limited, nearby public beach parking, shuttle recommended for large events
Accommodations: 15 guests with a week's rental
Telephone: use with approval
Outdoor Night Lighting: limited
Outdoor Cooking Facilities: through caterer
Cleanup: caterer
Other: pool, hot tub, jacuzzi

RESTRICTIONS:

Alcohol: through caterer
Smoking: outside only
Music: amplified OK

Wheelchair Access: mostly accessible
Insurance: extra liability required
Other: children must be supervised

---

*This is important! Tell facilities you're reading **Here Comes The Guide** and ask if our information is still current.*

Highlands Inn

Inn and Lodge

Highway 1, Carmel
(831) 622-5441, fax (831) 626-1574

www.highlands-inn.com
gm@highlands-inn.com

◆ Ceremonies   ◆ Special Events
◆ Wedding Receptions   ◆ Meetings
◆ Business Functions   ◆ Accommodations

Built in 1916 in the Carmel Highlands just south of Carmel, the Highlands Inn is one of the most sought-after event locations in California. Noted for its breathtaking views and extraordinary cliffside setting, the Inn provides an idyllic environment for any kind of celebration.

After its multi-million-dollar, award-winning renovation, Highlands Inn is more stunning than ever. Commanding one of the world's most spectacular vistas, with exploding waves crashing two hundred feet below, the Inn offers a variety of first class facilities for either business functions or weddings. For outdoor ceremonies, a redwood deck complete with contemporary gazebo is perched just above the rocky cliffs overlooking the Pacific. During inclement weather, ceremonies take place in front of one of two large stone fireplaces in the Fireside Room. The Room has a warm simplicity, with hardwood floors, nubby wool upholstery against butter-soft leathers and iron and polished granite appointments. A grand piano is also available for functions.

After the ceremony, guests are ushered into a variety of reception areas—each is elegant, with comfortable furnishings and outstanding views. The Inn's chefs are renowned for culinary excellence and the wine and champagne list is extensive. The staff can organize a traditional party or a more creative event for the adventuresome. If you are looking for a very special place for one of life's great moments, the incomparable Highlands Inn should be high on your list.

CEREMONY CAPACITY: The outdoor gazebo holds 95 seated or 125 standing. If the weather is uncooperative, the Fireside Room can be used. It holds 100 seated or 150 standing.

EVENT/RECEPTION CAPACITY:

Area	Seated	Standing
Yankee Point Room	50	75
Monarch Room	15	20
Surf Room	120	150
Fireside Room	—	180

Area	Seated	Standing
Gazebo & Deck	95	150
Wine Room	40	—

MEETING CAPACITY:

Area	Theater-style	Conference-style	Classroom-style
Yankee Point Room	80	28	50
Monarch Room	—	16	—
Surf Room	130	50	100
Groves North & South	80	40	50

FEES & DEPOSITS: The room rental fee is a non-refundable deposit, payable when your date is reserved. Rental fees are as follows and may vary depending on the season: Gazebo & Deck, $750; Monarch Room $175; Yankee Point Room and Gazebo $1,650; Wine Room $150, Grove Room $250 and Surf Room & Gazebo $1,950. A dance floor is an extra $150; wedding cakes vary in price. Luncheons start at $25/person, dinners at $30/person; alcohol, tax and an 18% service charge are additional. Half the estimated total is due 4 weeks prior and the balance is due 14 working days prior to the event. A final confirmed guest count is required 3 working days in advance of the event.

AVAILABILITY: Year-round, daily, any time.

SERVICES/AMENITIES:
Catering: provided, no BYO
Kitchen Facilities: n/a
Tables & Chairs: provided
Linens, Silver, etc.: provided
Restrooms: wheelchair accessible
Dance Floor: extra charge
Bride's Dressing Area: CBA
Meeting Equipment: full range CBA, extra fee

Parking: complimentary valet
Accommodations: 142 guest rooms
Telephone: pay phone
Outdoor Night Lighting: limited
Outdoor Cooking Facilities: BBQs
Cleanup: provided
View: Big Sur coastline and the ocean
Other: full service coordination, wedding cakes; marriage licenses issued

RESTRICTIONS:
Alcohol: provided
Smoking: outdoors only
Music: amplified restricted

Wheelchair Access: limited
Insurance: not required

The professionals in the back of the book are the best in the business! How do we know? Read page 831.

The Holly Farm

Private Home & Garden

Address withheld to ensure privacy. Carmel Valley
(831) 625-1926 or (831) 659-2139, fax (831) 625-1926

www.hollyfarm.com
hollyfarm@ibm.net

◆ Ceremonies	◆ Special Events
◆ Wedding Receptions	◆ Meetings
◆ Business Functions	◆ Accommodations

Here's a gem of a location that offers something rare—not only exclusive use, but the option to house your wedding or business guests overnight. First established over 100 years ago, The Holly Farm is a private three-and-a-half-acre estate which contains the last holly "farm" in the state: 49 enormous holly trees that flank both sides of the entrance drive to the property. Doyle and Mary Moses, The Holly Farm's owners, have transformed what used to be a worn out adobe building encircled by a jungle of plants into a chic hideaway, perfect for celebrity guests (who prefer its seclusion to the public atmosphere of hotels) and for those who'd like to have their special event in total privacy.

The old adobe home has been expanded and could easily grace the pages of *Architectural Digest*. Inside, you'll find a pleasing mix of California-style architecture and contemporary furnishings. Walls are a vibrant, warm apricot, floors are oak and Mexican tile. Guests can mingle in front of the fireplace in the roomy, country designer kitchen, and then sit down for a rehearsal dinner or other intimate celebration in the sun-filled sunken dining room. The living room offers a second fireplace, comfy couches and chairs, and a view of the Santa Lucia mountains. With four bedrooms, a honeymoon suite and additional homes, The Holly Farm can house plenty of guests overnight.

Outdoors, Doyle has created a picturesque and colorful landscape. Hundreds of annuals spill over flower beds and pots; a small pond and sparkling waterfall provide a lovely backdrop for a ceremony, wedding photos or company picnic. The adjacent Carriage House, with its impressive stone bar, provides a shady spot for cocktails, socializing and dancing. Holly Farm's talented French chef can prepare any type of cuisine, from a barbecue to a formal repast, and will be happy to customize your menu.

Only one event per week is scheduled so that you'll get a lot of personal attention. And no matter what services you request, your hosts will go out of their way to meet your needs, whether it's catering, photography, flowers or accommodations. For a unique experience in a genuinely charming environment, consider The Holly Farm for your next private event.

CEREMONY CAPACITY: The waterfall pond area holds 150 seated or standing guests; the lawn area can accommodate 200 seated guests.

EVENT/RECEPTION & MEETING CAPACITY: The Carriage House seats 50 comfortably; the lawn area holds 200 seated guests. The dining room in the house can hold up to 25 seated guests.

FEES & DEPOSITS: This is a package deal, so read the very long list of what's offered for weddings before you misjudge the $15,000 package price. The fee includes exclusive use of the property and all its facilities for 5 days and 5 nights (Thursday morning–Tuesday morning), sleeping accommodations for 18–20, dinner for 2 at Carmel's Casanova Restaurant, honeymoon suite for 5 nights, massage for bride and groom and 2 others, hair/makeup/nails for the bride, Monterey Strings Quartet for ceremony, Saturday morning brunch for bridal party, Monday offsite breakfast, daily continental breakfast, afternoon wine, cheese and fruit platter, all rental equipment for up to 200 guests, Sunday brunch for 15, assisted parking, and daily maid service.

A $2500 deposit plus a refundable $200 security deposit are due when reservations are confirmed. Catered meals are not included in the package, and start at $30/person for a buffet. Alcohol, tax and a 15% service charge (on food only) are additional. The adjacent property can accommodate 6 overnight guests at no additional charge.

Fees for corporate retreats or business meetings vary; call for more information.

AVAILABILITY: Larger weddings, May–November until 9pm. Smaller, off-season weddings can be arranged. Corporate retreats or business meetings, daily, November–April.

SERVICES/AMENITIES:

Catering: provided, no BYO
Kitchen Facilities: n/a
Tables & Chairs: provided
Linens, Silver, etc.: provided
Restrooms: most are wheelchair accessible
Dance Floor: in Carriage House
Bride's & Groom's Dressing Area: yes
Meeting Equipment: microphone

Parking: on site w/attendant
Accommodations: up to 18 guests
Telephone: CBA
Outdoor Night Lighting: yes
Outdoor Cooking Facilities: CBA
Cleanup: provided
View: Carmel hills, valley & Santa Lucia Mtns
Other: ping pong, darts, massage, ceremonial music, bride's hair/makeup/nails

RESTRICTIONS:

Alcohol: BYO, BWC only
Smoking: outside only
Music: provided or BYO, amplified OK, with volume restrictions until 9pm

Wheelchair Access: yes
Insurance: certificate required

---

*This is important! Tell facilities you're reading **Here Comes The Guide** and ask if our information is still current.*

613

Holman Ranch

Historic Ranch Estate & Garden

Address withheld to ensure privacy. Carmel Valley
(831) 659-2640, fax (831) 659-6055

◆ Ceremonies ◆ Special Events
◆ Wedding Receptions ◆ Meetings
◆ Business Functions ☐ Accommodations

When someone refers to their home as "heaven on earth," you're a bit skeptical, right? For all you know, their idea of paradise is a cabin with an outhouse in the wilderness. When Dorothy McEwen says it however, you can throw your skepticism out the window. She lives at Holman Ranch, a glorious 400-acre spread in Carmel Valley, that has often been called a miniature San Simeon.

Built in 1928 as a summer home for a Peninsula socialite, it soon became an exclusive getaway for Hollywood celebrities (the room where Charlie Chaplin often stayed is now a mini-museum/dressing room for brides). It was bought by the Holman family in 1943, who remodeled and enlarged the main residence, an architectural gem constructed of stone and oak from the property itself. After the Holmans died, the ranch suffered years of serious neglect, and who knows what would have become of it if Ms. McEwen hadn't purchased it in 1989 and brought it back to life.

The main house and grounds, which are perfect for all types of events, are on top of a hill with a truly breathtaking 360-degree view of the surrounding Santa Lucia Mountains. Many a wedding has taken place on the vast lawn adjacent to the house, where couples tie the knot in front of a quaint redwood gazebo, with the tree-covered mountains behind them. Naturally the lawn is also an option for a garden reception, but two other sites have their own charms. The redwood deck, just off the lawn, is reached via a small bridge spanning a trout pond, and is protected from the sun by a spreading oak tree growing up through the decking. At the far end of the house, the Rose Patio—named for the dozens of climbing rose bushes along its perimeter—can be set up for dining or dancing.

Keep in mind that the ranch has almost limitless possibilities for events. You can host a western-style barbecue with trail rides, a cow-milking contest and hobby horse relay, or a corporate retreat with a formal presentation and film in the Ranch Theatre followed by a picnic lunch. There's a game room with pool table, pinball and board games, a barn and rodeo arena and even a childcare room. Remarkably, Holman Ranch manages to be elegant, sophisticated, rustic and down home all at the same time, so whether you set your tables with linens or black-

and-white cowhide tablecloths, your party will fit in perfectly with the surroundings. And as for Ms. McEwen's claim that this place really is heaven on earth? Well, we'd be the last folks to argue with her.

CEREMONY CAPACITY: The site can accommodate 60–250 seated or 60–350 standing.

EVENT/RECEPTION CAPACITY:

Area	Seated	Standing	Area	Seated	Standing
Gazebo Lawn	250	350	Rose Patio*	150*	200
Theater	60	90	Living Room/Deck	50	150
Entire Site	450	450	Carriage House	100	150

with dancing

MEETING CAPACITY: The Theater holds 90 theater-style or 60 seated conference-style; the Carriage House holds 150 theater-style or 100 seated conference-style.

FEES & DEPOSITS: For weddings, two $500 non-refundable deposits are required: the first reserves your date, the second is due 90 days before the event; the balance is due the event day. For other events, 50% of the event total is payable 90 days prior; the balance is payable the day of the event. The site rental fee is $2,500–3,000 for Saturday events; $2,000–2,500 for Sunday–Friday events. Nonprofit rates are available. On average, catered functions run $25–45/person; alcohol, tax and service charges are additional.

AVAILABILITY. Feb–mid-Nov, 10am–10pm weekdays, 10am–11pm weekends; earlier hours for meetings can be arranged. Wedding receptions take place 10am–9pm. From mid-Nov–Jan, smaller parties can be specially arranged.

SERVICES/AMENITIES:

Catering: preferred list or BYO, licensed & insured
Kitchen Facilities: moderately equipped
Tables & Chairs: some provided
Linens, Silver, etc.: BYO
Restrooms: wheelchair accessible
Dance Floor: outdoor patio or in Theater
Bride's & Groom's Dressing Area: yes
Meeting Equipment: overhead, screen, microphone
Other: group trail, carriage, or hay rides; horse exhibits, demos, or riding lessons; western entertainment demos, ranch competitions

Parking: shuttle service, golf cart $30/hr/cart
Accommodations: no guest rooms
Telephone: pay phone & emergency use only office phone
Outdoor Night Lighting: limited, BYO extra lighting
Outdoor Cooking Facilities: BYO
Cleanup: caterer & renter
View: panoramic views of Carmel Valley & Santa Lucia Mtns.

RESTRICTIONS:

Alcohol: BYO, BWC only
Smoking: designated areas
Music: amplified OK w/restrictions

Wheelchair Access: yes
Insurance: required for certain activities
Other: children under 13 by arrangement; childcare activity area required

La Playa Hotel

Camino Real and 8th Street, Carmel
(800) 582-8900, (831) 624-6476, fax (831) 624-7966

Historic Hotel

- ◆ Ceremonies
- ◆ Wedding Receptions
- ◆ Business Functions
- ◆ Special Events
- ◆ Meetings
- ◆ Accommodations

Occupying several acres in the heart of residential Carmel, just two blocks from the beach, La Playa remains one of the loveliest and most inviting places we've had the pleasure to write about. Originally built in 1904 as a private residence, La Playa was converted and expanded into a hotel in 1916. Standing in front of the building, you feel a bit like you've been transported to Europe. The distinctly Mediterranean style, with earthy terra cotta tile roofs, soft pastel walls and a bright green, formal garden are reminiscent of Italy. Even though there's a lovely patina about La Playa, make no mistake—this is a full-service resort hotel offering a contemporary freshness as well as a romantic old-world appeal.

For outdoor celebrations, the wrought-iron gazebo is the spot, set amid brick patios, a fountain, technicolor annuals, manicured lawns and climbing bougainvillea. The entire setting is lush and private. Inside are rooms of various size for private functions, with antiques, lithographs and memorabilia of early Carmel. The hotel is a refreshing destination for a personal or business retreat—here tasteful furnishings, French doors, and magnificent views are standard amenities. We can't help but love this place. And if you can't drag yourself away, feel free to stay overnight, or have your honeymoon here too.

CEREMONY CAPACITY: The gazebo area holds 85 seated or 100 standing guests.

EVENT/RECEPTION CAPACITY & RENTAL FEES:

Room	Fee	Standing	Seated	Room	Fee	Standing	Seated
Poseidon Room	$750	150	100	Carmel Room	$500	80	64
Garden Room	350	50	36	Fireside Room	250	25	16
Patio Room	175	—	12	Gazebo	250	100	85

MEETING CAPACITY:

Room	Conf-style	Classroom-style	Theater-style
Poseidon Room	36	60	100
Carmel Room	30	56	110
Patio Room	12	12	15

FEES & DEPOSITS: For weddings, a $1,000 non-refundable deposit is required to confirm your date and banquet space. Half the estimated event total is due 6 weeks prior to the function; the remaining balance is due 3 weeks prior to the event. Menus can be customized; reception buffets and seated meals range $24–40/person. Room rental fees, alcohol, a 17% gratuity and tax are additional. For meeting or corporate event information, contact the sales and catering department.

AVAILABILITY: Year-round, daily.

SERVICES/AMENITIES:

Catering: provided, no BYO
Kitchen Facilities: n/a
Tables & Chairs: provided
Linens, Silver, etc.: provided
Restrooms: wheelchair accessible
Dance Floor: portable
Bride's Dressing Area: CBA
Meeting Equipment: CBA, extra fee

Parking: on street, valet
Accommodations: 75 guest rooms, 5 cottages
Telephone: pay phones, guest phones
Outdoor Night Lighting: limited
Outdoor Cooking Facilities: no
Cleanup: provided
View: ocean and gardens

RESTRICTIONS:

Alcohol: provided, no BYO
Smoking: outdoors only
Music: amplified OK til 10pm w/restrictions

Wheelchair Access: yes
Insurance: not required

The professionals in the back of the book are the best in the business! How do we know? Read page 681.

Mission Ranch

Historic Retreat

26270 Dolores, Carmel
(831) 624-3824, fax (831) 626-4163

◆ Ceremonies	◆ Special Events
◆ Wedding Receptions	◆ Meetings
◆ Business Functions	◆ Accommodations

Mission Ranch has been a Carmel tradition for over 50 years. Once a working dairy, the Ranch is a delightful and rustic retreat, extensively renovated in 1992. Situated on the grounds are a turn-of-the-century farmhouse, a bunkhouse, hotel rooms and triplex cottages with spectacular views of Carmel Beach and rugged Point Lobos. These historic buildings, surrounded by 100-year-old cypress trees and natural landscaping, offer the kind of quiet and peaceful ambiance not found in nearby bustling downtown Carmel.

Outdoor celebrations and ceremonies are often held on the brick patio of the Patio Party Barn or under the huge cypress trees on the lawns. The Party Barns are known for their friendly bars and great dance floors. The Patio Party Barn has a wall of full-length wood-framed glass doors opening onto a brick patio with a restful view of meadows and wetlands rolling down to Carmel River Beach. The Large Party Barn is ideal for larger parties with its lofty, three-story-high ceiling. Both barns feature stages for live music and built-in dance floors. The structures are painted white with an upbeat forest green trim. The Ranch Catering Department prides itself in designing specialty menus for any occas-on. If you're looking for a place to hold a relaxed event in a classic country setting, this is it.

CEREMONY CAPACITY: The Patio Barn and patio accommodate up to 110 seated, the Large Barn and Farmhouse Lawn hold 180.

EVENT/RECEPTION CAPACITY: The Patio Party Barn accommodates up to 110 guests seated. The Large Party Barn holds up to 180 seated. There is a required minimum of 50 guests in the barns.

MEETING CAPACITY:

Area	Theater-style	Conf-style	Area	Theater-style	Conf-style
Conference Room	—	14	Patio Barn	100	—
Large Barn	200	—			

FEES & DEPOSITS: The rental fee ($1,500 for the Patio Party Barn or $1,000 for the Large Party Barn) is required to reserve a date. A deposit in the amount of 60% of all estimated services is due 60 days prior to the event, with the remaining estimated balance due 10 days prior. Party Barn rental fees cover a 5-hour period. Buffet and dinner prices start at $30/person. Alcohol, tax and a 17% gratuity are additional. Please call for meeting room rates.

AVAILABILITY: Year-round, daily, 8am–10pm. On Sundays, events must end by 6pm.

SERVICES/AMENITIES:

Catering: provided, no BYO

Kitchen Facilities: n/a

Tables & Chairs: provided

Linens, Silver, etc.: some provided

Restrooms: wheelchair accessible

Dance Floor: in Barns

Bride's Dressing Area: no

Meeting Equipment: full range, extra charge

Parking: large lot

Accommodations: 31 guest rooms

Telephone: pay phones

Outdoor Night Lighting: CBA

Outdoor Cooking Facilities: CBA

Cleanup: provided

View: Pacific Ocean, Pt. Lobos & meadow

Other: full event planning services

RESTRICTIONS:

Alcohol: provided, no BYO

Smoking: not allowed in rooms

Music: amplified OK with restrictions

Wheelchair Access: yes

Insurance: not required

This is important! Tell facilities you're reading **Here Comes The Guide** and ask if our information is still current.

Quail Lodge Resort & Golf Club

8000 Valley Greens Drive, Carmel Valley
(831) 624-1581 ext. 360, fax (831) 626-8481

www.peninsula.com
qul@peninsula.com

Resort & Golf Club

◆ Ceremonies	◆ Special Events
◆ Wedding Receptions	◆ Meetings
◆ Business Functions	◆ Accommodations

So you've found the love of your life, and you're going to be married. Each of you has a vision of the perfect place for the Big Day: you've always pined for a site that combines serene elegance and the natural beauty of rolling meadows and wooded hills, while your intended is an avid golfer, whose wedding fantasies include a luxurious country club setting. Wondering if it's possible to satisfy both of your desires? Most definitely, if you choose Quail Lodge Resort & Golf Club for your wedding and reception! In addition to acres of lush gardens, tree-shaded lakes, and an assortment of banquet rooms, this exclusive resort also features a golf course designed by Robert Muir Graves.

Now that you've found the right location, you have a number of ceremony sites to choose from. Mallard Lake, a sparkling expanse of water divided by an arched bridge and embraced by well-groomed lawns and trees, is the resort's focal point. Two fountains, one at either end of the lake, add visual excitement. You can say your vows on the bridge, or anywhere around the lake's shore. The deck at the Covey Restaurant extends over the lake, and is the ideal spot for small weddings or receptions that want to take advantage of the lakeside ambiance. Picturesque Quail Meadows, with its lush lawns, tree-covered hillsides and peaceful lake, is also a favorite spot for weddings. Whether you let the scenery form the backdrop for your ceremony, or dress things up with a flower-laden bridal arch, this splendid venue will take your breath away. For an extra romantic touch, you can arrange for a horse-drawn carriage to take you to the wedding site.

Receptions, parties, dinners, or meetings can be accommodated at one of Quail Lodge's many banquet rooms, all with large windows to showcase views of the golf course or Lodge grounds. The dining room at the Country Club features a cathedral-beamed ceiling, wood paneling, and overlooks the golf course, Carmel Valley and the Carmel River. Special amenities like a built-in dance floor, private bar and lounge, and a wraparound deck make this room popular with weddings taking place at nearby Quail Meadows. Near the first fairway and driving range, the Fairway Room has a private entrance and bar, plus a projection screen and sound system for meetings and seminars. The Garden Room's glass walls and ceiling let you enjoy views of the 18th green and swimming pool, while air conditioning, ceiling fans and awnings keep you and your guests cool. The Sun Room at the Lodge, adjacent to the Covey Restaurant, is perfect for small meetings, dinners, or as a break-out room. The Valley Room is also great for meetings and dinners, and has its own patio. If you really want seclusion and privacy, plus lots of rustic charm, the Barn at Quail Meadows has plenty of both. Located five minutes from the hotel, it has an open-beamed ceiling and a loft.

What makes Quail Lodge so special is its combination of exceptional restaurants, top-notch staff, and luxurious accommodations—all in an atmosphere of unparalleled natural beauty. And it's only minutes away from Carmel-by-the-Sea and other attractions along Highway 1. So, if you and your fiance are having trouble deciding on a place for your wedding, why not plan a visit to Quail Lodge? Whether you're a golfing enthusiast, nature lover, or someone wanting to get away from it all, Quail Lodge is sure to have just what you're looking for.

CEREMONY CAPACITY: Outdoors, the Mallard Lake area holds 2–50 seated and the Quail Meadows area 50–500 seated guests. The deck at the Covey Restaurant holds up to 75 seated. Indoors, the Fairway Room holds up to 100, the Garden Room 75 seated. There are 3 other smaller rooms which can each accommodate 2–20 seated guests.

EVENT/RECEPTION CAPACITY:

Area	Seated	Standing	Area	Seated	Standing
Valley Room	50–70	50–70	Sun Room	20	25
Garden Room	50	70	Club Dining Room	300	400
Fairway Room	70	70–100	Barn at Quail Meadows	80	100
Quail Meadows	500	500			

MEETING CAPACITY:

Room	Theater	Boardroom	Classroom	Room	Theater	Boardroom	Classroom
Acacia Room	20	18	—	Garden Room	75	28	20
Valley Room	110	40	75	Glass House	—	10	—
Fairway Room	150	50	85				

FEES & DEPOSITS: For special events, a $250–3,500 refundable site fee (depending on the area selected) is required as a deposit. Half of the anticipated event total is payable 2 months prior to the event; any remaining balance is payable at the event's conclusion. Luncheons start $19/person, dinners at $35/person, and buffets at $59/person; tax, a 17% service charge and alcohol are additional. Wedding packages can be arranged.

For meetings and other business functions, customized menus and services are available; call for more information.

AVAILABILITY: Year-round, daily until 2am, including holidays.

SERVICES/AMENITIES:

Catering: provided, no BYO
Kitchen Facilities: n/a
Tables & Chairs: provided
Linens, Silver, etc.: provided
Restrooms: wheelchair accessible
Dance Floor: provided

Parking: large, ample lots
Accommodations: 100 guest rooms
Telephone: pay phones
Outdoor Night Lighting: CBA
Outdoor Cooking Facilities: BBQs CBA
Cleanup: provided

Bride's & Groom's Dressing Area: CBA
Meeting Equipment: full range, extra fee

RESTRICTIONS:

Alcohol: provided, or BYO corkage $15/bottle
Smoking: designated areas
Music: amplified OK indoors only

View: fairways, lakes, ponds, Valley hills
Other: baby grand piano, wedding & event coordination

Wheelchair Access: yes
Insurance: not required

The professionals in the back of the book are the best in the business! How do we know? Read page 681.

622

Club Del Monte

at Monterey Naval Postgraduate School

1 University Circle, Building 220, Monterey
(831) 656-1049, (831) 656-2170, fax (831) 656-3677

kandersen@monterey.nps.navy.mil

Historic Landmark

◆ Ceremonies   ◆ Special Events
◆ Wedding Receptions   ◆ Meetings
◆ Business Functions   ◆ Accommodations

Club Del Monte is an art deco jewel set amongst 25 acres of sprawling lawns dotted with oak, cypress, and pine. Originally built in 1880 as the grand Hotel del Monte, it was destroyed twice by fire and rebuilt. The present imposing structure (which is the 1926 incarnation) resembles a Spanish-Moorish fortress. It remained an elegant hotel until 1951, when it was acquisitioned for the Navy's Naval Postgraduate School. As you can see, this facility's history is long and illustrious, but what you might find most interesting is the fact that several of its sumptuous rooms are now available for special events to those with a military sponsor.

Your guests will step back in time and feel like royalty when welcomed with cocktails in the Quarterdeck Lounge. This majestic lobby was built on the scale of a castle foyer, with soaring 30-foot ceilings which are crosshatched with hand-painted wooden beams. Two stately rows of stone columns grace both sides of the room, framing a towering floor-to-ceiling window that overlooks the estate-like grounds. A fire in the elegant, carved-stone fireplace will warm the room and cast its flickering light across the highly polished terra cotta floors.

Proceed to the ballroom for a formal dinner-dance; you'll be transported back to the era when Jean Harlow, Clark Gable and Carole Lombard danced here, and when water cascaded down the room's main attraction: an ornately tiled fountain that dominates one wall. The fountain and the elaborate tilework bordering the floor-to-ceiling arched windows at either end of the room bring the Moorish influence inside, and give the space a spicy, exotic ambiance. Other art deco details include the lacy plasterwork ceiling, huge wrought-iron chandeliers, and matching wall sconces that add ambient light. French doors opening onto the terrace, and overlooking the European-style rose gardens, are the finishing touch.

For a buffet luncheon or catered business meeting, La Novia Room, with plaster walls and rich wood trim, offers the elegance of the ballroom but on a more intimate scale. It opens onto La Novia Terrace, a palm-filled atrium with a rustic brick fireplace, window benches and a brick floor. There are outdoor settings, too. The European-style rose garden with boxed hedge-lined flower beds, gravel paths, and sculpted trees begs for a romantic Victorian wedding. Or, if you're planning a western-theme party, we think the historical Arizona garden, planted with cacti, yucca, and lots of California natives, is just the place. Club Del Monte offers a treasure-trove of site options, and as you'd expect from a Naval facility, everything here is top rank.

CEREMONY CAPACITY:

Area	*Seated*	*Standing*	*Area*	*Seated*	*Standing*
Main Lawn Area	400	400	Ballroom	600	1,000
Quarterdeck	75	100	La Novia Room	80	100
La Novia Terrace	50	70	El Prado Room	150	200

EVENT/RECEPTION CAPACITY: For the Ballroom, La Novia Room, Terrace, and the El Prado Room, see above capacities. The Golf Course Club House is also available, which holds 50 seated or 75 standing guests.

MEETING CAPACITY: The Ballroom holds 600 seated theater-style or 400 conference-style; the La Novia Room holds 80 theater-style or 50 conference-style; and the La Novia Terrace holds 50, either style.

FEES & DEPOSITS: For weddings and receptions, a $200–500 non-refundable deposit, depending on the room reserved, is required to book the facility. 25% of the estimated event total is payable 6 weeks prior to the function, 50% of the remaining total is due 4 weeks prior, and the balance is due 1 week prior.

Catering is provided, starting at $13/person, with cake, wine and champagne included; a 15% service charge is additional.

Other facilities, such as baseball fields, picnic areas, or an Olympic-size pool are available for corporate or other special events in 5-hour blocks. Weekday meeting fees vary depending on catering services required.

AVAILABILITY: Year round, daily. Weddings can be booked 11am–4pm or 6pm–11pm; conferences or other special events, 7am–4pm or 6pm–11pm. Extra hours are available for an additional charge.

SERVICES/AMENITIES:

Catering: provided, no BYO
Kitchen Facilities: n/a
Tables & Chairs: provided
Linens, Silver, etc.: provided
Restrooms: wheelchair accessible
Dance Floor: CBA, extra charge
Bride's & Groom's Dressing Area: yes
View: of lawns and gardens
Meeting Equipment: CBA

Parking: on-base lot; weekday carpooling recommended for large events
Accommodations: for military only; 75 rooms
Telephone: pay phones
Outdoor Night Lighting: CBA upon request
Outdoor Cooking Facilities: BBQ
Cleanup: provided
Other: event coordination, ice sculptures, ballfields, swimming pool, theme parties

RESTRICTIONS:

Alcohol: provided
Smoking: outside only
Music: amplified OK

Wheelchair Access: yes
Insurance: certificate suggested
Other: no rice, birdseed, glitter, confetti or wall decorations

Monterey Beach Hotel

Waterfront Hotel

2600 Sand Dunes Drive, Monterey
(831) 394-2363, fax (831) 899-9160

www.montereybeachhotel.com
jodyl@montereybeachhotel.com

◆ Ceremonies   ◆ Special Events
◆ Wedding Receptions   ◆ Meetings
◆ Business Functions   ◆ Accommodations

Many hotels have the word "beach" in their name, even though sometimes all you really get is a glimpse of sand between parking lots and tall buildings. Not so at the Monterey Beach Hotel. This hotel has the delightful distinction of being the only one in the area located directly on the beach—and what a beach it is! Miles of pristine white sand, without a hotdog stand or condominium complex in sight, stretch in either direction behind the hotel. During the day, sailboats dot the white-capped waters of the bay, and at night the lights of Monterey glitter on the far shore.

Of course, it takes more than a beautiful beach to make a first-class event space, and the Monterey Beach Hotel has a variety of venues. The versatile Bayview Room is conveniently located on the first floor, and can be dressed up with a flowered-and-ribboned arch for a wedding ceremony, or hooked up with telephones for a business meeting. A wedding reception, corporate event, or any type of large gathering can be held in one of the two ballrooms on the fourth floor. The Point Room has Victorian floral curtains, subdued teal carpets, and plenty of windows with a sweeping view of Monterey Bay. Air walls allow the ballroom to be divided, if desired. The La Grande Room is smaller than the Point Room, but virtually identical to it in all other respects, including the panoramic view.

With all this stunning scenery, you'd expect outdoor events at the Monterey Beach Hotel to be popular, and they are. Adventurous couples can be married on the beach, and the hotel will provide a wedding arch, or rent a gazebo for the ceremony. Sunrises and sunsets are often breathtaking, so you might want to schedule your event to take advantage of the most spectacular light. The beach is best for informal weddings, however. As Jodi Hayes, Director of Sales for the hotel, warns brides, "if you're planning to dress to the nines, you'd better be prepared to get sand in your pantyhose!" You can have your reception on the beach, too, if you don't mind doing without amplified music, or dancing. Why not go for something casual and fun, like a luau or clambake? If you want to be married outdoors, but still crave a bit of formality, there's the Wedding Garden, an intimate, lushly planted lawn area, set up with a white runner and chairs. No matter what kind of event you envision, when you have it at the Monterey Beach Hotel, you not only have access to your very own "backyard" beach, you can stay over and enjoy all that this famous coastline region has to offer.

CEREMONY CAPACITY:

Area	Seated	Standing		Area	Seated	Standing
Bayview Room	125	150		Beach	150	300
Wedding Garden	75	125				

EVENT/RECEPTION CAPACITY:

Area	Seated	Standing		Area	Seated	Standing
La Grande Ballroom	50–150	300		Points Ballroom	125–350	1,000
Poolside	50	75		Captain's Table	40	50
Beach	—	300				

MEETING CAPACITY:

Area	Theater-style	Conf-style		Area	Theater-style	Conf-style
La Grande Ballroom	300	150		Points Ballroom	650	350
Executive Bayview	125	50		Captain's Table	50	40
Big Sur Boardroom	—	15		Little Sur Boardroom	—	12

FEES & DEPOSITS: For weddings, a non-refundable $1,000 deposit or 25% of the estimated event total is required to reserve your date. Half of the event balance is payable 30 days prior; any remaining balance is due 10 days prior to the event.

Catering is provided: breakfasts run $7–16/person, luncheons $17–27/person, dinners $20–35/person, and hors d'oeuvres start at $8/person. Alcohol, tax and an 18% service charge are additional.

Day rates for meeting rooms vary, and may be waived or reduced depending on event duration, food and beverage minimums or number of overnight accommodations reserved.

AVAILABILITY: Year-round, daily, 7am–10pm.

SERVICES/AMENITIES:

Catering: provided, no BYO
Kitchen Facilities: n/a
Tables & Chairs: provided
Linens, Silver, etc.: provided
Restrooms: wheelchair accessible
Dance Floor: provided
Bride's & Groom's Dressing Area: no
Meeting Equipment: CBA, extra charge

Parking: on-site garage
Accommodations: 196 guest rooms, 2 suites
Telephone: pay phones
Outdoor Night Lighting: yes, more CBA
Outdoor Cooking Facilities: BBQ
Cleanup: provided
View: Pacific Ocean and Monterey coastline
Other: event coordination, some decorations

RESTRICTIONS:

Alcohol: provided or corkage $9–18/bottle
Smoking: outside or balconies only
Music: amplified OK until 10pm

Wheelchair Access: yes, except to beach
Insurance: not required
Other: no rice, birdseed or confetti

Monterey Plaza

Waterfront Hotel

400 Cannery Row, Monterey
(831) 646-1700, fax (831) 646-5937

www.woodsidehotels.com
joysmith@montereyplazahotel.com

◆ Ceremonies ◆ Special Events
◆ Wedding Receptions ◆ Meetings
◆ Business Functions ◆ Accommodations

There's something about being next to the ocean that most of us find irresistible. Maybe it's the way the air smells, or the way the light glints off the waves. Whatever it is, you experience that "something" here. Built right at the water's edge, the Monterey Plaza Hotel takes advantage of a glorious oceanfront setting that's just a heartbeat away from the world-renowned Monterey Bay Aquarium and Cannery Row.

With its $6-million renovation and expansion in 1994 (which included six new banquet rooms, redecorated guest rooms and a sophisticated look enhanced by custom-designed furnishings from Italy), the Monterey Plaza reached a new level of hospitality design on the Monterey Peninsula.

Their latest and most exciting development is the addition of a full-service oceanfront health spa and four luxury suites, featuring fireplaces and outdoor decks. Now you can indulge in a relaxing massage, facial or sauna before (or even after) your event. And the large luxury suites can be used for intimate celebrations, dinners or cocktail parties.

Sun-splashed ceremonies take place on either of the terraces. Both have panoramic views of the Pacific and require minimal decoration. On the Lower Terrace, the bride will capture every eye as she descends the main staircase, while on the Upper Plaza, the processional walks beneath a white trellis, set off by terra-cotta planters filled with flowers. If you'd like to get married here, vows are exchanged under a simple arch with the ocean and sky as a blue-on-blue backdrop.

Afterwards, receptions are held in the Monterey Bay Room, adjacent to the Lower Terrace, or the Dolphins Room, next to the Upper Plaza. The former is so close to the water, you can see jellyfish floating by and hear the gentle lapping of the waves. Both rooms are easy to decorate, and each one has a gorgeous floor-to-ceiling view of the bay.

The Plaza emphasizes hospitality and service, and their event coordinator is one of the most congenial we've met. And if you'd like to extend your stay in the Monterey-Carmel area, you can always honeymoon at the hotel and take a few extra days to explore one of Northern California's most beautiful regions.

CEREMONY CAPACITY: The Lower Terrace can accommodate 190 guests seated in rows and more standing; the Upper Plaza holds over 400 seated in rows.

EVENT/RECEPTION CAPACITY:

Area	Seated	w/Dancing	Area	Seated	w/Dancing
Cypress Ballroom	350	250	Dolphins Room	250	190
Monterey Bay Room	175	120			

There are 9 additional rooms, some with ocean views, that accommodate 10–140 guests.

MEETING CAPACITY: There are 11 meeting rooms (16,000 square feet of meeting space) which can accommodate up to 400 guests.

FEES & DEPOSITS: The rental fee for a 5-hour event ranges $250–1,250 depending on the banquet room reserved. It is due, along with the $500 ceremony site fee (if applicable), when reservations are confirmed. The estimated food and beverage total is due 10 working days prior to the function. Luncheons start at $32/person, dinners at $38/person. Additional evening hours may be purchased at $200/hour. Wedding cake, alcohol, tax and an 18% service charge are additional. Note that overnight accommodations for the bride and groom can be arranged for $99/night with a 2-night maximum.

AVAILABILITY: For events, year-round, daily, until midnight; for meetings, 24 hours a day.

SERVICES/AMENITIES:

Catering: provided, no BYO
Kitchen Facilities: n/a
Tables & Chairs: provided
Linens, Silver, etc.: provided
Restrooms: wheelchair accessible
Dance Floor: provided
Bride's & Groom's Dressing Area: CBA
Meeting Equipment: some provided, other CBA extra fee

Parking: valet, extra fee
Accommodations: 285 guest rooms
Telephone: pay phone
Outdoor Night Lighting: additional CBA
Outdoor Cooking Facilities: CBA
Cleanup: provided
View: of Monterey Bay & Pacific Ocean
Other: event coordination

RESTRICTIONS:

Alcohol: provided, no BYO
Smoking: outside only
Music: amplified OK w/volume restrictions

Wheelchair Access: yes
Insurance: not required
Other: no glitter

---

*This is important! Tell facilities you're reading **Here Comes The Guide** and ask if our information is still current.*

628

Tarpy's Roadhouse

2999 Monterey Salinas Highway, Monterey
(831) 655-2999, fax (831) 655-2995

Restaurant in Historic Roadhouse

◆ Ceremonies   ◆ Special Events
◆ Wedding Receptions   ◆ Meetings
◆ Business Functions   Accommodations

Roadhouse? Okay, we know what you're thinking: How appealing can a place be with the word "roadhouse" in its name? Well, in this case, very appealing indeed. Though this historic stone building has a slightly raffish past (it sits on Tarpy Flats, the spot where Matt Tarpy was lynched for the murder of his neighbor, Sarah Nicholson in 1873), it's now known for its charming event

spaces, "Creative American Country" food, and eclectic, enticing atmosphere.

Pass under the vine-covered stone arch at the entrance, and you'll find yourself in the Courtyard, where a serene stone face peers out of a honeysuckle-draped grotto, and passion-flower vines ramble over a rustic stone-and-wood arbor. The walls of the building rise on two sides of this space, supporting still more vines and trailing flowers, as well as a bronze frieze of dancing figures. Wooden tables and metal chairs provide seating; market umbrellas and heat lamps make the space pleasant no matter what the weather. An intimate wedding, sunset cocktail party, or dinner lit by the soft glow of Craftsman-style lanterns and twinkling stars is sensational in this tantalizing spot. Other outdoor ceremony sites include the pleasant lawn in front of the restaurant, with pond and trees, or the tiny wishing-well garden.

Indoors, several dining rooms extend the pleasing ambiance found in the Courtyard. In the Shell Room, soft cream walls, white window mouldings and crisp white linens give the space a relaxed elegance; the natural wood-and-rush chairs echo the golden-brown tones of the room's focal point, a whimsical fireplace constructed entirely of shells. The Vintner's Room has displays of award-winning local wines, contemporary art, and views of the restaurant's lush gardens and wishing-well. Upstairs, the Library is a spacious, private room with off-white and natural stone walls, a large fireplace, brass chandeliers, distinctive metal-and-leather chairs, and bookshelves. Just off the Library is a private patio, where bougainvillea, fuchsias, jasmine and nasturtiums vie for the viewer's attention. One side of the patio is a wall, ingeniously built into the hillside, that provides a wealth of nooks and crannies for still more flowers and herbs to find a foothold. An enchanting *melange* of textures, colors and scents, this terra-cotta-paved terrace makes a lovely spot for pre-dinner cocktails or post-dinner dancing.

So, whether you're planning a formal wedding, business function, or casual celebratory dinner, Tarpy's is sure to fill the bill. And don't worry, you won't find any shady characters drinking bathtub gin at this roadhouse—just delighted diners, enjoying the restaurant's great wine, food and congenial ambiance.

CEREMONY CAPACITY: The on-property Monterey Stone Marriage Chapel holds 50 seated guests, maximum; the Library Patio holds 20 seated or more for a standing ceremony.

EVENT/RECEPTION & MEETING CAPACITY:

Area	Seated	Area	Seated
Tack Room	18	Shell Room	24
Vintner's Room	32	Library & Terrace	120
Restaurant w/buyout	300		

FEES & DEPOSITS: A $125 refundable deposit is required when you make your reservation. The event balance is payable at the event's conclusion. Luncheons start at $12/person, dinners at $27/person; an 18% service charge or minimum gratuity, tax and alcohol are additional. Room rental charges run $25–150 depending on the room. On-site ceremonies may require an additional charge.

For special events, arrangements can be made for exclusive use of the entire restaurant for a $10,000 food and beverage minimum. Buyouts are not available on Fridays, Saturdays or event weekends.

AVAILABILITY: Year-round, daily, 8am–11pm except July 4th, Thanksgiving and Christmas days.

SERVICES/AMENITIES:

Catering: provided, no BYO
Kitchen Facilities: n/a
Tables & Chairs: provided
Linens, Silver, etc.: provided
Restrooms: wheelchair accessible
Dance Floor: Terrace
Bride's & Groom's Dressing Area: CBA
Meeting Equipment: CBA, extra fee

Parking: large lot
Accommodations: no guest rooms
Telephone: pay phone
Outdoor Night Lighting: yes
Outdoor Cooking Facilities: yes
Cleanup: provided
View: gardens and landscaped hillside
Other: event coordination

RESTRICTIONS:

Alcohol: provided or BYO, corkage $10/bottle
Smoking: outside only
Music: amplified OK w/volume restrictions

Wheelchair Access: yes, ramp available
Insurance: not required
Other: no rice

---

*This is important! Tell facilities you're reading **Here Comes The Guide** and ask if our information is still current.*

Martine Inn

Bayfront Inn

255 Oceanview Boulevard, Pacific Grove
(800) 852-5588, (831) 373-3388, fax (831) 373-3896

www.martineinn.com

◆ Ceremonies ◆ Special Events
◆ Wedding Receptions ◆ Meetings
◆ Business Functions ◆ Accommodations

The Martine Inn is set high, right on the edge of Monterey Bay, overlooking the rocky coastline of Pacific Grove. Originally designed as an ocean-front Victorian mansion in 1899, it was remodeled as a Mediterranean villa by James and Laura Park (of the Park-Davis pharmaceutical company) when Victoriana went out of style in the early 1900s. Although the exterior is Mediterranean, the Inn's decor is strictly Victorian, in rose and pink hues. There are elegantly furnished rooms complete with museum-quality American antiques, and from interior windows, guests have wonderful views of waves crashing against the cliffs. The Martines can help you design your event to meet your specific requirements and will even provide a staff consultant to plan the food, music, decorations or entertainment.

CEREMONY CAPACITY:

Area	Standing	Seated	Area	Standing	Seated
Dining Room	15	10	Conference Room	30	20
Parlor	50	50	Courtyard	125	125
Library	20	15			

EVENT/RECEPTION CAPACITY: The Parlor holds 30–50 guests, the Courtyard up to 125. If you rent the entire Inn, it can accommodate 125 guests indoors.

MEETING CAPACITY: The Conference Rooms seats 20; 5 breakout rooms seat 5–30.

FEES & DEPOSITS: A non-refundable rental fee is required to book an event. The rental fee is $250 for under 10 guests or $500 for 10–50 guests. For more than 50 guests, there is a $950 rental fee, and you must reserve the entire Inn for approximately $5,300/night. A 2-night minimum applies to any weekend booking. For groups of fewer than 50 guests, the balance is payable when you make reservations; there is a 1-guest room minimum and a 5-guest room maximum. When booking the entire inn, a $1,500 deposit is required upon booking, and the guest room balance is due 6 months prior to the event.

Victorian luncheons or dinners range $35–150/person, and buffets $35–45/person; beverages, tax and a 15% service charge are additional. The balance is due at the end of the event. There is a 20-guest minimum for food service.

AVAILABILITY: Year-round, daily. If you book the entire Inn, the event hours are negotiable. If you reserve only a portion of the Inn, the hours are usually 1pm–4pm.

SERVICES/AMENITIES:

Catering: provided, no BYO
Kitchen Facilities: n/a
Tables & Chairs: provided
Linens, Silver, etc.: provided
Restrooms: wheelchair accessible
Dance Floor: yes
Bride's Dressing Area: guest room
Meeting Equipment: CBA, extra fee

Parking: on street, medium lot
Accommodations: 25 guest rooms
Telephone: guest phone
Outdoor Night Lighting: minimal
Outdoor Cooking Facilities: BBQ
Cleanup: provided
View: ocean or courtyard
Other: full wedding services

RESTRICTIONS:

Alcohol: provided, no BYO, WBC only
Smoking: restricted
Music: amplified OK w/volume limits

Wheelchair Access: yes
Insurance: not required

The professionals in the back of the book are the best in the business! How do we know? Read page 681.

632

The Lodge at Pebble Beach

17 Mile Drive, Pebble Beach
(831) 624-3811, fax (831) 622-8796

www.pebble-beach.com

Oceanfront Hotel & Conference Center

◆ Ceremonies	◆ Special Events
◆ Wedding Receptions	◆ Meetings
◆ Business Functions	◆ Accommodations

Since opening in 1919, The Lodge at Pebble Beach has welcomed thousands of guests to one of the world's premier and most challenging golf courses. Set on a gentle rise, the facility overlooks meticulously manicured, emerald-green fairways that slope down to the serpentine edge of Carmel Bay. But golf is not the only attraction—sweeping ocean panoramas and a relaxed elegance also make The Lodge one of Northern California's favorite places for business functions, parties and wedding receptions.

Couples who get married here usually tie the knot on the lawn overlooking the 18th hole. With a backdrop of the bay, boats bobbing in the harbor and tiers of coastal hills fading into the distance, it's clear why this is such a popular spot. For an intimate reception, reserve the Library Room. A marble fireplace, muted pastel decor and glassed-in bookcase give it a cozy ambiance, while a wall of floor-to-ceiling glass provides a view of the 18th green and the ocean just below. There's also an adjoining open-air terrace for cocktails or simply enjoying the surroundings.

For special events and business functions, The Lodge offers many options. The Pebble Beach Room, one of the larger spaces, is a lovely spot with a high, coffered ceiling and a wall of windows affording a partial view of the Pacific. It, too, has its own terrace where you can sip champagne and survey the fairway. Larger functions can be accommodated in the adjacent Conference Center, which overlooks the Lodge as well as a putting green.

And that's not all. Just a short walk from The Lodge, on the shores of Stillwater Cove, is the Beach & Tennis Club. If we had to list our favorite venues in California, this would certainly be among the top five. You couldn't pick a more gorgeous spot—it's located on the ocean's edge along one of the most stunning stretches of the Monterey coastline. The dining room has a glass conservatory and skylight that drench the room with light, and the views—we can hardly contain ourselves! You've got unobstructed vistas of the Pacific, Stillwater Cove and the renowned Pebble Beach Golf Links' 17th fairway. Even if you don't want to rent the Beach & Tennis Club for your special event, you might want to take a peek anyway.

CEREMONY CAPACITY: The lawn at the 18th hole can accommodate 250 seated or standing.

EVENT/RECEPTION CAPACITY:

Room	Seated		Room	Seated
Pebble Beach Room	120–150		Conference Center	250
Library Room	60		Card Room	30
Beach Club *(dinner only)*	125–200			

MEETING CAPACITY:

Room	Conf-style	Theater-style	Room	Conf-style	Theater-style
Conference Cntr	—	400	Council Room	60	275
Centre Room	20	25	Committee Room	36	100
Library	30	70	Card Room	20	35
Pebble Beach Room	70	250	*Other rooms are available.*		

FEES & DEPOSITS: For weddings, a non-refundable rental fee deposit is due within 2 weeks after making your reservation. Per-person rates for food: hors d'oeuvres start at $30, luncheons range $27–42 and dinners $53–80. Alcohol, tax and a 17% service charge are additional.

Room rental fees for all weddings, special events and business functions range from $1,500–$3,500. For ceremonies on the lawn overlooking the ocean, the fee is $2,000. Prices are for single-meal functions that take place in a 4-hour block; if more meals or time are required the price will increase.

AVAILABILITY: Year-round, daily, any time.

SERVICES/AMENITIES:

Catering: provided, no BYO
Kitchen Facilities: n/a
Tables & Chairs: provided
Linens, Silver, etc.: provided
Restrooms: wheelchair accessible
Dance Floor: yes
Bride's Dressing Area: no
Meeting Equipment: full range

Parking: large lots
Accommodations: 161 guest rooms
Telephone: pay phone
Outdoor Night Lighting: limited
Outdoor Cooking Facilities: CBA
Cleanup: provided
View: of Pacific Ocean, putting greens, panoramic views of Monterey Peninsula

RESTRICTIONS:

Alcohol: provided, no BYO
Smoking: not allowed
Music: amplified OK indoors until 10pm, outdoors w/volume limits until 10pm

Wheelchair Access: yes
Insurance: not required

*This is important! Tell facilities you're reading **Here Comes The Guide** and ask if our information is still current.*

634

san luis obispo area

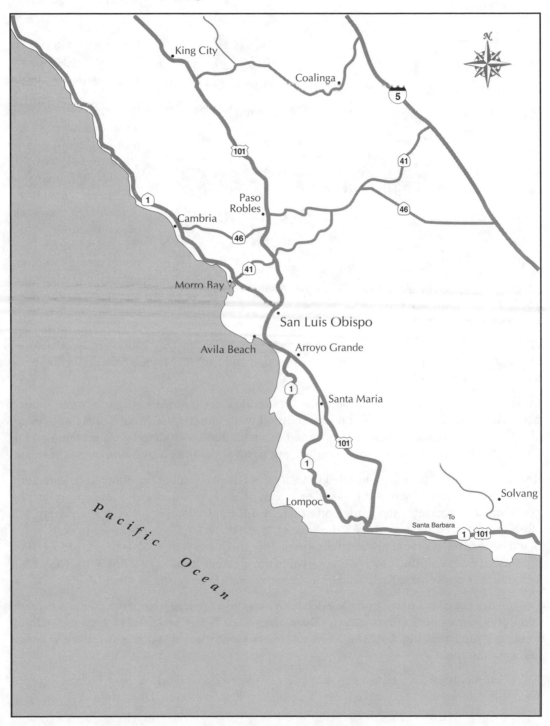

King City

Coalinga

5

101

41

Paso
Robles

46

Cambria

46

41

Morro Bay

San Luis Obispo

Avila Beach

Arroyo Grande

1

Santa Maria

101

1

Solvang

Lompoc

To
Santa Barbara

1 101

Pacific Ocean

N.

Crystal Rose Inn

Inn & Restaurant

789 Valley Road, Arroyo Grande
(805) 481-1854, (800) ROSE-INN, fax (805) 481-9541

www.centralcoast.com/crystalroseinn
stay@callamer.com

◆ Ceremonies   ◆ Special Events
◆ Wedding Receptions   Meetings
◆ Business Functions   Accommodations

Looking for a storybook location for a storybook wedding? Look no further than the Crystal Rose Inn, a Victorian jewel built in 1890. Extensively renovated in 1981 and 1994, this stately pink mansion has been chosen by *Sunset Magazine* as one of California's select "fantasies for rent." Envision yourself stepping out of the fast lane into another era, where the soothing tinkle of wind chimes, the refreshing splash of a garden fountain and the joyous song of birds replace the sound and fury that passes for normal life in the late 20th century.

Inside the Inn, the atmosphere is pure late 19th century. Each downstairs parlor room is filled with Victorian-era furnishings, and is suffused with the fragrance of roses. And every afternoon, the Inn indulges its guests' taste buds with that most Victorian of traditions: High Tea, featuring fresh-baked scones, sandwiches, pastries, and fresh fruit dipped in chocolate.

If you're interested in getting married here, try the Gazebo Garden for either your ceremony or reception. Graced by bright flowers, expanses of lawn, mature trees, fountains, reflecting pools and a lacy gazebo, the garden offers a refreshing environment for your special day. For more intimate ceremonies, there's the smaller "Secret Garden," where flower baskets and a petite lawn furnish a more private setting under the shady branches of a 100-year-old ash tree. For indoor events during the evening or when the weather turns cooler, the Inn's Hunt Club Restaurant is convenient for a rehearsal dinner, reception or business function.

The Inn has eight bedrooms, each one decorated around a favorite rose of the Innkeeper. Many couples commandeer the entire Inn for themselves, their family and guests for a long wedding weekend. After the "big day," the white rose-motif Honor Room is a magical place to spend the wedding night.

There are plenty of diversions nearby to keep everyone relaxed and happy, both before and after the celebration. You have your pick of beaches, wineries, lakes, two different golf courses, and an in-house masseuse. The Inn also offers everything you'll need for the wedding itself: in-house catering from the Hunt Club Restaurant and event coordination (help with finding a florist, videographer, musician or photographer or even a minister!). They'll even provide a lovely (and incredibly delicious) wedding cake, too.

With such a romantic setting (not to mention all the helpful services) you'll want to go out and meet that special someone (if you haven't already), just so you can use the Crystal Rose Inn for the wedding.

CEREMONY & EVENT/RECEPTION CAPACITY:

Space	Seated	Space	Seated
Sitting Room	20	Hunt Club Restaurant	60
Secret Garden	60	Gazebo Garden	400

MEETING CAPACITY: The Victorian Room can seat 12 people conference-style. The Sitting Room can accommodate up to 20 seated theater-style. The Restaurant holds 60 guests seated conference-style or 80 theater-style.

FEES & DEPOSITS: For weddings, half of the facility rental fee is required as a deposit to reserve your date. The balance of the rental fee and half of the estimated food and beverage total are due 6 weeks prior to the event. The final guest count is due 2 weeks prior to the event. The event balance is payable the day before the function. The 5-hour facility rental fee is $15/person in the afternoons, $30/person in the evenings. Minimum rental fees range $250–700, depending on space rented. Seated meals run $18–30/person or buffets $17–25/person; alcohol, tax and a 20% service charge are additional. Children under 10 years are 3/4 the adult price. A cake-cutting fee of $1.25/person is additional.

For other events, facility rental fees range $100–1,400. Seated meals run $11–30/person, buffets $17–25/person. All other pricing information is the same as above.

AVAILABILITY: Year-round, daily, 7am–11pm.

SERVICES/AMENITIES:

Catering: provided, no BYO
Kitchen Facilities: n/a
Tables & Chairs: provided
Linens, Silver, etc.: provided
Restrooms: wheelchair accessible
Dance Floor: cement pad outdoors
Bride's Dressing Area: yes
Meeting Equipment: BYO or CBA

Parking: large lots
Accommodations: 8 guest rooms
Telephone: room phones
Outdoor Night Lighting: yes
Outdoor Cooking Facilities: yes
Cleanup: provided
View: rolling hills, trees, flower garden
Other: event coordination, floral table arrangements

RESTRICTIONS:

Alcohol: provided or BYO, wine corkage $7/bottle
Smoking: outside only
Music: amplified OK until 9pm

Wheelchair Access: yes
Insurance: not required
Other: no rice or birdseed

The professionals in the back of the book are the best in the business! *How do we know? Read page 681.*

Avila Beach Resort

Avila Beach
(805) 595-4000 x503, fax (805) 595-4002
www.avilabeachresort.com

◆ Ceremonies ◆ Special Events
◆ Wedding Receptions ◆ Meetings
◆ Business Functions ◆ Accommodations

So...you're planning an intimate party for 1,000 of your closest friends. You want to be near the beach, and have gorgeous views, *and* you'd like someone to hold your hand while you're planning your event. Where on earth can you find such a place? Avila Beach Resort! This is a golf course *with* a special events facility, the largest on the Central Coast. It's an exceptional destination for banquets, weddings and other celebrations, affording breathtaking, panoramic views of the Avila Beach, Avila Valley and the Pacific Ocean.

The primary event area is an expansive, manicured lawn situated between the fairway's ninth and tenth holes. From here, you can see for miles, watch the water ebb and flow out of Avila Beach and take in a glorious sunset. The lawn can accommodate up to 3,000 guests! And if you'd like an outdoor event with an indoor feel, set up a tent (or two!) on the lawn. Using a little imagination, you can customize the mood inside the tent, from glitzy and elegant to sultry, nightclub chic. Tents come with clear-sided panels so you'll always have a guaranteed beach view. The Resort provides a portable dance floor, and ample electrical equipment to handle any size band. And the close proximity of the tent(s) to Mulligan's Restaurant means your guests will be served with a minimum of muss and fuss.

Nearby, inside Mulligan's Restaurant, you can host a more intimate reception or ceremony in the cozy banquet room which has a small fireplace. Mulligan's is also a terrific venue for rehearsal dinners and company meetings.

Avila Beach Resort can handle the grandest parties with ease. (Some of the events it plays host to every year are the KCBX Wine Classic, the Memorial Week Beer & Blues Festival, Pops by the Sea Concert, and many jazz concerts.) What brings them back time after time? The loveliness of the setting—especially at night, when the lighted tents glow like giant lanterns against the dark background of the ocean.

And the service. No matter how large or small your group is, your guests will always feel well taken care of. Much of the credit goes to event coordinator Linda Renfrow and her staff, who've worked together for years. They'll spare no effort to make sure everything is perfect, down to the tiniest detail. Recently, a classic roadster club rally was held at the Resort, with dozens of pristine show cars on display. To prevent any dirt from settling on those precious vehicles,

Renfrow's staff were busy hours before the rally, sweeping every drop of water from the entry drive with push brooms, so that nothing would splash up on the roadsters. If they'll do that for mere machines, imagine how they'll treat you!

As full-service caterers, they'll customize your menu, hunting down recipes if necessary to create the dishes you want. They'll also help newlyweds make their getaway in any one of several conveyances: limousine, horse-drawn carriage—even a hot air balloon! No wonder Renfrow and her crew were chosen by *Strictly Business Magazine* as the winner of their 1993 Best of Business Banquet Services Award. It's unusual for a facility that serves large numbers of people so effortlessly to retain its warm-and-cozy quality, but this one does. And that's the truth.

CEREMONY CAPACITY: The lawn can accommodate up to 1,000 seated or standing guests. Indoors, Mullilgan's holds up to 120 seated.

EVENT/RECEPTION CAPACITY: The patio tent holds 120 seated or 200 standing, the lawn without tents up to 3,000 seated, the lawn with tents 150–1,000 seated or 3,000 standing. Mulligan's Dining Room holds 50 seated guests.

FEES & DEPOSITS: For special events, a non-refundable $300 cancellation deposit is required when booking the site. The site rental fee ranges $400–2,000 depending on guest count. The anticipated food and beverage total and site rental fee are payable 7 business days prior to the event. Any menu can be customized: luncheons run $6–13/person, dinners $10–26/person; alcohol, tax and a 16% service charge are additional. Tent rentals can be arranged, and run $400–5,000 depending on tent size.

AVAILABILITY: Year-round, daily, 7am–midnight.

SERVICES/AMENITIES:

Catering: provided, no BYO
Kitchen Facilities: n/a
Tables & Chairs: provided up to 300
Linens, Silver, etc.: provided
Restrooms: wheelchair accessible
Dance Floor: CBA, extra fee
Bride's & Groom's Dressing Area: CBA
Meeting Equipment: BYO

Parking: large lots
Accommodations: no guest rooms
Telephone: pay phones
Outdoor Night Lighting: yes
Outdoor Cooking Facilities: CBA
Cleanup: provided
View: Pacific Ocean, fairways, Avila Beach
Other: event coordination

RESTRICTIONS:

Alcohol: provided or WC corkage 7.50/bottle
Smoking: outside only
Music: amplified OK until midnight

Wheelchair Access: yes
Insurance: required for concerts

This is important! Tell facilities you're reading **Here Comes The Guide** and ask if our information is still current.

639

Embassy Suites Hotel

Hotel

333 Madonna Road, San Luis Obispo
(805) 549-0800, (800) 864-6000, fax (805) 549-9138

www.embassy-suites.com

◆ Ceremonies ◆ Special Events
◆ Wedding Receptions ◆ Meetings
◆ Business Functions ◆ Accommodations

Over the last few years, the Embassy Suites has undergone a very successful transformation. It's not only become the largest conference center and indoor event site in San Luis Obispo County, it has a fresh, new look.

Its four-story Atrium is the heart of the hotel—a lovely spot for weekday dining or Saturday ceremonies and receptions. Light pours in through the gigantic skylight, warming the soft peach walls and nourishing the lush foliage. More greenery surrounds a three-tiered fountain and spills from planter boxes attached to railings above. Beneath white linen-clad tables, a teal-green patterned carpet adds to the serene, almost tropical ambiance of the room.

Large weddings, receptions and meetings are held in the San Luis Obispo Ballroom. Although this room can accommodate over 400 seated guests when used in its entirety, it can be divided into three sections for smaller groups. Each section has an elaborate shell chandelier set into a coffered ceiling, and recessed, adjustable lighting all around the room. With eleven meeting rooms to choose from, the total area of flexible meeting and banquet space tops 12,000 square feet!

Guest suites are also designed with business needs and comfort in mind. Each one has a private bedroom and spacious living room, and is fully equipped with two televisions, two telephones with data ports, a well-lit dining/work table, a refrigerator and microwave. Add to that a fitness center and heated indoor pool and spa, and you've got everything you need for a satisfying prolonged stay.

When it's time to relax after a special event or conference, there are dozens of local attractions and activities: golf courses, wineries, the spectacular coastline, historic missions and, of course, Hearst Castle. Complimentary shuttle service is provided to and from the San Luis Obispo Airport and the Amtrak station, both within five miles of the hotel.

So if you're planning a gala event with hundreds of friends and relatives coming from all over the state, or looking for a conference center conveniently located halfway between San

Francisco and Los Angeles, the Embassy Suites San Luis Obispo is the obvious choice. The staff—including the congenial and very accessible General Manager—is extremely service oriented and will make your visit to the central coast a pleasure.

CEREMONY CAPACITY: The Atrium seats 100–125 guests and the San Luis Obispo Ballroom seats up to 500 guests.

EVENT/RECEPTION CAPACITY:

Space	Seated	Standing	Space	Seated	Standing
San Luis Obispo Ballroom	500	600	Los Osos Room	80	125
SLO Ballroom South or North	110	175	Edna Room	80	125
SLO Ballroom Center	140	250			

MEETING CAPACITY:

Space	Theater-style	Classroom-style	Conference-style
San Luis Obispo Ballroom	550	275	—
SLO Ballroom South or North	130	75	50
Los Osos or Edna	100	60	32

FEES & DEPOSITS: For weddings, a $1,200 deposit is required to secure your date. The balance is due 3 days prior to the event. Luncheons start at $13/person, dinners at $20/person; alcohol, tax and an 18% service charge are additional. For ceremonies in the Atrium, a $300 charge applies.

For business functions, conferences or meetings, room charges vary based on room(s) and services selected. Embassy Suites offers a complete line of audio visual equipment and a variety of menus for meals, breaks and beverage service. Call for more specific information.

AVAILABILITY: Year-round, daily until midnight. After midnight, additional charges will apply.

SERVICES/AMENITIES:

Catering: provided, no BYO
Kitchen Facilities: n/a
Tables & Chairs: provided
Linens, Silver, etc.: provided
Restrooms: wheelchair accessible
Dance Floor: portable parquet floor, extra fee
Bride's & Groom's Dressing Area: CBA
Meeting Equipment: full range

Parking: large lots, complimentary self parking
Accommodations: 196 guest suites
Telephone: pay and guest phones
Outdoor Night Lighting: n/a
Outdoor Cooking Facilities: n/a
Cleanup: provided
View: no
Other: event coordination

RESTRICTIONS:

Alcohol: provided, or BYO w/corkage fee
Smoking: outside only
Music: amplified OK indoors until midnight

Wheelchair Access: yes
Insurance: not required
Other: no rice

The professionals in the back of the book are the best in the business! How do we know? Read page 681.

The Forum on Marsh

751 Marsh Street, San Luis Obispo
(805) 781-3403, fax (805) 781-3418

www.forum-on-marsh.com
bids@forum-on-marsh.com

◆ Ceremonies   ◆ Special Events
◆ Wedding Receptions   ◆ Meetings
◆ Business Functions   Accommodations

In ancient times, the forum was the town square where Roman citizens gathered for intelligent discourse and public activities. At the Forum on Marsh, they've expanded the concept of "the meeting place," and designed possibly the best (if not the only) full-service event facility in San Luis Obispo. What makes us say that? Only a whole list of features and services supported by an incredibly competent staff.

As you're driving down Marsh Street, you can easily spot the Forum by its Neoclassic facade, an architectural homage to its ancient predecessor. The Greco-Roman motif is carried indoors, too: a wonderful arch built into one wall of the Main Hall creates a visual centerpiece for the room, and columns inset around the perimeter further echo the theme. However, everything else about the Forum is thoroughly contemporary, and the combination of old and new styles works beautifully.

The Main Hall is a "chameleon room" in that it can become whatever you want it to be. The soft-hued color scheme makes a neutral background for decorating, while the specialized lighting and sound systems allow you to fine tune the atmosphere, going from bright to subdued or anywhere in between at the push of a button. You can actually make it look as though you're having a swanky evening affair in the middle of the day! At your request, the technically savvy staff will program a variety of lighting choices in advance, and execute them at the appropriate times.

The range of events that have been held here is extraordinary. Besides weddings, receptions, and seminars, the Forum has hosted concerts, operas and fashion shows. Two of the more unusual events were a Renaissance-theme party with tightrope walkers, and an East Indian wedding, where the hall was treated as sacred ground, tents were erected and the guests wore no shoes.

Just off the Main Hall is a gated courtyard, which can be tented for more privacy or strung with twinkle lights for glamour. Couples often have their ceremony or serve appetizers out here, then walk right into the Hall for the reception. If your event is very large, you can always tent the parking lot, too. Smaller gatherings are held in the Cuesta Room, a completely private room with foyer on its own floor. Its distinctive appointments, ergonomically designed chairs and adjustable lighting make it especially well-suited for meetings.

Whichever spaces you choose, the Forum will fill them with elegant touches: imported Bavarian china, real silver and crisp linens. Their staff—whose collective experience in theater, special events, floral arts and much more is impressive—will also help you with every aspect of your event. In addition to coordinating the food, a complete bar service, flowers, decor and entertainment, they'll assist you with overnight accommodations, ceremony arrangements at one of the local churches, and arrival by horse and buggy or 1929 Jaguar if you like. The event coordinator, Mark Padgett, is a joy to work with. We can tell you these folks are experts at putting on events, but their track record speaks for itself: out of their first 700 events, 697 were judged "excellent" by those filling out critiques afterward. The other three? Well, they were deemed merely "good." Clearly you have nothing to lose and everything to gain by entrusting your event to the Forum.

CEREMONY CAPACITY: The Courtyard holds 100 seated guests; the Main Hall can accommodate 150 seated guests.

EVENT/RECEPTION CAPACITY: The Main Hall holds 270 seated or 400 standing. The Cuesta Room, 32 seated or 40 standing guests.

MEETING CAPACITY: The Main Hall seats 150 classroom-style or 300 guests theater-style. The Cuesta Room holds 30 classroom-style or 45 theater-style.

FEES & DEPOSITS: A refundable $200 deposit is required when booking the site. One-fourth of the estimated event total is due 2 months after signing the contract, another one-fourth is due 2 months later. The balance is payable 1 week prior to the event. Luncheons range $10–20/person, dinners $23–45/person; tax, alcohol, waitstaff labor fees and an 18% service charge are additional. If you use the on-site caterer, a 25% discount on room rental fees applies. Room rental fees are as follows:

Day	Guest Count	Space	Rental fee
Mon–Fri	up to 300	Main Hall	$400–800/full day, $250–500/half day
Mon–Fri	up to 45	Cuesta Room	$200/full day, 150/half day
Sat/Sun	up to 400	Main Hall	$1,000–1,500
Sat–Sun	up to 40	Cuesta Room	$500
Any day	up to 100	Courtyard	$200

AVAILABILITY: Year-round, daily, 7:30am–11pm; closed Christmas Eve and Day.

SERVICES/AMENITIES:

Catering: provided, or select from list
Kitchen Facilities: prep only
Tables & Chairs: provided
Linens, Silver, etc.: provided
Restrooms: wheelchair accessible
Dance Floor: parquet floor provided
Bride's Dressing Area: CBA, extra charge
Meeting Equipment: full range, extra fee

Parking: small lot and nearby garage
Accommodations: no guest rooms
Telephone: pay phone
Outdoor Night Lighting: yes
Outdoor Cooking Facilities: through caterer
Cleanup: provided
View: no view
Other: event coordination, floral arrangements, grand piano, complete bar service

RESTRICTIONS:

Alcohol: provided, no BYO
Smoking: outside only
Music: amplified OK indoors, outside w/restrictions

Wheelchair Access: yes
Insurance: required for concerts only
Other: no red punch, glitter, nails or tacks

Sycamore Mineral Springs

Historic Resort & Spa

1215 Avila Beach Road, San Luis Obispo
(805) 595-7302 (800) 234-5831, fax (805) 781-2598

www.sycamoresprings.com
info@smsr.com

◆ Ceremonies ◆ Special Events
◆ Wedding Receptions ◆ Meetings
◆ Business Functions ◆ Accommodations

Just over a century ago, two men drilling for oil amongst the towering oaks and sycamores of Avila Valley struck a bonanza of a different sort: a piping hot spring of natural mineral water.

Thus was born Sycamore Mineral Springs, a luxurious Spanish stucco spa/resort that quickly became the favorite getaway for the "beautiful people" of Hollywood in the early days of the film industry. During the Roaring '20s, stars like Charlie Chaplin, Gloria Swanson and W.C. Fields regularly stopped by for a visit on their way to and from Hearst Castle at San Simeon.

Thanks to a lavish refurbishing during the 1970s, "The Spa" (as locals call it) looks much as it did when Charlie, Gloria and W.C. frolicked in its mineral waters. The accommodations are not only beautiful, they're restorative. Each guest room and suite is sumptuously furnished, and features its own, full-sized Jacuzzi on the balcony. Board-certified physical therapists and estheticians are also on hand to enhance the benefits of the hot mineral spas with therapeutic massage and facial therapy treatments.

Ah, brides, what could be more relaxing than to spend the night before the wedding pampering yourself with a long soak in one of the outdoor redwood hot tubs followed by a massage and facial? (This luxurious indulgence also makes an imaginative gift for your bridesmaids). And if you'd like to treat more of your family and friends to a warm, communal experience, the new "Oasis" spa can accommodate as many as 40 people at a time.

But it's on the day of the wedding that Sycamore Mineral Springs truly comes into its own. The lovely Gazebo Courtyard, set in the midst of a lush and fragrant garden, can easily accommodate large weddings and receptions. Smaller ceremonies and their festivities can take place in the delicate garden around the koi pond, a more intimate and romantic setting.

Sycamore Mineral Springs doesn't hold back on the creature comforts for non-wedding events, either. Indoors, the Palm Room, with its palm trees, arched windows and 20-foot-high mahogany ceiling, is a fresh, airy and appealing space for large meetings, business conferences and retreats; and the equally attractive Board Room, with its mahogany ceiling, silk Renaissance tapestries and dark wood, upholstered chairs, is an excellent site for smaller meetings. Both come with full audio-visual equipment, including TVs, VCRs, and movie screens.

Then there's the unique blend of cuisines offered by the Gardens of Avila Restaurant, located right at the resort. One of the most celebrated dining establishments in the area, it was recently named "The Most Romantic Restaurant in the Central Coast."

Once you've had your wedding here, where could you go for your honeymoon? Don't go anywhere. Stay and complete your already perfect day at one of Sycamore Mineral Springs two special suites nestled in the hillside where the two of you can sneak away to celebrate the beinning of your new life together. It's the perfect way to write a happy ending to a fairy tale wedding.

CEREMONY CAPACITY: The gazebo/courtyard area holds 250 seated and the Palm Room holds 100 seated guests indoors.

EVENT/RECEPTION CAPACITY: The gazebo/courtyard area can accommodate 250 seated or standing, the Palm Room 100–150 seated or 125 standing and the Board Room 25 seated guests.

MEETING CAPACITY: The Board Room holds 25 seated guests, conference-style; the Palm Room 100 seated guests.

FEES & DEPOSITS: For weddings, a non-refundable $300–1,000 deposit is required when booking the site. A final guest count is due 2 weeks prior and the event balance is payable 1 week before the event. Any menu can be customized. luncheons start at $10/person, buffets at $16.50/person, and dinners at $22/person; alcohol, beverages, tax and a 17% service charge are additional. Several wedding packages are available, and the price varies based on guest count and menu selection. Packages can be customized; coordination services are included for all weddings.

For other special events, retreats or business functions, rental fees vary depending on the type of event and accommodations selected. Food services are provided: breakfasts run $5–10/person and luncheons $8–12/person. Hors d'oeuvres start at $9/person, buffets at $16.50/person and dinners at $16–25/person.

AVAILABILITY: Year-round, daily. Indoor events 7am–11pm; extra hours may be negotiated. Outdoor events take place from dawn until dusk. If receptions include music in the Palm Room, it's only available until 5pm; without music, longer hours can be arranged.

SERVICES/AMENITIES:

Catering: provided, no BYO
Kitchen Facilities: n/a
Tables & Chairs: provided
Linens, Silver, etc.: provided
Restrooms: wheelchair accessible
Dance Floor: provided or CBA
Bride's & Groom's Dressing Area: yes
Meeting Equipment: full range, extra fee
Other: event coordination, full range of spa services, outdoor hot tubs

Parking: large lots
Accommodations: 26 guest rooms, 25 suites and 4 bed and breakfast rooms
Telephone: pay phones
Outdoor Night Lighting: no
Outdoor Cooking Facilities: no
Cleanup: provided
View: garden and wooded hillside

RESTRICTIONS:

Alcohol: provided, no BYO
Smoking: outside only
Music: amplified OK in courtyard until dusk, in Palm Room until 5pm, w/volume limits

Wheelchair Access: yes
Insurance: not required

gold country & yosemite

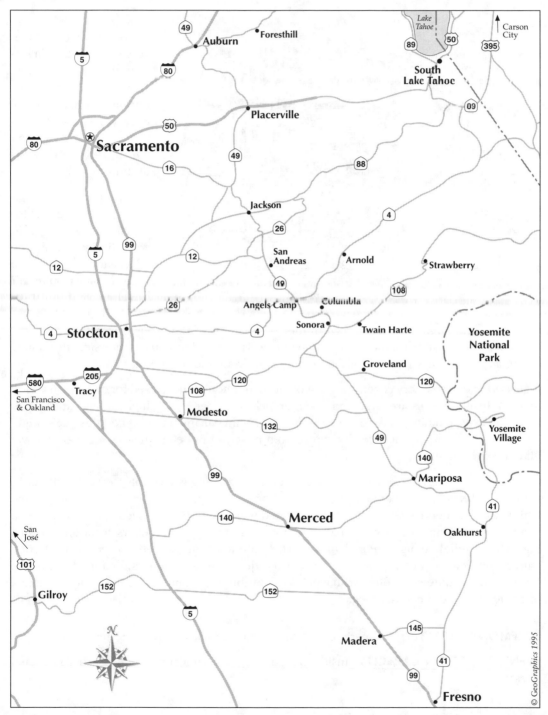

Monte Verde Inn

Inn & Garden

18841 Foresthill Road, Foresthill
(530) 888-8123, fax (530) 888-6260

◆ Ceremonies   ◆ Special Events
◆ Wedding Receptions   ◆ Meetings
◆ Business Functions   ◆ Accommodations

If you're looking for a very special place, it's in Foresthill, a small hamlet about forty minutes northeast of Sacramento. Here you'll find the historic Monte Verde Inn which is, in a word, wonderful.

The property was originally a gathering spot for Indians, and after gold was discovered in the 1850s, it became a toll station and respite for travelers. In the 1890s, the National Hotel was built here. Although it burned down in the 1920s, some of the original structure survived, forming the foundation for the Monte Verde Inn. Constructed during the depression, this stately Georgian-style manor is an old-fashioned, gracious reminder of the past.

A glassed-in conservatory covers the front of the manor house and is used for dancing in winter months. Inside, rooms are large and open. French doors, antiques, high ceilings and lots of labor-intensive detailing make the interior inviting. Unlike many older homes, this one's bright and cheerful, with an eclectic selection of both new and old elements—a sophisticated yet playful environment.

Outdoors, you'll feel like you're in the middle of an English country estate, with lush, manicured lawns and a veritable tapestry of flowers (changed seasonally according to the whim of the owners). The long entry drive, lined with venerable old cedars, draws you back in time. For ceremonies, try the patios, whose tall, surrounding cedars form an informal outdoor cathedral. At night, "fairy lights" and turn-of-the-century streetlights create a glittering halo around dancing couples. Hundred-year-old quince trees, a fountain dating back to the 1890s, and a granite pond filled with large koi contribute to Monte Verde Inn's successful mix of rustic charm and country elegance.

CEREMONY CAPACITY: The patio can accommodate 250 seated or standing guests.

EVENT/RECEPTION CAPACITY: Inside, 75 guests, maximum; outdoors, up to 250 seated guests.

MEETING CAPACITY: The Inn can accommodate up to 40 seated guests.

FEES & DEPOSITS: A refundable $500 cleaning/damage deposit is required to secure your date. Rates start at $37.50/person, which includes rental of the Inn for 4–5 hours, rehearsal, all setups for ceremony and reception, aisle runner, floral centerpieces for all dining, buffet and guest book tables, wedding cake, coffee, hors d'oeuvres and full buffet. Note that all food is prepared from fresh ingredients on the premises by a culinary trained chef. Beverages, alcohol, tax and a 17% service charge are additional.

AVAILABILITY: Events take place indoors 10am–midnight during winter months; outdoors 10am–midnight, May 15th–October 15th.

SERVICES/AMENITIES:

Catering: provided, no BYO
Kitchen Facilities: n/a
Tables & Chairs: provided
Linens, Silver, etc.: provided
Restrooms: wheelchair accessible
Dance Floor: patio
Bride's Dressing Area: yes; CBA for bridal party too
Meeting Equipment: BYO

Parking: 2 large lots
Accommodations: 2-bedroom carriage house
Telephone: house phone
Outdoor Night Lighting: yes
Outdoor Cooking Facilities: BBQ
Cleanup: provided
View: garden

RESTRICTIONS:

Alcohol: provided, BWC only
Smoking: outside only
Music: amplified OK

Wheelchair Access: outdoor access only
Insurance: not required
Other: decorations restricted

Gold Hill Vineyard

Winery & Park

5660 Vineyard Lane, Placerville
(530) 626-6522, fax (530) 642-1731

goldhill@cwnet.com

◆ Ceremonies ◆ Special Events
◆ Wedding Receptions ◆ Meetings
◆ Business Functions Accommodations

Set in the hills above the American River Canyon, Gold Hill Vineyard spreads out over 80 acres of some of the region's loveliest countryside. It's the dream-come-true for owner Hank Battjes, who bought the property in 1980 when he was still an electronic engineer working in Silicon Valley. For ten years he drove up here on weekends to plant grapes, until finally the call of the grape got the best of him, and he quit his city job to become a winemaker for good. Over the past nineteen years, he's not only produced award-winning wines, but created a Gold Country retreat that's custom-made for all types of events. When you call, you'll probably be greeted by John or Doug, the two ultra-friendly tasting room managers, who will help you arrange your event, and select from among Bordeaux, Chardonnay and Riesling wines or outstanding ales and stout—all made on the premises.

No matter where you hold your event—and there are three sites to choose from—you can't help but notice the beauty and quiet seclusion of your surroundings. The view is best from the Winery Hall, a peaked-roof building perched on a hill above the vineyards. The Hall was designed for parties, with a 40-foot redwood bar (beer and wine are on tap), a changing room for the bride, and a huge redwood deck. Triple-tiered and extending the width of the Hall, the deck provides an unobstructed panorama, extending from the bright green rows of vines below, all the way to the Coloma Hills and Mt. Murphy in the distance. If you reserve the Hall for your wedding reception, you can have your ceremony in the Winery Park on the knoll just above it. Guests are seated in a small meadow beneath a canopy of brush oaks, while you say your vows against the backdrop of the vineyards and hills.

A short drive through the vineyard takes you down property to the Upper Pond. Deep green and ringed by weeping willows, it's bordered by both sunny and shady spots for family get-togethers, parties, and small corporate picnics. Just a bit further down the road is Cornelia Meadows, Gold Hill's main outdoor site. Like the Hall, it's been designed for events, and you get the added benefits of the resident trees, lawn and pond. In the spring, wildflowers dot the grounds with color. Flexibility is built in here, making it possible to have any kind of celebration you like. Set up tables with umbrellas on the grass, or tent it for an afternoon or evening reception (indirect lighting is provided at night). A small building at the edge of the lawn houses the kitchen, restrooms, and dressing room; its deck accommodates a band, and the concrete pad in front of it was made for dancing. There's an outdoor bar off to one side, and a redwood platform just a few steps away was specially built for ceremonies under the pines. Just below the Meadows, a still, emerald pond makes a pretty setting for wedding photos. It's also available for fishing and picnicking around its shore.

The folks at Gold Hill have gone out of their way to make all areas of their facility not just wheelchair accessible, but wheelchair friendly, with parking areas near each event site, and ramps wherever necessary. They've also put in a hookup at Cornelia Meadows for an RV—just in case you're planning to stay overnight. And who wouldn't want to? Although you can't pan for gold here, you'll discover quite a few other riches at this peaceful winery in the heart of the Mother Lode.

CEREMONY & EVENT/RECEPTION CAPACITY: The Winery Hall holds 170 seated indoors; the deck holds an additional 80 seated. The Winery Park, across from the winery building, holds up to 300 seated guests; the lower pond area holds 300 seated or standing. For large events, plans are in the works for an amphitheater capable of holding 500 seated on lawn terraces (projected for the year 2000).

MEETING CAPACITY: The Winery Hall holds 200 seated theater-style.

FEES & DEPOSITS: A $350 refundable damage deposit is required to hold your date, the estimated event total is payable 2 months prior to the event.

Area	Guests	Rental Fee	Area	Rental Fee
Winery Hall	up to 100	$950	Winery Park	$250
	over 100	$950+$7.50	Amphitheater	inquire
		for each person over 100		
Upper Pond	up to 40	$150		
Lower Pond	up to 100	850		
	over 100	$850+$7.50		
		for each person over 100		

The Winery Hall rental fee includes tables and chairs for up to 100 guests; the Winery Park fee includes 80 chairs for the ceremony. Table umbrellas are available.

AVAILABILITY: Year-round, daily, 9am–11pm, except for Thanksgiving and Christmas. Events take place in 8-hour blocks; additional hours can be arranged at $100/hour.

SERVICES/AMENITIES:

Catering: select from preferred list or BYO, licensed & insured
Kitchen Facilities: prep only
Tables & Chairs: some provided, or CBA
Linens, Silver, etc.: BYO or caterer
Restrooms: wheelchair accessible
Dance Floor: patio or provided, extra fee
Bride's Dressing Area: yes
Meeting Equipment: podium, extra CBA

Parking: ample, large lot
Accommodations: no guest rooms
Telephone: pay phone
Outdoor Night Lighting: yes
Outdoor Cooking Facilities: BBQs, extra fee
Cleanup: provided, extra fee
View: vineyards, American River Canyon and Mt. Murphy
Other: event coordination, bartender

RESTRICTIONS:

Alcohol: beer/wine provided or corkage $6/bottle
Smoking: outdoors only
Music: amplified OK outdoors til 10pm, Ok indoors til 11pm w/volume restrictions

Wheelchair Access: yes
Insurance: not required
Other: no birdseed, glitter, rice or confetti

Strawberry Inn & Cabins

Inn & Cabins

Highway 108, Strawberry
(800) 965-3662, (888) 965-0885

www.StrawberryInn.com
info@StrawberryInn.com

◆ Ceremonies ◆ Special Events
◆ Wedding Receptions ◆ Meetings
◆ Business Functions ◆ Accommodations

The High Sierra is one of California's most spectacular regions, and the Strawberry Inn is steeped in the area's natural beauty. Surrounded by pines and overlooking the Stanislaus River, this family-owned and operated inn is a relaxed spot for a mountain wedding or special event.

Originally built in 1939 as a country inn for adventuresome mountain travelers, fishermen and hunters, the recently remodeled inn still retains a rustic charm. The building's exterior and many of its walls and ceilings are knotty pine, and as you walk through the hand-carved front doors, you can't help but notice the forest and mountain scene depicted on them. The Inn's interior is enhanced by sculptures, paintings and leaded glass panels created by local artists.

Ceremonies and meetings are often held in the octagonal two-story gazebo next to the restaurant. From here, you can watch the river waters tumble downstream over thousands of rocks worn smooth by time. An open-beamed roof provides shade, and dozens of pine trees filter the view. Another ceremony option is the lawn adjacent to the Inn. Bordered and partially shaded by tall pines, this open expanse of grass requires little decoration, and a staircase leading down to the lawn makes a convenient entrance for the bride.

Receptions take place either in the gazebo or on the lawn, and because both are outdoors, your guests will get the full experience of the scenery and fresh, mountain air. There are plenty of rooms for overnight guests, including several cabins nestled in the pines that the newlyweds might want to consider for themselves. For smaller indoor meetings and events, the Manzanita Room is perfect, and some of the cabins are large enough for small group sessions. After the wedding, go fly fishing or sunbathing in the Inn's backyard or hiking on nearby trails. Strawberry Inn offers the kind of hospitality you'd expect in the unspoiled High Sierra.

CEREMONY & EVENT/RECEPTION CAPACITY: The Gazebo area holds 120 seated or 180 standing; the lawn can accommodate 200 seated or standing guests.

MEETING CAPACITY: The Manzanita Room holds 12–15 conference style, 25 theater style. Additional meeting space can be arranged in the Gazebo or in any of the cabins.

FEES & DEPOSITS: For weddings and receptions, a signed contract and a $500 non-refundable deposit are required to reserve your date. 95% of the estimated event cost is payable 2 weeks prior to the event with a guest count guarantee due 7 days prior. The basic facility use fee (for all types of events) averages $500 and varies depending on the event. Events take place in 4-hour blocks; additional hours run $50/hour. Per person catering costs run: $7–12 for breakfasts, $9–15 for luncheons, $17–25 for dinners and $8–20 for hors d'oeuvres. Tax and service charges are included; alcohol is additional. The event balance is payable at the event's conclusion. Offsite fees and deposits for larger groups are quoted on an individual basis.

AVAILABILITY: Outdoor facilities are seasonal and usually available daily 9am–9pm, April through October. The Manzanita Room is available year-round, flexible hours.

SERVICES/AMENITIES:

Catering: provided, no BYO
Kitchen Facilities: n/a
Tables & Chairs: provided
Linens, Silver, etc.: provided
Restrooms: wheelchair accessible
Dance Floor: gazebo & lounge area
Bride & Groom's Dressing Area: yes
Meeting Equipment: CBA, extra fee

Parking: medium-sized lot
Accommodations: 14 guest rooms, 4 cabins
Telephone: pay phone; private phones CBA, extra fee
Outdoor Night Lighting: yes
Outdoor Cooking Facilities: n/a
Cleanup: provided
View: Stanislaus River, mountains, forest

RESTRICTIONS:

Alcohol: provided, corkage $6/bottle
Smoking: designated areas
Music: amplified OK

Wheelchair Access: limited
Insurance: not required
Other: no rice or confetti

The professionals in the back of the book are the best in the business! How do we know? Read page 681.

Yosemite

Yosemite National Park
(209)253-5673, fax (209) 456-0542

www.yosemitepark.com

National Park

◆ Ceremonies   ◆ Special Events
◆ Wedding Receptions   ◆ Meetings
◆ Business Functions   ◆ Accommodations

Have your wedding in the most beautiful place on earth—Yosemite. It never fails to leave its visitors with a sense of awe and wonder.

The park's unparalleled beauty is an inspiring backdrop for any function, whether it's a rehearsal dinner, anniversary celebration or wedding reception. Facilities here are a study in contrasts. Your choices range from the classically elegant and sophisticated Ahwahnee to the contemporary Yosemite Lodge or the casual Camp Curry to the stately and old-world Wawona Hotel.

After the festivities, your and your guests can enjoy a multitude of summer and winter activities. Savor Yosemite. It can transform any event into a special celebration.

CEREMONY CAPACITY: The Ahwahnee lawn can accommodate up to 200 seated or standing; the Wawona lawn up to 150 seated or standing. Lawns are only available for ceremonies if you have your reception at that site. Additional locations can be arranged through the National Park Service at (209) 379-1860.

EVENT/RECEPTION CAPACITY:

The Ahwahnee	*Seated*		*Seated*
Winter Club Room	10–40	Solarium	40–125
Mural Room	10–40	Rooms Combined	160
Yosemite Lodge			
Mountain Room	200	Falls Room	75
Cliff Room	75	Cliff & Falls Rooms	150
Wawona Hotel	*Seated*		*Seated*
Sunroom	50–75	Lawns	150
Curry Village Pavilion			
Poolside Room	10–40	Glacier Point Room	75–150
Main Room	150–250	Pavilion	500

MEETING CAPACITY: 5 rooms in the Ahwahnee Hotel can accommodate 20–100, 2 rooms in the Yosemite Lodge hold 100–200, the Curry Pavilion holds 150–500 and the Wawona Hotel Sunroom holds 20–60.

FEES & DEPOSITS: A $500 refundable deposit is required within 14 days after booking. At the Ahwahnee Hotel there is a room rental fee of $300 for the Solarium and $175 for either the Winter Club Room, Mural Room or the Underlounge for the first 3 hours of your event. A $150 room rental fee applies for any room at Yosemite Lodge, Wawona Hotel or Curry Village for the first 3 hours. A $150 rental fee will be applied for one additional hour at all properties. There is a 4-hour maximum for all private parties. Menu selection for groups must be submitted at least 8 weeks in advance and a final guest count must be submitted 72 hours prior to your party. The estimated total is due 4 weeks prior to the event and the final balance is payable before departure. Overnight accommodations vary; call for rates.

AVAILABILITY: For weddings, year-round, daily. Time frames vary depending on site and room selected; call for details. For meetings, space is available in the off season, mid-October to mid-April.

SERVICES/AMENITIES:

Catering: provided, no BYO
Kitchen Facilities: n/a
Tables & Chairs: provided
Linens, Silver, etc.: provided
Restrooms: wheelchair accessible
Dance Floor: several locations
Bride's Dressing Area: no
Meeting Equipment: projectors, flip charts

Parking: large lots, valet CBA at Awahnee
Accommodations: wide range of rooms
Telephone: pay phones
Outdoor Night Lighting: no
Outdoor Cooking Facilities: no
Cleanup: provided
View: Yosemite Park (various sights)
Other: event coordination

RESTRICTIONS:

Alcohol: all alcohol through Yosemite Concession Services Corporation
Smoking: restricted areas
Music: subject to approval, no amplified outdoors

Wheelchair Access: yes
Insurance: not required
Other: no rice, birdseed, or helium balloons; no horse-drawn carriages

---

This is important! Tell facilities you're reading **Here Comes The Guide** and ask if our information is still current.

Tahoe area

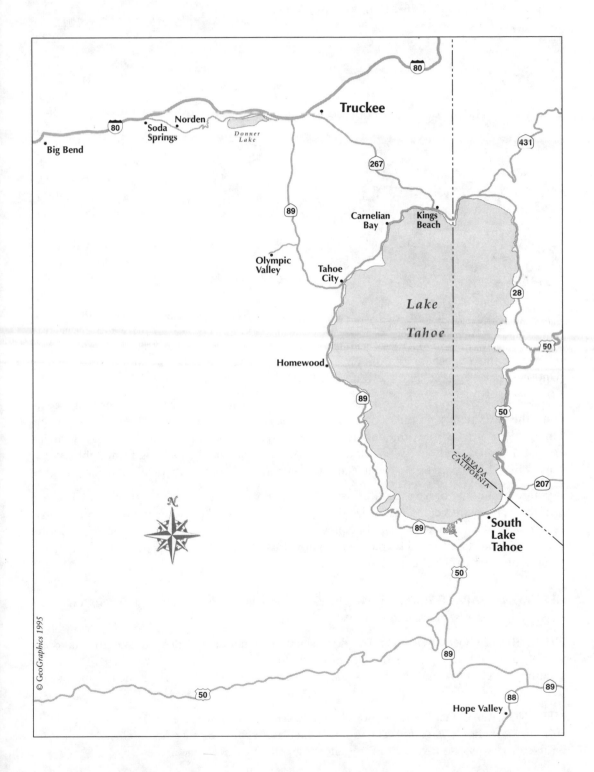

Gar Woods Grill and Pier

Lakefront Restaurant

5000 North Lake Boulevard, Carnelian Bay
(800) 298-2463, (530) 546-3366, fax (530) 546-2184

www.garwoods.com
garwoods@sierra.net

◆ Ceremonies ◆ Special Events
◆ Wedding Receptions ◆ Meetings
◆ Business Functions Accommodations

Gar Woods is a restaurant located right on the rim of Lake Tahoe. For outdoor parties or receptions, there's a substantial deck complete with blue, yellow and red umbrellas, wind screens and heat lamps for cool evenings. The deck has fabulous views of Gar Woods' public pier, the lake and the mountains beyond. If the weather is unfriendly, guests just relocate to the adjacent indoor dining room. Don't worry. The vistas through floor-to-ceiling windows make you feel like the water is only an arm's length away.

The interior is easy on the eyes: a cascading waterfall surrounded by ferns greets you as you enter the restaurant, and the decor is in soft, muted taupe and cream. The upstairs private dining rooms are favorites among the locals. Each has an "Old Tahoe" feeling: hickory chairs are hand-crafted, and photos of colorful, old Gar Wood racing boats hang from light, knotty pine walls. Dressed up for an event, Gar Woods presents a very pretty picture, inside and out.

If you're fun-loving or have an affinity for the water, wow your guests by arriving by boat or sea plane. If you're getting married, bride and groom can make a dramatic or surprise entry at Gar Woods' easily accessible public pier before heading to the altar. And if the South Shore is more to your taste, you'll be pleased to know that Gar Woods has opened a new lakefront restaurant, Riva Grill, on the other side of the lake.

CEREMONY CAPACITY: The upstairs private rooms hold 130 seated or 170 standing. The outside deck holds 130 seated or 170 standing.

EVENT/RECEPTION CAPACITY: The downstairs accommodates 120 seated or 200 standing guests. The upstairs private dining rooms hold 150 seated or 200 standing. The deck accommodates 180 seated, 200 for a standing reception. With exclusive use, the restaurant can hold up to 500 guests.

MEETING CAPACITY: The Riva Room accommodates 100 conference or theater style, and the Serrano Room holds 70 seated. The rooms (which are separated by a glass-enclosed foyer) can be used together to provide one large meeting or conference space.

FEES & DEPOSITS: For weddings, a non-refundable deposit equaling 25% of the estimated total is required upon reservation. A $7.50/person fee is charged for room setup, linens and cake cutting. Wedding buffets start at $23/person, seated luncheons at $15/person and dinners $18/person. The balance is due the day of the event; alcohol, tax and an 18–20% service charge are additional. There is a $200 setup charge for inside or deck ceremonies. For exclusive use, the restaurant can be reserved; call for more detailed information.

For meetings, there's a $50/hour (4-hour minimum) room rental fee. The fee includes use of the space, all equipment and some beverages.

AVAILABILITY: Year-round, daily, 10am–1am.

SERVICES/AMENITIES:

Catering: provided, no BYO
Kitchen Facilities: n/a
Tables & Chairs: provided, except on beach
Linens, Silver, etc.: provided
Restrooms: wheelchair accessible
Dance Floor: provided, extra fee
Bride's Dressing Area: no
Meeting Equipment: TV, VCR, microphone, screen, easels, overhead projector, podium

Parking: large lot
Accommodations: no guest rooms
Telephone: pay phone
Outdoor Night Lighting: yes
Outdoor Cooking Facilities: limited, more CBA
Cleanup: provided
View: Lake Tahoe and mountains

RESTRICTIONS:

Alcohol: provided, no BYO
Smoking: outside only
Music: amplified OK, volume restricted

Wheelchair Access: downstairs only
Insurance: not required

The professionals in the back of the book are the best in the business! How do we know? Read page 681.

Chambers Landing Restaurant & Bar

Lakefront Restaurant

6300 Chambers Lodge Road, Homewood
(530) 581-2199, fax (530) 581-5631

www.dinewine.com
graham@dinewine.com

◆ Ceremonies ◆ Special Events
◆ Wedding Receptions ◆ Meetings
◆ Business Functions ◆ Accommodations

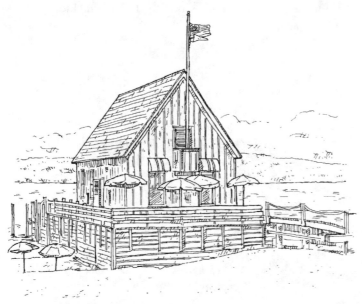

Although it's completely hidden from sight at the end of a narrow access road, Chambers Landing Restaurant & Bar still manages to be one of Tahoe's favorite places. It's set on a gentle rise at the edge of a lovely, white-sand beach, and it has an enviable view of the lake and the cloud-skimmed mountains in the distance. The restaurant is actually a charming pavilion with a large, sun-splashed terrace on one side and a smaller, awning-covered patio on the other. Connected to each by a set of folding French doors, the pavilion can be completely open to balmy breezes, or enclosed and heated if the weather turns cool. Its peaked, wood-beamed ceiling has a large skylight at its center, and the massive support columns and fireplace are fashioned from river rock.

From the restaurant, it's just a short walk down to the landing itself, where couples usually like to get married (and often arrive or depart in one of the many wooden boats available for rent on the lake). Standing at the end of the pier, there's nothing behind them except the vast blue lake and far-off mountains. Afterwards, everyone can mingle and sip champagne at the old boathouse on the landing. Built in 1867, this former post office, school house and general store now makes a delightful bar. A less dramatic ceremony option is a secluded lawn with gazebo next to the restaurant, where overhanging trees provide shade and filter the view.

Special events and receptions are most often held in the restaurant, and whether you're dining inside the pavilion or at umbrella-shaded tables on the terrace, the lake is always a welcome accompaniment to the meal. For a completely al fresco affair, have your reception on the pool patio off to one side of the restaurant, or on a lawn off to the other.

Owner Graham Rock can handle all the arrangements, and if you'd like to prolong the celebration, a full range of nearby accommodations are available for overnight stays. There's no denying the irresistible appeal of this setting, and by scheduling only one event a day and giving you exclusive use of the entire facility, Graham encourages you to enjoy it as long and as fully as possible.

CEREMONY CAPACITY: The pier holds up to 175 seated or standing; the lawn with gazebo holds 75 seated or 100 standing guests; the lakeside beach holds 175 seated or standing; the Pavilion's interior holds 175 seated.

EVENT/RECEPTION CAPACITY: The Pavilion holds up to 175 seated guests. Tenting can be arranged for an additional cost.

MEETING CAPACITY: The Main Dining Room can accommodate 60 seated theater style.

FEES & DEPOSITS: For all events, the rental fee ($2,500 Saturdays, $1,500 all other days), serves as your deposit and is required to book your date. It covers exclusive use of the facility for the entire day. Food costs start at $25/person; alcohol, tax and a 20% gratuity are additional. The final payment, which includes expenses other than the rental fee, is due at the end of the event.

AVAILABILITY: End of May through October 31st, flexible hours.

SERVICES/AMENITIES:

Catering: provided
Kitchen Facilities: n/a
Tables & Chairs: provided
Linens, Silver, etc.: provided
Restrooms: wheelchair accessible
Dance Floor: terrace
Bride's & Groom's Dressing Rooms: yes
Meeting Equipment: AV provided

Parking: lot
Accommodations: full range available
Telephone: guest phones
Outdoor Night Lighting: yes
Outdoor Cooking Facilities: n/a
Cleanup: provided
View: Lake Tahoe and mountains
Other: event coordination

RESTRICTIONS:

Alcohol: provided
Smoking: permitted
Music: acoustic only

Wheelchair Access: yes
Insurance: not required

---

*This is important! Tell facilities you're reading **Here Comes The Guide** and ask if our information is still current.*

Sorensen's Resort

14255 Highway 88, Hope Valley
(800) 423-9949 or (530) 694-2203

◆ Ceremonies ◆ Special Events
◆ Wedding Receptions ◆ Meetings
◆ Business Functions ◆ Accommodations

Although it's only a half hour from Lake Tahoe, at Sorensen's you feel as though you're in the middle of nowhere. "Nowhere" happens to be Hope Valley, a thinly populated alpine Eden that's remained largely unchanged since the 1800s, when the early settlers began coming through here. And fortunately for us, the resort suits its natural setting to a T.

What began over a hundred years ago as a modest cluster of cabins along the west fork of the Carson River is now a rustic—though quite civilized—Sierra getaway. No two of the 30 cabins are the same: some are classic log cabins, two are actually peaked-roof transplants from Santa's Village in Santa Cruz, and one is a replica of a thirteenth-century Norwegian lodging complete with hand-carved facade and sod roof. Many have knotty pine interiors or cedar siding, and most have wood-burning fireplaces and kitchens. Scattered among groves of rustling aspens, these little mountain "homes" give guests the refreshing experience of being out in the woods.

And what better place to have a company retreat or wedding than the great outdoors! Ceremonies are held on a gentle, aspen-and-pine-covered hillside, beneath a gazebo made of aspen trunks and branches. Not far below is the cafe and deck where receptions are held. The deck is sun-drenched by day, and sparkles with tivoli lights at night. In winter, you can put your wedding on skis, as did one couple who donned their tux and wedding dress and cross country skied about a mile into the valley with their entire entourage behind them. They were married in the snow, and warmed up afterwards with a long stint in the local hot springs.

Year round, Sorensen's is a fantastic place for a celebration, and no one comes up here for just a day—there's too much to enjoy. Depending on the season, you can fish, river raft, bike, birdwatch, ski, and hike—with or without llamas. Sorensen's has its own restaurant with home-cooked food, and owners Patty and John Brissenden have a knack for making everyone feel welcome. Sorensen's may be in the middle of nowhere, but as John put it, "Most of our guests feel like they're right in the middle of everything."

CEREMONY CAPACITY: The gazebo area holds 35 seated or 120 standing guests. Other ceremony sites are available on the grounds or nearby.

EVENT/RECEPTION CAPACITY:

Area	Seated	Standing	Area	Seated	Standing
Deck	100	175	Norway House	40	55
Cafe	30	50	*Other areas can be tented.*		

MEETING CAPACITY: The Norway House holds up to 40; other cabins can accommodate up to 15 each.

FEES & DEPOSITS: For weddings, a $250 non-refundable wedding consulting fee is due when you reserve your date. A site fee ranging $500–1,500, depending on guest count, is due within 5 days of booking, along with half the anticipated cost of food and lodging. The balance of the site fee is due the day of the event; the food and lodging balance is due on departure. Cabins run $65–350/night and catering costs run $13–30/person. Alcohol, tax and a 15% service charge are additional. If paying by credit card, the entire payment is due when the facility is booked. Fees for meetings and corporate events vary depending on the facilities and services used; there is a minimum $100 planning fee.

AVAILABILITY: Year-round, daily 8am–10pm, subject to weather. Closed Christmas Day.

SERVICES/AMENITIES:

Catering: provided
Kitchen Facilities: in individual cabins
Tables & Chairs: provided
Linens, Silver, etc.: provided or CBA, extra charge
Restrooms: wheelchair accessible 1 cabin only
Dance Floor: deck
Bride's Dressing Area: in cabin
Meeting Equipment: projector, easel, other CBA

Parking: large lot
Accommodations: 30 cabins, 26 campsites
Telephone: pay phone
Outdoor Night Lighting: yes
Outdoor Cooking Facilities: BBQs
Cleanup: provided
View: pine & aspen forest, mountains
Other: event coordination

RESTRICTIONS:

Alcohol: provided or BYO w/corkage fee
Smoking: outside only
Music: amplified OK until 10pm

Wheelchair Access: limited
Insurance: not required

The professionals in the back of the book are the best in the business! How do we know? Read page 681.

North Tahoe Conference Center

8318 North Lake Boulevard, Kings Beach
(530) 546-7249, fax (530) 546-7116
www.tahoeguide.com/go/ntccwedding

Lakeside Conference Center

◆ Ceremonies   ◆ Special Events
◆ Wedding Receptions   ◆ Meetings
◆ Business Functions   ◆ Accommodations

The North Tahoe Conference Center is one of those versatile places that's just as wonderful for weddings as it is for business functions. Located in an enviable spot on Tahoe's north shore, this modern facility has nothing between it and the deep blue waters of the lake except a wide stretch of beach.

During those glorious months from late spring to early fall, have your entire celebration on the center's expansive patio. Tie the knot beneath a majestic pine at one end, and dine and dance at the other. No matter where you are, gentle breezes flow off the water, and the panoramic view of the lake and surrounding mountains is stunning.

The center also has several options for indoor weddings and corporate events. Host cocktails and hors d'oeuvres in the foyer, a pleasant, skylit space with potted plants and colorful textile wall hangings. Receptions are usually held in the Lakeview Suites, four contemporary rooms which can be used individually or in combination. They overlook the brick patio through floor-to-ceiling windows, and their neutral decor—clean white walls, teal-tweed carpet and occasional ficus trees—doesn't distract from the mesmerizing view of the lake. The Timberline Room lacks a view, but its hardwood stage and audio-visual equipment are perfect for anyone who wants to put on a production. Other nice features are a special bride's dressing room and the fact that you can bring your own alcohol and caterer, who will definitely appreciate the spacious, commercial kitchen. With its prime location and flexibility, the North Tahoe Conference Center has developed quite a following not only for business functions, but for wedding celebrations, too.

CEREMONY CAPACITY:

Area	*Seated or Standing*	*Area*	*Seated or Standing*
Lakeview Deck	300	Lakeview Suite	175
Timberline Room	350	*Smaller rooms are available.*	

EVENT/RECEPTION & MEETING CAPACITY:

Area	Seated	Standing	Area	Seated	Standing
Lakeview Deck	220	250	Timberline Room	300	325
Lakeview Suite	40–120	40–150	*Other rooms are available.*		

FEES & DEPOSITS: A non-refundable $400 deposit (applied to the rental fee) is required within 3 weeks of reserving your date. Rental fees range $250–2,500 depending on guest count and space reserved. If you bring your own caterer, there is a $150–250 kitchen use fee. A discount is given for using the Conference Center caterer. In-house catering starts at $16/person; alcohol, tax and a 16% service charge are additional. The rental fee balance and all food and beverage costs are due 2 weeks prior to the event. Wedding packages are available; call for details.

AVAILABILITY: Year-round, daily, 9am–2am. Additional staffing fees apply on holidays.

SERVICES/AMENITIES:

Catering: provided or BYO
Kitchen Facilities: commercial
Tables & Chairs: provided
Linens, Silver, etc.: provided w/in-house caterer
Restrooms: wheelchair accessible
Dance Floor: deck or portable provided
Bride's Dressing Area: subject to availability
Meeting Equipment: full range
Other: wedding and event coordination

Parking: large lot, $5/car summer weekends until 5pm
Accommodations: guest rooms CBA
Telephone: office or pay phone
Outdoor Night Lighting: yes
Outdoor Cooking Facilities: BBQ grill
Cleanup: conference staff, caterer or renter
View: Lake Tahoe & Sierras

RESTRICTIONS:

Alcohol: provided or BYO
Smoking: designated areas
Music: amplified OK indoors, outdoors until 8pm

Wheelchair Access: yes
Insurance: not required
Other: no rice

This is important! Tell facilities you're reading **Here Comes The Guide** *and ask if our information is still current.*

Sugar Bowl Resort

Sierra Ski Resort

Sugar Bowl Ski Area, Norden
(530) 426-9000, fax (530) 426-3723

www.sugarbowl.com
info@sugarbowl.com

- ◆ Ceremonies
- ◆ Wedding Receptions
- ◆ Business Functions
- ◆ Special Events
- ◆ Meetings
- ◆ Accommodations

Grab your shades and sun block! If you're looking for an informal setting for a mountain retreat, wedding or rehearsal dinner, Sugar Bowl is the answer. Located off Interstate 80 at Donner Summit, this ski resort offers a high altitude deck (elevation 6,900 feet!) and creekside lawn for ceremonies and receptions.

You can have any kind of company event here, from an office getaway to a high-tech brainstorming session. Not only that, but you can also get married at Sugar Bowl—summer or winter. The south facing deck is really large—and a sun worshiper's dream! Backed on one side by the lodge and open on the other to snow-topped mountains and a picturesque stream, it offers plenty of space for dining, dancing and sunning.

During the summer, the flat, grassy area below the deck is highlighted by tall trees. We like it a lot because it's situated right next to a clear Sierra stream. If you're thinking of getting married here, take your vows by the stream—then head to the deck for a reception feast. At Sugar Bowl, cloudless blue skies, crisp mountain air and the smell of pine needles will guarantee to make you and your guests feel more alive.

CEREMONY CAPACITY: Outdoors, the lawn can accommodate over 400, the deck 300 guests. Indoors, the Resort can hold up to 150 seated guests.

EVENT/RECEPTION CAPACITY: The Resort can accommodate over 400 guests.

MEETING CAPACITY: The Resort has 9 rooms for meetings which can accommodate 20–100 people in various seating styles.

FEES & DEPOSITS: For weddings, a $500 non-refundable facility fee is required when reservations are confirmed. Buffets run approximately $20–30/person; seated service starts at $25/person. Half of the estimated event total is due 30 days in advance; the balance is payable the day of the function. Alcohol, tax and a 17% service charge are additional. For meetings and corporate events, fees vary depending on the facilities and services used.

AVAILABILITY: Year-round, daily, 7am–10pm.

SERVICES/AMENITIES:

Catering: provided, no BYO
Kitchen Facilities: fully equipped
Tables & Chairs: provided
Linens, Silver, etc.: CBA
Restrooms: wheelchair access limited
Dance Floor: deck or lounge
Bride's Dressing Area: yes
Meeting Equipment: TVs and VCRs

Parking: ample
Accommodations: 27 guest rooms
Telephone: pay phone
Outdoor Night Lighting: limited
Outdoor Cooking Facilities: BBQs
Cleanup: provided or renter
View: of mountain peaks
Other: event coordination and referrals

RESTRICTIONS:

Alcohol: provided
Smoking: designated areas
Music: amplified OK

Wheelchair Access: no
Insurance: not required

The professionals in the back of the book are the best in the business! *How do we know? Read page 681.*

Graham's at Squaw Valley

Restaurant

1650 Squaw Valley Road, Olympic Valley
(530) 581-0454, fax (530) 581-5631

www.dinewine.com
graham@dinewine.com

- ◆ Ceremonies
- ◆ Wedding Receptions
- ◆ Business Functions
- ◆ Special Events
- ◆ Meetings
- ◆ Accommodations

If you're like most people, you probably picture Squaw Valley as a winter wonderland, blanketed with snow and filled with skiers. What you may not realize is that the valley is just as lovely during summer months, and there's a wider variety of things to do: hiking, horseback riding, golf, tennis, theater, swimming and mountain biking for starters. If you add getting married to the list, the Christy Inn and its on-site restaurant, Graham's, may be just the place to help you take advantage of all that Squaw Valley has to offer.

Built over 50 years ago as the valley's first home, the Inn is now two separate entities—a lodge and restaurant—under one roof. Weddings take place in the restaurant and on the grounds, and guests can stay overnight in the Inn. The expansive lawn next to the Inn is a sunny spot for an alpine ceremony. Bordered by tall pines on one end, it overlooks tree-studded mountains on the other. The large redwood deck adjacent to the restaurant is covered by an awning and glassed in, and can be heated on cool nights. It's perfect for post-event cocktails, a small reception or dancing, while the restaurant itself provides an intimate ambiance for larger parties.

With its peaked pine ceiling and floor-to-ceiling river rock fireplace, Graham's feels a bit like a cozy mountain lodge. But unlike many a lodge, whose primary source of illumination day or night is a blazing fire, Graham's has skylights and picture windows that fill the room with soft, ambient light all afternoon. At night, firelight and candlelight cast their own warm glow. A changing art display on the walls and white table linens are sophisticated complements to the interior's rustic elements.

The restaurant's bar, with its river rock fireplace (hand-built by the original owners), is available for cocktails, and connects to both the deck and the lodge. The guest rooms themselves are pleasantly decorated in peach with floral bedspreads and wall art, and all have private baths. Surrounded by beautiful scenery and great sports facilities, and just a scant five miles from Lake Tahoe, Graham's Restaurant and the Christy Inn make it easy to take your vows *and* your vacation in Northern California's most popular playground.

CEREMONY CAPACITY: The lawn can accommodate 200 seated or standing, the fireplace area 70 seated or standing.

EVENT/RECEPTION CAPACITY: All areas can be used singly or combined; the lawn can be tented for an extra fee.

Area	Seated	Standing
Restaurant	70	100
Deck	35	70

Area	Seated	Standing
Lawn	200	300

MEETING CAPACITY: The Main Dining Room holds 60 and the Deck 40, both seated theater-style.

FEES & DEPOSITS: For all events, a $1,250 rental fee is required to secure your date; the final payment is due at the conclusion of the event. Rental includes exclusive use of the facility for the day. Food costs start at $25/person; alcohol, tax and a 20% gratuity are additional.

AVAILABILITY: Year-round, daily, one event per day, flexible hours.

SERVICES/AMENITIES:

Catering: provided
Kitchen Facilities: n/a
Tables & Chairs: provided
Linens, Silver, etc.: provided
Restrooms: wheelchair accessible
Dance Floor: deck
Bride's Dressing Area: rented guest room
Meeting Equipment: AV and conference chairs

Parking: large lot
Accommodations: 7 guest rooms
Telephone: guest phones
Outdoor Night Lighting: CBA, extra fee
Outdoor Cooking Facilities: n/a
Cleanup: provided
View: Squaw Valley peaks and meadow
Other: event coordination

RESTRICTIONS:

Alcohol: provided
Smoking: permitted
Music: amplified OK

Wheelchair Access: restaurant & lawn only
Insurance: not required

This is important! Tell facilities you're reading **Here Comes The Guide** and ask if our information is still current.

PlumpJack Squaw Valley Inn

1920 Squaw Valley Road, Olympic Valley

(530) 583-1576, fax (530) 583-1734

www.plumpjack.com

Inn & Conference Center

◆ Ceremonies   ◆ Special Events
◆ Wedding Receptions   ◆ Meetings
◆ Business Functions   ◆ Accommodations

During the 1960 Winter Olympics, athletes from all over the world called the Squaw Valley Inn home. They came here to compete in the Games, but couldn't help admiring the scenery: a quiet valley encircled by magnificently chiseled mountains, and a jewel of a lake just minutes away. But while Squaw Valley and Lake Tahoe still look much the same as they did then, the Inn has undergone a remarkable transformation.

A blend of mountain lodge and grand hotel, the "new" PlumpJack Squaw Valley Inn has a truly original look—one you won't find anywhere else in Tahoe. Public spaces and guest rooms all display an exceptional melding of decorative elements: earthy colors, rich fabrics, and innovative metal sculpture. Couches and chairs catch the eye with their sinuous shapes and textured, sheened upholstery; striking light fixtures combine whimsy with copper, glass and chrome. Copper is used liberally throughout, completely covering the bar in the lounge, and fashioned into fluid ceiling and wall sculptures. Even the floors in the foyer and lounge are unusual—poured concrete, laid out in geometric sections, each one tinted a different shade of muted brown.

The high style of the main Inn building makes an interesting contrast to the more relaxed ambiance of the adjacent banquet facility and pool patio, the two primary event sites. The main reception room takes up the entire first floor of the two-story banquet facility. Its neutral, light grey color scheme makes decorating a breeze—the addition of flowers, greenery and linens turns the room into a lovely space for a wedding reception or private party. If you're planning a conference or seminar, the room can be divided into four sections, handily outfitted with meeting equipment. The upstairs conference room is also multi purpose. Huge, natural wood beams crisscross beneath a high, peaked ceiling, giving the space the feeling of a large mountain cabin. Natural light, teal walls and blond wood wainscotting provide warmth and color. During a wedding, this room is often used for dancing or cutting the cake; for business functions it's great for large meetings or lectures.

Our favorite spot is the pool patio, a sun-splashed terrace that's wonderful for any kind of celebration. Sheltered on two sides by the banquet facility and the restaurant, it's bordered on the other two by aspens and pines, and ringed by Squaw Valley peaks. In spring, the pool patio is surrounded by colorful flowers, and an herb garden scents the air. Ceremonies are often held at one end of the pool, against a backdrop of mountains and the open sky. Many couples have their reception in the banquet facility, but you can also have it here, with umbrella-shaded tables set up on the raised patio level next to the pool. Note the huge copper, stainless steel and river rock woodfire pizza oven—it's so gorgeous, you might even consider serving pizza at your wedding!

PlumpJack's designers have created something unique: a mountain inn, banquet facility and restaurant with both the *avant garde* elegance and sophistication of a cosmopolitan city, and the fresh simplicity of a mountain retreat. The Inn's artsy interior may come as a bit of a shock to those used to the log-cabin decor of so many Tahoe places, but anyone who appreciates creativity and craftsmanship will love it.

CEREMONY CAPACITY: Each of the 2 banquet rooms can accommodate 180 seated or 300 standing guests; the pool patio can hold 150 seated or 300 standing.

EVENT/RECEPTION CAPACITY: Receptions can be held in any of the above areas as well as in the restaurant, which holds 60 seated or 100 standing guests.

MEETING CAPACITY: Each conference room holds 225 seated theater-style or 180 conference-style.

FEES & DEPOSITS: For weddings and special events, a $1,500 deposit is required to reserve your date. The rental fee for each floor of the banquet facility (including setup and breakdown) is $750; for both rooms it's $1,500. To rent the pool patio, the fee is $1,000. The restaurant rental fee ranges $3,000–10,000, depending on the season; with a $6,000 catering minimum, the rental fee may be waived.

Per person catering fees for weddings and special events run $25–45/person for luncheons, $45–75/person for 3-course dinners or buffets; 5-course dinners are by arrangement. Tax, alcohol and an 18% gratuity are additional. Meeting catering costs run $20–35/person for luncheons, with break and coffee service a la carte.

AVAILABILITY: Year round, daily. Weddings and special events take place in 4-hour blocks; additional time is negotiable. Corporate parties are in 4-hour blocks.

SERVICES/AMENITIES:

Catering: provided, no BYO
Kitchen Facilities: n/a
Tables & Chairs: provided
Linens, Silver, etc.: provided
Restrooms: wheelchair accessible
Dance Floor: CBA, $100 charge
Bride's Dressing Area: complimentary
Meeting Equipment: fully equipped

Parking: ample lot
Accommodations: 57 guest room, 4 suites
Telephone: pay phones
Outdoor Night Lighting: access only
Outdoor Cooking Facilities: n/a
Cleanup: provided
View: Sierra Nevada Mountains
Other: event coordination, tram rides, hikes, horsebackriding, other activities CBA

RESTRICTIONS:

Alcohol: provided, corkage $14/bottle
Smoking: outdoors only
Music: amplified OK

Wheelchair Access: yes
Insurance: not required
Other: no rice or balloon releases

Resort at Squaw Creek

Resort Hotel

400 Squaw Creek Road, Olympic Valley
(530) 583-6300, fax (530) 581-5407

◆ Ceremonies ◆ Special Events
◆ Wedding Receptions ◆ Meetings
◆ Business Functions ◆ Accommodations

Wow! That's the simplest word we could come up with to describe how impressed we were by the year-round Resort at Squaw Creek. You've got to come for a visit—this splendid, multi-million-dollar facility has to be seen to be fully appreciated. From its position slightly above the valley floor, views of the valley below and the surrounding mountains are refreshing. For a business function or wedding, we can hardly think of a more suitable spot. It's got everything—ballrooms, meeting rooms, multiple sun decks and restaurants, three pools and a 250-foot cascading waterfall, footbridge and stream.

Dressed for success, this facility is decked out in glass, wood and granite. Tasteful furnishings, fixtures and artwork accent beautifully designed interior spaces. Outdoor decks and patios are likewise appointed, with teak chairs and tables, huge umbrellas and distinctive paving underfoot. The level of detail here is awe-inspiring. Not only does the Resort offer top-notch spaces for events, but it also provides plenty of services to pamper guests. Have a sauna or a leisurely dip in the spa. An adjacent salon and massage room come fully staffed to keep guests relaxed and looking their best.

No matter what your culinary tastes, the Resort can arrange any menu to satisfy your needs. In-house restaurants include the elegant Glissandi, with world-class California cuisine in an Art Deco setting, the more casual Cascades, with a selection of regional food, Ristorante Montagna, an Italian *cucina* and Bullwhackers, a high-Sierra steakhouse and pub. Overnight guests? The Resort's 405 guest rooms can accommodate any size crowd, and if you get married here, the bride and groom are treated to a complimentary honeymoon suite. Definitely ask for the full tour because there are numerous places for picture-perfect ceremonies as well as receptions. With great skiing and ice skating in winter, and a golf course, swimming pools, tennis courts and horseback riding trails nearby in summer, you can turn your event into a vacation getaway. Your guests will be eternally thankful for the introduction to, and memories from, the Resort at Squaw Creek.

CEREMONY & EVENT/RECEPTION CAPACITY:

Area	Seated	Standing	Area	Seated	Standing
Grand Sierra Ballroom	660	950	Glissandi Deck	75	100
Squaw Peak Ballroom	350	475	Granite Chief	50	60
Ristorante Montagna	100	175	Cascades	240	—
Pavilion	400	550	Glissandi	80	120

MEETING CAPACITY: This facility has 30,000 square feet of meeting space; here are some of the larger rooms:

Area	Classroom-style	Theater-style	Conference-style
Grand Sierra Ballroom	644	936	—
Squaw Peak Ballroom	288	480	—
Emigrant Peak	88	100	24
Castle Peak	54	64	24
Papoose Peak	40	54	24

FEES & DEPOSITS: A $500–1,000 deposit (depending on room size) is due when reservations are confirmed. There is no rental fee for receptions with food service. Ceremonies cost $125–400, depending on chair setup. Per person rates for luncheons range from $25–30, dinners begin at $42. Alcohol, tax and an 18% service charge are additional. The estimated event total is payable 4 days prior to the function. All meeting rooms are complimentary for groups reserving 10 or more guest rooms per night.

AVAILABILITY: Year-round, daily, flexible hours between 6am–2am.

SERVICES/AMENITIES:

Catering: provided, no BYO
Kitchen Facilities: n/a
Tables & Chairs: provided
Linens, Silver, etc.: provided
Restrooms: wheelchair accessible
Dance Floor: provided
Bride's Dressing Area: guest room provided
Meeting Equipment: AV & ergonomic chairs

Parking: valet, extra fee or self parking
Accommodations: 405 guest rooms & suites
Telephone: pay phones
Outdoor Night Lighting: yes
Outdoor Cooking Facilities: n/a
Cleanup: provided
View: Sierra Mtns. and Squaw Valley
Other: event coordination, cakes, salon, massage

RESTRICTIONS:

Alcohol: provided, no BYO
Smoking: outside only
Music: amplified OK

Wheelchair Access: yes
Insurance: not required

The professionals in the back of the book are the best in the business! How do we know? Read page 681.

Riva Grill on the Lake

Restaurant

900 Ski Run Boulevard, South Lake Tahoe
(888) 734-2882, (530) 542-2600, fax (530) 542-3366

www.rivagrill.com
riva@sierra.net

◆ Ceremonies ◆ Special Events
◆ Wedding Receptions ◆ Meetings
◆ Business Functions Accommodations

One of South Shore's newest restaurants, Riva Grill would be considered a delightful place to dine, even if it didn't overlook Lake Tahoe. But it does, combining a gorgeous view with a beautifully designed interior.

One of the first things you notice when you step inside is the abundance of wood. Elegant, warm, gleaming wood. Used liberally throughout, it serves as a nostalgic homage to the lake's wooden boating era during the1960s and 70s, when Italian "Riva" boats were the all the rage. Anyone wanting to know what one of them looked like has only to glance at the walls, where a collection of Riva boat paintings, specially commissioned for the restaurant, is displayed. The unusual reception desk, an exact replica of a Riva bow, points the way to a graceful mahogany staircase leading up to the second-floor banquet rooms. Dark wood cabinets and wainscotting add to the feeling of richness. Yet despite the abundance of wood, the overall ambiance is never heavy. In fact, thanks to high ceilings, light walls and plenty of natural light, Riva Grill is refreshingly light and airy.

This is especially true upstairs, in the two banquet rooms. Separated by the stairwell and glass partitions, both spaces share the same decor—a sophisticated version of a contemporary loft. Twenty-foot ceilings are supported by a network of mahogany beams, varnished to a satiny shine. That same earthy color is echoed in the wainscotting and upholstered mahogany chairs. Striking hand-blown glass light fixtures drop from the ceiling, while windows just below the roofline and along the front of each room flood the spaces with daylight. Walls are faux-finished a pale yellow, and left unadorned, except for a couple of large boat-inspired paintings and a few sconces. Deep green leather banquettes and an occasional potted plant are the only other colorful accents, but no more is needed; the rooms' elements are in perfect harmony with each other. Lake Tahoe is visible from every table, and there's a long deck shared by the two rooms, affording guests a birds-eye view of the small marina below and the lake just beyond. Standing on the deck, you can feel the gentle breeze coming off the water, and you might catch a glimpse of the *Tahoe Queen,* a modern-day paddle-wheeler, taking on passengers for a cruise around the lake.

Have your ceremony in one room and your reception in the other, or host your entire celebration in just one room, inviting your guests down to the main dining room for cocktails after the ceremony, while the space upstairs is being readied for your party. The cuisine here is American with a Mediterranean flair, specializing in pasta, steaks and fresh seafood. When it comes to atmosphere, however, what you get is pure Lake Tahoe.

CEREMONY CAPACITY: The Riviera Room and the Gar Wood Room can each accommodate 120 seated guests or 150 standing. The deck holds 150 seated or 200 standing. The beach area holds 200 seated or 250 standing guests.

EVENT/RECEPTION CAPACITY: A restaurant buyout is possible to accommodate larger groups except on weekends, June–September. Deck availability is limited.

Area	Seated	Standing	Area	Seated	Standing
Restaurant	110	150	Riviera Room	100	150
Gar Wood Room	100	150	Deck	150	200
Beach	150	200			

MEETING CAPACITY: The Riviera and Gar Wood Rooms can each seat 120 theater-style.

FEES & DEPOSITS: 25% of the estimated food and beverage total is required as a deposit to secure your date. Additional deposits of 25% each are due at 60 days prior and 30 days prior to the event; the balance is due on the day of the event. For weddings, there is a $7.50/person set-up and cake-cutting fee. Buffets run $23–35/person, luncheons $12–17/person and dinners $18–25/person; tax, beverages, alcohol and a 15%–20% service charge are extra. For inside or deck ceremonies, there is a $250 setup fee, for beach ceremonies, a $350 fee plus extra for chairs. For business functions, a $50/hour room rental fee applies, with a 4-hour minimum. The fee includes meeting equipment and coffee/juices.

AVAILABILITY: Year-round, daily, 11am–2am.

SERVICES/AMENITIES:

Catering: provided, no BYO
Kitchen Facilities: n/a
Tables & Chairs: provided, except on beach
Linens, Silver, etc.: provided
Restrooms: wheelchair accessible
Dance Floor: CBA, extra charge
Bride's Dressing Area: no
Meeting Equipment: TV, VCR, easels, microphone & overhead projector

Parking: self and valet parking
Accommodations: no guest rooms
Telephone: pay phones
Outdoor Night Lighting: yes
Outdoor Cooking Facilities: no
Cleanup: provided
View: Lake Tahoe, mountains

RESTRICTIONS:

Alcohol: provided, no BYO
Smoking: outside only
Music: amplified OK indoors

Wheelchair Access: yes
Insurance: not required
Other: no nails, tacks or tape

Northstar-at-Tahoe

Mountain Resort

Hwy 267 at Northstar Drive, Truckee
(530) 562-2265, (800) GO-NORTH, fax (530) 562-2221
www.skinorthstar.com
northstar@boothcreek.com

◆ Ceremonies ◆ Special Events
◆ Wedding Receptions ◆ Meetings
◆ Business Functions ◆ Accommodations

We just love this place. Not only is it a beautiful setting for a wedding or conference, it's one of the most family-friendly facilities we've ever seen. Their brochure promises "all kinds of fun for all kinds of people" and they are true to their word.

Surrounded by tree-covered mountains, Northstar is an intimate resort, with all of their indoor event facilities, hotel-style lodging and shops clustered in a cozy, block-long "village." (Note that 5-bedroom houses are available for rent nearby.) From here, it's an easy walk to the many activities they offer. In winter, there's downhill and cross-country skiing, snowboarding, snowshoeing, sleigh rides, and snow tubing. During the summer you have another long list of options: golf, mountain biking, horseback riding, tennis, and an Adventure Park with a ropes course and climbing wall. And, if you're staying at Northstar, you can swim, sauna, work out and get a massage at their Swim & Racquet Club—any time of year. The absolutely terrific thing about Northstar is that in addition to all this wonderful stuff for grownups, there are lots of parallel activities tailored specifically for kids.

Kids or no kids, it's easy to see why people come up here for special events. Summer weddings are a delight. Ceremonies are held on a sun-dappled lawn, against a backdrop of towering fir trees. An arch is often set up in front of the trees, whose long shadows shade you and your guests. Receptions take place right behind the lawn, in the Chaparral Room or on the adjacent terrace. High, beamed ceilings and a rock fireplace give the room a casual ambiance, but a more sophisticated look is easily achieved with white linens and candles on the tables. Floor-to-ceiling windows afford a view of the terrace and the mountainside just beyond. On sunny days it's hard to resist the Chaparral terrace for an al fresco celebration. Broad, green market umbrellas provide shelter from the sun, while you savor your forested surroundings and the invigorating mountain air.

The Chaparral Room and terrace are available for conferences, too, along with several other light and airy meeting rooms. The Bracken Room, right off the Chaparral, has wraparound atrium windows with adjustable screens to regulate the inflow of light. The Martis, Sierra and

Laurel Rooms, which are separated by removable dividers, can be used individually or combined into one large meeting space. All three overlook the village's central walkway through large picture windows, and feature blond-wood slat walls, redwood beams and track lighting. Groups often hold their main meeting in the Chaparral Room, and use the terrace and smaller spaces as breakout rooms. Have your meals served in any of the rooms or, for a change of scenery, dine in one of Northstar's restaurants.

Northstar's staff is as friendly and flexible as the resort itself, and they'll help you coordinate all the essential elements of your event. During your free time you can relax on site, go to one of the North Shore casinos, take in a movie or cruise around Lake Tahoe on a paddle-wheel ferryboat. This really is the perfect place to mix business with pleasure, but don't feel guilty if all you're interested in is pleasure. Northstar was made for it.

CEREMONY CAPACITY: The lawn area holds up to 350 seated, the outdoor deck 100 seated, and the Chaparral Room, up to 150 seated guests.

EVENT/RECEPTION CAPACITY: The Deck can accommodate 75–120 seated or 150 standing; the Chaparral Room holds 200 seated or 300 standing guests.

MEETING CAPACITY:

Room	Theater	Classroom	Conference	Room	Theater	Classroom	Conference
Chaparral Room	250	100	30	Sierra Room	50	40	20
Martis Room	35	30	20	Laurel	35	30	20

FEES & DEPOSITS: For weddings, a partially refundable $750 wedding fee is required as the deposit to hold your date. The fee includes room rental, ceremony setup, custom signage, dry snacks at the bar, cake cutting, linens, table decorations, bartender for 4 hours, and coffee/tea service throughout the wedding. Ice carvings and a dance floor are available for an additional charge. The event balance is payable at the event's conclusion.

A variety of wedding meal packages are available, starting at $27.50/person, and include hors d'oeuvres, salad and entree. Any menu can be customized; luncheons start at $13/person, dinners at $22/person; tax, an 18% service charge and alcohol are additional.

For other social or business-related functions, room rental fees may apply; call for more information since pricing will vary depending on the rooms and services requested. Access to Northstar's Swim and Racquet Club plus on-site shuttle service are available on a complimentary basis to overnight guests.

AVAILABILITY: The Chaparral Room is available year-round, daily, any time; the Deck and meeting rooms, June–October, weather permitting.

SERVICES/AMENITIES:

Catering: provided, no BYO
Kitchen Facilities: n/a
Tables & Chairs: provided
Linens, Silver, etc.: provided
Restrooms: wheelchair accessible
Dance Floor: CBA, extra charge
Bride's & Groom's Dressing Area: CBA

Parking: large lots, ample
Accommodations: 260 units, from hotel rooms and homes to 5-bedroom condos
Telephone: pay phones
Outdoor Night Lighting: yes
Outdoor Cooking Facilities: BBQs
Cleanup: provided

Meeting Equipment: TV, VCR & overhead projector, AV; other equipment CBA, extra fee

RESTRICTIONS:

Alcohol: provided or BYO corkage $10/bottle
Smoking: outside only
Music: amplified OK indoors, outdoors until8pm

View: towering aspen trees & pines
Other: coordination; mountain bike/golf adventure park, swim & racquet club w/spa

Wheelchair Access: yes
Insurance: not required

Where can you find the best caterers, florists, cakemakers, photographers and other event professionals?

You can find them here...
turn the page—

Our service directory is
extraordinary!

Why?

Because we include only
the *best* event professionals
in the business.

Read This Page! This is important stuff!

#1 We only represent the best professionals in the biz.

The professionals featured in our service directory aren't plucked from the Yellow Pages. They're a carefully selected group of vendors who we'd recommend to our friends and business associates without hesitation.

#2 Because we're picky, you don't have to worry about who to hire.

We've thoroughly checked the professional track record of our advertisers so you can be as confident about their abilities as we are. The companies we highlight have passed our reference check with flying colors, and we're honored to represent each of them.

#3 Getting into *Here Comes The Guide* is tough.

The service providers we represent are top-notch. We put each one through a rigorous reference check which involves interviewing 15–30 other event professionals. We call every single reference and ask about the professionalism, technical competency and service orientation of the advertiser in question. Each interview may take as much as a half hour and when you invest 4–5 hours talking to that many professionals, you get a crystal clear picture of who's doing a superb job and who isn't. Those candidates who received consistent, rave reviews made it into the Guide. Those who didn't were (nicely) turned down.

Event Professionals by Service Category

Ministers · Rabbis · Celebrants · Officiants

We've received many requests for ministers, rabbis and non-denominational officiants for wedding ceremonies, so we did some research on your behalf.

Like the other service providers we've endorsed in *Here Comes The Guide*, each individual or group ministry has gone through a rigorous reference check. They've all been given high marks for professionalism, superior performance and integrity by numerous wedding professionals.

Even though these people come highly recommended, you still have to choose a celebrant that fits your personality. Balance, inspired counsel, perspective, humor, spirituality, joy and trust were some of the qualities mentioned in the testimonials we received. If you select someone who understands your lifestyle, beliefs and traditions, you'll be more likely to have a flawless ceremony, with not a dry eye in the house.

REVEREND REBECCA HERRERO, M.S., M. DIV.
A Creative and Meaningful Wedding
(800) 282-4983, (415) 721-1791

personalized services reflecting your own values and wishes • original or traditional weddings • large or small • non-denominational minister • licensed marital therapist • premarital counseling • sample services provided or created • keepsake copy of service in calligraphy

web: www.creativetransformation.com
email: rebecca@creativetransformation.com
serving: anywhere; willing to travel

SYDNEY BARBARA METRICK, PH.D., CET.
Creative Ceremonies
(510) 223-3882, fax (510) 223-3882

personalized ceremonies designed to express each couple's individual desires • spiritual and civil, traditional and non-traditional services • interfaith, intercultural ceremonies • commitment ceremonies • ordained, non-denominational minister

email: symetrick@aol.com
serving: greater Bay Area; office in the East Bay

ANN KEELER EVANS, M. DIV.
A Rite to Remember
(510) 654-3820

personalized ceremonies and vows which blend the traditional and the new • interfaith ceremonies • ceremonies of commitment • ordained, non-denominational minister • specializes in meaningful ritual for modern life

web: www.best.com/~emmettw/celebrate/ritetoremember.html
email: akeem@earthlink.net
serving: greater Bay Area

JOAN NELSON, M.A., ED.D.

(415) 453-6221, fax (415) 453-4821

humanist minister • individualized, spiritual and civil ceremonies • complimentary consultation with full ceremony • texts provided; also by email • board certified clinical sexologist • premarital counseling

email: aahajan@aol.com
serving: ceremonies throughout the greater Bay Area; office in Marin

T. MIKE WALKER
The Traveling Minister

(831) 425-5755

co-create a unique wedding ceremony to fit your special needs • secular or spiritual, traditional or personal • prenuptial consultation • laser copy of vows to make rehearsals easy • non-denominational

web: http://members.cruzio.com/~tmike/minister/html
email: tmike@cruzio.com
serving: Santa Cruz, Monterey, Gilroy, San Jose, Half Moon Bay and Salinas; willing to travel

HELEN WILLS BROWN

(415) 641-7691, fax (415) 641-1308

non-denominational • spiritual and civil, traditional and non-traditional ceremonies • custom ceremonies created • sings wedding songs or leads guests in song • eloquent speaker with a quality voice • warm, calm and gracious

email: hwb@dnai.com
serving: San Francisco Bay Area

REV. PHILLIP DAVENPORT & ASSOCIATES

(415) 460-9776

spiritual/humanistic, non-denominational and interfaith ceremonies • personalized, traditional and non-traditional ceremonies • premarital counseling

serving: Marin, San Francisco, East Bay, Wine Country and Peninsula

RABBI DAVID & RABBI SHOSHANA ROLLER

(800) 440-7046

ordained rabbis • traditional or personalized ceremonies • interfaith • will co-officiate experienced, versatile, accommodating • accept you as you are • counseling if desired

web: http://weddings-online.com/off/DavidRoller.html
email: DaveTarot@aol.com
serving: greater Bay Area and beyond; willing to travel

REV. JO ANN OSBORNE & REV. GEORGE FREASE
Personalized Weddings

(800) 382-8262, fax (415) 382-8262

warm, relaxed husband and wife officiant team • each ceremony is unique, personalized for the individual couple • present in the moment • each ceremony they officiate is both special and richly memorable

web: http://pages.prodigy.net/bikermom
email: bikermom@prodigy.net
serving: Northern California; nine Bay Area Counties

KIMBERLY A. THOMPSON
A Beautiful Ceremony

(707) 253-1492, (707) 256-0862

non-denominational, personalized vows to express each couples' special feelings and thoughts • unique and romantic ceremonies in desired locations • initial consultation • complimentary copy of ceremony if desired

web: http.//www.community.net/~weddings
email: weddings@community.net
serving: Wine Country, San Francisco and greater Bay Area locations

REV. BLANE W. ELLSWORTH
Coordinating Pastor, The Wedding Ministries

(800) 655-3677

on a mission to make ceremonies much more than just a ticket to the reception • truly concerned and respectful of your beliefs, values and desires • insightful • personable • a walking encyclopedia of ceremonial knowledge • access to The Wedding Ministries' 20 officiants

serving: greater Bay Area

REVEREND TIMOTHY MILLS, M.DIV., PH.D.

(510) 724-5250

ordained minister • church pastor • inter-denominational and interfaith weddings • personalized ceremonies • experienced, versatile, accommodating • quality voice * good sense of humor • strong sense of dignity • never late

web: http://www.california.com/~minister
email: minister@california.com
serving: all Bay Area locations

REVEREND RAY N. CAPPER, M.DIV.

(415) 924-8335

ordained minister • 20 years experience • personable • sense of humor • relaxed style • traditional non-traditional ceremonies • chapel or outdoor weddings • bilingual English/Spanish

serving: North Bay and Wine Country

REVEREND ED HOLT, M. DIV., M.B.A.
A Wedding Ministry

(650) 595-4225, fax (650) 593-3514

ordained, non-denominational minister • unique, customized traditional and non-traditional ceremonies • interfaith and cross cultural marriages • creative locations • complimentary initial consultation • premarital counseling • full ceremony text provided

web: www.batnet.com/revholt/
email: revholt@batnet.com
serving: San Mateo, San Francisco, San Mateo, San Francisco, Marin, Alameda, Santa Clara and Santa Cruz Counties

HENRY S. BASAYNE

(415) 567-7044, fax (415) 567-5306

senior humanist minister • individualized, humanistic, non-denominational and interfaith, secular and spiritual, traditional and contemporary ceremonies • 30 years of experience • co-author of book about personalizing wedding ceremonies • fees are all-inclusive; no extras for travel, rehearsals, etc. • structured premarital counseling

email: enfp@aol.com
serving: San Francisco, Marin, East Bay, Peninsula, Wine Country, Mendocino to Carmel

The rebirth of fine pastry making

RENAISSANCE
Pastry

PHOTO: BARBARA THOMPSON

Candace Weekly

Elegant Wedding Cakes & Specialty Desserts

San Francisco

by appointment

415-563-4099

DRAMATIC

ARTISTIC

SOPHISTICATED

...And they taste even better than they look

Extraordinary Wedding Cakes by

PERFECT ENDINGS

Tasting and Consultation by Appointment

Bay Area
(510) 724-4365

"Their name says it all... Perfection. <u>Inside and out</u>."
- Mary Ellen Murphy, Mary Ellen Murphy Weddings
The Wine Country's Premier Wedding Consultant

Wine Country
(707) 259-0500

Theobroma

Specialty Cakes, Catering & Events

Elegant Weddings,
Corporate Events,
Private Parties &
Event Planning Services

Visit us on The Web: **www.TheobromaCatering.com**
Call us for a complimentary tasting at (415) 695-1504

KATRINA ❀ ROZELLE

pastries and desserts

"… cakes so elegant they could pass for works of art."

"What do Barry Bonds, Danielle Steele, and Charlotte Swig have in common? They can afford any kind of wedding cake they want, and they all got theirs from Katrina Rozelle… But you don't have to be a millionaire to afford her creations." **Winner–Best Affordable Wedding Cake.**

– Diablo Magazine

Stylishly serving the greater Bay Area.
Free consultations by appointment.
Alamo 925-837-6337   Oakland 510-655-3209

Délices

Wedding Cakes that taste as good as they look
925-935-8070
1479 Newell Ave. • Walnut Creek, Ca 94596

Montclair Baking

+ Wedding Cakes

+ Dessert Buffets

+ Party Favors

+ Free Consultation

Hidden in the Montclair Hills of Oakland
2220 Mountain Blvd. Sweet #140
Oakland California 94611
510.530.8052

CAKEWORK

CUSTOM · WEDDING · AND · PARTY · CAKES

Cecile Gady

415-821-1333

By Appointment

Cakes

698

Catering and Event Planning Services

3310 Peralta Street Suite B Oakland, California 94608
510 658 8788 FAX 510 658 3537

Grapes of Wrath

Monterey Peninsula's
Premier Wedding & Special
Event Caterer

Awarded the 1997-98 Monterey Peninsula Chamber of Commerce Small Business of the Year • Coordination of Music, Flowers, Rentals, Locations, Photography, Cakes and Beverages • Specializing in Unique Wedding Locations and Site Tours

California Style Catering
831 • 649 • 3445

grapes@redshift.com ⟶ www.grapesofwrath.com
PO Box 5895, Monterey, Ca 93944

"MARTHA WISHES SHE COULD ENTERTAIN LIKE US"

CALL
888-A1-CATER
(888-212-2837)
winevalleycatering.com

Partytime Catering

distinctive
creative
& innovative catering

Specializing in Garden Weddings

Parties Individually Designed
From the Simplest to the Most Complex

Located at historic Rockefeller Lodge

Over 45 years of service and experience

510-235-7344

Closed Sunday & Monday

Fine Time Catering

From weddings and Bar Mitzvahs to corporate events, we offer services that encompass all your catering needs. We personalize our service and will work with you to create a menu that will delight both you and your guests. We look forward to being of service to you and would be pleased to offer you a complimentary sampling and consultation to discuss any of your future needs.

925.829.1126

Jon Wood & Pat English, Chefs
Annabel Wood, Event Planner, Service
Serving the Entire Bay Area

Great Receptions Start With

PERSONAL, PROFESSIONAL CATERING (408) 435-7337

780 Montague Expressway, Suite 706, San Jose, CA 95131
Phone: (408) 435-7337 • Fax: (408) 435-7454

CATERING

by Melissa Teaff

101 South Coombs, No. 4 • Napa, California 94559
707-254-8160

Every Event Is Special

Weddings·Corporate·Private

MELONS
CATERING

100 Ebbtide, Sausalito, CA 94965 415.331.0888 FAX 331.9504

You take care
of the guest list...

We'll take care
of everything else!

CALIFORNIA CAFE CATERING

ASK FOR THE EXTRAORDINARY...
IT'S OUR SPECIALTY!

CUSTOM CATERING & EVENT PLANNING
408.354.8300
800.440.4458

ANY SIZE * * SINCE 1949

THE ART OF GOOD FOOD

WINE COUNTRY SPECIALISTS

FULL SERVICE OR DELIVERY

ALEX'S CATERING

SERVING THE BAY AREA AND BEYOND
CHEF RAY VARELLA

Wine Country
707-944-1626

Marin
415-499-8707

East Bay
925-930-8387

* IMAGINATIVE MENUS * CREATIVE PRESENTATION *

When the Catering Coordinator at Campton Place Hotel was married, she selected **Event of the Season** to cater her wedding reception.

As did the Director of Catering at the Hyatt in Burlingame.

As have hundreds of other couples.

Perhaps **Event of the Season** should be part of your wedding plans too.

Event of the Season is on the recommended list of many of the most desirable sites in the Bay Area for one simple reason:

We consistently do an outstanding job.

Our food is an inspired fusion of Mediterranean, Asian and California cuisines made only from the finest and freshest ingredients, while our service is designed to make guests feel relaxed and comfortable.

We would be happy to design a menu just for you, one that not only reflects your good taste but also accommodates your budget.

**Please give us a call.
You will discover that we truly do cater.**

Event of the Season
Caterers

Tel. (415) 927-4721
148 Stetson Avenue, Corte Madera, CA 94925

CATERERS

EVENT OF THE SEASON

AnnWalkerCatering

If you want the **usual tired** and **trite** catering food, **don't call us**.

If you want exciting menus, planned to your tastes, we are ready to help. We believe the food should be at the top of the list when it comes to your catered event, whether it is a wedding, a corporate event or a private party. We have an attitude about our food. We think it's as good as anything you can find at the best restaurants. And our clients agree. You can ask them.

We do offer a complete catering service. We can help you select the right wine and spirits. Our bartenders can get real inventive with a cocktail shaker.

We know where to find the best flowers, the best music, the best site for your event. Call Ann Walker first. You may not have to call anyone else.

And most importantly, we **listen** to what you want.

After all, it's your party.

AnnWalkerCatering
P.O. Box 85, San Anselmo, CA 94979
415 . 460 . 9885
415 . 460 . 9886 fax
Email Ann directly at **foodwalker@aol.com**

Culinary Excellence

THE PROFESSIONAL CATERERS

Committed to Service
Dedicated to Excellence
since 1970

510/644-0612 ∿ 925/947-1090

FAX 925/682-1939

TRY OUR NEW
ESPRESSO
BAR SERVICE

VISA AND
MASTERCARD
ACCEPTED

**Our goal is to provide you exceptional
food and service
at affordable prices**

(415) 487-9244

www.premiercatering.com
e-mail: events@premiercatering.com

DESIGNERS OF
WEDDINGS AND
SPECIAL EVENTS
TO REFLECT
YOUR INDIVIDUAL
STYLE

La BOCCA Fina

FINE CATERING

PICNIC
PLEASURES TO
OPULENT
FEASTS

510 264 0276

Simply Fresh & Elegant

Debbie Raynor
EVENTS
CATERING

510.649.7700

catering and party planning

MON CHERI
CATERERS AND COOKING SCHOOL

✳

**"WE HAVE SERVED THE PRESIDENT OF THE UNITED STATES
AND SILICON VALLEY CEOs, AS WELL AS
THOUSANDS OF LUNCHES AND DINNERS."**

SHARON SHIPLEY
OWNER AND MASTER CHEF

✳

461 SOUTH MURPHY AVENUE, SUNNYVALE, CA 94086
(408) 736-0892
(408) 736-0932 FAX

www.monchericaterers.com ✳ sship25521@aol.com

CUSTOM POETIC ELEMENTS

The *Whole Big* Thing

Amy Lee Gillin, an event designer • tel: 415.752.8628 • fax: 415.831.7600 • twbt@well.com

TIE THE KNOT™

AWARD WINNING CONSULTANTS

Professional Planning and Coordination

Specializing In

CREATIVE ✿ THEME ✿ ETHNIC WEDDINGS

FABULOUS LOCATIONS

INVITATIONS

Vice President, June Weddings, Inc.®
Member: Association of Bridal Consultants

(650) 968-2564

Mountain View ✿ San Francisco

The Wedding Resource

Ceremony and Event Coordination since 1991

For Brochure or Interview, call (415) 928-8621

Diane Breivis & Kathryn Kenna

San Francisco

All Great Occasions

Event Planning

Large or small
local or remote,
for
stress-free entertaining
and
experienced event execution
call

Kimberly Bailey

Email: kbailey@napanet.net
P.O. Box 419 · Napa, CA 94559
Tel: 707.258.8006 · Fax: 707.255.0107

What our clients are saying about us...

"...thank you for making Janice and Brent's wedding day so very special.
Every detail was handled perfectly thanks to your great attention to detail.
All of our guests raved about the food, the wine, the great service.
Thank you so very much..." Fran A.

California Events

From Complete Weddings to only your Wedding Day

Expert in finding the Perfect Wedding and Reception Sites.

Laurie Anderson Wedding Consultant

Every Detail Orchestrated with your Vision in Mind

Customized Theme and Ethnic Wedding Design available.

(408) 559-4975 18 Years Experience

Unique Wedding Celebrations

Event Resource & Design

A Unique, Personalized
Approach to
**Wedding Catering, Design
& Management**

Purveyors of Inventive
Culinary Style
& Distinctive Locations:

**Elegant Mansions
Exclusive Wineries
Private Country Estates**

Serving the Bay Area
for over 17 years

by *Joan Freese*

800 . 457 . 2282

Coordinators

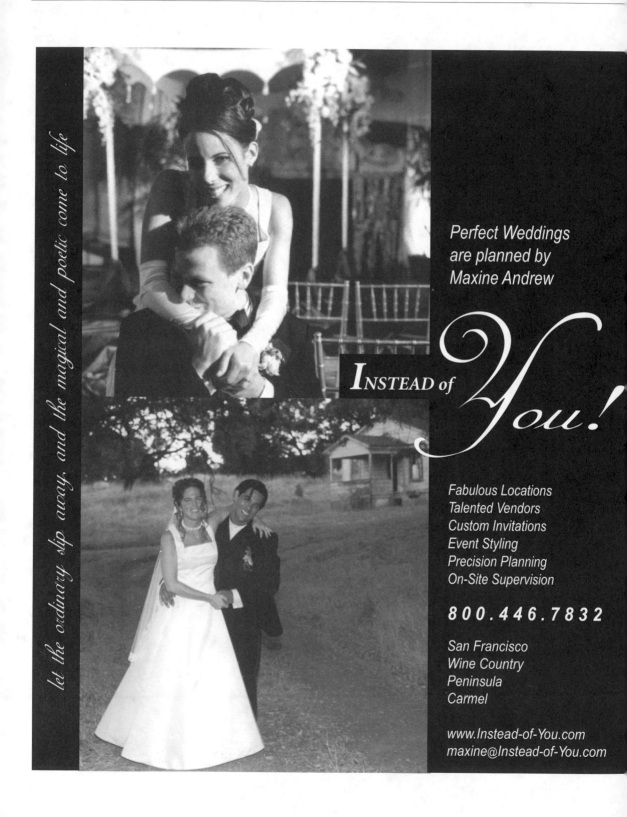

let the ordinary slip away, and the magical and poetic come to life

Perfect Weddings
are planned by
Maxine Andrew

INSTEAD of *You!*

Fabulous Locations
Talented Vendors
Custom Invitations
Event Styling
Precision Planning
On-Site Supervision

800.446.7832

San Francisco
Wine Country
Peninsula
Carmel

www.Instead-of-You.com
maxine@Instead-of-You.com

All Stars Productions

YOU FIND THE DRESS
...WE DO THE REST

LOCATIONS
- Hotels
- Wineries
- Resorts
- Yachts
- Gardens
- Museums
- Private Estates
- Art Galleries
- Historic Landmarks
- Country Clubs

ENTERTAINMENT

MENU PLANNING

PHOTOGRAPHY

VIDEO

FLOWERS

TRANSPORTATION

ETC.

ALL STARS PRODUCTIONS
Craig Sherwood, *Director*
phone 415-461-2200
fax 415-461-6962

Over 20 years experience | San Francisco Bay Area • Wine Country • Pebble Beach
Certified Chef – Beverly Hills • Maui • France • Holland | Musician/Bandleader since 1980

Decor & Coordination

i·de·as
the special events company™

Custom Floral Design

Entertainment

Catering

Custom Invitations

Unique Rentals

Event Design

Site Locations

Full Service Planner

Ideas develops, designs, and produces special events of distinction including weddings, theme events, charity galas, corporate functions and private gatherings.

Beginning with your vision, requirements and budget, Ideas can transform any event into an unforgettable affair.

Showroom available by appointment only

1302 Twenty Second Street
San Francisco, CA 94107

phone 1•888•ideas•88
      43327
fax 415•285•8688
email ideasSF@aol.com
url www.ideas-events.com

Breathtakingly beautiful chuppot
for sale or rental
in a variety of designs and fabrics

כול ששון וכול שמחה

PHOTO BY RICHARD MAYER

personalized "break the glass" bags, bridal purses, lace hankies,
challah covers, groom's vests, talit sets

Under the Chuppah — Carol Attia
(800) 661-4127

PHOTO: EVA GUSTON

VIP PRODUCTIONS
ONE NIGHT STAND ENTERTAINMENT

PENINSULA 650 571 5940
EAST BAY   925 833 0414

Mobile Disc Jockey Entertainment
Since 1988

Entertainment Ranging From
Formal to Festive

Thousands of Songs To Choose
From the 20's to 90's

 ICHARD OLSEN ORCHESTRAS

SWING

BIG BAND

MOTOWN

ROCK N' ROLL

LATIN

…"THE BAY AREA'S MOST VERSATILE BIG BAND" S.F. CHRONICLE

★ FIVE – 17 PIECE BANDS ★

EPUTATION FOR VERSATILITY, EXCELLENCE & PROFFESIONAL SERVICE

Also available:

SOLOISTS

TRIOS

STRING QUARTETS

" … It was a huge pleasure to have you playing at our reception, & we will always remember what wonderful music it was.

… Everyone was raving about how much they enjoyed dancing & listening to your orchestra, you are absolutely the best! … "

★ WEDDINGS   ★ PARTIES   ★ SPECIAL EVENTS

TELEPHONE ■ 415 831–3367   FAX ■ 415 831–3395

"The Bay Area's pre eminent swing band." SF Bay Guardian

Jazz ◆ Swing ◆ Big Band ◆ Latin ◆ Blues

20 Years Experience Playing Weddings, Parties, Concerts and Special Events

Veteran of 4 Black & White Balls, the Monterey Jazz Festival, and the
U.S. Mayor's Conference

(415) 459-2428

www.swingfever.com

We are also SWING FEVER ENTERTAINMENT
We represent a huge selection of professional, screened entertainers. Rock, Funk,
Blues, Motown, Variety, Classical, Jazz, DJs and Specialty Acts.

LEONARD NEIL ORCHESTRAS

over 2 decades producing the finest in dance music

all styles
888.453.1137

Eagan Photography

Magnolia Jazz Band

Bringing Fun, Elegance, and Excitement to Special Events!

*You will love the atmosphere we'll create for your next party —
rousing, danceable, or as an elegant background to the festivities.
Because we know how to get your guests into the swing of things,
they'll have a great time, and you'll enjoy a memorable event!*

Preview the fun you'll enjoy:
* *Visit our web site at **www.MagnoliaJazz.com**, or*
* *Call **(408) 245-9120** for your free information kit, or*
* *Check our schedule and catch us in action!*

Mention this ad for your special discount when you book the band.

Make Your Day Exceptional

MICHELLE K. SELL
H A R P I S T

WEDDINGS ~ RECEPTIONS
REHEARSAL DINNERS ~ PARTIES
SOLO HARP
HARP W/FLUTE OR CELLO OR VIOLIN

▸ PROFESSIONAL SINCE 1977
▸ SAN FRANCISCO CONSERVATORY
  ALUMNUS AND FACULTY
▸ STAFF HARPIST: GEORGE LUCAS'
  SKYWALKER STUDIOS
▸ 25 ALBUM DISCOGRAPHY
  W/ RADIO AIRPLAY
▸ REFERRED BY CATERERS AND CLERGY
▸ PERFORMED WITH SINATRA, MANCINI
  AND NUMEROUS KNOWN ARTISTS
▸ TV APPEARANCES INCLUDE:
  THE TONIGHT SHOW
  GOOD MORNING AMERICA
  LIVE WITH REGIS & KATHIE LEE

*"Her playing
on the harp is
impeccable."*

JOHN DILIBERTO
ECHOES,
AMERICAN PUBLIC RADIO

*"You sound so
beautiful. Let's
go on tour!"*

LINDA RONSTADT

(415) 457-3912

BOX 1002, FAIRFAX, CALIFORNIA 94978-1002
COMPETITIVE PRICES

Let me tell you about the

Music at my Reception

If I had worn more comfortable shoes, I could have danced all night.

We found the musicians for both our ceremony and reception through Angel Entertainment. They had a great selection of musicians and made choosing the entertainment easy.

We didn't have to worry about a thing. We'll be sure to use Angel Entertainment for all of our business and social occasions.

Angel Entertainment
800.836.5559

email: jessica@angelevent.com
www.angelevent.com

Savor the Melody

A favorite of the Monterey Peninsula for over ten years, the Scott & Peggy Brown band will travel anywhere in order to provide memory-making music from Broadway to Boogie with impeccable taste and style.

Scott & Peggy Brown Music

831 646-9051

photo: Scott & Peggy's wedding 1983

flute . violin . cello

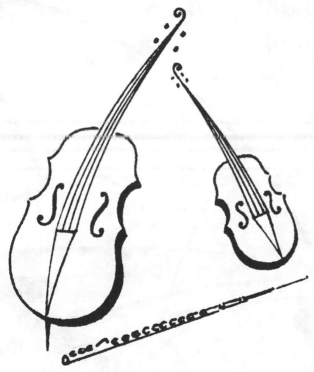

**Classical Music for your
Classic Event**
Janet Maestre (510) 524-2569

Elegant,
Romantic
Music

J OHN *T* URNER

Solo Piano for All Occasions

510-234-5646

Photo/Aribert Dormann

Eddie Pasternak

Music to Make Your Wedding Exceptional

 Playing Your Listening and Dancing
Favorites; Solo to Large Bands

 (510)655-5783

Planning A Special Event?

Innovative Entertainment Makes It One You Won't Forget!

Featuring the Bay Areas finest entertainers including:

- *Dick Bright Orchestra*
- *Dick Bright's SRO*
- *Pride & Joy*
- *Encore*
- *Big City Revue*
- *Napata Mero & the Kisses*
- *David Martin's House Party*
- *The Fundamentals*
- *String Ensembles*
- *Pianists*

**888 Brannan Street
Suite 615
San Francisco
California 94103
(415) 552-4276
Fax (415) 552-3545**

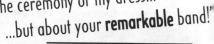

ALL STARS MUSIC
SEE & HEAR LIVE VIDEOS-TAPES-CD'S
OF ALL OUR GROUPS
DANCE BANDS • DJS
CLASSICAL GROUPS
ALL SIZES • ALL STYLES
• PARTY MUSIC
ROCK • BLUES • MOTOWN • JUMP SWING • DIXIE
BIG BAND • CAJUN • ZYDECO • REGGAE • JAZZ
VERSATILE • DANCE BANDS • STEEL DRUMS
MARIACHI • COUNTRY • ETC.
• CLASSICAL MUSIC
HARP • HARP & FLUTE • GUITAR • GUITAR & FLUTE
FLUTE VIOLIN & CELLO • STRING QUARTET
PIANO • BRASS • ETC.
FIND OUT WHY WE ARE THE MOST RECOMMENDED
MUSICIANS IN THE BAY AREA
CRAIG SHERWOOD, MUSICAL DIRECTOR
(415) 461-2200

For Music
Your Guests
Will Still Be
Talking About
Years Later

Nancy Carlin
Associates

A California Licensed Talent Agency

(925) 372-4260

Nancy Carlin Associates represents over 150
of the finest bands and musicians in the Bay
Area and has booked entertainment, since
1976. Call to discuss your wedding reception,
corporate event, or celebration for the finest
selection of Swing, Rock, Motown, Ethnic,
Classical and Popular Music.

P.O. Box 6499 Concord, CA 94521

LAURIE CHESTNUTT

F l o r a l s

"...my most treasured wedding memories have been of the absolutely gorgeous bridal and bridesmaids' bouquets you created. The flowers could not have been more beautiful, or have met my hopes and expectations more completely. I will always appreciate all of your personal assistance and care in helping us make our plans."

Letter from the bride
Katherine Olson
Hillsborough, California

There are artists who transform the sun into a yellow spot, but there are others who, with the help of their art and their intelligence transform a yellow spot into the sun.

Pablo Picasso

Photography by Joshua Ets-Hokin

*To schedule a consultation in your office or home **please call 650.325.9926***

Romantic Flowers

FOR ANY OCCASION

Laurel Ann Winzler
By Appointment Only
(415) 386-8360

Phone 650.652.9009
650.652.9007 Fax

Karen Baba

Floral and decorative planning for all occasions
Meeting all your individual needs

Specializing in Romantic and European Design

Plan Decor

BRANCH OUT
EVENT FLORAL DESIGN

Branch out (branch out)

v. **1**. to enlarge the scope of one's imagination.

2. diverse, unlike.

415.648.1887
BY APPOINTMENT

Your wedding should be like nobody else's. Custom designed wedding flowers from Hastings and Hastings are personalized to your individual taste, style and budget. Totally unique from bridal bouquet to matching floral head pieces, and a one-of-a-kind look for your ceremony and reception.

Please call us to make an appointment for a complimentary consultation.

© Rory Earnshaw 1994

Hastings & Hastings

FLORIST   27 Miller Avenue, Mill Valley, CA 94941
(415) 381-1272

PATRICIA GIBBONS

floral designer

Specializing in weddings, parties & events

COMPLIMENTARY CONSULTATIONS

"Your attention to detail is impeccable and your designs magical..."

extensive portfolio of styles including :

GARDEN BOUQUETS

FLORAL TOPIARIES

MODERN DESIGNS

custom built chuppas & pedestals

510.527.3197

FLORAMOR STUDIOS
florist

415.864.0145

Fax 415-864-3455 569 Seventh St., San Francisco, CA 94103

CREATIVE FLORAL DESIGNS
FOR ANY OCCASION

SALLY WHEELER
DESIGNS WITH FLOWERS
WEDDINGS · PARTIES · SPECIAL EVENTS
415 . 974 . 0727

...Simply the best.
Call for your complimentary floral consultation.
650-780-0111

Blossoms
by Jylene

1757 East Bayshore Rd., Ste. 16, Redwood City • Open: M-Sat. 9-5

TAPESTRY

BRIDAL & SPECIAL EVENT FLOWERS

PHOTO BY JOSHUA ETS-HOKIN

Natural. Hand-crafted. Intensely personal.

Karen Axel AIFD • 415·550·1015 • www.tapestryflowers.com

Floral Designers

specially designed
LINENS
CHUPPAS
& ARCHES

For flowers that speak
a language of their own

For weddings, parties & events in
European, traditional,
contemporary & custom styles

Mille Fleurs

AUDRA BOVIS TABER
510 237 8209

FANTASY FLORALS

SUMPTUOUS FLORAL DESIGN ~

EXQUISITE WEDDINGS & EVENTS
by susan barton

~ garden archways
magnificent chuppas ~
~ urn, topiary and glass rentals

415·456·0347

marin county ~ servicing the bay area ~ call for a complementary consultation to view extensive portfolios

In Full Bloom

Weddings ◆ Parties ◆ Events
English Garden Grandeur A Specialty

Susan Groves ◆ Menlo Park, California ◆ 650 ◆ 364 ◆ 1858

Flowers

Michaele Thunen

W E D D I N G S   P A R T I E S   E V E N T S

P L A N N I N G — C O O R D I N A T I O N

510·527·5279   BERKELEY · CALIFORNIA

Wedding Bouquet "On Flowers" — Chronicle Books

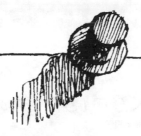

Why should you call one of our preferred event professionals?

Because it's so easy!

You don't have to ask your friends. You don't have to flip through the Yellow Pages. You don't have to go to a bridal fair or use a bridal magazine to locate a good wedding professional. Why? Because a directory with all of the region's best event professionals is right here! What could be easier?

Because you know our professionals are prequalified.

We've done the legwork for you! You don't have to worry about the professionalism of our clients because we've checked them out for you. The ones we feature in *Here Comes The Guide* have had to go through a rigorous screening process, and we've accepted only those that received "rave reviews" from their peers in the special events industry.

Because you know we're picky!

We're nuts about details. Picky, picky, picky. That's why *Here Comes The Guide* is so good. We don't cut corners when it comes to checking out event locations, and that goes for event professionals, too. And because we're picky, you won't have to spend as much time or effort in finding a fantastic cake maker, floral designer or caterer. We think you can find other things to do with the time you'll save!

ABCDEFGHIJKLMNOPQRSTUVWXYZ

· invitation design · envelopes · placecards · announcements · menus ·

· thank yous · monograms · stationery · moving cards · marriage vows ·

Calligraphy

english · עברית

Adrienne D. Keats

(415) 759·5678
fax: (415) 661·5249

abcdefghijklmnopqrstuvwxyzabcdefghijklmnopqrstuvw

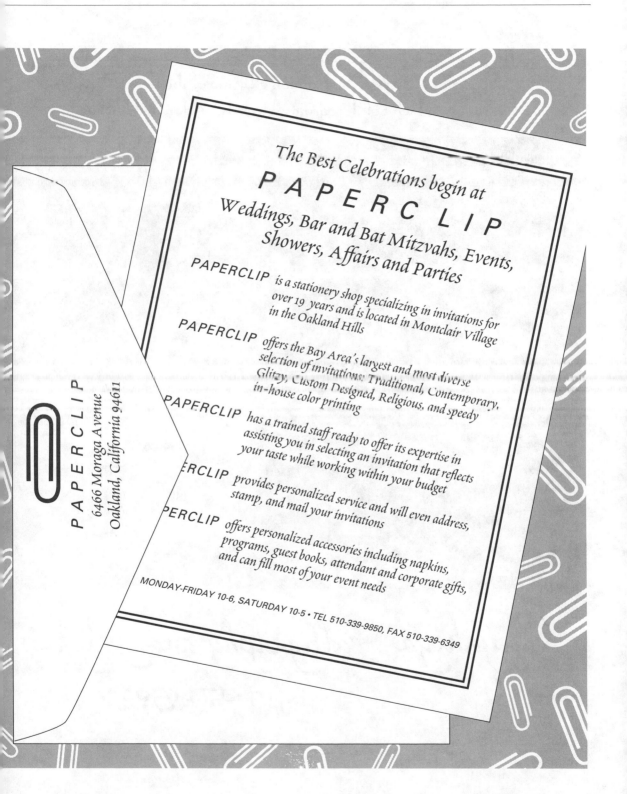

The Best Celebrations begin at

P A P E R C L I P

Weddings, Bar and Bat Mitzvahs, Events, Showers, Affairs and Parties

PAPERCLIP is a stationery shop specializing in invitations for over 19 years and is located in Montclair Village in the Oakland Hills

PAPERCLIP offers the Bay Area's largest and most diverse selection of invitations: Traditional, Contemporary, Glitzy, Custom Designed, Religious, and speedy in-house color printing

PAPERCLIP has a trained staff ready to offer its expertise in assisting you in selecting an invitation that reflects your taste while working within your budget

PAPERCLIP provides personalized service and will even address, stamp, and mail your invitations

PAPERCLIP offers personalized accessories including napkins, programs, guest books, attendant and corporate gifts, and can fill most of your event needs

MONDAY-FRIDAY 10-6, SATURDAY 10-5 • TEL 510-339-9850, FAX 510-339-6349

PAPERCLIP
6466 Moraga Avenue
Oakland, California 94611

ENGAGING

*For those
willing to make
a commitment . . .*

Custom Designed Jewelry

Designer Jewelry

Repair and Restoration

Appraisals

ALSO FEATURING FINE ARTS AND DISTINCTIVE CRAFTS

CHRISTENSEN HELLER GALLERY

*5831 College Avenue, Oakland • Near Rockridge BART • 510 655 5952
Tuesday through Saturday 11-6 • Sunday 12-5*

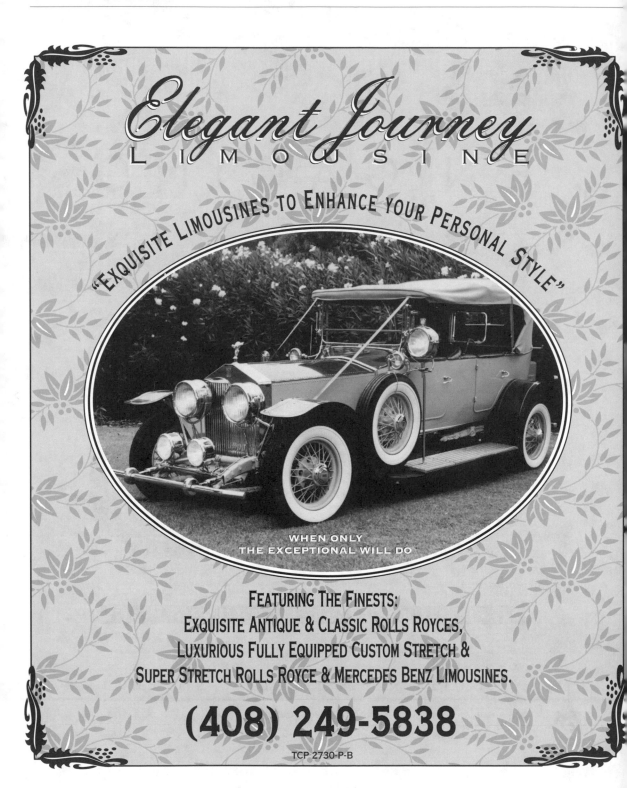

MICHAEL STEINBERG PHOTOGRAPHY

WWW.MICHAELSTEINBERG.COM

415.978.5499

S U Z A N N E   P A R K E R

distinctive
wedding photography

❧ 415.931.7151 ❧

LAWRENCE LAUTERBORN

PHOTOGRAPHY

SAN FRANCISCO STUDIO (415) 863-1132

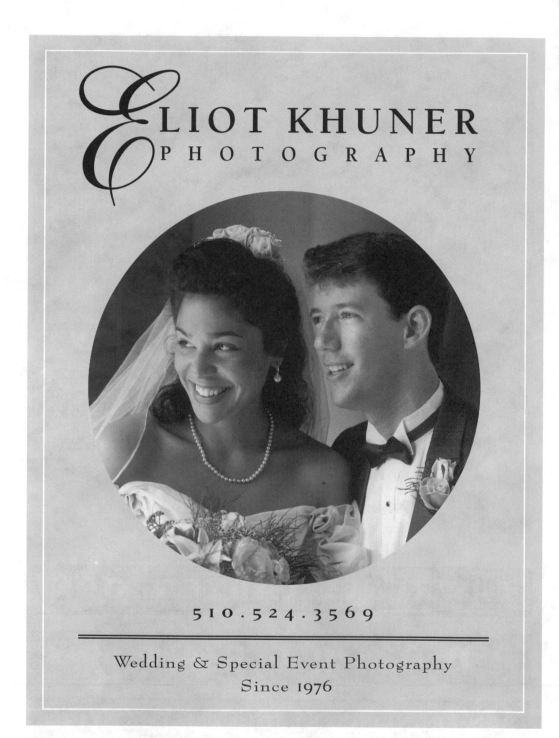

*Specializing in Wedding Photography
on the Monterey Peninsula...*

George C. McCullough
Monterey, California
831 · 373 · 8037

CAPTURE YOUR MAGIC MOMENT

With a spontaneous and imaginative style, Michael Loeb interprets your special moments with artistic flair.

Michael Loeb Photography
415.453.8755

VISIT OUR WEB SITE!: http://www.loebphotography.com

KIRA
GODBE
PHOTOGRAPHY
831/625-5799

MONTEREY BAY AREA · CARMEL · BIG SUR

P.O. BOX 222058
CARMEL, CA 93922
FAX 831/625-5820

Your Vision of a Perfect Celebration

RICHARD MILLER
PHOTOGRAPHY

415.388.3722

*With More than 25 Years
Event Experience, We will meet
and exceed your expectations.*

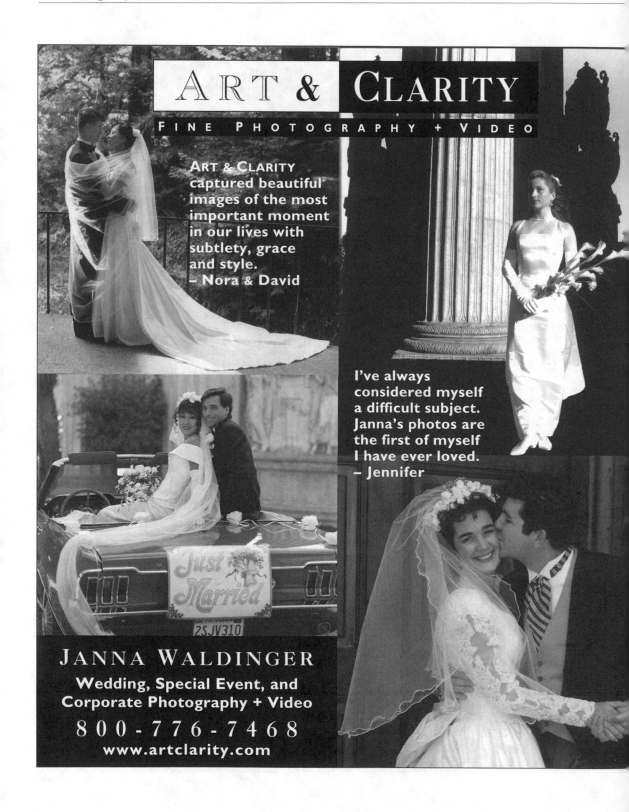

Distinctive Weddings by

Ben Janken Photography

510.482.9041

RANDY SILVER PHOTOGRAPHY

Natural Elegance...real people in real time

Bay Area
(650) 591-3056

Nevada City
(530) 265-2873

randy-silver-photo@juno.com

www.randysilverphotography.com

**CELEBRATIONS
PHOTOGRAPHY
AND VIDEO**

UNOBTRUSIVE STYLE
UNIQUE • REASONABLE • PROFESSIONAL
5999 WESTOVER DR. • OAKLAND, CA 94611 • 510-530-4480

Martina Konietzny

Master of Fine Arts

510.652.6563

martina@sirius.com

www.sirius.com/~martina

WITH THE

EYE OF AN ARTIST

AND SKILLS OF A

PHOTOJOURNALIST

LET

RICHARD MAYER

TELL

YOUR STORY.

"Thanks again for such great pictures. We just love the way you captured our wedding in the candids. It's like reliving all the excitement."
CHRISTINA MORRISON
Venture, CA

"We are totally happy with your photos. I have been showing them to everyone and people keep saying 'I wish I'd had him at my wedding'."
LUNDIE GUERARD
Kensington, CA

"You did a beautiful job. The pictures are fantastic!"
KARIE WHITMAN
San Rafael, CA

"I just wanted to let you know how pleased I am with my wedding pictures. Everyone just loves them."
FRAN REDFIELD
Rohnert Park, CA

Prichard Photography

Natural Style • Unobtrusive • Affordable

(510) 486-0905

1806 Blake St., Berkeley, CA 94703

PHOTOGRAPHY BY BILL STOCKWELL

napa valley 707 963 1179
san francisco 415 491 4575
BY APPOINTMENT
www.napaphotos.com/stockwell.html

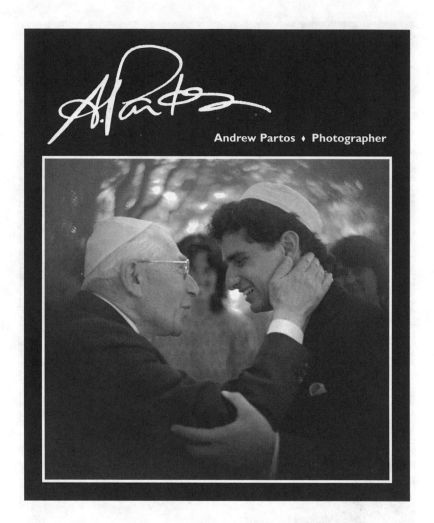

Andrew Partos ◆ Photographer

PHOTOGRAPHING WEDDINGS AND OTHER SIGNIFICANT OCCASIONS

*artistic professionalism for
more than 20 years*

Berkeley — 510.841.6727

Photography by Mark Stover
www.mstover.com
831 • 688 • 4143
Serving the Monterey and San Francisco Bay Areas Since 1983

Chin

KEVIN CHIN Photography 415.751.9248
www.kevinchin.com

AWARDS OF MERIT
CUSTOM WEDDINGS
SIGNATURE PORTRAITS

STEP UP TO

Avant Garde

PHOTOGRAPHY

Shirley Kerns Welcome
(707) 966-6026 • (707) 963-4201

Limo courtesy of Antique Tours, Napa Valley

NAPA VALLEY  BAY AREA

Jeffrey Davila Photography

Wine Country 707.544.9151
Bay Area 510.547.7531
www.jeffreydavila.com

MULTIVISION PRODUCTIONS

NATIONAL AWARD-WINNING
VIDEOGRAPHY
WEDDINGS & SPECIAL EVENTS

925 • 687 • 9999

Multivision creates a movie of your
wedding with classic taste and
personalized service.

Serving the Bay Area & Beyond

AMERICA'S MOST RESPECTED NAME IN WEDDING VIDEOGRAPHY

When your wedding is over,
the video is the first thing you'll want to see...
plan now to have the best!

**The Bay Area's most experienced team
18 years – 2600 weddings**

Creative
VIDEO SERVICES

510 252 9700

- Unobtrusive
  - Elegant
    - Technical Superiority

Winners of 5 National awards at the 1998 Wedding Video Expo
Voted best ceremony & reception videos in America

For complete information,
please visit our extensive website   **www.cvs-weddings.com**

Photo: Leslie Corrado

The Cake
  The Flowers
    The Dress
      The Groom's nervous "I do"

We capture it all...
    And you will never know we are there.

Thomas Hughes Video Productions

understated, elegant wedding videography

serving the Bay Area since 1985

415-925-8600

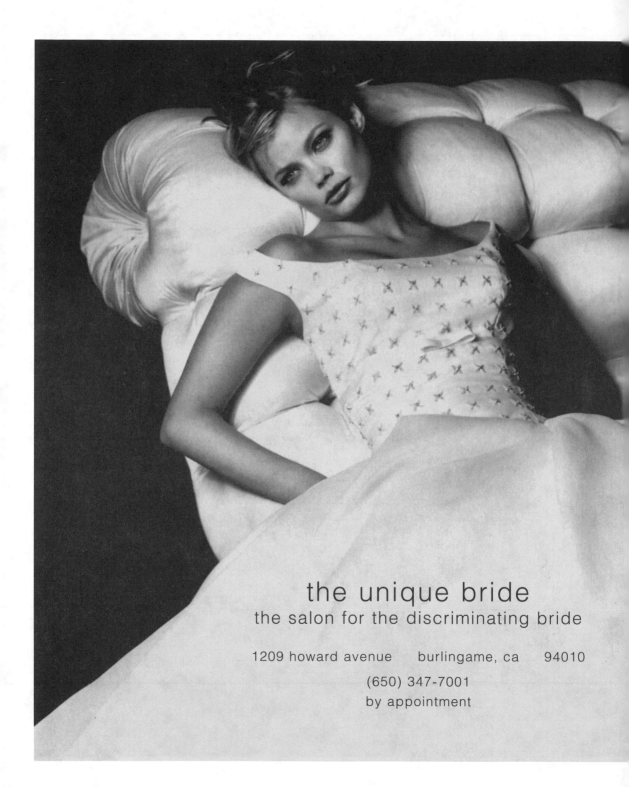

the unique bride
the salon for the discriminating bride

1209 howard avenue   burlingame, ca   94010

(650) 347-7001

by appointment

event location index

d

e

o

p

q

r

Y

professional index

Why Attend
A Bridal Fair?

If you're like most prospective brides and grooms, you'll want to shop around for wedding-related services and compare quality and price before making your final decisions. Bridal fairs offer an efficient way to review what's in the marketplace—you can check out florists and photographers, sample the wares of cakemakers and listen to the music of a variety of DJs. And if you haven't yet selected your wedding garb, there's always a lengthy production number with models showing off a wide range of wedding attire.

Most importantly, you'll be able to actually talk to event professionals and ask them your burning questions—namely what can they do for you and how much will it cost. You'll find out much more by chatting with experts in person than by calling them at random from the Yellow Pages.

The Bay Area's
Best Bridal Fairs

Here are our top picks in Bay Area bridal fairs and, in our usual Hopscotch Press fashion, we've been pretty selective—we've only chosen four out of about 50 locally produced fairs. Believe us when we tell you that all bridal fairs are not the same.

Here's why those below have garnered our highest endorsement: each is handled very professionally and attracts a wide range of high caliber vendors; the bridal fashion shows are very good, and the fair locations are well-maintained, including the restrooms.

If you're considering attending a bridal fair, we suggest you try these four first.

Bridal Fair Tips

You may not be able to plan your wedding in one day by going to a bridal fair, but you'll undoubtedly walk away with a better sense of what's out there, and the information you've gathered should help you streamline your planning.

- Leave plenty of time to browse. Although a large fair may be a bit overwhelming, if you keep your eyes open, you'll find products and services that will appeal to you. If you arrive at the last minute, you'll have to rush through the fair and you won't be able to enjoy the bridal fashion shows.

- Wear comfortable shoes and carry a big bag with handles for all the business cards and promotional materials you'll collect.

- Many companies offer freebies, discounts and other items if you give them your name and address—bring a stamp with your name and mailing address on it, and you won't have to write it down dozens of times.

- Bring a checkbook or credit card. Often there are specials offered on wedding favors, veils or cake tops and you can take advantage of bargains if you're prepared.

- Bring a friend. You'll find that it's more fun if you share the experience.

The Bridal Extravaganza

Jan 9/10, 1999	County Fairgrounds	San Jose
Jan 17, 1999	Marriott Hotel	Burlingame
Aug 22, 1999	Marriott Hotel	Santa Clara
Jan, 2000	County Fairgrounds	San Jose
Jan, 2000	Marriott Hotel	Burlingame
Aug, 2000	Marriott Hotel	Santa Clara

408/223-5683, 408/360-9333

Call for exact dates; weekends, 10am–4pm.
www.bestbridalshow.com

Modern Bridal Faire

Jan 31, 1999	San Jose Conv. Cntr.	San Jose
Feb 7, 1999	S.F. Concourse	San Francisco
Feb 21, 1999	Pleasanton Hilton	Pleasanton
Feb 28, 1999	Crown Plaza Cabana	Palo Alto
Mar 14, 1999	Concord Hilton	Concord
July 25, 1999	San Jose Fairmont	San Jose
Aug, 1999	S.F. Concourse	San Francisco
Aug, 1999	Pleasanton Hilton	Pleasanton
Aug, 1999	Concord Hilton	Concord
Sept, 1999	Crown Plaza Cabana	Palo Alto

800/400-2099, 925/253-8600

Schedule repeats for 2000 shows, call for exact dates.
Sundays only, 11am–4pm.

Bridal Network's Winter Wedding Faire

Jan 10, 1999	Claremont Hotel	Berkeley

Bridal Network's Palace Wedding Faire

Mar 7, 1999	Palace Hotel	San Francisco

510/339-3370

Schedule repeats for 2000 shows: call for exact dates. Sundays 11–4.

Party & Wedding Faire

Jan 17, 1999	San Ramon Marriott	San Ramon
Feb 7, 1999	Marriott Hotel	Walnut Creek
Feb 21, 1999	Centre Plaza	Modesto
Mar 7, 1999	Concord Sheraton	Concord
Sept 1999	San Ramon Marriott	San Ramon

510/370-9823

Schedule repeats for 2000 shows, call for exact dates; Sundays 11am–4pm, except Modesto show which is 12–5.

about the authors

Lynn Broadwell is an author, publisher and marketing professional for the special events industry. Her companies, Lynn Broadwell & Associates and Hopscotch Press provide consulting services, publications and products which are designed to meet the needs of the general public and special event professional. She's also a location scout and a veritable "clearing house" of information regarding locations for special events in California. She writes for metropolitan newspapers and industry-related journals and speaks on the topic of special events. Ms. Broadwell has been featured in many articles and appears on radio and TV frequently.

A graduate of UC Berkeley, with both an undergraduate degree in landscape architecture and a masters degree in business, Ms. Broadwell lives in the Berkeley hills with her husband, Doug, and son, Matthew.

Jan Brenner has co-authored all of Hopscotch Press' books. Although she received a BA in English from UC Berkeley, she backed into writing only after spending ten years in social work and four in publishing. Along the way she got a couple of other degrees which have never been put to official use. A lifelong dilettante, she's quasi-conversant in 3.1 languages, dabbles in domestic pursuits, pumps iron and travels whenever she gets the chance.

about the illustrator

In 1989, Michael Tse answered our "Artist Wanted" ad on the job board at the California College of Arts and Crafts, and he's been drawing for Hopscotch Press ever since. Still part of the under 30 crowd, he recently decided to try out "the marriage thing" (so far so good), and he's testing the waters of fatherhood with his canine kids, Moxie the boxer and Hugo the whippet. More importantly for Hopscotch Press, he's finally become a computer whiz verging on addict, and is handling our illustrations with more finesse than ever.

Get one directly from Hopscotch Press!

You can also get a Southern California edition by filling out this form.

☐ **YES!** Send me my own *Here Comes The Guide, Northern California!*

_____ copies @ $26.50 each (856 pages. Incl. tax, shipping & handling.)   Total $_____

☐ **YES!** I'd like *Here Comes The Guide, Southern California!*

_____ copies @ $26.50 each (696 pages. Incl. tax, shipping & handling.)   Total $_____

Shipping: we ship via UPS, which requires a street address. If you give us a PO box number, we will send your order Priority Mail, but we won't be able to track or replace lost shipments.

send my copies to:

Name _____

Address _____

City, State, Zip _____

Phone (   ) _____

MC/Visa # _____Exp._____

To phone in your order, call 510/525-3379 or fax 510/525-7793
Visa/MC cheerfully accepted.

Hopscotch Press • 1563 Solano Avenue, Suite 135 • Berkeley, CA 94707

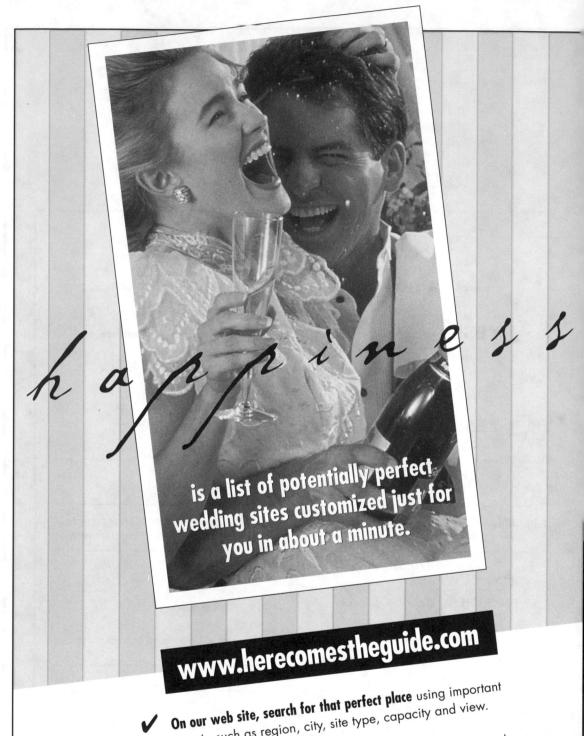